Introduction
to Old English

# Praise for the previous edition

'In its references to web-sites and computer-links, [*Introduction to Old English*] is very much a book of the twenty-first century; and many of its novel features – for example the chapter on the grammar of poetry, or the appendix on common spelling variants – will be extraordinarily helpful to teachers and students alike.'                    *Michael Lapidge, University of Notre Dame*

'Baker's Introduction is the kind of book that students of Old English – and their teachers – have been waiting for for a long time.'
*Hugh Magennis, Queen's University Belfast*

'This is a truly outstanding textbook for today's student of Old English. Written in lucid and friendly prose, Baker brings the language to life in a manner that will inspire students.'           *Elaine Treharne, University of Leicester*

'Peter Baker's *Introduction to Old English* offers an innovative combination of the traditional and the cutting edge. Beginning with the basics of the language, the chapters proceed through intelligently paced levels so that by the end the user is reading the most sophisticated literature in Old English.'
*Daniel G. Donoghue, Harvard University*

'. . . the fruit of years of sensitive, thoughtful and student-responsive teaching. [. . .] this work is a huge step forward in imaginative course design. It is accessible in manner and genuinely tries to address the needs of the modern student and teacher, taking them through a course step by step. [. . .] by far the best attempt yet to introduce Old English, and I enthusiastically recommend it to members.'                    *TOEBI Newsletter*

'Peter Baker's excellent new book, a combined grammar and reader, deserves to find a central place in the university teaching of Old English. It is unabashedly designed to be accessible to absolute beginners, but students who progress attentively through the whole book will in fact find themselves in command of a great deal of what makes Old English language and literature tick. [. . .] These chapters (on "Metre", "Poetic Style", "The Grammar of Poetry" and "Reading Old English Manuscripts") constitute the real novelty of the book in their lucid summation of some essential truths that have rarely if ever been so clearly set out for beginners; the sections on poetry in particular deserve to be read by all students beginning the translation of Old English for the first time.'                    *Notes and Queries*

# Introduction
# to Old English

Second Edition

## Peter S. Baker

© 2003, 2007 by Peter S. Baker

BLACKWELL PUBLISHING
350 Main Street, Malden, MA 02148-5020, USA
9600 Garsington Road, Oxford OX4 2DQ, UK
550 Swanston Street, Carlton Victoria 3053, Australia

The right of Peter S. Baker to be identified as the Author of this Work has been
asserted in accordance with the UK Copyright, Designs, and Patents Act 1988.

First edition published 2003
Second edition published 2007 by Blackwell Publishing Ltd

1   2007

*Library of Congress Cataloging-in-Publication Data*

Baker, Peter S. (Peter Stuart), 1952–
   Introduction to Old English / Peter S. Baker—2nd ed.
      p. cm.
   Includes bibliographical references and index.
   ISBN: 978-1-4051-5272-3 (pbk. : alk. paper)   1. English language—Old
English, ca. 450–1100.   2. English language—Old English, ca. 450–1100—
Grammar.   I. Title.
   PE135.B34 2007
   429′.82421—dc22

                                                      2006027497

A catalogue record for this title is available from the British Library.

Set in 10/12 $^1$/$_2$pt Minion
by Graphicraft Ltd, Hong Kong
Printed and bound in Singapore
by Markono Print Media Pte Ltd

The publisher's policy is to use permanent paper from mills that operate a
sustainable forestry policy, and which has been manufactured from pulp processed
using acid-free and elementary chlorine-free practices. Furthermore, the publisher
ensures that the text paper and cover board used have met acceptable
environmental accreditation standards.

For further information on
Blackwell Publishing, visit our website:
www.blackwellpublishing.com

# Contents

# Preface

This *Introduction to Old English* is for students whose interests are primarily literary or historical rather than linguistic. It aims to provide such students with a guide to the language that is detailed enough to enable them to read with facility, but it omits a great deal of the historical linguistic material that has traditionally been included even in beginning grammars. The linguistic material that the student needs in order to read Old English well is presented here as morphological feature rather than as historical 'sound change'. For example, *i*-mutation is understood as one of several ways of inflecting nouns, verbs, adjectives and adverbs. Its origin as a phonological change is treated briefly, as a sidelight rather than as an essential fact. Students who are interested in learning more about the history of the English language than is presented here may consult one of the grammars or linguistics texts listed in the References (pp. 377–83) and discussed under Further Reading (pp. 167–72).

This book assumes as little as possible about the student's knowledge of traditional grammar and experience of learning languages. Technical terminology is avoided where possible, and, where unavoidable, it is defined in simple terms. A brief grammar review is provided for those who need help with grammatical terminology.

The contents of this book are accessible via the Internet. The grammar may be consulted at the website of the Richard Rawlinson Center for Anglo-Saxon Studies at Western Michigan University (http://www.wmich.edu/medieval/researchrawl/index.html) and the texts in the anthology are available on-line at the *Old English Aerobics* website (http://www.engl.virginia.edu/OE/OEA/). Additional texts will be added to the *Old English Aerobics* website from time to time; these will be presented in such a way that they can either be used on-line or printed as a supplement to this book. The author and his publishers expect that students will find it a convenience to have this material available via the Internet as well as in printed form.

I would like to thank both the Rawlinson Center and Blackwell Publishing for agreeing to an innovative publishing venture. I would also like to thank James R. Hall of the University of Mississippi, Dan Wiley of Hastings College, and an anonymous reader for the Rawlinson Center for a number of valuable suggestions. Most of all I am indebted to my students at the University of Virginia who for the past two years have used this book and helped me to refine it. Among these students I am especially grateful to Samara Landers and John Bugbee for specific suggestions.

P. S. B.

## Preface to the Second Edition

This new edition includes many revisions intended to clarify obscure points in the grammar. In addition, four new texts have been added to the anthology: Ælfric's homily on the Book of Job from the Second Series of *Catholic Homilies*; the obituary of William the Conqueror from the *Peterborough Chronicle*, anno 1087; the voyages of Ohthere and Wulfstan from the Old English *Orosius*; and *The Battle of Maldon*. An innovation in the glossary is that entries for words with many definitions (e.g. *se*) have been subdivided so as to make it easier to determine the definition of any cited instance.

In this edition references to the on-line 'Old English Aerobics' exercises have been omitted, as the technology on which they depend has aged poorly. At the author's website instructors will find exercises intended to be downloaded and printed (http://www.engl.virginia.edu/OE/); all are welcome to make free use of this 'Old English Aerobics Workbook'. The 'Old English Aerobics Anthology' (http://www.engl.virginia.edu/OE/anthology/) still duplicates the anthology, and as it has a sturdy web interface it should continue to be a useful supplement to the book.

For extensive suggestions and corrections I am grateful to James R. Hall of the University of Mississippi and Nicole Guenther Discenza of the University of South Florida. For various corrections I would like to thank Daniel Donoghue of Harvard University, Claire Fennell of the University of Trieste and Pétur Knútsson of the University of Iceland.

P. S. B.

# How to use this book

This book can be read in any of several ways. If you have a great deal of experience learning languages, you may wish to read through from beginning to end, possibly skipping chapter 3. If you are like most students, though, reading about grammar is not your favourite activity, and you'd like to get started reading Old English texts as quickly as possible. In that case, you should first read the 'Quick Start' sections that begin most chapters. Then you may begin to read easy texts such as the 'minitexts' scattered through the book and 'The Fall of Adam and Eve' (reading 1 in the Anthology). As you read these Old English texts, go back and read the rest of chapters 2 and 5–12.

Once you have finished reading chapters 2–12, you are ready for the more advanced texts in the Anthology. Remember, as you read, that it is important to make liberal use of the glossary. Look up not only words you do not know, but also words you do know that seem to be used awkwardly, for these may not mean what you think they do. If you are not sure you have identified a word correctly, check the list of references in the glossary entry to see if it is there. The glossary lists the grammatical forms of words that can be inflected; you may check the number, person and other characteristics of words by locating forms in these lists, but remember that the glossary's 'parsing' is no substitute for learning inflections.

This book contains over 200 short passages illustrating grammatical and other points. As you encounter these passages, you may find it profitable to look up words exactly as if you were reading a minitext or one of the texts in the anthology – all words in even the shortest passages are registered in the glossary. Consult the accompanying translations to check your understanding of the grammar and sense of the Old English; if you find you have mis-understood a passage, use the translation to help you puzzle it out. Following this procedure will speed your acquisition of the language and improve your comprehension.

As you read, you will notice that some paragraphs are boxed with an exclamation mark in the margin. These paragraphs contain valuable tips and sometimes also alert you to possible pitfalls. You will also notice that some paragraphs are set in small type and marked with an *i* in a circle. These communicate useful or interesting information that you may not need to know right away. If one of these paragraphs looks confusing, skip it now and return to it later.

No one book on Old English has everything you need. Consult the list of references and Appendix C, 'Further Reading' to start reading in areas that interest you.

# Chapter 1

# The Anglo-Saxons and Their Language

## 1.1  Who were they?

'Anglo-Saxon' is the term applied to the English-speaking inhabitants of Britain up to the time of the Norman Conquest, when the Anglo-Saxon line of English kings came to an end. The people who were conquered in 1066 had themselves arrived as conquerors more than six centuries earlier.

According to the Venerable Bede, whose *Historia Ecclesiastica Gentis Anglorum* (Ecclesiastical History of the English People), completed in the year 731, is the most important source for the early history of England, the Anglo-Saxons arrived in the island of Britain during the reign of Martian, who in 449 became co-emperor of the Roman Empire with Valentinian III and ruled for seven years.

Before that time, Britain had been inhabited by Celtic peoples: the Scots and Picts in the north, and in the south various groups which had been united under Roman rule since their conquest by the emperor Claudius in AD 43. By the beginning of the fifth century the Roman Empire was under increasing pressure from advancing barbarians, and the Roman garrisons in Britain were being depleted as troops were withdrawn to face threats closer to home. In AD 410, the same year in which the Visigoths entered and sacked Rome, the last of the Roman troops were withdrawn and the Britons had to defend themselves. Facing hostile Picts and Scots in the north and Germanic raiders in the east, the Britons decided to hire one enemy to fight the other: they engaged Germanic mercenaries to fight the Picts and Scots.

It was during the reign of Martian that the newly hired mercenaries arrived. These were from three Germanic nations situated near the northern coasts of Europe: the Angles, the Saxons and the Jutes. According to Bede, the mercenaries succeeded quickly in defeating the Picts and Scots and then sent word to their homes of the fertility of the island and the cowardice of the Britons. They soon found a pretext to break with their employers, made an alliance with the Picts, and began to conquer the territory that would eventually be known as England – a slow-moving conquest that would take more than a century.

It is now difficult to measure the accuracy of Bede's account of the coming of the Anglo-Saxons. But Bede's story gives us essential information about how these people looked at themselves: they considered themselves a warrior people, and they were proud to have been conquerors of the territory they inhabited. Indeed, the warrior ethic that pervades Anglo-Saxon culture is among the first things that students notice on approaching the field.

But Europe had no shortage of warrior cultures in the last half of the first millennium. What makes Anglo-Saxon England especially worthy of study is the remarkable literature that flourished there. The Anglo-Saxon kingdoms converted to Christianity in the late sixth and seventh centuries, and by the late seventh and early eighth centuries had already produced two major authors: Aldhelm, who composed his most important work, *De Virginitate* (On Virginity), twice, in prose and in verse; and the Venerable Bede, whose vast output includes biblical commentaries, homilies, textbooks on orthography, metre, rhetoric, nature and time, and of course the *Historia Ecclesiastica*, mentioned above. A small army of authors, Bede's contemporaries and successors, produced saints' lives and a variety of other works in prose and verse, largely on Christian themes.

These seventh- and eighth-century authors wrote in Latin, as did a great many Anglo-Saxon authors of later periods. But the Anglo-Saxons also created an extensive body of vernacular literature at a time when relatively little was being written in most of the other languages of Western Europe. In addition to such well-known classic poems as *Beowulf, The Dream of the Rood, The Wanderer, The Seafarer* and *The Battle of Maldon*, they left us the translations associated with King Alfred's educational programme, a large body of devotional works by such writers as Ælfric and Wulfstan, biblical translations and adaptations, *The Anglo-Saxon Chronicle* and other historical writings, law codes, handbooks of medicine and magic, and much more. While most of the manuscripts that preserve vernacular works date from the late ninth, tenth and eleventh centuries, the Anglo-Saxons were producing written work in their own language by the early seventh century, and many scholars believe that *Beowulf* and several other important poems date from the eighth century. Thus we are in possession of five centuries of Anglo-Saxon vernacular literature.

To learn more about the Anglo-Saxons, consult Appendix C, 'Further Reading' and choose from the works listed there: they will give you access to a wealth of knowledge from a variety of disciplines. This book will give you another kind of access, equipping you with the skills you need to encounter the Anglo-Saxons in their own language.

## 1.2 Where did their language come from?

Bede tells us that the Anglo-Saxons came from *Germania*. Presumably he was using that term as the Romans had used it, to refer to a vast and ill-defined territory east of the Rhine and north of the Danube, extending as far east as the Vistula in present-day Poland and as far north as present-day Sweden and Norway. This territory was nothing like a nation, but rather was inhabited by numerous tribes which were closely related culturally and linguistically.[1]

The languages spoken by the inhabitants of *Germania* were a branch of the Indo-European family of languages, which linguists believe developed from a single language spoken some five thousand years ago in an area that has never been identified – perhaps, some say, the Caucasus. From this ancient language come most of the language groups of present-day Europe and some important languages of South Asia: the Celtic languages (such as Irish, Welsh and Scottish Gaelic), the Italic languages (such as French, Italian, Spanish and Romanian, descended from dialects of Latin), the Germanic languages, the Slavic languages (such as Russian and Polish), the Baltic languages (Lithuanian and Latvian), the Indo-Iranian languages (such as Persian and Hindi), and individual languages that do not belong to these groups: Albanian, Greek and Armenian. The biblical Hittites spoke an Indo-European language, or a language closely related to the Indo-European family, and a number of other extinct languages (some of them poorly attested) were probably or certainly Indo-European: Phrygian, Lycian, Thracian, Illyrian, Macedonian, Tocharian and others.

The Germanic branch of the Indo-European family is usually divided into three groups:

**North Germanic,** that is, the Scandinavian languages, Swedish, Danish, Norwegian, Icelandic and Faroese;

**East Germanic,** that is, Gothic, now extinct but preserved in a fragmentary biblical translation from the fourth century;

**West Germanic,** which includes High German, English, Dutch, Flemish and Frisian.

---

[1] For an early account of the Germanic tribes, see *Germania*, a work by the late first- and early second-century Roman historian Tacitus.

Within the West Germanic group, the High German dialects (which include Modern German) form a subgroup distinct from English and the other languages, which together are called 'Low German' because they were originally spoken in the low country near the North Sea.[2]

Surely the language spoken by the Germanic peoples who migrated to Britain was precisely the same as that spoken by the people they left behind on the Continent. But between the time of the migration and the appearance of the earliest written records in the first years of the eighth century, the language of the Anglo-Saxons came to differ from that of the people they had left behind. We call this distinct language Old English to emphasize its continuity with Modern English, which is directly descended from it.

## 1.3    What was Old English like?

We often hear people delivering opinions about different languages: French is 'romantic', Italian 'musical'. For the student of language, such impressionistic judgements are not very useful. Rather, to describe a language we need to explain how it goes about doing the work that all languages must do; and it is helpful to compare it with other languages – especially members of the language groups it belongs to.

Languages may be compared in a number of ways. Every language has its own repertory of sounds, as known by all students who have had to struggle to learn to pronounce a foreign language. Every language also has its own rules for accentuating words and its own patterns of intonation – the rising and falling pitch of our voices as we speak. Every language has its own vocabulary, of course, though when we're lucky we find a good bit of overlap between the vocabulary of our native language and that of the language we're learning. And every language has its own way of signalling how words function in utterances – of expressing who performed an action, what the action was, when it took place, whether it is now finished or still going on, what or who was acted upon, for whose benefit the action was performed, and so on.

The following sections attempt to hit the high points, showing what makes Old English an Indo-European language, a Germanic language, a West Germanic and a Low German language; and also how Old and Modern English are related.

---

[2]    The Low German languages are often called 'Ingvaeonic' after the *Ingvaeones*, a nation that, according to Tacitus, was located by the sea.

## 1.3.1   The Indo-European languages

The Indo-European languages do certain things in much the same way. For example, they share some basic vocabulary. Consider these words for 'father':

| | |
|---|---|
| Old English | *fæder* |
| Latin | *pater* |
| Greek | *patér* |
| Sanskrit | *pitṛ* |

You can easily see the resemblance among the Latin, Greek and Sanskrit words. You may begin to understand why the Old English word looks different from the others when you compare these words for 'foot':

| | |
|---|---|
| Old English | *fōt* |
| Latin | *pedem* |
| Greek | *póda* |
| Sanskrit | *pắdam* |

If you suspect that Latin *p* will always correspond to Old English *f*, you are right, more or less.[3] For now, it's enough for you to recognize that the Indo-European languages do share a good bit of vocabulary, though the changes that all languages go through often bring it about that the same word looks quite different in different languages.[4]

All of the Indo-European languages handle the job of signalling the functions of words in similar ways. For example, all add endings to words. The plural form of the noun meaning 'foot' was *pódes* in Greek, *pedēs* in Latin, and *pắdas* in Sanskrit – and English *feet* once ended with -*s* as well, though that ending had already disappeared by the Old English period. Most Indo-European languages signal the function of a noun in a sentence or clause by inflecting it for case[5] (though some languages no longer do, and the only remaining trace of the case system in Modern English nouns is the possessive *'s*). And most also classify their nouns by gender – masculine, feminine or neuter (though some have reduced the number of genders to two).

---

[3]   There is a complication, called 'grammatical alternation'; see §7.4.2.

[4]   For example, it's not at all obvious that Modern English *four* and Latin *quattuor*, or Modern English *quick* and Latin *vivus* 'alive', come from the same Indo-European word – but they do.

[5]   Inflection is the addition of an ending or a change in the form of a word (for example, the alteration of a vowel) to reflect its grammatical characteristics. See chapter 4 for a definition and explanation of case.

Indo-European languages have ways to inflect words other than by adding endings. In the verb system, for example, words could be inflected by changing their root vowels, and this ancient system of 'gradation' persists even now in such Modern English verbs as *swim* (past-tense *swam*, past participle *swum*). Words could also be inflected by shifting the stress from one syllable to another, but only indirect traces of this system remain in Old and Modern English.

## 1.3.2   The Germanic languages

Perhaps the most important development that distinguishes the Germanic languages from others in the Indo-European family is the one that produced the difference, illustrated above, between the *p* of Latin *pater* and the *f* of Old English *fæder*. This change, called 'Grimm's Law' after Jakob Grimm, the great linguist and folklorist, affected all of the consonants called 'stops' – that is, those consonants produced by momentarily stopping the breath and then releasing it (for example, [p], [b], [t], [d]):[6]

> **Unvoiced stops** ([p], [t], [k]) became unvoiced spirants ([f], [θ], [x]), so that Old English *fæder* corresponds to Latin *pater*, Old English *þrēo* 'three' to Latin *tres*, and Old English *habban* 'have' to Latin *capere* 'take'.
> **Voiced stops** ([b],[7] [d], [g]) became unvoiced stops ([p], [t], [k]), so that Old English *dēop* 'deep' corresponds to Lithuanian *dubùs*, *twā* 'two' corresponds to Latin *duo* and Old English *æcer* 'field' to Latin *ager*.
> **Voiced aspirated stops** ([bʰ] [dʰ], [gʰ])[8] became voiced stops ([b] [d], [g]) or spirants ([β], [ð], [ɣ]), so that Old English *brōðor* corresponds to Sanskrit *bhrā́tar-* and Latin *frater*, Old English *duru* 'door' to Latin *fores* and Greek *thúra*, and Old English *ġiest* 'stranger' to Latin *hostis* 'enemy' and Old Slavic *gosti* 'guest'.

Almost as important as these changes in the Indo-European consonant system was a change in the way words were stressed. You read in §1.3.1 that the Indo-European language sometimes stressed one form of a word on one

---

[6]   For the meanings of these International Phonetic Alphabet (IPA) symbols and of terms such as 'stop', 'spirant', 'voiced' and 'unvoiced', see Appendix B. IPA symbols in this book are enclosed in square brackets.

[7]   The consonant [b] for some reason was exceedingly rare in Indo-European, as a glance at the *b* entries in a Latin dictionary or the *p* entries in an Old English dictionary will show. Indo-European antecedents for Germanic words containing [p] are difficult to find.

[8]   An aspirated stop is a consonant that is accompanied by an *h*-like breathing sound. Most Indo-European languages altered the voiced aspirated stops in some way; for example, in Latin [bʰ] and [dʰ] became *f*, and [gʰ] became *h*.

syllable and another form on another syllable. For example, in Greek the nominative singular of the word for 'giant' was *gígās* while the genitive plural was *gigóntōn*. But in Germanic, some time after the operation of Grimm's Law, stress shifted to the first syllable. Even prefixes were stressed, except the prefixes of verbs and the one that came to Old English as *ġe-* (these were probably perceived as separate words rather than prefixes). The fact that words in Germanic were almost always stressed on the first syllable had many consequences, not least of which is that it made Old English much easier than ancient Greek for modern students to pronounce.

Along with these sound changes came a radical simplification of the inflectional system of the Germanic languages. For example, while linguists believe that the original Indo-European language had eight cases, the Germanic languages have four, and sometimes traces of a fifth. And while students of Latin and Greek must learn a quite complex verb system, the Germanic verb had just two tenses, present and past. Germanic did introduce one or two complications of its own, but in general its inflectional system is much simpler than those of the more ancient Indo-European languages, and the Germanic languages were beginning to rely on a relatively fixed ordering of sentence elements to do some of the work that inflections formerly had done.

### 1.3.3   West Germanic and Low German

The West Germanic languages differ from North and East Germanic in a number of features which are not very striking in themselves, but quite numerous. For example, the consonant [z] became [r] in North and West Germanic. So while Gothic has *hazjan* 'to praise', Old English has *herian*. In West Germanic, this [r] disappeared at the ends of unstressed syllables, with the result that entire inflectional endings were lost. For example, the nominative singular of the word for 'day' is *dagr* in Old Icelandic and *dags* in Gothic (where the final [z] was unvoiced to [s]), but *dæġ* in Old English, *dag* in Old Saxon, and *tac* in Old High German.

Low German is defined in part by something that *did not* happen to it. This non-event is the 'High German consonant shift', which altered the sounds of the High German dialects as radically as Grimm's Law had altered the sounds of Germanic. Students of Modern German will recognize the effects of the High German consonant shift in such pairs as English *eat* and German *essen*, English *sleep* and German *schlafen*, English *make* and German *machen*, English *daughter* and German *Tochter*, English *death* and German *Tod*, English *thing* and German *Ding*. Another important difference between High German and Low German is that the Low German languages did not distinguish person in plural verbs. For example, in Old High German one would say *wir nemumēs* 'we take', *ir nemet* 'you (plural) take', *sie nemant* 'they take', but in Old English one said *wē nimað* 'we take', *ġē nimað* 'you (plural) take', *hīe nimað* 'they take', using the same verb form for the first, second and third persons.

The most significant differences between Old English (with Old Frisian) and the other Low German languages have to do with their treatment of vowels. Old English and Old Frisian both changed the vowel that in other Germanic languages is represented as *a*, pronouncing it with the tongue farther forward in the mouth: so Old English has *dæg* 'day' and Old Frisian *dei*, but Old Saxon (the language spoken by the Saxons who didn't migrate to Britain) has *dag*, Old High German *tac*, Gothic *dags*, and Old Icelandic *dagr*. Also, in both Old English and Old Frisian, the pronunciation of a number of vowels was changed (for example, [o] to [e]) when [i] or [j] followed in the next syllable. This development, called *i*-mutation (§2.2.2), has implications for Old English grammar and so is important for students to understand.

Old English dramatically reduced the number of vowels that could appear in inflectional endings. In the earliest texts, any vowel except *y* could appear in an inflectional ending: *a, e, i, o, u, æ*. But by the time of King Alfred *i* and *æ* could no longer appear, and *o* and *u* were variant spellings of more or less the same sound; so in effect only three vowels could appear in inflectional endings: *a, e* and *o/u*. This development of course reduced the number of distinct endings that could be added to Old English words. In fact, a number of changes took place in unaccented syllables, all tending to eliminate distinctions between endings and simplify the inflectional system.

### 1.3.4   Old and Modern English

The foregoing sections have given a somewhat technical, if rather sketchy, picture of how Old English is like and unlike the languages it is related to. Modern English is also 'related' to Old English, though in a different way; for Old and Modern English are really different stages in the development of a single language. The changes that turned Old English into Middle English and Middle English into Modern English took place gradually, over the centuries, and there never was a time when people perceived their language as having broken radically with the language spoken a generation before. It is worth mentioning in this connection that the terms 'Old English', 'Middle English' and 'Modern English' are themselves modern: speakers of these languages all would have said, if asked, that the language they spoke was English.

There is no point, on the other hand, in playing down the differences between Old and Modern English, for they are obvious at a glance. The rules for spelling Old English were different from the rules for spelling Modern English, and that accounts for some of the difference. But there are more substantial changes as well. The three vowels that appeared in the inflectional endings of Old English words were reduced to one in Middle English, and then most inflectional endings disappeared entirely. Most case distinctions were lost; so were most of the endings added to verbs, even while the verb system became more complex, adding such features as a future tense, a perfect and a pluperfect. While the number of endings was reduced, the order of elements within clauses and sentences became more fixed, so that (for example) it came to sound archaic and awkward to place an object before the verb, as Old English had frequently done.

The vocabulary of Old English was of course Germanic, more closely related to the vocabulary of such languages as Dutch and German than to French or Latin. The Viking age, which culminated in the reign of the Danish king Cnut in England, introduced a great many Danish words into English – but these were Germanic words as well. The conquest of England by a French-speaking people in the year 1066 eventually brought about immense changes in the vocabulary of English. During the Middle English period (and especially in the years 1250–1400) English borrowed some ten thousand words from French, and at the same time it was friendly to borrowings from Latin, Dutch and Flemish. Now relatively few Modern English words come from Old English; but the words that do survive are some of the most common in the language, including almost all the 'grammar words' (articles, pronouns, prepositions) and a great many words for everyday concepts. For example, the words in this paragraph that come to us from Old English (or are derived from Old English words) include those in table 1.1.

**Table 1.1**   Some Modern English words from Old English

| | | | | |
|---|---|---|---|---|
| about | by | from | now | these |
| all | come | great | of | this |
| almost | Danish | in | old | thousand |
| and | do | into | or | time |
| are | England | it | some | to |
| as | English | king | speaking | was |
| at | everyday | many | such | were |
| borrowings | for | middle | ten | which |
| brought | French | more | than | word |
| but | friendly | most | the | year |

## 1.4   Old English dialects

The language spoken by the Anglo-Saxons at the time of their migration to Britain was probably more or less uniform. Over time, however, Old English developed into four major dialects: Northumbrian, spoken north of the river Humber; Mercian, spoken in the midlands; Kentish, spoken in Kent; and West Saxon, spoken in the southwest.

All of these dialects have direct descendants in modern England, and American regional dialects also have their roots in the dialects of Old English. 'Standard' Modern English (if there is such a thing), or at least Modern English spelling, owes most to the Mercian dialect, since that was the dialect of London.

Most Old English literature is not in the Mercian dialect, however, but in West Saxon, for from the time of King Alfred (reigned 871–99) until the Conquest Wessex dominated the rest of Anglo-Saxon England politically and culturally. Nearly all Old English poetry is in West Saxon, though it often contains spellings and vocabulary more typical of Mercian and Northumbrian – a fact that has led some scholars to speculate that much of the poetry was first composed in Mercian or Northumbrian and later 'translated' into West Saxon. Whatever the truth of the matter, West Saxon was the dominant language during the period in which most of our surviving literature was recorded. It is therefore the dialect that this book will teach you.

# Chapter 2

# Pronunciation

## 2.1 Quick start

No one knows exactly how Old English sounded, for no native speakers survive to inform us. Rather, linguists have painstakingly reconstructed the pronunciation of the language from various kinds of evidence: what we know of Latin pronunciation (since the Anglo-Saxons adapted the Latin alphabet to write their own language), comparisons with other Germanic languages and with later stages of English, and the accentuation and quantity of syllables in Old English poetry. We believe that our reconstruction of Old English pronunciation is reasonably accurate; but some aspects of the subject remain controversial, and it is likely that we will never attain certainty about them. The greatest Old English scholar in the world today might very well have difficulty being understood on the streets of King Alfred's Winchester.

Despite the uncertainties, you should learn Old English pronunciation and get into the habit of reading texts aloud to yourself. Doing so will give you a clearer idea of the relationship between Old and Modern English and a more accurate understanding of Old English metre, and will also enhance the pleasure of learning the language.

If you find any of the terminology or the phonetic symbols in this chapter unfamiliar, you should consult Appendix B, 'Phonetic Symbols and Terms' (pp. 164–6).

### 2.1.1 Vowels and diphthongs

Old English had seven simple vowels, spelled *a*, *æ*, *e*, *i*, *o*, *u* and *y*, and probably an eighth, spelled *ie*. It also had two diphthongs (two-part vowels), *ea* and *eo*. Each of these sounds came in short and long versions. Long vowels are always marked with macrons (e.g. *ā*) in modern editions for students, and also in some scholarly editions. However, vowels are never so marked in Old English manuscripts.

When we speak of vowel length in Old English, we are speaking of *duration*, that is, how long it takes to pronounce a vowel. This fact can trip up the modern student, for when we speak of 'length' in Modern English, we are actually speaking of differences in the *quality* of a vowel. If you listen carefully when you say *sit* (with 'short' *i*) and *site* (with 'long' *ī*), you'll notice that the vowels are quite different: the 'short' version has a simple vowel [ɪ],[1] while the 'long' version is a diphthong, starting with a sound like the *u* in *but* and ending with a sound like the *i* in *sit* [ʌɪ]. The same is true of other long/short pairs in Modern English: they are always qualitatively different. We do give some vowels a longer duration than others (listen to yourself as you pronounce *beat* and *bead*), but this difference in duration is never significant: that is, it does not make a difference in the meaning of a word. Rather, we pronounce some vowels long and others short because of the influence of nearby sounds.

> **!** Vowel length (that is, duration) is significant in Old English because it does make a difference in the meanings of words. For example, Old English *is* means 'is' while *īs* means 'ice', *ac* means 'but' while *āc* means 'oak', and *ge* means 'and' while *ġē* means 'you' (plural). The significance of length means that the macrons that appear in the texts you will be reading are not there only as guides to pronunciation, but also to help you decide what words mean. If you absent-mindedly read *mæġ* 'kinsman' as *mǣġ* 'may', you will never figure out the meaning of the sentence you are reading.

*Simple vowels*
The following list of vowels deals with quality only; you may assume that the short and long vowels sound alike except for a difference in duration. The list cites a number of Modern English words for comparison: these are from the

---

[1] This book frequently uses symbols from the International Phonetic Alphabet (IPA) for convenience of reference, though it also gives examples wherever possible. For a table of the IPA symbols relevant to the study of Old English, see Appendix B.

Mid-Atlantic dialect of American English and may not be valid for speakers of British English or other dialects.

*a* is pronounced [ɑ], as in Modern English *father*. Examples: *macian* 'make', *bāt* 'boat'.

*æ* is pronounced [æ], as in Modern English *cat*. *Bæc* 'back', *rǣdan* 'read'.

*e* is pronounced [e], as in Modern English *fate*; that is, it is like the *e* of a continental European language, not like the 'long' or 'short' *e* of Modern English (actually [i] or [ɛ]). *Helpan* 'help', *fēdan* 'feed'.

*i* is pronounced [i], as in Modern English *feet*; that is, it is like the *i* of a continental European language, not like the 'long' or 'short' *i* of Modern English (actually [ʌɪ] or [ɪ]). *Sittan* 'sit', *līf* 'life'.

*o* is pronounced [o], as in Modern English *boat*. *God* 'God', *gōd* 'good'.

*u* is pronounced [u], as in Modern English *tool*; it is never pronounced [ʌ] as in Modern English *but*. *Full* 'full', *fūl* 'foul'.

*y* is pronounced [y], like the *ü* in German *über* or *Füße*, or like the *u* in French *tu* or *dur*. Make it by positioning the tongue as you do to say *feet* while rounding the lips as you do to say *tool*. *Cyning* 'king', *brȳd* 'bride'.

*ie* which appears mainly in early West Saxon, is difficult to interpret. It was probably approximately [ɪ], like the *i* of Modern English *sit*. In late West Saxon, words that contained this vowel are rarely spelled with *ie*, but rather with *i* or *y*. *Ieldesta* 'eldest', *hīeran* 'hear'.

**ⓘ** Many grammars tell you to pronounce short *e* as [ɛ], like the *e* in Modern English *set*, short *i* as [ɪ], like the *i* of Modern English *sit*, and short *u* as [ʊ], like the *u* of Modern English *pull*. You can get away with these pronunciations, though they probably do not represent the Old English vowels accurately.

In most Modern English dialects, the 'long' vowels /eː/, /oː/ and sometimes /i/ and /u/ are pronounced as diphthongs, e.g. /eɪ/, /ou/. Old English long vowels probably were not diphthongized, so try to avoid pronouncing them as diphthongs.

In unaccented syllables, where few vowel sounds were distinguished (see §1.3.3), vowels were probably pronounced less distinctly than in accented syllables. In late Old English (*c.*1000 and later), frequent spelling confusion shows that by then the language was beginning to approach the Middle English situation in which all vowels in unaccented syllables were pronounced [ə] (a neutral schwa, like the *a* in *China*). But unaccented vowels *were* distinguished in Old English, and it is important to pronounce them, for vowel quality often is the only thing that distinguishes one ending from another. For example, dative singular *cyninge* and genitive plural *cyninga*, genitive singular *cyninges* and nominative plural *cyningas* are distinguished only by vowel quality.

*Diphthongs*

Old English has two digraphs (pairs of letters) that are commonly interpreted as diphthongs: *ea* and *eo*.[2]

Both *ea* and *eo* can represent short or long sounds, equivalent in length to the short and long vowels. Beyond this generally agreed fact, there is controversy about what sound these digraphs represent. Here we present the most widely accepted view.

> *eo* represents [eo] or [eʊ], a diphthong that started with [e] and glided to a rounded sound, [o] or [ʊ]. Examples: *ċeorl* 'freeman' (Modern English *churl*), *dēop* 'deep'.
>
> *ea* represents [æɑ], a diphthong that started with [æ] and glided to [ɑ] (as in *father*). *Feallan* 'fall', *rēad* 'red'.

Some grammar books say that the spelling *ie* also represents a diphthong, but this book interprets it as a simple vowel.

Perhaps the most common error students make when trying to pronounce Old English diphthongs is to break them into two syllables – for example, to pronounce *Bēowulf* as a three-syllable word when in fact it has only two syllables. Remember that there is a *smooth* transition between the two vowels of a diphthong, and this is as true of the unfamiliar diphthongs of Old English as it is of the familiar ones of Modern English (like those of *site* and *sound*).

## 2.1.2   Consonants

Most Old English consonants are pronounced as in Modern English, and most of the differences from Modern English are straightforward:

1   Old English scribes wrote the letters *þ* ('thorn') and *ð* ('eth') interchangeably to represent [θ] and [ð], the sounds spelled *th* in Modern English. Examples: *þing* 'thing', *brōðor* 'brother'.

2   There are no silent consonants. Old English *cniht* (which comes to Modern English as *knight*) actually begins with [k]. Similarly *hlāf* (Modern English *loaf*) and *hring* (*ring*) begin with [h], *gnæt* (*gnat*) with [g], and *wrīðan* (*writhe*) with [w]. Some Old English consonant combinations may be difficult to pronounce because they are not in Modern English. If you find this to be so, just do your best.

3   The consonants spelled *f*, *s* and *þ/ð* are pronounced as voiced [v], [z] and [ð] (as in *then*) when they fall between vowels or other voiced sounds.

---

[2]   A digraph *io* appears primarily in early texts, and for the student's purposes is best taken as a variant of *eo*.

For example, the *f* of *heofon* 'heaven', *hæfde* 'had' and *wulfas* 'wolves' is voiced. So are the *s* of *čēosan* 'choose' and the *ð* of *feðer* 'feather'. This distinction remains not only in such Modern English singular/plural pairs as *wolf/wolves*, but also in such pairs as noun *bath* and verb *bathe*, noun *cloth* and derivative *clothes*.

4    These same consonants were pronounced as unvoiced [f], [s] and [θ] (as in *thin*) when they came at the beginning or end of a word or adjacent to at least one unvoiced sound. So *f* is unvoiced in *ful* 'full', *cræft* 'craft' and *wulf* 'wolf'. Similarly *s* is unvoiced in *settan* 'set', *frost* 'frost' and *wulfas* 'wolves', and *þ/ð* is unvoiced in *þæt* 'that' and *strengð* 'strength'.

5    When written double, consonants must be pronounced double, or held longer. We pronounce consonants long in Modern English phrases like 'big gun' and 'hat trick', though never within words. In Old English, *wile* 'he will' must be distinguished from *wille* 'I will', and *freme* 'do' (imperative) from *fremme* 'I do'.

6    This book sometimes prints *c* with a dot (*ċ*) and sometimes without. Undotted *c* is pronounced [k]; dotted *ċ* is pronounced [ʧ], like the *ch* in Modern English *chin*. This letter is never pronounced [s] in Old English. It has a special function in the combination *sc* (see item 10 below).

7    The letter *g*, like *c*, is sometimes printed with a dot and sometimes without. Dotless *g* is pronounced [g], as in *good*, when it comes at the beginning of a word or syllable. Between voiced sounds dotless *g* is pronounced [ɣ], a voiced velar spirant.[3] This sound became [w] in Middle English, so English no longer has it. Dotted *ġ* is usually pronounced [j], as in Modern English *yes*, but when it follows an *n* it is pronounced [ʤ], as in Modern English *angel*.

8    The combination *cg* is pronounced [ʤ], like the *dge* of Modern English *sedge*. Examples: *hrycg* 'ridge, back', *brycg* 'bridge', *ecg* 'edge'.

9    Old English *h* is pronounced [h], as in Modern English, at the beginnings of syllables, but elsewhere it is pronounced approximately like German *ch* in *Nacht* or *ich* – that is, as a velar [x] or palatal [ç] unvoiced spirant (pronounced with the tongue against the velum [soft palate] or, after front vowels, against the hard palate). Examples: *nēah* 'near', *niht* 'night', *þēah* 'though', *dweorh* 'dwarf'.

10   The combination *sc* is usually pronounced [ʃ], like Modern English *sh*: *scip* 'ship', *æsc* 'ash (wood)', *wȳscan* 'wish'. But within a word, if *sc* occurs before a back vowel (*a, o, u*), or if it occurs after a back vowel at the end of a word, it is pronounced [sk]: *ascian* 'ask' (where *sc* was formerly followed by a back vowel), *tūsc* 'tusk'. When *sc* was pronounced [sk] it sometimes

---

[3]   Practise making this sound: raise the back of your tongue to the velum (the soft palate) as you do when pronouncing a *k*. Instead of a stop, though, pronounce a spirant, somewhat like the *ch* of German *Nacht*, but *voiced*. If you are sure you cannot pronounce the [ɣ], pronounce it [w] instead.

underwent metathesis (the sounds got reversed to [ks]) and was written *x*: *axian* for *ascian*, *tux* for *tusc*. Sometimes *sc* is pronounced [ʃ] in one form of a word and [sk] or [ks] in another: *fisc* 'fish', *fiscas/fixas* 'fishes'.

### 2.1.3 Sermonette

When students of Old English go wrong in translating, it is often because they have done a sloppy job of looking up words in a dictionary or glossary. Remember, when you look up words, that vowel length is significant, and so is the doubling of consonants. *Biddan* 'ask, pray' and *bīdan* 'await, experience' are completely different words, but some students mess up their translations because they look at them as equivalent. Don't fall into this trap!

On a related point, you will notice as you go along that the spelling of Old English is somewhat variable. Scribes at that time lacked our modern obsession with consistency. Rather than insisting that a word always be spelled the same way, they applied a set of rules for rendering the sounds of their language in writing, and these rules sometimes allowed them to get the job done in more than one way. Further, scribes sometimes mixed up the dialects of Old English, writing (for example) Mercian *þēostru* 'darkness' instead of West Saxon *þīestru*. These minor inconsistencies sometimes lead students to believe that *anything goes* in Old English spelling, and this belief leads them into error.

It is not true that anything goes in Old English spelling. Though you will have to get used to frequent variations, such as *ie/i/y* and *iung* for *ġeong* 'young', you *won't* often see confusion of *æ* and *ea*, or indeed of most vowels, or of single and double consonants, or of one consonant with another. For a list of spelling variants that you *will* frequently see, consult Appendix A.

Get into the habit of recognizing the distinctions that are important in Old English and doing an accurate job of looking up words, and you will avoid a lot of frustration.

## 2.2 More about vowels

### 2.2.1 Short a, æ and ea

The short sounds spelled *a*, *æ* and *ea* are all derived from the same vowel (spelled *a* in most other Germanic languages). The split of one vowel into two vowels and a diphthong, which occurred before the period of our written texts, was conditioned by the sounds that surrounded it in the word (the details are complex and controversial: see Lass [73], pp. 41–53). The effects of this split were not long-lasting; by the Middle English period *a*, *æ* and *ea* had coalesced into one vowel, spelled *a*.

The reason it is important for you to know about the relationship of *a*, *æ* and *ea* is that these sounds vary within paradigms. If *æ* or *ea* occurs in a short syllable (see §2.4) and a back vowel (*a, o, u*) follows, the *æ* or *ea* becomes *a*. Add the plural ending -*as* to *dæġ* 'day' and you get *dagas*; add plural -*u* to *ġeat* 'gate' and you get *gatu*.

### 2.2.2  I-*mutation*

*I*-mutation[4] is a shift in the quality of a vowel so that it is pronounced with the tongue higher and farther forward than usual – closer to its position when you pronounce the vowel [i] (as in *feet*). The correspondences between normal and mutated vowels are shown in table 2.1. Notice that the *i*-mutation of *a* produces a different result depending on whether a nasal consonant (*m* or *n*) follows.

**Table 2.1**    *i*-mutation

| *short* | | *long* | |
|---|---|---|---|
| *unmutated* | *mutated* | *unmutated* | *mutated* |
| a    *becomes*    æ | | ā    *becomes*    ǣ | |
| an/am | en/em | | |
| æ | e | | |
| e | i | | |
| ea | ie (i, y) | ēa | īe (ī, ȳ) |
| eo | ie (i, y) | ēo | īe (ī, ȳ) |
| o | e | ō | ē |
| u | y | ū | ȳ |

**ⓘ** *I*-mutation arose in prehistoric Old English when [i] or [j] followed in the next syllable. It is a subspecies of a common type of sound change called 'vowel harmony', in which one of a pair of neighbouring vowels becomes more like the other.

The vowels *ǣ*, *ē* and (long and short) *ĭ* are not subject to *i*-mutation.

The *ĭe* that arose by *i*-mutation of *ĕa* and *ĕo* occurs mainly in early West Saxon texts; *i* and *y* occur in later texts (see §2.1.1).

The results of *i*-mutation are sometimes different in dialects other than West Saxon. In these dialects, the *i*-mutation of *ĕa* was normally *ĕ*, and *i*-mutation did not affect *ĕo*; in Kentish, the *i*-mutation of *ŭ* was *ĕ*. You will sometimes meet with these spellings in West Saxon texts (see Appendix A).

---

[4]  German linguists call it *Umlaut*. Because of the great influence of German linguistics at the time when the historical evolution of the Germanic languages was being worked out, you will occasionally see this term even in grammars written in English.

The effects of *i*-mutation are still evident in Modern English. The vowels of such plurals as *men* (singular *man*), *lice* (*louse*) and *teeth* (*tooth*) exhibit *i*-mutation, as does the comparative adjective *elder* (*old*); and *i*-mutation accounts for most of the verbs that both change their vowels and add a past-tense ending (e.g. *sell/sold*, *buy/bought*, in which the present has *i*-mutation but the past does not).

All of these categories of Modern English words exhibiting *i*-mutation were already present in Old English. *I*-mutation also appears in some forms of certain nouns of relationship, some comparative adverbs, and many verb forms.[5] Examples: the nominative plural of *mann* 'man' is *menn*; the nominative plural of *lūs* 'louse' is *lȳs*; the comparative of *eald* 'old' is *ieldra*; the comparative of the adverb *feor* 'far' is *fier*; the third-person singular of the strong verb *ċēosan* 'choose' is *ċīest*.

ℹ️ Some Modern English words which we still perceive as being derived from other words have mutated vowels: for example, *length* from *long*, *feed* from *food*, *heal* from *whole*. These words and many more were present in Old English: *lengðu* from *lang*, *fēdan* from *fōda*, *hǣlan* from *hāl*.

### 2.2.3  Silent e; o *for* u

When *ċ*, *ġ* or *sc* (pronounced [ʃ]) occurs before a back vowel, it is sometimes followed by an *e*, which probably should not be pronounced, but merely indicates that the *ċ* should be pronounced [ʧ], the *ġ* [j] or [ʤ], and the *sc* [ʃ]. For example, you will see *sēċean* 'seek' as well as *sēċan*, *ġeþinġea* 'of agreements' as well as *ġeþinġa*, and *sceolon* 'must' (plural) as well as *sculon*.

Notice that *sceolon* has *o* in the first syllable while *sculon* has *u*. These two spellings do not indicate different pronunciations; rather, the Old English spelling system appears (for unknown reasons) to have prohibited the letter-sequence *eu*, and scribes sometimes wrote *eo* instead to avoid it. Other words that are spelled with *o* but pronounced [u] are *ġeō* 'formerly', *ġeong* 'young', *ġeoguð* 'youth' and *Ġeōl* 'Yule'. For these you may also encounter the spellings *iū*, *iung*, *iuguð*, *Ġiūl* and *Iūl*.

## 2.3  More about c and g

The dots that we print over *c* and *g* are not in the manuscripts that preserve the Old English language for us; rather, modern scholars have supplied them.

---

[5]  For the effects of *i*-mutation in these paradigms, see §§6.1.3, 6.3.2, 7.1.1, 7.3.2, 7.4, 8.4 and 10.2.1.

Further, the relationship between Old English pronunciation and Modern English outcome is not always straightforward, as you can see from Modern English *seek*, which comes from Old English *sēċan*. So what are the rules for the pronunciation of Old English *c* and *g*? We print dots over *c* and *g* when they come in these environments:

- Before the front vowels *i* and *ie* and the diphthongs *ea* and *eo*.
- Before *y* in late West Saxon, but only in words where it was spelled *ie* in early West Saxon.
- At the end of a syllable, we print *ġ* following any front vowel (*æ*, *e*, *i*), unless a back vowel (*a*, *o*, *u*) immediately follows. The same is true of *ċ*, but only after *i*.
- In a few words where *g* is not descended from an older [g] or [ɣ], as is usually the case, but rather from [j]: *ġeāra* 'of yore', *ġeoc* 'yoke', *ġeoguð* 'youth', *Ġeōl* 'Yule', *ġeōmor* 'unhappy', *ġeong* 'young'; internally, in *smēaġan* 'ponder', *frēoġan* 'set free' and a few other words.

Otherwise, we generally print plain *c* and *g*.

*C* was pronounced [k] in *camb* 'comb', *cǣġ* 'key', *cēne* 'keen, brave', *bacan* 'bake', *bōc* 'book'. It was pronounced [tʃ] in *ċeaf* 'chaff', *ċīdan* 'chide', *ċierran* (late West Saxon *ċyrran*) 'turn', *iċ* 'I'.

*G* was pronounced [g] in *gōd* 'good', *glæd* 'glad'. It was pronounced [ɣ] (the voiced velar spirant) in *dagas* 'days', *sorga* 'sorrows', *sīgan* 'descend'. It was pronounced [j] in *ġiestrandæġ* 'yesterday', *sleġen* 'slain', *mæġ* 'may', *seġl* 'sail' (noun), *seġlode* 'sailed'. It was pronounced [dʒ] in *enġel* 'angel', *senġe* 'I singe'.

As soon as you start to read Old English texts you will notice that these rules apply well enough at the beginnings of syllables, but don't always seem to work elsewhere. For example, the *c* in *sēċan* 'seek' has a dot even though it comes before a back vowel, and the *c* in *macian* 'make' lacks a dot even though it comes before a front vowel. Such anomalies arise from the fact that the changes that produced the sounds spelled *ċ* and *ġ* took place long before the time of our written texts, and the sounds that produced those changes often disappeared later as a result of the simplification of unaccented syllables that is characteristic of Old English (see §1.3.3).[6] This fact is inconvenient for students of Old English, for it means that you cannot be certain how to pronounce some words unless you know their prehistory.

Often it is enough to know about the grammar of a word to decide how to pronounce it. In class 1 weak verbs (§7.3), the root syllable had formerly been followed by [i], which either disappeared or came to be spelled *e*, or [j], which

---

[6] We can tell what these sounds were because they are often preserved unchanged in related languages. For example, in Old Saxon the word that appears in Old English as *sēċan* is *sōkian*, and in Gothic it is *sokjan* – the sound that produced *i*-mutation and changed [sk] to [tʃ] is still present in those languages.

usually disappeared; so *c* and *g* should generally be dotted at the ends of those syllables. Examples: *senġan* 'singe', *senċan* 'cause to sink', *sēċan* 'seek', *īeċan* 'increase', *bīeġan* 'bend'. In class 2 weak verbs, the root syllable had formerly been followed by a back vowel, even though that vowel often disappeared; so *c* and *g* at the ends of those root syllables should not be dotted. Examples: *macian* 'make', *bōgian* 'dwell', *swīgian* 'fall silent'.

When the vowel of any syllable has undergone *i*-mutation (§2.2.2), that is a sign that [i] or [j] once followed, and so *c* or *g* at the end of such a syllable should be dotted. Athematic nouns like *man/men*, which change their vowels (§6.1.3), do so as a result of *i*-mutation; so the plural of *bōc* 'book' is *bēċ*, and the plural of *burg* 'stronghold' is *byrġ*.

## 2.4   Syllable length

The *length* of a syllable (sometimes called its weight) is important in both Old English grammar and metre. A long syllable has a long vowel or diphthong or ends with at least one consonant. These one-syllable words are long: *sǣ* 'sea', *fæt* 'container', *blind* 'blind', *dǣd* 'deed', *hēng* 'hung'. A short syllable must have a short vowel or diphthong and must not end with a consonant. The demonstrative pronoun *se* (§5.1.3) is a short syllable.

When a single consonant falls between two syllables, it belongs to the second. Add an ending to *fæt* 'container', for example *fæte*, and the -*t*- no longer belongs to the first syllable, but rather to the second: *fæ-te*, in which the first syllable is now short rather than long. Add an ending to *dǣd* 'deed' (*dǣ-de*), and the first syllable is still long because it contains a long vowel.

Two short syllables may count as one long one, so a two-syllable word like *reċed* 'hall' behaves like a word with one long syllable. But when a two-syllable word begins with a long syllable – for example, *hēafod* 'head' – the second syllable counts as short, even if a consonant ends it. If you ponder this long enough, it may start to make some sense.

## 2.5   Accentuation

All Old English words are accented on the first syllable, except that words beginning with the prefix *ġe-* are accented on the second syllable, and verbs beginning with prefixes are accented on the next syllable after the prefix. It may seem odd, but it is a fact that nouns and adjectives with prefixes (except *ġe-*) are accented on the prefixes. The verb *forwéorðan* 'perish' is accented on the second syllable; a noun derived from it, *fórwyrd* 'destruction', is accented on the prefix.

Words borrowed from Latin are accented on the first syllable, despite Latin rules of accentuation. So *paradīsus* 'paradise' is accented on the first syllable (*páradısus*) instead of on the penultimate (*paradísus*), as in Latin.

## 2.6    On-line pronunciation practice

You will find pronunciation exercises at www.engl.virginia.edu/OE. Audio also accompanies the *Old English Aerobics* text 'The Fall of Adam and Eve'.

## 2.7    Summary

The table below presents the Old English pronunciation rules in summary form. Make a copy of it and keep it by your side as you practise reading aloud.

| Spelling | Pronunciation |
| --- | --- |
| *a* | [ɑ] as in Modern English *father* |
| *æ* | [æ] as in Modern English *cat* |
| *e* | [e] as in Modern English *fate* |
| *ea* | [æɑ] a diphthong, starting with [æ] and ending with [ɑ] |
| *eo* | [eo] or [eʊ] a diphthong, starting with [e] and ending with [o] or [u] |
| *i* | [i] as in Modern English *feet* |
| *ie* | [ɪ] as in Modern English *sit* |
| *o* | [o] as in Modern English *boat* |
| *u* | [u] as in Modern English *fool* |
| *y* | [y] as in German *über* or *Füße*, French *tu* or *dur* |
| *c* | [k] as in Modern English *cow* |
| *ċ* | [tʃ] as in Modern English *chew* |
| *cg* | [dʒ] like the *dge* in Modern English *edge* |
| *f* | [f] as in Modern English *fox*; between voiced sounds [v] |
| *g* | [g] as in Modern English *good*; between voiced sounds [ɣ], a voiced velar spirant |
| *ġ* | [j] as in Modern English *yes*; after *n* [dʒ] as in *angel* |
| *h* | within words or finally, [x] or [ç] like German *ch* |
| *s* | [s] as in Modern English *sin*; between voiced sounds [z] |
| *sc* | [ʃ] usually as in Modern English *show*; occasionally [sk] |
| *þ/ð* | [θ] as in Modern English *thin*; between voiced sounds, [ð] as in *then* |

# Chapter 3

# Basic Grammar: A Review

The remaining chapters of this book will often employ grammatical terminology. If you are not familiar with (or need to be reminded about) such terms as the names of the parts of speech and the elements of the sentence, or such concepts as the phrase and the clause, read this chapter.

## 3.1 Parts of speech

Traditional grammar defines eight parts of speech for English: nouns, pronouns, verbs, adjectives, adverbs, prepositions, conjunctions and interjections. Grammars often define these categories according to the meanings of the words they contain: a noun names a thing, a verb describes an action, and so forth. A better way to define a part of speech is by its morphology – the way its form can change (in English most commonly by adding an ending) or by its syntax – the rules that govern its relationship to other words in the sentence (in English, frequently, its position relative to other words). Words often slip out of the part of speech to which we assign them by their meaning, as when King Lear says:

when the thunder *would not peace* at my bidding.

The traditional grammarian shudders when anyone but Shakespeare makes a noun into a verb, as when a computer technician '*accesses* his hard drive'. But

if we think of the part of speech as defined by the word's grammatical characteristics rather than its meaning, we see that both Shakespeare and the computer technician are quite correct: *peace* is a verb when it comes in a periphrastic
verb construction, and *access* is a verb when it has a verb ending.

Words can move from one part of speech to another in Old English as they
can in Modern English: often the same word can function as a conjunction
or an adverb, for example, or as a pronoun or an adjective. In addition, Old
English, like Modern English, has rules for altering a word's part of speech.
In this section, and in the rest of this book, we will keep in mind that the 'part
of speech' is a grammatical and not a semantic category; but we will allude
to the more traditional way of defining parts of speech when it is helpful to
do so.

### 3.1.1   Nouns

A noun is the name of a person, place or thing. The 'thing' need not be
concrete: for example, it can be a thought, an activity or a principle.

The noun may be *inflected* (endings supplied or its form altered) to mark
its number (singular or plural) or case (in Modern English, subjective/
objective or possessive – but there are more cases in Old English).

### 3.1.2   Pronouns

According to the classic definition, a pronoun is a word used in place of a
noun. However, a pronoun can also work like an adjective, modifying the
meaning of a noun rather than replacing it. While the more familiar kind of
adjective may modify or limit the meaning of a noun in a novel way, creating,
just possibly, a concept that has never been spoken of before ('a transcend-
ental cow', 'a nuclear teapot'), the pronominal adjective modifies the sense of
the noun by narrowing its reference in a very limited and stereotyped way:
'*this* cow' (the one here with me), '*each* teapot' (all of them, but considered
one by one). As the 'classic' pronoun and the pronominal adjective generally
have the same form, this book treats them as equivalent.

Pronouns are of seven types: personal, demonstrative, interrogative, indefinite, relative, reflexive and reciprocal. Here is a rundown of these types:

**Personal.** The personal pronouns (Modern English *I, you, she, he, it,*
etc.) refer to specific objects and are inflected for person – the first
person referring to the speaker, the second person to someone or
something the speaker is addressing, and the third person to any other
person or thing.

**Demonstrative.** These pronouns point out specific things (Modern English *this*, *that*). The Modern English definite article *the* is in origin a demonstrative pronoun, and Old English used a demonstrative where we now use the definite article.

**Interrogative.** Interrogative pronouns introduce questions, either direct (e.g. '*Who* are you?') or indirect (e.g. 'He asked *who* you were').

**Indefinite.** This is a relatively large group of pronouns that indicate that we are speaking about one or more members of some category of things but do not specify exactly which. Modern English examples are *all*, *any*, *anyone*, *each*, *few*, *many*, *none*, *one* and *something*.

**Relative.** A relative pronoun introduces an adjective clause (also called a relative clause). In Modern English the most common relatives are *that* and *who*.

**Reflexive.** A reflexive pronoun is used as a direct object, indirect object, or object of a preposition to refer to the same thing as the subject. Examples:

> Direct object: The cat grooms *himself*.
> Indirect object: The president gave *himself* a raise.
> Object of a preposition: Look within *yourself*.

**Reciprocal.** These pronouns refer individually to the things that make up a plural antecedent and indicate that each of those things is in the position of object of the other as subject. That sounds complicated, and it is; but the idea is well known to speakers of Modern English, who use the phrases *each other* and *one another* to express it.

When a pronoun has an antecedent (a noun it refers back to), it agrees with that antecedent in gender and number. This rule holds in both Old and Modern English, though not without exception (see further §§11.3, 11.5).

### 3.1.3  Verbs

A verb usually describes an action (*they run*, *he jumps*, *we think*) or a state of being (*we lack*, *insects abound*, *I am*). In both Modern and Old English, verbs can be marked for person, number, tense and mood, and some forms can be used as nouns and adjectives.

There are several ways to divide up the paradigm (the list of inflectional forms) for any verb; the following scheme seems likely to be useful to students of Old English.

**Infinitive.** In both Old and Modern English, the infinitive is the form that dictionaries use as the headword for verb entries. In Modern English it is the same as the present form, sometimes preceded by *to* ('ride', 'to ride'), but in Old English it has its own endings that distinguish it from the present forms. It is in origin a noun built on the verbal root. In Modern English we can still see the noun-like quality of the infinitive in constructions where it functions as a subject, object or complement:

> *To marry* is better than *to burn.*
> Louis loves *to run.*
> The best course is usually *to ignore* insults.

These usages are also present in Old English. And both Old and Modern English use the infinitive to complete the sense of an auxiliary verb:

> We must *go.*
> He ought *to stay.*
> You may *do* as you like.

**Finite verb.** This verb form makes a statement about a subject: the subject *is* something, or *does* something:

> Larry *has* brains.
> Larry *is* a fool.
> Larry *thinks* clearly.

The finite verb can be inflected for person (first, second, third), number (singular, plural), tense (past, present, and in Modern English future) and mood (indicative, subjunctive, imperative). The other verb forms cannot be so marked.

The finite clause – the most common type – must contain a finite verb. In general, finding and understanding the finite verb is the key to decoding complex clauses and sentences in Old English, and so it is essential that you get familiar with the finite verb paradigms.

In Modern English, finite verbs are inflected for tense, but only minimally for person, number and mood: only the third person present singular is so inflected.[1] The Old English finite verb has only two tenses, past and present, but it is much more fully inflected than in Modern English for person, number and mood.

---

[1]   The Modern English verb *to be* differs from most others in distinguishing all three persons: *I am, you are, he is.* The modal auxiliaries, on the other hand, do not distinguish person at all: *I may, you may, she may.*

**Present participle.** This is an adjective-like verb form that generally expresses ongoing, repeated or habitual action. It is sometimes used as an adjective, sometimes as a noun and sometimes as part of a periphrastic[2] verb:

> the *flowing* water
> *bowling* is fun
> the Lord was *speaking*

**Past participle.** This verb form is so called because of the resemblance between it and the past-tense form of the verb. It is descended from an Indo-European verbal adjective.

In Old English and all the Germanic languages, the past participle retained its adjectival function; indeed, it is still easy to think of Modern English examples, e.g. 'I'll have a *boiled* egg'. The past participle is also used to form a periphrastic passive:

> The king was *slain.*
> Mistakes were *made.*

It may also be used to make periphrastic perfect and pluperfect forms (indicating that the action they describe has been completed), though in Old English there are other ways to do so as well:

> We have *begun* this work
> When God had *made* all things

These usages all arise from the perfective sense of the past participle: it expresses the state that is consequent upon an action having been completed.

Infinitives, past participles and present participles are collectively called *verbals*. They have in common that they are often used with auxiliaries (as you have seen) to make periphrastic constructions in which the auxiliary expresses person, number, tense and mood while the verbal conveys lexical information.

### 3.1.4   Adjectives

An adjective modifies or limits the meaning of a noun. If I speak of 'a car', I could be referring to any car in the world. But if I speak of 'a *green* car', I have modified the meaning of 'car' and limited the set of objects to which I am referring.

---

[2]   A periphrastic verb form is one that requires more than one word, such as 'to be' or 'have seen'.

In Indo-European languages generally, the adjective is inflected to agree with the grammatical characteristics (gender, case and number) of the noun it is modifying. In Modern English we have almost entirely stopped inflecting our adjectives: the only endings that remain are *-er* to make a comparative and *-est* to make a superlative. But in Old English the adjective has different endings depending on the gender, case and number of the noun it is modifying.

## 3.1.5   Adverbs

Adverbs are traditionally defined as words that modify adjectives, verbs and other adverbs. Adverbs like *finally*, *wonderfully* and *very* are easy to understand in both Old and Modern English. Conjunctive adverbs (also called transitional adverbs), which provide logical transitions between clauses, can be a little trickier. Examples of conjunctive adverbs in Modern English are *however*, *nevertheless*, *therefore*, *then* and *thus*. These are related to conjunctions in meaning and function, and in consequence are often confused with them by both speakers of Modern English and students of Old English.

## 3.1.6   Prepositions

A preposition introduces a prepositional phrase – that is, a word-group that functions (usually) as an adverb or adjective and consists of a preposition together with a noun, noun phrase or pronoun (the 'object of the preposition'). In such phrases, the preposition defines the relationship between the sentence-element the phrase is modifying and the object of the preposition.

In a sentence like this one

Fishes swim *in the water.*

the prepositional phrase 'in the water' acts as an adverb modifying 'swim'. The preposition 'in' tells us that the phrase has to do with space and, more precisely, location relative to 'the water'. Other prepositions work similarly, modifying nouns and verbs by defining the relationships between them and other things.

## 3.1.7   Conjunctions

Conjunctions are usually defined as words that link sentence elements. This definition can be a little misleading, since conjunctions often come at the beginnings of sentences where they do not appear to link anything.

*Coordinating conjunctions* join together words and clauses that are grammatically parallel. Modern English examples are *and, or* and *but*. *Subordinating conjunctions* introduce subordinate clauses: they are 'linking words' in the sense that they signal the relationship between the subordinate and the principal clause. Modern English examples are *when, where, although* and *as*. *Correlative conjunctions* come in pairs, for example, *either . . . or, both . . . and*.

### 3.1.8   Interjections

An interjection is an exclamation, usually expressing emotion or surprise or establishing a rhetorical level. Modern English examples are *Oh!* and *Gosh!* A justly famous interjection in Old English is *Hwæt*, which begins many poems (including *Beowulf*); it is sometimes interpreted as a call for attention and sometimes as a signal that what follows is in an elevated style.

## 3.2   Phrases

The function of a word in a sentence may be performed by a *phrase*, a group of words that forms a cohesive unit but lacks a subject and verb. The most important kinds of phrase to know about are these:

**Noun phrases** consist of a noun or pronoun with modifiers, including pronouns, adjectives, other phrases and clauses:

> *The archbishop of York* sent to the king.
> *He who laughs last* laughs best.
> So much depends upon *a red wheelbarrow*.

**Participial phrases** include present participles or past participles. They are called 'participial phrases' when they function as adjectives and 'gerund phrases' when they function as nouns, but there is no difference in form.

> It is a tale *told by an idiot*.
> *Giving alms* may help you get to heaven.

**Prepositional phrases** consist of prepositions and their objects. They function as adjectives or adverbs:

> Variety is the spice *of life*.
> We live *in Scottsville*.
> Never judge a book *by its cover*.

A phrase can contain any number of words and can also contain clauses and other phrases, which can in turn contain other clauses and phrases.

## 3.3   Clauses

A clause is a group of words that contains a subject and a finite verb. It is rather like a sentence in this respect, and in fact a simple declarative sentence (such as 'I like ice cream') is nothing more than an independent clause standing by itself – it is indeed the defining characteristic of an independent clause that it can stand by itself.

But a sentence of any complexity also contains one or more *subordinate clauses*. A subordinate clause is a sentence-like group of words (containing a subject and a verb) that functions as a word in another grammatical structure – in a sentence, clause or phrase. Subordinate clauses are classified according to the kinds of words they can stand in for: nouns, adjectives and adverbs.

**Noun clauses** in Modern English begin with such words as *that, which, what* and *whoever*. A noun clause may function as the subject or object of a verb, as a complement, or as the object of a preposition; in fact, a noun clause can come pretty much anywhere a noun can come. Examples:

You said *that you would be here today.*
*What you thought you saw* was an illusion.
*Whoever wins* will be a wealthy man.

**Adverb clauses** are extremely various and very common. They answer such questions as 'when?', 'where?', 'why?' and 'with what intention?' The types of adverb clauses that you should know about (with some – not all – of the Modern English conjunctions that introduce them) are conditional (*if*), concessive (*although*), temporal (*when, before, after*), causal (*because*), place (*where*), purpose (*in order that, so that*), result (*so that*) and comparison (*as*). A few examples:

*When it rains,* it pours.
We will be sorry *if you leave.*
*As I write* I keep looking for casualties.
I live *where the sun rises.*

**Adjective clauses** modify nouns or pronouns. The most common type is the 'relative clause', which commonly begins with the relative pronoun *that* or *who* (*whom*).

We do eat from all the trees *that are in paradise.*
Those *who cannot remember the past* are condemned to repeat it.

Adjective clauses can also begin with words such as *where, when* and other conjunctions that begin adverb clauses, which they often closely resemble.

In countries *where associations are free,* secret societies are unknown.
In the days *before there were trains,* people often travelled on horseback.

Like phrases, clauses can contain phrases and other clauses. We call a style that features much subordination *hypotactic;* we call a style that features the concatenation of clauses (either with or without *and*) *paratactic.* Some say that Old English literature generally is characterized by parataxis, but this is not true. Rather, some Old English works (such as the *Anglo-Saxon Chronicle*) tend to be paratactic, while others (such as King Alfred's Preface to his translation of Gregory's *Pastoral Care*) are rather more hypotactic. In poetry it can be difficult to tell independent clauses from subordinate clauses, and for that reason it is a matter of some controversy how paratactic or hypotactic Old English poetry is (see further §15.2.5).

## 3.4   Elements of the sentence or clause

Sentences and clauses are made up of elements such as subjects, verbs and objects. Such an element may be a single word, but a clause or phrase can also function as an element of a sentence or clause.

### 3.4.1   Subject

The subject names what the sentence or clause is about. It may be a noun, pronoun, noun phrase or a list (a compound subject):

Noun: *Warriors* should keep their swords sharp.
Pronoun: *They* won't do you any good if they're dull.
Noun phrase: *My sword* is razor sharp.
Noun phrase: *He who has a good sword* has a good friend.
List: *My sword and my shield* are friends in battle.

In the first sentence the subject is a single noun, and in the second it's a single pronoun. More often than not, though, the subject will be a noun phrase – and noun phrases come in many shapes and sizes. In the third sentence the subject consists of a possessive pronoun and a noun, and in the fourth it consists of a pronoun and a relative clause. The fifth shows a very simple example of a compound subject.

In Old English, as in Modern English, subjects can be simple or complex. Old English differs somewhat from Modern English in that a compound subject can be split. In Old English, a sentence structured like this one

My shield protects me and my sword.

could be interpreted as having a compound subject, 'my shield and my sword'. But in Modern English, 'and my sword' must be taken as part of a compound object, 'me and my sword'. Old English also differs from Modern English in that it often omits the subject when the context makes it obvious what it is.

### 3.4.2   Verb

The verb is both a part of speech and an essential element of the sentence. Grammarians classify Modern English verbs as *transitive*, *intransitive* or *linking*. We will use the first two of those terms, but we'll call the 'linking verb' a *copula*.

**A transitive verb** has a direct object (§3.4.3). For example, the verbs in these sentences are transitive:

In this year the Viking army *broke* the peace.
Sigebryht *slew* the nobleman who had stood by him longest.

In the first sentence, the object is 'the peace'; in the second it is a noun phrase consisting of an article with noun ('the nobleman') and an adjective clause modifying the noun ('who . . .').

**An intransitive verb** does not have a direct object, though it may be followed by an adverbial element (an adverb, a phrase or an adverb clause). Some examples:

In this year archbishop Wulfstan *died*.
This Cynewulf *reigned* for thirty-one years.

In the second sentence the verb is followed by an adverbial element (a prepositional phrase), but this is not a direct object.

**A copula** links the subject of a sentence to a *complement* (also called a predicate noun or predicate adjective), which characterizes the subject in some way. The verbs in these sentences are copulas:

Hrothgar *was* a good king.
They *were* the first ships of Danish men who sought the land of the English.

The copula is usually a form of the verb *to be*; the complement can be a noun, pronoun, adjective or noun phrase. In the first sentence the complement is a short noun phrase, 'a good king'; in the second sentence the complement is a long noun phrase containing several dependent elements.

In both Old and Modern English the verb may consist of an auxiliary ('helping') verb and an infinitive (e.g. 'may contribute', 'must pay') or, to make the passive, a form of the verb *to be* and a past participle (e.g. 'was arrested'). And of course these two constructions can be combined (e.g. 'must be excused').

### 3.4.3   Object

The 'direct object' is usually defined as the noun, pronoun or noun phrase that directly receives the action of a verb. Such definitions are usually followed by examples like these:

Rob painted *the house.*
Let us break *bread* together.

Here the verbs are 'action verbs', and the direct objects ('the house', 'bread') are actually affected by the actions that the verbs specify.

But it is always dangerous to bind grammatical concepts too closely to the logical relationships expressed by language. Here is another example of a direct object:

Newton pondered *the nature of the universe.*

Few persons would claim that Newton affected 'the nature of the universe' by pondering it; the direct object in this sentence does not 'receive the action of the verb' in anything like the sense in which 'the house' and 'bread' received the actions of the verbs 'painted' and 'break'. Further, the sentence about Newton might easily be rewritten thus, with little change of sense:

Newton thought deeply about the nature of the universe.

Here the verb 'thought' is followed by a prepositional phrase, 'about the nature of the universe' – not a direct object. And yet it says the same thing about Newton that the other sentence says.

What all our examples of direct objects have in common is their *grammatical* relationships to their verbs: in Modern English, the direct object usually follows the verb and never has a preposition in front of it.

In Old English, the direct object *may* follow the verb, but may also precede it (especially when the object is a pronoun). It is generally in the accusative case, though some verbs have their direct objects (or what we translate as direct objects) in the dative or genitive case.

An 'indirect object' is a thing that has some indirect relationship to the action of a verb. Such relationships are extremely various: one may, for example, benefit from or be disadvantaged by some action, witness some action, or be the destination of some movement. Examples:

Papa's going to buy *you* a mockingbird.
Let me tell *you* a story.

### 3.4.4 *Complement*

The complement was defined above in §3.4.2; here we will expand on that definition a little. The complement restates the subject of a sentence or clause, characterizing it in some way, for example describing or renaming. It usually follows the verb *to be*, but it may follow other verbs as well:

Æthelflæd was *the ruler of the Mercians.*
Beowulf was *brave.*
Greek is considered *a difficult language.*
This plant is called *cinquefoil.*

Notice that the complement may be a noun, pronoun, adjective or noun phrase.

### 3.4.5 *Predicate*

The *predicate* is the finite verb together with the direct object or complement, any other elements (such as indirect objects) that are governed by the verb, and any elements (such as adverbs or prepositional phrases) that modify the verb. In short, it includes everything in the clause except the subject. Predicates may be compound – they may contain more than one verb:

Suzy *grabbed her bag, threw a kiss to her mother, and ran out the door.*

# Chapter 4

# Case

## 4.1   What is case?

Case is the inflection of nouns, pronouns and adjectives to signal their functions in sentences and clauses. Those who have studied Latin or German
know the concept of case well, for it is important in those languages.

In Modern English, however, case has nearly disappeared. Adjectives have
no case endings at all. Nouns are generally inflected for case only when singular,
and then only by adding 's to form the possessive.[1] In these sentences, the
difference in form between the two italicized words is one of case:

> The *king* is in the hall.
> The *king's* bodyguard is in the tavern.

We make more case distinctions with pronouns than we do with nouns. We
use one form for subjects:

> *We* will learn this language.
> *She* sold lemon platt.

We use another form for direct objects, indirect objects and objects of
prepositions:

---

[1]   The plural possessive, *s'*, is for the most part merely a graphical convention, though we do
occasionally make an *audible* possessive plural by adding 's to an anomalous plural form like *men*.

They beat *us* at bridge.
Don't lie to *me*.
Reader, I married *him*.

And we use still another form for possessives:

*Our* swords are better than *your* swords.
*My* mother warned me about *their* wiles.

Modern English distinctions such as *king/king's*, *I/me/my*, *he/him/his* and *we/us/our* have descended to us directly from Old English, though over the centuries the number of distinct case forms, and even the number of cases, has declined. Modern English pronouns have at most three cases, which grammarians call *subjective*, *objective* and *possessive*. Old English, on the other hand, has five: *nominative*, *accusative*, *genitive*, *dative* and *instrumental*.

ⓘ  The Modern English subjective case is descended from the Old English nominative, and the Modern English possessive is from the Old English genitive. The Modern English objective has taken over the functions of the Old English accusative, dative and instrumental; it has distinct forms only in pronouns, and these forms are from the Old English dative.

## 4.2   Uses of the cases

Case, as mentioned above, tells us something about the function of a noun, adjective or pronoun in a sentence or clause. You will find that quite often you must recognize the case of a word before you can decide whether it is a subject, object or something else, just as you may have to recognize the distinction between *king* and *king's* to understand a Modern English sentence.

But it is worth pointing out as well that you will not always be able to recognize the case of a word by its ending. For example, the nominative singular form of the Old English word for 'name' is *nama*, but the other singular forms are all *naman*, and the nominative and accusative plural forms are also *naman*. That there are five cases in Old English and that any noun can be either singular or plural might lead you to expect ten distinct forms of every noun. But there are only *four* distinct forms of the word *nama* 'name', and no Old English noun has more than *six* distinct forms.

Obviously, Old English must have had some feature other than case to help speakers and listeners decide what a noun, adjective or pronoun was doing in a sentence. In Modern English, word-order tells us most of what we need to know. In the sentence 'Rover bit Fido', we understand that the subject of the sentence is *Rover*, the verb is *bit*, and the object is *Fido* because the standard word-order in a declarative English sentence is Subject–Verb–Object. There are more permissible word-orders in Old English than in Modern English, but Old English word-order is not at all 'free', as some sources may tell you. In fact there are just a few common word-orders. If you learn what to expect, you will find that word-order is a help in Old English, just as it is in Modern English.

Word-order will be discussed more fully in chapter 12. The point we are making here is that case is only one of the signals, along with word-order and your feeling for what makes sense in a particular context, that tell you how a word is functioning in a sentence.

Before we throw a lot of case forms at you (in the next chapter), we will discuss the functions of each case.

### 4.2.1   Nominative

The nominative case has few functions, and since there are few complications in its use, it is very easy to understand.

> **Subject.** The subject of any sentence or clause will be in the nominative case.
> **Complement.** The complement (the word on the other side of a copula or 'linking verb', usually 'to be') is always in the nominative. In this sentence:
>
>> Sēo sunne is swīðe *brād*
>> [The sun is very *broad*]
>
> both *sunne* (the subject) and *brād* (the complement) are in the nominative case.
> **Direct address.** When the speaker addresses someone directly, the name or title by which he calls the person he is speaking to is nominative. In this sentence
>
>> Ġeseoh þū, *cyning*, hwelċ þēos lār sīe
>> [See, *king*, what kind of teaching this is]
>
> *cyning* 'king' is nominative.

### 4.2.2   Accusative

Direct objects of transitive verbs are usually in the accusative case. Thus in this sentence:

His āgen swustor bebyrġde his *līċ*
[His own sister buried his *corpse*]

*līċ* 'corpse' is accusative. Objects of certain prepositions are sometimes or always accusative, and the accusative can be used adverbially in certain expressions of time.

In Old English the accusative has partly fallen together with the nominative. For example, nominative and accusative are never distinguished in the plural or in any neuter noun, pronoun or adjective, and they have also fallen together in the singular of strong masculine nouns.

## 4.2.3  Genitive

To put it very broadly indeed, the genitive modifies or limits a word (usually a noun) by associating it with something. For example, in the phrase *þæs cyninges* sweord 'the king's sword', the sense of *sweord* is modified by our saying that it belongs to the king: we're not speaking of just any sword. In this respect, a word in the genitive case is like an adjective, limiting the reference of the word it is associated with.

Most genitives fall into one of three categories:

**Possessive.** This is the ancestor of the Modern English 'possessive case'. It does not always indicate actual possession, but often some other kind of association. For example, **sanctes Ēadmundes** *mæssedæġ* 'the feast *of St Edmund*' does not mean that the day actually belongs to St Edmund, but rather that he is venerated on that day.

**Partitive.** The partitive genitive represents the whole collection of things to which a particular thing or subset of things belongs, for example, *ǣlċ* **þāra manna** 'each of *the men*', **ealra cyninga** *betst* 'best *of all kings*'. As the translations with 'of' suggest, Modern English has a roughly similar construction made with the preposition *of*; but Old English used the partitive genitive much more extensively than we use this partitive construction, for example, *maniġ* **manna** 'many *men*', *twelf* **mīla** *lang* 'twelve *miles* long'. Expect to find the partitive genitive used with any word that expresses number, quantity or partition.

**Descriptive.** This genitive attributes a quality to a thing, for example,

þæt lamb sceal bēon *hwītes hīwes*
[the lamb must be *of a white colour*]

Here the translation with *of* echoes the genitive construction and shows that similar constructions are still possible in Modern English, but it is now more idiomatic to say 'white in colour'.

A few prepositions sometimes have objects in the genitive case (see §10.5), and some verbs have genitive direct objects. Genitive constructions may also be used adverbially, especially in expressions of time (see §10.2).

### 4.2.4   Dative

In all of the Germanic languages the dative case is an amalgam of several older cases that have fallen together: dative, locative, ablative and instrumental. Old English retains traces of the instrumental case (see §4.2.5), but for the most part that too has fallen together with the dative.

In view of its diverse origins, it should be no surprise that the dative case has a variety of functions. Of these, the easiest for the speaker of Modern English to understand is that of object of a preposition. The objects of certain prepositions (*æfter, æt, be, fram, mid, of, tō*) are usually or always in the dative case. With other prepositions the case may be either dative or accusative, depending on the writer's dialect or the meaning of the preposition.

But the dative can be used without prepositions, and then the modern reader must be aware of its possible meanings:

> **Interest.** Here the dative signifies that one is in some way interested in the outcome of an action. This category includes the 'indirect object':
>
>> Ġif *him* his sweord
>> [Give *him* his sword]
>
> But the dative of interest also covers situations in which something has been taken away:
>
>> Benam hē *him* his bisceopscīre
>> [He took his bishopric away *from him*]
>
> **Direct object.** Some verbs have their direct objects in the dative case. It is not always easy to tell the difference between a direct and an indirect object: for example, should we translate **him** *hīerde* as 'obeyed him' or 'was obedient to him'? But in this matter it is sufficient for the student to be guided by modern usage and leave the technical aspects to the linguists.
>
> **Possession.** The dative often indicates possession, for example:
>
>> *Him* wæs ġeōmor sefa
>> [*Theirs* was a sad mind (i.e. Their minds were sad)]

Often the dative of possession may also be interpreted as a dative of interest.

**Comparison.** The dative may express likeness or equality:

and ġē bēoð þonne *englum* gelīċe
[and you will then be like *the angels*]

The dative that expresses unlikeness is rare enough that beginners probably should not worry about it.

**Instrument, means, manner.** These senses of the dative overlap, and so are grouped together here. In Modern English we generally express them with prepositions like 'with' and 'by', for example, 'Ecgferth struck Æthelbryht with his sword'; 'He was wounded by a spear'; 'We sing the mass with joy'. In Old English, too, instrument, means and manner can be expressed with prepositions, especially *mid* and *fram*. But they are very commonly expressed by the dative alone, for example:

for þan iċ hine *sweorde* swebban nelle[2]
[therefore I will not kill him *with a sword*]

þū scealt *yfelum dēaðe* sweltan
[you must die *by a wretched death*]

This usage is especially common in poetry (see §15.2.2). To express the instrument, Old English may use the instrumental case (which exists only in the masculine and neuter singular), but it may equally well use the dative.

When translating the dative, it is often necessary to supply a preposition, because in Modern English prepositions very commonly express what used to be expressed by the dative alone.

## 4.2.5 Instrumental

The instrumental case was disappearing during the centuries when Old English was being written. It has a distinct form only in masculine and neuter singular adjectives and pronouns; everywhere else the dative is used.

**Instrument, means, manner.** These uses occur mainly in early texts, for example:

---

[2] *Beowulf*, l. 679.

hē forðon *fǣ̇gre ǣnde* his lif betȳnde
[he therefore concluded his life *with a beautiful end*]

**Accompaniment.** This usage is not common, but it does occur in the *Chronicle* entry for 755, which students often read:

Ond þā ġeascode hē þone cyning *lȳtle werode*
[And then he learned of the king (being) *with a little force*]

**Expressions of time.** Such expressions are largely formulaic, for example, *ǣlċe dǣ̇ge* 'each day', *þȳ ilcan ġēare* 'in the same year'. They occur frequently in both early and late texts.

# Chapter 5

# Pronouns

## 5.1 Quick start

Before you read any farther, download the 'Magic Sheet' (a one-page summary of Old English inflections, http://www.engl.virginia.edu/OE/courses/handouts/ magic.html) and print it out on the best colour printer you can find. Keep this sheet by your side as you read Old English.

The pronouns[1] you will meet with most often are the personal pronouns (with the closely related possessive adjectives) and the demonstratives.

### 5.1.1 Personal pronouns

You will find the personal pronouns easy to learn because of their resemblance in both form and usage to those of Modern English. The first-person pronouns (table 5.1) are quite similar to those of Modern English, especially in prose, where you will generally see accusative singular *mē* rather than *mec*.

The second-person pronouns, on the other hand, have changed radically since the Old English period (table 5.2). Modern English does not distinguish number or any case but the possessive; in fact there are now only two forms of the pronoun, *you* and *your*. By contrast, the second-person pronouns of Old English look a lot like the first-person pronouns, distinguishing number

---

[1] For a general discussion of pronouns, see §3.1.2.

**Table 5.1**   First-person pronouns

|            | *singular*      | *plural*       |
|------------|-----------------|----------------|
| nominative | iċ 'I'          | wē 'we'        |
| accusative | mē, mec 'me'    | ūs 'us'        |
| genitive   | mīn 'my'        | ūre 'our'      |
| dative     | mē 'me'         | ūs 'us'        |

and at least three of the cases. Old English does not use the second-person singular as a 'familiar' form, the way Middle English, French and German do: *þū* is simply singular. Like *mec*, accusative singular *þec* is mainly poetic.

**Table 5.2**   Second-person pronouns

|            | *singular*      | *plural*        |
|------------|-----------------|-----------------|
| nominative | þū 'you'        | ġē 'you'        |
| accusative | þē, þec 'you'   | ēow 'you'       |
| genitive   | þīn 'your'      | ēower 'your'    |
| dative     | þē 'you'        | ēow 'you'       |

The third-person pronouns, unlike the first- and second-person pronouns, are inflected for gender, but only in the singular (table 5.3).

**Table 5.3**   Third-person singular pronouns

|            | *masculine*   | *neuter*    | *feminine*   | *plural*       |
|------------|---------------|-------------|--------------|----------------|
| nominative | hē 'he'       | hit 'it'    | hēo 'she'    | hīe 'they'     |
| accusative | hine 'him'    | hit 'it'    | hīe 'her'    | hīe 'them'     |
| genitive   | his 'his'     | his 'its'   | hire 'her'   | hira 'their'   |
| dative     | him 'him'     | him 'it'    | hire 'her'   | him 'them'     |

> **!**   Notice that several singular forms are repeated in table 5.3. As you study the pronouns, nouns and adjectives, you will find that forms repeat themselves in the same pattern:
>
> • Neuter nominative and accusative singular forms are the same
> • Neuter and masculine genitive singular forms are the same

- Neuter and masculine dative singular forms are the same
- Feminine genitive and dative singular forms are the same

If you learn these patterns you will save yourself some of the labour of memorizing paradigms.

The third-person plural pronouns may cause some difficulty at first, because they don't start with *th-* the way their Modern English counterparts do. Also confusing is that dative plural *him* is exactly the same as the masculine/neuter dative singular pronoun. You will need to take extra care in memorizing these plural pronouns.

## 5.1.2   Possessive adjectives

Possessive adjectives are the pronoun-like forms we use with nouns to signal possession:

*my* sword
the sword is *mine*
*your* shield
the shield is *yours*
*her* spear
the spear is *hers*

These are closely related to the genitive personal pronouns, but we call them adjectives because they modify nouns. In Old English the third-person genitive pronouns are used as possessive adjectives:

*his* hring [*his* ring]
*hire* healsbēag [*her* necklace]
*hira* fatu [*their* cups]

These work like Modern English possessives in that they agree in gender and number with their antecedents, not with the nouns they modify. To make first- and second-person possessive adjectives, strong adjective endings (§8.2) are added to the genitive pronoun forms; these agree with the nouns they modify, not with their antecedents:

*mīnum* scipe [*my* ship (dative)]
*þīnne* wæġn [*your* wagon (accusative)]
*ēowru* hors [*your* horses (nominative plural)]

### 5.1.3   *Demonstrative pronouns*

There are two demonstrative pronouns, *se/þæt/sēo* (table 5.4) and *þes/þis/þēos* (table 5.5). The first does the job of Modern English *that/those* and also that of the definite article *the*. The second does the same job as Modern English *this/these*. As with the third-person pronouns, gender is distinguished only in the singular.

**Table 5.4**   Demonstrative pronoun 'the', 'that', 'those'

|  | *masculine* | *neuter* | *feminine* | *plural* |
| --- | --- | --- | --- | --- |
| nominative | se | þæt | sēo | þā |
| accusative | þone | þæt | þā | þā |
| genitive | þæs | þæs | þǣre | þāra, þǣra |
| dative | þām | þām | þǣre | þām |
| instrumental | þȳ, þon | þȳ, þon |  |  |

**Table 5.5**   Demonstrative pronoun 'this', 'these'

|  | *masculine* | *neuter* | *feminine* | *plural* |
| --- | --- | --- | --- | --- |
| nominative | þes | þis | þēos | þās |
| accusative | þisne | þis | þās | þās |
| genitive | þisses | þisses | þisse, þisre | þisra |
| dative | þissum | þissum | þisse, þisre | þissum |
| instrumental | þȳs | þȳs |  |  |

Modern English *that* comes from the neuter nominative/accusative form. Notice that the same patterns occur here as in the third-person pronouns: neuter nominative and accusative forms are the same, masculine and neuter forms are the same in the genitive and dative cases, and feminine genitive and dative forms are the same.

The instrumental case is distinguished only in the masculine and neuter singular; elsewhere you will see the dative instead.

## 5.2   More about personal and demonstrative pronouns

### 5.2.1   *The dual number*

The first- and second-person pronouns have dual as well as singular and plural forms (table 5.6). Dual pronouns are used to refer to two things:

'we two', 'you two'. Use of the dual is optional: the plural will do just as well. It is used to emphasize that two persons or things are being discussed, as in Riddle 85:

Ġif wit unc ġedǣlað,    mē bið dēað witod
[If the two of us part from each other, death is ordained for me]

There is no dual verb form; dual pronouns agree with plural verbs.

**Table 5.6**    Dual pronouns

|  | *first person* | *second person* |
| --- | --- | --- |
| nominative | wit 'we two' | ġit 'you two' |
| accusative | unc 'us two' | inc 'you two' |
| genitive | uncer 'of us two' | incer 'of you two' |
| dative | unc 'us two' | inc 'you two' |

*5.2.2    Common spelling variants*

Personal and demonstrative pronouns receive relatively little stress in most sentences, and as a result they may be pronounced somewhat indistinctly. Long vowels are frequently shortened (though this book always marks them with their etymologically correct lengths), and *i*, *ie* and *y* are frequently confused. Thus you will see not only *hine* (for example), but also *hyne* and *hiene*, and not only *hīe*, but also *hī* and *hȳ*. For *hīe* you will also see occasional *hiġ* and *hēo*. For *him* you will see not only *hym*, but also, in the plural, *heom*.

In *þām*, *ǣ* varies with *ā*. In late Old English you will also see *þane* for *þone*. You may expect to see occasional *y* or *eo* for *i* in forms of *þes* (e.g. *þysne*, *þeossa*), and also occasional variation between -*s*- and -*ss*-.

## 5.3    Interrogative pronouns

There are three common interrogative pronouns: *hwā* (table 5.7), the ancestor of Modern English *who/what*; *hwelċ/hwilċ/hwylċ*, which gives Modern English *which*; and *hwæþer* 'which of two'. *Hwā* has only a singular form; there is no distinction between masculine and feminine. The instrumental form is the ancestor of Modern English *why*, and is used to mean 'why'.

### Minitext A. Psalm I

King Alfred reportedly translated the first fifty psalms into Old English; this version of Psalm I may be his. For the rest of this prose translation, see O'Neill [91].

[1] Ēadiġ bi se wer þe ne gǣ on ġeþeaht unrihtwīsra,[a] ne on þām weġe ne stent synfulra, ne on heora wōlbǣrendum[b] setle ne sitt; [2] ac his willa bi on Godes ǣ, and ymb his ǣ hē bi smēaġende dæġes and nihtes. [3] Him bi swā þām trēowe[c] þe bi āplantod nēah wǣtera rynum, þæt sel his wæstmas tō rihtre tīde, and his lēaf and his bladu ne fealwia ne ne sēaria;[d] eall him cym tō gōde þæt þæt hē dē. [4] Ac þā unrihtwīsan ne bēo nā swelċe, ne him ēac swā ne limp;[e] ac hīe bēo dūste ġelīcran, þonne hit wind tōblǣw. [5] Þ ne ārīsa þā unrihtwīsan on dōmes dæġ, ne þā synfullan ne bēo on ġeþeahte þǣra rihtwīsena; [6] for þām God wāt hwelċne weġ þā rihtwīsan ġeearnedon, ac þā unrihtwīsan cuma tō wītum.

[a]  unrihtwīsra: of the unrighteous.

[b]  *Wōlbærendum* translates *pestilentiae* 'destructive', the reading of most Anglo-Saxon psalters; the reading of the 'Hebrew' version, *derisorum* 'of the scornful ones', is closer to that of most modern translations.

[c]  It is for him as (it is) for the tree.

[d]  The translator here adds a note: *swā bý þām men þe wē ǣr ymb sprǣcon* 'so it is for the man whom we spoke of before'.

[e]  *ne him ēac swā ne limp*: nor does it happen to them thus.

**Table 5.7**  Interrogative pronoun

|              | *masculine and feminine* | *neuter*        |
| ------------ | ------------------------ | --------------- |
| nominative   | hwā 'who'                | hwæt 'what'     |
| accusative   | hwone, hwæne             | hwæt            |
| genitive     | hwæs                     | hwæs            |
| dative       | hwām, hwǣm               | hwām, hwǣm      |
| instrumental | hwȳ, hwon                | hwȳ, hwon       |

The other two interrogative pronouns mentioned above are inflected as strong adjectives (§8.2).

## 5.4  Indefinite pronouns

The interrogative pronouns can also be used as indefinite pronouns: you must judge which is intended from the context. The addition of the prefix ġe- to these pronouns alters the meaning somewhat:

*hwā* 'anyone'               *ġehwā* 'each, everyone, someone'
*hwelċ* 'any, anyone'       *ġehwelċ* 'each'
*hwæþer* 'either, both'     *ġehwæþer* 'both'

These pronouns can also be modified by placing them in the phrases *swā hwā swā* 'whoever', *swā hwēlċ swā, swā hwæþer swā* 'whichever'. Yet another indefinite pronoun may be made by prefixing *nāt-*, a negative form of the verb 'to know': *nāthwelċ* 'someone or other', 'something or other' (literally 'I don't know who', 'I don't know which'). Here are a few examples:

wite *ġehwā* þæt þā yfelan ġeþōhtas ne magon ūs derian
[let *everyone* know that those evil thoughts may not harm us]

Swā *hwylċe* swā ne woldon hlāfordas habban
[*Whoever* did not wish to have lords]

þāra banena byre *nāthwylċes*[2]
[the son *of one or another* of those killers]

Other indefinite pronouns are inflected like adjectives.


## 5.5   Relative pronouns

There are several ways to make a relative pronoun. One is simply with the indeclinable particle *þe*:

Þā bēoð ēadiġe *þe* ġehȳrað Godes word
[They are blessed *who* obey God's word]

Another is to use a form of the demonstrative *se* with *þe*:

Hē lifode mid þām Gode *þām þe* hē ǣr þēowode
[He lived with that God *whom* he earlier had served]

A third way is to use a form of the demonstrative pronoun alone, without *þe*:

Danai þǣre ēa, *sēo* is irnende of norþdæle
[the river Don, *which* flows from the north]

---

[2]   *Beowulf,* l. 2053.

When a demonstrative is used, its case and number will usually be appropriate to the following adjective clause. That is the case with both of the examples above, since *þēowian* takes the dative and nominative *sēo* is the subject of the clause that it introduces. Sometimes, though, the demonstrative will agree with the word that the adjective clause modifies:

> Uton wē hine ēac biddan þæt hē ūs ġescylde wið grimnysse *myssenlicra yfela and wīta þāra þe* hē on middanġeard sendeð for manna synnum.
> [Let us also entreat him that he shield us from the severity *of various evils and punishments that* he sends to the earth because of men's sins.]

The relative pronoun *þāra þe* agrees with the genitive plural noun phrase *myssenlicra yfela and wīta*, which lies outside the adjective clause (*þāra þe . . . synnum*).

## 5.6   Reflexive pronouns

The personal pronoun can be used by itself as a reflexive, and *self/sylf* can be added for emphasis. Examples:

> Iċ ondrēd *mē*
> [I was afraid]
>
> Iċ ðā sōna eft *mē selfum* andwyrde
> [I then immediately afterwards answered *myself*]

Old English sometimes uses a reflexive pronoun where it would make no sense to use one in Modern English: when this happens the translator may simply ignore it.

## 5.7   Reciprocal pronouns

There are several ways to express what Modern English usually expresses with the phrase *each other*. One may simply use a plural personal pronoun where we say *each other*, optionally adding *self* to the pronoun for emphasis. Or one can use a construction such as *ǣġðer . . . ōðer* or *ǣġhwylċ . . . ōðer* 'each . . . other'. An example of each style:[3]

---

[3]    From *Beowulf*, l. 2592, and *The Battle of Maldon*, l. 133.

þæt ðā āglæcan    *hȳ* eft ġemētton
[that the contenders met *each other* again]

*ǣ́ġðer* hyra *ōðrum*    yfeles hogode
[*each* of them intended harm *to the other*]

In the first sentence you must rely on context to tell you that the pronoun is reciprocal.

# Chapter 6

# Nouns

## 6.1 Quick start

In Modern English almost all nouns[1] are declined[2] in pretty much the same way: we add -s to make plurals and -'s to make possessives. There are notable exceptions, however. The plural of *ox* is not *oxes*, but *oxen*, and the plural of *child* has the same ending, but preceded by -r-. And of course several very common nouns make plurals by changing their vowels: for example, *tooth/ teeth* and *mouse/mice*.

Our nouns with -s plurals, nouns with -en plurals, the noun with -r-, and the nouns that change their vowels belong to different *declensions* – classes of nouns that are declined in similar ways. Though we have just one major declension in Modern English and a few minor ones, in Old English there were several major declensions and several more minor ones. You must learn the forms for each of the major declensions, and you should acquire enough knowledge of the minor ones to enable you to be on the lookout for them.

In Modern English we do not think of nouns as having gender; rather, the things they refer to have gender (or they do not, in which case they are 'neuter'). But gender is an attribute of every Old English noun, and the *grammatical gender* of a noun does not necessarily correspond to the *natural*

---

[1]  For a general discussion of nouns, see §3.1.1.
[2]  To decline a noun is to list all of its possible forms.

*gender* of the thing it refers to. For example, *wīf* 'woman' is neuter and *wīfman* 'woman' is masculine; and nouns that refer to inanimate objects are very often masculine or feminine (for example, masculine *stān* 'stone', feminine *benċ* 'bench'). Further, different endings are added to nouns of different gender (for example, the nominative plural of masculine *wer* 'man' is *weras*, of neuter *scip* 'ship' *scipu*, and of feminine *cwēn* 'queen' *cwēna*).

---

**!** You can make the job of learning the nouns easier by looking for patterns within the paradigms. Take particular note of these:

- Neuter and masculine genitive singular forms are the same within each major declension
- All dative singular forms are the same within each major declension
- All genitive plural forms end in *-a*
- All dative plural forms end in *-um*

You should also look for resemblances between the noun and pronoun paradigms. The more patterns and resemblances you find, the less you'll have to memorize.

---

Most nouns fall into one of two major declensions, conventionally called 'strong' and 'weak'. There are also several minor declensions; we'll look at one of these (the 'athematic' nouns) in the Quick Start section and save the others for later.

### 6.1.1  Strong nouns

Table 6.1 shows the basic endings of the strong nouns. Notice how much duplication there is in this table. Often one cannot tell the gender of a noun from its ending: strong masculines and neuters differ only in the nominative/ accusative plural, and gender is never distinguished in the dative singular or in the genitive and dative plural. Further, one cannot always tell the case: nominative and accusative singular are not distinguished in masculine and neuter nouns, accusative, genitive and dative singular are not distinguished in feminine nouns, and nominative and accusative plural are never distinguished at all.

Table 6.2 adds these endings to several common masculine and neuter nouns. It also shows that the neuter nominative/accusative plural ending *-u* appears only after short syllables (see §2.4); neuters with long syllables have no ending.

**Table 6.1** Strong noun endings

|          |                     | *masculine* | *neuter* | *feminine* |
|----------|---------------------|-------------|----------|------------|
| singular | nominative          | –           | –        | -u/–       |
|          | accusative          | –           | –        | -e         |
|          | genitive            | -es         | -es      | -e         |
|          | dative              | -e          | -e       | -e         |
| plural   | nominative/accusative | -as       | -u/–     | -a         |
|          | genitive            | -a          | -a       | -a         |
|          | dative              | -um         | -um      | -um        |

**Table 6.2** Strong masculines and neuters

|          |                       | *masculine* | *short neuter* | *long neuter* |
|----------|-----------------------|-------------|----------------|---------------|
| singular | nominative/accusative | stān 'stone' | scip 'ship'   | þing 'thing'  |
|          | genitive              | stānes      | scipes         | þinges        |
|          | dative                | stāne       | scipe          | þinge         |
| plural   | nominative/accusative | stānas      | scipu          | þing          |
|          | genitive              | stāna       | scipa          | þinga         |
|          | dative                | stānum      | scipum         | þingum        |

**!** An endingless plural may seem a great inconvenience at first – how will you be able to tell a plural when you see it? In practice, you'll find that one of three things will be true when you come across an endingless neuter: (1) a nearby pronoun will tell you what you need to know (*þæt þing* singular, *þā þing* plural); (2) the context will make clear whether the noun is singular or plural; or (3) it won't matter. If you stay alert to the likelihood that some plural nouns will lack endings, you won't get into trouble.

Although the nominative and accusative are always the same for strong masculines and neuters, you may often find the case of a masculine singular noun by looking at the pronoun in front of it (if there is one): *se stān* or *þes stān* is nominative, while *þone stān* or *þisne stān* is accusative. Since the nominative and accusative are the same for *all* neuter words – nouns, pronouns and adjectives – you must rely on context to tell whether a neuter is nominative or accusative.

The nominative/accusative singular of masculine and neuter nouns often ends in -e: *ende* 'end', *wine* 'friend', *spere* 'spear', etc. These forms look the same as the dative singular; do not be confused by the resemblance.

Feminine nouns (table 6.3) look much less familiar than masculines or even neuters. The feminines do not have the masculine/neuter genitive -es or the masculine plural -as, which give us the dominant Modern English noun endings, and so the strong feminine declension seems to be furnished with none of the comforts of home. The good news, on the other hand, is that the strong feminines have relatively few endings, so you have less to memorize.

**Table 6.3**    Strong feminines

|          |                      | short stem | long stem     |
|----------|----------------------|------------|---------------|
| singular | nominative           | ġiefu 'gift' | sorg 'sorrow' |
|          | accusative           | ġiefe      | sorge         |
|          | genitive/dative      | ġiefe      | sorge         |
| plural   | nominative/accusative | ġiefa      | sorga         |
|          | genitive             | ġiefa      | sorga         |
|          | dative               | ġiefum     | sorgum        |

Like the strong neuters, the strong feminines come in short and long varieties. The ending -u appears in the nominative singular after short syllables, but is dropped after long ones. Sometimes, however, the ending gets restored, for example, in *lenġu* 'length', *iermðu* beside *iermð* 'misery', and *brǣdu* beside *brǣd* 'breadth'.

Among the strong feminine nouns are a great many that represent abstract concepts, made from adjectives and other nouns. These include nouns ending in -þ such as *strengþ* 'strength' and *hǣlþ* 'health', those ending in -ness such as *clǣnness* 'cleanness' and *ġīferness* 'greed', and those ending in -ung such as *leornung* 'learning' and *ġeōmrung* 'groaning'.

## 6.1.2    Weak nouns

Table 6.4 shows the endings of the weak declension, ancestor of the Modern English nouns with anomalous plural -en. These nouns make even fewer distinctions of gender and case than the strong nouns do: the rule that neuter words do not distinguish between nominative and accusative (mentioned in §5.1.1) accounts for its having accusative singular -e where the masculine and feminine have -an;[3] otherwise, the only difference among the genders is that

---

[3]    Weak neuters are actually quite rare: only *ēage* 'eye' and *ēare* 'ear' are attested.

**Table 6.4**  Weak noun endings

|          |                       | *masculine* | *neuter* | *feminine* |
|----------|-----------------------|-------------|----------|------------|
| singular | nominative            | -a          | -e       | -e         |
|          | accusative            | -an         | -e       | -an        |
|          | genitive              | -an         | -an      | -an        |
|          | dative                | -an         | -an      | -an        |
| plural   | nominative/accusative | -an         | -an      | -an        |
|          | genitive              | -ena        | -ena     | -ena       |
|          | dative                | -um         | -um      | -um        |

**Table 6.5**  Weak nouns

|          |                       | *masculine*    | *neuter*      | *feminine*        |
|----------|-----------------------|----------------|---------------|-------------------|
| singular | nominative            | nama 'name'    | ēage 'eye'    | tunge 'tongue'    |
|          | accusative            | naman          | ēage          | tungan            |
|          | genitive              | naman          | ēagan         | tungan            |
|          | dative                | naman          | ēagan         | tungan            |
| plural   | nominative/accusative | naman          | ēagan         | tungan            |
|          | genitive              | namena         | ēagena        | tungena           |
|          | dative                | namum          | ēagum         | tungum            |

the masculine nominative singular ends in -a while the neuter and feminine end in -e. Most case endings are simply -an. Table 6.5 adds these endings to three common nouns.

> **!**  The fact that most forms end in -an can cause problems for the student who expects to be able to find out the case and number of a noun from its inflection. When in doubt about a weak noun ending in -an, look first for a pronoun or adjective that agrees with it. The noun in þæs guman can only be genitive singular, and the phrase should thus be translated 'the man's'; in godfyrhte guman, the strong nominative/accusative plural adjective tells us that the phrase must be translated 'God-fearing men'.
>
> But what about a noun that lacks modifiers, as in the phrase eorðan bearnum?[4] A noun that, like eorðan, comes just before another noun

[4]  *Cædmon's Hymn*, l. 5.

has a good chance of being a genitive, and in fact this phrase should be translated 'the children of earth'. But ultimately the context will help you decide. If you haven't yet found the subject of the clause you're reading and the verb is plural, consider the possibility that the noun in -*an* is a plural subject:

þæs ne wēndon ǣr   witan Scyldinga[5]
[the wise men of the Scyldings had not expected that]

Similarly, if the verb wants an object, consider that as a possibility. In short, find out what's missing in the clause and try the noun in that function. Don't lose heart: remember that writers of Old English, when they wanted to be understood, did not write clauses containing unresolvable ambiguities. After you've puzzled out a few difficult instances of weak nouns, you should start to get the hang of them.

### 6.1.3   Athematic nouns

The athematic nouns[6] are those that sometimes have *i*-mutation (§2.2.2) of the root vowel instead of an ending; they are the ancestors of Modern English nouns like *man/men* and *tooth/teeth* (see table 6.6).

**Table 6.6**   Athematic nouns

|          |                      | *masculine* | *short feminine* | *long feminine* |
|----------|----------------------|-------------|------------------|-----------------|
| singular | nominative/ accusative | mann 'man'  | hnutu 'nut'      | bōc 'book'      |
|          | genitive             | mannes      | hnyte            | bēċ             |
|          | dative               | menn        | hnyte            | bēċ             |
| plural   | nominative/ accusative | menn        | hnyte            | bēċ             |
|          | genitive             | manna       | hnuta            | bōca            |
|          | dative               | mannum      | hnutum           | bōcum           |

---

[5]   *Beowulf*, l. 778.
[6]   The inflections of Indo-European nouns were generally added to a 'stem' built from a 'root' syllable and a 'thematic element' (a sort of suffix). The athematic nouns are so called because they are descended from a class of Indo-European nouns that lacked thematic elements.

> ! The distribution of mutated forms differs in Old and Modern English: some mutated forms appear in the singular, while some plurals are unmutated. Also, as you might guess from the presence in the table of *hnutu* and *bōc*, which are no longer athematic, this declension once contained more nouns than it does now. In fact, in the Old English period some of the athematic nouns were already beginning to move into the strong declensions: feminine *āc* 'oak', for example, has for the dative singular both *ǣċ* and strong *āce*.

Several nouns that end in -nd, especially frēond 'friend', fēond 'enemy', are declined like the athematic nouns, though they are not, technically speaking, members of this declension. Several of these have partly or entirely gone over to the strong declension; for example, you are about as likely to encounter the plural *frēondas* as *frīend*.

## 6.2 More about strong nouns

### 6.2.1 Two-syllable nouns

Two-syllable nouns have syncopation (loss of a vowel) in the second syllable when the first syllable is long and an ending follows, as table 6.7 shows. The syncopated vowel often gets restored, so you should not be surprised to see *enġeles* or *hēafodes*.

**Table 6.7**  Two-syllable strong nouns

|  |  | *masculine* | *neuter* | *feminine* |
|---|---|---|---|---|
| singular | nominative/accusative | enġel 'angel' | hēafod 'head' | sāwol 'soul' |
|  | genitive | enġles | hēafdes | sāwle |
|  | dative | enġle | hēafde | sāwle |
| plural | nominative/accusative | enġlas | hēafdu | sāwla |
|  | genitive | enġla | hēafda | sāwla |
|  | dative | enġlum | hēafdum | sāwlum |

**ⓘ** Notice that the nominative/accusative plural of *hēafod* ends in -u even though the first syllable is long. Two-syllable neuters follow the rule in §2.4: if the first syllable is short, the ending -u is dropped; if it is long, the ending remains (syncopation in the second syllable does not affect this rule). Thus you will see the plurals *hēafdu* 'heads' and *reċed* 'halls'. But two-syllable feminines generally lack *-u* in the nominative singular, whatever the length of the first syllable.

### 6.2.2   Nouns with changes in the stem syllable

The consonant that ends a noun may change if an ending follows. A simple example of this kind of change is Modern English *wolf*, plural *wolves*. The same change, from an unvoiced to a voiced spirant ([f] to [v], [s] to [z], [θ] to [ð]), takes place in Old English whenever a voiced sound precedes and an ending follows, though this change is rarely reflected in the spelling (see §2.1.2, item 3).

In addition, as you read in §2.3, *c* alternates with *ċ* and *g* with *ġ* depending on whether the inflectional syllable contains a back vowel, and the *sc* pronounced [ʃ] (like Modern English *sh*) alternates with the *sc* pronounced [sk].

When an ending begins with a back vowel (*a, o, u*), *æ* or *ea* in a short root syllable becomes *a* (§2.2.1). That is why *dæġ* 'day' alternates with *dagas* 'days' and *ġeat* 'gate' with *gatu* 'gates' in table 6.8. The *a* of the plural is sometimes changed back to *æ* or *ea* by analogy with the singular, so you will see *æscas* as well as *ascas* and *hwælas* 'whales' as well as *hwalas*.

Feminines like *sacu* 'strife' should have -*æ*- rather than -*a*- in the root syllable before the ending -*e*: accusative singular *sæce*, etc. Such forms do occur, but one frequently finds -*a*- before -*e* as well.

**Table 6.8**   Masculines and neuters with changed stems

|  |  | *masculine* | *masculine* | *neuter* |
|---|---|---|---|---|
| singular | nominative/accusative | dæġ 'day' | æsc 'ash tree' | ġeat 'gate' |
|  | genitive | dæġes | æsces | ġeates |
|  | dative | dæġe | æsce | ġeate |
| plural | nominative/accusative | dagas | ascas | gatu |
|  | genitive | daga | asca | gata |
|  | dative | dagum | ascum | gatum |

Old English does not permit *h* to fall between voiced sounds; it is always dropped in that environment, and the preceding vowel is lengthened. The loss of *h* produces nouns like those in table 6.9. A vowel at the beginning of an ending is always dropped when no consonant remains after the loss of *h*; so you'll see forms like dative singular *fēo*. We expect the genitive plural to look exactly like the dative singular, but Old English resolves the ambiguity by borrowing the ending -*ena* from the weak declension (§6.1.2).

**Table 6.9**   Masculines ending in *h*

| singular | nominative/accusative | wealh 'foreigner' | feoh 'money' |
|---|---|---|---|
| | genitive | wēales | fēos |
| | dative | wēale | fēo |
| plural | nominative/accusative | wēalas | – |
| | genitive | wēala | fēona |
| | dative | wēalum | – |

## 6.2.3   Nouns with -w- or -ġ- before the ending

Some nouns add *-w-* or *-ġ-* before the ending; but when there is no ending the *w* appears as *-u* or *-o* (lost after a long syllable – see §6.1.1) and the *ġ* as *-e*. These nouns are illustrated in table 6.10. Words like *here* are quite rare, and nouns with *-w-* are usually neuter or feminine. These nouns will cause you little trouble if you remember that the headword form in your glossary or dictionary lacks the *-w-*.

ⓘ   Sometimes what is rather unattractively called a 'parasite vowel' gets inserted before *ġ* or *w*, and we then end up with forms like *heriġas* and *beaduwa*.

**Table 6.10**   Nouns with *-ġ-* and *-w-*

| | | *masculine* | *neuter* | *feminine* |
|---|---|---|---|---|
| singular | nominative | here 'army' | searu 'skill' | beadu 'battle' |
| | accusative | here | searu | beadwe |
| | genitive | herġes | searwes | beadwe |
| | dative | herġe | searwe | beadwe |
| plural | nominative/accusative | herġas | searu | beadwa |
| | genitive | herġa | searwa | beadwa |
| | dative | herġum | searwum | beadwum |

## 6.3    Minor declensions

The minor declensions contain relatively few nouns, but the ones they contain tend to be common. As a declension is disappearing from a language, the nouns it contains move into the major declensions. The last nouns to leave these minor declensions are usually the ones in daily use, like Modern English *man/men*, *tooth/teeth* and *child/children*, for the familiarity of the words keeps their inflections from coming to seem strange. So although the minor declensions contain few nouns, you are likely to encounter most of them in the course of your reading.

### 6.3.1    u-*stem nouns*

This declension contains only masculines and feminines, and they are declined alike. There is, on the other hand, a distinction between short stems and long stems in the nominative singular (see §6.1.1), so table 6.11 illustrates one short stem and one long stem without regard to gender.

**Table 6.11**    *u*-stem nouns

|          |                       | short stem | long stem |
|----------|-----------------------|------------|-----------|
| singular | nominative/accusative | sunu       | hand      |
|          | genitive/dative       | suna       | handa     |
| plural   | nominative/accusative | suna       | handa     |
|          | genitive              | suna       | handa     |
|          | dative                | sunum      | handum    |

Often *u*-stem nouns use a mix of forms, some of them being from the strong declensions. For example, *winter* was originally a *u*-stem, but one frequently sees strong genitive singular *wintres*.

### 6.3.2    Nouns of relationship

The nouns of relationship that end in -*r* belong here: *fæder* 'father', *mōdor* 'mother', *brōðor* 'brother', *sweostor* 'sister', *dohtor* 'daughter'. These have endingless genitive singulars and usually *i*-mutation (§2.2.2) in the dative singular (table 6.12). The feminines here are exceptions to the rule that the genitive and dative singular must always be the same in feminine words.

*Fæder* and *mōdor* have partly gone over to the strong declensions, in that the nominative/accusative plurals are *fæderas* and *mōdra*. *Fæder* and *sweostor* lack mutated vowels in the dative singular.

**Table 6.12**   Nouns of relationship

|  |  | *masculine* | *feminine* |
|---|---|---|---|
| singular | nominative/accusative | brōðor | dohtor |
|  | genitive | brōðor | dohtor |
|  | dative | brēðer | dehter |
| plural | nominative/accusative | brōðor | dohtor |
|  | genitive | brōðra | dohtra |
|  | dative | brōðrum | dohtrum |

### 6.3.3   Nouns with -r- plurals

The *-r-* of Modern English *children* shows that it once belonged to this declension, and in fact we find a plural *ċilderu* or *ċildra* in early West Saxon and similar forms in some other dialects. But in late West Saxon the word *ċild* has gone over to the strong neuters. Several neuter nouns remain in this declension, though, even in late West Saxon (table 6.13). Like *lamb* are *ċealf* 'calf' and *ǣġ* 'egg'. Scattered instances of other words (including *ċild* in early texts) show that this declension was once somewhat larger.

**Table 6.13**   Nouns with *-r-* plurals

|  | *singular* | *plural* |
|---|---|---|
| nominative/accusative | lamb 'lamb' | lambru |
| genitive | lambes | lambra |
| dative | lambe | lambrum |

### 6.3.4   Nouns with -þ- endings

The genitive/dative singular and all plural forms of these nouns contain the element *-þ-*, as you can see in table 6.14, which shows poetic words for 'man, warrior' and 'maiden'. In these nouns the *-þ-* element is in the process of being re-analysed as part of the word's stem rather than as part of the inflectional

**Minitext B. A Miracle of St Benedict**

From Bishop Wærferth of Worcester's Old English translation of the *Dialogues* of Pope Gregory the Great. See Hecht [56], pp. 122–3.

[1] Ēac hit ġelamp sume dæġe þæt þā ġebrōðru timbredon þæs mynstres hūs. [2] And þā læġ þǣr ān stān tōmiddes, þone hīe mynton hebban ūp on þæs hūses timbrunge, ac hine ne mihton twēġen men ne þrīe onstyrian. [3] Þā ēodon þǣr mā manna tō, ac hē swā þēah wunode fæst and unwendedliċ, efne swelċe hē wǣre hæfd be wyrtwalan in þǣre eorðan. [4] And ēac hit openlīċe mihte bēon onġieten þæt se ealda fēond sæt ofer þām stāne, þone ne mihton swā maniġra wera handa onstyrian. [5] Þā for þǣre earfoþnesse wæs sended tō þām Godes were, and þā brōðru bǣdon þæt hē cōme and mid his ġebedum þone fēond onweġ ādrife, þæt hīe mihten þone stān ūp āhebban. [6] Þā sōna swā se Godes wer þider cōm, hē dyde þǣr his ġebed and his bletsunge. [7] And þā wearð se stān mid swā miċelre hrædnesse ūp āhafen, swelċe hē ǣr nǣniġe hefiġnesse on him næfde.

ending; that is why we find -*þ*- in the nominative singular (often for *hæle*, always for *mæġþ*). Other nouns belonging to this declension are *ealu* 'ale' (genitive/dative singular *ealoþ*) and *mōnaþ* 'month', which has entirely gone over to the strong nouns except in the nominative/accusative plural, where we find *mōnaþ* as well as *mōnþas*.

**Table 6.14** Nouns with -*þ*- endings

|          |                     | 'man, warrior' | 'maiden' |
|----------|---------------------|----------------|----------|
| singular | nominative/accusative | hæle, hæleþ   | mæġþ     |
|          | genitive            | hæleþes        | mæġþ     |
|          | dative              | hæleþe         | mæġþ     |
| plural   | nominative/accusative | hæleþ        | mæġþ     |
|          | genitive            | hæleþa         | mæġþa    |
|          | dative              | hæleþum        | mæġþum   |

# Chapter 7

# Verbs

## 7.1   Quick start

Old English verbs[1] can be daunting, for a typical verb appears in more forms than a typical pronoun, noun or adjective. While no noun has more than six distinct forms, most verbs have fourteen. (Modern English verbs, by contrast, normally have four or five forms.) Further, while some nouns, like *mann* 'man', have two different vowels in the root syllable, some verbs have as many as five. (The Modern English maximum, leaving aside the verb *to be*, is three.)

This multiplicity of forms may cause you difficulty when looking up verbs in the dictionary or figuring out their grammatical characteristics. But you can see from the 'Magic Sheet' that, despite its inevitable complications, the Old English verb system is really quite orderly. If you keep that orderliness in view as you work through the 'Quick start' section and the rest of this chapter, you will find the verbs to be much easier than they look.

### 7.1.1   Strong and weak verbs

Table 7.1 shows all the forms of two common verbs. *Fremman*[2] 'do' belongs to the so-called 'weak' class of Old English verbs, those that make the past

---

[1]   For a general discussion of verbs, see §3.1.3.

[2]   By convention, glossaries and dictionaries use the infinitive as the headword for verb entries, and when citing verbs we cite the infinitive.

**Table 7.1**    Basic verb paradigms

|  | *weak* | *strong* |
|---|---|---|
| infinitives | fremman 'do' | helpan 'help' |
|  | tō fremmanne | tō helpanne |
| present indicative | iċ fremme | iċ helpe |
|  | þū fremest | þū hilpst |
|  | hēo fremeþ | hē hilpþ |
|  | wē fremmaþ | wē helpaþ |
| past indicative | iċ fremede | iċ healp |
|  | þū fremedest | þū hulpe |
|  | hēo fremede | hē healp |
|  | ġē fremedon | ġē hulpon |
| present subjunctive | hē fremme | iċ helpe |
|  | hīe fremmen | hīe helpen |
| past subjunctive | iċ fremede | þū hulpe |
|  | wē fremeden | wē hulpen |
| imperative | freme | help |
|  | fremmaþ | helpaþ |
| participles | fremmende | helpende |
|  | fremed | holpen |

tense by adding a dental consonant (-*d*- or -*t*-) as a suffix. The Old English weak verbs correspond roughly to the Modern English 'regular' verbs. *Helpan* 'help' is a 'strong' verb, one that does not add a dental suffix to make its past tense, but rather changes the vowel of its root syllable. The Old English strong verbs correspond to Modern English 'irregular' verbs such as *sing* (past *sang*, past participle *sung*).

Take note of these points about the paradigms for *fremman* and *helpan* (further details will come later in the chapter):

1   There are just two tenses, past and present. Old English has various strategies for referring to future time: it uses auxiliary verbs (including *willan*), explicit references to time (e.g. *tōmorgen* 'tomorrow'), and the simple present, relying on context to express futurity.
2   Similarly, Old English has no settled way of expressing what Modern English expresses with the perfect and pluperfect – that is, that an action is now complete or was complete at some time in the past. It can use forms of the verb *habban* 'to have' with the past participle, as Modern English does (*hæfð onfunden* 'has discovered', *hæfde onfunden* 'had discovered'), it can use the adverb *ǣr* 'before' with the simple past (*ǣr onfand* 'had

**Table 7.2**   Personal endings

| present indicative | singular | | plural |
|---|---|---|---|
| first person | -e | | |
| second person | -st | | -aþ |
| third person | -þ | | |
| *past indicative* | *strong* | *weak* | |
| first person | -e | – | |
| second person | -st | -e | -on |
| third person | -e | – | |
| *all subjunctives* | | | |
| all persons | -e | | -en |

discovered'), or it can use the past tense alone, in which case you must infer the correct translation from the context.

3   While the Modern English verb has only one personal ending (-*s* for the third-person singular), most Old English verb forms have several such endings. These are mostly the same for both weak *fremman* and strong *helpan*, but notice that in the singular past indicative the endings are different. The personal endings are shown separately in table 7.2.

4   Person is distinguished only in the indicative singular, never in the plural or subjunctive. For example, table 7.1 gives the present first-person plural indicative form *wē fremmaþ*, but the second person is *ġē fremmaþ* and the third person *hīe fremmaþ*, with the same verb forms. Further, only the second person is distinguished in the singular past indicative: the first- and third-person forms are the same.

5   The root vowels of strong verbs undergo *i*-mutation (§2.2.2) in the present second- and third-person singular indicative: thus the second-person singular of *helpan* is *hilpst*, that of *faran* 'travel' is *færst*, and that of *ċēosan* 'choose' is *ċīest*. The same does not occur in the weak paradigms or in those of strong verbs whose vowels are not subject to *i*-mutation (e.g. *wrītan* 'write', second-person singular *wrītst*).

6   While a Modern English verb descended from the strong verbs never has more than one vowel in the past tense, most Old English strong verbs have *two* past forms with different vowels, distributed as in table 7.1. The form used for the first- and third-person singular past indicative (e.g. *healp*) is called the 'first past', and the form used everywhere else in the past tense (e.g. *hulpon*) is called the 'second past'.

7   The present participle ending in -*ende* is used where Modern English uses the present participle in -*ing*: in constructions that express continuing action (for example, 'was living') and as adjectives ('the living God').

## 7.1.2   Bēon 'to be'

The verb *bēon* 'to be' in Old English is a mess, but so is 'to be' in Modern English. To the extent that the Old and Modern English verbs look alike, *bēon* will be easy to learn for students who are native speakers of English.

The forms in table 7.3 are an amalgam of three different verbs: one that accounts for the present forms in the first column, one that accounts for all the *b-* forms, and one that accounts for all the *w-* forms. Paradigms derived from these three verbs overlap, so that there are two complete sets of present forms,[3] two sets of imperatives, two infinitives and two present participles.

The *b-* forms are often used with reference to future time, as in this sentence on the Day of Judgement:

On þām dæġe ūs *bi̇ð* ætēowed se opena heofon and enġla þrym.
[On that day *will be* revealed to us the open heaven and the host of angels.]

But the *b-* forms sometimes are simple presents, as here:

Ðēos wyrt þe man betonican nemneð, hēo *biþ* cenned on mædum and on clǣnum dūnlandum.
[This herb that one calls betony *is* produced in meadows and in open hilly lands.]

**Table 7.3**   *bēon*

| infinitives | bēon, wesan | | | |
|---|---|---|---|---|
| present indicative | iċ eom | iċ bēo | past indicative | iċ wæs |
| | þū eart | þū bist | | þū wǣre |
| | hē is | hēo bi̇ð | | hit wæs |
| | hīe sind, sindon | wē bēoð | | ġē wǣron |
| present subjunctive | hē sīe | þū bēo | past subjunctive | iċ wǣre |
| | wē sīen | ġē bēon | | hīe wǣren |
| imperative | bēo, wes | | | |
| | bēoð, wesað | | | |
| participles | bēonde, wesende | | | |
| | ġebēon | | | |

---

[3]   Present forms of the verb *wesan* (*weseð*, *wesað*) are also attested, but they are rare.

You'll have to look to the context to tell you whether to translate a *b-* form of *bēon* as a future.

### 7.1.3  Preterite-present verbs

Some of the Modern English auxiliary verbs (also called 'helping verbs') are descended from a class of Old English verbs called 'preterite-presents'. They are so called because the present tense of these verbs looks like the past tense (what many grammar books call the 'preterite') of the strong verbs. Most of these Modern English preterite-presents come in pairs, one member of which was originally a present tense and the other originally past: *can/could, may/might* and *shall/should*. The original past-tense forms *could, might* and *should* have come to be used mainly as presents with specialized meanings, and two verbs of this class, *must* and *ought*, have lost their original present tenses altogether: their old pasts are now used as presents.

The conjugation of the Old English preterite-present verbs will be laid out in §7.6. For now it is enough to know that many of the Old English preterite-presents look reassuringly like their Modern English descendants: *hē mæġ* 'he may', *hēo sceal* 'she shall, she must', *iċ can* 'I can, I know', *ġē mihton* 'you might, you were able to', *wē scoldon* 'we should, we had to'.

## 7.2  More about endings

### 7.2.1  Assimilation

When the personal ending *-st* or *-þ* or the *-d-* of the weak past immediately follows a consonant, the result may be a sequence of consonants that is difficult to pronounce. In such cases, one or both consonants are altered so that they are more similar to each other, an effect called assimilation:

1   The ending *-d-* becomes *-t-* when it immediately follows an unvoiced consonant. The singular past of *slǣpan* 'sleep' is *slǣpte*, and that of *mētan* 'meet' is *mētte*. The same change occurs in Modern English, though it is not always reflected in the spelling (say *reached* aloud: what is the final consonant?).
2   The ending *-ð* becomes *-t* when it immediately follows *d, s* or *t*. For example, the third-person singular of *rǣdan* 'read' is *rǣtt* (see also item 3), of *rǣsan* 'rush' *rǣst*, and of *grētan* 'greet' *grētt*.
3   When a *d* or *g/ġ* at the end of a root syllable comes in contact with the ending *-st* or *-ð*, it is changed to *t* or *h*: for example, the second-person singular of *fēdan* 'feed' is *fētst*, and the third-person singular of *bīeġan* 'bend' is *bīehð*.

4   Whenever one of these rules has produced a double consonant at the end
of a word, or when the ending -ð follows a root ending in ð, the double
consonant may be simplified. For example, the third-person singular of
čīdan 'chide' can be čītt or čīt, and that of cȳðan 'make known' may be
cȳðð or cȳð. A double consonant will always be simplified when preceded
by another consonant: so the past singular of sendan 'send' is sende, not
*sendde (an asterisk marks a form that does not occur).

### 7.2.2   Plurals ending in -e

Before the pronouns wē 'we' and ġē 'you', any plural ending may appear as
-e. For example:

> Nū bidde wē þē, lēof, þæt ðū ġebidde for hȳ, and hȳ eft āwende tō ðām þe
> hēo ǣr wæs.
> [Now we ask you, sir, that you pray for her, and turn her back into what
> she was before.]

Here the verb in the main clause would be biddaþ if it did not immediately
precede the pronourn wē.

### 7.2.3   Subjunctive plural endings

In Old English of the tenth century you will frequently see subjunctive plural
-on (sometimes -an) as well as -en, and in Old English of the eleventh century
subjunctives in -en are quite rare. Thus an early text will normally have present
subjunctive plural bidden 'ask', but a later one will have biddon. In the past
tense, where the indicative plural personal ending is already -on, the distinction between indicative and subjunctive plural is lost: for biddan 'ask', both
forms are bǣdon in late Old English.

## 7.3   More about weak verbs

Germanic weak verbs fall into three classes: the first two of these are well
represented in Old English and the third has almost disappeared (the few
remaining class 3 verbs are discussed below, §7.3.4). Of the four weak verbs
in table 7.4, sceþþan, herian and hǣlan belong to class 1, and lufian belongs
to class 2.

**Table 7.4**   Weak verbs

| | Class 1 | | | Class 2 |
|---|---|---|---|---|
| | *'injure'* | *'praise'* | *'heal'* | *'love'* |
| infinitives | sceþþan | herian | hǣlan | lufian |
| | tō sceþþanne | tō herianne | tō hǣlanne | tō lufianne |
| present indicative | iċ sceþþe | iċ herie | iċ hǣle | iċ lufie |
| | þū sceþest | þū herest | þū hǣlst | þū lufast |
| | hēo sceþeþ | hē hereþ | hit hǣlþ | hē lufað |
| | wē sceþþaþ | ġē heriaþ | hīe hǣlaþ | wē lufiað |
| past indicative | iċ sceþede | iċ herede | iċ hǣlde | iċ lufode |
| | þū sceþedest | þū heredest | þū hǣldest | þū lufodest |
| | hit sceþede | hē herede | hēo hǣlde | hēo lufode |
| | ġē sceþedon | hīe heredon | wē hǣldon | hīe lufodon |
| present subjunctive | hē sceþþe | iċ herie | þū hǣle | hēo lufie |
| | hīe sceþþen | ġē herien | wē hǣlen | ġē lufien |
| past subjunctive | iċ sceþede | þū herede | hē hǣlde | hēo lufode |
| | hīe sceþeden | wē hereden | ġē hǣlden | ġē lufoden |
| imperative | sceþe | here | hǣl | lufa |
| | sceþþaþ | heriaþ | hǣlaþ | lufiað |
| participles | sceþende | heriende | hǣlende | lufiende |
| | sceþed | hered | hǣled | lufod |

## 7.3.1   Classes 1 and 2

Class 1 is marked by *i*-mutation (§2.2.2) in the root syllable of the present tense, and usually of the past tense as well (see §7.3.2 for the exceptions). If the root syllable is short (§2.4), gemination (the doubling of the consonant at the end of the root syllable) occurs in certain forms, including the infinitive; but if the consonant is *r*, you will find *-ri-* or *-rġ-* instead of *-rr-*. The *-i-* or *-ġ-* represents a consonant [j], so *herian* is a two-syllable word: [her-jɑn].

ⓘ The geminated form of *f* is *bb* (*swebban* 'put to sleep', third-person singular *swefeþ*); that of *g* is *cg* (*bycgan* 'buy', third-person singular *byġeð*).

Class 2 lacks *i*-mutation. Wherever you find gemination in class 1 verbs with short root syllables, you will find an element spelled *-i-* or *-iġ-* after the root syllable of the class 2 verb.[4] This -*i*- is a syllable all by itself – weighty enough, in fact, to be capable of bearing metrical stress, as we see in this line:

```
×   × /    / ×      × ×  / \ ×
```
Him þā secg hraðe        ġewāt sīðian[5]
[The man then quickly departed journeying]

where stress falls on both the first and second syllables of *sīðian*.

---

! The present third-person singular of the class 2 weak verb looks like the present plural of the other major verb classes (for example, *hē lufað* 'he loves', *wē sceþþað* 'we injure'). To avoid being confused by this resemblance, you should learn to recognize a class 2 weak verb when you see one. If your glossary (unlike the one in this book) doesn't tell you the class of the verb, then look at the headword. If the root syllable ends with any consonant but *r* and is followed by -*i*-, chances are it is a class 2 weak verb, and the present third-person singular will end with -*að*.

---

In some verbs, a vowel is inserted before the endings that do not begin with vowels (-*st*, -*ð*, -*d*-). In verbs like *sceþþan* and *herian* this vowel is -*e*-, in verbs like *hǣlan* the vowel is absent, and in all class 2 weak verbs it is -*a*- or -*o*-. Often the vowel is omitted in class 1 verbs with short root syllables, so you can expect to see (for example) *fremst* and *fremþ* as well as *fremest* and *fremeþ*. This is the rule rather than the exception when the root syllable ends with *d* or *t*: so the past tense of *āhreddan* 'rescue' is *āhredde* and that of *hwettan* 'urge' is *hwette*.

### 7.3.2  Class 1 weak verbs that change their vowels

Verbs like Modern English *buy/bought*, which both change their vowels in the past tense and add the dental consonant characteristic of the weak past, should not be confused with verbs like *swim/swam*, which are descended from the Old English strong verbs. *Buy/bought* belongs to a group of class 1 weak verbs in which the vowels of the present tense are subject to *i*-mutation (§2.2.2) while the vowels of the past tense are not. Table 7.5 illustrates with *cwellan* 'kill', *sēċan* 'seek' and *þenċan* 'think'.

---

[4]  This element did not cause *i*-mutation because it did not begin with *i* at the time that *i*-mutation took place. Rather, it was a long syllable [oːj], which later became the syllable spelled -*i*-.

[5]  *Genesis A*, l. 2018. For the metrical notation, see chapter 13.

**Table 7.5** Class 1 weak verbs that change their vowels

|  | 'kill' | 'seek' | 'think' |
|---|---|---|---|
| infinitive | cwellan | sēċan | þenċan |
| present indicative | iċ cwelle | iċ sēċe | iċ þenċe |
|  | þū cwelest | þū sēċst | þū þenċst |
|  | hēo cweleþ | hē sēċþ | hit þenċþ |
|  | wē cwellaþ | ġē sēċaþ | hīe þenċaþ |
| past indicative | iċ cwealde | hēo sōhte | hē þōhte |
| present subjunctive | hē cwelle | iċ sēċe | þū þenċe |
| past subjunctive | iċ cwealde | hēo sōhte | hē þōhte |
| imperative | cwele | sēċ | þenċ |
|  | cwellaþ | sēċaþ | þenċaþ |
| participles | cwellende | sēċende | þenċende |
|  | cweald | sōht | þōht |

A ċ, cg or ġ at the end of the root syllable of one of these weak verbs is always changed to h before the past-tense ending -t-. Old English also has a rule that when n precedes h, it is dropped and the preceding vowel is lengthened. Thus the past tense of þenċan is þōhte and that of brenġan 'bring' is brōhte.

ⓘ The vowels of cwellan are not as predicted in table 2.1 (p. 17) because the unmutated vowel in the forms with e was actually æ, not ea. Similar verbs include cweċċan 'shake' (past cweahte), reċċan 'narrate' (reahte), sellan 'give' (sealde) and tellan 'count, relate' (tealde).

## 7.3.3  Contracted verbs

The rule that h is always dropped between vowels (already mentioned in connection with nouns, §6.2.2) introduces some complications in the verb paradigm. Table 7.6 illustrates this with the class 2 weak verb smēaġan 'ponder'.

The underlying (and unattested) verb is *smēahian or *smēahiġan, but the h has been lost in all forms, since it always comes between vowels. Notice the -ġ- that comes before the ending in certain forms: it is a remnant of the syllable spelled -i- or -iġ- in normal class 2 weak verbs. Like smēaġan are þrēaġan 'chastise', twēoġan 'doubt' and frēoġan 'set free'.

**Table 7.6**   Contracted weak verbs

| 'ponder' | singular | plural |
|---|---|---|
| infinitive | smēaġan | |
| present indicative | iċ smēaġe | |
| | þū smēast | wē smēaġaðð |
| | hēo smēaðð | |
| past indicative | iċ smēade | ġē smēadon |
| present subjunctive | hēo smēaġe | hīe smēaġen |
| past subjunctive | hē smēade | wē smēaden |
| imperative | smēa | smēaġaðð |
| present participle | smēaġende | |
| past participle | smēad | |

### 7.3.4   Class 3 weak verbs

Obeying the rule that the most common words are the last to leave a dying class (§6.3), class 3 contains only *habban* 'have', *libban* 'live', *secgan* 'say' and *hycgan* 'think' (table 7.7), together with a few odd remnants. Each of these verbs has partly gone over to other classes, and the resulting confusion makes it impractical to describe the characteristics of the class. The best course is to study the paradigms and be prepared to encounter these anomalous verbs in your reading.

## 7.4   More about strong verbs

Most strong verbs are inflected in pretty much the same way as *helpan* (table 7.1, p. 63). You will be able to predict the present paradigm of almost any strong verb if you know how *i*-mutation affects the vowels of root syllables (§2.2.2) and how the endings -*st* and -*ðð* interact with consonants at the ends of root syllables (the rules outlined at §7.2.1 apply to both weak and strong verbs). Once you have learned the gradation patterns for the strong verbs, you will easily master the past paradigms as well.

### 7.4.1   The strong verb classes

The Germanic languages have seven classes of strong verbs, each characterized by its own gradation pattern. Gradation is an Indo-European grammatical

**Table 7.7**  Class 3 weak verbs

| | infinitive · | | |
|---|---|---|---|
| habban | libban, lifġan | secgan | hycgan |

| | present indicative | | |
|---|---|---|---|
| iċ hæbbe | iċ libbe, lifġe | iċ secge | iċ hycge |
| þū hæfst, hafast | þū lifast, leofast | þū seġst, sagast | þū hyġst, hogast |
| hēo hæfð, hafað | hē lifað, leofað | hēo seġð, sagað | hē hyġ(e)ð, hogað |
| wē habbaþ | ġē libbað | wē secgaþ | ġē hycgað |

| | past indicative | | |
|---|---|---|---|
| iċ hæfde | hē lifde, leofode | hēo sæġde | iċ hog(o)de, hyġde |

| | present subjunctive | | |
|---|---|---|---|
| hē hæbbe | iċ libbe, lifġe | þū secge | iċ hycge |

| | past subjunctive | | |
|---|---|---|---|
| iċ hæfde | þū lifde, leofode | hēo sæġde | hē hog(o)de, hyġde |

| | imperative | | |
|---|---|---|---|
| hafa | leofa | sæġe, saga | hyġe, hoga |
| habbaþ | libbaþ, lifġaþ | secgaþ | hycgaþ |

| | participles | | |
|---|---|---|---|
| hæbbende | libbende, lifġende | secgende | hycgende |
| ġehæfd | ġelifd | ġesæġd | ġehogod |

feature whereby the root vowels of words are altered to signal changes in grammatical function. For example, if the present tense of a Modern English verb contains 'short' *i* followed by *n* or *m*, the past-tense form will usually have *a* and the past participle *u*: *drink, drank, drunk*; *ring, rang, rung*; *swim, swam, swum*.

Old English has some variations within the Germanic classes, as table 7.8 shows. This table includes the present third-person singular indicative so that you can see how *i*-mutation affects each class. You should understand, however, that the vowel of this form is not part of the gradation pattern inherited from Indo-European, but rather a relatively recent phenomenon. Eventually the English language would discard the *i*-mutation of the second- and third-person singular, but the ancient gradation patterns of the strong verbs are still with us.

**Table 7.8**    Classes of strong verbs

| | *infinitive* | *3rd pers. sg.* | *first past* | *second past* | *past participle* |
|---|---|---|---|---|---|
| 1 | wrītan | writt | wrāt | writon | writen |
| 2a | ċēosan | ċīesð | ċēas | curon | coren |
| 2b | lūcan | lȳcð | lēac | lucon | locen |
| 3a | singan | singð | sang | sungon | sungen |
| 3b | helpan | hilpð | healp | hulpon | holpen |
| 3c | hweorfan | hwierfð | hwearf | hwurfon | hworfen |
| 4a | stelan | stilð | stæl | stǣlon | stolen |
| 4b | niman | nimð | nam | nōmon | numen |
| 5 | sprecan | spricð | spræc | sprǣcon | sprecen |
| 6 | bacan | bæcð | bōc | bōcon | bacen |
| 7a | hātan | hætt | hēt | hēton | hāten |
| 7b | flōwan | flēwð | flēow | flēowon | flōwen |

! Students often ask if they should memorize the strong verb classes. The answer is a qualified 'yes'. The qualification is that you should take note of patterns within these classes and use them as mnemonic devices. Most of the vowels of classes 1–5, especially, are derived from a single gradation pattern, and though these vowels have been altered by the influence of surrounding sounds, they still resemble each other:

1 The vowels of the present tense are mid or high vowels – that is, pronounced with the tongue at or near the roof of the mouth ( [e,i] ) – or diphthongs that begin with these vowels.

2 The vowels of the first past are low vowels – that is, pronounced with the tongue and jaw lowered ( [ɑ,æ] ) – or diphthongs that begin with these vowels.

3 The vowels of the second past, though their original resemblance to each other has been obscured, are mostly short; in classes 4–5 they are long and low.

4 The vowels of the past participle are mostly variations on the short vowels of the second past, but in class 5 the vowel is the same as the present.

The gradation patterns of classes 6–7 differ from those of 1–5 and must be memorized separately.

ⓘ Class 2 verbs like *lūcan* 'lock' do not conform to the standard gradation pattern; the *ū* of the present tense has never been satisfactorily explained.

A few class 3 verbs have *u* in the present tense. Of these, the one you will meet most frequently is *murnan* 'mourn' (first past *mearn*, second past *murnon*).

The *ō* of class 4b appears before nasal consonants. *Cuman* 'come' belongs to this subclass, but its present tense is anomalous.

The present tense of class 6 sometimes has *æ* or *ea*.

Class 7 has a variety of vowels in the present tense, not just *ā* and *ō*. The past-tense vowels *ē* and *ēo* are what distinguish this class.

You may observe the same gradation patterns you have seen here in families of words derived from the same root. For example, *lēof* 'beloved' has the same vowel as a class 2 present, *ġelēafa* 'belief' has the same vowel as the first past, *ġelīefan* 'believe' has the first past vowel with *i*-mutation, and *lufian* 'love' and *lof* 'praise' have the vowels of the second past and past participle.

## 7.4.2  Verbs affected by grammatical alternation

Grammatical alternation[6] is an alternation between one consonant and another to mark the grammar of a word. Only three pairs of consonants alternate in this way:

*þ* : *d*      *h* : *g*/*ġ*      *s* : *r*

Grammatical alternation affects the paradigms of most strong verbs whose roots end with the consonants *þ*, *h* and *s*: three such verbs are shown in table 7.9.

At the end of the root syllable *h* is often dropped, in verbs like *tēon* 'accuse' (see next section), but enough forms with *h* remain to show the alternation clearly.

ⓘ Although the Modern English strong verbs no longer show the effects of grammatical alternation, it remains in some fossilized past participles such as *forlorn* (from *forlēosan*, past participle *forloren*) and *sodden* (from the past participle of *sēoðan*).

---

[6] A translation of the German phrase 'der grammatische Wechsel'. In grammars written in English you will usually see it referred to as 'Verner's Law' after the Danish linguist Karl Verner, who described its origin. Here we prefer the German term as more descriptive of its function in the recorded language.

**Table 7.9**  Grammatical alternation

|  | *'seethe'* | *'accuse'* | *'choose'* |
|---|---|---|---|
| infinitive | sēoðan | tēon | cēosan |
| present indicative | iċ sēoðe | iċ tēo | iċ ċēose |
|  | þū sīeðst | þū tīehst | þū ċiest |
| past indicative | iċ sēað | iċ tāh | iċ cēas |
|  | þū sude | þū tige | þū cure |
|  | ġē sudon | hīe tigon | wē curon |
| present subjunctive | hē sēoðe | iċ tēo | þū cēose |
| past subjunctive | iċ sude | þū tige | hē cure |
| past participle | soden | tigen | coren |

You will notice this alternation not only in verb paradigms, but also in families of words derived from the same root; for example, *hliehhan* 'laugh' and *hlagol* 'inclined to laugh', *nēah* 'near' and *nǣġan* 'approach', *lēosan* 'lose' and *lor* 'loss', *cweðan* 'say' and *cwide* 'saying'.

## 7.4.3  Contracted verbs

As you have just seen, some strong verbs are subject to contraction as a result of the loss of *h* between voiced sounds – the same rule that produces contracted weak verbs (§7.3.3). Table 7.10 illustrates with three very common verbs, *sēon* 'see', *slēan* 'slay' and *fōn* 'take'. The contraction affects only some present-tense forms, the infinitives and the present participle; past-tense forms that might have been affected have *g* (by grammatical alternation) instead of *h*. Verbs of classes 1, 2 and 5 have *ēo* in contracted forms; those of class 6 have *ēa*; those of class 7 have *ō*.

🛈 The alternation *h/w* in *sēon* is the result of a rare anomaly in the rule of grammatical alternation, the result of which is that *ġ* varies with *w* in the second past and past participle. For example, the usual past participle is *sewen*, but you may sometimes see *seġen* instead.

The *-n-* that appears in some forms of *fōn* (and also *hōn* 'hang') was at one time distributed throughout the paradigm. But the rule that *n* cannot appear before *h* (§7.3.2) caused it to be dropped in all forms but those with *g*. *Fōn* is also unusual in that the form with *g* has been extended to the first past (whose vowel is also the same as that of the second past).

**Table 7.10**　Contracted strong verbs

|  | 'see' | 'slay' | 'take' |
|---|---|---|---|
| infinitive | sēon | slēan | fōn |
| present indicative | iċ sēo | iċ slēa | iċ fō |
|  | þū siehst | þū sliehst | þū fēhst |
|  | hēo siehþ | hē sliehð | hit fēhþ |
|  | wē sēoð | ġē slēað | hīe fōð |
| past indicative | iċ seah | hēo slōh | hē fēng |
|  | hīe sāwon | wē slōgon | ġē fēngon |
| present subjunctive | hē sēo | iċ slēa | þū fō |
| past subjunctive | iċ sāwe | þū slōge | hē fēnge |
| imperative | seoh | sleah | fōh |
|  | sēoþ | slēað | fōð |
| participles | sēonde | slēande | fōnde |
|  | sewen, seġen | slagen | fangen |

## 7.4.4　Tips on strong verbs

!　This would be a good time to go over all the verb paradigms you have
seen so far, noting basic similarities. Notice particularly that in the
present tense the second- and third-person singular forms are usually
different from all the others. These are the forms in which the personal
ending does not begin with a vowel.

Present-tense strong verbs cause few difficulties, since the endings
make them easy to identify; past plurals are easy as well, for the same
reason. But past singulars, which either lack an ending or end only in
-e, are easy to confuse with nouns and adjectives. As you gain experience
with the language, this kind of confusion will become less likely. But in
the meantime, here are some tips to help you get it right.

- Look up words carefully. Learn what kind of spelling variations you
  can expect in Old English (see §2.1.3 and Appendix A); when two
  words look alike but their spelling differences are not what you'd
  expect, you may conclude that they are different words. *Wearð*
  'became' looks like *weorð* 'value, price', but *ea* normally does not
  vary with *eo*; *nam* 'took' looks like *nama* 'name', but endings are

rarely lost in Old English. If the glossary you're using has a great many references to the texts you're reading, check to see if the glossary entry you're looking at has a reference to the word you're trying to figure out. If it doesn't, look for an entry that does.

- Examine the grammatical context of the sentence or clause you're reading. Have you located a subject? a verb? an object? If the word you're looking at is *bēag* and you need a verb, try it as the first past of *būgan* 'bow'; if you need a noun, try it as 'ring'.
- Examine the word-order (see chapter 12). Is the word in a place where you'd normally expect to find a subject, an object or a verb?
- Once you've got a tentative translation, apply a sanity test: does it make sense? If it seems ungrammatical, or grammatical but absurd, try something else.

If you're using the on-line texts in *Old English Aerobics*, you won't have any difficulty distinguishing nouns and verbs because every word is clearly marked with its part of speech and a good bit of other grammatical information. *Don't let this feature make you complacent!* Pay attention to the form of the words you're looking up and ask yourself how the editor knew this word was a verb or that word plural. Remember that very few Old English texts are marked up the way the ones in *Old English Aerobics* are. The transition from on-line to printed texts will be very difficult if you have abused the convenience of *Old English Aerobics*.

## 7.5   Verbs with weak presents and strong pasts

A few verbs have the characteristics of the first weak class in the present tense and of strong class 5 or 6 in the past tense. For example, *hebban* 'lift' has a present tense like that of *fremman* 'do' or *sceþþan* 'injure' (tables 7.1, 7.4): *iċ hebbe, hē hefeð*, etc. But the past third-person singular indicative of this verb is *hōf*, the plural is *hōfon*, and the past participle is *hafen* (the vowel is the same as that of the present, but without *i*-mutation).

Some common verbs behave in this way, for example, *biddan* 'ask', *licgan* 'lie', *scieppan* 'make, create', *sittan* 'sit'. The dual nature of these verbs (which most glossaries, including the one in this book, classify as strong) is a curiosity, but it will cause you little difficulty.

## 7.6 More about preterite-present verbs

Many forms of the preterite-present verbs (introduced in §7.1.3) look anomalous, but fortunately their resemblance to some of the most common Modern English auxiliary verbs makes them easy to understand. (However, not all Old English preterite-presents are auxiliaries.) By way of illustration, paradigms for four of the most common verbs in this group are presented in table 7.11. Here are some notes to help you make sense of these paradigms.

1    The present tense is an old strong past-tense form that has come to be used as a present: compare these present-tense forms with the strong pasts in table 7.8. But the second-person singular of these verbs differs from that of the strong verbs in two respects: a) it has the first past vowel in its root syllable rather than the second past vowel; and b) it has an ending -*st* or -*t* rather than -*e*.

2    The past tense is usually built on the second past root, with -*d*- or -*t*- added. In fact, it often looks like the past tense of the class 1 weak verbs

**Table 7.11**    Preterite-present verbs

| 'know how to' | 'be able to' | 'be obliged to' | 'know' |
|---|---|---|---|
| | infinitive | | |
| cunnan | *magan | sculan | witan |
| | present indicative | | |
| ić cann | ić mæġ | ić sceal | ić wāt |
| þū canst | þū meaht | þū scealt | þū wāst |
| hēo cann | hē mæġ | hit sceal | hēo wāt |
| wē cunnon | ġē magon | hīe sculon | ġē witon |
| | past indicative | | |
| ić cūðe | hēo meahte, mihte | hit sceolde | hē wisse, wiste |
| þū cūðest | þū meahtest, mihtest | þū sceoldest | þū wistest |
| wē cūðon | ġē meahton, mihton | hīe sceoldon | wē wisson, wiston |
| | present subjunctive | | |
| ić cunne | hēo mæġe | þū scyle, scule | hē wite |
| | past subjunctive | | |
| ić cūðe | hēo meahte, mihte | þū sceolde | hē wisse, wiste |
| | participles | | |
| | | | witende |
| -cunnen, cūð | | | witen |

described in §7.3.2, though sometimes the forms have been subjected to phonological changes that make them look anomalous.

3 When the root syllable ends in *g* (as in *āgan, dugan* and *magan*), past *-d-* becomes *-t-*; *g* becomes *h* before this past ending and before the second-person singular present *-t* (compare §7.2.1, items 1 and 3).

Here is a list of the preterite-present verbs with their principal present and past forms. Infinitives preceded by asterisks are not attested, though speakers and writers presumably used them.

**āgan.** *possess.* iċ **āh,** þū **āhst,** hīe **āgon;** past **āhte.**
**cunnan.** *know (how to).* iċ **can,** hīe **cunnon;** past **cūðe.**
**dugan.** *be good (for something).* iċ **dēag,** hīe **dugon;** subjunctive **duge, dyġe;** past **dohte.**
*****durran.** *dare.* iċ **dearr,** hīe **durron;** subjunctive **durre, dyrre;** past **dorste.**
**magan.** *may.* iċ **mæġ,** þū **meaht,** hīe **magon;** past **meahte, mihte.**
*****mōtan.** *must, be allowed.* iċ **mōt,** þū **mōst,** hīe **mōton;** past **mōste.**
**ġemunan.** *remember.* iċ **ġeman,** hīe **ġemunon;** subjunctive **ġemune, ġemyne;** past **ġemunde.**
*****ġe-,** *****benugan.** *be enough.* hit **ġeneah,** hīe **ġenugon;** past **benohte.**
**sculan.** *must.* iċ **sceal,** þū **scealt,** hīe **sculon;** subjunctive **scyle, scule;** past **sceolde.**
**þurfan.** *need.* iċ **þearf,** þū **þearft,** hīe **þurfon;** subjunctive **þurfe, þyrfe;** past **þorfte.**
**unnan.** *grant, give, allow.* iċ **ann,** hīe **unnon;** past **ūðe.**
**witan.** *know.* iċ **wāt,** þū **wāst,** hīe **witon;** past **wisse, wiste.**

## 7.7 *Dōn, gān, willan*

The verbs *do, go* and *will* (table 7.12) are still anomalous in Modern English, and in much the same way as in Old English: *dōn* 'do' has a past form that is paralleled in no other verb; *gān* 'go' lacks a past form of its own and has apparently borrowed the past of another verb, now disappeared; and *willan* 'desire' has distinctive inflections in the present tense.

The present forms of *dōn* and *gān* look like those of normal strong verbs (see §7.4). But the past tense of *dōn* is built on a syllable that looks somewhat like a weak past (though its origin is a mystery), and *gān* has a past tense that also looks weak and in any case does not belong to the same root that gives us the present forms. *Willan* looks a bit like a preterite-present verb, but it is not; and its first- and third-person singular present and plural present are quite different from the preterite-present forms.

**Table 7.12** dōn, gān, willan

|  | *'do'* | *'go'* | *'will'* |
|---|---|---|---|
| infinitive | dōn | gān | willan |
| present indicative | iċ dō | iċ gā | iċ wille |
|  | þū dēst | þū gǣst | þū wilt |
|  | hēo dēð | hit gǣð | hē wile |
|  | wē dōð | ġē gāð | hīe willað |
| past indicative | iċ dyde | hit ēode | hēo wolde |
|  | þū dydest | þū ēodest | þū woldest |
|  | wē dydon | ġē ēodon | hīe woldon |
| present subjunctive | iċ dō | hēo gā | þū wille |
| past subjunctive | iċ dyde | hēo ēode | þū wolde |
| participles | dōnde | —— | willende |
|  | ġedōn | ġegān | —— |

# 7.8 Negation

Most verbs are negated very simply by placing the adverb *ne* 'not' directly in front of them. In independent clauses, the word-order that follows will normally be Verb–Subject (see §12.3):

> Se þe mē *ne lufað, ne hylt* hē mīne sprǣċe.
> [He who *does not love* me *does not keep* my sayings.]

*Ne* is contracted with certain verbs, for example, *nis* 'is not', *næs* 'was not' (from *bēon*), *næfð* 'does not have', *næfde* 'did not have' (*habban*), *nyllað* 'will not', *noldon* 'would not' (*willan*), *nāh* 'does not have', *nāhte* 'did not have' (*āgan*), *nāt* 'does not know' (*witan*). Notice that all of the verbs so contracted begin with a vowel, *h* or *w*. Not all verbs beginning with those sounds are contracted, but only the more common ones; and those common verbs need not be contracted. You will also see *ne wæs*, *ne hæfð* and so on.

The Modern English rule that two negatives make a positive does not apply in Old English; rather, the addition of more negative adverbs to a sentence adds emphasis to its negativity:

> *Ne* bēo ġē *nāteshwōn* dēade, ðēah ðe ġē of ðām trēowe eton.
> [You will *certainly not* be dead, though you eat from the tree.]

Here the additional negative adverb *nāteshwōn* makes the sentence more emphatic than it would be with *ne* alone; since we cannot use double negatives the same way in Modern English, we must resort to a different strategy to represent this emphasis in our translations. Common negative adverbs are *nā*, *nales*, *nāteshwōn* and *nātōþæshwōn*.

## 7.9   The verbals

Old English forms periphrastic verbs much as Modern English does, with auxiliary verbs and verbals (infinitives or participles – see §3.1.3):

auxiliary + infinitive (will find, may find, etc.)
auxiliary + past participle (has found, had found, was found)
*to be* + present participle (is finding)

This section lists a few ways in which the infinitives and participles of Old English differ from those of Modern English.

### 7.9.1   Infinitives

Verbs of knowing, seeing, hearing and commanding may be followed by an accusative object and an infinitive expressing what that object is doing or should do. The construction remains in sentences like 'I saw him dance', but in Old English it is more frequent and it comes where we no longer use it. Examples:

Ġewīt fram mē, forþon þe iċ *ġesēo þē* on forhæfdnesse *þurhwunian.*
[Depart from me, for I *see you are persevering* in abstinence.]

Hǣlend fērde þǣr forþ and þā *ġehȳrde þone blindan cleopian.*
[The Savior went forth there and then *heard the blind man call out.*]

Drihten, ġyf þū hyt eart, *hāt mē cuman* tō þē ofer þās wæteru.
[Lord, if it is you, *command me to come* to you over these waters.]

The object is often unexpressed, especially after verbs of commanding:

And se cyng þā *hēt niman* Sīferðes lāfe and ġebringan hī binnan Mealdelmesbyriġ.
[And then the king *commanded* [*someone*] *to take* Siferth's widow and bring her into Malmesbury.]

It is sometimes appropriate to translate such sentences with a passive construction ('commanded her to be brought') even though the Old English construction is not passive.

The inflected infinitive is often used with bēon to express obligation, necessity or propriety. It can usually be translated with *should* or *must* and an infinitive:

hyt ys ġȳt ġeornlīċe tō āsmēaġeanne
[it should further be diligently investigated]

## 7.9.2   Participles

The Old English present participle (§3.1.3, p. 26) is often used as a noun denoting the performer of an action, e.g. *rodora Rǣdend* 'Ruler of the heavens' (*Rǣdend* being the present participle of *rǣdan* 'rule'). You will often find such forms listed separately as nouns in glossaries and dictionaries.

**ⓘ** The Modern English participle in *-ing* can also be used as a noun (the 'gerund') denoting the action of a verb (e.g. 'living well is the best revenge'), but for this purpose Old English uses the infinitive.

A construction consisting of a noun or pronoun and participle, both in the dative case, is occasionally used where one would expect an adverb clause or another construction expressing time or cause. This noun phrase may sometimes be introduced by a preposition.

And Offa ġefēng Myrċena rīċe, *ġeflȳmdum Beornrede*.
[And Offa seized the kingdom of the Mercians *after Beornred had been driven out.*]

Æfter Agustini fyliġde in biscophāde Laurentius, þone hē forðon *bi him lifiġendum* ġehālgode, þȳ lǣs *him forðfērendum* se steall æniġe hwīle būton heorde taltriġan ongunne.
[After Augustine, Lawrence followed in the bishopric, whom he consecrated *while he was still alive* for this reason: lest *by his passing away* the position should for any time, being without a guide, begin to be unstable.]

**ⓘ** Those who know Latin will recognize the similarity between this construction and the ablative absolute, of which it is generally thought to be an imitation.

## 7.10   The subjunctive

Because speakers of Modern English seldom use the subjunctive mood, the Old English subjunctive is difficult for us to get used to. We do still use it when stating conditions contrary to fact, as in

> If I *were* a carpenter,
> and you were a lady,
> would you marry me anyway?

Here the subjunctive *were* (the indicative would be *was*) suggests that the speaker is not in fact a carpenter. We also use the subjunctive in noun clauses following verbs of desiring and commanding. For example:

The king desired that the knight *go* on a quest.
The king commanded that the knight *go* on a quest.
I suggest that you *be* a little quieter.
I move that the bypass *be* routed east of town.
I wish that I *were* wiser.

Here the subjunctives tell us that the condition described in the noun clause is not a present reality or a future certainty, but a possibility mediated by someone's desire. Some of these usages are disappearing: the first two examples above sound a little archaic, and it would now be more idiomatic to say 'The king wanted the knight to go on a quest' and 'The king commanded the knight to go on a quest', using infinitive constructions rather than subjunctives.

Aside from these common uses, the subjunctive now appears mainly in fixed or formulaic expressions, for example, 'come what may', 'thanks be to God'.

The subjunctive is far more common in Old English than in Modern English, and you must get used to seeing it in environments where you do not expect it. As in Modern English, the subjunctive is used for conditions contrary to fact. A made-up example:

Ġif iċ *wǣre* trēowwyrhta . . .
[If I *were* a carpenter . . . ]

It is also used in noun clauses following verbs of desiring and commanding:

Iċ wȳsce þæt iċ wīsra *wǣre*.
[I wish that I *were* wiser.]

But the subjunctive is also used in noun clauses where we would not now use it:

Hīe cwǣdon þæt hē *wǣre* wīs.

Here the subjunctive in the noun clause following *Hīe cwǣdon* 'They said' does not signal a condition contrary to fact, and *cwǣdon* 'said' is hardly a verb of desiring or commanding. In fact, the fairest translation of this sentence would be

They said that he *was* wise.

making no attempt at all to reproduce the subjunctive. What then does the subjunctive express?

Think of it as implying a point of view towards the action of the verb. In clauses following verbs of desire, the point of view is obvious. In *Hīe cwǣdon þæt hē wǣre wīs*, it is merely that the speaker is reporting an opinion. He is not necessarily taking a position on the rightness or wrongness of that opinion. It may indeed be obvious that he is in complete agreement:

Þæt folc ðā ðe þis tācen ġeseah cwæð þæt Crist *wǣre* sōð wītega.
[The people who saw this sign said that Christ *was* a true prophet.]

The following sentence is similar, but it uses the indicative:

Be him āwrāt se wītega Isaias þæt hē *is* stefn clipiendes on wēstene.
[Concerning him (John the Baptist) the prophet Isaiah wrote that he *is* the voice of one crying in the wilderness.]

The choice between subjunctive and indicative may often be a matter of individual preference or rhetorical emphasis.

Another common environment in which the subjunctive does not necessarily indicate doubt or unreality is the concessive clause introduced by *þēah* or *þēah þe* 'though', which always takes the subjunctive whether or not the statement it contains is known to be true. For example:

Ne sceal nān man swā þēah, þēah hē synful *sīe*, ġeortrūwian.
[Nevertheless, no man must despair, though he *be* sinful.]

Here *þēah* has a sense something like 'even if', implying that the man may or may not be sinful; the subjunctive is appropriate (if a little archaic) even in Modern English. But compare:

God is mildheort, þēah ðe ūre yfelnes him oft *ābelge*.
[God is merciful, though our wickedness often *angers* him.]

## Minitext c. Wulfstan's Translation of the Apostles' Creed

From the sermon 'To Eallum Folke' by Wulfstan, Bishop of Worcester and Archbishop of York. See Bethurum [9], pp. 166–8.

[1] Wē ġelȳfað on ǣnne God ælmihtiġne þe ealle þing ġesceōp and ġeworhte. [2] And wē ġelȳfað and ġeorne witon þæt Crist Godes sunu tō mannum cōm for ealles mancynnes ðearfe. [3] And wē ġelȳfað þæt hine clǣne mǣden ġebǣre, Sancta Maria, þe nǣfre nāhte weres ġemānan. [4] And wē ġelȳfað þæt hē miċel ġeðolode and stīðlīċe þrōwode for ūre ealra nēode. [5] And wē ġelȳfað þæt hine man on rōde āhēnge and hine tō dēaðe ācwealde and hine siððan on eorðan bebyriġde. [6] And wē ġelȳfað þæt hē tō helle fērde and ðǣrof ġehergode eal þæt hē wolde. [7] And wē ġelȳfað þæt hē siððan of dēaðe ārise. [8] And wē ġelȳfað þæt hē æfter þām tō heofonum āstige. [9] And wē ġelȳfað and ġeorne witon þæt hē on dōmes dæġ tō ðām miċlan dōme cymð. [10] And wē ġelȳfað þæt ealle dēade men sculon þonne ārīsan of dēaðe and þone miċlan dōm ealle ġesēċan. [11] And wē ġelȳfað þæt ðā synfullan sculon þanon on ān[a] tō helle faran and ðǣr ā siððan mid dēoflum wunian on byrnendum fȳre and on ēċan forwyrde, and ðæs æniġ ende ne cymð æfre tō worulde. [12] And wē ġelȳfað þæt ðā gōdan and wel Cristenan þe hēr on worulde Gode wel ġecwēmdon þonne on ān sculon intō heofonum faran and ðǣr siððan wununge habban mid Gode selfum and mid his enġlum ā on ēċnesse. Amen.

[a] immediately.

Here the writer can have no doubt that we do often anger God, but the verb *ābelge* is still in the subjunctive mood.

In general, you can expect relative clauses, clauses of place, and 'when' and 'while' clauses to take the indicative. Concessive clauses and 'before' and 'until' clauses more often take the subjunctive. But the mood in many kinds of clause varies as it does in noun clauses, and linguists argue ceaselessly about the meaning of the subjunctive and the indicative in several common constructions.

> ! Beginners (and scholars too!) sometimes feel that they must always translate the Old English subjunctive with a Modern English subjunctive or with a subjunctive-like construction such as the conditional ('would anger'). But it is often best, as the discussion above shows, to translate the subjunctive with a plain indicative. You must determine as nearly as you can what the subjunctive is doing in each instance and decide what Modern English construction best renders that sense.

The Old English subjunctive is often used to make a first- or third-person imperative, and then the best translation usually converts the subject of the verb into an object of 'let'. In plural constructions, the -*n* of the ending is generally dropped.

*Sīe* hē āmānsumod.
[Let him be excommunicated.]

*Ete* hīe hrædlīce.
[Let them eat quickly.]

*Lufie* wē ūre nēxtan.
[Let us love our neighbours.]

This usage survives in some formulaic phrases such as 'God be thanked'.

# Chapter 8

# Adjectives

## 8.1 Quick start

Surely the oddest grammatical feature belonging to the Germanic languages is that they can inflect almost any adjective in either of two very different ways. If the adjective follows a demonstrative pronoun (§5.1.3), possessive adjective (§5.1.2), or genitive noun or noun phrase, one of the so-called 'weak' endings is added to it; otherwise it is given a 'strong' ending. This distinction is widespread (all the early Germanic languages have it) and surprisingly durable: strong and weak adjectives were still distinguished in Chaucer's English, and they are distinguished even now in German.

At this point you may be grumbling that we have arbitrarily doubled the amount of memorization required to learn the adjectives. If so, calm down: adjectives are really quite easy. The weak adjectives are almost exactly the same as the weak nouns (§6.1.2). Most of the strong adjective endings resemble those of either the strong nouns (§6.1.1) or the demonstrative pronouns. In this chapter you will see almost no endings that you have not seen before.

Indeed (though some Old English teachers may not approve of our telling you so), you may find it possible to read Old English prose pretty well without having put in a lot of work on adjectives. In a noun phrase like *þæs æðelan bōceres* 'the noble scholar's', you can get the information that the phrase is genitive singular from either the demonstrative pronoun or the noun. The weak adjective *æðelan* doesn't tell you much. In a phrase like *ġeonge prēostas* 'young priests', the strong ending of the adjective *ġeonge* is less ambiguous, but it is also redundant: you can get all the information you need from the noun. It becomes important to recognize the adjective's ending when it gets separated from its noun:

> hē lēt him þā of handon    *lēofne* flēogan
> *hafoc* wið þæs holtes[1]
> [he then let his *beloved hawk* fly from his
> hands towards the woods]

Here *hafoc* 'hawk' is the accusative direct object of *lēt* 'let'. The adjective *lēofne* 'beloved' is separated from this noun by the infinitive *flēogan* 'fly', and so it is helpful that *lēofne* has the masculine accusative singular ending *-ne* so that you can associate it correctly with its noun. You will run into this kind of situation more often in poetry than in prose.

Table 8.1 summarizes the adjective endings.

**Table 8.1**    Adjective endings

|  |  | *masculine* | *neuter* | *feminine* |
|---|---|---|---|---|
|  |  | Strong | | |
| singular | nominative | – | – | -u / – |
|  | accusative | -ne | – | -e |
|  | genitive | -es | -es | -re |
|  | dative | -um | -um | -re |
| plural | nominative/accusative | -e | -u / – / -e | -a / -e |
|  | genitive | -ra | -ra | -ra |
|  | dative | -um | -um | -um |
|  |  | Weak | | |
| singular | nominative | -a | -e | -e |
|  | accusative | -an | -e | -an |
|  | genitive | -an | -an | -an |
|  | dative | -an | -an | -an |
| plural | nominative/accusative | -an | -an | -an |
|  | genitive | -ra / -ena | -ra / -ena | -ra / -ena |
|  | dative | -um | -um | -um |

---

[1]  *The Battle of Maldon*, ll. 7–8.

## 8.2   Strong adjectives

Table 8.2 shows the strong endings attached to an adjective with a long stem. (Forms in **bold** type should be compared with the demonstrative pronouns (§5.1.3), others with the strong nouns (§6.1.1).) The adjectives are subject to the same kinds of transformations that affect the nouns. Those with long stems differ from those with short stems (table 8.3) in that the feminine nominative singular and the neuter nominative/accusative plural end in *-u* (see §6.1.1 for an explanation). Table 8.3 also shows that when the vowel of an adjective with a short stem is *æ* or *ea*, it alternates with *a* (§§2.2.1, 6.2.2). In some other adjectives, *h* is dropped between voiced sounds (§6.2.2), so, for example, the masculine accusative singular of *hēah* 'high' is *hēane* and the feminine nominative singular is *hēa*.

**Table 8.2**   Strong adjectives (long stems)

| *'good'* | | *masculine* | *neuter* | *feminine* |
|---|---|---|---|---|
| singular | nominative | gōd | gōd | gōd |
| | accusative | **gōdne** | gōd | gōde |
| | genitive | gōdes | gōdes | **gōdre** |
| | dative | **gōdum** | **gōdum** | **gōdre** |
| | instrumental | gōde | gōde | |
| plural | nominative/accusative | **gōde** | gōd, **gōde** | gōda, -e |
| | genitive | | **gōdra** | |
| | dative | | gōdum | |

**Table 8.3**   Strong adjectives (short stems)

| *'vigorous'* | | *masculine* | *neuter* | *feminine* |
|---|---|---|---|---|
| singular | nominative | hwæt | hwæt | hwatu |
| | accusative | **hwætne** | hwæt | hwate |
| | genitive | hwætes | hwætes | **hwætre** |
| | dative | **hwatum** | **hwatum** | **hwætre** |
| | instrumental | hwate | hwate | |
| plural | nominative/accusative | **hwate** | hwatu, **-e** | hwata, -e |
| | genitive | | **hwatra** | |
| | dative | | hwatum | |

> **!**   The masculine/neuter dative singular ending -*um* may cause confusion, for this is also the ending of the dative plural nouns and adjectives, and you may already have come to think of it as plural. Remember it this way: -*um* is always dative, and in nouns it is always plural.

**ⓘ**   The second syllable of a two-syllable adjective, like that of a two-syllable noun (§6.2.1), may be syncopated, so the dative plural of *hāliġ* 'holy' is *hālgum* but the masculine accusative singular is *hāliġne*.

The nominative and accusative plural ending -*e* is very frequent for both feminines and neuters in late Old English, when -*e* becomes the dominant ending for all genders. You will also see occasional -*a* in nominative and accusative plural neuters.

Possessive adjectives (§5.1.2) are always declined strong, and so is *ōðer* 'other, second', regardless of context.

## 8.3   Weak adjectives

The weak adjectives (table 8.4) are almost exactly like the weak nouns (§6.1.2). The difference is that the ending of the genitive plural of a weak adjective is usually the same as that of a strong adjective.

**Table 8.4**   Weak adjectives

| *'good'* | | *masculine* | *neuter* | *feminine* |
|---|---|---|---|---|
| singular | nominative | gōda | gōde | gōde |
| | accusative | gōdan | gōde | gōdan |
| | genitive | gōdan | gōdan | gōdan |
| | dative | gōdan | gōdan | gōdan |
| plural | nominative/accusative | gōdan | gōdan | gōdan |
| | genitive | | gōdra, -ena | |
| | dative | | gōdum | |

There is no distinction between long and short stems, except that *æ* or *ea* in a short root syllable always becomes *a* (§2.2.1), so the weak masculine nominative singular of *hwæt* 'vigorous' is *hwata*. Because all weak endings begin with vowels, *h* is always dropped at the end of a root syllable (§6.2.2), so the weak nominative/accusative plural of *hēah* 'high' is *hēan*. As with nouns and

**Minitext D. On Danish Customs**

From a letter by Ælfric, Abbot of Eynsham, to an unidentified 'Brother Edward', complaining of certain Englishmen who cut their hair in the Danish fashion (long in front, short behind). This scandalous hairstyle (England was at this time fighting off Viking armies) seems similar to the Norman style depicted in the Bayeux tapestry. For the full text, see Clayton [31].

[1] Iċ secge ēac ðē, brōðor Ēadweard, nū ðū mē þisses bǣde, þæt ġē dōð unrihtlīċe þæt ġē ðā Engliscan þēawas forlǣtað þe ēowre fæderas hēoldon, and hǣðenra manna þēawas lufiað þe ēow ðæs līfes ne unnon,[a] [2] and mid ðām ġeswuteliað þæt ġē forsēoð ēower cynn and ēowre yldran mid þām unþēawum, þonne ġē him on tēonan[b] tysliað ēow on Denisc,[c] ābleredum hneccan and āblendum ēagum. [3] Ne secge iċ nā māre embe ðā sceandlican tyslunge, būton þæt ūs secgað bēċ þæt se bēo āmānsumod þe hǣðenra manna þēawas hylt on his līfe and his āgen cynn unwurþað mid þām.

[a] *þe ēow ðæs līfes ne unnon*: who do not allow you life; who wish you ill.
[b] *him on tēonan*: as an injury to them.
[c] *on Denisc*: in Danish fashion.

strong adjectives (§§6.2.1, 8.2), the second syllable of a two-syllable adjective can be syncopated, so the weak nominative/accusative plural of *hāliġ* 'holy' is *hālgan*.

Comparative adjectives and ordinal numbers (except for *ōðer* 'second') are always declined weak.

# 8.4   Comparison of adjectives

The comparative adjective is made by adding *-r-* between the root syllable and the inflectional ending, which is always weak regardless of context. The superlative is made by adding *-ost*, which may be followed by either a weak or a strong inflection. Examples:

| | | |
|---|---|---|
| heard 'hard, fierce' | heardra | heardost |
| milde 'kind' | mildra | mildost |
| hāliġ 'holy' | hāliġra | hālgost |
| sweotol 'clear' | sweotolra | sweotolost |

Some adjectives have *i*-mutation (§2.2.2) in the comparative and superlative forms, and in these cases the superlative element is usually *-est*. For example:

| | | |
|---|---|---|
| eald 'old' | ieldra | ieldest |
| ġeong 'young' | ġinġra | ġinġest |
| hēah 'high' | hīera | hīehst |
| lang 'long' | lenġra | lenġest |
| strang 'strong' | strenġra | strenġest |

You may occasionally encounter unmutated forms, e.g. *strangost* 'strongest'.

A few adjectives have anomalous comparative and superlative forms; these are still anomalous in Modern English, though sometimes in different ways:

| | | |
|---|---|---|
| gōd 'good' | betera | betst |
| | sēlra | sēlest |
| lȳtel 'small' | lǣssa | lǣst |
| miċel 'large' | māra | mǣst |
| yfel 'bad' | wiersa | wierrest, wierst |

Modern English has lost the alternative comparative and superlative *sēlra* 'better' and *sēlest* 'best'.

---

**!**  Comparative adjectives sometimes cause problems for students who are not on the lookout for them, or who confuse comparative *-r-* with the *-r-* of the feminine genitive/dative singular ending *-re* or the genitive plural *-ra*. The Old English comparative *-r-* may not look enough like the Modern English comparative *-er* to be easy for you to detect. The only solution to the problem is to be alert when you read.

# Chapter 9

# Numerals

## 9.1 Quick start

Numbers are of two kinds, *cardinal* and *ordinal*. Cardinal numbers (such as Modern English *one, two . . .* ) may function either as nouns or as adjectives:

As noun:
*Fēower* sīðon *seofon* bēoð *eahta and twentiġ*
[*Four* times *seven* are *twenty-eight*]

As adjective:
On *ānum* dæġe bēoð *fēower and twentiġ* tīda
[In *one* day there are *twenty-four* hours]

Ordinal numbers (such as Modern English *first, second . . .* ) are always adjectives, and all of them are declined weak (§8.3) except for *ōðer* 'second', which is always strong (§8.2):

Þone *forman* dæġ hīe hēton Sunnandæġ
[They called the *first* day Sunday]

Þone *ōðerne* dæġ hīe hēton Mōnandæġ
[They called the *second* day Monday]

**Minitext E. Weeks of the Year**

From the *Enchiridion* by Byrhtferth, a monk of Ramsey. See Baker and Lapidge [5], pp. 30–3.

[1] Efne seofon bēoð seofon; twīa seofon bēoð fēowertȳne; þrīwa seofon bēoð ān and twēntiġ; fēower sīðon seofon bēoð eahta and twēntiġ; fīf sīðon seofon bēoð fīf and þrīttiġ; syx sīðon seofon bēoð twā and fēowertiġ; seofon sīðon seofon bēoð nigon and fēowertiġ; eahta sīðon seofon bēoð syx and fīftiġ; nigon sīðon seofon bēoð þrēo and syxtiġ; tȳn sīðon seofon bēoð hundseofontiġ. [2] Twēntiġ sīðon seofon bēoð ān hund and fēowertiġ; þrīttiġ sīðon seofon bēoð twā hundred and tȳn; fēowertiġ sīðon seofon bēoð twā hundred and hundeahtatiġ; fīftiġ sīðon seofon bēoð þrēo hundred and fīftiġ. [3] Ġīt þær sind fīftȳne tō lāfe; tōdǣlað þā eall swā þā ōðre. [4] Twīa seofon bēoð fēowertȳne; nū þær is ān tō lāfe.

## 9.2 Cardinal numbers

Here are the cardinal numbers one–twelve:

| | | | |
|---|---|---|---|
| ān | fēower | seofon | tīen |
| twēġen, twā | fīf | eahta | endleofan |
| þrīe, þrēo | siex | nigon | twelf |

The cardinal *ān* is usually declined as a strong adjective; when it is declined weak (*āna*) it means 'alone': *hē āna læġ* 'he lay alone'. The cardinals *two* and *three* have their own peculiar inflectional system, shown in table 9.1. If you substitute a b- for the *tw-* of *twēġen*, you will get *bēġen* (*bā*, *bū*, etc.) 'both'.

**Table 9.1** The numerals *twēġen* and *þrīe*

| | | masculine | neuter | feminine |
|---|---|---|---|---|
| 'two' | nominative/accusative | twēġen | twā, tū | twā |
| | genitive | | twēġa, twēġra | |
| | dative | | twǣm, twām | |
| 'three' | nominative/accusative | þrīe | þrēo | þrēo |
| | genitive | | þrēora | |
| | dative | | þrim | |

Cardinals above three occasionally have grammatical endings, but generally are not declined at all. The numbers thirteen through nineteen are made by adding -*tīene* to the numbers *þrēo* through *nigon*: *þrēotīene*, *fēowertīene*, etc. From twenty through to the sixties, numbers are in the form *ān and twentiġ* 'twenty-one'.

Starting with seventy, Old English prefixes *hund-* to the expected forms: *hundseofontiġ* 'seventy', *hundeahtatiġ* 'eighty', *hundnigontiġ* 'ninety', *hundtēontiġ* or *ān hund* 'one hundred', *hundtwelftiġ* or *hundtwentiġ* 'one hundred and twenty'. These curious forms seem to reflect a number system, common to all the earliest Germanic languages, in which counting proceeded by twelves and sixty was a significant number in much the same way that one hundred is now.

## 9.3   Ordinal numbers

Here are the ordinal numbers first–twelfth:

| | | | |
|---|---|---|---|
| forma, fyrmest | fēorða | seofoða | tēoða |
| ōðer | fīfta | eahtoða | endlyfta |
| þridda | siexta | nigoða | twelfta |

For 'first' you may also find *ǣrest*, but *fyrst* is not common.

For 'thirteenth' to 'nineteenth', add the element -*tēoða* in place of ordinal -*tīene*: for example, *þrēotēoða* 'thirteen'. For 'twentieth' and higher, add -*tigoða*, -*tegoða* or -*teogoða*: *fīfteogoða* 'fiftieth', *fīf and hundeahtatigoða* 'eighty-fifth'.

# Chapter 10

# Adverbs, Conjunctions and Prepositions

## 10.1 Quick start

Adverbs, conjunctions and prepositions[1] are relatively easy because they are not inflected. Many of them, however, have changed their meanings since the end of the Old English period; further, some have been lost and others have taken their places, so many of these exceedingly common words will be unfamiliar to you at first. You should memorize the most common of them early on, especially the adverbs *ǣr* 'before', *ēac* 'also', *siððan* 'afterwards' and *þā* 'then'; the conjunctions *ac* 'but', *for þām þe* 'because', *oð þæt* 'until' and *þā* 'when'; and the prepositions *be* 'by, near', *mid* 'with', *of* 'from', *wið* 'opposite, against' and *ymb(e)* 'near, by'.

## 10.2 Adverbs

An adverb may be made from an adjective by adding *-e*; since many adjectives are made by adding *-lić* to nouns or other adjectives, you will often see adverbs ending in *-līċe*.[2] Examples: *wearme* 'warmly' from *wearm* 'warm',

---

[1]   For general discussions of these parts of speech, see §§3.1.5, 3.1.6, 3.1.7.
[2]   The suffix *-lić* is generally thought to have had a long vowel when an ending followed, but otherwise a short vowel.

*sārlīċe* 'painfully' from *sār*, *sārliċ* 'painful'. The adverb corresponding to *gōd* 'good', however, is *wel*.

Adverbs may also be made by adding case endings to nouns, for example, genitive *dæġes* 'by day', *unþances* 'unwillingly'; dative *nēode* 'necessarily', *hwīlum* 'at times'. Some of the most common adverbs are conjunctive or prepositional: that is, they are related (and sometimes identical) to certain conjunctions and prepositions. Such adverbs often relate to place, time, extent, degree, negation or affirmation.

Some of the most common adverbs are listed in table 10.1.[3] Adverbs marked with ☆ have corresponding conjunctions that are identical in form and related in meaning; for these, see further §§10.3 and 10.4.

**Table 10.1** Common adverbs

| | | |
|---|---|---|
| ā 'always' | heonan 'hence' | sōna 'immediately' |
| ādūn(e) 'down' | hēr 'here' | ☆ swā 'so' |
| æfre 'ever' | hider 'hither' | ☆ swelċe 'likewise' |
| æfter 'after' | hūru 'indeed' | swīðe 'very' |
| ☆ ǣr 'before' | hwæðre 'nevertheless' | tō 'too' |
| ætgædere 'together' | hwīlum 'at times' | ☆ þā 'then' |
| ēac 'also' | in 'in' | ☆ þanon 'thence' |
| eall 'entirely' | innan 'from within' | ☆ þǣr 'there' |
| eft 'afterwards' | nā 'not at all' | þæs 'afterwards' |
| fela 'much' | næfre 'never' | ☆ þēah 'nevertheless' |
| feor 'far' | ne 'not' | ☆ þenden 'while' |
| forð 'forwards' | neoðan 'from below' | ☆ þider 'thither' |
| ☆ for þām 'therefore' | nese 'no' | ☆ þonne 'then' |
| ful 'very' | niðer 'down' | þus 'thus' |
| furðum 'even' | ☆ nū 'now' | ufan 'from above' |
| ġēa 'yes' | ofdūne 'down' | ūp 'up' |
| ġeāra 'formerly' | oft 'often' | ūt 'out' |
| ġīese 'yes' | on 'on, in, forward' | ūtan 'from outside' |
| ġīet 'yet' | ☆ siððan 'afterwards' | wel 'well' |

Interrogative adverbs, used (of course) in asking questions, are listed in table 10.2. The Modern English interrogatives (*where*, *when*, etc.) can be used to introduce adverb clauses (e.g. 'I know *where* you live') or adjective clauses (e.g. 'on the street *where* you live'), but the same is rarely true for Old English, which instead will use one of the conjunctions listed in §10.3 or the relative particle *þe*.

---

[3]  The word-lists in this chapter do not display all definitions of the words they contain. For complete collections of definitions, you must consult a dictionary.

**Table 10.2**   Interrogative adverbs

| | |
|---|---|
| hū 'how' | hwǣr 'where' |
| hwider 'whither' | hwonne 'when' |
| hwanon 'whence' | hwȳ 'why' |

### 10.2.1   Comparison of adverbs

Adverbs made from adjectives normally add -*or* to make the comparative and -*ost* to make the superlative: *ġearwor* and *ġearwost* from *ġearwe* 'readily' (adjective *ġearo* 'ready'), *lēoflīcor*, *lēoflīcost* from *lēoflīċe* 'lovingly' (adjective *lēof*, *lēoflīċ* 'beloved').

Other adverbs may add -*rra* or -*ra* for the comparative and -*mest* for the superlative (e.g. *norþerra*, *norþmest* from *norþ* 'northwards').

A few common adverbs make their comparatives by applying *i*-mutation to the root vowel (omitting the ending); the superlatives may or may not have *i*-mutation:

| | | |
|---|---|---|
| ēaðe 'easily' | īeð | ēaðost |
| feorr 'far' | fierr | fierrest |
| lange 'long' | leng | lenġest |
| sōfte 'softly' | sēft | sōftost |

Others are anomalous:

| | | |
|---|---|---|
| lȳtle, lȳt 'a little' | lǣs | lǣst, lǣsest |
| miċle 'much' | mā | mǣst |
| nēah 'near' | nīer | nīehst, nēxt |
| wel 'well' | bet, sēl | betst, sēlest |
| yfle 'badly' | wiers(e) | wierrest, wierst |

## 10.3   Conjunctions

The coordinating conjunctions *and/ond* 'and', *ac* 'but' and *oððe* 'or' will cause you no difficulty. The subordinating conjunctions are more difficult, for they do not always resemble the Modern English words to which they correspond in function. The most common subordinating conjunctions are listed in table 10.3. Here, as in table 10.1, conjunctions with matching adverbs are marked ✮.

! The ambiguity of some of the conjunctions with matching adverbs may optionally be resolved by adding the particle *þe*, which marks the word as a conjunction: these are indicated in the table. A few others may be doubled to mark them as conjunctions: *swā* may mean 'so' or 'as', but *swā swā* always means 'as'; similarly *þā þā* means 'when' and *þǣr þǣr* means 'where'.

**Table 10.3**  Subordinating conjunctions

| | | |
|---|---|---|
| æfter þām (þe) 'after' | ☆ nū 'now that' | ☆ þǣr 'where' |
| ☆ ǣr 'before' | oð þæt 'until' | þæs þe 'after' |
| ǣr þām (þe) 'before' | ☆ siððan 'after' | þæt 'that, so that' |
| būtan 'unless' | ☆ swā 'as' | ☆ þēah (þe) 'though' |
| ☆ for þām (þe) 'because' | ☆ swelċe 'as if' | ☆ þenden 'while' |
| ġif 'if' | ☆ þā 'when' | ☆ þider (þe) 'whither' |
| hwæðer 'whether' | þā hwīle þe 'while' | ☆ þonne 'when' |
| nemþe 'unless' | ☆ þanon 'whence' | wið þām þe 'provided that' |

The correlative conjunctions (like Modern English *both . . . and*) are as follows:

ǣġðer . . . ġe 'both . . . and'
hwæðer . . . oððe 'whether . . . or'
nā þæt ān . . . ac ēac swilċe 'not only . . . but also'
nāðor . . . ne 'neither . . . nor'
ne . . . ne 'neither . . . nor'
þȳ . . . þȳ 'the . . . the' (as in 'the more, the merrier')

## 10.4  Correlation

Correlation is a construction in which an adverb at the beginning of an independent clause recapitulates or anticipates an adverb clause. The conjunction that begins the adverb clause is related in sense to the adverb in the independent clause (e.g. 'when . . . then'); these two words are said to be correlative.

Correlation is much rarer in Modern English than in Old English, but it is still fairly common with conditional clauses:

*If* you were in Philadelphia, *then* you must have seen Independence Hall.

## Minitext f. A Vision of Hell

The resemblance between this passage from a homily on Michaelmass and *Beowulf* ll. 1357–66 has often been remarked. For the complete text of the homily, see Morris [84], pp. 196–211.

[1] Swā Sanctus Paulus wæs ġesēonde on norðanweardne þisne middanġeard, þǣr ealle wæteru niðer ġewītað, and hē þǣr ġeseah ofer ðām wætere sumne hārne stān. [2] And wǣron norð of ðām stāne āweaxene swīðe hrīmiġe bearwas, and ðǣr wǣron þӯstru ġenipu, and under þām stāne wæs nicra eardung and wearga. [3] And hē ġeseah þæt on ðām clife hangodon on ðām īsiġean bearwum maniġe swearte sāwla be heora handum ġebundne, and þā fӯnd þāra on nicra onlīċnesse heora grīpende wǣron, swā swā grǣdiġ wulf. [4] And þæt wæter wæs sweart under þām clife nēoðan, and betweox þām clife on ðām wætere wǣron swelċe twelf mīla. [5] And ðonne ðā twigu forburston þonne ġewiton þā sāwla niðer þā þe on ðām twigum hangodan, and him onfēngon ðā nicras. [6] Ðis ðonne wǣron ðā sāwla þā ðe hēr on worulde mid unrihte ġefirenode wǣron, and ðæs noldon ġeswīcan ǣr heora līfes ende. [7] Ac uton nū biddan Sanctus Michael ġeornlīċe þæt hē ūre sāwla ġelǣde on ġefēan, þǣr hīe mōton blissian ā būton ende on ēċnesse.

Other correlations can be used in Modern English for emphasis or rhetorical effect. The King James Bible (1611) has

For *where* your treasure is, *there* will your heart be also.

We understand this perfectly well, though it sounds a bit archaic.

Most instances of correlation in Old English will cause you no difficulty. Here are some examples:

And *ðēah ðe* hē ġehēran ne wolde, *hwæðre* hē ġeðyldelīċe wæs from him eallum ārǣfned.
[And *though* he would not obey, *nevertheless* he was patiently tolerated by all of them.]

*þider þe* hē sylfa tōweard wæs æfter dēaþe, *þider* hē his ēagan sende ǣr his dēaðe, þæt hē þӯ blīþelīcor þrōwade.
[*where* he himself was headed after death, *there* he directed his eyes before his death, so that he could suffer more happily.]

Correlation can cause difficulties when the conjunction and adverb have the same form, as they often do (see tables 10.1 and 10.3):

þā . . . þā 'when . . . then'
þonne . . . þonne 'when . . . then'
þǣr . . . þǣr 'where . . . there'
swā . . . swā 'as . . . so'

In such cases you must sometimes allow context to guide you to the correct reading. But with certain conjunction/adverb pairs, word-order can help you decide which is the conjunction and which the adverb: see further §§12.5 and 15.2.5.

## 10.5   Prepositions

Here we will briefly list the most common prepositions and offer notes on their usage. The information you will need about each preposition, in addition to its meanings, is what case the object of the preposition may take and whether the case of that object influences the meaning of the preposition. This information is usually, but not always, supplied by glossaries and dictionaries.

**æfter,** *after, according to,* usually with dative, sometimes with accusative.
**ǣr,** *before* (in time), usually with dative, sometimes with accusative.
**æt,** with dative, *at, from*; with accusative, *until, up to.*
**be,** *by, near, along, about, in relation to,* with dative.
**beforan,** *before, in front of, in the presence of, ahead of,* with dative or (usually with an added sense of motion) accusative.
**betweox,** *between, among,* with dative or accusative.
**binnan,** with dative, *within*; with accusative, *to within.*
**bufan,** with dative, *above*; with accusative, *upwards.*
**būtan,** *outside, except, without,* with dative or accusative.
**ēac,** *besides, in addition to,* with dative.
**for,** *before, in front of, because of, in place of, for the sake of,* usually with dative, sometimes with accusative.
**fram,** *from, by,* with dative.
**ġeond,** *throughout, through,* usually with accusative, sometimes with dative.
**in,** with dative, *in*; with accusative, *into.*
**innan,** with dative, *in, within, from within*; with accusative, *into.*
**mid,** *with, and, by means of,* usually with dative, sometimes with accusative.
**of,** *from, of,* with dative.
**ofer,** with dative, *over, upon, throughout*; with accusative (usually with an added sense of motion), *over, across, throughout, more than.*
**on,** with dative, *in, on*; with accusative, *into, onto.* In West Saxon, *on* is usual where you would expect *in.*

**onġēan,** *opposite, towards, in opposition to,* with dative or (usually with an added sense of motion) accusative.

**oð,** *up to, as far as, until,* usually with accusative, sometimes with dative.

**tō,** with dative, *to, towards, at, for;* with genitive, *at.* With dative, *tō* often forms an idiom to be translated with 'as': *tō ġefēran* 'as a companion'.

**tōġēanes,** *towards, in preparation for, in opposition to,* with dative.

**þurh,** *through, by means of,* usually with accusative, sometimes with dative or genitive.

**under,** *under,* with dative or (usually with an added sense of motion) accusative.

**wið,** *towards, opposite, against, in exchange for,* with accusative, dative or genitive.

**ymb(e),** *near, by, about, after,* usually with accusative, sometimes with dative.

Some prepositions have the same meaning whatever the case of the object: for, these, some authors favour the dative while others favour the accusative. But several prepositions have different meanings depending on the case of the object. For these, the dative is generally associated with location while the accusative is associated with movement towards.

Study this list of prepositions carefully, for you will meet with a number of these words in every text you read.

# Chapter 11

# Concord

## 11.1 Quick start

Concord is agreement in gender, case, number or person between different words that share a reference. For example, if a sentence contains a proper noun 'Paul' and somewhat later a pronoun 'he', and they refer to the same person, we say that they agree in number (for both are singular) and gender (for both are masculine).

As speakers or writers of a language we experience concord as a set of rules to learn and follow (and sometimes complain about). As listeners or readers we recognize that concord helps us decode sentences.

> Elizabeth Bennet had been obliged, by the scarcity of gentlemen, to sit down for two dances; and during part of that time, Mr Darcy had been standing near enough for *her* to overhear a conversation between *him* and Mr Bingley, who came from the dance for a few minutes, to press *his* friend to join it.

In this passage two grammatical rules help us to determine the reference of the pronouns 'her', 'him' and 'his'. The first of these is that a pronoun must agree with its antecedent in gender and number; this rule associates 'her' with Elizabeth Bennet (rather than Darcy, who would otherwise be a possible antecedent) and prevents our associating 'him' or 'his' with Elizabeth Bennet. The second is that a pronoun must be associated with the most recent possible antecedent; by this rule we understand 'his friend' to mean 'Bingley's friend' rather than 'Darcy's friend'.

We work out the reference of the pronouns in a passage like the one above without conscious effort. Indeed the Modern English rules of concord are few and relatively simple:

- The subject must agree with its verb in person and number. For most Modern English verbs this simply means that we must remember that a third-person singular subject generally takes a special verb form ending in -*s*. The verb *to be*, however, distinguishes all three persons in the present singular (*I am*, *you are*, *she is*) and the second person in the past singular (*I was*, *you were*, *he was*).
- The pronoun must agree with its antecedent in gender and number. If you speak of a woman named Ruth in one clause and then in the next clause want to refer to her with a pronoun, the pronoun must be both feminine and singular.
- The pronouns *that* and *this*, when used adjectivally, must agree in number with the nouns they modify: *that wolf*, *those wolves*; *this horse*, *these horses*. These pronominal adjectives are not inflected for gender.

The first two Modern English rules of concord are largely the same as in Old English. The third Modern English rule is a remnant of an Old English rule that a noun and all its modifiers (adjectives and pronouns used adjectivally) must agree in gender, case and number. All three of these rules are a little more complex in Old English than in Modern English, so you will have to pay careful attention to the rules of concord – at first, anyway.

## 11.2   Subject and verb

The Old English verb must agree with its subject in person and number. The Old English finite verb always distinguished number and often distinguished person, and this relatively great degree of expressiveness can help you locate hard-to-find subjects, as here:

> Þæt wæs yldum cūþ,
> þæt hīe ne mōste,  þā Metod nolde,
> se scynscaþa   under sceadu breġdan.[1]
> [It was known to men
> that the demonic foe could not, if God did not wish it,
> drag them under the shadows.]

---

[1]   *Beowulf*, ll. 705–7.

In the noun clause that begins in the second line of this passage, the nominative/accusative third-person plural pronoun *hīe* comes before the verb *mōste* 'could', where Modern English grammar leads us to expect the subject. But the verb is plainly singular, so plural *hīe* cannot be the subject. Looking further, we find the nominative singular noun phrase *se scynscaþa* 'the demonic foe'; this is the subject.

A verb's personal ending is actually a statement or restatement of the subject, conveying much of the information that a personal pronoun can convey. In fact, in situations where Modern English uses a pronoun subject, the Old English finite verb can sometimes express the subject all by itself:[2]

Hēt þā bord beran,   beornas gangan
[(He) then commanded the men to bear their shields (and) to go]

Ġewiton him þā fēran
[Then (they) departed travelling]

Nū sculon heriġean   heofonrīċes Weard
[Now (we) must praise the Guardian of the kingdom of heaven]

In these fragments, the subjects of the verbs *hēt* 'commanded', *ġewiton* 'departed' and *sculon* 'must' are unexpressed, but context and the form of the verb together give us enough information to figure them out for ourselves.

Compound subjects may be split in Old English, one part divided from the others by the verb or some other sentence element. When this happens, the verb will typically agree with the first part of the subject. Consider these sentences:

Hēr Henġest ond Horsa fuhton wiþ Wyrtgeorne þām cyninge
[Here Hengest and Horsa fought with King Vortigern]

Hēr cuōm Ælle on Bretenlond ond his þrīe suna, Cymen ond Wlenċing ond Ċissa
[Here Ælle and his three sons, Cymen and Wlencing and Cissa, came to Britain]

In the first, the compound subject is arranged as in Modern English and the verb (*fuhton*) is plural. In the second, however, the first part of the compound subject, *Ælle*, is divided from the other parts by a prepositional phrase (*on Bretenlond* 'to Britain'), and the verb (*cuōm*, an archaic form of *cōm* 'came') is singular. A spectacular example of this sort of construction is at the beginning of Riddle 46:

---

[2]   Passages from *The Battle of Maldon*, l. 62, *Beowulf*, l. 301, and *Cædmon's Hymn*, l. 1.

Wer sæt æt wīne   mid his wīfum twām
ond his twēġen suno   ond his twā dohtor,
swāse ġesweostor,   ond hyra suno twēġen,
frēolicu frumbearn.

To the Modern English eye it looks as if *Wer* 'A man' is the sole subject of the singular verb *sæt* 'sat', and that everything following *mid* 'with' is part of a long prepositional phrase ('with his two wives and his two sons . . .'). But in fact the whole of the prepositional phrase is *mid his wīfum twām*; everything that follows is nominative and therefore part of a compound subject. The correct translation (rearranging the sentence so that the parts of the subject come together) is as follows: 'A man, his two sons, his two daughters (beloved sisters), and their two sons (noble first-borns) sat at wine with his two wives'.

### 11.2.1   Impersonal verbs

Impersonal verbs are those that lack a subject, or that have only *hit* 'it' as a 'placeholder' subject. We still have such verbs in Modern English:

*It rained* yesterday.
*It seems* to me that the world has grown smaller.
*It is fitting* that children obey their parents.

Old English has many more such verbs than Modern English, and they often lack the subject *hit*:

Nāp nihtscūa,   norþan *snīwde*[3]
[The night-shadow darkened, *(it) snowed* from the north]

*Hit gedafenað* þæt hē wel ġelǣred sȳ mid godcundre lāre.
[*It is fitting* that he be well taught in divine doctrine.]

Frequently what looks to us like the *logical* subject of the impersonal verb is in the dative or the accusative case:

*Mē hingrode* and ġē mē sealdon etan; *mē þyrste* and ġē me sealdon drincan.
[*I was hungry* and you gave me something to eat; *I was thirsty* and you gave me something to drink.]

Ġehȳrað mīn swefn, ðe *mē mǣtte*.
[Hear my dream, which *I dreamed*.]

---

[3]   *The Seafarer*, l. 31.

Þā ongan *hine* eft *langian* on his cȳþþe.
[Then *he* began *to long* for his homeland again.]

In such cases it makes no sense to translate with an impersonal construction; you may translate the dative or accusative as the subject of the verb.

## 11.3    Pronoun and antecedent

A pronoun typically restates a noun, called its *antecedent*; it must agree with this antecedent in gender and number.[4] Modern English pronouns obey the same rule, but the Old English rule behaves a little differently because of the way the language handles gender. Consider this passage:

Sēo sunne gǣð betwux heofenan and eorðan. On ðā healfe ðe *hēo* scīnð þǣr bið dæġ, and on ðā healfe ðe *hēo* ne scīnð þǣr bið niht.
[The sun goes between heaven and earth. On the side where *it* shines there is day, and on the side where *it* does not shine there is night.]

Students sometimes ask whether the use of the feminine pronoun *hēo* to refer to the sun means that it is being personified. It doesn't mean that at all; rather, the pronoun is simply agreeing with the feminine noun *sunne* 'sun' and must be translated 'it', not 'she'.

On the other hand, when the pronoun refers to a human being, it will very likely take on the 'natural gender' of its antecedent rather than its grammatical gender:

Abrames wīf wæs ðā ġȳt wuniġende būtan ċildum, and *hēo* hæfde āne þīnene, ðā Eġyptiscan Agar.
[Abraham's wife continued still to be without children, and *she* had a maid-servant, the Egyptian Agar.]

The grammatical gender of *wīf* is neuter, but the pronoun *hēo*, which refers to it, is feminine.

When a pronoun anticipates the noun it refers to, it may appear as neuter singular, regardless of the gender and number of the noun. We do something like this in Modern English:

Who's there? It's Bob.

---

[4]    When a pronoun is used as an adjective, it obeys the rule for modifiers (§11.4) rather than the rule for pronouns.

A famous Old English example comes near the beginning of *Beowulf* (l. 11):

> þæt wæs gōd cyning!
> [*that* was a good king!]

where we get neuter singular *þæt* instead of masculine singular *se*. A stranger example is in a passage quoted below (p. 110), *Þæt synt fēower sweras* 'They are four columns', where the same pronoun refers to a masculine plural noun.

## 11.4    Noun and modifiers

A noun and all its modifiers must agree in gender, case and number. Though this rule has all but disappeared in Modern English, it is very important in Old English. Every time a demonstrative pronoun is used as an 'article', for example, it agrees with its noun:

> Þā þæs on merġen *se* mæsseprēost ābēad *þæs* mædenes word *þām* mǣran bisceope . . .
> [When, the morning after, *the* priest reported *the* virgin's words to *the* famous bishop . . . ]

Here the demonstrative is used three times to modify a noun:

> se mæsseprēost: masculine nominative singular
> þæs mædenes: neuter genitive singular
> þām mǣran bisceope: masculine dative singular

and each time, it matches its noun exactly in gender, case and number. What is true of pronouns is equally true of adjectives:

> Đā ārison sōna of þām *sweartan* flocce *twēġen eġesliċe* dēoflu mid *īsenum* tōlum.
> [Then from that *dark* company *two terrifying* devils instantly arose with *iron* tools.]

Here the adjectives agree with their nouns as follows:

> þām sweartan flocce: masculine dative singular
> twēġen eġesliċe dēoflu: masculine[5] nominative plural
> īsenum tōlum: neuter dative plural

---

[5]    In a rare anomaly, the plural of *dēofol* 'devil' is neuter in form, but may agree with either masculine or neuter pronouns and adjectives.

The adjective is frequently separated from its noun, especially in poetry. When this happens, the rules of concord will help you to match up the adjective with its noun:

> Slōh ðā wundenlocc
> þone fēondsceaðan    fāgum mēċe,
> *heteþoncolne*,    þæt hēo *healfne* forċearf
> þone swūran him.[6]
> > [Then the wavy-haired one struck
> > the *hostile-minded* enemy with a decorated sword,
> > so that she cut through *half*
> > of his neck.]

In the main clause of this sentence, *þone fēondsceaðan* 'the enemy' is the direct object of the verb *slōh* 'struck'. We can tell by its ending that the adjective *heteþoncolne* 'hostile-minded', in the next line, agrees with accusative *fēondsceaðan*; since an adjective normally comes before its noun in Modern English, we must move it in our translation, making a noun phrase 'the hostile-minded enemy'. In the clause of result that follows (*þæt hēo . . . swūran him*), the adjective *healfne* 'half' agrees with *þone swūran* 'the neck', though it is separated from it by the verb *forċearf* 'cut through'. Once again we must gather the fragments of a noun phrase in our translation: 'half of his neck'.

Past and present participles are often inflected as adjectives, even when they form periphrastic verb forms:

> ēowre ġefēran þe mid þām cyninge *ofslæġene* wǣrun
> [your companions who were *slain* with the king]

> Dryhten, hwænne ġesāwe wē þē *hingriġendne* oððe *þyrstendne*?
> [Lord, when did we see you *hungering* or *thirsting*?]

Here the participles *ofslæġene*, *hingriġendne* and *þyrstendne* all have adjective endings.

**ⓘ** When participles are inflected, the ending *-e* is added to the nominative/accusative plural of all genders and may occasionally be omitted. Feminine nominative singular *-u* also may be omitted.

## 11.5   Bad grammar?

It is probably fair to say that the schools of Anglo-Saxon England offered little or no instruction in Old English grammar and that vernacular texts generally

---

6   *Judith*, ll. 103–6.

## Minitext G. From *Solomon and Saturn*

*Solomon and Saturn* is a dialogue between the biblical king Solomon and the pagan god Saturn, in which Solomon answers questions posed by Saturn concerning God and the nature of creation. For the complete text, see Cross and Hill [34].

[1] Hēr cȳð hū Saturnus and Saloman fettode ymbe heora wīsdōm.

[2] Þā cwæð Saturnus tō Salomane: Saga mē hwǣr God sǣte þā hē ġeworhte heofonas and eorðan. Iċ þē secge, hē sætt ofer winda feðerum.

[3] Saga mē, hwelċ wyrt ys betst and sēlost? Iċ þē secge, liliġe hātte sēo wyrt, for þām þe hēo ġetācnað Crist.

[4] Saga mē, hwelċ fugel ys sēlost? Iċ ðē secge, culfre ys sēlost; hēo ġetācnað þone hālgan gāst.

[5] Saga mē, hwanon cymð līġetu? Iċ secge, hēo cymð fram winde and fram wætere.

[6] Saga mē, hwelċ man ǣrost wǣre wið hund sprecende? Iċ þē secge, Sanctus Petrus.

[7] Saga mē, hwæt ys hefegost tō berenne on eorðan? Iċ þē secge, mannes synna and hys hlāfordes yrre.

[8] Saga mē, for hwan bið sēo sunne rēad on ǣfen? Iċ þē secge, for ðām hēo lōcað on helle.

[9] Saga mē, hwȳ scīnð hēo swā rēade on morgene? Iċ þē secge, for ðām hire twēonað hwæðer hēo mæġ oþþe ne mæġ þisne middaneard ġeondscīnan swā hire beboden is.

did not pass through the hands of copy-editors on their way to 'publication'. Old English was an unpoliced language for which 'correct' grammar was governed by usage rather than by the authority of experts. Under these circumstances we should expect to find what look to the rigorously trained modern grammarian rather like errors. Consider this passage, for example, by a learned author:

Þæt synt fēower sweras, þā synd þus ġecīġed on Lȳden: iustitia, þæt ys rihtwīsnys; and *ōðer* hātte prudentia, þæt ys snoternys; *þridde* ys temperantia, þæt ys ġemetgung; *fēorðe* ys fortitudo, þæt ys strengð.
[They (the cardinal virtues) are four columns, which are called thus in Latin: *iustitia*, or righteousness; and the *second* is called *prudentia*, or prudence; the *third* is *temperantia*, or temperance; the *fourth* is called *fortitudo*, or strength.]

Notice the sequence of ordinal numbers here: *ōðer, þridde, fēorðe*. The first of these could be any gender, but *þridde* and *fēorðe* have the neuter/feminine weak nominative singular ending -*e* (§8.3). They do not agree in gender with masculine *sweras*, their grammatical antecedent, but rather with feminine nouns such as *rihtwīsnys* and *snoternys*. Editors of an earlier age tended to 'fix' such 'errors'; modern editors, on the other hand, are more likely to conclude that what looks like 'bad grammar' to us did not necessarily look so to the Anglo-Saxons. If the text is readable, there is little reason to emend.

Another example of what we are talking about comes at *Beowulf*, ll. 67–70, where Hrothgar decides to build his great hall Heorot:

> Him on mōd bearn
> þæt healreċed    hātan wolde,
> medoærn miċel    men ġewyrċean
> *þone* yldo bearn    æfre ġefrūnon
> [It came into his mind
> that he would command men to build
> a hall – a great mead-hall
> *which* the children of men would always hear about]

Here the problem is with *þone* in the last line, which looks as if it should be a masculine relative pronoun 'which', but does not agree in gender with the nearest antecedent, neuter *medoærn* 'mead-hall'. Early editors emended *þone* to *þon*[*n*]*e* 'than', creating yet another problem by positing an 'unexpressed comparative'. The better solution is to recognize that writers of Old English were less punctilious than we are about concord. Further, masculine nouns are more common in Old English than either feminines or neuters; when you find an otherwise unmotivated disagreement of gender, it is likely to involve a shift from feminine or neuter to masculine.

Do not get carried away with finding 'errors' in the Old English texts you read. Violations of the rules of concord are relatively rare, and generally you will be able to see why they happened, as in the examples above.

# Chapter 12

# Word-order

## 12.1    Quick start

You may read in some sources, especially older ones, that Old English word-order is 'free' compared to that of Modern English, and you may conclude that writers of Old English could mix up their words in any order at all. But though word-order was freer then than now, there are just a few common word-orders in Old English clauses. Learn these and the job of learning the language will become much easier. The main Old English word-orders are these:

> **Subject–Verb.** This, of course, is how most Modern English sentences are arranged.
>
> **Verb–Subject.** This word-order still occurs in Modern English sentences like 'There are plenty of fish in the sea', and often in questions, such as 'Are you sleeping?'
>
> **Subject . . . Verb.** The finite verb is delayed until the end of the clause.

Each of these can occur in several different environments, but, as you will see, each is also typical of particular kinds of clause.

## 12.2    Subject–Verb

Since this is the standard word-order of the Modern English clause, you'll be glad to know that it is very common in Old English. It is typical of independent clauses, though it also occurs frequently in subordinate clauses. Sometimes you'll be able to translate a sentence that uses this word-order almost word-for-word:

> Ēac swylċe ðā nȳtenu of eallum cynne and eallum fugolcynne cōmon tō Noe, intō ðām arce, swā swā *God bebēad.*
> [Also *the beasts* of each species and (of) each species of bird *came* to Noah, into the ark, as *God commanded.*]

The direct object, when it is a noun or noun phrase, will generally follow the verb:

> *God bletsode* ðā *Noe and his suna* and cwæð him tō: 'Weaxað and bēoð ġemenifylde and āfyllað ðā eorðan.'
> [*God* then *blessed Noah and his sons* and said to them: 'Increase and be multiplied and fill the earth.']

Old English has a tendency to place pronoun objects – direct and indirect – early in the clause. A pronoun object will usually come between the subject and the verb:

> And iċ *hine ġesēo* and bēo ġemyndiġ ðæs ēċean weddes ðe ġeset is betwux Gode and eallum libbendum flǣsce.
> [And I *will see it* and be mindful of the eternal covenant that is established between God and all living flesh.]

If the clause has both a direct and an indirect object, and one of them is a pronoun, the pronoun will come first:

> Hēr ġē magon ġehȳran þæt hē ġyfð *ūs anweald,* ġif wē on hine ġelȳfað, Godes bearn tō bēonne.
> [Here you may hear that he gives *us the power,* if we believe in him, to be God's children.]

If the indirect object had been a noun and the direct object a pronoun, the direct object would have come first.

Though you will most frequently find a noun object after the verb and a pronoun before, there is no hard-and-fast rule for the placement of objects. Sometimes you will find a pronoun object after the verb, and sometimes the object will come before the subject:

> and iċ *fordō hī* mid ðǣre eorðan samod.
> [I *will destroy them* together with the earth.]

*Ðone cyning* hī brōhton cucene tō Iosue.
[They brought *the king* alive to Joshua.]

Since the location of the direct object in Modern English is fixed after the verb, its mobility in Old English may occasionally cause problems. Keep an eye on the inflections and, when they don't help you, let the context guide you to the correct reading.

Adverbial elements, including prepositional phrases and adverb clauses, occur in various places in the sentence. Though such elements are also mobile in Modern English, you will often find them where we cannot now put them, as in *God bletsode ðā Noe*, quoted above, which we can translate 'God *then* blessed Noah', '*then* God blessed Noah' or 'God blessed Noah *then*', but not 'God blessed *then* Noah'. Similarly, *ġif wē **on hine** ġelȳfa*ð, also quoted above, must be translated 'if we believe *in him*', not 'if we *in him* believe'.

## 12.3   Verb–Subject

This word-order is common in independent clauses introduced by the adverbs *þā* 'then', *þonne* 'then', *þǣr* 'there', *þanon* 'thence', *þider* 'thither', the negative adverb *ne*, and the conjunctions *and/ond* and *ac* 'but'.

Since Old English narrative often advances in a series of *þā*-clauses, you'll find the Verb–Subject word-order quite frequent in narrative:

Ðā *cwæð Drihten* tō Caine: 'Hwǣr is Abel ðīn brōðor?'
Ðā *andswarode hē* and cwæð: 'Iċ nāt; seġst ðū, sceolde iċ mīnne brōðor healdan?'
Ðā *cwæð Drihten* tō Caine: 'Hwæt dydest ðū? Þīnes brōðor blōd clypað tō mē of eorðan'.
[Then *the Lord said* to Cain: 'Where is Abel, your brother?'
Then *he answered* and said: 'I don't know: do you say I must look after my brother?'
Then *the Lord said* to Cain: 'What have you done? Your brother's blood cries to me from the earth.']

This word-order also occurs in independent clauses not introduced by an adverb or adverbial element:

*Wǣron hī* ēac swȳþe druncene, for ðām þǣr wæs brōht wīn sūðan.
[They were also very drunk, for wine had been brought from the south.]

When the clause contains a direct object, it will usually follow the subject, but it may also come first in the clause, as in §12.2.

The Verb–Subject word-order is also characteristic of questions, whether or not introduced by an interrogative word:

Him cwæð Nicodemus tō: 'Hū *mæ̇g se ealda mann* eft bēon ācenned? *Mæ̇g hē*, lā, inn faran tō his mōdor innoðe eft, and swā bēon ġeedcenned?'
[Nicodemus said to him, 'How *can the old man* be born again? *May he*, indeed, go into his mother's womb again, and thus be reborn?']

In Modern English this word-order is used mostly in questions, but, as you have seen, in Old English it is also used in declarative sentences. You must therefore be careful not to make assumptions about the kind of clause you are reading based on this word-order. When Unferth makes fun of a youthful exploit that Beowulf undertook with Breca, he begins his speech thus:

Eart þū se Bēowulf,   se þe wið Brecan wunne[1]

The Verb–Subject word-order has suggested to most editors that the line is a question, to be translated 'Are you the Beowulf who contended with Breca?' But it has been plausibly suggested that it is instead a statement, to be translated 'You're *that* Beowulf, the one who contended with Breca!'

Commands also generally have the Verb–Subject word-order unless the subject is omitted, as happens more often than not when the command is positive:

Ne *wyrċ ðū* ðē āgrafene godas.
[Do not *make* graven gods for yourself.]

*Ārwurða* fæder and mōdor.
[*Honour* (your) father and mother.]

## 12.4   Subject . . . Verb

The Subject . . . Verb word-order is commonly found in subordinate clauses and clauses introduced by *and/ond* or *ac* 'but', though it does sometimes occur in independent clauses. The subject comes at the beginning of the clause and the finite verb is delayed until the end (though it may be followed by an adverbial element such as a prepositional phrase).

Gode ofðūhte ðā ðæt *hē* mann ġeworhte ofer eorðan.
[Then it was a matter of regret to God that *he had made* man upon the earth.]

---

[1] *Beowulf*, l. 506.

In the noun clause (ðæt ... eorðan), the direct object of ġeworhte comes between the subject and the verb. You may also find indirect objects, complements, adverbial elements and various combinations of these in the same position:

Adverbial element:

Se Iouis wæs swā swīðe gāl þæt *hē* on hys swustor *ġewīfode*.
[This Jove was so very lustful that *he married* his sister.]

and þā bēċ ne magon bēon āwǣġede, þe *þā ealdan hǣðenan* be him *āwriton* þuss.
[and the books that *the old heathens wrote* thus about them may not be nullified.]

Complement:

Nū secgað þā Deniscan þæt se Iouis wǣre, þe *hī* Þōr *hātað*, Mercuries sunu.
[Now the Danes say that this Jove, whom *they call* Thor, was Mercury's son.]

Indirect object and object:

and *Adam* him eallum naman *ġescēop*
[and *Adam made* names for them all]

---

**!**  If you find you are having difficulty locating the end of a clause and the word-order appears to be Subject . . . Verb, consider the possibility that the finite verb marks the end of the clause.

---

## 12.5   Correlation

When a subordinate clause and an independent clause are correlated (§10.4), and are introduced by an ambiguous conjunction/adverb pair (especially þā 'when, then', þonne 'when, then' and þǣr 'where, there'), you can usually tell the subordinate clause from the independent clause by looking at the word-order. In this situation, the tendency of the independent clause introduced by an adverb to have the word-order Verb–Subject and that of the subordinate clause to have the order Subject–Verb or Subject . . . Verb will usually tell you which clause is which.

## Minitext H. Orosius on the Reign of Caligula

From the Old English translation of the *History in Reply to the Pagans* by Paulus Orosius (see Bately [6]).

[1] Æfter ðām þe Rōmeburg ġetimbred wæs seofon hunde wintra ond hundnigontiġ, wearþ Gaius Gallica[a] cāsere fēower ġēar. [2] Hē wæs swīþe ġefylled mid unþēawum ond mid firenlustum, ond ealle hē wæs swelċe Rōmāne þā wyrþe wǣron, for þām þe hīe Cristes bebod hyspton ond hit forsāwon. [3] Ac hē hit on him swīþe wræc, ond hīe him swā lāðe wǣron þæt hē oft wȳscte þæt ealle Rōmane hæfden ǣnne swēoran, þæt hē hine raþost forċeorfan meahte. [4] Ond mid unġemete mǣnde[b] þæt þǣr þā næs swelċ sacu swelċ þǣr oft ǣr wæs; ond hē self fōr oft on ōþra lond ond wolde ġewin findan, ac hē ne meahte būton[c] sibbe.

[a]  An error for Caligula, the nickname of the infamous emperor Gaius Julius Caesar (AD 12–41).
[b]  The subject *hē* is omitted; see §11.2.
[c]  *ne meahte būton*: could not [find anything] but.

---

**!**  Simply put, the rule is this: when two clauses are correlated, the subordinate clause will have the subject before the verb, while the independent clause will have the verb before the subject. Examples:

Ðonne *sēo sunne ūp ārīst*, þonne *wyrċð hēo* dæġ.
[When *the sun rises*, then *it brings about* day.]

Ðǣr *ēower goldhord is*, ðǣr *bið ēower* heorte.
[Wherever *your treasure is*, there *is your heart*.]

Þā hē þā *se cyning* þās word *ġehȳrde*, þā *hēt hē* hī bīdan on þǣm ēalonde þe hī ūp cōmon.
[When *the king heard* these words, then *he commanded* them to wait on the island where they had come ashore.]

In each of these examples, the subordinate clause has the word-order Subject–Verb while the independent clause has Verb–Subject.

Unfortunately, this rule does not work in poetry. In prose it will work most of the time, but you cannot count on it absolutely.

## 12.6 Anticipation

When a noun clause functions as a subject or object it must follow the verb; but often a pronoun (usually *þæt*, but sometimes *hit*) appears before the verb, anticipating the coming clause. This pronoun occurs in the position that a pronoun subject or object would normally take (see §12.2). In the first sentence below, the pronoun and clause are the subject of *ġelimpe*, and in the second they are the object of the paired verbs *onġeat and ġeseah*.

> Ġeheald þū mīn word, and þū hī nǣnigum ōþrum men ne secge, ġif *þæt* ġelimpe *þæt þū wið hine ġesprece.*
> [Hold fast my words, and do not tell them to any other man, if *it* should happen *that you speak to him.*]

> Hē Drihten *þæt* onġeat and ġeseah *þæt se dēofol þone Iudas lǣrde þæt hē hine belǣwde.*
> [He, the Lord, perceived and saw *that the devil was persuading Judas that he should betray him.*]

The translation of the first sentence shows that Modern English does something similar with certain verbs when a clause is the subject. If the verb takes an object in a case other than accusative, the anticipatory pronoun will be in that case, but the conjunction that begins the noun clause (*þæt*, *hū* or some other) will remain the same. For example, the verb *wēnan* 'expect, believe' takes a genitive object:

> Hē *þæs* wēnde *þæt his wamb wǣre his Drihten God.*
> [He believed that his belly was his Lord God.]

This construction usually cannot be translated word for word: you will normally have to omit the anticipatory pronoun, as in the second and third translations above.

## 12.7   Periphrastic verbs

In Modern English auxiliary and verbal may be separated by an adverbial element, but usually we keep them together. In Old English, on the other hand, they may come together or be widely separated. Here are some typical patterns:

Subject–Verb:

ond ēac se miċla here *wæs* þā þærtō *cumen*
[and also the great (Viking) army *had* then *come* to that place]

Þǣr man *meahte* þā *ġesēon* ermðe þǣr man oft ǣr ġeseah blisse[2]
[There one *might* then *see* misery where before one had often seen bliss]

Verb–Subject:

*Hæfde* se cyning his fierd on tū *tōnumen*
[The king *had divided* his army in two]

Ðǣr *mihton ġesēon* Winċeasterlēode rancne here and uneargne
[There the people of Winchester *could see* the bold and uncowardly (Viking) army]

Subject . . . Verb:

Ac sōna swā hīe tō Bēamflēote cōmon, ond þæt ġeweorc *ġeworht wæs*
[But as soon as they came to Benfleet, and the fortification *had been constructed*]

The splitting of periphrastic verb forms and the placement of verbals and finite verbs at the ends of clauses can give Old English a 'foreign' look. But there are sources of comfort here: when finite verb and verbal are separated, the last one will usually mark the end of a clause, helping you with the problem of finding clause boundaries. When they are not separated, your Modern English sense of how clauses are constructed will generally serve you well.

---

[2] This sentence illustrates the point made in §12.5 that you cannot absolutely count on word-order to tell you which clause is independent and which subordinate.

# Chapter 13

# Metre

The Anglo-Saxons wrote what we call *alliterative poetry* after its most salient feature, the system of alliteration that binds its verses together and is largely responsible for its distinctive sound. Similar metrical systems are found in Old Icelandic, Old Saxon and Old High German: all of these cultures inherited a common Germanic metre, which they adapted as their languages and cultures changed. English poets continued to write alliterative poetry as late as the fifteenth century, and the metre has often been revived – most notably by the twentieth-century poet Ezra Pound.

There is more to Old English metre than alliteration. The poetry also employed a strict rhythmic scheme, which you will find to be markedly different from the rhythms employed by later poets such as Chaucer and Shakespeare. These later rhythms are based on the regularly timed recurrence of stressed syllables in the line. In Old English metre, the line consists of two *verses* (also called *half-lines*) divided by a syntactical boundary called a *caesura*. Each verse must conform to one of five rhythmic patterns (or *types*, as they are generally called), which we designate with the letters A–E. Verses of all types have in common that they always (well, *almost* always) contain two stressed syllables, called *lifts*, and two or more groups of unstressed syllables, called *drops*. The arrangement of lifts and drops depends on the type. The lifts do not necessarily come at regular intervals.

Why some rhythmic patterns were permissible in Old English poetry while others were forbidden is a subject of vigorous debate among scholars. The answer, if we had it, might tell us why the permissible rhythms sounded 'good', or sounded 'like poetry'. At present the most plausible theory is that the rhythms of poetry were based on those of ordinary speech, but with added rules that enabled listeners to recognize the boundaries between verses and lines. In much the same way, we can recognize the organization of Shakespearean blank verse when we hear actors recite it, even though there are no rhymes to tell us where the lines end.

Modern editions of Old English poetry print it as you have seen it in this book, in long lines with the caesura marked by a space. You should be aware, though, that in Old English manuscripts the poetry is not broken into lines, but rather written continuously, like prose. Like other editorial conventions (such as the use of modern capitalization and punctuation), the arrangement of poetic lines in printed editions is a compromise: it makes Old English texts more accessible to modern readers, but it conceals some interesting characteristics of Old English manuscript culture. You should track down a facsimile of the manuscript of a poem you are reading (follow the references in Further Reading, §8) and compare it with the printed edition.

**ⓘ** The term 'line' refers to the way poetry is broken into lines in modern books. Since Old English poetry is not broken into lines on the page, our speaking of 'lines' would probably seem strange to an Old English poet. We retain the term here, however, for want of a better one.

The first verse in a line is generally called the *on-verse* or *a-verse* and the second verse is called the *off-verse* or *b-verse*. When referring to specific verses, use the line number plus *a* for the on-verse and *b* for the off-verse: 'l. 11a', 'll. 234b–236a'. If you don't need that degree of precision in referring to passages of poetry, it is perfectly all right to use the line number alone.

## 13.1   Alliteration

Alliteration is the repetition of a consonant sound at the beginning of a syllable. In addition, any syllable that begins with a vowel alliterates with any other syllable that begins with a vowel. In Old English poetry, only the alliteration of lifts is significant. The combinations *sc*, *sp* and *st* may alliterate only with themselves. In most poems, however, *ġ* can alliterate with *g* and *ċ* with *c*. The ·italic letters in this list alliterate:

| | |
|---|---|
| *c*lyppe | *c*ysse |
| *ġe*þōht | *þ*enċan |
| *ē*adiġ | *ġe*endod |
| *f*oremihtiġ | *f*ēond |
| *ġe*cunnod | *ċ*ēole |
| *g*ōd | *ġe*ogoð |

These words, on the other hand, contain sounds that you might expect to alliterate, but do not:

| | |
|---|---|
| ġehāten | ġēar |
| foremihtig | mǣre |
| forweorðan | fēond |
| stān | sāriġ |
| scōp | sǣ |

In each poetic line, one or two lifts in the on-verse must alliterate with the first lift in the off-verse. The second lift in the off-verse normally does not alliterate with any of the three other stressed syllables in the line. These lines illustrate the three patterns:[1]

        × (/) × / × / \ × /
xa|ay:  þæt biþ in eorle  indryhten þēaw

        × × × / \ × / × / ×
ax|ay:  þæt hē his ferðlocan  fæste binde.

        × × / / × / × × / ×
aa|ax:  ne se hrēo hyġe  helpe ġefremman

🛈 It is customary to mark a lift with a stroke. A backward stroke (\) marks a half-lift, and × marks an unstressed syllable, part of a drop. In this book, a stroke in parentheses marks a syllable that one would expect to receive metrical stress even though the rules of Old English accentuation indicate that it should not be stressed (see §13.2.1).

The pattern xa|ay occurs mostly when the first lift in a verse is weak (as when it is a syllable of a finite verb). When the first lift is strong (as when it is a syllable of a noun, adjective or verbal), it normally *must* alliterate, so the pattern will be ax|ay or aa|ax. A competent poet would not write a line like this one:

        × × / / × / × × / ×
ne se wō hyġe  helpe ġefremman

Occasionally you will meet with *transverse alliteration* (the pattern ab|ab) and *crossed alliteration* (ab|ba). These probably were regarded as especially ornate:[2]

---

[1] *The Wanderer*, ll. 12–13, 16. Since the quotations in this chapter are intended only to illustrate metrical principles, translations are omitted.
[2] *Beowulf*, ll. 32, 2615.

Þǣr æt hȳðe stōd    hringedstefna
brūnfāgne helm,    hringde byrnan

Other unusual kinds of alliteration (such as syllables in the drop alliterating
with a lift) are probably incidental and without metrical significance.

## 13.2  Rhythm

### 13.2.1  Lifts, half-lifts and drops

We mentioned at the head of this chapter that a verse generally has two lifts,
or stressed syllables. A lift will normally be a long syllable (for the distinction
between long and short syllables, see §2.4). The italicized syllables in these
words are long:

   *hlēoð*rode     *heal*le
   *frēo*lic       *weġ*

But the italicized syllables in these words are short and so will not normally be
lifts, even though they are the stressed syllables of their words:

   *we*ra      *du*ru
   *da*gas     ā*bro*cen

Two short syllables can, however, add up to what is called a *resolved lift*, which
we mark with a tie between a stroke and an × (/̮×). For example, in this line,

   /̮×   ×   /   ×    /̮×  \ × × /
   monegum mǣġþum    meodosetla oftēah[3]

the first two syllables of *monegum* and *meodosetla* make resolved lifts. In
addition, a lift may consist of a single short syllable when it immediately
follows another lift.

There is a strong tendency in Old English poetry to group weakly stressed
words that are not proclitic[4] at the beginning of a clause or immediately after
the first lift in a clause. These weakly stressed words include conjunctions,

---

[3]  *Beowulf*, l. 5.
[4]  A proclitic word is normally found immediately before another word. Adjectives and adjectival pronouns ('*green* cheese', '*this* cow') are normally proclitic, and so are prepositions ('*in* the
scabbard').

finite verbs, adverbs and pronouns; you will often find them clustered right at the beginning of a verse, before the first lift, as here,

$$\times \quad \times \quad \times \times \times \quad / \quad \times \quad \times \quad /$$

syþðan hē hire folmum æthrān[5]

where a conjunction and two pronouns (five syllables in all) constitute the drop that comes before the first lift. When a word that normally is weakly stressed occurs somewhere other than its accustomed position, it acquires stress. Thus a finite verb, adverb or pronoun will be stressed if it does not come before or immediately after the first lift, and a proclitic, such as a preposition, will be stressed if it follows the word it normally precedes:[6]

$$/\times \quad \times \quad \times \quad / \quad \times$$

Hete wæs onhrēred

$$\times \quad \times \quad \times / \quad \times \quad /$$

ðā hē ġebolgen wæs

$$\times \quad \times \quad \times \quad \times \quad / \quad / \times$$

for ðon iċ mē on hafu

$$/ \quad \backslash \quad / \quad \times$$

grundwong þone

In the first of these examples, the finite verb *wæs*, coming right after the first lift (*hete*), remains unstressed, but in the second example *wæs* at the end of the clause is stressed. In the third example, a preposition (*on*) comes after its object (*mē*), and in the fourth example, a pronoun used as an adjectival 'article' follows the noun it modifies. Both the preposition and the pronoun are lifts. The preposition even participates in the alliterative pattern of the line.

The second element of a compound noun normally has a half-stressed syllable, or half-lift (this is still true: say 'the flashlight' aloud to yourself and listen to the relative stress levels of *the*, *flash* and *light*). In Old English metre, a half-stress may sometimes be treated as part of the drop and sometimes as the lift:[7]

$$/\times \quad \backslash \quad / \quad \times$$

medudrēam māran

$$/ \quad \times \backslash \quad \times$$

bēodġenēatas

---

[5]  *Beowulf*, l. 722b.
[6]  *Beowulf*, ll. 2556a, 723b, 2523b, 2588a.
[7]  *Beowulf*, ll. 2016a, 1713b.

In the first example, the half-stress -*drēam* comes where you expect a drop, while in the second the half-stress -*nēa*- comes where you expect a lift.

## 13.2.2  Rhythmic types

Every correctly constructed verse belongs to one of the five rhythmic types. The rhythmic patterns of these types are not fixed, but rather flexible. Each type has a basic form and a range of variations on that form. The rhythmic patterns of modern verse also have variations. In this line, for example,

The whiskey on your breath

which we perceive as having three iambs ($\times/|\times/|\times/$), we in fact pronounce the second iamb as two unstressed syllables ($\times/|\times\times|\times/$). The phonetic realization of a poetic line can differ quite a bit from its basic form; in fact, any poem in which the two do not differ is certain to strike us as monotonous. The differences between basic form and phonetic realization are themselves governed by rules that ensure that the verse retains its integrity so that we can still recognize it as poetry.

**A. Basic form: lift, drop, lift, drop.** This is the most common type of verse. Examples:[8]

```
/   ×   /   ×
ēower lēode
```

```
/   ×  ×  /×   ×
sorge ġefremede
```

Notice that the drop may consist of more than one unstressed syllable. Either or both of the drops may also be replaced by a half-lift. The second lift may also be replaced by a half-lift, but half-lifts cannot replace both drops and lifts in the same verse.

> ⓘ Many metrists believe that verses were subdivided into feet. If so, the first line above would be divided /×|/× and the second would be divided /×|/×× . Not all scholars agree that verses were so divided. This book takes no position on that question, but omits the division into feet as unlikely to be of much use to students beginning to read poetry.

---

[8]  *Beowulf*, ll. 596b, 2004b.

An extra syllable may precede the first lift in an A-type verse; this phenomenon, called *anacrusis*, occurs only in on-verses. This line exhibits anacrusis:

× / × × / ×
in mǣġþa ġehwǣre[9]

You will frequently encounter A-type verses in which the first lift is so weak that you may have difficulty locating it at all. These 'light' A-type verses typically occur at the beginnings of clauses. They are always on-verses. Examples:[10]

(/) × × × × / ×
hī hyne þā ætbǣron

(/) × × / ×
Ðā cōm of mōre

**B. Basic form: drop, lift, drop, lift.** B-type verses are especially common as off-verses, though they also occur as on-verses:[11]

× × / × /
Ne scel ānes hwæt

× × / × /
þæt se sīð ne ðāh

The first drop may have as many as five syllables, but the second can have no more than two.

**C. Basic form: drop, lift, lift, drop.** Verses of this type, in which the clashing stresses are rather startling to the modern ear, are more often than not off-verses. Examples:[12]

× / / ×
Oft Scyld Scēfing

× × × / / ×
þēah hē him lēof wǣre

---

[9]   *Beowulf*, l. 25a.
[10]  *Beowulf*, ll. 28, 118a.
[11]  *Beowulf*, ll. 3010b, 3058b.
[12]  *Beowulf*, ll. 4a, 203b.

Though the first drop may have as many as five syllables, the second drop may have only one. The second lift is often a short syllable, since it immediately follows the first (see §13.2.1):

× × / / ×
þæt hīe ǣr drugon[13]

**D. Basic forms: lift, lift, half-lift, drop; lift, lift, drop, half-lift.** D-type verses often consist of a word of one long or two short syllables followed by a word of three syllables; alternatively, a D-type verse may be a compound whose second element has three syllables. The drop at or near the end of the verse never has more than one syllable. Examples:[14]

/× / \ ×
sunu Ecglāfes

/ / \ ×
fletsittendum

/ / × \
hār hilderinc

Some D-type verses are 'extended', with a one- or two-syllable drop after the first lift:[15]

/ × / \ ×
wēoldon wælstōwe

/× / × \
hwīlum hildedēor

**E. Basic form: lift, half-lift, drop, lift.** The E-type verse is the inverse of the D-type, frequently consisting of a three-syllable word followed by a word of one long syllable or two short ones:[16]

/ \ × /
edwenden cwōm

/ \ × /
stefn in becōm

---

[13]   *Beowulf*, l. 15a.
[14]   *Beowulf*, ll. 590b, 1788a, 1307a.
[15]   *Beowulf*, ll. 2051a, 2107a.
[16]   *Beowulf*, ll. 1774b, 2552b.

### Minitext ı. Riddle 80

This is one of ninety-five riddles preserved in the Exeter Book (see textual note for reading 11 in the anthology). For an edition of the Riddles, see Williamson [116]. This source (and others as well) will give you the solution to this riddle, but try to figure it out for yourself before looking it up.

|   | |
|---|---|
| | Iċ eom æþelinges   eaxlġestealla, |
| | fyrdrinces ġefara,   frēan mīnum lēof, |
| | cyninges ġeselda.   Cwēn mec hwīlum |
| | hwītloccedu   hond on leġeð, |
| 5 | eorles dohtor,   þēah hīo æþelu sȳ. |
| | Hæbbe mē on bōsme   þæt on bearwe ġewēox.[a] |
| | Hwīlum iċ on wloncum   wicge rīde |
| | herġes on ende;   heard is mīn tunge. |
| | Oft iċ wōðboran   wordlēana sum |
| 10 | āġyfe æfter ġiedde.   Good is mīn wīse |
| | ond iċ sylfa salo.   Saga hwæt iċ hātte. |

[a]   This line probably refers to mead, made of honey from beehives kept in the woods.

The drop may consist of two short syllables (never more):

/    \    ×  ×/
feorhswenġ ne oftēah[17]

### 13.2.3   Hypermetric verses

Occasionally you will encounter clusters of lines in which the verses appear to be exceptionally long. These extended verses, which we call *hypermetric*, occur rarely in *Beowulf*, but frequently in *The Dream of the Rood* and *Judith*. Here is a sample:

Þurhdrifan hī mē mid deorcum næġlum.   On mē syndon þā dolg ġesīene,
opene inwidhlemmas.   Ne dorste iċ hira nǣnigum sceððan.
Bysmeredon hīe unc būtū ætgædere.   Eall iċ wæs mid blōde bestēmed,
begoten of þæs guman sīdan,   siððan hē hæfde his gāst onsended.[18]
[They drove dark nails through me. The wounds, open wicked wounds,
are visible on me. I did not dare to harm any of them.
They reviled both of us together. I was entirely drenched with blood,
poured from the man's side after he had sent forth his spirit.]

[17]   *Beowulf*, l. 2489b.
[18]   *The Dream of the Rood*, ll. 46–9.

Exactly what is going on in this kind of verse is a matter of some disagreement. The traditional view is that hypermetric on-verses are normal verses with a prefix that usually takes the form /×× or /× (but is sometimes longer), while hypermetric off-verses have an extra-long drop before the first lift, thus:

```
/x   x /   \   /     x
opene inwidhlemmas

  x  x   x    x   /  x  x  /  x
Eall ić wæs mid blōde bestēmed
```

We may interpret the first of these verses as an A-type with /×× prefixed and the second as another A-type with ×××× prefixed.

Some scholars have argued that this traditional view provides an inadequate explanation of the hypermetric verses. It is beyond the scope of a grammar book to discuss in detail the competing theories regarding these verses. You may take the traditional view as a starting point, read further, and decide for yourself what stylistic effect these verses may have had.

# Chapter 14

# Poetic Style

Reading poetry is always more challenging than reading prose. Poets employ figurative language more intensively than most prose writers do, they leave much for readers to infer, and in many poetic traditions (including those of England and America in the relatively recent past) their language is deliberately archaic. Here, for example, are the first two stanzas of Thomas Gray's *Elegy Written in a Country Churchyard*:

> The curfew tolls the knell of parting day,
>  The lowing herd wind slowly o'er the lea,
> The ploughman homeward plods his weary way,
>  And leaves the world to darkness and to me.
>
> Now fades the glimmering landscape on the sight,
>  And all the air a solemn stillness holds,
> Save where the beetle wheels his droning flight,
>  And drowsy tinklings lull the distant folds.

Gray's eighteenth-century masterpiece has stylistic features rarely found in prose of that time. The contraction *o'er* 'over', dialectal in origin, is rare outside of poetry, and *lea*, from Old English *lēah* 'pasture, meadow', had been an almost exclusively poetic word for centuries.

Further, the word-order of this passage makes it look strange to the modern eye. In line 3 an adverbial element (*homeward*) comes where it does not normally occur, line 5 has the word-order Verb–Subject, and line 6 has Subject . . . Verb. These three divergences from Modern English word-order would make good Old English, as you remember from chapter 12. Gray's use of such archaisms is typical of the poetic idiom of his time, and although that idiom is now out of favour, we still recognize it with no difficulty.

Old English poetry employs a number of words that are rarely or never found in prose, and its syntax differs from that of prose in several respects. The result of these differences is that there is a distinctively poetic Old English idiom, which probably was as easily recognizable to English people of that time as Gray's poetic idiom is to us.

## 14.1 Vocabulary

A large number of words are found exclusively, or almost exclusively, in poetry. Some of these are dialectal in origin (much Old English poetry, whether written in the north or the south, displays northern dialect features), while others are presumably archaisms. You might expect most poetic words to represent unusual concepts, but frequently they appear in place of quite common words, as these examples show:[1]

**āwa,** adv. *always* (for usual *ā*).
**æfnan,** wk. 1. *perform, do* (for *fremman*).
**benn,** fem. *wound* (for *wund*).
**ellor,** adv. *elsewhere* (for *elles ġehwǣr*).
**elra,** pron. adj. *another* (for *ōðer*).
**fricgan,** st. 5. *ask* (for *ascian, axian*).
**gamol,** adj. *old* (for *eald*).
**ġeador,** adv. *together* (for *ætgædere* or *tōgædere*).
**grēotan,** st. 2. *weep* (for *wēpan*).
**holm,** masc. *sea* (for *sǣ*).

**mearh,** masc. *horse* (for *hors*).
**ōr,** neut. *beginning, origin* (for *fruma* or *anġinn*).
**sǣlan,** wk. 1. *fasten, moor* (for *fæstnian*).
**siġel,** masc. or neut. *sun* (for *sunne*).
**sīn,** possessive adj. *his* (for *his*).
**swefan,** st. 5. *sleep* (for *slǣpan*).
**til,** adj. *good* (for *gōd*).
**welhwylċ,** indefinite pron. *every* (for *ġehwylċ*).
**wītiġ,** adj. *wise* (for *wīs*).

Poetic vocabulary has an especially large number of words for human beings, and most of the words within this group mean 'man', 'warrior' or both:

---

[1] This and other lists of poetic words in this chapter are largely based on the glossary in Klaeber [67], which indicates which words occur only or mostly in poetry and which are unique to *Beowulf*. These lists present words found in *Beowulf* and at least one other poem. The abbreviations are those used in this book's glossary (p. 269).

**beorn,** masc. *man, noble, warrior.*
**byre,** masc. *son, young man.*
**eafora,** masc. *son, heir.*
**freca,** masc. *warrior.*
**guma,** masc. *man, warrior.*
**hæle, hæleð,** masc. *man, warrior.*
**hyse,** masc. *young man.*
**ides,** fem. *woman, lady.*

**mago,** masc. *son, young man.*
**mæġð,** fem. *maiden, woman.*
**niþðas,** masc. *men.*
**rinc,** masc. *man, warrior.*
**secg,** masc. *man, warrior.*
**wiga,** masc. *warrior.*
**ylde,** masc. *men.*

Old English is a compounding language, frequently making new words by forming compounds from old ones. Most of the words in the list above can appear as elements of compounds, greatly expanding the group of words for human beings. Here, for example, are the compounds of *rinc*:

**beadorinc,** masc. *battle-warrior.*
**fyrdrinc,** masc. *army-warrior.*
**gumrinc,** masc. *man-warrior.*
**gūþrinc,** masc. *war-warrior.*
**heaðorinc,** masc. *war-warrior.*

**hererinc,** masc. *army-warrior.*
**hilderinc,** masc. *war-warrior.*
**magurinc,** masc. *son-warrior, young warrior.*
**sǣrinc,** masc. *sea-warrior.*

Most of these compounds are redundant, or they state the obvious: that a warrior goes to war, or is a man, or someone's son. Normally we expect a compound noun to consist of a base word (the second element) with a modifier (the first element); but the only compound in the list that fits this pattern is *sǣrinc* 'warrior who goes to sea'. Compounds in which the first element does not modify the second are common enough in Old English poetry that we have a specialized term to describe them: *poetic compounds*. In these the first element fills out the rhythm of a line and supplies alliteration. The poetic compounds you are most likely to meet have first elements meaning 'war', 'battle', 'slaughter' or 'army': *beadu-, gūð-, here-, hild(e)-, wæl-, wīġ-*. For example, here are the compounds in *Beowulf* with the first element *beadu-*:

**beadufolm,** fem. *battle-hand,* i.e. a hand used in battle.
**beadogrīma,** adj. *battle-mask,* i.e. helmet with mask.
**beadohræġl,** neut. *battle-garment,* i.e. coat of mail.
**beadulāc,** neut. *war-play,* i.e. battle.
**beadolēoma,** masc. *battle-light,* i.e. sword (which gleams in battle).

**beadomēċe,** masc. *battle-sword.*
**beadorinc,** masc. *battle-warrior.*
**beadurōf,** adj. *battle-bold.*
**beadurūn,** fem. *battle-speech, hostile speech.*
**beaduscearp,** adj. *battle-sharp* (describing a weapon).
**beaduscrūd,** neut. *battle-garment.*
**beaduserċe,** fem. *battle-corslet.*

Some of these (*beadomēċe, beadorinc, beaduserċe*) are true poetic compounds, while in others the first element does modify the second: a *beadohræġl* is not just any garment, but one worn to battle, i.e. a coat of mail. But more striking than this compound is *beadolēoma* 'battle-light', in which the first element provides a clue to the riddle of the second, a metonymic reference to a gleaming sword. This kind of compound is called a *kenning*, and it is one of the most striking features of Old English poetic style. A good poet may coin his own kennings (*Beowulf* has many unique ones), but a number of them appear to belong to a common stock of poetic terms. Here are some kennings that appear in *Beowulf* and at least one other poem:

**bāncofa,** masc. *bone-chamber*, i.e. body.

**bānfæt,** neut. *bone-container*, i.e. body.

**bānhūs,** neut. *bone-house*, i.e. body.

**bānloca,** masc. *locked bone-enclosure*, i.e. body.

**brēosthord,** neut. *breast-hoard*, i.e. feeling, thought, character.

**frumgār,** masc. *first spear*, i.e. chieftain.

**hronrād,** fem. *whale-road*, i.e. sea.

**merestræt,** fem. *sea-street*, i.e. the way over the sea.

**nihthelm,** masc. *night-helmet*, i.e. cover of night.

**sāwoldrēor,** masc. or neut. *soul-blood*, i.e. life-blood.

**sundwudu,** masc. *sea-wood*, i.e. ship.

**swanrād,** fem. *swan-road*, i.e. sea.

**wordhord,** neut. *word-hoard*, i.e. capacity for speech.

*Sāwoldrēor* and *sundwudu* are like *beadolēoma* in being metonymic; others (like the *bān-* compounds) are metaphorical, while some are even more complex: a *hronrād* is metaphorically a road over the sea, and metonymically for use by whales (and other sea-creatures, but especially ships). Kennings are not always compounds: they can be compound-like phrases consisting, generally, of two nouns, the first in the genitive case, as in *hwæles ēþel* 'the whale's home' or *bēaga brytta* 'giver of rings'.

The best glossaries will give you both a literal translation of a kenning and an interpretation of it:

**flæschoma,** masc. *flesh-covering*, i.e. the body.

But you must be on your guard, for some glossaries may supply only an interpretation. To do so, of course, is to rob poetry of much of what makes it poetry. If you suspect that the definition of a compound is not literal but rather an interpretation, go to a dictionary and look up its elements separately.

To give you an idea of how many poetic words may be available for a single concept, we end this section with a list of poetic words meaning 'king, lord' used in *Beowulf* and at least one other poem:

bēaggyfa, masc. *ring-giver.*
bealdor, masc. *lord.*
brego, masc. *lord, ruler.*
folcāgend, masc. *possessor of the people.*
folccyning, masc. *king of the people.*
folctoga, masc. *leader of the people.*
frēa, masc. *lord.*
frēadrihten, masc. *lord-lord.*
frumgār, masc. *first spear.*
goldgyfa, masc. *gold-giver.*
goldwine, masc. *gold-friend.*
gūðcyning, masc. *war-king.*
herewīsa, masc. *leader of an army.*
hildfruma, masc. *battle-first.*
hlēo, masc. *cover, shelter.*

lēodfruma, masc. *first of a people.*
lēodgebyrgea, masc. *protector of a people.*
mondryhten, masc. *lord of men.*
rǣswa, masc. *counsellor.*
sigedryhten, masc. *lord of victory.*
sincgifa, masc. *treasure-giver.*
sinfrēa, masc. *great lord.*
þengel, masc. *prince.*
þēodcyning, masc. *people-king.*
þēoden, masc. *chief, lord.*
wilgeofa, masc. *joy-giver.*
wine, masc. *friend.*
winedryhten, masc. *friend-lord.*
wīsa, masc. *guide.*
woroldcyning, masc. *worldly king.*

## 14.2   Variation

Variation is the repetition in different words of an element of a sentence, clause or phrase. In Old English poetry you should expect to meet frequently with sentences whose subjects, objects or other elements are repeated one or more times. In the simplest case an element may appear twice, perhaps on either side of another element:[2]

> þǣr hē *dōme* forlēas
> *ellenmǣrðum.*
> [There he lost *glory,*
> *the reputation for valour.*]

> Hæfde ðā forsīðod    *sunu Ecgþēowes*
> under gynne grund    *Gēata cempa*
> nemne him heaðobyrne    helpe gefremede
> [Then *the son of Ecgtheow, the champion of the Geats,*
> would have fared badly under the spacious earth
> if (his) battle-corslet had not given him help]

> Ðā se gist onfand
> þæt se beadolēoma    *bītan* nolde,
> aldre *scepðan*
> [Then the stranger found
> that the battle-light would not *bite,*
> *injure* (her) life]

---

2  *Beowulf*, ll. 1471–2, 1550–2, 1522–4.

In the first passage, two dative objects of *forlēas* appear on either side of that verb; in the second, two subjects appear on either side of a prepositional phrase. In the third, two infinitives governed by *nolde* are separated by that verb; the second infinitive, used transitively, is accompanied by its object.

> **!** Take note of these points about variation:
>
> - The elements in variation, when they are nouns, are different from compound noun phrases, which are sometimes split (§11.2), because here each element has the same referent. 'Glory' and 'the reputation for valour' both name the thing that Unferth lost, and 'the son of Ecgtheow' and 'the champion of the Geats' are the same person. In a compound subject like *Hengest ond Horsa*, the two nouns refer to two different persons.
> - We say that variation is 'the repetition of a sentence element' rather than 'the repetition of an idea' to emphasize that variation is a grammatical as well as a stylistic phenomenon. The grammatical construction in which a sentence element gets repeated is called *apposition*.
> - In the classical definition of apposition, appositive elements are grouped together, as in the translations above. In Old English poetry, though appositive elements *may* be grouped together, they are more likely to be separated. Because of this difference you must often rearrange sentence elements when translating passages of poetry that contain variation.

Variation can be much more complicated – and interesting – than in the examples quoted above. Study this passage, in which Beowulf describes how he once survived an attack by a school of sea-monsters:

> Næs hīe ðære fylle   ġefēan hæfde,
> mānfordædlan,   þæt hīe mē þēgon,
> symbel ymbsæton   sægrunde nēah.[3]
> [They did not, the evil destroyers,
> have joy of that meal, that they devoured me,
> sat around the feast near the sea-bottom.]

Let's count the variations in these three lines. First, the subject of the sentence, *hīe* 'they', is repeated in the next line with *mānfordædlan* 'evildoers'. Next, the verb *hæfde* 'had' has two objects, the first a noun, *ġefēan* 'joy', and the

---

[3]   *Beowulf*, ll. 562–4.

second a noun clause, þæt . . . nēah. (Did anyone say that elements in variation all had to be the same part of speech, or even that they all had to be words?) Within that noun clause there are two predicates: first, mē þēgon 'devoured me' states the matter plainly; then symbel . . . nēah 'sat around the feast near the sea-bottom' restates the same action, but more elaborately.

So far you have seen variations consisting of just two elements. But variations can have more elements than that. A poet may easily line up five of them:

> hlehhan ne þorftun
> þæt hēo *beaduweorca*   beteran wurdun
> on campstede   *cumbolġehnastes,*
> *gārmittinge,   gumena ġemōtes,*
> *wǣpenġewrixles* . . .[4]
>       [they had no need to laugh
> that they were better *at battle-works*
> on the battlefield, *at the clash of banners,*
> *at the meeting of spears, at the gathering of men,*
> *at the exchange of weapons* . . . ]

Clearly this poet has allowed his enthusiasm for variation to get the better of his sense of proportion. Further, his piling up of conventional terms for battle adds nothing to our sense of what this battle was about. Let's see what a better poet can do with variation:

> Calde ġeþrungen
> wǣron mīne fēt,   forste ġebunden
> caldum clommum,   þǣr þā ċeare seofedun
> hāt ymb heortan . . .[5]
>       [My feet were
> oppressed by cold, bound with frost,
> with cold fetters, where cares sighed,
> heat around my heart . . . ]

In this passage a seafarer describes conditions at sea. There are three variations here: the past participles ġeþrungen 'pressed, pinched' and ġebunden 'bound', both modifying fēt 'feet', the datives calde 'cold', forste 'frost' and caldum clommum 'cold fetters', which go with them, and the nominatives ċeare 'cares' and hāt 'heat'. Through these variations, the speaker incrementally introduces the metaphor of cold and frost as shackles which constrain him; we are unprepared for the sudden introduction of his 'cares', whose

---

[4]   *The Battle of Brunanburh,* ll. 47–51.
[5]   *The Seafarer,* ll. 8–11.

temperature contrasts sharply with what has gone before, and which tell us in the most dramatic way that the cold is not so much a physical as an emotional hardship. Here, as often happens, careful attention to the variations you meet will be repaid with greater appreciation of the poet's artistry.

## 14.3  Formulas

If you were to search for 'o'er the lea' (from Gray's *Elegy*, quoted above, p. 130) in a reasonably complete database of English poetry, you would find that it occurs frequently in poems of the eighteenth and nineteenth centuries.[6] It is a *formula*, a set phrase used in a conventional way. When a poem – or a poetic tradition – uses formulas frequently, we say it is *formulaic*. Homeric poetry, as is well known, is formulaic: every student who has ever read the *Iliad* remembers the 'rosy-fingered dawn'.

It has long been recognized that Old English poetry is also formulaic. We will discuss Old English formulas under two headings: phrases and themes.

### 14.3.1  Phrases

Look at these lines from *Beowulf*, all of which introduce speeches:[7]

Hrōðgār maþelode,   helm Scyldinga
[Hrothgar, helmet of the Scyldings, spoke]

Unferð maþelode,   Ecglāfes bearn
[Unferth, the son of Ecglaf, spoke]

Bēowulf maþelode,   bearn Ecgþēowes
[Beowulf, the son of Ecgtheow, spoke]

Such lines are common in *Beowulf*: clearly we are dealing with a formula here, but it differs from 'o'er the lea' in being variable, not fixed. From the examples above, we might hazard a guess at the principles by which it was constructed: it consisted of the name of the person who was about to speak, the verb *maþelode* 'spoke, made a speech' and, in the second half-line, a noun phrase consisting of a noun and a genitive modifier, in variation with the proper name.

---

[6]  For example, a search of the Chadwyck-Healey database of English poetry, 600–1900 (http://www.chadwyck.com) yields 118 instances of the phrase.
[7]  Lines 456, 499, 529.

So far so good; and it is easy to find additional examples of formulas on exactly that pattern:

Wīġlāf maðelode,   Wēohstānes sunu[8]
[Wiglaf, the son of Weohstan, spoke]

But it is not hard to find formulas that belong to the same *formulaic system* but diverge from the pattern:[9]

Weard maþelode   ðǣr on wicge sæt
ombeht unforht
[The guard spoke where he sat on his horse,
a fearless officer]

Wulfgār maþelode   (þæt wæs Wendla lēod;
wæs his mōdsefa   manegum ġecȳðed,
wīġ ond wīsdōm)
[Wulfgar spoke (he was a man of the Wendels;
his character, his warfare and wisdom
were known to many)]

Now we know that the first word in the formula does not have to be a name, and that the verb can be followed not only by a noun phrase, but also by a clause or even a parenthetical statement. There is a good bit of flexibility in this formulaic system. You will find it to be generally true that the Old English poetic formula is not a set phrase, but rather a syntactical pattern built around a word or short phrase.

An analysis of the first fifty half-lines of *Beowulf*, in a classic article by Francis P. Magoun [77], showed that about three quarters of them were paralleled in other Old English poems. Although a parallel in another poem does not guarantee that a phrase is a formula, it is nevertheless clear that *Beowulf* is heavily formulaic. So, it should be added, is most Old English poetry.

Magoun's article has often been reprinted, and so you are very likely to encounter it in your study of Old English poetry. Magoun made some rather sweeping claims in that article, of which the most influential was that the formulaic character of Old English poetry showed that it had been composed orally. His argument is simple, logical and compelling; but you should be aware that a central claim on which Magoun's 'oral-formulaic theory' rests, that 'the recurrence in a given poem of an appreciable number of formulas

---

[8]   *Beowulf*, l. 2862.
[9]   *Beowulf*, ll. 286–7, 348–50.

or formulaic phrases brands the latter as oral, just as a lack of such repetitions marks a poem as composed in a lettered tradition', has long since been shown to be false. It turns out that a number of Old English poems that are unlikely to have been composed orally, such as translations of Latin poems, are every bit as formulaic as *Beowulf*. Many scholars still hold that *Beowulf* and other important poems were composed orally, but few now rest their arguments to that effect entirely on the formulaic character of these poems.

## 14.3.2  Themes

One of the better Old English poems is a paraphrase of that part of Exodus which narrates the escape of the Hebrews from Egypt. As the Hebrews race towards the Red Sea, pursued by the doomed Egyptians, we find these lines:

> Hrēopon herefugolas,    hilde grǣdiġe,
> dēawiġfeðere,    ofer drihtnēum,
> wonn wælċēasega.    Wulfas sungon
> atol ǣfenlēoð    ǣtes on wēnan,
> carlēasan dēor,    cwyldrōf beodan
> on lāðra lāst    lēodmæġnes fyl;
> hrēopon mearcweardas    middum nihtum.[10]
> [The dewy-feathered war-birds, greedy
> for battle, and the dark corpse-picker
> screamed over the corpses. Wolves, careless
> wild animals, expecting a meal, sang
> a terrible evening song; the slaughter-bold awaited
> the fall of the army on the path of the hated ones;
> the border-wardens screamed in the middle of the nights.]

This grisly passage, which depicts carrion-eating birds and wolves hungrily awaiting the outcome of a battle, has no parallel in the poem's biblical source. It may, however, remind readers of *The Battle of Maldon* of this passage, which occurs just as the battle is getting underway:

> Þǣr wearð hrēam āhafen,    hremmas wundon,
> earn ǣses ġeorn;    wæs on eorþan ċyrm.[11]
> [There an outcry was raised up, ravens circled
> and the eagle eager for carrion; there was an uproar upon the earth.]

---

[10]  *Exodus*, ll. 162–8.
[11]  Lines 106–7.

And those who have read *The Battle of Finnsburg* may be reminded of these two half-lines:

> Hræfen wandrode,
> sweart and sealobrūn.[12]
> [The dark and deep brown
> raven wandered]

In fact, whenever men gather to do battle in Old English poetry, it is customary for some combination of ravens, eagles and wolves to gather as well, in expectation of a feast of human flesh. Their doing so is a formulaic *theme*, a motif or narrative element that occurs, generally at predictable moments, in various poems.

Readers of Old English elegies such as *The Wanderer*, *The Seafarer* and *The Wife's Lament* will recognize such a theme in the storms and frost that symbolize the speakers' emotional state. Readers of *Beowulf* should know that the Unferth episode (ll. 499–607) is a formulaic narrative element called a *flyting* with parallels in several poetic traditions, especially the Norse. Indeed, formulaic themes are pervasive in Old English poetry, though they tend to be harder to spot than formulaic phrases.

The formulaic theme, like the formulaic phrase, is a flexible form, allowing expanded, leisurely treatments like the one in the Old English *Exodus* or extremely compressed treatments like the one in *The Battle of Finnsburg*. The choices these poets made were consonant with their other stylistic choices: *Exodus* is an ornate and much-elaborated treatment of the biblical story while *The Battle of Finnsburg* is spare and fast-paced.

### 14.3.3   Originality and quality

Naive readers of Old English poetry sometimes worry that, if poets were required by the tradition in which they worked to use formulaic diction, motifs and narrative elements, they must have had difficulty saying anything new. And if they could say nothing new, how could they say anything good? Keep the following points in mind when thinking about the implications of formulaic diction and themes.

First, although Old English poetry is formulaic, few scholars, if any, now believe Magoun's assertion that a poem such as *Beowulf* must have been made up entirely of formulas. On the contrary, it is probable that the *Beowulf* poet not only composed a great many lines that conformed to no formulaic

---

[12]   Lines 34–5.

## Minitext J. Extract from *Maxims I*

The poem from which this extract is taken is a collection of proverbs and gnomes preserved in the Exeter Book. The present excerpt, ll. 81–92, addresses the duties and proper behaviour of a queen.

>       Cyning sceal mid ċēape   cwēne ġebicgan,
>       bunum ond bēagum;   bū sceolon ǣrest
>       ġeofum gōd wesan.   Gūð sceal in eorle,
>       wīġ ġeweaxan,   ond wīf ġeþēon
> 85    lēof mid hyre lēodum,   leohtmōd wesan,
>       rūne healdan,   rūmheort bēon
>       mēarum ond māþmum,   meodorǣdenne,[a]
>       for ġesīðmæġen   symle ǣġhwǣr
>       eodor æþelinga   ǣrest ġegrētan,
> 90    forman fulle   tō frēan hond
>       ricene ġerǣcan,   ond him rǣd witan[b]
>       boldāgendum   bǣm ætsomne.

[a]  *meodorǣdenne*: in the assembly. The dative here expresses location, a relatively rare usage.
[b]  *ond him rǣd witan*: know what is good advice for them. The pronoun *him* is dative plural.

pattern, but also coined a great many of his own kennings. The same is no doubt true of other poets as well.

Second, as we have seen, both the formulaic phrase and the formulaic theme were flexible: the materials that Old English poets worked with were not building blocks of fixed shape, size and colour, but rather a generous set of malleable shapes and flexible rules for the construction of poetry, rather like the vocabulary and grammar of a language.

Third, it is clear that Anglo-Saxon audiences valued originality in poetry less than we do – or at least they evaluated the 'originality' of poetry differently from the way we do now. The formulas of *Beowulf* and other poems, together with such features as frequent use of the phrase *iċ ġefræġn* 'I have heard', seem to have assured the audience that both the matter and manner of these poems were traditional, and the poet was not presuming to try anything new. Old English poets avoided the appearance of originality.

But if an entertainer must offer some kind of novelty to keep an audience engaged, the best poets certainly did so – sometimes by playing with the formulaic elements of style. Here is what becomes of the 'Beasts of Battle' theme in the hands of the *Beowulf* poet, as a messenger, having announced Beowulf's death to the waiting Geats, predicts that a time of strife is nearly upon them:

> Forðon sceall gār wesan
> moniġ morgenċeald   mundum bewunden,
> hæfen on handa,   nalles hearpan swēġ
> wīġend weċċean,   ac se wonna hrefn
> fūs ofer fǣġum   fela reordian,
> earne secgan   hū him æt ǣte spēow,
> þenden hē wið wulf   wæl rēafode.[13]
>       [Therefore must many a
> morning-cold spear be grasped in fists,
> raised in the hand, not the sound of the harp
> wake the warriors, but the dark raven,
> greedy over the doomed, talking away,
> saying to the eagle how it went for him at his meal,
> while, with the wolf, he plundered the slain.]

We imagine a morning scene, announced to us by an attribute applied to the chill of the spears that warriors must grasp. Then we are told what will awaken the warriors that morning: not the sound of the harp, as in peacetime, but the excited 'talking' of the raven as he describes to the eagle how he and the wolf 'plundered' (that is, ate) the corpses on the battlefield. We have traded direct statement ('the raven wheeled above') for indirection: we do not see the raven eat, but rather enter the warriors' minds as they hear him croak and imagine what he is saying. Their terror makes this passage by far the darkest of all the 'Beasts of Battle' passages in Old English poetry.

These lines are untraditional in a way, but an audience could hardly fail to respond to them.

---

[13]   Lines 3021–7.

# Chapter 15

# The Grammar of Poetry

You are already aware of some of the grammatical differences between prose and poetry. You know, for example, that Old English poetry has some rules of its own for the ordering of sentence elements (§13.2.1), and you know that poetry makes heavy use of apposition (§14.2). Here we will discuss the grammar of poetry in greater detail.

## 15.1 Inflections

### 15.1.1 Pronouns

You will frequently see accusative singular *þec* 'you' and *mec* 'me' where prose has *þē* and *mē* (see §5.1.1).

Instead of the genitive singular pronoun *his*, you will sometimes see *sīn* 'his' used as a possessive adjective. It takes strong adjective endings.

### 15.1.2 Verbs

You may (rarely) see a present first-person singular verb with the archaic ending *-o* or *-u*: for example *fullǣstu* 'assist' in *Beowulf*, l. 2668, but more often *hafo*, *hafu* 'I have' instead of West Saxon *habbe*.

The present second-person singular and third-person singular endings are
-*st* and -*ð* in West Saxon (see table 7.2, p. 64). But in poetry, which frequently
displays northern dialect features, you will often see -*est* and -*eð* instead. And
where West Saxon has *i*-mutation of the root vowel (§7.4), these longer forms
generally lack it. For example, the West Saxon present third-person singular
of *healdan* 'hold' is *hielt* (for the -*t*, see §7.2.1, item 2), but you will see *healdeð*
in poetry; and the West Saxon present third-person singular of *brūcan* 'make
use of' is *brȳcð*, but you will see *brūceð* in poetry.

Certain archaic and dialectal verb forms occur in both prose and poetry,
but more often in poetry. These include *cwōm* (past tense of *cuman* 'come'),
*sǣgon, sēgon* (past plural of *sēon* 'see'), *ġēong* (past tense of *gangan* 'to
go'), and alternate forms of third-class weak verbs (see §7.3.4), especially
*hafast, hafað* beside *hæfst, hæfð*.

### 15.1.3   Adjectives

In poetry, weak adjectives are frequently found where you would normally
find strong adjectives in prose – that is, where no demonstrative pronoun
or possessive adjective precedes (for the usual rule, see the beginning of
chapter 8). Example:

> wolde blondenfeax    beddes nēosan
> *gamela* Scylding.[1]
> [the grey-haired one, the *old* Scylding, wished
> to seek his bed.]

The strong form corresponding to *gamela* 'old' would be *gamol*.

The reverse does not happen: strong adjectives are not used with preceding
pronouns or possessive adjectives. You will never see such phrases as \**þone
gōdne cyning*.

## 15.2   Syntax

### 15.2.1   Omission of subjects and objects

You learned in §11.2 that a pronoun subject may be omitted in Old English.
In fact, when reading poetry you will frequently encounter clauses with

---

[1]   *Beowulf*, ll. 1791–2.

unexpressed subjects. Often it is no more than a matter of one subject belonging with two predicates:

Ðā ārās mæniġ goldhladen ðeġn,  ġyrde hine his swurde.[2]
[Then many a gold-laden thegn arose (and) girded his sword on himself.]

As the translation suggests, we can do much the same thing in Modern English, though we usually say *and* between the two predicates. But sometimes it is not so easy to figure out the reference of an unexpressed subject:

Sceolde lǣndaga
æþeling ǣrgōd  ende ġebīdan,
worulde līfes,  ond se wyrm somod,
þēah ðe hordwelan  hēolde lange.[3]
[The good old prince
had to experience the end of his transitory days,
of his life in the world, and the worm along with him,
though (he) had held the hoard-wealth for a long time.]

The subject of the clause in the last line is evidently the dragon (which has been guarding the only treasure that interests us in the last third of *Beowulf*), but the subject of the preceding clause, being compound, does not match it precisely.

In the examples above, the reference of the unexpressed subject is someone or something that has recently been mentioned. But the unexpressed subject need not have an antecedent:

Þǣr mæġ nihta ġehwǣm  nīðwundor sēon
fȳr on flōde.[4]
[There every night (one) may see an evil wonder,
fire in the water.]

Here it is a simple matter to supply a pronoun subject.

Direct objects may also be omitted. Usually the object will be expressed in a nearby clause (though not always *as* an object):

Ðā ġȳt hīe him āsetton  seġen gyldenne
hēah ofer hēafod,  lēton holm beran,
ġēafon on gārsecg.[5]

---

[2]  *The Battle of Finnsburh*, l. 13.
[3]  *Beowulf*, ll. 2341–4.
[4]  *Beowulf*, ll. 1365–6.
[5]  *Beowulf*, ll. 47–9.

[Then further they set up for him a golden standard,
high over head, let the sea bear (him),
gave (him) unto the sea.]

There can be no doubt as to whom they are sending out onto the sea; it is the one for whom they set up the standard.

### 15.2.2   Omission of prepositions

You will remember from an earlier chapter (§4.2.4) that words in the dative case are often used by themselves where Modern English would use a preposition. This tendency is even more pronounced in poetry than in prose. Examples:

> Weorða ðē selfne
> gōdum dǣdum   ðenden ðīn God recce.[6]
> [Honour yourself
> *with good deeds* for as long as God cares for you.]

> þonne hand wereð
> feorhhord *fēondum*.[7]
> [when my hand defends
> my life-hoard *from enemies*.]

> seġe *þīnum lēodum*   miċċle lāþre spell[8]
> [say *to your people* a much more hateful message]

As you can see, you will frequently have to supply a preposition when you encounter a word in the dative that lacks one. But there is no one Modern English preposition that is always appropriate. You will have to judge from the context what the dative is doing and how best to translate it.

In the first passage above, notice also the clause *ðenden ðīn God recce* 'for as long as God cares for you'. Here the verb *reċċan* takes the genitive of what one cares for, and we supplied a preposition in translating it. Verbs that govern words in the genitive case are common in both verse and prose. For example, *ġielpan* 'boast' takes the genitive of what one is boasting of (you must supply the preposition *of* or *about*) and *þancian* 'thank' takes the genitive of what one is grateful for (you must supply the preposition *for*). A good glossary or dictionary will tell you about the cases that verbs govern.

---

[6]   *Waldere*, I, ll. 22–3.
[7]   *Waldere*, II, ll. 21–2.
[8]   *The Battle of Maldon*, l. 50.

### 15.2.3 Adjectives used as nouns

In Modern English, when we wish to name a thing by mentioning one of its attributes, we use an adjective with a placeholder noun: 'the wise one', 'the big one'. In Old English poetry it is more common to use a demonstrative pronoun with a weak adjective:

> Þā wæs Nerġendes
> þēowen þrymful,  þearle ġemyndiġ
> hū hēo *þone atolan*  ēaðost mihte
> ealdre benǣman  ǣr *se unsȳfra,*
> *womfull* onwōce.[9]
>
> [Then the Saviour's handmaiden
> was filled with glory, vigorously thoughtful
> how she could most easily deprive
> *the terrible one* of life before *the unclean one,*
> *the impure one* awoke.]

Here Holofernus (about to be beheaded by Judith) is *þone atolan* 'the terrible one', *se unsȳfra* 'the unclean one', and finally *womfull* 'the impure one'. The last of these is a strong adjective unaccompanied by either a demonstrative or a noun. Strong adjectives are used as nouns less often than weak adjectives are, but it happens often enough that you should be prepared for it.

### 15.2.4 Word-order

The basic patterns of Old English word-order that you learned in chapter 12 apply as well for poetry as they do for prose. To illustrate, here is a short passage with the word-order of each clause indicated:

1 **Verb–Subject:**
Ðā *wearð breahtm* hæfen.
2 **Verb–Subject:**
>  Beorg *ymbstōdan*
hwearfum *wræcmæcgas.*
3 **Subject–Verb:**
>  *Wōð* ūp *āstāg*
ċearfulra ċirm.
4 **Verb–Subject:**
>  *Cleopedon* moniġe
*fēonda foresprecan,*  firenum gulpon:

---

[9] *Judith,* ll. 73–7.

## Minitext κ. Grendel's *mere*

In this extract from *Beowulf*, Hrothgar describes to Beowulf the watery home of Grendel and his mother (the *hīe* of the first line) just before he asks him to pursue and kill Grendel's mother. The punctuation and capitalization of the passage are those of the manuscript, though the diacritics, word-division and lineation are modern. See if you can find the boundaries of the clauses and their types without benefit of modern punctuation. Hints: remember that the caesuras and line breaks are also a kind of punctuation; look for the conjunctions and adverbs that begin clauses: *ðǣr*, *þæt* and others (see §10.2–3).

Hīe dȳgel lond
warigeað wulfhleoþu   windiġe næssas
frēcne fenġelād   ðǣr fyrġenstrēam

1360   under næssa ġenipu   niþer ġewīteð
flōd under foldan   nis þæt feor heonon
mīlġemearces   þæt se mere standeð
ofer þǣm hongiað   hrinde bearwas
wudu wyrtum fæst   wæter oferhelmað

1365   þǣr mæġ[a] nihta ġehwǣm   nīðwundor sēon
fȳr on flōde   nō þæs frōd leofað
gumena bearna   þæt[b] þone grund wite
ðēah þe hǣðstapa   hundum ġeswenċed
heorot hornum trum   holtwudu sēċe

1370   feorran ġeflȳmed   ǣr hē feorh seleð
aldor on ōfre   ǣr[c] hē in wille
hafelan beorgan   nis þæt hēoru stōw.

[a]   The subject of this verb is unexpressed; see §15.2.1.
[b]   *þæs frōd . . . þæt*: so wise . . . that.
[c]   *ǣr . . . ǣr*: first . . . before (correlated).

5 **Subject–Verb:**
'Oft *wē ofersēgon*   bi sǣm twēonum
þēoda þēawas,   þrǣce mōdiġra
6 **Subject . . . Verb:**
þāra þe in ġelimpe   līfe *wēoldon*'.[10]
[*1* Then a cry was raised. *2* The devils stood
around the mound in crowds. *3* The noise, the uproar
of the miserable ones rose up. *4* Many advocates
for the enemies called out, boasted criminally:

[10]   *Guthlac*, ll. 262–8.

5 'Often we have observed, between the two seas,
the customs of the nations, the power of those proud ones
6 who lived their lives in prosperity'.]

Each clause in this passage (chosen nearly at random) uses a standard word order. If the passage seems difficult, that is because the poet is vigorously taking advantage of the flexibility of these standard word orders. For example, in (1) the finite verb is an auxiliary, and the verbal (a past participle) is delayed to the end of the clause (§12.6), and in (2) the direct object comes before the verb instead of after the subject (§12.3).

Variation (§14.2) or, to use the grammatical term, apposition, would seem likely to violate the norms of Old English word order. In (3) the subject *Wōð* is varied by *ċearfulra ċirm*, and thus a subject follows as well as precedes the verb: the word-order is really Subject–Verb–Subject. But you will often find that it is possible to look at such clauses as hybrids of two standard word-orders: in this case Subject–Verb and Verb–Subject. Clause (4), where the word-order is Verb–Subject–Verb, can also be seen as a hybrid. It is as if poets saw the clause as containing several positions where a subject, verb or other element would be permissible and set out to fill up those positions.

It would be nice if you could always count on elements in variation coming in 'normal' positions, but sometimes they do not:

Hē ǣrest sceōp    eorðan bearnum
heofon tō hrōfe,    hāliġ Scyppend.[11]
[he, the holy Creator, first created
heaven as a roof for the children of men.]

The beginning of this sentence, with its order Subject–Verb . . . Object, looks normal enough, but the variation *hāliġ Scyppend* comes where a subject normally does not come (as part of a sequence Verb . . . Object–Subject). This example should serve as a reminder that you must be especially attentive to grammatical form and context when reading poetry. We can tell that *hāliġ Scyppend* is a subject, in variation with *Hē*, because it is nominative in form and because the poem has been talking about God.

### 15.2.5  Independent and subordinate clauses

In §§10.2–10.4 you learned that some adverbs have the same form as conjunctions and that the two occur together in correlative constructions. In §12.5 you learned further that word-order will often tell you which clause of

---

[11]   *Cædmon's Hymn*, ll. 5–6.

a correlative construction is independent and which is subordinate. We also warned you there, however, that the word-order rule does not work in poetry. So how can you tell, in a sentence like the one that follows, whether we have a correlative construction, and if we do, which clause is independent? (We omit editorial punctuation to discourage you from prejudging the case.)

> Ðā wæs on ūhtan    mid ǣrdæġe
> Grendles gūðcræft    gumum undyrne
> þā wæs æfter wiste    wōp up āhafen
> miċel morgenswēġ[12]
> [When/Then Grendel's warcraft was manifest
> to men at dawn, early in the day,
> when/then after the feasting weeping, a great morning-sound,
> was raised up.]

Even where we don't have ambiguous adverb/conjunction pairs, it can be difficult to distinguish independent and subordinate clauses:

> Nū ēow is ġerȳmed    gāð ricene tō ūs
> guman tō gūþe[13]

If *Nū* is an adverb, the translation should go like this:

> Now the way is open to you; go quickly to us,
> men to battle.

But if *Nū* is a conjunction, it should go like this instead:

> Now that the way is open to you, go quickly to us,
> men to battle.

How to read such sentences as these is a matter of controversy. Until around the middle of the twentieth century, editors more often than not interpreted ambiguous clauses as independent and supplied punctuation to match that interpretation. In any case, editors showed an aversion to sentences in which subordinate clauses preceded independent clauses. In a passage like the following, we have a choice of translating *Þā* as 'then' and punctuating the first clause with a semicolon or translating *Þā* as 'when' and punctuating with a comma:

---

[12]    *Beowulf*, ll. 126–9.
[13]    *The Battle of Maldon*, ll. 93–4.

Þā of wealle ġeseah    weard Scildinga
se þe holmclifu    healdan scolde
beran ofer bolcan    beorhte randas
fyrdsearu fūslicu    hine fyrwyt bræc
mōdġehygdum    hwæt þā men wæron.[14]
[then/When the guardian of the Scyldings, he who
had to hold the sea-cliffs, saw from the wall
(them) bearing their bright shields, their ready army-trappings,
over the gangway;/ curiosity tormented him
in his mind-thoughts (to know) what those men were.]

Early editors and translators would almost invariably choose 'then' and the semicolon. Recent editors are more likely to interpret the first clause as subordinate and punctuate with a comma.

Our decision whether to interpret a clause as independent or subordinate rarely makes much difference in the sense of a passage, but it does make a significant difference in the way we perceive its style. A paratactic style (one with relatively few subordinate clauses – see §3.3) was once thought to be 'primitive', especially by scholars who were interested in recovering, in Old English poetry, a genuine experience of English or Germanic cultural origins. Now, on the other hand, scholars are more likely to deny the possibility (and perhaps also the value) of recovering the origins of a culture, and further to deny that parataxis is in any way 'primitive'. Such modern scholars have been open to arguments that Old English poetry is less paratactic than formerly believed.

But how can you decide, in a particular passage, whether a clause is independent or subordinate? The following rule seems to work for clauses that contain an auxiliary and a verbal: if the auxiliary precedes the verbal and is unstressed, the clause is independent, but if the auxiliary follows the verbal and is stressed, the clause is subordinate. So this clause, in which the auxiliary *wearð* precedes the verbal *ġeġearewod* and is unstressed, is independent:

Þā wearð snelra werod    snūde ġeġearewod,
cēnra tō campe.[15]
[Then the host of the bold and the brave was quickly
prepared for battle.]

This clause, on the other hand, in which a stressed auxiliary (*hafað*) follows the verbal (*ġetācnod*), is subordinate:

---

[14]    *Beowulf*, ll. 229–33.
[15]    *Judith*, ll. 199–200.

> swā ēow ġetācnod hafað
> mihtiġ Dryhten    þurh mīne hand.[16]
> [as the mighty Lord
> has signalled to you through my hand.]

It may be uncertain whether clauses in which stressed auxiliaries precede verbals, or which do not contain auxiliaries, are independent or subordinate – unless, of course, the context tells us, as it often does.

The existence of clauses that may be either independent or subordinate has occasioned debate, some holding that Old English had a type of clause that fell somewhere between independent and subordinate while others believe that Old English clauses were always one or the other, even if we do not always know how to distinguish them. In this connection it is worth noting that the rule for distinguishing independent and subordinate clauses that contain auxiliaries was not discovered until relatively recently (see Donoghue [36]). It is not inconceivable that a rule for distinguishing other clauses has yet to be discovered.

---

[16]  *Judith*, ll. 197–8.

# Chapter 16

# Reading Old English Manuscripts

If you continue long enough in your study of Old English, you will sooner or later want to consult one or more of the roughly four hundred manuscripts (complete books and fragments) in which the language is recorded. Some 65 per cent of these manuscripts are owned by just three libraries: the British Library in London, the Bodleian Library in Oxford, and the Parker Library in Corpus Christi College, Cambridge. These and most other libraries will grant you access to their collections if you come with the proper credentials and have a legitimate research interest in Old English manuscripts. A great many manuscripts have been published in facsimile editions: these include all of the poetic manuscripts along with some of the most important of the prose ones. Eventually the series Anglo-Saxon Manuscripts in Microfiche Facsimile will include every manuscript that contains even a word of Old English (see Further Reading §8 for references). The availability of so many facsimiles means that you can work with Old English manuscripts even if your circumstances do not allow you to consult the real thing.

## 16.1   Construction of the manuscript

Most Anglo-Saxon manuscripts were written on vellum (Old English *fell*) made of calf skin. This was stretched, scraped smooth, whitened with chalk, cut into sheets, ruled with a stylus, and folded into quires of eight leaves (four sheets), or sixteen pages. After the scribes had done their work, the quires were sewn together and bound.

## 16.2   The Old English alphabet

The Anglo-Saxons adopted the styles of script employed by the Irish missionaries who had been instrumental in the conversion of the northern kingdoms. These styles included Insular half-uncial, used for fine books in Latin, and the less formal minuscule, used for both Latin and the vernacular. Beginning in the tenth century Anglo-Saxon scribes began to use caroline minuscule (developed in Francia during the reign of Charlemagne) for Latin while continuing to write Old English in Insular minuscule. Thereafter Old English script was increasingly influenced by caroline minuscule even as it retained certain distinctively Insular letter-forms. Once you have learned these letter-forms you will be able to read Old English manuscripts of all periods without difficulty.

Here are the basic letter-forms of Old English script, illustrated in a late Old English style:

a b c ꝺ e ꝼ ᵹ h ı k l m n o p ꝑ ꞃ ſ s τ þ ð u p x ẏ

Take particular note of these features:

- the rounded shape of ꝺ (**d**);
- the ꝼ (**f**) that extends below the baseline instead of sitting on top of it;
- the distinctive Insular ᵹ (**g**);
- the dotless ı (**i**);
- the ꝑ (**r**) that extends below the baseline;
- the three shapes of **s**, of which the first two (the Insular long ꞃ and the high ſ) are most common;
- the τ (**t**) that does not extend above the cross-stroke;
- the p ('wynn'), usually transliterated as **w** but sometimes printed as ƿ, derived from the runic letter ᚹ;
- the ẏ (**y**), usually dotted, which comes in several different shapes.

Old English has no use for **q** or **z**. **J** and **v** do not have the status of separate letters but are occasional variant shapes of **i** and **u** (more common in roman numbers than elsewhere). Old English scribes used **k** rarely, and only to represent the [k] sound, never the [ʧ] (ċ).

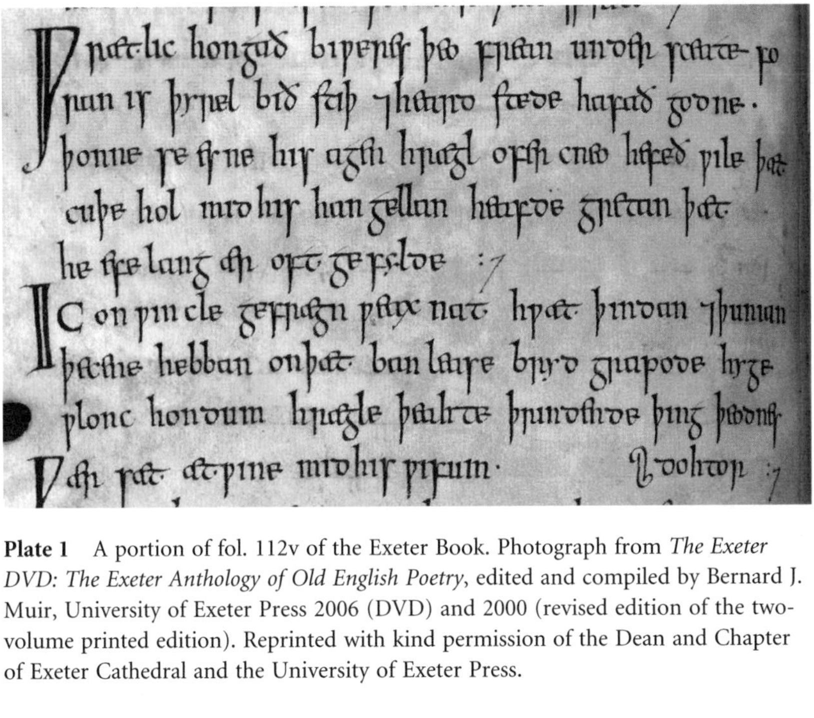

**Plate 1**  A portion of fol. 112v of the Exeter Book. Photograph from *The Exeter DVD: The Exeter Anthology of Old English Poetry*, edited and compiled by Bernard J. Muir, University of Exeter Press 2006 (DVD) and 2000 (revised edition of the two-volume printed edition). Reprinted with kind permission of the Dean and Chapter of Exeter Cathedral and the University of Exeter Press.

### Minitext L. Two Riddles

Plate 1 shows a portion of fol. 112v of the Exeter Book, containing Riddles 44 and 45. Read and transcribe these, normalizing punctuation and capitalization and arranging them in poetic lines.

### Minitext M. Two Laws of Ine

Plate 2 shows two sections of the Laws of Ine, king of Wessex (688–728), preserved in Cambridge, Corpus Christi College, MS 173, the Parker Chronicle and Laws (for a complete facsimile see Flower and Smith [40]). The part of the manuscript containing these laws was written around the middle of the tenth century.

## 16.3    Abbreviations

Old English scribes used only a few abbreviations, of which the most common is ⁊ (= *and*, *ond*), a sign (Latin *nota*) from the shorthand system developed by Cicero's assistant M. Tullius Tiro, and hence called the Tironian *nota*. Another common abbreviation is ꝥ for *þæt*. A stroke over a letter often signals that an *m* or *n* has been omitted; thus **bocū** stands for *bocum* and **ᵹumā** for *guman*. The *ġe-* prefix can also be abbreviated with a stroke (ᵹ̄), as can *þonne* (**þoñ**).

## 16.4    Punctuation and capitalization

Writers of Modern English follow a rather strict set of rules for punctuation – for example, placing a semicolon between independent clauses that are not coordinated with *and* and a comma between independent clauses that are so coordinated. Such punctuation guides the reader through the syntax of the sentence. Where the rules give us a choice, say, among comma, semicolon and dash, we use punctuation as a rhetorical device, marking the intensity of a pause or the formality of a clause boundary.

Old English scribes did not have so strict a set of rules to follow, and usage varies widely even among books produced at the same time and place. Some scribes used punctuation with fair reliability to mark clause- and sentence-boundaries, while others punctuated so lightly that their work is, for practical purposes, unpunctuated. To meet the expectations of readers accustomed to modern rules of punctuation, it has long been the practice of editors to

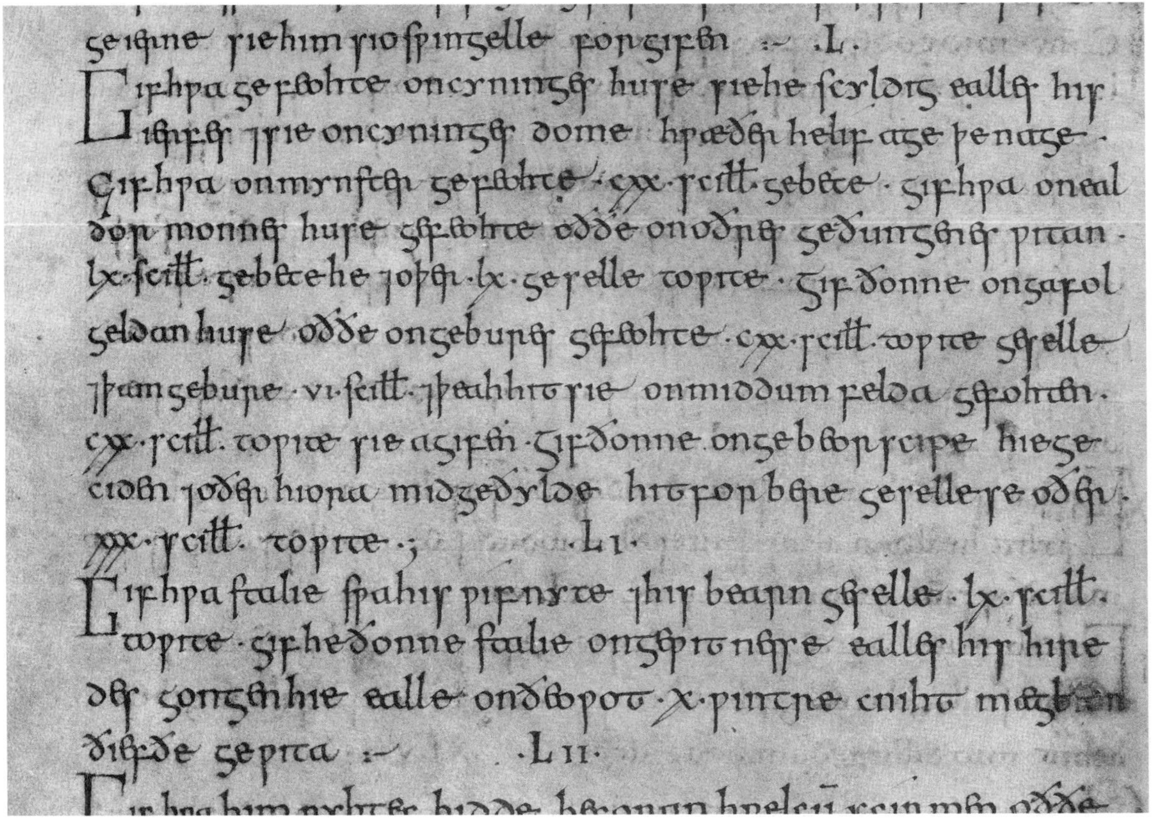

geirne sie him sio swingelle forgifen :- L.
Gif hwa gefeohte on cyninges huse sie he scyldig ealles his
ierfes 7 sie on cyninges dome hwæðer he lif age þe nage.
Gif hwa on mynster gefeohte ·cxx· scill. gebete. Gif hwa on eal
dormonnes huse gefeohte oððe on oðres geðungenes witan.
lx scill. gebete he 7 oðer ·lx· geselle to wite. Gif ðonne on gafol
geldan huse oððe on gebures gefeohte ·cxx· scill. to wite geselle
7 þam gebure ·vi· scill. 7 ðeah hit sie on middum felda gefohten.
cxx scill. to wite sie agifen. Gif ðonne on gebeorscipe hie ge
ciden 7 oðer hiora mid geðylde hit forbere geselle se oðer
xxx scill. to wite :; ·LI·
Gif hwa forstele swa his wif nyte 7 his bearn geselle ·lx· scill.
to wite. Gif he ðonne forstele on gewitnesse ealles his hiredes
gongen hie ealle on ðeowot. x winter cniht mæg bion
ðiefðe gewita :- ·LII·
Gif hwa him ryhtes bidde beforan hwelcum scirmen oððe

**Plate 2** Two sections of the Laws of Ine, king of Wessex (688–728). Reprinted with kind permission of the Master and Fellows of Corpus Christi College, Cambridge.

modernize the punctuation of Old English works. Editors have debated how heavy this editorial punctuation should be, how much it should be influenced by the punctuation of the manuscript, and whether modern punctuation is adequate for representing Old English syntax.

Here is a passage from a manuscript of Ælfric's homilies, illustrating the punctuation used by one good scribe.[1]

Ic ðancige þa ælmihtigū scyppende mid ealre heortan · þ he me ryngfullū þær geuðe · þ ic ðas tpa bec him to lofe ꝛ to pundmynte angelcynne onppeah ðam ungelæꝛedū · ða gelæꝛedan ne beðurfon þyrrera boca · for ðan þe him mæg heora agen lar genihtꝛumian;

[I thank the almighty Creator with all my heart that he has granted to me, a sinful one, that I have, in praise and worship of him, revealed these two books to the unlearned English nation; the learned have no need of these books because their own learning can suffice for them.]

The most common mark of punctuation is the point, which sometimes is placed on the baseline (as in Modern English) and sometimes, as here, somewhat above the line. The semicolon is used where a heavier syntactical or rhetorical break is indicated (here at the end of a pair of related sentences, which the translation coordinates with a semicolon). You may also occasionally see ⸵ (the *punctus elevatus*, marking a lighter pause than the semicolon but a heavier one than the point), and sometimes the ⸮ (the *punctus interrogativus* or question mark – but marking the end of a question is optional). At the ends of sections you may see some combination of punctuation marks used as an ornament.

**ⓘ** The function of acute accents, such as those in the preceding and following quotations, is uncertain. They are more often than not found over long vowels, but they also appear over short ones. They are especially common on one-syllable words.

In some poetic manuscripts punctuation is used to separate verses and lines – a convenience to modern readers, since scribes always wrote poetry from margin to margin, as if it were prose. Here are the first lines of *The Battle of*

---

[1]    Cambridge, University Library, MS. Gg. 3. 28, fol. 255r. A facsimile of this page is printed as the frontispiece to Henel [57]. The passage is printed as in the manuscript, except that word- and line-division have been normalized (see §16.5 below). In this and the other quotations in this chapter, the style of script is not intended to reproduce that of the manuscripts being quoted.

*Brunanburh* from the oldest manuscript of that poem[2] (the original line-breaks have been retained here):

Añ ꝺccc.xxxvii her æþelſtan cýnınᵹ · eorla ꝺryhten · beorna
beahᵹıfa · ⁊ hıſ broþor eac · eaꝺmunꝺ æþelınᵹ · ealꝺorlanᵹne tír ·
ᵹeſloᵹon æt ſæcce · ſpeorꝺa ecᵹum · ẏmbe brunanburh ·

[Anno 937. Here King Æthelstan, lord of warriors, ring-giver of men, and also his brother, Prince Edmund, struck life-long glory in battle with the edges of swords near Brunanburh.]

As you can see from these passages, proper names are not capitalized. Some scribes capitalized words for God and the beginnings of sentences, but most did not do so with any consistency. Those editors who modernize punctuation usually do the same with capitalization.

## 16.5   Word- and line-division

Word-division is far less consistent in Old English than in Modern English; it is, in fact, less consistent in Old English manuscripts than in Latin written by Anglo-Saxon scribes. You may expect to see the following peculiarities:[3]

- spaces between the elements of compounds, e.g. aldor mon;
- spaces between words and their prefixes and suffixes, e.g. be æftan, ᵹeriht nette;
- spaces at syllable divisions, e.g. len ᵹet;
- prepositions, adverbs and pronouns attached to the following words, e.g. uuiþbræc palū, hehæþe;
- many words, especially short ones, run together, e.g. þæt þehepuce hæþde.

The width of the spaces between words and word-elements is quite variable in most Old English manuscripts, and it is often difficult to decide whether a scribe intended a space. 'Diplomatic' editions, which sometimes attempt to reproduce the word-division of manuscripts, cannot represent in print the variability of the spacing on a hand-written page.

---

[2]   Cambridge, Corpus Christi College, MS. 173, fol. 26r. This is the Parker manuscript of the *Anglo-Saxon Chronicle* (see reading 3), in which the poem is the entry for the year 937. For a facsimile of this manuscript see Flower and Smith [40].

[3]   Most of the examples in the following list are from reading 3.

Most scribes broke words freely at the ends of lines. Usually the break takes place at a syllable boundary, e.g. ofſlæ̃ʒen (= *ofslægen*), ſū̃ne (= *sumne*), heo‑fenum. Occasionally, however, a scribe broke a word elsewhere, e.g. ſoþhaf‑ðnerre. Some scribes marked word-breaks with a hyphen, but many did not mark them in any way.

## 16.6   Errors and corrections

Everyone who writes makes mistakes, and it is probably safe to say that every Old English text of any length at all contains errors. Most manuscripts also contain corrections, either by the scribe himself or by a later corrector. But the correction of texts was often inconsistently carried out, and may not have taken into account errors already present in the copy from which corrections were being entered. In general you should not assume that a corrected text retains no uncorrected errors.

When a corrector added words to a text, he usually placed a comma below the line at the insertion point and wrote the addition above the line; longer additions might be written in the margin, very long ones on an added leaf. To delete a letter, the scribe would place a point under it; to delete a word or phrase he would underline it. Some correctors erased text, but erasure roughened the vellum, making it difficult to write on; so erasure was most suitable when no substitute text was to be supplied.

# Appendix A

# Common Spelling Variants

## A.1 Vowels of accented syllables

| Sounds | Environments | Examples |
|--------|--------------|----------|
| a ~ ea | When back vowel follows (or once followed) in next syllable. | *gatu ~ ġeatu* 'gates'; *gladian ~ gleadian* 'gladden'. |
| a ~ o | Before *m* and *n*. | *maniġ ~ moniġ* 'many'. |
| e ~ eo | When back vowel follows (or once followed) in next syllable. | *medo ~ meodo* 'mead'; *werod ~ weorod* 'troop'. |
| e ~ y | Late; between *s* and *l*. | *self ~ sylf* 'self'; *sellan ~ syllan* 'give'. |
| ea ~ a | Mercian and Northumbrian; before *l* + consonant. | *ealdor ~ aldor* 'life'; *healdan ~ haldan* 'hold'. |
| ĕa ~ ĕ | Late; before *c*, *g* and *h* or after *ċ*, *sc* and *ġ*. | *sceal ~ scel* 'must'; *seah ~ seh* 'saw'. |
| ĕo ~ ĭo | Frequent in a variety of texts. | *Bēowulf ~ Bīowulf*. |
| eo ~ u/o | Late; between *w* and *r*. | *weorðan ~ wurðan* 'become'; *weorold ~ woruld* 'world'. |
| eo/i ~ u | Late; after *w* when next syllable contains a back vowel; *w* may be lost. | *sweostor ~ swustor* 'sister'; *cwicu ~ cucu* 'alive'. |

| Sounds | Environments | Examples |
| --- | --- | --- |
| i ~ eo/io | When back vowel follows (or once followed) in next syllable. | *clipian* ~ *cleopian* 'call'; *ġewritu* ~ *ġewriotu* 'writings'. |
| i ~ y | Late; near labial consonants (*b*, *m*, *p*, *w*) and *r*. | *clipian* ~ *clypian* 'call'; *miċel* ~ *myċel* 'large'. |
| ĭe ~ ĭ/ў | Late and widespread. | *nīed* ~ *nȳd*/*nīd* 'necessity'; *iernan* ~ *irnan*/*yrnan* 'run'. |
| ĭe/ĭ/ȳ ~ ĕo/ĭo | Non-West Saxon; when *ĭe/ĭ/ȳ* is from *i*-mutation of *ĕo/ĭo*. | *þīestru* ~ *þēostru* 'darkness'; *āfierran* ~ *āfeorran* 'remove'. |
| ĭe/ĭ/ȳ ~ ĕ | Kentish; when *ĭe/ĭ/ȳ* is from *i*-mutation of *ĕa*. | *hliehhan* ~ *hlehhan* 'laugh'; *hīeran* ~ *hēran* 'hear'. |

## A.2   Unaccented syllables

| Sounds | Environments | Examples |
| --- | --- | --- |
| -an ~ -a | Late; weak noun and adjective ending. | *mōnan* ~ *mōna* genitive singular 'of the moon'. |
| -iġ ~ -ī | Adjective ending. | *maniġ* ~ *manī* 'many'. |
| -ness ~ -niss/-nyss | Feminine suffix. | *ēadiġness* ~ *ēadiġniss* ~ *ēadiġnyss* 'prosperity'. |
| -od- ~ -ad- | Past and past participle of second-class weak verbs. | *wunode* ~ *wunade* 'dwelled, remained with'. |
| -on ~ -an/-un | Late; plural verb ending. | *writon* ~ *writan* 'wrote'; *wǣron* ~ *wǣrun* 'were'. |
| -u ~ -o | Feminine nominative singular and neuter nominative plural. | *scipu* ~ *scipo* 'ships'. |
| -um ~ -on/-un | Late; dative ending. | *sīðum* ~ *sīðon* 'times'; *ārum* ~ *ārun* 'oars'. |

## A.3    Consonants

| Sounds | Environments | Examples |
|---|---|---|
| doubling | Before *l* or *r*. | *miċle* ~ *miċċle* 'large'; *nædre* ~ *næddre* 'serpent'. |
| undoubling | At the ends of words; after consonants; in unaccented syllables. | *mann* ~ *man* 'man'; *ġeornness* ~ *ġeorness* 'zeal'; *gyldenne* ~ *gyldene* 'golden'. |
| fn ~ mn/mm | Late. | *stefn* ~ *stemn* 'voice'; *hrefnas* ~ *hremmas* 'ravens'. |
| g ~ h | At the ends of words. | *sorg* ~ *sorh* 'sorrow'; *burg* ~ *burh* 'city'. |
| ġ ~ i/iġ | Late; after front vowels. | *dæġ* ~ *dæi* 'day'; *þeġn* ~ *þeiġn* 'thegn'. |
| ġeo ~ iu | At the beginnings of words. | *ġeong* ~ *iung* 'young'; *ġeogoð* ~ *iugoð* 'youth'. |
| r | Undergoes metathesis in syllables ending in *n* or *s*. | *irnan* ~ *rinnan* 'run'; *forst* ~ *frost* 'frost'. |
| sc ~ x | When *sc* is pronounced [sk] (see §2.1.2, item 10). | *ascian* ~ *axian* 'ask'; *fiscas* ~ *fixas* 'fishes'. |
| sco/scu ~ sceo | At the beginnings of words. | *sculan* ~ *sceolan* 'must'; *scort* ~ *sceort* 'short'. |

# Appendix B

# Phonetic Symbols and Terms

## B.1 International Phonetic Alphabet symbols

| Symbol | Description | Example |
|---|---|---|
| ɑ | open back unrounded vowel | mann 'man' |
| ɑː | long open back unrounded vowel | ān 'one' |
| æ | open-mid to open front unrounded vowel | bæc 'back' |
| æː | long open-mid to open front unrounded vowel | rǣdan 'read' |
| ʌ | open-mid back unrounded vowel | Modern English *but* |
| b | voiced bilabial stop | bōc 'book' |
| β | voiced bilabial spirant | |
| ç | voiceless palatal spirant | niht 'night' |
| d | voiced dental/alveolar stop | dēofol 'devil' |
| ʤ | voiced postalveolar affricate | enġel 'angel' |
| ð | voiced dental spirant | feðer 'wing' |
| e | close-mid front unrounded vowel | etan 'eat' |
| eː | long close-mid front unrounded vowel | hēr 'here' |
| ə | mid central unrounded vowel | Modern English *China* |
| ɛ | open-mid front unrounded vowel | Modern English *set* |
| f | voiceless labiodental spirant | feorr 'far' |
| g | voiced velar stop | gōd 'good' |
| ɣ | voiced velar spirant | āgan 'own' |

| Symbol | Description | Example |
|---|---|---|
| h | voiceless glottal spirant | hand 'hand' |
| i | close front unrounded vowel | sittan 'sit' |
| iː | long close front unrounded vowel | bītan 'bite' |
| ɪ | close to close-mid front unrounded vowel | iernan 'run' |
| ɪː | long close to close-mid front unrounded vowel | hīeran 'hear' |
| j | voiced palatal approximant | ġē 'you' |
| k | voiceless velar stop | camb 'comb' |
| l | alveolar lateral approximant | lamb 'lamb' |
| m | bilabial nasal | mann 'man' |
| n | dental/alveolar nasal | nū 'now' |
| ŋ | velar nasal | singan 'sing' |
| o | close-mid back rounded vowel | open 'open' |
| oː | long close-mid back rounded vowel | ōr 'origin' |
| p | voiceless bilabial stop | prēost 'priest' |
| r | alveolar trill | rǣdan 'read' |
| s | voiceless alveolar spirant | sittan 'sit' |
| ʃ | voiceless postalveolar spirant | scip 'ship' |
| t | voiceless dental/alveolar stop | twēġen 'two' |
| ʧ | voiceless postalveolar affricate | ċild 'child' |
| θ | voiceless dental spirant | þēaw 'custom' |
| u | close back rounded vowel | burg 'stronghold' |
| uː | long close back rounded vowel | būgan 'bow' |
| ʊ | close to close-mid back rounded vowel | Modern English *put* |
| v | voiced labiodental spirant | heofon 'heaven' |
| w | voiced labio-velar approximant | weall 'wall' |
| x | voiceless velar spirant | beorht 'bright' |
| y | close front rounded vowel | yfel 'evil' |
| yː | long close front rounded vowel | brȳd 'bride' |
| z | voiced alveolar spirant | rīsan 'rise' |

## B.2 Phonetic terms

**back vowel.** A vowel pronounced towards the back of the mouth, e.g. [ɑou].

**front vowel.** A vowel pronounced towards the front of the mouth, e.g. [ieæ].

**high vowel.** A vowel pronounced with the tongue raised, e.g. [iuy].

**liquid.** A term applied to the consonants [l] and [r].

**low vowel.** A vowel pronounced with the tongue and jaw lowered, e.g. [æɑ].

**nasal.** A consonant pronounced by passing air through the nose: [m] and [n].

**rounded vowel.** A vowel pronounced with the lips rounded, e.g. [uoy].

**spirant.** A consonant produced by passing air through a narrow opening in the mouth, e.g. [fsθvz]; also called a fricative.

**stop.** A consonant produced by momentarily stopping the breath, e.g. [bgkp]; also called a plosive.

**unvoiced.** Pronounced while the vocal chords are not vibrating, e.g. [fhkpst].

**voiced.** Pronounced while the vocal chords are vibrating. A vowel is always voiced; so are the consonants [bdgvz].

# Appendix C

# Further Reading

## C.1 General works

For a well-illustrated general account of the Anglo-Saxons, consult Campbell et al. [28]. If you have a specific query, consult Lapidge et al. [70], which is also good for browsing. Szarmach et al. [110], which covers England through the Middle Ages, also has many useful entries relating to Anglo-Saxon England.

## C.2 Grammars

Several scholarly grammars will give you far more information about Old English than this book does. Campbell [26] is the standard grammar for English speakers; although a bit dated, it is still a mine of information, especially on the pre-history of the language. For those who know German, Brunner [19] is also invaluable, especially for its information on Old English dialects. A more recent grammar than either of these, Hogg [58] is informed by recent linguistic theory; only vol. 1 (Phonology) has appeared so far.

The field of Old English syntax is mapped by Mitchell [80]. Since the appearance of Mitchell's work, now a standard reference, there has been a torrent of useful work on the subject. Two important and accessible books on Old English syntax are Blockley [14] and Donoghue [36].

Lass [73] is a well-written tour of the history of Old English for students who know at least a little about linguistics. For a survey of the other Germanic languages, see Robinson [99].

## C.3   Dictionaries and concordances

The standard dictionary of Old English is Bosworth et al. [15]. Its quality is uneven, largely because Bosworth, who was responsible for the letters A–G, was not quite up to the job of compiling an Old English dictionary. However, Toller was an excellent lexicographer, and if one remembers always to check his *Supplement* for words beginning A–G, the dictionary is still quite serviceable (Campbell's contribution is a thin supplement published about fifty years after the dictionary was complete). This venerable dictionary is being superseded by Cameron et al. [23], now complete through F; it was originally issued on microfiche, but is now issued on CD-ROM instead. Clark Hall [30] is an excellent compact dictionary for students. The standard etymological dictionary is Holthausen [59].

The 'Old English Aerobics Glossary' (http://www.engl.virginia.edu/OE/glossary/) is not as complete as the printed dictionaries, but it allows a user to look up words by headword, attested form, or definition (and thus can function as a reverse dictionary).

The entire corpus of Old English was concorded by the Dictionary of Old English Project at the University of Toronto; the result is Healey and Venezky [55], published on microfiche. Those whose libraries subscribe to the Old English Corpus on line (for information, see http://www.press.umich.edu/), however, should generally prefer that as a much more flexible tool for researching the language. If you want a concordance of the poetry only, consult Bessinger [8].

## C.4   Bibliographies

Greenfield and Robinson [51] is a comprehensive bibliography of publications on Old English literature up to 1972. For annotated bibliographies of Beowulf scholarship, see Short [105] and Hasenfratz [54]. For a bibliography of Anglo-Saxon history, see Keynes [65]. The home page of the Richard Rawlinson Center for Anglo-Saxon Studies and Manuscript Research (http://www.wmich.edu/medieval/rawl/index.html) has several useful bibliographies, including an on-line version of Keynes and 'A Bibliography of *The Battle of Maldon*' by Wendy E. J. Collier.

Comprehensive annual bibliographies are published in two journals, *Old English Newsletter* and *Anglo-Saxon England*. The poetry section of the bibliography in *Old English Newsletter* is classified by work and therefore very useful for literary research.


## C.5    Old English texts and translations

Several published collections contain texts for students of Old English. Especially good ones, aside from the one in this book, are Marsden [78], Mitchell and Robinson [81], Whitelock [115] and Pope and Fulk [95]. Methuen's Old English Library, which published student-oriented editions of prose and poetry, has been discontinued, but its editions have been reissued (with additional bibliography) in the series Exeter Medieval English Texts, which has also published several Old English editions of its own. Mitchell and Robinson [82] is a good edition of *Beowulf* for students. *Old English Aerobics* includes a growing collection of on-line texts of Old English prose and poetry with complete glossaries and full grammatical information about each word and clause.

To locate scholarly editions of Old English texts, see Greenfield and Robinson [51]. For editions published after 1972, consult the annual bibliographies listed in C.4. The standard edition of almost all the Old English poetry is Krapp and Dobbie [69]. For the poems of the Exeter Book, see also Muir [85], and for *Beowulf* see Klaeber [67] (the standard scholarly edition, now showing its age) and Kiernan [66].

Several series have published significant numbers of Old English texts. The Early English Text Society have been publishing Old English and Middle English texts since 1864; most Old English editions published up to around 1900 are accompanied by translations. A German series, Bibliothek der angelsächsischen Prosa, published editions of Old English prose in the late nineteenth and early twentieth centuries; several of these are still useful.

In addition to the translations included with some of the editions mentioned above, the student should know of two important collections, Bradley [16] for poetry (supersedes Gordon [49], which is nevertheless still useful) and Swanton [109] for prose.


## C.6    Literary criticism; sources and analogues; metre

To get started reading about Old English literature, you would do well to consult Donoghue [37], which provides a broad overview. Fulk and Cain [43] provide a more detailed survey. Older but still useful surveys include Greenfield and Calder [50] and Alexander [2]. Liuzza [75], Pulsiano [97], Godden and Lapidge [45] and O'Keeffe [89] are collections of essays usefully broken down by topic. All of these books contain bibliographies.

The series Basic Readings in Anglo-Saxon England collects useful essays on individual topics, authors and works: see Baker [4], O'Keeffe [88], Bjork [11], Szarmach [111] and Liuzza [76]. Fulk [41] is a good collection of criticism on *Beowulf*, and Bjork and Niles [12] surveys the history of *Beowulf* scholarship. Orchard [92] is another good guide to *Beowulf*.

Sources and analogues of Old English poetry have been conveniently collected in Calder and Allen [21] and Calder et al. [22]; for analogues of *Beowulf*, see Garmonsway and Simpson [44].

There have been many books on metre, especially in recent decades. Particularly important studies include Bliss [13], Russom [100], Cable [20] and Fulk [42].

## C.7   History and culture

Readers interested in Anglo-Saxon history should consult Keynes [65]. Here we list a few works of general interest. The standard history of Anglo-Saxon England (if there is such a thing) is Stenton [107]. Two good general introductions to the history and culture are Hunter Blair [60] and Campbell et al. [28]. See Fell [39] for an account of women in Anglo-Saxon England. Pelteret [94] is a collection of useful recent essays.

## C.8   Manuscripts, art and archaeology

The indispensable guide to the manuscripts containing Old English is Ker [63] (which also contains a brief and lucid introduction to Old English palaeography, pp. xxiii–xlii); see also Ker [64], the supplement to his *Catalogue*. For a survey of illuminated manuscripts, see Alexander [1] and Temple [112], and for a collection of useful essays, Richards [98]. For a useful guide to the terminology used by palaeographers, see Brown [18], and for a comprehensive survey of Western palaeography, see Bischoff [10].

The series Early English Manuscripts in Facsimile has published twenty-six volumes of high-quality facsimiles of Anglo-Saxon manuscripts. Pulsiano et al. [96] aims to produce descriptions and microfiche facsimiles of all manuscripts containing Old English. Important printed facsimiles of individual manuscripts and works include Zupitza and Davis [119] for *Beowulf*,

Chambers et al. [29] for the Exeter Book, Gollancz [48] for the Junius Manuscript (formerly called the 'Cædmon Manuscript') and Flower and Smith [40] for the oldest manuscript of the Anglo-Saxon Chronicle.

Electronic manuscript facsimiles are becoming increasingly important, both because of the research advantages of having images that can be manipulated and because they are relatively cheap to produce. Kiernan [66], a pioneer in this area, contains a facsimile of the *Beowulf* manuscript and the 'Thorkelin transcripts' from which editors restore damaged passages of that poem, along with a rich selection of supplementary material and an on-line edition. Muir [86] is a high-quality electronic facsimile of the Junius Manuscript; as of this writing Muir's electronic facsimile of The Exeter Book is soon to be released.

A good (and copiously illustrated) introduction to the art of Anglo-Saxon England is Wilson [118]. For the archaeology, see Wilson [117], and the essays in Karkov [62].


## C.9    On-line aids

For World Wide Web browsing, you should add several pages to your list of bookmarks:

www.georgetown.edu/cball/oe/old_english.html Cathy Ball's 'Old English Pages' offers a wide-ranging collection of links to Anglo-Saxon sites. (It appears to be no longer maintained.)

http://www.hcu.ox.ac.uk/toebi/ 'Teachers of Old English in Britain and Ireland' is similar, and may load faster for European users.

www.trin.cam.ac.uk/sdk13/sdk13home.html Simon Keynes's homepage contains a comprehensive collection of links for historians.

www.ucalgary.ca/UofC/eduweb/engl401/ Murray McGillivray of the University of Calgary offers an on-line course in Old English; the site for the course contains a good bit of publicly available material.

www.georgetown.edu/cball/hwaet/hwaet_toc.html Cathy Ball's 'Hwæt' is a basic vocabulary drill.

http://www.labyrinth.georgetown.edu/ 'The Labyrinth' is a collection of links and materials for medievalists; it offers a good collection of Old English electronic texts.

http://www.wmich.edu/medieval/research/rawl/ The Richard Rawlinson Center for Anglo-Saxon Studies and Manuscript Research at Western Michigan University has published several original on-line editions of Old English texts on its site and is the home of or has links to a number of other scholarly projects.

## C.10   On-line amusements

http://www.rochester.edu/englisc/ A website for 'Englisc', a mailing list for people who like to write Old English. Follow the links to 'Ðæt Gettysburg Gemaþel' or 'The New Anglo-Saxon Chronicles' (current events narrated in Old English).

http://ang.wikipedia.org/ An Old English version of Wikipedia, the free encyclopedia. An excellent place to exercise your Old English composition skills.

http://www.georgetown.edu/faculty/ballc/englisc/instant-oe.html 'Instant Old English: A Conversational Phrasebook: a help if you need to ask directions while visiting tenth-century Winchester.

http://www.mun.ca/Ansaxdat/vocab/wordlist.html 'Modern English to Old English Vocabulary': an aid to composition.

http://www.u.arizona.edu/~ctb/wordhord.html 'Circolwyrde Wordhord': a glossary of Old English computer terminology.

# Anthology

## 1 The Fall of Adam and Eve

This reading is from a translation of the first several books of the Old Testament by two writers – one anonymous, the other Ælfric, pupil of St Æthelwold, monk of Cerne, and later Abbot of Eynsham. The present extract is from Ælfric's section of the work. For a facsimile of the magnificently illustrated manuscript, see Dodwell and Clemoes [35], and for a complete text see Crawford [33].

If your class is using the *Guide to Old English*, compare the text in that book (printed from a different manuscript) with this one. Can you spot the substantive differences?

[1] Ēac swylċe¹ sēo nǣddre wæs ġēapre ðonne ealle ðā ōðre nȳtenu ðe God ġeworhte ofer eorðan. And sēo nǣddre cwæð tō ðām wīfe: 'Hwī forbēad God ēow ðæt ġē ne ǣton of ǣlcum trēowe binnan Paradīsum?'

[2] Þæt wīf andwyrde: 'Of ðǣra trēowa wæstme ðe synd on Paradīsum wē etað:

[3] and of ðæs trēowes wæstme þe is onmiddan neorxnawange, God bebēad ūs ðæt wē ne ǣton, ne wē ðæt trēow ne hrepodon, ðī lǣs ðe wē swelton.'²

[4] Ðā cwæð sēo nǣdre eft tō ðām wīfe: 'Ne bēo³ ġē nāteshwōn dēade, ðēah ðe ġē of ðām trēowe eton.

---

¹ *Ēac swylċe*: likewise, moreover.
² A subjunctive. In this late text the plural subjunctive ending is -*on* rather than -*en* (see §7.2.3).
³ *Ne bēo*: will not be. Before *wē* or *ġē* a plural verb sometimes ends in -*e* (see §7.2.2). Here the -*e* has disappeared because the root syllable ends in a vowel.

[5] Ac God wāt sōðlīċe ðæt ēowre ēagan bēoð ġeopenode on swā hwylċum dæġe swā[4] ġē etað of ðām trēowe; and ġē bēoð ðonne englum ġelīċe, witende ǣġðer ġe gōd ġe yfel.'

[6] Ðā ġeseah ðæt wīf ðæt ðæt trēow wæs gōd tō etenne, be ðām ðe hyre ðūhte, and wlitiġ on ēagum and lustbǣre on ġesyhðe; and ġenam ðā of ðæs trēowes wæstme and ġeǣt, and sealde hyre were: hē ǣt ðā.

[7] And heora bēġra ēagan wurdon ġeopenode: hī oncnēowon ðā ðæt hī nacode wǣron, and sȳwodon him fīclēaf and worhton him wǣdbrēċ.

[8] Eft ðā ðā God cōm and hī ġehȳrdon his stemne ðǣr hē ēode on neorxnawange ofer midne dæġ, ðā behȳdde Adam hine, and his wīf ēac swā dyde, fram Godes ġesihðe onmiddan ðām trēowe neorxnawonges.

[9] God clypode ðā Adam, and cwæð: 'Adam, hwǣr eart ðū?'

[10] Hē cwæð: 'Ðīne stemne iċ ġehīre, lēof, on neorxnawange, and iċ ondrǣde mē, for ðām ðe iċ eom nacod, and iċ behȳde mē.'

[11] God cwæð: 'Hwā sǣde ðē ðæt ðū nacod wǣre, ġyf ðū ne ǣte of ðām trēowe ðe iċ ðē bebēad ðæt ðū ne ǣte?'

[12] Adam cwæð: 'Ðæt wīf ðe ðū mē forġēafe tō ġefēran sealde mē of ðām trēowe, and iċ ǣtt.'

[13] God cwæð tō ðām wīfe: 'Hwī dydestū[5] ðæt?' Hēo cwæð: 'Sēo nǣdre bepǣhte mē and iċ ǣtt.'

[14] God cwæð tō ðǣre nǣddran: 'For ðan ðe ðū ðis dydest, ðū bist[6] āwyrġed betweox eallum nȳtenum and wildēorum. Ðū gǣst on ðīnum brēoste and ytst ðā eorðan eallum dagum ðīnes līfes.[7]

[15] Iċ sette fēondrǣdenne betwux ðē and ðām wīfe and ðīnum ofspringe and hire ofspringe; hēo tōbrȳtt ðīn hēafod and ðū syrwst onġēan hire hō.'

[16] Tō ðām wīfe cwæð God ēac swylċe: 'Iċ ġemǣnifylde ðīne yrmða and ðīne ġeēacnunga; on sārnysse ðū ācenst ċild, and ðū bist under weres anwealde and hē ġewylt ðē.'

[17] Tō Adame hē cwæð: 'For ðān ðe ðū ġehȳrdest ðīnes wīfes stemne and ðū ǣte of ðǣm trēowe ðe iċ ðē bebēad ðæt ðū ne ǣte, is sēo eorðe āwyrġed on ðīnum weorce. On ġeswyncum ðū ytst of ðǣre eorðan eallum dagum ðīnes līfes.

[18] Ðornas and brēmelas hēo āspryt ðē, and ðū ytst ðǣre eorðan wyrta.

[19] On swāte ðīnes andwlitan[8] ðū brȳċst ðīnes hlāfes oð ðæt ðū ġewende tō eorðan, of ðǣre ðe ðū ġenumen wǣre, for ðan ðe ðū eart dūst and tō dūste ġewyrst.'

---

4  *swā hwylċum dæġe swā*: whatever day. For this construction, see §5.4.
5  A contraction of *dydest þū*.
6  *ðū bist*: you will be. All of the following present tense verbs should be translated as futures.
7  *ðīnes līfes*: of your life.
8  *ðīnes andwlitan*: of your face.

# 2   The Life of St Æthelthryth

St Æthelthryth, the seventh-century Abbess of Ely, was one of Anglo-Saxon England's most widely venerated saints. This life of her by Ælfric (see headnote to reading 1) was written in the last years of the tenth century. Ælfric's collection of saints' lives is edited in Skeat [106].

VIIII KALENDAS IULII. NATALE SANCTE ÆÐELDRYÐE VIRGINIS.

[1] Wē wyllað nū āwrītan, þēah ðe hit wundorlic sȳ, be ðǣre hālgan sancte Æðeldrȳðe[1] þām Engliscan mǣdene, þe wæs mid twām werum and swā ðēah wunode mǣden, swā swā þā wundra ġeswuteliað þe hēo wyrcð ġelōme. [2] Anna[2] hātte hyre fæder, Ēastengla cynincg, swȳðe Cristen man, swā swā hē cȳdde mid weorcum, and eall his tēam wearð ġewurðod þurh God. [3] Æðeldrȳð wearð þā forġifen ānum ealdormenn[3] tō wīfe. [4] Ac hit nolde se ælmihtiga God þæt hire mæġðhād wurde mid hǣmede ādylegod, ac hēold hī on clǣnnysse, for ðan þe hē is ælmihtiġ God and mæġ dōn eall þæt hē wile, and on manegum wīsum his mihte ġeswutelað.

[5] Se ealdorman ġewāt þā ðā hit wolde God, and hēo wearð forġifen Ecfride cynincge,[4] and twelf ġēar wunode unġewemmed mǣden on þæs cynincges synscype, swā swā swutele wundra hyre mǣrða cȳðaþ and hire mæġðhād ġelōme. [6] Hēo lufode þone Hǣlend þe hī hēold unwemme, and Godes ðēowas wurðode. [7] Ān þēra wæs Wilfrid bisceop,[5] þe hēo swȳðost lufode, and hē sǣde Bēdan þæt se cyning Ecfrid him oft behēte myċel on lande and on fēo, ġif hē lǣran mihte Æðeldrȳðe his ġebeddan þæt hēo bruce his synscipes. [8] Nū cwæð se hālga Bēda, þe þās bōc ġesette, þæt se ælmihtiga

---

[1]   Æthelthryth (d. 679), founder of the monastery at Ely, was daughter of King Anna of the East Angles. She is one of the royal and noble women who played an important role in the development of the Church in Anglo-Saxon England and whose numbers include Æthelthryth's sister Seaxburh, Eafe and Mildrith of Minster-in-Thanet, Hild of Whitby, and others. Bede's account of Æthelthryth in his *Ecclesiastical History*, Bk. IV ch. 19, is the source of the present life of her.

[2]   Anna was king of the East Angles from c.636 to c.654; he was killed in battle with Penda, the pagan king of Mercia.

[3]   According to Bede, one Tondberct of the South Gyrwas. According to the Life of St Æthelthryth in the *Liber Eliensis*, Tondberct gave her Ely as part of her 'dowry' (i.e. bride-price or morning-gift).

[4]   Ecgfrith, king of the Northumbrians (670–85), who plays a major role in Bede's *Ecclesiastical History*. Ecgfrith later married one Eormenburg, who after his death took orders and became an abbess herself.

[5]   Wilfrid (634–709), the wilful and controversial Bishop of York (664–709), whose conflicts with King Ecgfrith of Northumbria are told both by Bede and by Wilfrid's biographer, Eddius Stephanus (see Colgrave [32]).

God mihte ēaðe ġedōn nū on ūrum dagum þæt Æðeldrȳð þurhwunode unġewemmed mǣden, þēah ðe hēo wer hæfde, swā swā on ealdum dagum hwīlon ǣr ġetīmode þurh þone ylcan God þe ǣfre þurhwunað mid his ġecorenum hālgum, swā swā hē sylf behēt.

[9] Æðeldrȳð wolde ðā ealle woruldþincg forlǣtan, and bæd ġeorne þone cynincg þæt hēo Criste mōste þēowian on mynsterliċre drohtnunge, swā hire mōd hire tō spēon. [10] Þā lȳfde hire se cynincg, þēah þe hit embe lang wǣre, þæs þe hēo ġewilnode, and Wilfrid bisceop þā hī ġehādode tō myneċene, and hēo syððan on mynstre wunode sume twelf mōnað swā, and hēo syððan wearð ġehādod eft tō abudissan on Eliġmynstre, ofer manega myneċena, and hēo hī mōdorlīċe hēold mid gōdum ġebysnungum tō þām gāstlican līfe.

[11] Be hire is āwryten þæt hēo wel drohtnode tō ānum mǣle fæstende, būtan hit frēolsdæġ wǣre, and hēo syndriġe ġebedu swȳðe lufode[6] and wyllen weorode, and wolde seldhwænne hire līċ baðian būtan tō hēahtīdum, and ðonne hēo wolde ǣrest ealle ðā baðian þe on ðām mynstre wǣron, and wolde him ðēnian mid hire þīnenum, and þonne hī sylfe baðian.

[12] Þā on þām eahteoðan ġeare siððan hēo abbudisse wæs, hēo wearð ġeuntrumod, swā swā hēo ǣr wītegode, swā þæt ān ġeswel wēox on hire swūran myċel under þām ċynnbāne, and hēo swīðe þancode Gode þæt hēo on þām swūran sum ġeswinc þolode. [13] Hēo cwæð: ‘iċ wāt ġeare þæt iċ wel wyrðe eom þæt mīn swūra bēo ġeswenċt mid swylċere untrumnysse, for ðan þe iċ on iugoðe frætwode mīnne swūran mid mæniġfealdum swūrbēagum, and mē is nū ġeþūht þæt Godes ārfæstnyss þone gylt āclǣnsiġe, þonne mē nū þis ġeswel scȳnð for golde, and þes hāta bryne for hēalicum ġymstānum.’

[14] Þā wæs þǣr sum lǣċe on ðām ġelēaffullum hēape, Cynefrȳð ġehāten, and hī cwǣdon þā sume þæt se lǣċe sceolde āscēotan þæt ġeswell. [15] Þā dyde hē sōna swā, and þǣr sāh ūt wyrms. [16] Wearð him þā ġeðūht swilċe hēo ġewurpan mihte, ac hēo ġewāt of worulde mid wuldre tō Gode on þām ðriddan dæġe syððan se dolh wæs ġeopenod, and wearð bebyrġed swā swā hēo bæd sylf and hēt, betwux hire ġeswustrum, on trēowenre ċyste.

[17] Þā wearð hire swustor Sexburh[7] ġehādod tō abbudissan æfter hire ġeendunge, sēo ðe ǣr wæs cwēn on Cantwarebyriġ. [18] Þā wolde sēo Sexburh æfter syxtȳne ġēarum dōn hire swustor bān of ðǣre byrġene ūp and beran intō þǣre ċyrċan; and sende þā ġebrōðra tō sēċenne sumne stān tō swilċere nēode, for ðan þe on þām fenlande synd fēawa weorcstāna. [19] Hī rēowan þā tō Grantanċeastre, and God hī sōna ġehradode, swā þæt hī þǣr ġemētton āne

---

[6] That is, she prayed by herself as well as communally at the canonical hours. According to Bede, she prayed each day from the hour of matins (between midnight and 3 a.m.) until dawn unless prevented by illness.

[7] Seaxburg, Anna’s eldest daughter, was married to Erconberht, king of Kent (640–64) before joining her sister at Ely. She was the mother of St Ercongota, celebrated by Bede in his *Ecclesiastical History*, Bk. III ch. 8.

mǣre þrūh wið þone weall standende, ġeworht of marmstāne eall hwītes blēos
bufan þǣre eorðan, and þæt hlyd ðǣrtō ġelimplīce ġefēġed, ēac of hwītum
marmstāne, swā swā hit macode God.

[20] Þā nāman ðā ġebrōðra blȳðelīce þā ðrūh and ġebrōhton tō mynstre,
myċċlum ðanciġende Gode; and Sexburh sēo abbudisse hēt slēan ān ġeteld
bufan ðā byrġene, wolde þā bān gaderian. [21] Hī sungon ðā ealle sealmas
and līċsang þā hwīle þe man ðā byrġene bufan ġeopenode. [22] Þā læġ hēo on
ðǣre ċyste swilċe hēo lǣġe on slǣpe, hāl eallum limum, and se lǣċe wæs ðǣr
ðe þæt ġeswell ġeopenode, and hī scēawode ġeorne. [23] Þā wæs sēo wund
ġehǣled þe se lǣċe worhte ǣr; ēac swilċe þā ġewǣda þe hēo bewunden wæs
mid wǣron swā ansunde swylċe hī eall nīwe wǣron.[8]

[24] Sexburh þā hyre swuster swīðe þæs fæġnode, and hī þwōgon ðā syððan
þone sāwllēasan līċhaman, and mid nīwum ġewǣdum bewundon ārwurðlīce,
and bǣron into ðǣre ċyrċan, blyssiġende mid sangum, and lēdon hī on ðǣre
þrȳh, þǣr ðǣr hēo līð oð þis on myċelre ārwurðnysse, mannum tō wundrunge.

[25] Wæs ēac wundorlīc þæt sēo ðrūh wæs ġeworht þurh Godes forescēawunge
hire swā ġemǣte, swylċe hēo hyre sylfre swā ġesceapen wǣre, and æt hire
hēafde wæs āhēawen se stān ġemǣte þām hēafde þæs hālgan mǣdenes.

[26] Hit is swutol þæt hēo wæs unġewemmed mǣden, þonne hire līċhama
ne mihte formolsnian on eorðan, and Godes miht is ġeswutelod sōðlīce þurh
hī, þæt hē mǣġ ārǣran ðā formolsnodan līċhaman, se ðe hire līċ hēold hāl on
ðǣre byrġene ġīt oð þisne dæġ; sȳ him ðæs ā wuldor. [27] Þǣr wǣron ġehǣlede
þurh ðā hālgan fēmnan fela ādliġe menn, swā swā wē ġefyrn ġehȳrdon; and
ēac ðā þe hrepodon þæs rēafes ǣniġne dǣl þe hēo mid bewunden wæs wurdon
sōna hāle; and manegum ēac fremode sēo ċyst miċċlum þe hēo ǣrest on læġ,
swā swā se lārēow Bēda on ðǣre bēċ sǣde þe hē ġesette be ðysum.

[28] Oft woruldmenn ēac hēoldon, swā swā ūs bēċ secgað, heora clǣnnysse
on synscipe for Cristes lufe, swā swā wē mihton reċċan ġif ġē rohton hit tō
ġehȳrenne. [29] Wē secgað swā ðēah be sumum ðeġne, se wæs þrȳttiġ ġēara
mid his wīfe on clǣnnysse. [30] Þrȳ suna hē ġestrȳnde, and hī siððan būta
ðrīttiġ ġēara wǣron wuniġende būtan hǣmede and fela ælmyssan worhton
oð þæt se wer fērde tō munucliċere drohtnunge; and Drihtnes enġlas cōmon
eft on his forðsīðe and feredon his sāwle mid sange tō heofonum, swā swā
ūs secgað bēċ. [31] Manega bysna synd on bōcum be swylċum, hū oft weras
and wīf wundorlīce drohtnodon and on clǣnnysse wunodon tō wuldre þām
Hǣlende þe þā clǣnnysse āstealde, Crist ūre Hǣlend, þām is ā wurðmynt and
wuldor on ēċnysse. Amen.

---

[8]   It is a frequent motif in hagiographical literature for the saint's body to be discovered undecayed
after years, or even decades. It was included in the lives to provide evidence of the saint's sanctity.

# 3 Ælfric on the Book of Job

Ælfric's homily on the Book of Job is the first treatment in English of an Old Testament book whose compelling narrative and intensely lyrical meditation on the meanings of misfortune have influenced Western authors as diverse as Geoffrey Chaucer, Franz Kafka and Toni Morrison. The early Middle Ages, informed by Gregory the Great's massive commentary, *Moralia in Iob*, understood Job as a prefigurement of Christ. Ælfric considers this figurative interpretation too difficult for the lay audience of this homily. Further, he worries here, as in some of his other writings, that laymen may pick up erroneous notions from an Old Testament text such as this, since we are not now permitted to practise some of the customs depicted, such as animal sacrifice. However, Ælfric, like many other authors, finds in Job an irresistible moral exemplar: in patiently bearing his afflictions without losing his faith, he teaches us to bear patiently the adversities that God sends upon us. Ælfric seems also to recognize in the Book of Job an opportunity to exercise his own considerable ability as a storyteller: whereas the original is a 'wisdom book' in which the narrative component is subordinated to the long and meditative conversation between Job and his friends, Ælfric's version has it the other way around. The meditative element has been radically abbreviated and now appears not so much as an exploration of the problem of evil, but rather as a justification of Job as an ideal servant of God.

This text belongs to a lengthy work called the *Catholic Homilies*, which presents two series of forty homilies each, most of them intended to be read on particular dates in the liturgical calendar. The homily on Job is the thirtieth in the second series, intended for the first Sunday in September. For a scholarly edition of the second series of *Catholic Homilies* see Godden [46], and for commentary Godden [47].

DOMINICA I IN MENSE SEPTEMBRI, QUANDO LEGITUR IOB.[1]
[1] Mīne ġebrōðra, wē rǣdað nū æt Godes ðēnungum be ðān ēadigan were Iob. [2] Nū wille wē ēow hwæt lȳtles be him ġereċċan, for ðan þe sēo dēopnys ðǣre race oferstīhð ūre andġit and ēac swīðor þǣra unġelǣredra. [3] Man sceal lǣwedum mannum secgan be heora andġites mǣðe, swā þæt hī ne bēon ðurh ðā dēopnysse ǣmōde ne ðurh ðā langsumnysse ġeǣðrytte.

[4] Sum wer wæs ġeseten on þām lande þe is ġehāten Hus; his nama wæs Iob. [5] Se wer wæs swīðe bilewite and rihtwīs and ondrǣdende God and forbūgende yfel. [6] Him wǣron ācennede seofan suna and ðrēo dohtra. [7] Hē hæfde seofon ðūsend sċēapa and ðrēo ðūsend olfenda, fíf hund ġetȳmu oxena and fíf hund assan and ormǣte miċelne hīred. [8] Se wer wæs swīðe mǣre betwux eallum ēasternum, and his suna fērdon and ðēnode ǣlċ ōðrum[2]

---

[1] The first Sunday in September, when Job is read.
[2] *ðēnode ǣlċ ōðrum*: each served the others.

mid his gōdum on ymbhwyrfte æt his hūse, and þǣrtō heora swustru
ġelaðodon. [9] Iob sōðlīċe ārās on ðām eahteoðan dæġe on ǣrnemeriġen and
offrode Gode seofonfealde lāc for his seofon sunum, ðȳ lǣs ðe hī wið God on
heora ġeðance āgylton. [10] Ðus dyde Iob eallum dagum for his sunum, and
hī swā ġehālgode.[3]

[11] Hit ġelamp on sumum dæġe, ðā ðā Godes enġlas cōmon and on his
ġesihðe stōdon, ðā wæs ēac swylċe se scucca him betwux. [12] Tō ðām cwæð
Drihten, 'Hwanon cōme ðū?' [13] Se sceocca andwyrde, 'Iċ fērde ġeond þās
eorðan and hī beēode.' [14] Drihten cwæð, 'Ne behēolde ðū,[4] lā, mīnne ðēowan
Iob, þæt nān man nis his ġelīca on eorðan, bilewite man and rihtwīs,
ondrǣdende God and yfel forbūgende?'

[15] Swā stōd se dēofol on Godes ġesihðe swā swā dēð se blinda on sunnan.[5]
[16] Sēo sunne ymbscīnð þone blindan, and se blinda ne ġesihð þǣre sunnan
lēoman. [17] God ġeseah ðone dēofol, and se dēofol swā ðēah wæs bedǣled
Godes ġesihðe and his wuldres.[6] [18] Eorðe is ġecweden Godes fōtsceamel,
and sēo heofen is his ðrymsetl. [19] Nū stōd se sceocca swilċe æt Godes
fōtsceamele upon ðǣre eorðan ðā ðā se ælmihtiga hine axode hwanon hē
cōme. [20] Hē cwæð þæt hē fērde ġeond þās eorðan for ðan ðe hē færð swā
swā Pētrus se apostol cwæð: 'Bēoð sȳfre and wacole, for ðan ðe se dēofol
ēower wiðerwinna færð onbūtan swā swā grymetende lēo, sēċende hwæne hē
ābīte.[7] Wiðstandað þām, strange on ġelēafan.'

[21] Miċele wǣron þises mannes ġeearnunga þā se ælmihtiga be him cwæð
þæt his ġelīca nǣre on eorðan. [22] Ġē magon ġehȳran sume his ðēawas, swā
swā hē be him sylfum āwrāt.[8] [23] Iob cwæð, 'Iċ ālȳsde hrȳmende þearfan,
and ðām stēopbearne þe būton fultume wæs iċ ġehēolp, and wydewan heortan
iċ ġefrēfrode. [24] Iċ wæs ymbscrȳd mid rihtwīsnysse. [25] Iċ wæs blindum
men ēage[9] and healtum fōt and þearfena fæder. [26] Of flȳsum mīnra sċēapa
wǣron ġehlȳwde ðearfena sīdan, and iċ ðearfum ne forwyrnde þæs ðe hī
ġyrndon, ne iċ ne æt āna mīnne hlāf būton stēopbearne, ne iċ ne blissode on
mīnum meniġfealdum welum. [27] Ne fæġnode iċ on mīnes fēondes hryre, ne
læġ ælðeodiġ man wiðūtan mīnum heġum, ac mīn duru ġeopenode symle

---

[3] *hī swā ġehālgode*: thus sanctified them.

[4] *Ne behēolde ðū*: Have you not beheld.

[5] Ælfric emphasizes the limitations of Satan's power and his exclusion from God's presence.
The biblical text positions Satan *coram Domino* 'in the presence of God', but Ælfric carefully
explains that the devil cannot actually be situated in heaven or see God. Similarly, he explains
later that Satan's apparently hurling fire from heaven is a trick: the fire comes from above, but
not from heaven.

[6] *bedǣled Godes ġesihðe and his wuldres*: separated from God's sight and his glory.

[7] *hwæne hē ābīte*: someone he can devour.

[8] Gregory thought it likely that Job himself was the author of the Book of Job, though he
emphasized that the true author was the Holy Spirit.

[9] *blindum men ēage*: an eye for the blind man.

weġfērendum. [28] Ne behȳdde iċ mīne synna, ne iċ on mīnum bōsme ne bedīġlode mīne unrihtwīsnysse.' [29] Ne sǣde Iob ðis for ġylpe, ac for ðan ðe hē wæs eallum mannum tō bysne ġeset.

[30] Þus mǣrne man wolde se mānfulla dēofol þurh ðām micclum costnungum ðe hē him tō dyde fram Gode ġewēman, and cwæð tō Drihtne, [31] 'Ne ondrǣt Iob on īdel God: þū ymbtrymedest hine and ealle his ǣhta, and his handġeweorc þū bletsodest, and his ǣhta wēoxon on eorðan. [32] Ac āstreċe hwōn ðīne hand and ġetill ealle ðā ðing þe hē āh, and hē ðē on ansȳne wyriġð.'

[33] Drihten cwæð tō ðām sceoccan, 'Efne nū ealle ðā ðing þe hē āh sindon on ðīnre handa būton ðām ānum,[10] þæt ðū on him sylfum ðīne hand ne āstreċċe.' [34] Ne derode Iobe nāht þæs dēofles costnung, ac fremode, for ðan ðe hē wæs fulfremedra on ġeðincðum and Gode nēar æfter þæs sceoccan ēhtnysse.

[35] Se dēofol ġewende ðā fram Godes ġesihðe and ācwealde ealle his ǣhta ānes dæġes[11]. [36] Sum ǣrendraca cōm tō Iobe and cwæð, 'Þīne syll ēodon and ðā assan wið hī lǣswodon; þā fǣrlīċe cōmon Sabei, and hī ealle ūs benāmon[12] and ðīne yrðlingas ofslōgon, and iċ āna ætbærst þæt iċ ðē þis cȳdde.' [37] Mid þām ðe se yrðling þis sǣde, ðā cōm sum ōðer and cwæð, 'Fȳr cōm fǣrlīċe of heofenum and forbærnde ealle ðīne scēp and ðā hyrdas samod, and iċ āna ætwand þæt iċ ðē ðis cȳdde.' [38] Þā cōm se ðridda ǣrendraca and cwæð, 'Ðā Chaldeiscan cōmon on ðrim floccum and ūre olfendas ealle ġelǣhton, and ðā hyrdas mid swurde ofslōgon. Iċ āna ætflēah þæt iċ ðē þis cȳdde.' [39] Efne ðā ġȳt cōm se fēorða ǣrendraca inn and cwæð, 'Ðīne suna and ðīne dohtra ǣton and druncon mid heora yldestan brēðer, and efne þā fǣrlīċe swēġde swīðlic wind of ðām wēstene and tōslōh þæt hūs æt ðām fēower hwemmum þæt hit hrēosende ðīne bearn ofðrihte and ācwealde. Iċ āna ætbærst þæt iċ ðē þis cȳdde.'

[40] Hwæt ðā Iob ārās and tōtær his tunecan and his loccas forċearf and fēol tō eorðan and cwæð, [41] 'Nacod iċ cōm of mīnre mōdor innoðe, and nacod iċ sceal heonan ġewendan. [42] Drihten mē forġeaf ðā ǣhta, and Drihten hī mē eft benam; swā swā him ġelīcode[13] swā hit is ġedōn. Bēo his nama ġebletsod.'

[43] On eallum ðisum ðingum ne syngode Iob on his welerum[14] ne nān ðing dyslīċes[15] onġēan God ne spræc. [44] Eal ðis dyde se ealda dēofol tō gremienne þone gōdan man, and symle hē lǣfde ǣnne cucenne him tō cȳðenne

---

[10] *būton ðām ānum*: except for that one thing only.

[11] *ānes dæġes*: in a single day.

[12] *ealle ūs benāmon*: took everything from us.

[13] *him ġelīcode*: it pleased him.

[14] That is, Job did not sin in his speech.

[15] *nān ðing dyslīċes*: nothing of what is foolish; nothing foolish.

his æhta lyre, þæt his mōd wurde fram Gode āwend ðā ðā hē ðā unġelimp ġeaxod hæfde. [45] Þæt fȳr cōm ufan ðe þā scēp forbærnde, ac hit ne cōm nā of heofenum, þēah ðe hit swā ġehīwod wære, for ðan ðe se dēofol næs on heofenum næfre siððan hē ðanon þurh mōdiġnysse āfēol mid his ġefērum. [46] Eall swā dēð[16] Antecrist ðonne hē cymð: hē āsent[17] fȳr ufan swilċe of heofenum tō bepǣċenne þæt earme mancynn ðe hē on bið. [47] Ac wite ġehwā[18] þæt se ne mæġ nān fȳr of heofenum āsendan se ðe on heofenum sylf cuman ne mōt.

[48] On eallum ðisum ðingum ne syngode Iob on his welerum. [49] On twā wīsan men syngiað on heora welerum, þæt is ġif hī unriht sprecað oþþe riht forsuwiað; ac Iob ne syngode on his welerum, for ðan ðe hē dyslīċe onġēan God ne spræc, ne ēac Godes herunge ne forsuwade. [50] Hē cȳdde þæt hē būton ġȳtsunge swā miċele æhta hæfde ðā ðā hē hī swā ēaðelīċe būton unrōtnysse forlēt.

[51] Eft siððan on sumum dæġe, þā þā Godes englas stōdon on his ġesihðe, þā wæs ēac se scucca him betwȳnan, and Drihten him cwæð tō, [52] 'Hwæt lā, ne behēolde ðū mīnne ðēowan Iob, þæt his ġelīca nis on eorðan, and ġȳt hē hylt his unscæððiġnysse. [53] Þū āstyredest mē tōġēanes him þæt iċ ðearflēas hine ġeswenċte.'

[54] Se scucca andwyrde, 'Fel sceal for felle, and swā hwæt swā[19] man hæfð hē sylð for his līfe. [55] Āstreċe nū ðīne hand and hrepa his bān and his flæsc; ðonne ġesīhst ðū þæt hē ðē on ansȳne wiriġð.'

[56] Drihten cwæð tō ðān scuccan, 'Efne hē is nū on ðīnre handa; swā ðēah hwæðere heald his sāwle.' [57] Ne ġeðafode God þis tō forwyrde[20] þām ēadigan were, ac þæt hē wære tō bysne eallum ġelēaffullum mannum and wurde swīðor ġemærsod þurh his miċċle ġeðyld and earfoðnyssum.

[58] Ðā ġewende se dēofol of Drihtnes ġesihðe and slōh Iob mid þære wyrstan wunde fram his hnolle ufewerdum oð his ilas neoðewerde. [59] Iob sæt ðā sārlīċe eal on ānre wunde[21] upon his mixene and āscræp ðone wyrms of his līċe mid ānum crocscearde. [60] His wīf him cwæð tō, 'Ġȳt ðū þurhwunast on ðīnre bilewitnysse. Wyriġ God and swelt.'

[61] Iob hire andwyrde, 'Þū sprǣce swā swā ān stunt wīf. [62] Ġif wē gōd underfēngon of Godes handa, hwī ne sceole wē ēac yfel underfōn?' [63] On eallum ðisum ðingum ne syngode Iob on his welerum. [64] Se swicola dēofol ġenam þæt wīf him tō ġefylstan þæt hē ðone hālgan wer ðurh hī beswice swā

---

16   *dēð*: will do.
17   *āsent*: will send.
18   *wite ġehwā*: let everyone know; let everyone understand.
19   *swā hwæt swā*: whatever.
20   *tō forwyrde*: for the destruction of.
21   *eal on ānre wunde*: just one great wound.

swā hē ǣr Adam þurh Euan beswāc,[22] ac se ylca God ðe ġeðafode þæt hē swā ġecostnod wǣre hēold hine wið þæs dēofles syrwungum and wið his sāwle lyre.

[65] Witodlīċe ðā ġeaxodon þrȳ cyningas ðe him ġesibbe wǣron[23] eal his unġelimp and cōmon him tō of heora rīċe þæt hī hine ġenēosodon. [66] Heora naman wǣron ðus ġecīġde: Elifaz, Baldað, Sofar. [67] Hī ġecwǣdon þæt hī samod cumende hine ġenēosodon and ġefrēfrodon. [68] Hī ðā cōmon and hine ne oncnēowon for ðǣre ormǣtan untrumnysse, and hrȳmdon þærrihte wēpende. [69] Hī tōtǣron heora rēaf and mid dūste heora hēafod bestrēowodon and him mid sǣton manega dagas. [70] Hit wæs swā ġewuneliċ on ealdum dagum þæt ġif hwām sum fǣrliċ sār becōme, þæt hē his rēaf tōtǣre, swā swā Iob dyde and ēac ðās ðrȳ cyningas.

[71] Hī cōmon hine tō ġefrēfriġenne; ðā āwendon hī heora frōfer tō edwīte and hine mid heora wordum tiriġdon, swilċe hē for synnum swā ġetūcod wǣre, and cwǣdon, [72] 'Wīte cōm ofer ðē, and ðū ātēorodest; sārnys ðē hrepode, and ðū eart ġeunrōtsod. [73] Hwǣr is nū ðīn Godes eġe[24] and ðīn strencð? [74] Hwǣr is ðīn ġeðyld and ðīnra dǣda fulfremednys? [75] And mid managum ðrafungum hine ġeswenċton.

[76] Iob cwæð, 'Ēalā, ġif mīne synna and mīn yrmð þe iċ ðoliġe wǣron āweġene on ānre wǣgan, þonne wǣron hī swǣrran ġesewene[25] ðonne sandcorn on sǣ. [77] Tō ðrēaġenne ġē lōgiað ēowere sprǣce, and ġē ðenċað tō āwendenne ēowerne frēond. [78] Mannes līf is campdōm ofer eorðan, and swā swā mēdġildan dagas, swā sind his dagas.' [79] Hē cwæð þæt mannes līf wǣre campdōm ofer eorðan for ðan þe ælċ ðǣra ðe Gode ġeðīhð bið on ġewinne wið ðone unġesewenlican dēofol and ongēan his āgenum lustum þā hwīle ðe hē on līfe[26] bið. [80] And swā swā se hȳrman his edlēanes anbidað, swā ġeanbidað se gāstlica cempa his edlēanes æt ðām ælmihtigan Gode. [81] Godes ġecorenan sind on ġewinne on ðyssere worulde, and ðā ārlēasan on hire blissiað, ac ðǣra rihtwīsra ġewinn āwent tō blisse and ðǣra ārlēasra bliss tō biterum sārnyssum on ðǣre ēċan worulde þe ġewelgað ðā þolmōdan. [82] Ealle ðās dēofles costnunga and ðǣra ǣhta lyre, his bearna dēað and his āgen untrumnys, his wīfes ġewitlēast and his frēonda edwīt ne mihton āwecgan Iob of his mōdes ānrǣdnysse ne fram his miċċlan ġelēafan ðe hē tō þām ælmihtigan Gode symle hæfde, ac se scucca wearð ġescynd þe hine beswīcan wolde.

---

[22] The assertion that Satan attempted to use Job's wife as he had used Eve to deceive Adam comes from Gregory, who further says that Job manfully disciplined his wife's weaker mind. The moral weakness of woman's mind as exemplified by Eve was a commonplace among medieval theologians.

[23] According to Godden, the idea that the three kings were Job's kinsmen appears to be unique to Ælfric.

[24] ðīn Godes eġe: your fear of God.

[25] wǣron hī swǣrran ġesewene: they would seem heavier.

[26] on līfe: alive.

[83] Iob cwæð eft, 'Mīn flæsc is ymbscrȳd mid forrotodnysse and mid dūstes horwum. Mīn hȳd forsēarode and is forscruncen. Mē habbað ġeswenċednysse dagas, and on niht mīn bān bið mid sārnysse ðurhðȳd, and ðā ðe mē etað ne slāpað. [84] Iċ eom lāme wiðmeten and yslum and axum ġeanlīcod.' [85] Eft hē cwæð, 'Āra mē Drihten; ne sind mīne dagas nāhte.' [86] Eft hē cwæð, 'Iċ wāt sōðlīce þæt mīn ālȳsend leofað, and iċ on ðām endenēxtan dæġe of eorðan ārīse,²⁷ and iċ bēo eft mid mīnum felle befangen, and iċ on mīnum flæsce God ġesēo, iċ sylf and nā ōðer. [87] Þes hiht is on mīnum bōsme ġelēd.'

[88] Wē sædon ēow and ġȳt secgað þæt wē ne magon ealle ðās race ēow be endebyrdnysse²⁸ secgan, for ðan ðe sēo bōc is swīðe miċel, and hire dīgele andġyt is ofer ūre mǣðe tō smēaġenne. [89] Ðā ðrȳ cyningas þā hæfdon langsume sprǣce wið þone ġedrehtan Iob and ġewendon him hām syþþan. [90] Ac God him ġesprǣc þā and cwæð þæt hē him eallum ðrim gram wære for þan ðe hī swā rihtlīce ætforan him ne sprǣcon swā swā Iob his ðeġen. [91] God cwæð him tō, 'Nimað ēow nū seofon fearras and seofon rammas and farað eft onġēan tō mīnum ðēowan Iobe, and ġeoffriað þās lāc for ēow. [92] Iob sōðlīce mīn ðēowa ġebit for ēow, and iċ his ansȳne underfō,²⁹ þæt ēow ne bēo tō dysiġe ġeteald³⁰ þæt ġē swā rihtlīce tō mē ne sprǣcon swā swā mīn ðēowa Iob.' [93] Hit wæs ġewunelіċ on ealdum dagum þæt man Gode ðyllіċe lāc offrode on cucan orfe and ðā ācwealde, ac sēo offrung is nū unālȳfedlіċ æfter Cristes ðrōwunge.

[94] Elifaz ðā and Baldað and Sofar fērdon onġēan tō heora mǣġe Iobe and didon swā swā him God bebēad, and Drihten underfēng Iobes ansȳne and heora synne ðurh his ðingrǣdene forġeaf. [95] Ðēah þe Iobes ansȳn wære atelіċe tōswollen, and his līc eal maðum wēolle, swā þēah is āwriten þæt se ælmihtiga underfēng his ansȳne þā þā hē for his frēondum ġebæd.

[96] Drihten ēac ðā ġeċyrde tō Iobes behrēowsunge ðā ðā hē for his māgum ġebæd,³¹ and hine ġehǣlde fram eallum his untrumnyssum, and his æhta him ealle forġeald be twyfealdum.³² [97] Be ðisum is tō understandenne þæt se ðe for ōðrum ġebit fremað him sylfum micclum, swā swā þæt hāliġe ġewrit seġð, þæt ðā ðā Iob for his frēondum ġebæd, þā ġeċyrde God tō his behrēowsunge and swā ēaðelīce hine eft ġehǣlde swā hē hine ær ġeuntrumode.

[98] Iob hæfde ær his untrumnysse seofon ðūsend sċēapa and ðrēo ðūsend olfenda, fīf hund ġetȳme oxena and fīf hund assan. [99] Him wæron eft

---

²⁷  *ārīse*: will arise.

²⁸  *be endebyrdnysse*: completely.

²⁹  That is, 'I will accept his prayer'.

³⁰  *ēow ne bēo tō dysiġe ġeteald*: it may not be considered as a folly in you.

³¹  Compare the Douay-Reims translation of the Latin Vulgate: 'The Lord also was turned at the penance of Job, when he prayed for his friends.' The general sense is that God was moved to reverse Job's fortunes.

³²  *be twyfealdum*: doubly; two times over.

forgoldene fēowertȳne þūsend scēapa and six ðūsend olfenda, þūsend ġetȳme oxena and ðūsend assan, and Drihten hine bletsode swīðor on ende ðonne on anġynne.

[100] Hē hæfde seofon suna and ðrēo dohtra ǣr, and siððan eft eal swā fela.[33] [101] Hwī nolde God him forġyldan his bearn be twyfealdum swā swā hē dyde his ǣhta? [102] Hē nolde for ðī þe his bearn nǣron forlorene swā swā his ǣhta wǣron. [103] His ǣhta wǣron ealle āmyrrede and his tȳn bearn ācwealde, ac ðā bearn wǣron swā ðēah ġehealdene on ðām dīgelan līfe[34] betwux hālgum sāwlum, and hē for ðī underfēng þǣra bearna ġetel be ānfealdon[35] for ðan þe ðā ōðre him wǣron ġehealdene ðe þurh þæs dēofles ēhtnysse ācwealde wǣron.

[104] Hwæt ðā Iobes ġebrōðra and ġeswustru and ealle ðā ðe hine ǣr cūðon cōmon him tō and hine ġefrēfrodon and his micclum wundrodon[36] and him ġife ġēafon. [105] Nǣron ġemētte on ealre eorðan swā wlitiġe wimmen swā swā wǣron Iobes dohtra. [106] Hē sōðlīce leofode æfter his swingle ān hund ġēara and fēowertiġ ġēara and ġeseah his bearna bearn oð ðā fēorðan mǣġðe. [107] On eallum his līfe hē leofode twā hund ġēara and eahta and fēowertiġ ġēara. [108] Hē wæs se fifta man æfter Abrahame þām hēahfædere. On ðām tīman wæs swīðe langsum līf on mancynne.

[109] Ġif hwilc ġelǣred man þās race oferrǣde oððe rǣdan ġehȳre,[37] þonne bidde ic þæt hē ðās scyrtinge ne tǣle. [110] Him mæġ his āgen andġyt secgan fullīce be ðisum, and ēow lǣwedum mannum is ðis ġenōh, ðēah ðe ġē ðā dēopan dīgelnysse ðǣron ne cunnon. [111] Hit ġelamp ðus sōðlīce be Iobe,[38] swā swā hē sylf āwrāt, ac swā ðēah sēo gāstlīce ġetācnung þǣre ġereccednysse belimpð tō Cristes menniscnysse and tō his ġelaðunge, swā swā lārēowas trahtnodon. [112] Ġif ūre ǣnigum sum unġelimp becume, ðonne sceole wē bēon ġemyndiġe þises mǣran weres, and ġeðyldiġe bēon on ðām ðwȳrnyssum þe ūs se ælmihtiga on besent, and habban māran care ūrre sāwle[39] þonne ðǣre scortan ġesǣlðe þe wē sceolon forlǣtan. [113] Sȳ wuldor and wurðmynt ðām welwyllendan Scyppende ealra his wundra and his weldǣda, se ðe āna is God ā on ēcnysse. Amen.

---

[33] *eal swā fela*: just as many.
[34] That is, in the afterlife.
[35] *be ānfealdon*: singly; one time.
[36] *his micclum wundrodon*: wondered at him greatly.
[37] *rǣdan ġehȳre*: hear being read.
[38] Ælfric asserts the historical truth of Job's narrative and contrasts its historicity with its spiritual meaning.
[39] *ūrre sāwle*: for our soul.

# 4   Cynewulf and Cyneheard

This selection, the entry for the year 755 (an error for 757) in the *Anglo-Saxon Chronicle*, offers a detailed account of the deaths of two feuding members of the West-Saxon royal family. The wealth of detail here is remarkable for such an early *Chronicle* entry (the final paragraph, on the Mercian succession, is much more typical of the eighth-century entries). Presumably the chronicler thought this exemplary tale of loyalty in extreme circumstances compelling enough to justify a radical departure from his usual style.

For a complete text of the earliest manuscript of the *Chronicle*, see Bately [7].

**Anno .dcc.lv.** [1] Hēr Cynewulf benam Siġebryht his rīċes ond Westseaxna wiotan[1] for unryhtum dǣdum, būton Hamtūnscīre, ond hē hæfde þā oþ hē ofslōg þone aldormon þe him lenġest wunode. [2] Ond hiene þā Cynewulf on Andred[2] ādrǣfde, ond hē þǣr wunade oþ þæt hiene ān swān ofstang æt Pryfetesflōdan; ond hē wræc þone aldormon Cumbran.[3] [3] Ond se Cynewulf oft miċlum ġefeohtum feaht uuiþ Bretwālum, ond ymb .xxxi. wintra þæs þe hē rīċe hæfde hē wolde ādrǣfan ānne æþeling se was Cyneheard hāten, ond se Cyneheard wæs þæs Siġebryhtes brōþur. [4] Ond þā ġeascode hē[4] þone cyning lȳtle werode on wīfcȳþþe on Merantūne,[5] ond hine þǣr berād ond þone būr[6] ūtan beēode ǣr hine þā men onfunden þe mid þām kyninge wǣrun. [5] Ond þā onġeat se cyning þæt, ond hē on þā duru ēode ond þā unhēanlīċe hine werede oþ hē on þone æþeling lōcude, ond þā ūt rǣsde on hine[7] ond hine miċlum ġewundode. [6] Ond hīe[8] alle on þone cyning wǣrun feohtende oþ þæt hīe hine ofslæġenne hæfdon. [7] Ond þā on þæs wīfes ġebǣrum onfundon þæs cyninges þeġnas þā unstilnesse, ond þā þider urnon swā hwelċ

---

[1]   *Ond Westseaxna wiotan* is the remainder of a compound subject. See also sentence [10].

[2]   Also called *Andredesweald*, this is the area of Sussex now known as The Weald. According to the *Anglo-Saxon Chronicle* for 893, Andred was a great forest, 120 miles long and 30 miles broad.

[3]   Cumbra is the name of the loyal *ealdorman* whom Sigebryht had slain.

[4]   I.e. Cyneheard.

[5]   Suggested identifications of this place include Merton, Surrey, and Marten, Wiltshire. But this *Merantūne* has never been identified with certainty.

[6]   A *būr* is usually an interior chamber, especially a bed-chamber. It could be a cottage, however, and that seems to be the sense here, as it is difficult to imagine how Cyneheard's men could surround an interior chamber. The action suggests that Cynewulf is in a cottage with his mistress while his men are together in a hall some distance away.

[7]   The doorway was easy for Cynewulf to defend because none of his attackers could get behind him. His rushing out at Cyneheard, while understandable, was a strategic error.

[8]   I.e. Cyneheard and his men.

swā þonne ġearo wearþ ond radost. [8] Ond hiera se æþeling ġehwelċum feoh ond feorh ġebēad, ond hiera nǣniġ hit ġeþicgean nolde, ac hīe simle feohtende wǣran oþ hīe[9] alle lǣgon būtan ānum Bryttiscum ġīsle,[10] ond se swīþe ġewundad wæs.

[9] Ðā on morgenne ġehīerdun þæt þæs cyninges þeġnas þe him beæftan wǣrun þæt se cyning ofslæġen wæs. [10] Þā ridon hīe þider ond his aldormon Ōsriċ ond Wīferþ his þeġn ond þā men þe hē beæftan him lǣfde ǣr, ond þone æþeling on þǣre byriġ mētton þǣr se cyning ofslæġen læġ (ond þā gatu him tō belocen hæfdon),[11] ond þā þǣrtō ēodon.[12] [11] Ond þā ġebēad hē[13] him hiera āgenne dōm fēos ond londes ġif hīe him þæs rīċes ūþon, ond him cȳþdon þæt hiera mǣgas him mid wǣron þā þe him from noldon.[14] [12] Ond þā cuǣdon hīe þæt him nǣniġ mǣġ lēofra nǣre þonne hiera hlāford, ond hīe nǣfre his banan folgian noldon. [13] Ond þā budon hīe[15] hiera mǣgum þæt hīe ġesunde from ēodon, ond hīe[16] cuǣdon þæt tæt[17] ilce hiera ġefērum ġeboden wǣre þe ǣr mid þām cyninge wǣrun. [14] Þā cuǣdon hīe þæt hīe hīe þæs ne onmunden[18] 'þon mā þe ēowre ġefēran þe mid þām cyninge ofslæġene wǣrun.'[19] [15] Ond hīe þā ymb þā gatu feohtende wǣron oþ þæt hīe þǣrinne fulgon ond þone æþeling ofslōgon ond þā men þe him mid wǣrun, alle būtan ānum, se wæs þæs aldormonnes godsunu,[20] ond hē his feorh ġenerede, ond þēah hē wæs oft ġewundad. [16] Ond se Cynewulf rīcsode .xxxi. wintra, ond his līċ līþ æt Wintanċeastre ond þæs æþelinges æt Ascanmynster, ond hiera ryhtfæderencyn gǣþ tō Ċerdiċe.[21]

---

9    I.e. Cynewulf's men.

10   A *ġīsle* (a hostage, exchanged between warring groups as a pledge of peace) also aids his captors in *The Battle of Maldon*, ll. 265–72.

11   The unexpressed subject of this parenthetical clause is 'Cyneheard and his men'.

12   That is, Cynewulf's men proceeded to the *byriġ* at *Merantūne*.

13   I.e. Cyneheard.

14   *him from noldon*: did not wish to leave him.

15   I.e. Cynewulf's men, who are offering their kinsmen the opportunity to leave.

16   I.e. Cyneheard's men, who will refuse the offer to allow them to leave unharmed. Presumably it is clear to all present that Cynewulf's men now have the upper hand.

17   I.e. *þæt*. The initial *þ* has become assimilated to the *t* at the end of the preceding word. This presumably happened more often in speech than is represented in writing.

18   *hīe þæs ne onmunden*: did not consider themselves worthy of that (offer).

19   The sudden shift into direct discourse seems awkward to the modern reader, and presumably seemed so to some medieval scribes as well: three of the five manuscripts of this entry in the *Anglo-Saxon Chronicle* read *heora* for *ēowre*, converting the passage to indirect discourse.

20   The sole survivor among Cyneheard's men was saved by his godfather, the *ealdorman* Osric. The chronicler is careful to establish that special circumstances attended the survival of Osric's godson and the British hostage in the earlier battle: neither could be accused of cowardice.

21   Cerdic is the legendary founder of the kingdom of Wessex. His arrival (with his son Cynric) is recorded in the *Anglo-Saxon Chronicle* for 495.

[17] Ond þȳ ilcan ġēare mon ofslōg Æþelbald Mierċna cyning[22] on Seccandūne, ond his līċ līþ on Hrēopadūne; ond Beornrǣd fēng tō rīċe ond lȳtle hwīle hēold ond unġefēalīċe. [18] Ond þȳ ilcan ġēare Offa[23] fēng tō rīċe ond hēold .xxxviiii. wintra, ond his sunu Ecgferþ[24] hēold .xli. daga ond .c. daga. [19] Se Offa wæs Þincgferþing,[25] Þincgferþ Ēanwulfing, Ēanwulf Ōsmōding, Ōsmōd Ēawing, Ēawa Pybing, Pybba Crēoding, Crēoda Cynewalding, Cynewald Cnebing, Cnebba Iceling, Icel Ēomǣring, Ēomǣr Angelþowing, Angelþēow Offing, Offa Wǣrmunding, Wǣrmund Wyhtlǣging, Wihtlǣġ Wōdening.[26]

# 5   The Martyrdom of Ælfheah

This extract from the *Anglo-Saxon Chronicle* recounts events of the years 1011 and 1012, when a Viking war-band besieged and entered Canterbury, sacked the city and captured many of its inhabitants, including monks and nuns. Among their captives was Ælfheah, Archbishop of Canterbury, whom they seem to have expected the Church to ransom. When Ælfheah refused to allow ransom to be paid for him (perhaps because the Church's finances were straitened at the time), the Vikings brutally killed him. The present chronicler (probably a monk of St Augustine's, Canterbury) saw the attack on Canterbury as a blow aimed at the very heart of the kingdom. The English responded to the murder by proclaiming the archbishop a martyr and saint; his day (19 April) was widely observed during the eleventh century.

For an edition of the manuscript from which this reading is taken, see O'Keeffe [90].

[22]   Æthelbald was king of Mercia for a remarkably long time, 716–57 (this entry incorrectly dates his death to 755).

[23]   Offa was the greatest of the Mercian kings, ruling not only his own kingdom, but also Sussex, Kent and East Anglia. He was responsible for the construction of Offa's dike, an earthen fortification that runs almost 150 miles along the Welsh border.

[24]   The entry is looking far ahead: Ecgferþ didn't get his chance to rule until 794, according to the *Anglo-Saxon Chronicle* (actually 796).

[25]   The words *Se Offa wæs Þincgferþing* begin a genealogy of the kind often found in the *Anglo-Saxon Chronicle*. The suffix *-ing* is a patronymic: thus this phrase should be translated 'this Offa was the son of Þincgferþ'.

[26]   Woden was one of the chief gods in the pre-Christian pantheon of Anglo-Saxon England and also, according to legend, the founder of several Anglo-Saxon royal lines, including those of Kent, Wessex, Northumbria and Mercia. His name appeared in genealogies long after the Anglo-Saxons had embraced Christianity.

**Mille .xi.** [1] Hēr on þissum ġēare sende se cyning[1] and his witan tō ðām here[2] and ġyrndon friðes, and him gafol and metsunge behēton wið þām ðe hī hiora herġunge ġeswicon. [2] Hī hæfdon þā ofergān (.i.) Ēastengle and (.ii.) Ēastsexe and (.iii.) Middelsexe and (.iiii.) Oxenafordscīre and (.v.) Grantabricscīre and (.vi.) Heortfordscīre and (.vii.) Buccingahāmscīre and (.viii.) Bedefordscīre and (.ix.) healfe Huntadūnscīre and miċel (.x.) on Hamtūnscīre, and be sūþan Temese ealle Kentingas and Sūðsexe and Hæstingas and Sūðrīġe and Bearrocscīre and Hamtūnscīre and miċel on Wiltūnscīre. [3] Ealle þas unġesælða ūs ġelumpon þuruh unrædas, þæt man nolde him a tīman gafol bēodon oþþe wið ġefeohtan. [4] Ac þonne hī mæst tō yfele[3] ġedōn hæfdon, þonne nam mon frið and grið wið hī, and naþelæs, for eallum þissum griðe and gafole, hī fērdon æġhweder flocmælum and heregodon ūre earme folc and hī rȳpton and slōgon. [5] And þā on ðissum ġēare betweox Natiuitas Sancte Marie[4] and Sancte Michaeles mæssan[5] hī ymbsǣton Cantwareburuh, and hī intō cōmon þuruh syruwrenċas, for ðan Ælmǣr[6] hī beċyrde, þe se arcebisceop Ælfēah[7] ǣr ġenerede æt his līfe.[8] [6] And hī þǣr ðā ġenāman þone arcebisceop Ælfēah and Ælfweard cynges ġerēfan and Lēofrūne abbatissan and Godwine bisceop;[9] and Ælfmǣr abbud[10] hī lēton āweġ. [7] And hī ðǣr ġenāmon inne ealle þā ġehādodan men and weras and wīf, þæt wæs unāsecgendliċ ǣnigum men hū miċel þæs folces wæs,[11] and on þǣre byriġ syþþan wæron

---

[1]    Æthelræd, whose reign began in 978 after the murder of his half-brother Edward, would be driven from the country in 1013 by the Viking army led by Swein Forkbeard. Æthelræd returned to England after Swein's death the following year and died in 1015; he was succeeded by Swein's son Cnut. Æthelræd is often called 'the Unready' ('Unready' rendering Old English *unræd* 'folly') on account of his supposed incompetence as king. His bad reputation may not be fully deserved, but his reign was marked by increasingly severe Viking incursions and infighting among his nobles. His reign was also one of the most productive periods of Old English literature, for Ælfric and Wulfstan were his contemporaries, and a great many vernacular manuscripts (including, probably, the one that contains *Beowulf*) were produced during his time.

[2]    In the *Anglo-Saxon Chronicle* the word *here* is usually used of a Viking army. This one was under the command of Thorkell the Tall, who is reputed to have tried to save Ælfheah's life and was among those who joined Æthelræd in 1012.

[3]    *mæst tō yfele*: the greatest harm.

[4]    The feast of the birth of St Mary (8 Sept.).

[5]    Michaelmass (29 Sept.).

[6]    Not the abbot Ælfmær mentioned later (though the names are equivalent), but rather, according to another source, an archdeacon. Nothing more is known of him.

[7]    Ælfheah had been Bishop of Winchester before being appointed Archbishop of Canterbury in 1006. As far as we know, his short tenure as archbishop was distinguished only by the spectacular nature of its end.

[8]    *ġenerede æt his līfe*: saved his life.

[9]    Godwine was Bishop of Rochester.

[10]    Ælfmær was abbot of St Augustine's monastery in Canterbury. The identities of the other persons mentioned here are uncertain.

[11]    *hū miċel þæs folces wæs*: how much of the population it was.

swā lange swā hī woldon. [8] And ðā hī hæfdon þā buruh ealle āsmēade, wendon him þā tō scypan and lǣddon þone arcebisceop mid him. [9] Wæs ðā rǣpling, se ðe ǣr wæs hēafod Angelkynnes and Cristendōmes. [10] Þǣr man mihte ðā gesēon yrmðe þǣr man oft ǣr geseah blisse on þǣre earman byrig þanon cōm ǣrest Cristendōm and blis for Gode and for worulde.[12] [11] And hī hæfdon þone arcebisceop mid him swā lange oð þǣne tīman þe hī hine gemartiredon.

**Mille .xii.** [12] Hēr on þissum gēare cōm Ēadric ealdorman[13] and ealle þā yldestan witan, gehādode and lǣwede, Angelcynnes tō Lundenbyrig tōforan þām Ēastron. [13] Þā wæs Ēasterdæg on þām datarum Idus Aprilis.[14] [14] And hī ðǣr þā swā lange wǣron oþ þæt gafol eal gelǣst wæs ofer ðā Ēastron, þæt wæs ehta and fēowertig þūsend punda. [15] Ðā on þæne Sæternesdæg wearð þā se here swȳðe āstyred angēan þone bisceop, for þām ðe hē nolde him nān feoh behātan, ac hē forbēad þæt man nān þing wið him syllan ne mōste. [16] Wǣron hī ēac swȳþe druncene, for ðām þǣr wæs brōht wīn sūðan. [17] Genāmon þā ðone bisceop, lǣddon hine tō hiora hūstinge on ðone Sunnanǣfen octabas Pasce,[15] þā wæs .xiii. kalendas Mai,[16] and hine þǣr ðā bysmorlīce ācwylmdon, oftorfedon mid bānum and mid hrȳþera hēafdum. [18] And slōh hine ðā ān hiora mid ānre æxe yre[17] on þæt hēafod, þæt mid þām dynte hē nyþer āsāh, and his hālige blōd on þā eorðan fēol, and his hāligan sāwle tō Godes rīce āsende.[18] [19] And mon þone līchaman on mergen ferode tō Lundene, and þā bisceopas Ēadnōþ and Ælfūn[19] and sēo buruhwaru hine underfēngon mid ealre ārwurðnysse and hine bebyrigdon on Sancte Paules mynstre, and þǣr nū God sutelað þæs hālgan martires mihta. [20] Ðā þæt gafol gelǣst wæs and friðaþas āsworene wǣron, þā tōfērde se here wīde swā hē ǣr gegaderod wæs. [21] Ðā bugon tō þām cynge of ðām here fīf and fēowertig scypa, and him behēton þæt hī woldon þysne eard healdan, and hē hī fēdan sceolde and scrȳdan.

---

[12]  *for Gode and for worulde*: both religious and secular.

[13]  Eadric Streona, the powerful and treacherous *ealdorman* of Mercia, was now suspected of sympathy for the Danes and would in fact join Cnut in 1016. He was murdered in London in 1017 ('very justly', according to one chronicler).

[14]  13 April.

[15]  The octave of Easter, i.e. a week after Easter.

[16]  19 April.

[17]  Possibly 'the back of an axe'; but the meaning of *yre* is uncertain.

[18]  The unexpressed subject of *āsende* is *hē* (i.e. Ælfheah).

[19]  Eadnoth (d. 1016) was Bishop of Dorchester. Ælfun was Bishop of London; in 1013 Æthelræd sent him to Normandy with his sons Edward and Alfred a short time before he fled there himself.

# 6    William the Conqueror

William I ruled England for twenty-one years after the Norman Conquest. His reign is notable for the ruthlessness with which he secured his hold upon the throne; but also for his remarkable construction programme (Canterbury, Ely, Lincoln, Rochester, Winchester and Worcester Cathedrals were all begun during his reign), the church reforms he instituted, and the Domesday Book, the ambitious survey of English landholding undertaken towards the end of his life. Though William was rapacious, he was no kleptocrat: he poured tremendous energy and resources into the development of his new acquisition.

His reign is memorably chronicled in a manuscript of the *Anglo-Saxon Chronicle* written at Peterborough around 1121. This is a copy of a manuscript (now lost) probably borrowed from Christ Church, Canterbury, to replace one that had perished by fire in 1116. The ultimate origin of this text is of more than passing interest, both because of the author's firmly stated views and because of the tantalizing clues he left to his identity. He was not friendly towards William, though he was willing to be fair to him. He was certainly a churchman, and one who ranked high enough not only to have 'looked upon' William, but also to have lived in his household. His English is grammatical and idiomatic: almost certainly he was an Anglo-Saxon, not a Norman. Though William had placed Normans in the highest positions in the English church (both the Archbishop of Canterbury and the prior of Christ Church were Normans), Anglo-Saxons remained influential. The noted hagiographer Osbern, for example, was active in Canterbury around the time of William's death, and the historian Eadmer, then a young man, was also there. It is unlikely that we will ever know the name of this contributor to the *Chronicle*, but whoever he was, he gave us an unusually vivid portrait of William on the occasion of his death in 1087. It is rare that an early medieval writer pays much attention to what modern readers think of as 'personality'; but interest in the interior life was on the rise throughout Europe in the late eleventh and the twelfth centuries: this text is an early example of that interest.

The present text is part of the entry for 1087 (misdated 1086 in the manuscript), and was presumably written shortly after that date. The Old English written around this time is conservative – still very far from the Middle English of Chaucer or Laȝamon, or even the mid-twelfth-century entries of the Peterborough Chronicle. The scribe of 1121 did a reasonably good job of preserving the usage of the older manuscript that he was copying, but introduced a number of late features. Here the inflectional endings and some spellings have been normalized to make the language more like what the original author probably wrote. For an edition of the Peterborough Chronicle, see Irvine [61].

[1] Rēowliċ þing hē dyde,[1] and rēowlicor him ġelamp. [2] Hū rēowlicor?[2] Him ġeyfelade and þæt him stranglīċe eġlade. [3] Hwæt mæġ iċ tellan? Se scearpa

---

[1]    According to the chronicler, William had just harried the lands of his overlord, King Philip of France, killing a great many people, and had burned the town of Mantes. The chronicler considers his illness and death to be divine retribution for these acts.

[2]    *Hū rēowlicor*: how much more more grievous; how much more more cruel.

dēað, þe ne forlēt ne rīċe menn ne hēane, se hine ġenam. [4] Hē swealt on Normandiġe on þone nēxtan dæġ æfter Natiuitas Sancte Marie,[3] and man bebyrġede hine on Caþum æt sancte Stephanes mynstre.[4] [5] Ǣror hē hit ārǣrde, and syððan mænifealdlīċe ġegōdade.

[6] Ēalā, hū lēas and hū unwrēst is þysses middaneardes wela! [7] Se þe wæs ǣror rīċe cyng and maniġes landes[5] hlāford, hē næfde þā ealles landes[6] būton seofon fōtmǣl; and se þe wæs hwīlon ġescrīd mid golde and mid ġimmum, hē læġ þā oferwrogen mid moldan. [8] Hē lǣfde æfter him þrȳ suna. [9] Rodbeard[7] hēt se yldesta, se wæs eorl on Normandiġe æfter him. [10] Se ōðer hēt Willelm,[8] þe bær æfter him on Englalande þone cynehelm. [11] Se þridda hēt Hēanriċ,[9] þām se fæder becwæð gersuman unātellendliċe.

[12] Ġif hwā ġewilniġað tō ġewitanne hū ġedōn[10] mann hē wæs oððe hwilċne wurðscipe hē hæfde oððe hū fela landa hē wǣre hlāford, ðonne wille wē be him āwrītan swā swā wē hine āġēaton ðe him on lōcodon and ōðre hwīle[11] on his hīrede wunodon. [13] Se cyng Willelm, þe wē embe specað, wæs swīðe wīs man and swīðe rīċe, and wurðfulra and strengra þonne æniġ his foregenġa wǣre. [14] Hē wæs milde þām gōdum mannum þe God lufodon and ofer eall ġemett stearc þām mannum þe wiðcwǣdon his willan. [15] On ðām ilcan stede þe God him ġeūðe þæt hē mōste Englaland ġegān, hē ārǣrde mǣre mynster[12] and munecas þǣr ġesette and hit well ġegōdade. [16] On his dagum wæs þæt mǣre mynster on Cantwarebyriġ ġetymbrad[13] and ēac swīðe maniġ ōðer ofer eall Englaland. [17] Ēac þis land wæs swīðe āfylled mid munecum, and þā leofodan

---

[3]   *Natiuitas Sancte Marie*: Feast of St. Mary (8 Sept.).

[4]   The monastery of St Étienne. William promised to found St-Étienne as a condition of winning papal approval for his marriage to his cousin, Matilda of Flanders, who founded a house for women, Ste Trinité, also at Caen.

[5]   *maniġes landes*: of many a land.

[6]   *ealles landes*: of all his land.

[7]   Robert Curthose was estranged from his father at the time of his death because he had attempted to seize the duchy of Normandy for himself. According to one source, William intended to disinherit Robert but was persuaded not to do so as he lay dying. After William's death Robert tried unsuccessfully to conquer England.

[8]   William Rufus, or William II of England (r. 1087–1100).

[9]   Though he inherited no land from his father, Henry used much of the treasure bequeathed to him to purchase a part of Normandy from his brother Robert. After the death of William Rufus he reigned (1100–1135) as Henry I of England. In 1106 he conquered Normandy and thereafter kept Robert prisoner until his death in 1134.

[10]   *hū ġedōn*: what kind of.

[11]   *ōðre hwīle*: sometimes.

[12]   Battle Abbey, which is reputed to have been founded as penance for the bloodshed associated with the Conquest.

[13]   The Anglo-Saxon cathedral in Canterbury burned in 1067. Construction of the Norman replacement began around 1070, and work was probably ongoing at the time of William's death.

heora līf æfter Sanctus Benedictus regule;[14] and se Cristendōm wæs swilċ on his dæġe þæt ælċ man hwæt his hāde tō belumpe folgade se þe wolde.[15]

[18] Ēac hē wæs swȳðe wurðful. [19] Þrīwa hē bær his cynehelm[16] ælċe ġeare, swā oft swā[17] hē wæs on Englalande: [20] on Ēastron hē hine bær on Winċeastre, on Pentecosten on Westmynstre, on middanwintre on Glēaweċeastre; [21] and þænne wæron mid him ealle þā rīċe men ofer eall Englaland: arcebiscopas and lēodbiscopas, abbodas and eorlas, þeġnas and cnihtas.[18]

[22] Swilċe hē wæs ēac swȳðe stearc man and rēðe, swā þæt man ne dorste nān þing onġēan his willan dōn. [23] Hē hæfde eorlas on his bendum þe dydon onġēan his willan. [24] Biscopas hē sette of heora biscoprīċe and abbodas of heora abbodrīċe and þeġnas on cweartern; and æt nēxtan hē ne sparode his āgenne brōðor, Odo hēt. [25] Hē wæs swīðe rīċe biscop on Normandīġe. [26] On Baius wæs his biscopstōl, and wæs manna fyrmest tōēacan þām cynge; and hē hæfde eorldōm on Englalande, and þonne se cyng wæs on Normandīġe, þonne wæs hē mǣst on þisum lande; and hine hē sette on cweartern.[19]

[27] Betwyx ōðrum þingum nis nā tō forġytanne þæt gōde frið þe hē macode on þisum lande, swā þæt ān man þe him sylf āht wǣre mihte faran ofer his rīċe mid his bōsum full goldes unġederad, [28] and nān man ne dorste slēan ōðerne man, næfde hē nǣfre swā myċel yfel ġedōn wið þone ōðerne. [29] And ġif hwilċ carlman hǣmde wið wimman hire unðances,[20] sōna hē forlēas þā limu þe hē mid plegode.

[30] Hē rīxade ofer Englaland and hit mid his ġēapscipe swā þurhsmēade þæt næs ān hīd landes innan Englalande þæt hē nyste hwā hī hæfde oððe hwæs hēo wurð wæs, and syððan on his ġewrit ġesette. [31] Brytland him wæs on ġewealde and hē þǣrinne castelas ġewrohte and hæfde þæt manncynn mid ealle[21] on ġewealde. Swilċe ēac Scotland hē him underþēodde for his myċele strengþe. [32] Normandīġe þæt land wæs his ġecynd, and ofer þone eorldōm þe Mans is ġehāten hē rīxade, and ġif hē mōste þā ġȳt twā ġear libban hē hæfde Yrland mid his werscipe ġewunnen, and wiðūtan ælcum wǣpnum.

---

[14] The monastic establishments in Anglo-Saxon England were already Benedictine; but the Normans who took them over during William's reign introduced Cluniac reforms.

[15] *ælċ man . . . se þe wolde*: each man who wished (to do so) observed what pertained to his order.

[16] *bær his cynehelm*: wore his crown.

[17] *swā oft swā*: as often as.

[18] This is the first recorded use of the word *cniht* in its later medieval sense. Up to this time, a *cniht* had been a young man, a servant, or a retainer. Here it designates one who serves the king militarily and is bound to him by feudal ties.

[19] Odo was Bishop of Bayeux and Earl of Kent under William; he commissioned the Bayeux Tapestry to commemorate his brother's conquest of England. The reason for Odo's imprisonment in 1082 or 1083 is not clear: he may have misappropriated English troops as part of a plot to march to Rome and make himself pope. Odo was released by William when he was dying.

[20] *hire unðances*: against her will.

[21] *mid ealle*: completely.

[33] Witodlīċe on his tīman hæfdon men myċel ġeswinc and swīðe maniġe tēonan.

[34] Castelas hē lēt wyrċean[22] and earme men swīðe swenċean.

[35] Se cyng wæs swā swīðe stearc and benam of his underþēoddan[23]
maniġ marc goldes and mā hundred punda seolfres
ðæt hē nam be wihte and mid myċlum unrihte
of his landlēode[24] for lȳtelre nēode.

[36] Hē wæs on ġītsunge befeallen and grǣdinesse hē lufode mid ealle.

[37] Hē sette myċel dēorfrið[25] and hē læġde laga þǣrwið,
þæt swā hwā swā slōge heort oððe hinde, þæt hine man sceolde blendian.

[38] Hē forbēad þā heortas, swylċe ēac þā bāras;
swā swīðe hē lufode þā hēadēor swilċe hē wǣre heora fæder.

[39] Ēac hē sette be þām haran þæt hī mōston frēo faran.

[40] His rīċe men hit mǣndon and þā earme men hit beċeorodon,
ac hē wæs swā stīð þæt hē ne rōhte heora eallra nīð;
ac hī mōston mid ealle þæs cynges willan folgian
ġif hī woldon libban oððe land habban,
land oððe ǣhta oððe wel his sehte.

[41] Wā lā wā,[26] þæt ǣniġ man sceolde mōdiġan swā,
hine sylfne ūpp āhebban and ofer ealle men tellan.[27]

[42] Se ælmihtiga God cȳþe his sāule mildheortnisse
and dō him his synna forġifenesse.

[43] Ðās þing wē habbað be him ġewritene, ǣġðer ġe gōde ġe yfele, þæt þā gōdan men nimon æfter þǣre gōdnesse and forlēon mid ealle yfelnesse,[28] and gān on ðone weġ þe ūs lǣtt tō heofonan rīċe.

---

[22]   *hē lēt wyrċean*: he had (someone) build (see §7.9.1). The following passage, while divided into metrical lines, is vastly different from the other verse printed in this book. The metre does not conform strictly to either the rhythmical or the alliterative conventions of Old English verse. Note also the frequent use of rhyme, which anticipates the conventions of Middle English poetry. The syntax of the poem is more that of prose than of earlier verse. For a discussion of late Old English verse, see Bredehoft [17], pp. 70–98; and for this passage, pp. 93–5. Here Bredehoft's lineation is adopted.

[23]   *of his underþēoddan*: from his subjects.

[24]   Apparently *landlēode* is a collective singular: 'from his tenants'.

[25]   William established the New Forest (now a national park) as a game preserve for royal use. As this text makes plain, the Anglo-Saxons were not used to the kinds of restrictions on hunting described here and resented them strongly.

[26]   *Wā lā wā*: alas, alas!

[27]   *ofer ealle men tellan*: consider himself above all men.

[28]   A conventional disclaimer by authors describing the bad behaviour of historical figures. It was already employed by Bede in the preface to his *Ecclesiastical History*: 'if history records good things of good men, the thoughtful hearer is encouraged to imitate what is good: or if it records evil of wicked men, the devout, religious listener or reader is encouraged to avoid all that is sinful and perverse and to follow what he knows to be good and pleasing to God' (Sherley-Price [104], p. 33).

# 7 *Sermo Lupi ad Anglos*

Wulfstan (d. 1023) was Bishop of London until 1002 and then Bishop of Worcester and Archbishop of York (the two titles had been held by the same person since 972 because York under the Viking kings was barely a functional see). He was an adviser to Æthelræd during the later years of his reign and wrote several of that king's law codes; he also wrote law codes for Cnut. Wulfstan was not primarily a writer of homilies; he wrote many fewer than his contemporary and correspondent Ælfric (see Bethurum [9]). The *Sermo Lupi ad Anglos*, however, reveals him as a writer of extraordinary power. As you read, notice the strong binary rhythms, the many rhymes and alliterations, and the chains of grammatically parallel words and phrases.

For editions of this homily, see Bethurum [9], pp. 255–75 (which presents three different versions), Whitelock [114] (especially valuable for its very full annotations), and Melissa J. Bernstein, ed., The Electronic *Sermo Lupi ad Anglos* (http://www.cif. rochester.edu/˜mjbernst/wulfstan/). In this text, *-an* is often written for *-um* and *-on*, and the *-o-* of class 2 weak verbs often appears as *-e-*.

**Sermo Lupi ad Anglos, quando Dani maxime persecuti sunt eos, quod fuit anno millesimo .xiiii. ab incarnatione Domini nostri Iesu Cristi**[1]
[1] Lēofan men, ġecnāwað þæt sōð is. [2] Ðēos worold is on ofste, and hit nēalǣċð þām ende, and þȳ hit is on worolde aa swā lenġ swā wyrse.[2] [3] And swā hit sceal nȳde for folces synnan ǣr antecristes tōcyme yfelian swȳþe, and hūru hit wyrð þænne eġesliċ and grimliċ wīde on worolde. [4] Understandað ēac ġeorne þæt dēofol þās þēode nū fela ġēara dwelode tō swȳþe, and þæt lȳtle ġetrēowþa wǣran mid mannum, þēah hȳ wel spǣcan, and unrihta tō fela rīcsode on lande. [5] And næs ā fela manna þe smēade ymbe þā bōte swā ġeorne swā man scolde, ac dæġhwāmlīċe man īhte yfel æfter ōðrum[3] and unriht rǣrde and unlaga maneġe ealles tō wīde ġynd ealle þās þēode. [6] And wē ēac for þām habbað fela byrsta and bysmara ġebiden, and ġif wē ǣniġe bōte ġebīdan scylan, þonne mōte wē þæs tō Gode earnian bet þonne wē ǣr þysan dydan, [7] for þām mid miċlan earnungan wē ġeearnedan þā yrmða þe ūs onsittað, and mid swȳþe miċelan earnungan wē þā bōte mōtan æt Gode ġerǣċan ġif hit sceal heonanforð gōdiende weorðan. [8] Lā hwæt, wē witan ful ġeorne þæt tō miċlan bryċe sceal miċel bōt nȳde, and tō miċlan bryne wæter

---

[1] 'The Sermon of *Lupus* to the English, when the Danes were persecuting them most, which was in the year 1014 from the incarnation of our Lord Jesus Christ.' Latin *Lupus* 'wolf' is Wulfstan's *nom de plume*. In 1013 Æthelræd had been driven from his throne by the Danish king Swein; after Swein's death in 1014 Æthelræd was restored to his throne, but Swein's son Cnut remained a threat.
[2] *swā lenġ swā wyrse*: worse and worse.
[3] *yfel æfter ōðrum*: one evil after another.

unlȳtel, ġif man þæt fȳr sceal tō āhte[4] ācwenċan. [9] And miċel is nȳdþearf manna ġehwilċum þæt hē Godes lage ġȳme heonanforð ġeorne and Godes ġerihta[5] mid rihte ġelæste. [10] On hæþenum þēodum ne dear man forhealdan lȳtel ne miċel þæs þe ġelagod is tō ġedwolgoda weorðunge, and wē forhealdað æġhwær Godes ġerihta ealles tō ġelōme. [11] And ne dear man ġewanian on hæþenum þēodum inne ne ūte æniġ þæra þinga þe ġedwolgodan brōht bið and tō lācum betæht bið, and wē habbað Godes hūs inne and ūte clæne berȳpte, and Godes þēowas syndan mæþe and munde ġewelhwær bedælde. [12] And ġedwolgoda þēnan ne dear man misbēodan on æniġe wīsan mid hæþenum lēodum, swā swā man Godes þēowum nū dēð tō wīde þær Cristene scoldan Godes lage healdan and Godes þēowas griðian.

[13] Ac sōð is þæt iċ secge: þearf is þære bōte, for þām Godes ġerihta wanedan tō lange innan þysse þēode on æġhwylċan ende,[6] and folclaga wyrsedan ealles tō swȳþe, and hāliġnessa syndan tō griðlēase wīde, and Godes hūs syndan tō clæne berȳpte ealdra ġerihta and innan bestrȳpte ælċra ġerisena. [14] And wydewan syndan fornȳdde on unriht[7] tō ċeorle, and tō mæneġe foryrmde and ġehȳnede swȳþe, and earme men syndan sāre beswicene and hrēowlīċe besyrwde and ūt of þysan earde wīde ġesealde, swȳþe unforworhte,[8] fremdum tō ġewealde, [15] and cradolċild ġeþēowede þurh wælhrēowe unlaga for lȳtelre þȳfþe[9] wīde ġynd þās þēode, and frēoriht fornumene and þrælriht[10] ġenyrwde and ælmæsriht ġewanode; and, hrædest is tō cweþenne,[11] Godes laga lāðe and lāra forsāwene. [16] And þæs[12] wē habbað ealle þurh Godes yrre bysmor ġelōme, ġecnāwe se ðe cunne; and se byrst wyrð ġemæne, þēh man swā ne wēne, eallre þysse þēode, būtan God beorge.

[17] For þām hit is on ūs eallum swutol and ġesēne þæt wē ær þysan oftor bræcan þonne wē bēttan, and þȳ is þysse þēode fela onsæġe. [18] Ne dohte hit nū lange inne ne ūte, ac wæs here and hunger, bryne and blōdgyte on ġewelhwylċan ende oft and ġelōme. [19] And ūs stalu and cwalu, strīċ and steorfa, orfcwealm and uncoþu, hōl and hete and rȳpera rēaflāc derede swȳþe

---

4  *tō āhte*: in any way.

5  These *gerihta* are compulsory payments to the Church such as tithes and Peter's Pence.

6  *on æġhwylċan ende*: in every part.

7  *on unriht*: unjustly.

8  Those who were guilty of certain crimes could be enslaved. Here Wulfstan condemns the selling of persons who have committed no crimes; he is thought also to have opposed all selling of persons to foreigners. For a useful commentary on Wulfstan's views on slavery as represented in the *Sermo Lupi*, see Pelteret [93].

9  Under Anglo-Saxon law, any member of a family found to be complicit in a crime could be enslaved along with the actual perpetrator. Here Wulfstan condemns the enslavement of children so young they could not be complicit, and adds that the crime is sometimes petty theft. The laws of Cnut would forbid the penal enslavement of children under the age of twelve.

10  Slaves had the right to earn money for themselves on various religious holidays during the year. Some slaves were able by this means to purchase their own freedom.

11  *hrædest is tō cweþenne*: to put it briefly; in short.

12  *þæs*: because of that.

þearle, and ūs unġylda[13] swȳþe ġedrehtan, and ūs unwedera foroft wēoldan unwæstma. [20] For þām on þysan earde wæs, swā hit þinċan mæġ, nū fela ġēara unriht fela and tealte ġetrȳwða æġhwær mid mannum. [21] Ne bearh nū foroft ġesib ġesibban þē mā þe fremdan, ne fæder his bearne, ne hwīlum bearn his āgenum fæder, ne brōþor ōþrum; ne ūre æniġ his līf ne fadode swā swā hē scolde, ne ġehādode regollīċe, ne læwede lahlīċe.[14] [22] Ac worhtan[15] lust ūs tō lage ealles tō ġelōme, and nāþor ne hēoldan ne lāre ne lage Godes ne manna swā swā wē scoldan. [23] Ne æniġ wið ōþerne ġetrȳwlīċe þōhte swā rihte swā hē scolde, ac mæst ælċ swicode and ōþrum derede wordes and dæde,[16] and hūru unrihtlīċe mæst ælċ ōþerne æftan hēaweþ sceandlican onscytan, dō māre ġif hē mæġe.[17]

[24] For þām hēr syn[18] on lande unġetrȳwþa miċle for Gode and for worolde,[19] and eac hēr syn on earde on mistlīċe wīsan hlāfordswican maneġe. [25] And ealra mæst hlāfordswice se bið on worolde þæt man his hlāfordes sāule beswīce, and ful miċel hlāfordswice ēac bið on worolde þæt man his hlāford of līfe forræde oððon of lande lifiendne drīfe; and æġþer is ġeworden on þysan earde: [26] Ēadweard man forrædde and syððan ācwealde and æfter þām forbærnde.[20] [27] And godsibbas and godbearn tō fela man forspilde wīde ġynd þās þēode tōēacan ōðran ealles tō manegan þe man unscyldiġe forfōr ealles tō wīde. [28] And ealles tō maneġe hāliġe stōwa wīde forwurdan þurh þæt þe[21] man sume men ær þām ġelōgode, swā man nā ne scolde ġif man on Godes griðe mæþe witan wolde.[22] [29] And Cristenes folces tō fela

---

[13] The reference is probably to the Danegeld, a tax levied so that tribute could be paid to marauding Vikings. Beginning in 991 this tax was collected as needed, and in the reign of Cnut it became a regular tax for the support of the king's army. It was discontinued in the reign of Edward the Confessor.

[14] It is a commonplace in Wulfstan's works that those in religious orders should obey the rule of their order and those in secular life should obey the law.

[15] The unexpressed subject of this verb is *wē*.

[16] *wordes and dæde*: in word and in deed.

[17] *dō māre ġif hē mæġe*: [and] would do more if he could.

[18] This text occasionally has *syn* for *synd*, the indicative present plural of the verb *bēon*.

[19] *for Gode and for worolde*: both religious and secular.

[20] In 978, King Edward, whom the chronicles described as *ċild unweaxen* on his accession in 975, was murdered by members of the household of his half-brother Æthelræd, who succeeded him as king. No other source claims that Edward's body was burned; rather, he was buried without ceremony and later translated to the nunnery at Shaftesbury, where miracles were reported at his tomb. He is known to history as Edward the Martyr. An earlier version of this sermon adds after the sentence on Edward's murder: *and Æþelræd man dræfde ūt of his earde* 'and Æthelræd was driven out of his land'. Perhaps the circumstances surrounding the later revisions made it impolitic to allude to Æthelræd's exile.

[21] *þurh þæt þe*: because.

[22] *on Godes griðe mæþe witan wolde*: were willing to honour God's sanctuary. The circumspect wording of this passage tells us little about the unsuitable admissions that had caused harm to monasteries.

man ġesealde ūt of þysan earde nū ealle hwīle;[23] and eal þæt is Gode lāð, ġelȳfe se þe wille. [30] And scandliċ is tō specenne þæt ġeworden is tō wīde, and eġesliċ is tō witanne þæt oft dōð tō maneġe þe drēogað þā yrmþe, þæt scēotað tōgædere and āne cwenan ġemǣnum ċēape[24] bicgað ġemǣne, and wið þā āne fȳlþe ādrēogað, ān æfter ānum[25] and ælċ æfter ōðrum, hundum ġelīccast þe for fȳlþe ne scrīfað, [31] and syððan wið weorðe syllað of lande fēondum tō ġewealde Godes ġesceafte and his āgenne ċēap þe hē dēore ġebōhte.

[32] Ēac wē witan ġeorne hwær sēo yrmð ġewearð þæt fæder ġesealde bearn wið weorþe and bearn his mōdor, and brōþor sealde ōþerne fremdum tō ġewealde;[26] and eal þæt syndan miċle and eġeslīċe dǣda, understande se þe wille. [33] And ġīt hit is māre and ēac mæniġfealdre þæt dereð þysse þēode. [34] Mæniġe synd forsworene and swȳþe forlogene, and wed synd tōbrocene oft and ġelōme, and þæt is ġesȳne on þysse þēode þæt ūs Godes yrre heteliċe onsit, ġecnāwe se þe cunne.

[35] And lā, hū mæġ māre scamu þurh Godes yrre mannum ġelimpan þonne ūs dēð ġelōme for āgenum ġewyrhtum? [36] Ðēh þrǣla hwylċ hlāforde ætlēape and of Cristendōme tō wīċinge weorþe, and hit æfter þām eft ġeweorþe þæt wǣpnġewrixl weorðe ġemǣne þeġene and þrǣle,[27] ġif þrǣl þæne þeġen fullīċe āfylle,[28] licge ǣgylde ealre his mǣġðe.[29] [37] And ġif se þeġen þæne þrǣl þe hē ǣr āhte fullīċe āfylle, ġylde þeġenġylde.[30] [38] Ful earhlīċe laga and scandlīċe nȳdġyld þurh Godes yrre ūs syn ġemǣne, understande se þe cunne, and fela unġelimpa ġelimpð þysse þēode oft and ġelōme. [39] Ne dohte hit nū lange inne ne ūte, ac wæs here and hete on ġewelhwilċan ende oft and ġelōme, and Engle nū lange eal siġelēase and tō swȳþe ġeyriġde þurh Godes yrre, and flotmen swā strange þurh Godes þafunge þæt oft on ġefeohte ān fēseð tȳne and hwīlum lǣs, hwīlum mā, eal for ūrum synnum. [40] And oft tȳne oððe twelfe, ælċ æfter ōþrum, scendað tō bysmore þæs þeġenes cwenan and hwīlum his dohtor oððe nȳdmāgan þǣr hē on lōcað þe lǣt hine sylfne rancne and rīċne and ġenōh gōdne ǣr þæt ġewurde. [41] And oft þrǣl þæne þeġen þe ǣr wæs his hlāford cnyt swȳþe fæste and wyrċð him[31] tō þrǣle þurh Godes yrre. [42] Wā lā þǣre yrmðe and wā lā þǣre woroldscame þe nū habbað Engle, eal þurh Godes yrre. [43] Oft twēġen sǣmen oððe þrȳ hwīlum drīfað þā drāfe Cristenra manna fram sǣ tō sǣ ūt þurh þās þēode ġewelede tōgædre, ūs eallum tō woroldscame, ġif wē on eornost ǣniġe cūþon āriht understandan.

---

23  *ealle hwīle*: all the while.
24  *ġemǣnum ċēape*: as a joint purchase.
25  *ān æfter ānum*: one after another.
26  The sale of family members would have been caused by economic distress.
27  *ġemǣne þeġene and þrǣle*: between the thegn and the slave.
28  *fullīċe āfylle*: kill outright.
29  *ealre his mǣġðe*: for all of his family.
30  The *werġild* for a thegn was twenty-five pounds; that of a slave was one pound.
31  *him*: for himself.

[44] Ac ealne þæne bysmor þe wē oft þoliað wē ġyldað mid weorðscipe þām þe ūs scendað. [45] Wē him ġyldað singallīċe, and hȳ ūs hȳnað dæġhwāmlīċe. [46] Hȳ hergiað and hȳ bærnað, rȳpaþ and rēafiað and tō scipe lædað; and lā, hwæt is æniġ ōðer on eallum þām ġelimpum būtan Godes yrre ofer þās þēode, swutol and ġesæne?

[47] Nis ēac nān wundor þēah ūs mislimpe, for þām wē witan ful ġeorne þæt nū fela ġēara menn nā ne rōhtan foroft hwæt hȳ worhtan wordes oððe dæde,[32] ac wearð þes þēodscipe, swā hit þinċan mæġ, swȳþe forsyngod þurh mæniġfealde synna and þurh fela misdæda: [48] þurh morðdæda and þurh mándæda, þurh ġitsunga and þurh ġīfernessa, þurh stala and þurh strūdunga, þurh mannsylena and þurh hæþene unsida, þurh swicdōmas and þurh searacræftas, þurh lahbryċas and þurh æswicas, þurh mæġræsas and þurh manslyhtas, þurh hādbryċas and þurh æwbryċas, þurh sibleġeru and þurh mistliċe forliġru. [49] And ēac syndan wīde, swā wē ær cwædan, þurh āðbriċas and þurh wedbryċas and þurh mistliċe lēasunga forloren and forlogen mā þonne scolde, and frēolsbriċas and fæstenbryċas wīde ġeworhte oft and ġelōme. [50] And ēac hēr syn on earde apostatan ābroþene and ċyriċhatan hetole and lēodhatan grimme ealles tō maneġe, and oferhogan wīde godcundra rihtlaga and Cristenra þēawa, and hocorwyrde dysiġe[33] æġhwær on þēode – oftost on þā þing þe Godes bodan bēodaþ and swȳþost on þā þing þe æfre tō Godes lage ġebyriað mid rihte. [51] And þȳ is nū ġeworden wīde and sīde tō ful yfelan ġewunan, þæt menn swȳþor scamað nū for[34] gōddædan þonne for misdædan, for þām tō oft man mid hocere gōddæda hyrweð and godfyrhte lehtreð ealles tō swȳþe; [52] and swȳþost man tæleð and mid olle ġegrēteð ealles tō ġelōme þā þe riht lufiað and Godes eġe habbað be æniġum dæle.[35] [53] And þurh þæt þe[36] man swā dēð þæt man eal hyrweð þæt man scolde herian and tō forð lāðet þæt man scolde lufian, þurh þæt man ġebringeð ealles tō maneġe on yfelan ġeþance and on undæde, swā þæt hȳ ne scamað nā þēh hȳ syngian swȳðe and wið God sylfne forwyrċan hȳ mid ealle,[37] [54] ac for īdelan onscytan hȳ scamað þæt hȳ bētan heora misdæda, swā swā bēċ[38] tæċan, ġelīċe þām dwæsan þe for heora prȳtan lēwe nellað beorgan[39] ær hȳ nā ne magan, þēh hȳ eal willan.[40]

[55] Hēr syndan þurh synlēawa, swā hit þinċan mæġ, sāre ġelēwede tō maneġe on earde. [56] Hēr syndan mannslagan and mæġslagan and mæsserbanan and

---

[32]  *wordes oððe dæde*: in word or deed.

[33]  *hocorwyrde dysiġe*: derisive foolish [people].

[34]  *menn swȳþor scamað nū for*: one is now more ashamed of.

[35]  *be æniġum dæle*: in any part; at all.

[36]  *þurh þæt þe*: because.

[37]  *mid ealle*: entirely.

[38]  More specifically, penitential manuals, which assigned penances for various sins.

[39]  *lēwe nellað beorgan*: will not guard against an injury.

[40]  People who are not ashamed of their sins but are ashamed of empty calumnies directed against them are, according to Wulfstan, like those foolish persons who will not protect themselves from injury until it is too late to do so even if they want to.

mynsterhatan; and hēr syndan mānsworan and morþorwyrhtan; and hēr syndan myltestran and bearnmyrðran and fūle forleġene hōringas maneġe; and hēr syndan wiċċan and wælcyrian; and hēr syndan rȳperas and rēaferas and woroldstrūderas and, hrædest is tō cweþenne, māna and misdǣda unġerīm ealra. [57] And þæs ūs ne scamað nā, ac þæs ūs scamað swȳþe þæt wē bōte āġinnan swā swā bēċ tǣċan, and þæt is ġesȳne on þysse earman forsyngodon þēode. [58] Ēalā, miċel magan maneġe ġȳt hērtōēacan ēaþe beþenċan⁴¹ þæs þe ān man ne mehte on hrǣdinge⁴² āsmēaġan, hū earmlīċe hit ġefaren is nū ealle hwīle wīde ġynd þās þēode. [59] And smēaġe hūru ġeorne ġehwā hine sylfne and þæs nā ne latiġe ealles tō lange. [60] Ac lā, on Godes naman wutan dōn swā ūs nēod is, beorgan ūs sylfum⁴³ swā wē ġeornost magan þe lǣs wē ætgædere ealle forweorðan.

[61] Ān þēodwita wæs on Brytta tīdum, Gildas hātte.⁴⁴ [62] Se āwrāt be heora misdǣdum hū hȳ mid heora synnum swā oferlīċe swȳþe God ġegrǣmedan þæt hē lēt æt nȳhstan Engla here heora eard ġewinnan and Brytta dugeþe fordōn mid ealle. [63] And þæt wæs ġeworden, þæs þe hē sǣde, þurh rīċra rēaflāc and þurh ġītsunge wōhgestrēona, ðurh lēode unlaga and þurh wōhdōmas, ðurh biscopa āsolcennesse and þurh lȳðre yrhðe Godes bydela þe sōþes ġeswugedan ealles tō ġelōme and clumedan mid ċeaflum þǣr hȳ scoldan clypian. [64] Þurh fūlne ēac folces gǣlsan and þurh oferfylla and mæniġfealde synna heora eard hȳ forworhtan and selfe hȳ forwurdan. [65] Ac utan dōn swā ūs þearf is, warnian ūs be swilċan; and sōþ is þæt iċ secge, wyrsan dǣda wē witan mid Englum þonne wē mid Bryttan āhwār ġehȳrdan. [66] And þȳ ūs is þearf miċel þæt wē ūs beþenċan and wið God sylfne þingian ġeorne. [67] And utan dōn swā ūs þearf is, ġebūgan tō rihte and be suman dǣle⁴⁵ unriht forlǣtan and bētan swȳþe ġeorne þæt wē ǣr brǣcan. [68] And utan God lufian and Godes lagum fylġean, and ġelǣstan swȳþe ġeorne þæt þæt wē behētan þā wē fulluht underfēngan, oððon þā þe æt fulluhte ūre forespecan wǣran. [69] And utan word and weorc rihtlīċe fadian and ūre inġeþanc clǣnsian ġeorne and āð and wed wǣrlīċe healdan and sume ġetrȳwða habban ūs betwēonan būtan uncræftan. [70] And utan ġelōme understandan þone miċlan dōm þe wē ealle tō sculon, and beorgan ūs ġeorne wið þone weallendan bryne hellewītes, and ġeearnian ūs þā mǣrða and þā myrhða þe God hæfð ġeġearwod þām þe his willan on worolde ġewyrċað. [71] God ūre helpe.⁴⁶ Amen.

---

⁴¹ *miċel magan maneġe ġȳt hērtōēacan ēaþe beþenċan*: in addition, many could call to mind much
. . . The *þæs þe* that begins the next clause is a partitive genitive with *miċel*; translate it 'that'.

⁴² *on hrǣdinge*: briefly.

⁴³ *ūs sylfum*: ourselves.

⁴⁴ Gildas is the sixth-century author of *De Excidio Britanniae* 'On the Ruin of Britain', which, as Wulfstan reports, views the coming of the Angles, Saxons and Jutes to Britain as divine punishment for the sins of the Britons.

⁴⁵ *be suman dǣle*: to some degree.

⁴⁶ *God ūre helpe*: God help us. *Helpan* takes a genitive object.

# 8    Ohthere and Wulfstan

One of the major Old English works produced during the reign of King Alfred (d. 899) was a translation of a history of the world written by Paulus Orosius (d. 420) as a defence against the charge that the adoption of Christianity and the neglect of the old gods had brought catastrophe upon the Roman Empire. Orosius's work is more polemic than history – a dreary recital of the many calamities that had befallen the earth while Rome worshipped pagan gods. Nevertheless, it was enthusiastically read in the Middle Ages, which regarded it as an authoritative history of the world. The Old English translation was formerly ascribed to King Alfred, but is now thought to be the work of a contemporary writing at the king's direction or urging.

Orosius's *History* begins with an account of the geography and peoples of the ancient world. The Old English translator greatly expanded this with a survey of the Germanic nations and other matter; embedded in this survey are the narratives of two travellers, Ohthere and Wulfstan. Ohthere was a Norwegian (the Old Norse form of his name would have been Óttarr) who lived by hunting, whaling and trading; we are told that he 'sought' the court of King Alfred, presumably as a market for his goods. He had travelled over the top of present-day Norway, above the Arctic Circle, then around the Kola Peninsula and into the White Sea, where he had encountered the Bjarmians. He had been to the Norse ports of Skiringssal and Hedeby. Less is known about Wulfstan: we are not told his nationality or anything about his business. But we are told that he sailed from Hedeby east into the Baltic Sea, where he visited the city of Truso near the coast of present-day Poland and the Ests (the ancient *Aestii*) in the region beyond the Vistula. Someone at Alfred's court – perhaps the king himself – was impressed enough by these travellers that he engaged a scribe or scribes to take down their narratives. The scribe responsible for Wulfstan's narrative seems, in places at least, to have taken down his very words.

It is difficult to verify much of what is in these accounts, which seem to have been inserted into the translation of Orosius's *History* with little or no editing. The trickiness of memory, the frequent inaccuracy of second-hand reporting, and, in the case of Ohthere at least, the difficulty of communication between Englishman and Norseman, cause us to question some details. But the narratives of Ohthere and Wulfstan are plainly different from many of the travellers' tales that circulated in the Middle Ages, which were long on the fantastic and short on fact. Despite our questions about the details, there is little reason to doubt that we have here a rare and valuable glimpse of life outside the royal courts and monasteries of Viking-age Europe.

The standard edition of the Old English Orosius is by Bately [6], who cites many useful studies of the places and peoples mentioned here. In this text, sentences 1–18 are from a manuscript nearly contemporary with King Alfred. This early manuscript is unfortunately defective, so the remainder is from an eleventh-century copy: see the Textual Note for details.

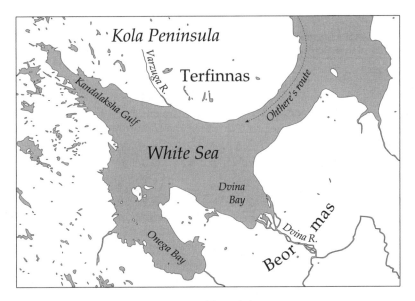

1. The White Sea, with places visited by Ohthere

[1] Ōhthere sǣde his hlāforde, Ælfrede cyninge, þæt hē ealra Norðmonna norþmest būde.[1] [2] Hē cwæð þæt hē būde on þǣm lande norþweardum wiþ þā Westsǣ. [3] Hē sǣde þēah þæt þæt land sīe swīþe lang norþ þonan, ac hit is eal wēste, būton on fēawum stōwum styċċemǣlum wīciað Finnas[2] on huntoðe[3] on wintra and on sumera on fiscaþe be þǣre sǣ.

[4] Hē sǣde þæt hē æt sumum ċirre wolde fandian hū longe þæt land norþryhte[4] lǣġe, oþþe hwæðer ǣniġ mon benorðan þǣm wēstenne būde. [5] Þā fōr hē norþryhte be þǣm lande. [6] Lēt him ealne weġ[5] þæt wēste land on ðæt stēorbord[6] and þā wīdsǣ on ðæt bæcbord þrīe dagas; þā wæs hē swā feor

---

[1]  Later in the narrative we learn that Ohthere came from Hālgoland (Norse Hålogaland), the northernmost province of Viking-age Norway, extending from modern Nord-Trøndelag (above Trondheim) to Troms, well above the Arctic Circle. If the transcriber has recorded Ohthere's words accurately, he comes from the northern part of Hālgoland.

[2]  By *Finnas* Ohthere means the Sami, or Lapps.

[3]  *on huntoðe*: by hunting.

[4]  *Norþryhte* is usually translated 'direct north,' but Bately points out that in Old Norse words for 'north' might point anywhere in the northern quadrant. In the early Middle Ages 'north,' 'south,' 'east' and 'west' were more often thought of as regions than as directions, so to 'travel north' was to travel into the northern region.

[5]  *ealne weġ*: the whole way.

[6]  The *stēorbord* 'starboard' is the side of the ship on which the rudder (the steering mechanism) was attached: compare Old English *stēoran* 'steer'. The *bæcbord* 'larboard, port' was so called because the steersman had his back to that side of the ship.

norþ swā þā hwælhuntan firrest faraþ. [7] Þā fōr hē þā ġīet norþryhte swā feor swā hē meahte on þǣm ōþrum þrim dagum ġesiġlan. [8] Þā bēag þæt land þǣr ēastryhte, oþþe sēo sǣ in on ðæt lond, hē nysse hwæðer, būton hē wisse ðæt hē ðǣr bād westanwindes and hwōn norþan[7] and siġlde ðā ēast be lande swā swā hē meahte on fēower dagum ġesiġlan. [9] Þā sceolde hē ðǣr bīdan ryhtnorþanwindes, for ðǣm þæt land bēag þǣr sūþryhte,[8] oþþe sēo sǣ in on ðæt land, hē nysse hwæþer. [10] Þā siġlde hē þonan sūðryhte be lande swā swā hē mehte on fīf dagum ġesiġlan.[9] [11] Ðā lǣġ þǣr ān miċel ēa ūp in on þæt land. [12] Þā ċirdon hīe ūp in on ðā ēa, for þǣm hīe ne dorston forþ bi þǣre ēa siġlan for unfriþe, for þǣm ðæt land wæs eall ġebūn on ōþre healfe þǣre ēas.[10] [13] Ne mētte hē ǣr nān ġebūn land siþþan hē from his āgnum hām fōr, ac him wæs ealne weġ wēste land on þæt stēorbord, būtan fiscerum and fugelerum and huntum, and þæt wǣron eall Finnas,[11] and him wæs ā wīdsǣ on ðæt bæcbord.

[14] Þā Beormas hæfdon swīþe wel ġebūd hira land, ac hīe ne dorston þǣron cuman. [15] Ac þāra Terfinna[12] land wæs eal wēste, būton ðǣr huntan ġewīcodon oþþe fisceras oþþe fugeleras. [16] Fela spella him sǣdon þā Beormas ǣġþer ġe of hiera āgnum lande ġe of þǣm landum þe ymb hīe ūtan wǣron, ac

---

[7]    As Ohthere was changing direction, he would have had to wait for a favourable wind. Rounding the top of Norway, he would have headed east while trending somewhat south towards the Kola Peninsula; thus he wanted a wind from a little north of east.

[8]    Ohthere is rounding the end of the Kola Peninsula (in present-day Russia) and entering the White Sea. It must have been summer or autumn, or the entrance to the White Sea would have been frozen.

[9]    Very likely the scribe who recorded Ohthere's narrative missed something here. If Ohthere kept sailing with land on his starboard, he would have turned west along the southern coast of the Kola Peninsula, probably as far as the Varzuga River; but it is not impossible that he sailed around much of the periphery of the White Sea, reaching some unidentified river that served as the border of Bjarmian territory. If he continued to sail south, he would have left the land behind on his starboard, and, presumably following the eastern coast of the White Sea on his larboard, would reach the Dvina, which is indeed, as Ohthere says, a very large river. Since he encountered both the Ter Sami (*Terfinnas*) in the eastern Kola Peninsula and the Bjarmians (*Beormas*) around the Dvina River, he must have reached both places; but it seems impossible to reconstruct the details of his voyage.

[10]    As the next sentence shows, Ohthere does not consider land occupied by any variety of *Finnas* to be *ġebūn* 'inhabited' or 'cultivated' (one implies the other in both a Norse and an Anglo-Saxon context). As it seems exceedingly unlikely that he would have encountered any but *Finnas* around the Varzuga River, the river mentioned here is very likely the Dvina, which forms a delta in which much of the land is under cultivation today. However, a river to the north or west of the Dvina is also a possibility.

The genitive singular *ēas* is unusual for feminine *ēa*, but not unknown. The expected form of this athematic noun is *īe*, which is attested elsewhere in the Old English Orosius, but the word is in the process of moving into the strong feminine declension (see dative singular *ēa* in sentence 12 above).

[11]    For *þæt wǣron*, see §11.3. Here *eall* agrees with *þæt* rather than *Finnas*.

[12]    The *Terfinnas* are almost certainly the Ter Sami, who lived in the eastern portion of the Kola Peninsula.

hē nyste hwæt þæs sōþes wæs,[13] for þæm hē hit self ne ġeseah. [17] Þā Finnas, him þūhte, and þā Beormas spræcon nēah ān ġeþēode.[14] [18] Swīþost hē fōr ðider, tōēacan þæs landes sċēawunge, for þæm horshwælum, for ðæm hīe habbað swīþe æþele bān on hiora tōþum (þā tēð hīe brōhton sume þæm cyninge), and hiora hȳd[15] bið swīðe gōd tō sciprāpum. [19] Se hwæl bið miċle læssa þonne ōðre hwalas: ne bið hē lenġra ðonne syfan elna[16] lang. [20] Ac on his āgnum lande is se betsta hwælhuntað: þā bēoð eahta and fēowertiġes elna lange, and þā mæstan fiftiġes elna lange. [21] Þāra hē sæde þæt hē syxa sum[17] ofslōge syxtiġ[18] on twām dagum.

[22] Hē wæs swȳðe spēdiġ man on þæm æhtum þe heora spēda on bēoð, þæt is on wildrum. [23] Hē hæfde þā ġȳt, ðā hē þone cyningc sōhte, tamra dēora unbebohtra syx hund. [24] Þā dēor hī hātað hrānas; þāra wæron syx stælhrānas, ðā bēoð swȳðe dȳre mid Finnum, for ðæm hȳ fōð þā wildan hrānas mid.[19] [25] Hē wæs mid þæm fyrstum mannum on þæm lande; næfde hē þēah mā ðonne twentiġ hrȳðera and twentiġ sċēapa and twentiġ swȳna, and þæt lȳtle þæt hē erede hē erede mid horsan.[20] [26] Ac hyra ār is mæst on þæm gafole þe ðā Finnas him ġyldað. [27] Þæt gafol bið on dēora fellum and on fugela feðerum and hwales bāne and on þæm sciprāpum þe bēoð of hwæles hȳde ġeworht and of sēoles. [28] Æġhwilċ ġylt be hys ġebyrdum. [29] Se byrdesta sceall ġyldan fīftȳne mearðes fell and fīf hrānes and ān beran fel and tȳn ambra feðra and berenne kyrtel oððe yterenne and twēġen sciprāpas; æġþer sȳ syxtiġ elna lang: ōþer sȳ of hwæles hȳde ġeworht, ōþer of sīoles.

[30] Hē sæde ðæt Norðmanna land wære swȳþe lang and swȳðe smæl. [31] Eal þæt his man āþer oððe ettan oððe erian mæġ, þæt lið wið ðā sæ; and þæt is þēah on sumum stōwum swȳðe clūdiġ. [32] And licgað wilde mōras wiðēastan and wiðuppon, emnlange þæm bȳnum lande; on þæm mōrum

---

[13]  *hwæt þæs sōþes wæs*: how much of it was the truth.

[14]  The Sami languages are Finno-Ugric (belonging to the same language family as Finnish and Hungarian). If, as some argue, the Bjarmians are the ancestors of the modern Karelians, they also spoke a Finno-Ugric language; but Bjarmian and the Sami languages would not have been mutually intelligible.

[15]  After *hȳd* some pages are missing from the earlier manuscript of the Old English Orosius; the remainder of the text is from an eleventh-century copy. Be on the lookout for spelling differences (e.g. *y* for *ie*) and differences of usage (e.g. *(ġe)seġlian* for *(ġe)siġlan*).

[16]  The ell was not a fixed unit of measure: Bately suggests that it was probably twenty-two to twenty-four inches in Anglo-Saxon England at this time.

[17]  *syxa sum*: as one of six (whalers).

[18]  Sixty is an exceedingly improbable number. Either the English recorder of Ohthere's narrative has misunderstood him or he has exaggerated his success as a whaler.

[19]  The Sami continued to use tame decoy reindeer to catch wild ones well into the modern period. At this time the Sami did not assemble large herds of reindeer and breed them, as they did later, but rather followed wild reindeer herds.

[20]  In Anglo-Saxon England oxen were usually used for ploughing.

eardiað Finnas. [33] And þæt bȳne land is ēasteweard[21] brādost and symle swā norðor swā smælre.[22] [34] Ēastewerd hit mæġ bīon syxtiġ mīla brād oþþe hwēne brǣdre; and middeweard þrītiġ oððe brādre. [35] And norðeweard, hē cwæð, þǣr hit smalost wǣre, þæt hit mihte bēon þrēora mīla brād tō þǣm mōre, and se mōr syðþan on sumum stōwum swā brād swā man mæġ on twām wucum oferfēran, and on sumum stōwum swā brād swā man mæġ on syx dagum oferfēran. [36] Þonne is tōemnes þǣm lande sūðeweardum, on ōðre healfe þæs mōres, Swēoland,[23] oþ þæt land norðeweard; and tōemnes þǣm lande norðeweardum Cwēna land.[24] [37] Þā Cwēnas hergiað hwīlum on ðā Norðmen ofer ðone mōr, hwīlum þā Norðmen on hȳ. [38] And þǣr sint swīðe miċle meras fersce ġeond þā mōras, and berað þā Cwēnas hyra scypu ofer land on ðā meras and þanon hergiað on ðā Norðmen; hȳ habbað swȳðe lȳtle scypa and swȳðe lēohte.

[39] Ōhthere sǣde þæt sīo scīr hātte Hālgoland þe hē on būde. [40] Hē cwæð þæt nān man ne būde benorðan him. [41] Þonne is ān port on sūðeweardum þǣm lande þone man hǣt Scīringesheal.[25] [42] Þyder hē cwæð þæt man ne mihte ġeseġlian on ānum mōnðe ġyf man on niht wīcode and ælċe dæġe hæfde ambyrne wind. [43] And ealle ðā hwīle hē sceal seġlian be lande. [44] And on þæt stēorbord him bið ǣrest Īraland[26] and þonne ðā īġland þe synd betux Īralande and þissum lande.[27] [45] Þonne is þis land on þæt stēorbord oð hē cymð tō Scīringesheale, and ealne weġ on þæt bæcbord Norðweġ.

[46] Wiðsūðan þone Scīringesheal līð swȳðe myċel sǣ[28] ūp in on ðæt lond; sēo is brādre þonne æniġ man ofersēon mæġe, and is Gotland on ōðre healfe onġēan and siððan Sillende.[29] [47] Sēo sǣ līð mæniġ hund mīla ūp in on þæt

---

[21] By *ēasteweard* Ohthere means the southern part of Norway, especially the south-eastern coast.

[22] *swā norðor swā smælre*: the farther north, the narrower.

[23] The *Swēon* or Swedes occupied the southern part of present-day Sweden except for Halland and Skåne, which belonged to Denmark.

[24] The *Cwēnas* (Old Norse *Kvenir*, Finnish *Kainulaiset*) at this time occupied roughly the north-eastern quarter of present-day Sweden.

[25] Skiringssal, an area of Vestfold. As a trader, Ohthere would have visited Kaupang, a trading centre considered to be the first town in Norway.

[26] A glance at a map of the area shows that Ireland is not on the starboard (in the usual sense) as one sails from Hålogaland to Skiringssal. The commonly accepted interpretation of this passage is that to reach Ireland from the Norwegian coast one would turn to the starboard and head west, clearing the Shetland Islands to the north, before turning south towards Ireland.

[27] Probably the Shetlands and Orkneys, possibly also the Hebrides, which lie between Britain and Ireland in the same sense that Ireland is on the starboard when journeying from Hålogaland to Skiringssal.

[28] The Baltic Sea. From Skiringssal one approaches it through the northern part of the Skagerrak and the Kattegat.

[29] By *Sillende* most scholars understand an area on the east coast of the Jutland Peninsula, though its exact boundaries are unknown.

land. [48] And of Scīringesheale hē cwæð þæt hē seġlode on fīf dagan tō þæm porte þe mon hæt æt Hæþum;[30] se stent betuh Winedum, and Seaxum, and Angle, and hȳrð in on Dene. [49] Ðā hē þiderweard seġlode fram Scīringesheale, þā wæs him on þæt bæcbord Denamearc,[31] and on þæt stēorbord wīdsǣ þrȳ dagas; and þā, twēġen dagas ǣr hē tō Hæþum cōme, him wæs on þæt stēorbord Gotland, and Sillende, and īġlanda fela.[32] [50] On þǣm landum eardodon Engle, ǣr hī hider on land cōman.[33] [51] And hym wæs ðā twēġen dagas on ðæt bæcbord þā īġland þe in Denemearce hȳrað.

[52] Wulfstān sǣde þæt hē ġefōre of Hǣðum, þæt hē wǣre on Truso[34] on syfan dagum and nihtum, þæt þæt scip wæs ealne weġ yrnende under seġle. [53] Weonoðland[35] him wæs on stēorbord, and on bæcbord him wæs Langaland and Lǣland and Falster and Scōneġ; and þās land eall hȳrað tō Denemearcan. [54] And þonne Burgenda land wæs ūs on bæcbord, and þā habbað him sylf cyning.[36] [55] Þonne æfter Burgenda lande wǣron ūs þās land þā synd hātene ǣrest Blecinga ēġ, and Meore and Eowland and Gotland on bæcbord;[37] and þās land hȳrað tō Swēon. [56] And Weonodland wæs ūs ealne weġ on stēorbord oð Wislemūðan.

[57] Sēo Wisle is swȳðe myċel ēa, and hīo tōlīð Witland and Weonodland, and þæt Witland belimpeð tō Ēstum.[38] [58] And sēo Wisle līð ūt of Weonodlande and līð in Ēstmere, and se Ēstmere is hūru fīftēne mīla brād. [59] Þonne cymeð Ilfing ēastan[39] in Ēstmere of ðǣm mere ðe Truso standeð

[30]  Hedeby, a major trading centre (later abandoned) on the Schlei, near the south-eastern coast of the Jutland Peninsula. In early Old English it is common for a place-name to consist of *æt* followed by a dative form.

[31]  Not modern Denmark, but Halland and Skåne, which then belonged to Denmark.

[32]  Ohthere's statement that there were many islands on his starboard suggests that he approached Hedeby by way of the Great Belt, the strait that runs between Zealand and Funen.

[33]  The *Engle* who settled in Britain (§1.1) are generally associated with Angeln, an area in the lower Jutland Peninsula. The text here suggests that they also came from the islands to the east of Angeln.

[34]  Truso was a seaport near the north coast of present-day Poland. It is sometimes identified with the modern city of Elbląg, but the text below seems to suggest that Truso stood on the shores of Lake Druzno, a little south of Elbląg.

[35]  The land of the Wends (the Slavic peoples of the southern Baltic), according to this text, stretched from the base of the Jutland Peninsula to the Vistula.

[36]  *þā habbað him sylf cyning*: they have their own king.

[37]  The text seems to suggest that one could see these places on the larboard, but of course if Wulfstan was sailing along the south coast of the Baltic he could not: he simply indicates that they are there by way of marking progress by citing familiar landmarks.

[38]  The *Ēstas* are the *Aestii* mentioned by Tacitus in his *Germania*. According to Tacitus, they used clubs instead of iron weapons and gathered and sold amber without understanding its value.

[39]  The Elbląg River flows more north than east; but it connects *Ēstland* in the east to the Vistula Lagoon (*Ēstmere*).

**2.**  The Baltic Sea, with places visited by Ohthere and Wulfstan

in staðe, and cumað ūt samod in Ēstmere, Ilfing ēastan of Ēstlande and Wisle
sūðan of Winodlande, and þonne benimð Wisle Ilfing hire naman,[40] and ligeð
of þǣm mere west and norð on sǣ; for ðȳ hit man hǣt Wislemūða.
    [60] Þæt Ēstland is swȳðe myċel, and þǣr bið swȳðe maniġ burh, and on
ǣlċere byriġ bið cynincg. [61] And þǣr bið swȳðe myċel huniġ and fiscað; and
se cyning and þā rīcostan men drincað myran meolc, and þā unspēdigan and
þā þēowan drincað medo. [62] Þǣr bið swȳðe myċel ġewinn betwēonan him.
[63] And ne bið ðǣr nǣniġ ealo ġebrowen mid Ēstum, ac þǣr bið medo ġenōh.
    [64] And þǣr is mid Ēstum ðēaw, þonne þǣr bið man dēad, þæt hē līð inne
unforbærned mid his māgum and frēondum mōnað, ġe hwīlum twēġen; and þā
kyningas and þā ōðre hēahðungene men swā miċle lencg swā hī māran spēda

---

[40]  A much discussed passage. Wulfstan seems to be thinking of the Elblą̨g as the more important river, since it flows from Truso, an important trading centre. He thinks of the route from the
emergence of the Elblą̨g (near the Vistula) to the opening from the Vistula Lagoon into the Baltic
as belonging to the Elblą̨g; but it takes the name of the Vistula (in a colourful formulation it
'deprives the Vistula of its name'), and so this route is called 'the Mouth of the Vistula'.

habbað, hwīlum healf ġēar þæt hī bēoð unforbærned; and licgað bufan eorðan on hyra hūsum. [65] And ealle þā hwīle þe þæt līċ bið inne, þǣr sceal bēon ġedrync and plega, oð ðone dæġ þe hī hine forbærnað. [66] Þonne þȳ ylcan dæġe þe hī hine tō þǣm āde beran wyllað, þonne tōdǣlað hī his feoh[41] þæt þǣr tō lāfe[42] bið æfter þǣm ġedrynce and þǣm plegan on fīf oððe syx, hwȳlum on mā, swā swā þæs fēos andefn bið. [67] Ālecgað[43] hit ðonne forhwǣga on ānre mīle þone mǣstan dǣl fram þǣm tūne, þonne ōðerne, ðonne þæne þriddan, oþ þæt hyt eall ālēd bið on þǣre ānre mīle; and sceall bēon se lǣsta dǣl nȳhst þǣm tūne ðe se dēada man on līð.

[68] Ðonne sceolon bēon ġesamnode ealle ðā menn ðe swyftoste hors habbað on þǣm lande, forhwǣga on fīf mīlum oððe on syx mīlum fram þǣm fēo. [69] Þonne ærnað hȳ ealle tōweard þǣm fēo; ðonne cymeð se man se þæt swiftoste hors hafað tō þǣm ǣrestan dǣle and tō þǣm mǣstan, and swā ǣlċ æfter ōðrum, oþ hit bið eall ġenumen; and se nimð þone lǣstan dǣl se nȳhst þǣm tūne þæt feoh ġeærneð. [70] And þonne rīdeð ǣlċ hys weġes[44] mid ðān fēo, and hyt mōtan habban eall;[45] and for ðȳ þǣr bēoð þā swiftan hors ungefōge dȳre. [71] And þonne hys ġestrēon bēoð þus eall āspended, þonne byrð man hine ūt and forbærneð mid his wǣpnum and hrǣġle. [72] And swīðost ealle hys spēda hȳ forspendað mid þān langan leġere þæs dēadan mannes inne, and þæs þe hȳ be þǣm wegum ālecgað, þe ðā fremdan[46] tō ærnað and nimað.

[73] And þæt is mid Ēstum þēaw þæt þǣr sceal ǣlċes ġeðēodes man bēon forbærned; and ġyf þār man ān bān findeð unforbærned, hī hit sceolan miċlum ġebētan. [74] And þǣr is mid Ēstum ān mǣġð þæt hī magon ċyle ġewyrċan;[47] and þȳ þǣr licgað þā dēadan men swā lange and ne fūliað, þæt hȳ wyrċað þone ċyle hine on. [75] And þēah man āsette twēġen fætelsas full ealað oððe wæteres, hȳ ġedōð þæt ōþer bið oferfroren, sam hit sȳ sumor sam winter.

---

[41]    As the subsequent text makes clear, the treasure is divided into unequal portions, each one smaller than the one before. The largest portion is placed first along the course of the race, then the next largest, and so on; so the rider of the fastest horse takes first prize.

[42]    *tō lāfe*: left over.

[43]    The subject of *ālecgað* (*hȳ*) is implicit.

[44]    *hys weġes*: on his way.

[45]    *hyt mōtan habban eall*: they may have all of it.

[46]    Wulfstan or the writer emphasizes that those running the race may be quite unrelated to the dead man. To any Germanic visitor the most remarkable aspect of the funerary customs of the *Ēstas* would be the distribution of the dead man's wealth to persons outside the family.

[47]    Making cold is of course a remarkable achievement at this early date, if Wulfstan is reporting accurately. It is not known how the *Ēstas* made cold.

# 9  The Story of Cædmon

The story of Cædmon, the illiterate cowherd who received the gift of song from God, is told in Book Four, Chapter 24 of Bede's *Ecclesiastical History of the English People*. It was translated into Old English, probably during the reign of King Alfred the Great, by an anonymous Mercian scholar.

For a complete edition of the Old English Bede, see Miller [79]. For an edition of *Cædmon's Hymn* in all its versions, with extensive commentary, see O'Donnell [87].

[1] In ðeosse abbudissan[1] mynstre wæs sum brōðor syndriġlīċe mid godcundre ġife ġemǣred ond ġeweorðad, for þon hē ġewunade ġerisenliċe lēoð wyrċan þā ðe tō ǣfestnisse ond tō ārfæstnisse belumpen, swā ðætte swā hwæt swā hē of godcundum stafum þurh bōceras ġeleornode, þæt hē æfter medmiċlum fæce in scopġereorde mid þā mǣstan swētnisse ond inbryrdnisse ġeglǣnġde ond in Engliscġereorde wel ġeworht forþbrōhte. [2] Ond for his lēoþsongum moniġra monna mōd oft tō worulde forhogdnisse ond tō ġeþēodnisse þæs heofonlican līfes[2] onbǣrnde wǣron. [3] Ond ēac swelċe[3] moniġe ōðre æfter him in Ongelþēode ongunnon ǣfeste lēoð wyrċan; ac nǣniġ hwæðre him þæt ġelīċe dōn meahte, for þon hē nales from monnum ne þurh mon ġelǣred wæs, þæt hē þone lēoðcræft leornade, ac hē wæs godcundlīċe ġefultumed ond þurh Godes ġife þone songcræft onfēng. [4] Ond hē for ðon nǣfre nōht lēasunge ne īdles lēoþes wyrċan meahte, ac efne þā ān þā ðe tō ǣfestnisse belumpon, ond his þā ǣfestan tungan ġedeofanade singan.

[5] Wæs hē se mon in weoruldhāde ġeseted oð þā tīde þe hē wæs ġelȳfdre ylde,[4] ond nǣfre nǣniġ lēoð ġeleornade. [6] Ond hē for þon oft in ġebēorscipe, þonne þǣr wæs blisse intinga ġedēmed,[5] þæt hēo ealle sceoldon þurh ende-byrdnesse[6] be hearpan singan, þonne hē ġeseah þā hearpan him nēalēċan, þonne ārās hē for forscome[7] from þǣm symble ond hām ēode tō his hūse. [7] Þā hē

---

[1]  Hild (d. 680), daughter of Hereric, a nephew of Edwin, the first Christian king of Northumbria, and his wife Breguswith. She was baptized with Edwin in 627 and entered the religious life in 647, very likely after being widowed. In 657 she became abbess of the double monastery of Whitby, where she hosted the famous Synod of Whitby, at which the English Church decided to follow Roman practice in calculating the date of Easter.

[2]  *ġeþēodnisse þæs heofonlican līfes*: membership in the heavenly life.

[3]  *ēac swelċe*: likewise; moreover.

[4]  *ġelȳfdre ylde*: of an advanced age.

[5]  *blisse intinga ġedēmed*: judged to be cause for merriment.

[6]  *þurh endebyrdnesse*: in order.

[7]  It is tempting to emend *forscome* to *scome*, as the word *forscome* is not attested elsewhere and the other, later manuscripts have *for scome* (in various spellings) where this one has *for forscome*. But the related word *forscamung* is attested as a gloss to the Latin word *pudor* 'modesty', and the sense 'modesty' works well here.

þæt þā sumre tīde dyde, þæt hē forlēt þæt hūs þæs ġebēorscipes ond ūt wæs gongende tō nēata scipene, þāra heord him wæs þǣre neahte beboden, þā hē ðā þǣr in ġelimpliċe tīde his leomu on reste ġesette ond onslēpte, þā stōd him sum mon æt þurh swefn ond hine hālette ond grētte ond hine be his noman nemnde: 'Cedmon, sing mē hwæthwugu.' [8] Þā ondswarede hē ond cwæð: 'Ne con iċ nōht singan; ond iċ for þon of þeossum ġebēorscipe ūt ēode ond hider ġewāt, for þon iċ nāht singan ne cūðe.' [9] Eft hē cwæð, se ðe wið hine sprecende wæs: 'Hwæðre þū meaht singan.' [10] Þā cwæð hē: 'Hwæt sceal iċ singan?' Cwæð hē: 'Sing mē frumsceaft.'

[11] Þā hē ðā þās andsware onfēng, þā ongon hē sōna singan in herenesse Godes Scyppendes þā fers ond þā word þe hē nǣfre ġehȳrde, þāra endebyrdnes[8] þis is:

> [12] Nū sculon[9] heriġean   heofonrīċes weard,
> Meotodes meahte   ond his mōdġeþanc,
> weorc wuldorfæder,   swā hē wundra ġehwæs,
> ēċe Drihten,   ōr onstealde.
> [13] Hē ǣrest sceōp   eorðan bearnum[10]
> heofon tō hrōfe,   hāliġ Scyppend;
> þā middanġeard   monncynnes weard,
> ēċe Drihten,   æfter tēode
> fīrum foldan,[11]   Frēa ælmihtiġ.

[14] Þā ārās hē from þǣm slǣpe, ond eal þā þe hē slǣpende song fæste in ġemynde hæfde, ond þǣm wordum sōna moniġ word in þæt ilce ġemet Gode wyrðes[12] songes tōġeþēodde. [15] Þā cōm hē on morgenne tō þǣm tūnġerēfan þe his ealdormon wæs; sǣgde him hwylċe ġife hē onfēng; ond hē hine sōna tō

---

[8]   The word *endebyrdnes* 'order' suggests that the text is quoting Cædmon's poem exactly; Bede's original Latin here says *quorum iste est sensus* (of which this is the sense). After his Latin paraphrase of the hymn, Bede adds, 'This is the sense, but not the very order [*ordo*] of the words which he sang while sleeping; for songs may not, however well composed they are, be translated literally from one language to another without harm to their beauty and dignity.' The Old English translator has omitted this sentence, for an obvious reason. In two eighth-century copies of the Latin text of Bede's *Ecclesiastical History* a version of *Cædmon's Hymn* in the Northumbrian dialect is written in the margin; it is not impossible that it was Bede's intention that the Old English poem should be transmitted with his text.

[9]   The unexpressed subject of *sculon* is *wē*. The omission of first-person subjects is not unusual in Old English (see §15.2.1). Both of the eighth-century copies and two of the earliest of the West-Saxon copies that accompany the Old English Bede omit the pronoun; a number of copies dating from the tenth century and later insert *we*, presumably because the text as originally recorded was by then beginning to look a little cryptic.

[10]   *eorðan bearnum*: for the children of earth.

[11]   *fīrum foldan*: the earth for the people.

[12]   *Gode wyrðes*: worthy of God.

þǣre abbudissan ġelǣdde ond hire þā cȳðde ond sæġde. [16] Þā hēht hēo ġesomnian ealle þā ġelǣredestan men ond þā leorneras, ond him ondweardum hēt secgan þæt swefn ond þæt lēoð singan, þæt ealra heora dōme[13] ġecoren wǣre, hwæt oððe hwonon þæt cumen wǣre.

[17] Þā wæs him eallum ġeseġen, swā swā hit wæs, þæt him wǣre from Drihtne sylfum heofonliċ ġifu forġifen. [18] Þā rehton hēo him ond sæġdon sum hāliġ spell ond godcundre lāre word; bebudon him þā, ġif hē meahte, þæt hē in swinsunge lēoþsonges þæt ġehwyrfde. [19] Þā hē ðā hæfde þā wīsan onfongne, þā ēode hē hām tō his hūse, ond cwōm eft on morgenne,[14] ond þȳ betstan lēoðe ġeglenġed him āsong ond āġeaf þæt him beboden wæs.

[20] Ðā ongan sēo abbudisse clyppan ond lufiġean þā Godes ġife in þǣm men; ond hēo hine þā monade ond lǣrde þæt hē woruldhād ānforlēte ond munuchād onfēnge, ond hē þæt wel þafode. [21] Ond hēo hine in þæt mynster onfēng mid his gōdum ond hine ġeþēodde tō ġesomnunge þāra Godes þēowa; ond hēht hine lǣran[15] þæt ġetæl þæs hālgan stǣres ond spelles. [22] Ond hē eal þā hē in ġehȳrnesse ġeleornian meahte mid hine ġemyndgade, ond swā swā clǣne nēten eodorcende in þæt swēteste lēoð ġehwerfde. [23] Ond his song ond his lēoð wǣron swā wynsumu tō ġehȳranne þætte þā seolfan his lārēowas[16] æt his mūðe wreoton ond leornodon. [24] Song hē ǣrest be middanġeardes ġesceape ond bi fruman moncynnes ond eal þæt stǣr Genesis (þæt is sēo ǣreste Moyses booc), ond eft bi ūtgonge Israhēla folces of Ægypta londe ond bi ingonge þæs ġehātlandes, ond bi ōðrum monegum spellum þæs hālgan ġewrites canōnes bōca,[17] ond bi Crīstes menniscnesse ond bi his þrōwunge ond bi his ūpāstīġnesse in heofonas, ond bi þæs Hālgan Gāstes cyme ond þāra apostola lāre, ond eft bi þǣm dæġe þæs tōweardan dōmes ond bi fyrhtu þæs tintreġlican wiites, ond bi swētnesse þæs heofonlecan rīċes hē moniġ lēoð ġeworhte. [25] Ond swelċe ēac ōðer moniġ be þǣm godcundan fremsumnessum ond dōmum hē ġeworhte. [26] In eallum þǣm hē ġeornlīċe ġēmde þæt hē men ātuge from synna lufan ond māndǣda, ond tō lufan ond tō ġeornfulnesse āwehte gōdra dǣda, for þon hē wæs se mon swīþe ǣfest ond regollecum þēodscipum ēaðmōdlīċe underþēoded. [27] Ond wið þǣm þā ðe

---

[13]　*ealra heora dōme*: by the judgement of them all.

[14]　The text does not say whether Cædmon dreamed another song or composed it while waking. The later metaphor of a ruminating animal suggests silent meditation. The Icelandic *Egil's Saga* depicts the poet Egil composing his 'Head-Ransom' poem to placate the Viking king Eirik of York, who intended to put him to death. He stayed up all night to do it, and so important was concentration to the process of composition and memorization that his friend Arinbjorn had to sit up with him to keep away a sparrow that had been distracting him with its singing.

[15]　*hēht hine lǣran*: commanded (one) to teach him.

[16]　*þā seolfan his lārēowas*: his teachers themselves.

[17]　*þæs hālgan ġewrites canōnes bōca*: of the books of the canon of holy scripture.

in ōðre wīsan dōn woldon hē wæs mid welme miċelre ellenwōdnisse onbærned, ond hē for ðon fæġre ænde[18] his līf betȳnde ond ġeendade.[19]

[28] For þon þā ðǣre tīde nēalǣċte his ġewītenesse ond forðfōre, þā wæs hē fēowertȳnum dagum ǣr þæt hē wæs līċhomlicre untrymnesse þryċċed ond hefgad, hwæðre tō þon[20] ġemetlīċe þæt hē ealle þā tīd meahte ġe sprecan ġe gongan. [29] Wæs þǣr in nēaweste untrumra monna hūs, in þǣm heora þēaw wæs þæt hēo þā untrumran ond þā ðe æt forðfōre wǣron inlǣdon sceoldon ond him þǣr ætsomne þeġnian. [30] Þā bæd hē his þeġn on ǣfenne þǣre neahte þe hē of worulde gongende wæs þæt hē in þǣm hūse him stōwe ġeġearwode, þæt hē ġerestan meahte. [31] Þā wundrode se þeġn for hwon[21] hē ðæs bæde, for þon him þūhte þæt his forðfōr swā nēah ne wǣre; dyde hwæðre swā swā hē cwæð ond bibēad.

[32] Ond mid þȳ[22] hē ðā þǣr on reste ēode ond hē ġefēonde mōde sumu þing mid him sprecende ætgædere ond glēowiende wæs þe þǣr ær inne wǣron, þā wæs ofer midde neaht þæt hē fræġn hwæðer hēo æniġ hūsl inne hæfdon. [33] Þā ondswarodon hēo ond cwǣdon: 'Hwylċ þearf is ðē hūsles? Ne þīnre forþfōre swā nēah is, nū þū þus rōtlīċe ond þus glædlīċe tō ūs sprecende eart.' [34] Cwæð hē eft: 'Berað mē hūsl tō.' [35] Þā hē hit þā on honda hæfde, þā fræġn hē hwæþer hēo ealle smolt mōd ond, būton eallum incan, blīðe tō him hæfdon. [36] Þā ondswaredon hȳ ealle ond cwǣdon þæt hēo nǣniġne incan tō him wiston, ac hēo ealle him swīðe blīðemōde wǣron; ond hēo wrixendlīċe hine bǣdon þæt hē him eallum blīðe wǣre. [37] Þā ondswarade hē ond cwæð: 'Mīne broðor, mīne þā lēofan, iċ eom swīðe blīðemōd tō ēow ond tō eallum Godes monnum.' [38] Ond swā wæs hine ġetrymmende mid þȳ heofonlecan weġneste ond him ōðres līfes ingong ġeġearwode.

[39] Þā ġȳt hē fræġn hū nēah þǣre tīde wǣre þætte þā brōðor ārīsan scolden ond Godes lof rǣran ond heora ūhtsong[23] singan. [40] Þā ondswaredon hēo: 'Nis hit feor tō þon.'[24] [41] Cwæð hē: 'Teala: wuton wē wel þǣre tīde bīdan.' [42] Ond þā him ġebæd ond hine ġeseġnode mid Crīstes rōdetācne ond his hēafod onhylde tō þām bolstre ond medmiċel fæc onslēpte, ond swā mid stilnesse his līf ġeendade.

---

[18]  *fæġre ænde*: with a beautiful end.

[19]  Here Bede's account of Cædmon starts to take on some of the characteristics of a saint's life. As in many saints' lives, his equanimity and confidence in the face of death was a sign of unusual faith, and his ability to foresee the time of his death was taken as a sign of divine favour.

[20]  *tō þon*: to that extent.

[21]  *for hwon*: for what reason; why.

[22]  *mid þȳ*: when.

[23]  *Ūhta* is dawn. *Ūhtsong* corresponds to Bede's *laudes nocturnas*, 'lauds' or 'nocturns', one of the canonical hours, or eight daily services, observed by monks living under the Benedictine Rule. *Ūhtsang* was ordinarily timed to end at dawn; Cædmon would have participated in this service every day since becoming a monk.

[24]  *tō þon*: until then.

[43] Ond swā wæs ġeworden þætte swā swā hlūttre mōde ond bilwitre ond smyltre wilsumnesse Drihtne þēode, þæt hē ēac swylċe swā smylte dēaðe middanġeard wæs forlǣtende ond tō his ġesihðe becwōm. [44] Ond sēo tunge þe swā moniġ hālwende word in þæs Scyppendes lof ġesette, hē[25] ðā swelċe ēac þā ȳtmæstan word in his herenisse, hine seolfne seġniende ond his gāst in his honda bebēodende, betȳnde. [45] Ēac swelċe þæt is ġeseġen þæt hē wǣre ġewis his seolfes forðfōre of þǣm we nū secgan hȳrdon.

# 10   Boethius on Fame

King Alfred, who ruled the West Saxons from 870 to 899, is chiefly remembered for two accomplishments, either of which would have been sufficient to earn him his epithet 'the Great': he stopped the advance of the Vikings in England, inaugurating a century of relative peace and stability, and he instituted and led a programme of educational reform, initiating a tradition of vernacular literary prose that lasted until the Conquest. As part of this reform, Alfred himself translated several works: the *Pastoral Care* of Pope Gregory the Great (in the preface to which, edited in Mitchell and Robinson [81], he outlines his educational programme), *The Consolation of Philosophy* by the sixth-century philosopher Boethius, the *Soliloquies* of St Augustine, and the first fifty psalms.

Alfred generally treated his source quite freely; you may wish to consult either the Latin text or one of the numerous available translations to spot the passages that he added or altered. He renders the allegorical figure *Philosophia* as *Wīsdōm* 'Wisdom' or *Ġesceādwīsnes* 'Reason'; the figure which in the source is understood to be Boethius himself is here allegorized as *Mōd* 'Mind'. The present selection, corresponding to Book II, Prose vii and Metre vii of the source, follows the discourse of *Philosophia/Wīsdōm* on temporal power, which closes with a metre on the disastrous reign of Nero.

The standard edition of King Alfred's Boethius is Sedgefield [103]; the metres have been edited separately in Krapp and Dobbie [69], vol. 5, and, with commentary and glossary, in Griffiths [53].

[1] Ðā se Wīsdōm ðā þis lēoð āsungen hæfde, ðā ġesūgode hē, ond þā andswarode þæt Mōd ond þus cwæð: [2] 'Ēalā, Ġesceādwīsnes, hwæt, þū wāst þæt mē nǣfre sēo ġītsung ond sēo ġemǣġð þisses eorðlican anwealdes forwel

---

[25] Clearly the Old English translator has lost track of his sentence here. The noun phrase with included adjective clause, *Ond sēo tunge ... lof ġesette* should function as the subject of the whole sentence; but the subject awkwardly changes from 'the tongue' to 'he' (i.e. Cædmon) at this point.

ne līcode, ne iċ ealles forswīðe ne ġirnde þisses eorðlican rīċes,[1] būton tōla iċ wilnode þēah ond andweorces tō þām weorce þe mē beboden was tō wyrċanne, þæt was þæt iċ unfracoðlīċe ond ġerisenlīċe meahte stēoran ond reċċan þone anwald þe mē befæst wæs. [3] Hwæt, þū wāst þæt nān mon ne mæġ nænne cræft cȳðan ne nænne anweald reċċan ne stīoran būtan tōlum ond andweorce; þæt bið ælċes cræftes andweorc þæt mon þone cræft būton wyrċan ne mæġ. [4] Þæt bið þonne cyninges andweorc ond his tōl mid tō rīcsianne þæt hē hæbbe his lond full monnad: hē sceal habban ġebedmen ond ferdmen[2] ond weorcmen.[3] [5] Hwæt, þū wāst þætte būtan þissum tōlum nān cyning his cræft ne mæġ cȳðan. [6] Þæt is ēac his ondweorc þæt hē habban sceal tō ðǣm tōlum, þām þrim ġefērscipum, bīwiste. [7] Þæt is þonne heora bīwist: land tō būgianne ond ġifa ond wǣpnu ond mete ond ealu ond clāþas ond ġehwæt þæs ðe þā þrē ġefērscipas behofiġen.[4] [8] Ne mæġ hē būtan þisum þās tōl ġehealdan ne būton þisum tōlum nān þāra þinga wyrċan þe him beboden is tō wyrċenne.

[9] 'For þȳ iċ wilnode andweorces þone anweald mid tō reċċenne, þæt mīne cræftas ond anweald ne wurden forġitene ond forholene, for þām[5] ælċ cræft ond ælċ anweald bið sōna forealdod ond forsugod ġif hē bið būton wīsdōme. [10] For ðǣm ne mæġ nōn[6] mon nænne cræft bringan būton wīsdōme, for ðǣm þe swā hwæt swā[7] þurh dysiġ ġedōn bið, ne mæġ hit mon nǣfre tō cræfte ġereċċan. [11] Þæt is nū hraðost tō secganne[8] þæt iċ wilnode weorðfullīċe tō libbanne þā hwīle þe[9] iċ lifde ond æfter mīnum līfe þǣm monnum tō lǣfanne þe æfter mē wǣren mīn ġemyndiġ[10] on gōdum weorcum.'

[12] Ðā ðis þā ġesprecen was, þā ġesūgode þæt Mōd, ond sēo Ġesceādwīsnes ongon sprecan ond þus cwæþ: [13] 'Ēalā, Mōd, ēalā, ān yfel is swīðe swīðe tō

---

[1]   From this point most of *Mōd*'s speech has been added by Alfred to his source.

[2]   The first element of *ferdmen* is a word for 'army', usually spelled *fierd* (in early West Saxon) or *fyrd* (in late West Saxon). The vowel of this word, which arises from the *i*-mutation of *ea* (see §2.2.2), is often spelled *e* in this text, e.g. *onġetan* 16 (spelled *ongietan*, *ongitan* and *ongytan* elsewhere in this anthology) and *nēten* 18 (spelled *nīeten* in early West Saxon and *nȳten* in the later texts in this anthology). This spelling is characteristic of non-West Saxon dialects; if you keep it in mind as you read this text you may save yourself some trips to the glossary.

[3]   It is a commonplace in medieval literature that society is composed of three 'estates': those who pray (the clergy and those in monastic orders), those who fight (the nobility) and those who work (the commoners).

[4]   *ġehwæt . . . behofiġen*: literally 'everything of that which the three fellowships require'; but translate 'everything that the . . .'.

[5]   The adverb *for þȳ* at the beginning of this sentence is correlated with the conjunction *for þām* here (see §10.4).

[6]   A peculiarity of this text is its occasional spelling of *ō* for *ā* before *n*.

[7]   *swā hwæt swā*: whatever (see §5.4).

[8]   *Þæt is nū hraðost tō secganne*: to put it briefly.

[9]   *þā hwīle þe*: for as long as.

[10]   *wǣren mīn ġemyndiġ*: remembered me.

anscunianne: þæt is þæt þætte swīðe singallīċe ond swīðe hefiġlīċe beswīcð ealra þāra monna mōd þe bēoð on heora ġecynde ġecorene, ond þēah ne bēoð tō þām hrōfe þonne ġīt cumen fulfremedra mæġena; þæt is þonne wilnung lēases ġilpes ond unryhtes anwealdes ond unġemetliċes hlīsan gōdra weorca[11] ofer eall folc. [14] For þon wilnigað moniġe woruldmen anwealdes þē[12] hīe woldon habban gōdne hlīsan, þēah hī his unwyrðe sīen; ġe furðum se ealra forcūþesta wilnað þæs ilcan. [15] Ac se þe wile wīslīċe ond ġeornlīċe æfter þām hlīsan spyrian, þonne onġit hē swīðe hræðe hū lȳtel hē bið, ond hū læne, ond hū tēdre, ond hū bedæled ælċes gōdes.

[16] 'Ġif þū nū ġeornlīċe smēaġan wilt ond witan wilt ymb ealre þisse eorðan ymbhwyrft from ēasteweardum ðisses middanġeardes oð westeweardne, ond from sūðeweardum oð norðeweardne, swā swā þū liornodest on þǣre bēċ þe Astralogium hātte,[13] ðonne meaht þū onġetan þæt hē is eal wið þone heofon tō metanne swilċe ān lȳtlu price on brādum brede, oðþe rondbēag on scelde, æfter wīsra monna dōme. [17] Hū ne wāst þū[14] þæt ðū leornodest on Ptolomeus bōcum, se tōwrāt ealles þises middanġeardes ġemet on ānre bēċ?[15] [18] Þær þū meaht on ġesēon þæt eall moncynn ond ealle nētenu ne notiġað furðum nāwer nēah fēorðan dæles þisse eorðan, ðæs þe[16] men ġefaran magan, for þæm þe hȳ hit ne magon eall ġebūgian, sum for hæte, sum for ċile; ond þone mæstan dæl his hæfð sæ oferseten. [19] Dō nū of ðām fēorðan dæle an þīnum mōde eall þæt sēo sæ his ofseten hæfð, ond eal þā sceard þe hīo him[17] on ġenumen hæfð, ond eall þæt his fennas ond mōras ġenumen habbað, ond eall þæt on eallum þīodum wēstes liġeð[18]. [20] Þonne meaht þū onġitan þætte þæs ealles nis monnum þonne māre læfed tō būgianne, būton swelċe ōn lȳtel cafertūn. [21] Is þæt þonne fordysliċ ġeswinc þæt ġē winnað ēowre worulde[19] tō ðon[20] þæt ġē wilniað ēowerne hlīsan unġemetlīċe tō brædanne ofer swelċne cafertūn swelċe þæt is ðætte men būgiað þisse worulde[21] – ful nēah swilċe

---

[11]   hlīsan gōdra weorca: fame (or approbation) for good deeds.

[12]   The adverb for þon at the beginning of this sentence is correlated with the conjunction þē (more often spelled þȳ) here.

[13]   The Latin text does not allude to a specific work, but rather in a general way to 'astrological [that is, astronomical] accounts'.

[14]   Questions beginning Hū ne are generally to be translated 'Do not . . . ?' In this sentence Hū ne wāst þū means 'Do you not know . . . ?'

[15]   Ptolemy (fl. first half of second century) is best known for his Almagest, which summarized Greek astronomy; however, the allusion here is to his Geography. The Anglo-Saxons had no first-hand knowledge of Ptolemy's works.

[16]   Genitive ðæs þe agrees with dæles.

[17]   The antecedent of hīo is sæ; that of him (and the other masculine pronouns in this sentence) is dæle. The gender of the pronouns prevents their being ambiguous.

[18]   The genitive wēstes is adverbial: translate 'lies waste'.

[19]   winnað ēowre worulde: struggle all your lives.

[20]   tō ðon: for the purpose.

[21]   Take the genitive phrase þisse worulde with cafertūn: 'a little courtyard (or vestibule) of this world'.

ān price for þæt ōðer. [22] Ac hwæt rūmedlíċes oððe miċelliċes oððe weorðfulliċes[22] hæfð se ēower ġilp[23] þe ġē þær būgiað on þām fiftan dæle healfum[24] londes ond unlondes, mid sæ, mid fænne, mid ealle,[25] swā hit is ġenerwed. [23] Tō hwon[26] wilniġe ġē þonne tō unġemetlīċe þæt ġē ēowerne naman tōbrǣden ofer þone tēoðan dæl, nū his māre nis mid sæ, mid fænne, mid ealle?

[24] 'Ġeðenċað ēac þæt on ðisum lȳtlan pearroce þe wē ǣr ymb sprǣcon būgiað swīðe manega þēoda ond swīðe mislica ond swīðe unġelica, ǣġþer ġe on sprǣċe ġe on þēawum ġe on eallum sidum ealra þāra þēoda þe ġē nū wilniað swīðe unġemetlīċe þæt ġē scylen ēowerne naman ofer tōbrǣdan. [25] Þæt ġē nǣfre ġedōn ne magon, for ðon hiora sprǣċ is tōdǣled on twā ond on hundseofontiġ, ond ǣlċ þāra sprǣċa is tōdǣled on manega þīoda, ond þā sint tōleġena ond tōdǣlda mid sæ ond mid wudum ond mid muntum ond mid fennum ond mid manegum ond mid mislicum wēstenum ond unġefērum londum, þæt hit furðum ċēpemen ne ġefarað. [26] Ac hū mag ðǣr þonne synderlīċe ānes rīċes monnes nama cuman, þonne þǣr mon furðum þǣre burge naman ne ġehērð ne þǣre þēode þe hē on hāmfæst bið? [27] Þȳ iċ nāt hwelċe dysiġe[27] ġē ġirnað þæt ġē woldon ēowerne naman tōbrǣdan ġeond ealle eorþan; þæt ġē nǣfre ġedōn ne magon, ne furðum nāwer nēah.

[28] 'Hwæt, þū wāst hū miċel Rōmāna rīċe wæs on Marcuses dagum þæs heretogan, se wæs ōðre naman hāten Tullius ond þriddan Cicero. [29] Hwæt, hē cȳðde on sumre his bōca[28] ðætte þā ġēt Rōmāna nama ne cōme ofer þā muntas þā wē hātað Caucaseas, ne ðā Sciððeas þe on ōðre healfe þāra munta būgiað furðum þǣre burge naman ne þæs folces ne ġehērdon, ac þā hē cōm ǣrest tō Parðum, ond wæs þǣr swīðe nīwe; ac hē[29] wæs þēah þǣrymbūtan manegum folce swīðe eġeful. [30] Hū ne onġite ġē nū hū nearo se ēower hlīsa bīon wile þe ġē þǣr ymb swincað ond unrihtlīċe tioliað tō ġebrǣdanne? [31] Hwæt wēnstū hū miċelne hlīsan[30] ond hū miċelne weorðscipe ān Rōmānisc man mæġe habban on þām lande þǣr mon furðum ðǣre burge naman ne ġehērde, ne ealles ðæs folces hlīsa ne cōm?

[32] 'Þēah nū hwelċ mon unġemetlīċe ond unġedafenlīċe wilniġe þæt hē scyle his hlīsan tōbrǣdan ofer ealle eorþan, hē ne mæġ þæt forðbringan, for

---

22  The genitives are partitive with *hwæt*. A literal translation would be 'what of that which is generous . . .'.

23  *se ēower ġilp*: that fame of yours.

24  *on þām fiftan dæle healfum*: on half of the fifth part.

25  *mid ealle*: and so forth.

26  *Tō hwon*: for what purpose (*hwon* being an alternate instrumental form of *hwā* – see §5.3).

27  *hwelċe dysiġe*: an instrumental phrase, 'for what folly'.

28  Cicero's *De Republica*, known even to Boethius mainly through the commentary on a part of it in Macrobius, *In Somnium Scipionis*, which was very likely known to the Anglo-Saxons in Alfred's time.

29  The antecedent of *hē* is *nama*.

30  *Hwæt wēnstū hū miċelne hlīsan*: how much fame do you think.

þām þe þāra ðēoda þēawas sint swīðe unġelīċe ond hiora ġesetenessa swīðe mislica, swā ðætte þæt on ōðrum lande betst līcode, þætte þæt bið hwīlum on ðǣm ōðrum tǣlwyrðlicosð,[31] ond ēac miċles wītes wyrðe. [33] For ðǣm ne mæġ nān mon habban ġeliċ lof on ǣlċum londe, for þon ðe on ǣlċum londe ne līcað þæt on ōðrum līcað. [34] For ðȳ sceolde ǣlċ mon bīon on ðǣm wel ġehealden þæt hē on his āgnum earde līcode. [35] Þēah hē nū māran wilniġe, hē ne mæġ furðum þæt forðbringan, for þǣm þe seldhwonne bið þætte āuht monegum monnum ānes hwæt[32] liciġe. [36] For þȳ wyrð oft gōdes monnes lof āleġen inne in þǣre ilcan þēode þe hē on hāmfæst bið, ond ēac for þām þe hit oft swīðe sārlīċe ġebyrede þurh þā heardsælþa þāra wrītera ðæt hī for heora slǣwðe ond for ġīmelēste ond ēac for reċċelēste forlēton unwriten þāra monna ðēawas ond hiora dǣda, þe on hiora dagum formǣroste ond weorðġeornuste wǣron. [37] Ond þēah hī nū eall hiora līf ond hira dǣda āwriten hæfden, swā swā hī sceoldon ġif hī dohten, hū ne[33] forealdodon þā ġewritu þēah ond losodon þonēcan þe hit wǣre,[34] swā some swā þā wrīteras dydon, ond ēac þā ðe hī ymb writon? [38] Ond ēow þinċð þēah þæt ġē hæbben ēċe āre ġif ġē mæġen on ealre ēowerre worulde[35] ġeearniġan þæt ġē hæbben gōdne hlīsan æfter ēowrum dagum.

[39] 'Ġif þū nū ġetelest þā hwīla þisses andweardan līfes ond þisses hwīlendlican wið þæs unġeendodan līfes hwīla, hwæt bið hit þonne? [40] Tele nū þā lenġe þǣre hwīle þe þū þīn ēage on beprēwan mæġe wið tēn ðūsend wintra; þonne habbað þā hwīla hwæthwugu onlīċes,[36] þēah hit lȳtel sīe, þæt is þonne þæt heora ǣġþer hæfð ende. [41] Tele nū þonne þæt tēn þūsend ġēara, ġe ēac mā ġif þū wille,[37] wið þæt ēċe ond þæt unġeendode līf. [42] Þonne ne findst þū þǣr nāuht anlīċes, forðām þæt tēn ðūsend ġēara, þēah hit lang ðinċe, āscortaþ, ond þæs ōðres nǣfre ne cymð nān ende.[38] [43] For þǣm hit nis nō tō metanne[39] þæt ġeendodlīċe wið ðæt unġeendodlīċe. [44] Þēah þū nū telle from þises middanġeardes fruman oð ðone ende, ond mete þonne þā ġēar wið þæt ðe nǣnne ende nǣfð, þonne ne bið þǣr nāuht anlīċes. [45] Swā bið ēac se hlīsa þāra formǣrra monna; þēah hē hwīlum lang sīe, ond fela ġēara þurhwuniġe, hē bið þēah swīðe scort tō metanne wið ðone þe nǣfre ne ġeendað.

---

[31]  The letter-sequence *sð* sometimes appears instead of *st* in early manuscripts.

[32]  *ānes hwæt*: any one thing.

[33]  *hū ne*: would not . . . ?

[34]  *þonēcan þe hit wǣre*: as soon as it was done.

[35]  *on ealre ēowerre worulde*: for you whole lives.

[36]  *hwæthwugu onlīċes*: literally 'something of what is similar'; translate 'some similarity'.

[37]  For *ġe ēac mā ġif þū wille* the Bodley text (Cotton is unavailable here and Junius is no help) has *ge þeah þu ma wille* 'and although you want more' or 'and nevertheless you want more', neither of which makes sense in this context. There is no equivalent phrase in the Latin source.

[38]  *Nān ende* governs the partitive genitive *þæs ōðres* at the beginning of this clause.

[39]  For *þǣm hit nis nō tō metanne*: 'Therefore one ought not to compare'. For this use of the inflected infinitive, see §7.9.1.

[46] Ond ġē ne reċċað ðēah hweðer ġē āuht tō gōde dōn wið ǣnegum ōþrum þingum būton wið þām lӯtlan lofe þæs folces, ond wið þǣm scortan hlīsan þe wē ǣr ymb sprǣcon. [47] Earniað⁴⁰ þæs ond forsīoð þā cræftas ēoweres inġeðonces ond ēowres andġietes ond ēowre⁴¹ ġesceādwīsnesse, ond woldon habban ēowerra gōdena weorca mēde æt fremdra monna cwiddunge. [48] Wilniað þǣrtō þǣre mēde þe ġē tō Gode sceolden.⁴²

[49] 'Hwæt, þū ġehērdest þætte ġiōdagum ġelomp þæt ān swīðe wīs mon ond swīðe rīċe ongan fandian ānes ūðwitan ond hine bismrode for ðǣm hē hine swā orgellīċe ūp āhōf ond bodode þæs þæt hē ūðwita wǣre. [50] Ne cӯðde hē hit mid nǣnum cræftum, ac mid lēasum ond ofermōdlicum ġelpe. [51] Þā wolde se wīsa mon his fandian hwæðer hē swā wīs wǣre swā hē self wēnde þæt hē wǣre. [52] Ongon hine þā hyspan ond hearmcwidian. [53] Þā ġehērde se ūðwita swīðe ġeþyldelīċe þæs wīsan monnes word sume hwīle, ac siððan hē his hispinge ġehēred hæfde, þā scylde hē ongēan swīðe unġeþyldelīċe, þēah hē ǣr līċette þæt hē ūðwita wǣre; ahsode⁴³ hine þā eft hwæðer him þūhte þæt hē ūþwita wǣre þe nǣre. [54] Ðā andswarode se wīsa mon him ond cwæð, "iċ wolde cweþan þæt þū ūðwita wǣre, ġif þū ġeðyldiġ wǣre ond ġesūgian meahte".⁴⁴ [55] Hū langsum wæs him se hlīsa þe hē ǣr mid lēasungum wilnode? [56] Hū ne forbǣrst hē þā þǣrrihte for ðǣm ānum andwyrde? [57] Hwæt forstōd þonne þǣm betstum monnum þe ǣr ūs wǣron þæt hī swā swīðe wilnodon þæs īdelan ġelpes ond þæs hlīsan æfter heora dēaþe, oððe hwæt forstent hit þǣm þe nū sindon? [58] Þӯ wǣre ǣlcum men māre þearf þæt hē wilnode gōdra cræfta þonne lēases hlīsan. [59] Hwæt hæfð hē æt þām hlīsan æfter þæs līċhoman ġedāle ond þǣre sāwle? [60] Hū ne witon wē þæt ealle men līċhomlīċe sweltað, ond þēah sīo sāwl bið libbende? [61] Ac sīo sāwl færð swīðe frīolīċe tō hefonum siððan hīo ontīġed bið ond of þǣm carcerne þæs līċhoman onlēsed bið. [62] Hēo forsihð þonne eall ðās eorðlican þing ond fæġnað þæs þæt hīo mōt brūcan þæs heofonlican⁴⁵ siððan hīo bið ābrogden from ðǣm eorðlican. [63] Þonne þæt mōd him selfum ġewita bið Godes willan.'

[64] Ðā se Wīsdōm þā þis spel āreaht hæfde, ðā ongan hē ġyddian ond ðus singende cwæð:

---

⁴⁰ The unexpressed subject of *earniað* (*not* an imperative), and of the other verbs in this and the following sentence, is *ġē*.

⁴¹ Feminine genitive singular; compare dative *ēowerre* 38. When the vowel of the second syllable of *ēowerre* is dropped, double -rr- gets simplified following another consonant (see §7.2.1, item 4).

⁴² *þǣrto*: from that source. *tō Gode*: from God. The infinitive that one expects to find with *sceolden* is unexpressed.

⁴³ The unexpressed subject of *ahsode* is the false philosopher.

⁴⁴ The translation alters the story somewhat. In Boethius's version the false philosopher sits patiently through the man's harangue and then says, 'can you see now that I'm a philosopher?' – thereby proving that he is not. Alfred's version, in which the false philosopher first defends himself and then asks the question, is less concise.

⁴⁵ Understand *þinges* with *heofonlican*.

[65] Ġif nū hæleða hwone    hlīsan lyste,
unnytne ġelp    āgan wille,
þonne iċ hine wolde    wordum biddan
þæt hē hine ǣghwonon ūtan    ymbeþōhte,[46]
sweotole ymbsāwe    sūð, ēast and west,
hū wīdġil sint    wolcnum ymbūtan
heofones hwealfe.[47]    [66] Hiġesnotrum mæġ
ēaðe ðinċan    þæt þēos eorðe sīe
eall[48] for ðæt ōðer    uniġmet[49] lȳtel,
þēah hīo unwīsum    wīdġel þinċe,
on stede strongliċ    stēorlēasum men.
[67] Þēah[50] mæġ þone wīsan    on ġewitlocan
þǣre ġitsunge    ġelpes scamian[51]
ðonne hine þæs hlīsan    heardost lysteð,
and hē þēah ne mæġ    þone tōbrēdan
ofer ðās nearowan    nǣniġe ðinga[52]
eorðan sċēatas:    is ðæt unnet ġelp!
[68] Ēalā, ofermōdan,    hwī ēow ā lyste
mid ēowrum swīran    selfra willum[53]
þæt swǣre ġioc    symle underlūtan?
[69] Hwȳ ġē ymb ðæt unnet    ealniġ swincen,
þæt ġē þone hlīsan    habban tiliað
ofer ðīoda mā    þonne ēow þearf sīe?
[70] Þēah ēow nū ġesǣle    þæt ēow sūð oððe norð
þā ȳtmestan    eorðbūende
on moniġ ðīodisc    miċlum herien,
ðēah hwā ǣðele sīe    eorlġebyrdum,
welum ġeweorðad,    and on wlenċum ðīo,
duguðum dīore,    dēað þæs ne scrīfeð
þonne him rūm forlǣt    rodora Waldend,

---

[46]    *hine ǣghwonon utan ymbeþōhte*: consider everywhere all around himself. *Utan* is often paired either with the preposition or the verb prefix *ymb(e)* to mean 'round about'. Here the combination has the force of a preposition with *hine* as its object.

[47]    The subject of this clause is *hwealfe*; *wolcnum* is the object of the preposition *ymbūtan*. The 'vaults' of the heavens are the heavenly spheres, which revolve around the earth and contain the moon, the sun, the planets and the fixed stars.

[48]    *Eall* here modifies *eorðe* in the preceding line.

[49]    For *unġemet*; -*iġ*- (probably pronounced [iː]) is a simplified version of the prefix *ġe*-, which appears in Middle English as *y-*.

[50]    *Þēah*: That is, despite their being wise enough to recognize the insignificance of the earth.

[51]    The genitive phrase *þǣre ġitsunge* is governed by *scamian*; the genitive *ġelpes* is governed by *ġitsunge*. Translate 'be ashamed of the greed for fame'.

[52]    *nǣniġe ðinga*: by no means; by any means.

[53]    *selfra willum*: by your own desires; of your own volition.

ac hē þone welegan    wǣdlum ġelīċe
efnmǣrne ġedēð    ǣlċes þinges.[54]
[71] Hwǣr sint nū þæs wīsan    Wēlandes[55] bān
þæs goldsmiðes,    þe wæs ġeō mǣrost?
[72] For þȳ iċ cwæð 'þæs wīsan    Wēlandes bān'
for ðȳ ængum ne mǣġ    eorðbūendra
se cræft losian    þe him Crist onlǣnð.
[73] Ne mǣġ mon ǣfre þȳ ēð    ǣnne wræċċan
his cræftes beniman    þe mon onċerran mǣġ
sunnan onswīfan[56]    and ðisne swiftan rodor[57]
of his rihtryne    rinca ǣniġ.
[74] Hwā wāt nū þæs wīsan    Wēlandes bān,
on hwelċum hī hlǣwa    hrūsan þeċċen?
[75] Hwǣr is nū se rīċa    Rōmāna wita
and se aroda    þe wē ymb sprecað,
hiora heretoga,    se ġehāten wæs
mid þǣm burgwarum    Brūtus nemned?[58]
[76] Hwǣr is ēac se wīsa    and se weorðġeorna
and se fæstrǣda    folces hyrde,
se wæs ūðwita    ǣlċes þinges
cēne and cræftiġ,    ðǣm[59] wæs Cāton nama?[60]
[77] Hī wǣron ġefyrn    forðgewitene;
nāt nǣniġ mon    hwǣr hī nū sindon.
[78] Hwæt is hiora here[61]    būton se hlīsa ān?

[54]  *ǣlċes þinges*: in all respects.

[55]   In Germanic legend, Weland the goldsmith was captured and enslaved by Niðhad, but killed his captor's two sons, impregnated his daughter, and escaped by making a pair of wings for himself. Boethius's text here asks the whereabouts of the bones of Fabricius, a military hero; presumably Alfred thought Weland a good substitute because of the etymological connection between the name Fabricius and Latin *fabricor* 'make, build'.

[56]   The auxiliary verb *mǣġ* governs two infinitives, *onċerran* and *onswīfan*; *sunnan* is the common object of both infinitives.

[57]   In ancient and medieval cosmology, the position of the earth is fixed and the heavens revolve around it once each day; that is why the *rodor* is here described as *swift*.

[58]   Either Lucius Junius Brutus, who expelled the Tarquins from Rome, or Marcus Junius Brutus, one of the assassins of Julius Caesar. The prose version of this metre shows that King Alfred thought this the latter Brutus and confused him with his inciter, Gaius Longinus Cassius. Notice that *nemned* is redundant, since this clause already contains a past participle *ġehāten*.

[59]   *Ðǣm* is a dative of possession (see §4.2.4).

[60]   Cato the Elder, whom Boethius here calls *rigidus Cato*; he was well known to the Anglo-Saxons as the supposed author of a collection of wise sayings, which circulated in both Latin and Old English.

[61]   *Here* 'army' does not normally have a sense that would be appropriate here; but 'glory' is a possibility, on the model of such words as *þrym* 'army, might, splendour'. However, since the line is unmetrical as well as difficult to understand, it is likely that the text is corrupt here.

[79] Se is ēac tō lȳtel    swelċra lārīowa,[62]
for ðǣm þā magorincas    māran wyrðe
wǣron on worulde.    [80] Ac hit is wyrse nū
þæt ġeond þās eorðan    ǣghwǣr sindon
hiora ġelīcan    hwōn ymbsprǣċe,
sume openlīċe    ealle forġitene,
þæt hī se hlīsa    hīwcūðe ne mæġ
foremǣre weras    forð ġebrenġan.[63]
[81] Þēah ġē nū wēnen    and wilniġen
þæt ġē lange tīd    libban mōten,
hwæt īow ǣfre þȳ bet    bīo oððe þinċe?[64]
[82] For ðǣm þe nāne forlēt,    þēah hit[65] lang ðinċe,
dēað æfter dogorrīme,    þonne hē hæfð Drihtnes lēafe,
hwæt þonne hæbbe    hæleþa ǣniġ,
guma æt þǣm ġilpe,    ġif hine ġegrīpan mōt
se ēċa dēað    æfter þissum?[66]

# 11   A Lyric for Advent

This is the fifth in a collection of twelve Advent lyrics (the first a fragment), based on a group of antiphons sung at vespers during the Advent season. The antiphon that is the source of this lyric reads, *O Oriens, splendor lucis aeternae et Sol iustitiae, veni et illumina sedentes in tenebris et umbra mortis*: 'O Rising Sun, radiance of eternal light and Sun of righteousness, come and illuminate those who sit in darkness and the shadow of death.'

You may consult this poem in its context in one of the editions of the Exeter Book (see textual note, p. 266): Krapp and Dobbie [69] vol. 3 and Muir [85]. The lyrics were edited separately (with a translation) by Campbell [27].

Ēalā earendel,    enġla beorhtast,
ofer middanġeard    monnum sended,
ond sōðfæsta    sunnan lēoma,

[62]  *swelċra lārīowa*: for such teachers.
[63]  These two lines are difficult. With an assist from the Latin (*nec fama notos efficit*) and Alfred's prose translation (*þæt se hlīsa hīe furðum cūþe ne ġedēð*), translate 'that fame cannot bring forth very famous men as familiar', that is, make famous men familiar to us.
[64]  'What will ever be or seem better for you because of that?'
[65]  That is, life.
[66]  The Cotton text has *worulde* after the last word. It is presumably someone's gloss, which a scribe has incorporated, for it is unmetrical, ungrammatical and unnecessary.

torht ofer tunglas,  þū tīda ġehwane
5  of sylfum þē  symle inlīhtes.[1]
Swā þū, God of Gode  ġearo ācenned,
sunu sōþan fæder,  sweġles in wuldre
būtan anġinne  ǣfre wǣre,
swā þec nū for þearfum  þīn āgen ġeweorc
10  bideð þurh byldo  þæt þū þā beorhtan[2] ūs
sunnan onsende,  ond þē sylf[3] cyme
þæt ðū inlēohte  þā þe longe ǣr,
þrosme beþeahte  ond in þēostrum hēr,
sǣton sinneahtes,  synnum bifealdne,
15  deorc dēaþes sceadu  drēogan sceoldan.
Nū wē hyhtfulle  hǣlo ġelȳfað
þurh þæt word Godes  weorodum brungen,
þe on frymðe wæs  fæder ælmihtigum
efenēċe mid God,  ond nū eft ġewearð
20  flǣsc firena lēas  þæt sēo fǣmne ġebær
ġeōmrum tō ġēoce.  God wæs mid ūs
ġesewen būtan synnum;  somod eardedon
mihtiġ Meotudes bearn  ond se monnes sunu
ġeþwǣre on þēode.  Wē þæs þonc magon
25  secgan siġedryhtne  symle bi ġewyrhtum,[4]
þæs þe hē hine sylfne ūs  sendan wolde.

# 12  The Battle of Maldon

In August 991 Byrhtnoth, *ealdorman* of Essex, encountered an army of Vikings camped on Northey Island in the estuary of the River Blackwater near the town of Maldon,

---

[1]  The second-person singular ending -*s* is common in early texts and in some non-West Saxon dialects. Although the language of the Exeter Book is predominantly West Saxon, the Advent Lyrics may originally have been written in an Anglian dialect (Mercian or Northumbrian).

[2]  This adjective modifies *sunnan* in the next line (see §8.1).

[3]  *Þē* is a dative, apparently an unusual (and untranslatable) reflexive with *cuman*. *Sylf* is the nominative subject of *cyme* and should be translated 'you yourself'. An alternative to this rather awkward reading, suggested by an early editor, is to emend *þē* to *þū* and read the phrase *þū sylf* as the subject: 'you yourself'.

[4]  *Bi ġewyrhtum* is often translated 'for his acts' or the like (i.e. we thank God for his acts): but *ġewyrht* generally refers either to one's merits or deserts or to one's deeds as deserving of praise, blame or recompense, and the phrase *be ġewyrhtum* elsewhere means 'according to one's deserts'. The thought here seems to be that we are grateful to God in that his coming has enabled us to be rewarded according to our deserts.

Essex. This island was (as it still is) connected to the mainland by a causeway which was covered at high tide. As the causeway was flooded when the armies met, battle could not be joined; when the tide went out, uncovering the causeway, the English were able to keep the Vikings bottled up on the island. Then, in a notable tactical blunder, Byrhtnoth decided to allow the Viking army to cross to the mainland, presumably so as to break the stalemate. In the battle that followed, Byrhthnoth was slain, much of his army routed, and many (perhaps most) of those who remained slaughtered.

*The Battle of Maldon*, which commemorates this disaster, is one of a number of poems that find inspiration in defeat: others include *The Song of Roland*, a fictionalized account of the annihilation of a Frankish army by Saracens; a number of Serbian epics, which dwell upon the fourteenth-century defeat of the Serbs at the Battle of Kosovo and their subsequent domination by the Ottomans; and of course Tennyson's *Charge of the Light Brigade*, written on the occasion of one of the most famous military disasters in English history. The poetry of defeat, in giving voice to a nation's grief, can stir nationalist sentiment and rouse soldiers to deeds of valour (Tennyson's poem, famously, was distributed in pamphlet form to soldiers in the Crimea). It can also express nostalgia for the values of a supposedly greater national past. *The Battle of Maldon* does all these things. The anonymous poet is largely uninterested either in demonizing the Vikings or in the carnage of the battle, and his treatment of the cowards who run away is cursory. Rather, he focuses intensely on the thoughts and words of the men who stay, often juxtaposing their own resolute statements with foreshadowings or spare notices of their deaths. These doomed warriors are predominantly young (one of the most common words that describe them is *hyse* 'young man'): and yet they cast their lot with the aged Byrhtwold, whose sole remaining wish is to lie by the side of his lord. Even as defeat grows more certain, they hold their ground or, more often, advance. Indeed, *forð* 'forth, forward' is the poem's most prominent adverb, being used ten times of the English troops. But *forð* is also associated with death in Old English: in *The Wanderer* (81), death is *forðweġ* 'the way forward', while in *The Dream of the Rood* (132–3) the narrator laments that his friends *forð ġewiton* 'have gone forward' into death; and the most common euphemism meaning 'to die' is *forðfēran* 'go forth', attested hundreds of times in the *Anglo-Saxon Chronicle* and elsewhere. The young warriors who go *forð* to the next life subscribe to the code of absolute loyalty to one's lord described as early as the second century by the Roman historian Tacitus and celebrated in the *Anglo-Saxon Chronicle* entry for 755 (see 'Cynewulf and Cyneheard', no. 4 above). As English fortunes declined during the decades following 991, partly because of English treachery, this code of loyalty must have seemed more and more to be a thing of the past.

The poem was already fragmentary, its opening and closing lines lost, when the unique manuscript was destroyed in the Cotton Library fire of 1731. Fortunately a transcript had been made by Deputy-Librarian David Casley; all subsequent editions are based on this transcript. The standard recent edition is Scragg [101]; the editions in Pope and Fulk [95] and Mitchell and Robinson [81] are also valuable. For a collection of useful studies of the battle and its context, see Scragg [102].

The language of this poem is late and fairly easy. You should be aware that the ending -*um* sometimes appears as -*on* or -*an* and that there is no formal distinction between indicative and subjunctive in the past plural.

brocen wurde.[1]

Hēt[2] þā hyssa hwæne hors forlǣtan,
feor āfȳsan and forð gangan,
hicgan tō handum and tō hiġe gōdum.

5 Þā þæt Offan mǣġ ǣrest onfunde
þæt se eorl[3] nolde yrhðo ġeþolian,
hē lēt him þā of handon[4] lēofne flēogan
hafoc[5] wið þæs holtes and tō þǣre hilde stōp.
Be þām man mihte oncnāwan þæt se cniht nolde

10 wācian æt þām wīġe þā hē tō wǣpnum fēng.[6]
Ēac him wolde Ēadriċ his ealdre gelǣstan
frēan tō ġefeohte; ongan þā forð beran
gār tō gūþe. Hē hæfde gōd ġeþanc
þā hwīle þe[7] hē mid handum healdan mihte

15 bord and brād swurd; bēot hē ġelǣste
þā hē ætforan his frēan feohtan sceolde.

    Ðā þǣr Byrhtnōð ongan beornas trymian,
rād and rǣdde, rincum tǣhte
hū hī sceoldon standan and þone stede healdan

20 and bæd þæt hyra randas rihte hēoldon[8]
fæste mid folman and ne forhtedon nā.
Þā hē hæfde þæt folc fæġere ġetrymmed,
hē līhte þā mid lēodon þǣr him lēofost wæs,
þǣr hē his heorðwerod[9] holdost wiste.

[1] No plausible guess has ever been made as to the content of the sentence that ended with these two words. As the surviving fragment takes up before the beginning of the battle, presumably little has been lost: perhaps one leaf of the original manuscript, or about fifty-four lines.

[2] The subject of *Hēt* is Byrhtnoth.

[3] In this poem, *eorl* always refers to Byrhtnoth. Before the late tenth century the word can be used of any nobleman or warrior (see, for example, *Wanderer* 12); only in the later period does it specify rank or position – in this case a nobleman appointed by the king to rule a territory, at this period usually called an *ealdorman*.

[4] *him þā of handon*: then from his hands. The dative of possession (§4.2.4) is often used in connection with the body and its parts: see also ll. 119, 145, 152 and 318.

[5] The adjective *lēofne* modifies *hafoc*. Nouns and their modifiers are separated by other sentence elements more often in poetry than in prose. Various sources show that hawking was a favourite sport among the Anglo-Saxon nobility. Releasing the hawk shows that the young man has ceased to think of this day's outing as a lark.

[6] *tō wǣpnum fēng*: took up weapons.

[7] The clause beginning *þā hwīle þe* 'for as long as' suggests that the time will come when Ēadriċ will be unable to hold shield and sword: this is the first of many hints of the impending disaster.

[8] The missing subject of *hēoldon* is *hī* 'they'. The context tells us that the verb is subjunctive; but by this time there is no longer a formal distinction between indicative and subjunctive in the past plural (§7.2.3).

[9] The *heorðwerod* is the troop of retainers who share Byrhtnoth's hearth: they are members of his household, who attend him in his hall.

25        Þā stōd on stæðe,   stīðlīċe clypode
          wīċinga ār,   wordum mælde;
          se on bēot[10] ābēad   brimlīþendra[11]
          ærænde tō þām eorle   þær hē on ōfre stōd:
          'Mē sendon tō þē   sæmen snelle,
30        hēton ðē secgan[12]   þæt þū mōst sendan raðe
          bēagas wið ġebeorge;   and ēow[13] betere is
          þæt ġē þisne gārrǣs   mid gafole forġyldon
          þonne wē swā hearde   hilde dǣlon.
          Ne þurfe wē ūs spillan   ġif ġē spēdaþ tō þām;[14]
35        wē willað wið þām golde   grið fæstnian.
          Ġyf þū þat ġerǣdest   þe hēr riċost eart
          þæt þū þīne lēoda   lȳsan wille,
          syllan sǣmannum   on hyra sylfra dōm[15]
          feoh wið frēode   and niman frið æt ūs,
40        wē willaþ mid þām sceattum   ūs tō scype gangan,
          on flot fēran   and ēow friþes healdan.'[16]
                  Byrhtnōð maþelode,   bord hafenode,
          wand wācne æsc,   wordum mælde,
          yrre and ānrǣd   āġeaf him andsware:
45        'Gehȳrst þū, sǣlida,   hwæt þis folc seġeð?
          Hī willað ēow tō gafole   gāras syllan
          ǣttrynne ord[17]   and ealde swurd,
          þā hereġeatu[18]   þe ēow æt hilde ne dēah.[19]

[10]  on bēot: boastingly.
[11]  brimlīþendra: 'of the seafarers'. An adjective is here used as a noun, as is common in poetry (§15.2.3).
[12]  hēton ðē secgan: 'commanded (me) to say to you'. For the construction, see §7.9.1.
[13]  Notice the shift from the second-person singular pronoun (addressing only Byrhtnoth) to a plural pronoun (addressing the whole English army).
[14]  tō þām: to that extent; enough.
[15]  on hyra sylfra dōm: 'according to their own judgement'. This is a Nordic legalism, illustrated frequently in the Icelandic family sagas: 'self-judgement' is a right granted to one party in a dispute to decide the terms of a settlement. The equivalent Old English phrase is āgen dōm (see 'Cynewulf and Cyneheard', 4/11).
[16]  ēow friþes healdan: probably 'maintain you in peace'. The messenger seems to be proposing that the English become the vikings' dependants.
[17]  The motif of the poisoned weapon is attested in Old English poetry (see Beowulf, l. 1459), but especially common in Old Norse. It is unknown if this is a figure of speech (ǣttrene meaning 'deadly') or reflective of some actual practice.
[18]  War-equipment would presumably make up part of the payment if the English were to pay off the vikings. But hereġeatu also means 'heriot', a tax (usually of armaments) paid to a lord on the death of a dependant. If Byrhtnoth has this meaning in mind as well as the literal 'war-equipment', he is choosing a rhetorically sophisticated way to reject the dependent relationship offered by the Vikings.
[19]  We expect a plural verb to agree with hereġeatu; but see §11.5.

Brimmanna boda, ābēod eft onġēan:

50 seġe þīnum lēodum miċċle lāþre spell,

þæt hēr stynt unforcūð eorl mid his werode

þe wile ġealgean ēþel þysne,

Æþelrēdes[20] eard ealdres mīnes

folc and foldan. Feallan sceolon

55 hæþene æt hilde! Tō hēanliċ mē þinċeð

þæt ġē mid ūrum sceattum tō scype gangon

unbefohtene, nū ġē þus feor hider

on ūrne eard in becōmon.

Ne sceole ġē swā sōfte sinc ġegangan;

60 ūs sceal ord and ecg ǣr ġesēman

grim gūðplega ǣr wē gofol syllon.'

Hēt þā bord beran, beornas gangan[21]

þæt hī on þām ēasteðe ealle stōdon.

Ne mihte[22] þǣr for wætere werod tō þām ōðrum;

65 þǣr cōm flōwende flōd æfter ebban,

lucon lagustrēamas. Tō lang hit him þūhte

hwænne hī tōgædere gāras bēron.

Hī þǣr Pantan strēam mid prasse bestōdon

Ēastseaxena ord and se æschere.

70 Ne mihte hyra ǣniġ ōþrum derian

būton hwā þurh flānes flyht fyl ġenāme.

Se flōd ūt ġewāt.[23] Þā flotan stōdon ġearowe

wīċinga fela, wīges ġeorne.

Hēt þā hæleða hlēo healdan þā bricge[24]

75 wigan wīġheardne, se wæs hāten Wulfstān,

cāfne mid his cynne;[25] þæt wæs Ċeolan sunu

þe ðone forman man mid his francan[26] ofscēat

þe þǣr baldlīcost on þā bricge stōp.

Þǣr stōdon mid Wulfstāne wigan unforhte,

---

[20] For a brief account of Æthelræd and his reign, see 'The Martyrdom of Ælfheah', n. 1.

[21] The phrases *bord beran* and *beornas gangan* appear to be grammatically parallel; but the first is the construction seen in l.30 (*bord* being the object of *beran*), while in the second *beornas* is the object of *Hēt* and the subject of *gangan*.

[22] The expected infinitive for this auxiliary, *gān* or *gangan*, is missing. Verbs meaning 'to go' are frequently omitted in constructions like this one.

[23] The receding tide uncovers the causeway between the island and the mainland.

[24] The causeway that links the island with the mainland is sometimes referred to as a *bricg* (here, 78, 85) and sometimes as a *ford* (81, 88).

[25] *mid his cynne*: like the rest of his family.

[26] A *franca* was originally a spear in the Frankish style; but in this text and elsewhere *franca* appears to be a generic term for 'spear'.

80     Ælfere and Maccus,    mōdiġe twēġen,
          þā noldon æt þām forda    flēam ġewyrċan,[27]
          ac hī fæstliċe    wið ðā fȳnd weredon
          þā hwīle þe hī wæpna    wealdan mōston.

          Þā hī þæt onġēaton    and ġeorne ġesāwon
85     þæt hī þær briċgweardas    bitere fundon,
          ongunnon lytegian þā    lāðe ġystas:
          bædon þæt hī ūpgang    āgan mōston,
          ofer þone ford faran,    fēþan lædan.
          Ðā se eorl ongan    for his ofermōde[28]
90     ālȳfan landes tō fela    lāþere ðēode.
          Ongan ċeallian þā    ofer cald wæter
          Byrhtelmes bearn    (beornas ġehlyston):
          'Nū ēow is ġerȳmed;    gāð riċene tō ūs,
          guman tō gūþe.    God āna wāt
95     hwā þære wælstōwe    wealdan mōte.'
          Wōdon[29] þā wælwulfas    (for wætere ne murnon),
          wīċinga werod    west ofer Pantan,
          ofer scīr wæter    scyldas wēgon,
          lidmen tō lande    linde bæron.
100    Þær onġēan gramum[30]    ġearowe stōdon
          Byrhtnōð mid beornum;    hē mid bordum hēt
          wyrċan þone wīhagan[31]    and þæt werod[32] healdan
          fæste wið fēondum.    Þā wæs feohte nēh
          tīr æt ġetohte.    Wæs sēo tīd cumen

---

[27] *flēam ġewyrċan*: take flight.

[28] The precise meaning of *ofermōd* in this line has been much discussed. *Ofermōd* occurs as both noun and adjective in Old English, and several related words (e.g. *ofermōdiġness*) are also well attested, always in the sense 'pride', 'proud', and always used pejoratively. Some scholars have attempted to find a meaning for *ofermōd* that does not imply criticism of Byrhtnoth, basing their arguments on the frequent non-pejorative use of *mōd* and *mōdiġ* in secular texts: 'spirit, courage'; 'spirited, courageous'. It must be admitted that, since *ofermōd* is otherwise found only in religious texts, we cannot be certain of its meaning in this secular context. It is possible that the element *mōd* here means 'spirit, courage'. But the prefix *ofer-* must mean 'excessive': whatever the precise sense of *mōd*, there can be no doubt that Byrhtnoth has too much of it. The phrase *landes tō fela* in the next line also suggests criticism of Byrhtnoth's judgement.

[29] Though Old English *wadan* comes to Modern English as 'wade', its sense here is 'advance': it does not suggest that the Vikings are wading to battle.

[30] *gramum*: the fierce ones.

[31] *hēt wyrċan þone wīhagan*: 'commanded (someone) to form the shield-wall' (for the construction, see note to l. 30). The shield-wall is a defensive formation in which men stand in a line close enough so that their shields overlap. The formation is also called a *scyldburh* (l. 242) and a *bordweall* (l. 277).

[32] *Þæt werod* is the object of *hēt* (101), not of *healdan*.

105      þæt þǣr fǣġe men    feallan sceoldon.
        Þǣr wearð hrēam āhafen.    Hremmas wundon,
        earn ǣses ġeorn.[33]    Wæs on eorþan ċyrm.
        Hī lēton þā of folman    fēolhearde speru,
        ġegrundene   gāras flēogan.
110      Bogan wǣron bysiġe;    bord ord onfēng.
        Biter wæs se beadurǣs.    Beornas fēollon
        on ġehwæðere hand,    hyssas lāgon.
        Wund wearð Wulfmǣr,    wælrǣste ġeċēas
        Byrhtnōðes mǣġ;    hē mid billum wearð
115      his swuster sunu[34]    swīðe forhēawen.
        Þǣr wearð wīċingum    wiþerlēan āġyfen.
        Ġehȳrde iċ þæt Ēadweard    ānne slōge
        swīðe mid his swurde,    swenġes ne wyrnde
        þæt him æt fōtum fēoll    fǣġe cempa.
120      Þæs him his ðēoden    þanc ġesǣde
        þām būrþēne    þā hē byre hæfde.
            Swā stemnetton[35]    stīðhicgende
        hysas æt hilde;    hogodon ġeorne
        hwā þǣr mid orde    ǣrost mihte
125      on fǣġean men    feorh ġewinnan,
        wigan mid wǣpnum.    Wæl fēol on eorðan.
        Stōdon stædefæste;    stihte hī Byrhtnōð,
        bæd þæt hyssa ġehwylċ    hogode tō wīġe
        þe on Denon[36] wolde    dōm ġefeohtan.
130         Wōd þā wīġes heard,[37]    wǣpen ūp āhōf,
        bord tō ġebeorge,    and wið þæs beornes stōp.
        Ēode swā ānrǣd    eorl tō þām ċeorle;
        ǣġþer hyra ōðrum    yfeles hogode.
        Sende ðā se sǣrinc    sūþerne gār[38]

---

[33] For the 'beasts of battle' theme, see §14.3.2.

[34] A man's relationship with his sister's son was particularly close in early Germanic societies, as noted already by the second-century historian Tacitus (*Germania* 20).

[35] *Stemnetton* is attested only here, and its meaning is uncertain. It is usually connected with *stefn* 'root, trunk' and taken to mean 'stand firm'. Another possible connection is *stefn* 'voice' with a meaning 'fall silent'.

[36] *Dene* yields Modern English 'Dane', but in Old English it is used of any Norseman. Other records of the military activity in 991 suggest that this Viking army was led by Norwegians.

[37] *wīġes heard*: 'the one fierce in battle'. This is presumably one of the Vikings, and the *beorn* of l. 131 is Byrhtnoth. The lack of clarity in the text at this point suggests the possibility of textual corruption.

[38] Spears of southern make or southern design (Frankish or English) were especially prized by the Vikings.

135   þæt ġewundod wearð wigena hlāford.
     Hē scēaf þā mid ðām scylde þæt se sceaft tōbærst
     and þæt spere sprenġde þæt hit sprang onġēan.[39]
     Ġegremod wearð se gūðrinc; hē mid gāre stang
     wlancne wīċing þe him þā wunde forġeaf.
140   Frōd wæs se fyrdrinc: hē lēt his francan wadan
     þurh ðæs hysses hals, hand wīsode[40]
     þæt hē on þām færsceaðan feorh ġeræhte.
     Ðā hē ōþerne[41] ofstlīċe scēat
     þæt sēo byrne tōbærst; hē wæs on brēostum wund
145   þurh ðā hringlocan; him æt heortan stōd
     ætterne ord. Se eorl wæs þē blīþra;
     hlōh þā mōdi man, sæde Metode þanc
     ðæs dæġweorces þe him Drihten forġeaf.
      Forlēt þā drenga[42] sum daroð of handa
150   flēogan of folman þæt se tō forð ġewāt
     þurh ðone æþelan Æþelrēdes þeġen.[43]
     Him be healfe stōd hyse unweaxen,
     cniht on ġecampe, se full cāflīċe
     bræd of þām beorne blōdiġne gār,
155   Wulfstānes bearn, Wulfmǣr se ġeonga
     forlēt forheardne[44] faran eft onġēan;
     ord in ġewōd þæt se on eorþan læġ
     þe his þēoden ǣr þearle ġeræhte.
     Ēode þā ġesyrwed secg tō þām eorle;
160   hē wolde þæs beornes bēagas ġefetiġan
     rēaf and hringas and ġerēnod swurd.[45]

---

[39] Interpretation of these ll. 136–7 is complicated by the verb *sprenġan*, which elsewhere in Old English means 'scatter, sprinkle', definitions which are not appropriate here. Etymologically, however, *sprenġan* is a causative verb from *springan* 'spring', and so might mean 'cause to spring'. The passage plainly states that Byrhtnoth struck the spear lodged in his body violently with his shield, causing it to burst; then it appears to say that this action made the spear spring so that it sprang out of the wound.

[40] *hand wīsode*: his hand guided it.

[41] 'Another Viking', not 'another spear': there is little point in wounding a man in the body when you have just driven a spear through his neck.

[42] This is the earliest attestation of the Norse loan *dreng*, which the poet perhaps thought an appropriate choice of words for a Viking warrior. The word is common in Middle English.

[43] That is, Byrhtnoth, now wounded again.

[44] *forheardne*: the very hard (spear).

[45] To strip the body of a fallen enemy was standard practice, and there was no dishonour in doing so (Beowulf returns from battle in Frisia carrying the armour of thirty men he has killed). Such looting is depicted in the borders of the Bayeux Tapestry. Here, of course, the *ġesyrwed secg* is attempting to do so prematurely.

Þā Byrhtnōð brǣd   bill of scēðe
brād and brūneccg   and on þā byrnan slōh.
Tō raþe hine ġelette   lidmanna sum
165  þā hē þæs eorles   earm āmyrde.
Fēoll þā tō foldan   fealohilte swurd;
ne mihte hē ġehealdan   heardne mēċe,
wǣpnes wealdan.   Þā ġȳt þæt word ġecwæð
hār hilderinc,[46]   hyssas bylde,
170  bæd gangan forð   gōde ġefēran;
ne mihte þā on fōtum lenġ   fæste ġestandan.
Hē tō heofenum wlāt:[47]
'Ġeþancie[48] þē,   ðēoda Waldend,
ealra þǣra wynna   þe iċ on worulde ġebād.
175  Nū iċ āh, milde Metod,   mǣste þearfe
þæt þū mīnum gāste   gōdes ġeunne
þæt mīn sāwul tō ðē   sīðian mōte
on þīn ġeweald,   þēoden engla,
mid friþe fēran.   Iċ eom frymdi tō þē[49]
180  þæt hī helsceaðan   hȳnan ne mōton.'[50]
Ðā hine hēowon   hǣðene scealcas
and bēġen þā beornas   þe him biġ stōdon:
Ælfnōð and Wulmǣr[51]   bēġen lāgon
ðā onemn hyra frēan   feorh ġesealdon.
185      Hī bugon þā fram beaduwe   þe þǣr bēon noldon.
Þǣr wearð Oddan bearn   ǣrest on flēame
Godriċ fram gūþe   and þone gōdan forlēt
þe him mæniġne oft   mearh ġesealde.
Hē ġehlēop þone eoh   þe āhte his hlāford
190  on þām ġerǣdum   þe hit riht ne wæs,[52]
and his brōðru mid him   bēġen ærndon,
Godwine and Godwīġ   gūþe ne ġȳmdon,

---

[46]  Hār hilderinc is a common formula meaning 'old warrior'. Byrhtnoth was probably more than sixty years old at the time of this battle.

[47]  The metre indicates that one or more verses is missing here, though the sense seems reasonably complete.

[48]  The subject of ġeþancie (iċ) is omitted. Compare the first line of Cædmon's Hymn (9/12); but the construction is unusual, especially in so late a text as this. The subject may have been lost in the confusion that produced the error ġeþance for ġeþancie.

[49]  Iċ eom frymdi tō þē: I entreat you.

[50]  It was commonly believed that the fate of the soul after death would be decided by a battle fought by devils and angels.

[51]  The same as Wulfmǣr (above, 155). Contraction and the dropping of consonants were common in late Old English personal names.

[52]  þe hit riht ne wæs: (on) which it was not right (to ride).

ac wendon fram þām wīġe    and þone wudu sōhton,
flugon on þæt fæsten    and hyra fēore burgon,
195    and manna mā    þonne hit æniġ mæð wære[53]
ġyf hī þā ġeearnunga    ealle ġemundon
þe hē him tō duguþe    ġedōn hæfde.[54]
Swā him Offa on dæġ    ær āsæde
on þām meþelstede    þā hē ġemōt hæfde
200    þæt þær mōdiġlīċe    manega spræcon
þe eft æt þearfe    þolian noldon.
    Þā wearð āfeallen    þæs folces ealdor,
Æþelrēdes eorl;    ealle ġesāwon
heorðġenēatas    þæt hyra heorra læġ.
205    Þā ðær wendon forð    wlance þeġenas,
unearge men    efston ġeorne;
hī woldon þā ealle    ōðer twēġa,[55]
līf forlætan    oððe lēofne ġewrecan.
    Swā hī bylde forð    bearn Ælfriċes,
210    wiga wintrum ġeong    wordum mælde;
Ælfwine þā cwæð,    hē on ellen spræc:
'Gemunon[56] þā mæla    þe wē oft æt meodo spræcon,
þonne wē on benċe    bēot āhōfon[57]
hæleð on healle,    ymbe heard ġewinn.
215    Nū mæġ cunnian[58]    hwā cēne sȳ.
Iċ wylle mīne æþelo    eallum ġecȳþan,
þæt iċ wæs on Myrcon    miċċles cynnes:[59]
wæs mīn ealda fæder[60]    Ealhelm hāten,
wīs ealdorman    woruldġesæliġ.
220    Ne sceolon mē on þære þēode    þeġenas ætwītan
þæt iċ of ðisse fyrde    fēran wille,
eard ġesēċan,    nū mīn ealdor liġeð

---

[53]  þonne hit æniġ mæð wære: than would have been at all fitting.
[54]  A lord has a right to expect that his retainers will repay his gifts of money, armaments and land with loyal service: see Beowulf, ll. 20–4, 2864–72.
[55]  ōðer twēġa: one of two things.
[56]  Gemunon: Let us remember.
[57]  From this passage and 289–93 it is plain that Ælfwine and Offa consider a bēot made before a battle to be a binding vow, not an empty boast. But anxiety that some might not carry out their vow is frequently expressed in Old English poetry: see ll. 198–201 above, The Wanderer, ll. 70–2, and, famously, Beowulf, ll. 2864–72. Beowulf, ll. 2884–91 outlines the penalty to be paid by those whose courage has failed them.
[58]  mæġ cunnian: one may find out.
[59]  on Myrcon miċċles cynnes: of a great family in Mercia.
[60]  ealda fæder: grandfather.

forhēawen æt hilde.    Mē is þæt hearma mæst:
hē wæs ǣġþer mīn mǣġ    and mīn hlāford.'
225   Þā hē forð ēode,    fǣhðe ġemunde,
þæt hē mid orde    ānne ġerǣhte
flotan on þām folce,    þæt se on foldan læġ
forweġen mid his wǣpne.    Ongan þā winas manian
frȳnd and ġefēran    þæt hī forð ēodon.
230       Offa ġemǣlde,    æscholt āsceōc:
'Hwæt þū, Ælfwine, hafast    ealle ġemanode
þeġenas tō þearfe,[61]    nū ūre þēoden līð
eorl on eorðan.    Ūs is eallum þearf
þæt ūre ǣġhwylċ    ōþerne bylde
235   wigan tō wīġe    þā hwīle þe hē wǣpen mæġe
habban and healdan    heardne mēċe,
gār and gōd swurd.    Ūs Godriċ hæfð,
earh Oddan bearn,    ealle beswicene.
Wēnde þæs[62] formoni man,    þā hē on mēare rād
240   on wlancan þām wicge,    þæt wǣre hit ūre hlāford;
for þan wearð hēr on felda    folc totwǣmed,
scyldburh tōbrocen.[63]    Ābrēoðe his anġin,[64]
þæt hē hēr swā maniġne    man āflȳmde!'
       Lēofsunu ġemǣlde    and his linde āhōf,
245   bord tō ġebeorge;    hē þām beorne oncwæð:
'Iċ þæt ġehāte    þæt iċ heonon nelle
flēon fōtes trym,[65]    ac wille furðor gān,
wrecan on ġewinne    mīnne winedrihten.
Ne þurfon mē embe Stūrmere    stedefæste hælæð
250   wordum ætwītan,    nū mīn wine ġecranc,
þæt iċ hlāfordlēas    hām sīðie,
wende fram wīġe,    ac mē sceal wǣpen niman
ord and īren.'    Hē ful yrre wōd,
feaht fæstliċe,    flēam hē forhogode.
255       Dunnere þā cwæð,    daroð ācwehte
unorne ċeorl,    ofer eall clypode,
bæd þæt beorna ġehwylċ    Byrhtnōð wrǣce:

---

[61]   *tō þearfe*: to do what is necessary.
[62]   *Þæs* anticipates the noun clause beginning with *þæt* in the next line. It is similar to the construction found (for example) in ll. 5–6, but here the pronoun that anticipates the clause is in the genitive because *wēnan* takes a genitive object.
[63]   To 'break' the shield-wall is to create a gap in it so that warriors can attack from behind.
[64]   Apparently a mild curse, not reported elsewhere: 'May his initiative fail'. The following noun clause expands upon *anġin*.
[65]   *fōtes trym*: the length of one foot.

'Ne mæġ nā wandian    se þe wrecan þenċeð
frēan on folce,    ne for fēore murnan.'

260          Þā hī forð ēodon,    fēores hī ne rōhton.
Ongunnon þā hīredmen[66]    heardlīċe feohtan
grame gārberend    and God bædon
þæt hī mōston ġewrecan    hyra winedrihten
and on hyra fēondum    fyl ġewyrċan.

265    Him se ġȳsel[67] ongan    ġeornlīċe fylstan:
hē wæs on Norðhymbron    heardes cynnes,
Ecglāfes bearn,    him wæs Æscferð nama.
Hē ne wandode nā    æt þām wīġplegan,
ac hē fȳsde forð    flān ġenehe.

270    Hwīlon hē on bord scēat,    hwīlon beorn tæsde;
æfre embe stunde[68]    hē sealde sume wunde[69]
þā hwīle ðe hē wæpna    wealdan mōste.

          Þā ġȳt on orde stōd    Ēadweard se langa,
ġearo and ġeornful    ġylpwordum spræc

275    þæt hē nolde flēogan    fōtmæl landes,
ofer bæc[70] būgan    þā his betera leġ.
Hē bræc þone bordweall    and wið þā beornas feaht
oð þæt hē his sincġyfan    on þām sæmannum
wurðlīċe wrec    ær hē on wæle læġe.

280    Swā dyde Æþeriċ,    æþele ġefēra,
fūs and forðġeorn    feaht eornoste.
Sībyrhtes brōðor    and swīðe mæniġ ōþer
clufon cellod bord,    cēne hī weredon.

                          *  *  *

          bærst bordes læriġ,    and sēo byrne sang
285    gryrelēoða sum.[71]    Þā æt gūðe slōh
Offa þone sælidan    þæt hē on eorðan fēoll,

---

[66]    The appearance here of *hīredmen* 'household retainers' (perhaps the *heorðwerod* of l. 24) breaks the apparent progression of fighters from persons of high degree (Ælfwine and Offa) to the humble (Dunnere) followed by one who is bound to a lesser degree by the ties of lordship (the hostage). Scragg [101] p. 49 n. 95 suggests that *hīredmen* might mean simply 'soldiers'; another possibility is that the word is miswritten for *hȳrmen* or *hȳriġmen* 'mercenaries'.

[67]    To judge from this passage and 'Cynewulf and Cyneheard' (4/8), the hostage who fights loyally for his captor is likely to have been a stock narrative element.

[68]    *æfre embe stunde*: every so often.

[69]    Notice the end-rhyme *stunde . . . wunde*: this effect is unusual but not unknown in Old English alliterative poetry. See also l. 282.

[70]    *ofer bæc*: backwards.

[71]    Some matter has been lost before l. 284; the text resumes in the midst of Offa's fight with a viking (see note to these lines in Pope and Fulk [95]). It is not entirely clear whose shield has burst and whose corslet sings a terrible song.

and ðǣr Gaddes mǣġ[72]    grund ġesōhte.

Raðe wearð æt hilde    Offa forhēawen;

hē hæfde ðēah ġeforþod    þæt hē his frēan ġehēt

290    swā hē bēotode ǣr    wið his bēahġifan

þæt hī sceoldon bēġen    on burh rīdan

hāle tō hāme,    oððe on here crincgan,

on wælstōwe    wundum sweltan;

hē læġ ðeġenlīċe    ðēodne ġehende.

295        Ðā wearð borda ġebræc.    Brimmen wōdon

gūðe ġegremode;    gār oft þurhwōd

fǣġes feorhhūs.    Forð þā ēode Wīstān,

Þurstānes sunu    wið þās secgas feaht;

hē wæs on ġeþrange    hyra þrēora bana

300    ǣr him Wīġelmes bearn    on þām wæle læġe.

        Þǣr wæs stīð ġemōt.    Stōdon fæste

wigan on ġewinne.    Wīġend cruncon

wundum wēriġe.[73]    Wæl fēol on eorþan.

Ōswold and Ēadwold    ealle hwīle[74]

305    bēġen þā ġebrōþru    beornas trymedon,

hyra winemāgas    wordon bǣdon

þæt hī þǣr æt ðearfe    þolian sceoldon,

unwāclīċe    wǣpna nēotan.

        Byrhtwold maþelode,    bord hafenode

310    (se wæs eald ġenēat),    æsc ācwehte;

hē ful baldlīċe    beornas lǣrde:

'Hiġe sceal þē heardra,    heorte þē cēnre,

mōd sceal þē māre    þē ūre mæġen lȳtlað.[75]

Hēr līð ūre ealdor    eall forhēawen

---

[72]  Gadd is usually understood to be a kinsman of Offa; but the context in which Offa strikes a blow and then the kinsman of Gadd falls suggests that Gadd may be the Norseman who has been fighting with Offa. The argument against this position is that no other Viking is named in the extant poem; whether Gadd is the kinsman of Offa or of a Viking, then, is an open question.

[73]  *wundum wēriġe*: made weary by wounds. This is the rhetorical figure litotes, much favoured by Old English poets. It consists of irony (to feel weary you must be alive, but these warriors are dead), combined with understatement that nudges the ironic statement towards the literal (they are less alive for being tired). *The Dream of the Rood* 65 is similar: there the dead Christ is described as weary.

[74]  *ealle hwīle*: all the time; for the whole time.

[75]  The first three instances of *þē* (for earlier *þȳ*) are adverbs: 'therefore'; but we usually translate 'the'. The last *þē* is the conjunction: 'because'. The conjunction is usually translated 'as', but the statement is a causal one (as it still is in Modern English – §10.3): 'our mental strength must be greater *because* our physical strength is diminishing'. Indeed, mental qualities are now worth more than physical ones: none of the English warriors expects to live, and the only possible victory is the moral one of simply staying on the field.

315   gōd on grēote. Ā mæġ gnornian
     se ðe nū fram þisum wīġplegan wendan þenċeð.
     Iċ eom frōd fēores;[76] fram iċ ne wille,
     ac iċ mē be healfe mīnum hlāforde,
     be swā lēofan men licgan þenċe.'
320     Swā hī Æþelgāres bearn ealle bylde
     Godriċ tō gūþe. Oft hē gār forlēt
     wælspere windan on þā wīċingas;
     swā hē on þām folce fyrmest ēode,
     hēow and hȳnde oð þæt hē on hilde ġecranc.
325   Næs þæt nā se Godriċ þe ðā gūðe forbēah

# 13 The Wanderer

This poem is one of the finest of the Old English 'elegies', laments for the transitory nature of worldly goods. Most of the poem is in the voice of a man who, following the death of his lord, has been wandering the earth in search of another. He laments his own loss and the inevitability of loss with a poignancy that is not balanced by the brief introduction and conclusion in the voice of a Christian moralist.

 *The Wanderer* is preserved in the Exeter Book (see textual note for reading 11). It has been edited separately by Dunning and Bliss [38]; see also Klinck [68].

    Oft him ānhaga āre ġebīdeð,
    Metudes miltse, þēah þe hē mōdċeariġ
    ġeond lagulāde longe sceolde
    hrēran mid hondum hrīmċealde sæ,
5   wadan wræclāstas. Wyrd bið ful ārǣd.[1]
    Swā cwæð eardstapa, earfeþa ġemyndiġ,
    wrāþra wælsleahta, winemǣga hryre:[2]

---

[76] *frōd fēores*: advanced in life.

[1] *Arǣd* is the past participle form of the verb *ārǣdan*, which has a range of meanings such as 'arrange', 'determine', 'decree', 'appraise', 'explain', 'interpret', 'read (aloud)', 'utter'. Though the meaning of the past participle is generally 'determined, resolute', in this line it is often glossed 'predetermined, foreordained, inexorable'. But that sense of the word is not otherwise attested in Old English, and the idea of 'fate' as 'inexorable' is not characteristic of Old English literature. The gloss 'resolute' offered here suggests that *wyrd* is a powerful force (or a strong tendency of events to turn out in certain ways), but not inexorable.

[2] We expect the ending *hryra* for the genitive plural, but the vowels of unaccented syllables are often confused in late Old English.

Oft³ iċ sceolde āna    ūhtna ġehwylċe
mīne ċeare cwīþan.    Nis nū cwicra nān
10  þe iċ him mōdsefan    mīnne durre
sweotule āsecgan.    Iċ tō sōþe wāt
þæt biþ in eorle    indryhten þēaw
þæt hē his ferðlocan    fæste binde,
healde his hordcofan,    hycge swā hē wille.⁴
15  Ne mæġ wēriġ mōd    wyrde wiðstondan,
ne se hrēo hyġe    helpe ġefremman.
For ðon dōmġeorne    drēoriġne⁵ oft
in hyra brēostcofan    bindað fæste;
swā iċ mōdsefan    mīnne sceolde,
20  oft earmċeariġ,    ēðle bidæled,
frēomǣgum feor,    feterum sǣlan,
siþþan ġeāra iū    goldwine mīnne
hrūsan heolstre biwrāh,    ond iċ hēan þonan
wōd winterċeariġ    ofer waþema ġebind,
25  sōhte seledrēoriġ    sinces bryttan,
hwǣr iċ feor oþþe nēah    findan meahte
þone þe in meoduhealle    mīne⁶ wisse,
oþþe mec frēondlēasne    frēfran wolde,
wenian mid wynnum.    Wāt⁷ se þe cunnað
30  hū slīþen bið    sorg tō ġefēran
þām þe⁸ him lȳt hafað    lēofra ġeholena.
Warað hine wræclāst,    nales wunden gold,
ferðloca frēoriġ,    nalæs foldan blǣd.
Ġemon hē selesecgas    ond sincþeġe,
35  hū hine on ġeoguðe    his goldwine
wenede tō wiste.    Wyn eal ġedrēas.
For þon wāt se þe sceal    his winedryhtnes

---

³  It is generally agreed that a speech begins with this line. Most editors consider this the wanderer's first speech and place a quotation mark before *Oft*. Dunning and Bliss, however, consider lines 1–5 to be spoken by the wanderer as well. In view of the disagreements among scholars, and following the example of the Old English manuscript, this edition omits quotation marks altogether.

⁴  *hycge swā hē wille*: whatever he may think.

⁵  The adjectives *dōmġeorne* and *drēoriġne* are both used as nouns (see §15.2.3). Translate 'those who are *dōmġeorn*'; 'something *drēoriġ*'.

⁶  *mīne*: my people.

⁷  The verb *witan* 'to know' lacks an object here and in line 37. Read 'He understands (my situation) who . . .'.

⁸  *þām þe*: for him who.

leofes lārcwidum   longe forþolian.
Đonne sorg ond slǣp⁹   somod ætgædre
40   earmne ānhogan   oft ġebindað,
þinceð him on mōde   þæt hē his mondryhten
clyppe ond cysse   ond on cnēo lecge
honda ond hēafod,¹⁰   swā hē hwīlum ǣr
in ġeārdagum   ġiefstōlas brēac.¹¹
45   Đonne onwæcneð eft   winelēas guma,
ġesihð him biforan   fealwe wēgas,
baþian brimfuglas,   brǣdan feþra,
hrēosan hrīm ond snāw,   hagle ġemenġed.
Þonne bēoð þȳ hefiġran   heortan benne,
50   sāre æfter swǣsne.   Sorg bið ġenīwad
þonne māga ġemynd   mōd ġeondhweorfeð;
grēteð glīwstafum,¹²   ġeorne ġeondscēawað
secga ġeseldan.   Swimmað eft on weġ.¹³
Flēotendra¹⁴ ferð   nō þǣr fela bringeð
55   cūðra cwideġiedda.   Ċearo bið ġenīwad
þām þe sendan sceal   swīþe ġeneahhe
ofer waþema ġebind   wēriġne sefan.
For þon iċ ġeþenċan ne mæġ   ġeond þās woruld
for hwan¹⁵ mōdsefa   mīn ne ġesweorce,
60   þonne iċ eorla līf   eal ġeondþenċe,
hū hī fǣrlīċe   flet ofġēafon,
mōdġe maguþeġnas.   Swā þes middanġeard
ealra dōgra ġehwām   drēoseð ond fealleþ.
For þon ne mæġ weorþan wīs   wer, ǣr hē āge

---

⁹   The hypothetical person who has experienced loneliness and so 'knows' or 'understands' the speaker's state of mind is here imagined falling asleep and dreaming of happier days in the hall. The verb *þyncan* (line 41) is often used in Old and Middle English to introduce the contents of dreams.

¹⁰   These are generally interpreted as formal gestures of fealty rather than as informal gestures of affection. However, it must be admitted that we know almost nothing about the ceremony that would have accompanied a thegn's swearing fealty to his lord.

¹¹   For a thegn to 'use' or 'benefit from' the 'gift-seat' or 'throne' was presumably to receive gifts from his lord.

¹²   *glīwstafum*: with joy; joyfully.

¹³   Lines 51–3 are more difficult to interpret than to read. Having just awakened from a dream of the now-departed joys of the hall, the man thinks of his kinsmen, eagerly greets them and peers at them (*secga geseldan*) intently. But either they recede from his memory like the birds floating on the sea, or he has been imagining (in his half-awake state) that he actually sees them, and now perceives that they are only sea-birds floating on the water.

¹⁴   That is, of the sea-birds, which do not speak to him.

¹⁵   *for hwan*: for what reason; why.

65  wintra dǣl in woruldrīċe.   Wita sceal[16] ġeþyldiġ;
    ne sceal nō tō hātheort   ne tō hrǣdwyrde
    ne tō wāc wiga   ne tō wanhȳdiġ
    ne tō forht ne tō fǣġen   ne tō feohġīfre
    ne nǣfre ġielpes tō ġeorn,   ǣr hē ġeare cunne.
70  Beorn sceal ġebīdan,   þonne hē bēot spriceð,
    oþ þæt collenferð   cunne ġearwe
    hwider hreþra ġehyġd   hweorfan wille.[17]
    Onġietan sceal glēaw hæle   hū gǣstliċ[18] bið,
    þonne ealre þisse worulde wela   wēste stondeð,
75  swā nū missenlīċe   ġeond þisne middanġeard
    winde biwāune   weallas stondaþ,
    hrīme bihrorene,   hrȳðġe þā ederas.
    Wōriað þā wīnsalo,   waldend licgað
    drēame bidrorene,   duguþ eal ġecrong,
80  wlonc bī wealle.   Sume wīġ[19] fornom,
    ferede in forðweġe:   sumne fugel oþbær
    ofer hēanne holm,   sumne se hāra wulf
    dēaðe ġedǣlde,   sumne drēoriġhlēor
    in eorðscræfe   eorl ġehȳdde.
85  Ȳþde swā þisne eardġeard   ælda Scyppend
    oþ þæt burgwara   breahtma lēase
    eald enta ġeweorc[20]   īdlu stōdon.
    Se þonne þisne wealsteal   wīse ġeþōhte
    ond þis deorce līf   dēope ġeondþenċeð,

---

[16]  *sceal*: should be. Forms of the verbs *gān* and *bēon* are often omitted after auxiliaries.

[17]  This passage reflects what appears to have been a common anxiety that one could make impressive vows before a battle and yet lose one's nerve at the hour of greatest need (compare *The Battle of Maldon*, ll. 198–201). It is better not to boast at all, the speaker says, until one is thoroughly acquainted with oneself.

[18]  This instance of *gǣstliċ* is almost universally glossed as 'terrifying' or the like, an extension of a presumed meaning 'ghastly' or 'spectral'. But although *Gǣstliċ, gāstliċ* is a common word, the meaning 'terrifying' is nowhere else attested for it; its usual meaning is 'spiritual'. The notion that it is 'terrifying' when the earth stands in ruins would be rather blandly predictable, if the poet were saying that; but it makes at least as much sense to take the common meaning 'spiritual' here: and indeed meditating on death and ruination does lead the speaker's mind to higher concerns.

[19]  Notice that *wīġ* is the subject and *sume* the object. What follows is one of the better variations on the common 'Beasts of Battle' formula, which imagines the raven, the eagle and the wulf feasting on the corpses of the slain (see §14.3.2). Here the bird bearing a corpse away over the sea recalls one's sending one's 'weary spirit' out over the sea.

[20]  The formula *enta ġeweorc* is used of magnificent artifacts from the distant past. In *Beowulf* it is used of the giant sword with which Beowulf kills Grendel (1679) and the dragon's barrow and its contents (2717, 2774). In *The Ruin* 2 it is used of the Roman ruins at Bath, and similarly in *Andreas* 1495 it is used of an ancient edifice.

90    frōd in ferðe,    feor oft ġemon
      wælsleahta worn,    ond þās word ācwið:
      Hwǣr cwōm²¹ mearg? Hwǣr cwōm mago?    Hwǣr cwōm māþþumġyfa?
      Hwǣr cwōm symbla ġesetu?    Hwǣr sindon seledrēamas?
      Ēalā beorht bune!    Ēalā byrnwiga!
95    Ēalā þēodnes þrym!    Hū sēo þrāg ġewāt,
      ġenāp under nihthelm,    swā hēo nō wǣre.
      Stondeð nū on lāste    lēofre duguþe
      weal wundrum hēah,    wyrmlīcum fāh.
      Eorlas fornōman    asca þrȳþe,
100   wǣpen wælġīfru,    wyrd sēo mǣre,
      ond þās stānhleoþu    stormas cnyssað,
      hrīð hrēosende    hrūsan bindeð,
      wintres wōma,    þonne won cymeð,
      nīpeð nihtscūa,    norþan onsendeð
105   hrēo hæġlfare    hæleþum on andan.
      Eall is earfoðliċ    eorþan rīċe;
      onwendeð wyrda ġesceaft    weoruld under heofonum.

---

²¹  This phrase, meaning 'what has become of', echoes the Latin formula *ubi sunt* 'where are', often used in sermons to convey the theme of the transitoriness of worldly goods. A similar echo of the *ubi sunt* formula occurs in Blickling Homily viii, speaking of the riches of past ages:

Ac hwyder gewiton þa welan and þa glengas and þa idlan blissa? Oþþe hwyder gewiton þa mycclan weorod þe him ymb ferdon and stodon? And hwær syndon þa þe hie heredan and him olyhtword sprecan? And hwær com seo frætwodnes heora husa and seo gesomnung þara deorwyrþra gimma oþþe þæt unmæte gestreon goldes and seolfres oþþe eal se wela þe him dæghwamlice gesamnodan ma and ma and nystan ne ne gemdon hwonne hie þæt eall anforlætan sceoldon? Oþþe hwær com heora snyttro and seo orþonce glaunes, and se þe þa gebregdnan domas demde, and seo wlitignes heora ræsta and setla, oþþe se manigfealde licetung heora freonda and seo myccle menigo heora þeowa and seo scylfring heora leohtfata þe him beforan burnon and ealle þa mycclan þreatas þe him mid ferdon and embþrungon?

But where has the wealth gone, and the adornments and the idle pleasures? Or where have the great armies gone, which travelled and stood about them? And where are those who praised them and spoke flattering words to them? And what has become of the ornamentation of their houses and the collection of valuable gems or the immense treasure of gold and silver or all the wealth of which they daily collected more and more for themselves and neither knew nor cared when they would have to abandon it all? Or what has become of their cleverness and their ingenious wisdom, or him who rendered false judgements, and the beauty of their beds and seats, or the manifold hypocrisies of their friends and the great company of their servants and the swinging of the lamps that burned before them and all the great hosts that travelled with them and pressed about them?

While the prevailing tone of the sermon is scorn for worthless riches, the speaker in *The Wanderer* seems to feel something more akin to regret for the loss of a good thing. One wonders whether any of the sermon's scorn echoed in the minds of the audience of this poem.

Hēr bið feoh lǣne,    hēr bið frēond lǣne,
hēr bið mon lǣne,    hēr bið mǣġ lǣne,
110    eal þis eorþan ġesteal    īdel weorþeð.
Swā cwæð snottor on mōde;    ġesæt him sundor æt rūne.[22]
Til biþ se þe his trēowe ġehealdeþ;    ne sceal nǣfre his torn tō ryċene
beorn of his brēostum ācȳþan,    nemþe hē ǣr þā bōte cunne
eorl mid elne ġefremman.    Wel bið þām þe him āre sēċeð,
115    frōfre tō Fæder on heofonum,    þǣr ūs eal sēo fæstnung stondeð.

# 14    The Dream of the Rood

*The Dream of the Rood* is a dream-vision in which the cross tells the story of the crucifixion. Here Christ appears as a young hero-king, confident of victory as he rushes to mount the cross. By contrast, the cross itself (now stained with blood, now encrusted with gems in the manner of a reliquary) feels all the agony of crucifixion, and its physical pain is more than matched by the pain of its being forced to kill its young lord.

The text is from the tenth-century Vercelli Book (see textual note, p. 267); a portion of it is also carved in runes on an eighth-century stone cross in Ruthwell, Dumfriesshire. The earliness of the Ruthwell Cross guarantees the earliness of the poem, or at least the part of it that recounts the crucifixion (ll. 1–78).

For the poems of the Vercelli Book, see Krapp and Dobbie [69], vol. 2. Both the Vercelli and the Ruthwell texts have been edited separately, with full notes and glossary, in Swanton [108].

Hwæt,[1] iċ swefna cyst    secgan wylle,
hwæt mē ġemǣtte    tō midre nihte
syðþan reordberend    reste wunedon.
Þūhte mē þæt iċ ġesāwe    syllicre[2] trēow

---

[22]    Lines 111–15 are hypermetric – that is, they have an expanded rhythmic pattern (see §13.2.3). Most editions print hypermetric lines as here, set into the left margin.

[1]    The interjection *hwæt*, which begins many Old English poems, is often interpreted as a call for attention (and performed as a shout, followed by a long pause). But the word often comes within speeches (as at l. 90 below), where we suppose that the speaker already has the listener's attention. Rather than calling for attention, *hwæt* probably marks what follows as especially significant or signals an upward shift in rhetorical level.

[2]    *Syllicre* may be intensified by the comparative ending (as Modern English often does with the superlative, e.g. 'a most wonderful tree'), or an actual comparison may be implied ('more wonderful [than any other tree]').

5    on lyft lǣdan,[3]   lēohte bewunden,
      bēama beorhtost.   Eall þæt bēacen wæs
      begoten mid golde;  ġimmas stōdon
      fæġere æt foldan scēatum;[4]  swylċe þǣr fīfe wǣron[5]
      uppe on þām eaxleġespanne. Behēoldon þǣr enġel Dryhtnes ealle
10   fæġere þurh forðġesceaft.[6]  Ne wæs ðǣr hūru fracodes[7] ġealga,
      ac hine þǣr behēoldon  hāliġe gāstas,
      men ofer moldan,  ond eall þēos mǣre ġesceaft.
      Syllìc wæs se siġebēam  ond iċ synnum fāh,
      forwunded mid wommum.  Ġeseah iċ wuldres trēow
15   wǣdum ġeweorðode,  wynnum scīnan,
      ġeġyred mid golde;  ġimmas hæfdon
      bewriġene weorðlīċe  Wealdendes trēow.
      Hwæðre iċ þurh þæt gold  onġytan meahte
      earmra[8] ǣrġewin,  þæt hit ǣrest ongan
20   swǣtan on þā swīðran healfe.[9]  Eall iċ wæs mid sorgum ġedrēfed;
      forht iċ wæs for þǣre fæġran ġesyhðe.  Ġeseah iċ þæt fūse bēacen
      wendan wǣdum ond blēom;  hwīlum hit wæs mid wǣtan bestēmed,
      beswyled mid swātes gange,  hwīlum mid since ġeġyrwed.
      Hwæðre iċ þǣr licgende  lange hwīle
25   behēold hrēowċeariġ  Hǣlendes trēow,
      oð ðæt iċ ġehȳrde  þæt hit hlēoðrode.
      Ongan þā word sprecan  wudu sēlesta:
      'Þæt wæs ġeāra iū  (iċ þæt ġȳta ġeman)
      þæt iċ wæs āhēawen  holtes on ende,

---

[3]  The construction with accusative and infinitive following a verb of perceiving or commanding is discussed in §7.9.1. A strict translation would be 'It seemed to me that I saw [someone] lead a wonderful tree into the air'; a more idiomatic translation would employ the passive voice: 'It seemed to me that I saw a wonderful tree being led into the air.' See also ll. 51–2.

[4]  *Scēatum* has occasioned some difficulty, but there seems little doubt that the plural noun refers to a singular object, the earth's surface (compare l. 37, where the context is a greater help in interpreting the word).

[5]  This line begins the first of several groups of hypermetric verses (for which see §13.2.3). Others are at ll. 20–3, 30–4, 39–49, 59–69, 75 and 133.

[6]  Lines 9b–10a are puzzling, since one expects the Lord's angels to observe the cross, rather than (as the grammar insists) 'all, fair through eternity' to observe an angel. But the cross may plausibly be described as an angel, especially as its role in this poem is the essentially angelic one of messenger. *Ealle* then refers to the heavenly host, who are observing the cross: 'All who are fair through eternity beheld the Lord's angel there.'

[7]  *fracodes*: of a criminal. The adjective is used as a noun: see §15.2.3.

[8]  *earmra*: of wretched ones. Compare l. 10.

[9]  According to legend, it was Christ's right side that the soldier of John 19:34 pierced with his spear. Notice that it is the cross, not Christ, who is imagined as having received the wound.

30 āstyred of stefne mīnum.  Ġenāman mē ðǣr strange fēondas,
   ġeworhton[10] him þǣr tō wǣfersȳne,  hēton mē heora wergas hebban.
   Bǣron mē ðǣr beornas on eaxlum  oð ðæt hīe mē on beorg āsetton;
   ġefæstnodon mē þǣr fēondas ġenōge.  Ġeseah iċ þā Frēan mancynnes
   efstan elne myċle  þæt hē mē wolde on ġestīgan.
35 Þǣr iċ þā ne dorste  ofer Dryhtnes word
   būgan oððe berstan,  þā iċ bifian ġeseah
   eorðan sċēatas.  Ealle iċ mihte[11]
   fēondas ġefyllan,  hwæðre iċ fæste stōd.
   Onġyrede hine þā ġeong hæleð  – þæt wæs God ælmihtiġ,
40 strang ond stīðmōd.  Ġestāh hē on ġealgan hēanne,
   mōdiġ on maniġra ġesyhðe,[12]  þā hē wolde mancyn lȳsan.
   Bifode iċ þā mē se beorn ymbclypte.  Ne dorste iċ hwæðre būgan tō
   eorðan,
   feallan tō foldan sċēatum,  ac iċ sċeolde fæste standan.
   Rōd wæs iċ ārǣred.  Āhōf iċ rīċne Cyning,
45 heofona Hlāford,  hyldan mē ne dorste.
   Þurhdrifan hī mē mid deorcan næġlum.  On mē syndon þā dolg ġesīene
   opene inwidhlemmas.  Ne dorste iċ hira nǣnigum sceððan.
   Bysmeredon hīe unc būtū ætgædere.  Eall iċ wæs mid blōde bestēmed,
   begoten of þæs guman sīdan  siððan hē hæfde his gāst onsended.
50 Feala iċ on þām beorge  ġebiden hæbbe
   wrāðra wyrda.  Ġeseah iċ weruda God
   þearle þenian.[13]  Þȳstro hæfdon
   bewriġen mid wolcnum  Wealdendes hrǣw,
   sċīrne sċīman;  sceadu forðēode
55 wann under wolcnum.  Wēop eal ġesceaft,
   cwīðdon Cyninges fyll.  Crist wæs on rōde.
   Hwæðere þǣr fūse  feorran cwōman
   tō þām æðelinge;  iċ þæt eall behēold.
   Sāre iċ wæs mid sorgum ġedrēfed;  hnāg iċ hwæðre þām secgum tō
   handa,
60 ēaðmōd, elne myċle.  Ġenāmon hīe þǣr ælmihtiġne God,
   āhōfon hine of ðām hefian wīte.  Forlēton mē þā hilderincas
   standan stēame bedrifenne.  Eall iċ wæs mid strǣlum forwundod.
   Ālēdon hīe ðǣr limwēriġne,  ġestōdon him æt his līċes hēafdum;
   behēoldon hīe ðǣr heofenes Dryhten,  ond hē hine ðǣr hwīle reste,

---

[10]  The unexpressed object of *geworhton* is *mē*.
[11]  *mihte*: might have.
[12]  *maniġra ġesyhðe*: the sight of many.
[13]  Translate 'I saw [someone] severely stretch out the God of hosts' or 'I saw the God of hosts severely stretched out.' Compare ll. 4–5.

65 mēðe æfter ðām miċlan ġewinne.    Ongunnon him[14] þā moldern wyrċan
   beornas on banan[15] ġesyhðe.    Curfon hīe ðæt of beorhtan stāne;
   ġesetton hīe ðǣron sigora Wealdend.    Ongunnon him þā sorhlēoð galan
   earme on þā ǣfentīde.    Þā hīe woldon eft sīðian
   mēðe fram þām mǣran þēodne;    reste hē ðǣr mǣte weorode.[16]

70    Hwæðere wē ðǣr grēotende    gōde hwīle
      stōdon on staðole    syððan stefn ūp ġewāt
      hilderinca.    Hrǣw cōlode
      fæġer feorgbold.    Þā ūs man fyllan ongan
      ealle tō eorðan.    Þæt wæs eġesliċ wyrd!

75 Bedealf ūs man on dēopan sēaþe;    hwæðre mē þǣr Dryhtnes þeġnas,
   frēondas ġefrūnon,[17]
      ġyredon mē    golde ond seolfre.
      Nū ðū miht ġehȳran,    hæleð mīn se lēofa,
      þæt iċ bealuwara weorc    ġebiden hæbbe,
80    sārra sorga.[18]    Is nū sǣl cumen
      þæt mē weorðiað    wīde ond sīde
      menn ofer moldan    ond eall þēos mǣre ġesceaft,
      ġebiddaþ him tō þyssum bēacne.    On mē bearn Godes
      þrōwode hwīle;    for þan iċ þrymfæst nū
85    hlīfiġe under heofenum,    ond iċ hǣlan mæġ
      ǣġhwylċne ānra    þāra þe him bið eġesa tō mē.[19]
      Iū iċ wæs ġeworden    wīta heardost,
      lēodum lāðost,    ǣr þan iċ him līfes weġ
      rihtne ġerȳmde    reordberendum.

90    Hwæt, mē þā ġeweorðode    wuldres Ealdor
      ofer holtwudu,    heofonrīċes Weard,
      swylċe swā[20] hē his mōdor ēac,    Marian sylfe,
      ælmihtiġ God    for ealle menn
      ġeweorðode    ofer eall wīfa cynn.
95    Nū iċ þē hāte,    hæleð mīn se lēofa,

---

[14]  *Him* in ll. 65 and 67 is probably to be translated 'for him' (that is, for Christ). Some editors read them as reflexives with *ongunnon*, but this usage is without precedent.

[15]  The killer of Christ is the cross itself.

[16]  'With a small troop', i.e. quite alone. The figure in which one understates the contrary is called litotes. Here the poet states the contrary of the fact (Christ is not alone, but 'with a troop') but understates it (Christ is 'with a *small* troop').

[17]  The line is metrically defective, but as the sense is complete it is difficult to guess what is missing. Therefore most editors do not emend here.

[18]  The first object of *ġebiden* (which can take either an accusative or a genitive object) is accusative *weorc*, the second a genitive phrase, *sārra sorga*. This mixed construction was probably introduced by a scribe, who perhaps altered accusative *sāra sorga* to a genitive.

[19]  *ǣġhwylċne . . . tō mē*: each of those for whom there is fear of me.

[20]  *swylċe swā*: in the same way as.

þæt ðū þās ġesyhðe   secge mannum,
onwrēoh wordum   þæt hit is wuldres bēam
se ðe ælmihtiġ God   on þrōwode
for mancynnes   manegum synnum
100   ond Adomes   ealdġewyrhtum.
Dēað hē þǣr byriġde;   hwæðere eft Dryhten ārās
mid his miċlan mihte   mannum tō helpe.
Hē ðā on heofenas āstāg,   hider eft fundaþ
on þysne middanġeard   mancynn sēċan
105   on dōmdæġe   Dryhten sylfa,
ælmihtiġ God   ond his enġlas mid,²¹
þæt hē þonne wile dēman,   se āh dōmes ġeweald,
ānra ġehwylcum   swā hē him ǣrur hēr
on þyssum lǣnum   līfe ġeearnaþ.
110   Ne mæġ þǣr æniġ   unforht wesan
for þām worde   þe se Wealdend cwyð.
Frīneð hē for þǣre mæniġe   hwǣr se man sīe,
se ðe for Dryhtnes naman   dēaðes wolde
biteres onbyriġan,   swā hē ǣr on ðām bēame dyde.
115   Ac hīe þonne forhtiað,   ond fēa þenċaþ
hwæt hīe tō Criste   cweðan onġinnen.
Ne þearf ðǣr þonne æniġ   anforht wesan
þe him ǣr in brēostum bereð   bēacna sēlest,
ac ðurh ðā rōde sceal   rīċe ġesēċan
120   of eorðweġe   æġhwylċ sāwl
sēo þe mid Wealdende   wunian þenċeð.'
Ġebæd iċ mē þā tō þān bēame   blīðe mōde,
elne myċle,   þǣr iċ āna wæs
mǣte werede.   Wæs mōdsefa
125   āfȳsed on forðweġe;   feala ealra ġebād
langunghwīla.²²   Is mē nū līfes hyht
þæt iċ þone siġebēam   sēċan mōte
āna oftor   þonne ealle men,
well weorþian.   Mē is willa tō ðām
130   myċel on mōde,   ond mīn mundbyrd is
ġeriht tō þǣre rōde.²³   Nāh iċ rīċra feala

---

²¹   *mid*: with him.
²²   *feala . . . langunghwīla*: I endured many of all times of longing.
²³   *Mundbyrd* is a legal term denoting the guardianship of a person (not just a minor, for nearly everyone had a *mundbora* or protector), and also the compensation paid to the protector for an offence committed against his ward. It is frequently used in religious contexts, where it implies a comparison between the protection of a king or the head of a family and God's protection of the faithful soul.

frēonda on foldan,   ac hīe forð heonon
ġewiton of worulde drēamum,   sōhton him wuldres Cyning,
lifiaþ nū on heofenum   mid hēahfædere,
135   wuniaþ on wuldre,   ond iċ wēne mē
daga ġehwylċe   hwænne mē Dryhtnes rōd
þe iċ hēr on eorðan   ǣr sċēawode
on þysson lǣnan   līfe ġefetiġe
ond mē þonne ġebringe   þǣr is blis myċel,
140   drēam on heofonum,   þǣr is Dryhtnes folc
ġeseted tō symle,   þǣr is singal blis,
ond mē þonne āsette   þǣr iċ syþþan mōt
wunian on wuldre,   well mid þām hālgum
drēames brūcan.   Sī mē Dryhten frēond,
145   se ðe hēr on eorþan   ǣr þrōwode
on þām ġealgtrēowe   for guman synnum.
Hē ūs onlȳsde   ond ūs līf forġeaf
heofonlicne hām.   Hiht wæs ġenīwad²⁴
mid blēdum ond mid blisse   þām þe þǣr bryne þolodan.
150   Se Sunu wæs sigorfæst   on þām sīðfate,
mihtiġ ond spēdiġ   þā hē mid maniġeo cōm,
gāsta weorode,   on Godes rīċe,
Anwealda ælmihtiġ,   englum tō blisse
ond eallum ðām hālgum   þām þe on heofonum ǣr
155   wunedon on wuldre   þā heora Wealdend cwōm,
ælmihtiġ God,   þǣr his ēðel wæs.

# 15   Wulf and Eadwacer

*Wulf and Eadwacer* is one of the most enigmatic Old English poems, since the story it alludes to is not known to us. It has given rise to many theories, of which perhaps the most widely credited is that the speaker (a woman, as *rēotugu* in l. 10 tells us) is being held prisoner on an island by Eadwacer, while Wulf (her lover or husband) is in exile, perhaps being hunted by the speaker's people. For accounts of the scholarship on the poem, see Klinck [68] and Muir [85].

---

²⁴   The poem ends with a brief account of the Harrowing of Hell, Christ's release of the souls of the righteous from hell between the time of the crucifixion and that of the resurrection. The theme is a popular one in Old English homilies and religious poetry. Here the emphasis is on Christ's triumphal entrance into heaven with a host of souls.

Lēodum is mīnum[1]   swylċe him mon lāc ġife;
willað hȳ hine āþecgan[2]   ġif hē on þrēat[3] cymeð.
Unġelīċ is ūs.[4]
Wulf is on īeġe,   iċ on ōþerre.

5      Fæst is þæt ēġlond,   fenne biworpen.
Sindon wælrēowe   weras þǣr on īġe;
willað hȳ hine āþecgan   ġif hē on þrēat cymeð.
Unġelīċe is ūs.
Wulfes iċ mīnes wīdlāstum   wēnum hogode,[5]

10     þonne hit wæs rēniġ weder   ond iċ rēotugu sæt,
þonne mec se beaducāfa[6]   bōgum bileġde,
wæs mē wyn tō þon,   wæs mē hwæþre ēac lāð.[7]
Wulf, mīn Wulf!   wēna mē þīne
sēoce ġedydon,   þīne seldcymas,

15     murnende mōd,   nales metelīste.
Ġehȳrest þū, Ēadwacer?   Uncerne eargne[8] hwelp
bireð wulf[9] tō wuda.
Þæt mon ēaþe tōslīteð   þætte nǣfre ġesomnad wæs,[10]
uncer ġiedd ġeador.

[1]  The possessive adjective is divided from its noun here and in ll. 9 and 13 (see §8.1).

[2]  A weak first-class causative from *þicgan* 'to receive, take, eat, consume'. The literal meaning is 'to serve, feed' with accusative of the person served and dative of the things served, but a figurative meaning 'kill' is also attested.

[3]  The probable meaning of *on þrēat* here and in l. 7 is 'to (upon) a band of men'. A less likely (though still possible) reading would be to take *on þrēat* as an adverbial phrase meaning 'violently'.

[4]  'It is different with us.' There is little practical difference between the usages with adjective and adverb (in l. 8). Perhaps the adjective describes a static state, while the adverb describes a course of events.

[5]  MS. *dogode* is attested nowhere else in Old English; the best solution proposed has been to emend to *hogode*: 'I thought with hope of my Wulf's long journey'.

[6]  Probably Eadwacer, who will be mentioned by name in l. 16.

[7]  The syntax of ll. 9–12 is difficult. *Þonne* in l. 10 may mean 'when' and be subordinated to l. 9, and *þonne* in l. 11 may mean 'when' and be subordinated to l. 12. Or l. 9 may be a complete sentence, with ll. 10 and 11 coordinated, 'when . . . then'. Or ll. 10 and 11 may be 'when' clauses subordinated to l. 12.

[8]  MS. *earne* makes no sense. The only other plausible emendation is to *earmne* 'poor, pitiful'.

[9]  The common noun 'wolf' fits best with the image of a cub being carried off to the wood, but Old English manuscripts make no distinction between proper and common nouns, and it is probable that a pun is intended here. It is unfortunate that modern editorial procedures force us to make distinctions that the poet may not have intended.

[10]  The line echoes Matthew 19:6, *Quod ergo Deus coniunxit, homo non separet*: 'What therefore God hath joined together, let not man put asunder'.

# 16   The Wife's Lament

This poem from the Exeter Book is spoken by a woman whose husband has been outlawed because of his involvement in a feud. She followed him into exile, but for unknown reasons her husband's kinsmen schemed to separate them, with the result that she now finds herself living in a remote and desolate place with dark, pagan associations. Here she laments her own emotional torment, but also that of her husband, whom she imagines suffering from cold and loneliness.

Such is the dominant interpretation of *The Wife's Lament*, but the text contains a number of ambiguities, and is in fact a good example of how an editor can steer a reader's interpretation by including or omitting a comma, or placing a sentence break here or there. The edition in Pope and Fulk [95] provides an excellent guide to the various ways in which the poem can be read.

<br>

         Iċ þis ġiedd wrece    bi mē ful ġeōmorre,[1]
         mīnre sylfre sīð.[2]   Iċ þæt secgan mæġ,
         hwæt iċ yrmþa ġebād,   siþþan iċ ūp wēox,
         nīwes oþþe ealdes,   nō mā þonne nū.
5      Ā iċ wīte wonn   mīnra wræcsīþa.
         Ǣrest mīn hlāford ġewāt   heonan of lēodum
         ofer ȳþa ġelāc;   hæfde iċ ūhtċeare
         hwǣr mīn lēodfruma   londes[3] wǣre.
         Ðā iċ mē fēran ġewāt[4]   folgað[5] sēċan,
10    winelēas wræċċa,   for mīnre wēaþearfe,
         ongunnon þæt þæs monnes   māgas hycgan
         þurh dyrne[6] ġeþōht   þæt hȳ tōdǣlden unc,
         þæt wit ġewīdost   in woruldrīċe
         lifdon lāðlicost,   ond mec longade.

[1]   The feminine dative singular ending of *ġeōmorre* announces unambiguously that the speaker in this poem is a woman.

[2]   Rather than make the possessive pronoun *mīn* agree with masculine accusative singular *sīð*, as one would expect, the poet makes it agree with the feminine genitive singular form of the pronoun *sylf*; so a literal translation of this verse would be 'the plight of my self'. The effect is to emphasize the feminine endings, in case any listener or reader had missed the ending of *ġeōmorre* in the preceding line.

[3]   *londes*: In the land. The genitive sometimes indicates the place where; see also l. 47.

[4]   *iċ mē fēran ġewāt*: I departed journeying; I departed on a journey.

[5]   Presumably the speaker was seeking to perform the 'office' of wife with her *hlāford*, or husband. The terminology used of this marriage is the same as what would be used of the relationship between a thegn and his lord.

[6]   For *dyrnne*, a strong masculine accusative singular. But a double consonant is frequently simplified when it follows another consonant (see Appendix A).

15       Hēt mec hlāford mīn   herheard niman.[7]
          Āhte iċ lēofra[8] lȳt   on þissum londstede,
          holdra frēonda;   for þon is mīn hyġe ġeōmor.
          Ðā iċ mē ful ġemæcne   monnan funde—[9]
          heardsæliġne,   hyġeġeōmorne,
20       mōd mīþendne,   morþor hycgendne—
          blīþe ġebæro   ful oft wit bēotedan
          þæt unc ne ġedælde   nemne dēað āna
          ōwiht elles.[10]   Eft is þæt onhworfen;
          is nū ġeworden[11]   swā hit nō wǣre
25       frēondscipe uncer.   Sceal iċ feor ġe nēah
          mīnes felalēofan   fǣhðe drēogan.[12]
          Heht mec mon wunian   on wuda bearwe,
          under āctrēo   in þām eorðscræfe.
          Eald is þes eorðsele;   eal iċ eom oflongad.

---

[7]   Editors do not agree on the interpretation of this line. *Herheard* is often glossed 'dwelling in the woods,' but a *herh* (the more standard spelling is *hearh* or *hearg*) is a pagan shrine or sanctuary. Once the word is used of a sacred grove, but the principal attribute of such a grove is not that it is wooded, but rather that it is a place of worship. Some have emended to *hēr eard niman* 'take up residence here'; Pope and Fulk [95] emends to *hēr hīred niman* 'set up a household here.'

This edition retains the manuscript reading *herheard* in its obvious sense; the verse should be translated 'take up residence in a pagan shrine'. That the resulting verse is difficult to interpret does not make the reading wrong, but only means that we do not know enough to interpret it. An arresting parallel is *Beowulf* 3072, where we read that a curse on the dragon's treasure specifies that whoever plunders the hoard should be *hergum ġeheaðerod, hellbendum fæst* 'confined in a pagan shrine, fast in hellish bonds'. Why being 'confined in a pagan shrine' should implicitly be compared to damnation is no longer clear; but what the hoard-robber of *Beowulf* is threatened with resembles the present reality of this poem's speaker.

[8]   This adjective is used as a noun. See §15.2.3 and compare ll. 26, 34 and 53.

[9]   The first and third person past indicative of *findan* is usually *funde* rather than expected *fand* (though the latter is attested).

[10]   The punctuation of ll. 18–23a is problematic, and editors' decisions about it influence the interpretation of the poem in important ways. At issue is whether the passage speaks of the man who has already been mentioned or introduces a new one, and whether the action described took place before or after the speaker was forced to take up residence in a pagan place. The punctuation adopted here is that of Pope and Fulk [95], the implication of which is that these lines refer to the time when the speaker first found her husband. Though he was already secretly plotting the crime that would bring about his outlawry, the two of them made happy and optimistic vows to each other.

[11]   *Ġeworden* is not in the manuscript. The line is metrically defective without some word in this place, and yet the sense is clear enough; in such a case an unobtrusive emendation like *ġeworden* seems best.

[12]   The speaker probably is forced to endure not her husband's enmity, but rather the consequences of his having become involved in a feud.

30   Sindon dena dimme, dūna ūphēa,
    bitre burgtūnas[13] brērum beweaxne,
    wīċ wynna lēas. Ful oft mec hēr wrāþe beġeat
    fromsīþ frēan. Frȳnd sind on eorþan
    lēofe lifġende, leġer weardiað
35   þonne iċ on ūhtan āna gonge
    under āctrēo ġeond þās eorðscrafu.
    Þǣr iċ sittan mōt sumorlangne dæġ;
    þǣr iċ wēpan mæġ mīne wræcsīþas,
    earfoþa fela, for þon iċ ǣfre ne mæġ
40   þǣre mōdċeare mīnre ġerestan,
    ne ealles þæs longaþes þe mec on þissum līfe beġeat.
    Ā scyle ġeong mon wesan ġeōmormōd,[14]
    heard heortan ġeþōht; swylċe habban sceal
    blīþe ġebǣro, ēac þon[15] brēostċeare,
45   sinsorgna[16] ġedreag. Sȳ[17] æt him sylfum ġelong[18]
    eal his worulde wyn, sȳ ful wīde fāh
    feorres folclondes,[19] þæt mīn frēond siteð
    under stānhliþe storme behrīmed,
    wine wēriġmōd, wætre beflōwen
50   on drēorsele, drēogeð[20] se mīn wine[21]
    miċle mōdċeare. Hē ġemon tō oft
    wynlicran wīċ. Wā bið þām þe sceal
    of langoþe lēofes ābīdan.

---

[13] *Burgtūnas* refers figuratively to the surrounding hills. The imagery in this and the following lines dramatizes the speaker's confinement. Here the *burgtūnas* serve not to defend, but rather to imprison her; so too the briars that grow all around and her husband's departure, which 'seizes' her.

[14] Of the various interpretations offered of this and the following lines (to 45a), the most persuasive is that they are gnomic – a statement of a universal truth. Such gnomic statements are common in Old English poetry: see, for example, *The Wanderer*, ll. 65–77. Subjunctive *scyle* is frequent in such statements, though it should be translated as an indicative.

[15] *ēac þon*: in addition to that.

[16] Strong feminine nouns sometimes have weak endings in the genitive plural.

[17] Translate the two clauses beginning with *sȳ* 'whether . . . or'.

[18] *æt him sylfum ġelong*: dependent on himself. *Ġelong* agrees with *wyn* in the next line.

[19] *feorres folclondes*: in a distant nation.

[20] After the *sȳ* clauses, which speculate about the current condition of the speaker's husband (45b–47a) and a long clause of result (*þæt . . . drēorsele*, 47b–50a) that goes with the second *sȳ* clause, the main clause of this sentence begins here.

[21] *se mīn wine*: that friend/love of mine.

# 17    The Husband's Message

This poem is found near the end of the Exeter Book, whose final folios have been badly damaged by fire. Despite the damage to the text, the situation it describes is clear: a husband has had to leave his country and his wife because of a feud; this poem is spoken by the rune staff he sends to his wife pledging his fidelity and asking her to join him. The poem seems to supply a happy ending to the darker narratives implied by *Wulf and Eadwacer* and *The Wife's Lament*.

Damaged places in the text are signalled with square brackets. These gaps are filled in where scholars have offered plausible reconstructions; however, a complete reconstruction of this poem is not possible.

For full editions of *The Husband's Message*, see Leslie [74] and Klinck [68]. The latter includes facsimiles of the manuscript pages, permitting the reader to visualize the damage to the text.

Nū iċ onsundran þē    secgan wille
[ . . . . . ] trēocyn    iċ tūdre āwēox
in mec æld[a . . .    . . . ] sceal
ellor londes¹ setta[n    . . . . . . . . . ]c
5    sealte strēamas    [ . . . . . . . . . . ]sse.
Ful oft iċ on bātes [ . . .    . . . . . ] ġesōhte,
þǣr mec mondryhten    mīn [onsende
o]fer hēah hafu;    eom nū hēr cumen
on ċēolþele,    ond nū cunnan scealt²
10    hū þū ymb mōdlufun    mīnes frēan
on hyġe hycge.    Iċ ġehātan dear
þæt þū þǣr tīrfæste    trēowe findest.
Hwæt, þec þonne biddan hēt³    se þisne bēam āgrōf
þæt þū sinchroden    sylf ġemunde
15    on ġewitlocan    wordbēotunga
þe ġit on ǣrdagum    oft ġesprǣcon,
þenden ġit mōston    on meoduburgum
eard weardiġan,    ān lond būgan,⁴
frēondscype fremman.    Hine fǣhþo ādrāf

---

¹  *ellor londes*: in another land.
²  The unexpressed subject of *scealt* is *þū*.
³  The unexpressed object of *hēt* is *mec* (see §7.9.1).
⁴  *Būgan* is sometimes written for *būan* in late Old English, perhaps signalling that *g* between back vowels had already become [w], as in Middle English.

20        of siġeþēode;   heht⁵ nū sylfa þē  
           lustum lǣran   þæt þū lagu drēfde  
           siþþan þū ġehȳrde   on hliþes ōran  
           galan ġeōmorne   ġēac on bearwe.  
           Ne lǣt þū þec siþþan   sīþes ġetwǣfan,  
25        lāde ġelettan   lifġendne monn.⁶  
           Onġin mere sēċan,   mǣwes ēþel,  
           onsite sǣnacan   þæt þū sūð heonan  
           ofer merelāde   monnan findest  
           þǣr se þēoden is   þīn on wēnum.⁷  
30        Ne mæġ him worulde   willa ġelimpan  
           māra on ġemyndum,   þæs þe hē mē sæġde,  
           þonne inc ġeunne   alwaldend God  
           [þæt ġit] ætsomne   siþþan mōtan  
           secgum ond ġesīþum   s[inc brytnian]  
35        næġlede bēagas.   Hē ġenōh hafað  
           fǣttan goldes,   [feohġestrēona  
           þæt hē mi]d elþēode   ēþel healde,⁸  
           fǣġre foldan   [ . . . . . . . . . .  
           . . . ]ra hæleþa,   þēah þe hēr mīn wine⁹  
40        [ . . . . . . . . . ]  
           nȳde ġebǣded,   nacan ūt āþrong  
           ond on ȳþa ġelagu   [āna] sceolde  
           faran on flotweġ,   forðsīþes ġeorn,  
           menġan merestrēamas.   Nū se mon hafað  
45        wēan oferwunnen;   nis him wilna gād,  
           ne mēara ne māðma   ne meododrēama,  
           ǣnġes ofer eorþan   eorlġestrēona,  
           þēodnes dohtor,   ġif hē þīn beneah.  
           Ofer eald ġebēot   incer twēġa¹⁰

---

⁵   The subject of *heht* is *sylfa*; the unexpressed object is *mec*. *Þē* in this line goes with *lǣran* in the next.

⁶   The object of the imperative *lǣt* is *lifġendne monn* (notice the accusative ending of the participle). The object of *getwǣfan* is *þec*: 'hinder you from your journey'.

⁷   *þīn on wēnum*: waiting for you.

⁸   The indicative is more frequent than the subjunctive in adjective clauses. The subjunctive *healde* here may indicate that we are to consider the present sentence as continuing the indirect discourse of ll. 30–5.

⁹   Though the text of the clause that begins here is too damaged to be recovered with any certainty, it evidently introduces an allusion to the time when the husband was forced to flee to the land that he now inhabits. We return to the present with *Nū* in l. 44.

¹⁰   *incer twēġa*: of the two of you.

50   ġehȳre[11] iċ ætsomne   ᛋ.ᚱ[12] ġeador,
    ᛇ.ᚹ ond ᛗ  āþe benemnan
    þæt hē þā wǣre   ond þā winetrēowe
    be him lifġendum[13]   lǣstan wolde
    þe ġit on ǣrdagum   oft ġesprǣconn.[14]

# 18   Judith

In this poem the biblical book of Judith (considered canonical by the Catholic Church but not by Protestants) has been recast in an unmistakably Anglo-Saxon mould, and with the characteristic theme that God rewards those who believe and trust in him with victory, glory and wealth.

The missing beginning of the poem presumably followed, in greater or lesser detail, the biblical account in telling how Holofernes, a general of the Assyrian army, has besieged the Judean city of Bethulia, whose leaders are preparing to surrender when Judith, a widow, ventures with a single maidservant to the Assyrian encampment. She pretends to defect and stays with the Assyrians for three days. By the fourth day, Holofernes is inflamed with desire for the beautiful widow, and here our fragment begins.

[11] The third letter of this word was erased, presumably as the first step in a correction that was never completed. *Gehȳre* is the most plausible of several suggestions that have been made as to the intended reading. This verb introduces a construction like the one discussed in §7.9.1, in which a verb of perceiving is followed by an accusative object and an infinitive expressing what that object is doing. In this case the speaker 'hears' the runes in ll. 50–1 taking a vow (*āþe benemnan*).

[12] In the Old English runic alphabet (called the *fuþorc* after the first six runes in the sequence) each rune has a name that usually corresponds to an Old English word. In poetic manuscripts runes are sometimes used to represent these words. Here we are to understand that the husband's message to his wife consists of five runes cut on a staff:

ᛋ.   *siġel* 'sun' or *seġl* 'sail'
ᚱ.   *rād* 'road' or 'riding'
ᛇ.   usually *ēar* (of uncertain meaning), but here perhaps *eard* 'country', 'land'
ᚹ.   *wyn* 'joy'
ᛗ.   *man* 'man'

A plausible interpretation of these runes (and thus of the husband's message itself) might be 'take the sail-road [ᛋ.ᚱ *seġlrād*] to the land [ᛇ *eard*] where you will find joy [ᚹ *wyn*] with your husband [ᛗ *man*].' These runes and the message they express constitute the vow of fidelity spoken of in the final lines of the poem: they may have been intended as a riddle for the audience to puzzle out.

[13] *be him lifġendum*: while he is living (see §7.9.2).

[14] A doubled consonant at the end of an inflectional syllable is highly unusual. At the end of the poem, this one (if not a simple error) may be a flourish of sorts.

For an edition with in-depth commentary and glossary, see Griffith [52]. Interested students may wish to consult other treatments of the story by the Anglo-Saxon writers Aldhelm (in Latin, translated by Lapidge and Herren [71], pp. 126–7, and Lapidge and Rosier [72], p. 159) and Ælfric (ed. Assmann [3], pp. 102–16). All who read this poem should also read the biblical book, available in Bibles published under Catholic auspices and also in separate editions of the Old Testament Apocrypha.

---

                                                twēode

    ġifena in ðȳs ġinnan grunde.[1]   Hēo ðār ðā ġearwe funde[2]
    mundbyrd æt ðām mǣran Þēodne   þā hēo āhte mǣste þearfe,
    hyldo þæs hēhstan Dēman,   þæt hē hīe wið þæs hēhstan brōgan
5  ġefriðode, frymða Waldend.   Hyre ðæs Fæder on roderum
    torhtmōd tīðe ġefremede,   þe[3] hēo āhte trumne ġelēafan
    ā tō ðām ælmihtigan.[4]   Ġefræġen iċ ðā Hōlofernus
    wīnhātan wyrċean ġeorne   ond eallum wundrum þrymliċ
    ġirwan ūp swæsendo.   Tō ðām hēt se gumena baldor
10 ealle ðā yldestan ðeġnas.   Hīe ðæt ofstum miċlum
    ræfndon rondwiġġende,   cōmon tō ðām rīċan þēodne
    fēran, folces ræswan.   Þæt wæs þȳ fēorðan dōgore
    þæs ðe Iūdith hyne,   glēaw on ġeðonce
    ides ælfscīnu,   ǣrest ġesōhte.


       .X.
15  Hīe ðā tō ðām symle   sittan ēodon
    wlance tō wīnġedrince   ealle his wēaġesīðas,
    bealde byrnwiġġende.   Þǣr wǣron bollan stēape
    boren æfter benċum ġelōme,   swylċe ēac bunan ond orcas
    fulle fletsittendum.[5]   Hīe þæt fǣġe þēgon
20 rōfe rondwiġġende,   þēah ðæs se rīċa ne wēnde
    eġesful eorla dryhten.   Ðā wearð Hōlofernus,
      goldwine gumena   on gytesālum,
      hlōh ond hlȳdde,   hlynede ond dynede,
      þæt mihten fīra bearn   feorran ġehȳran

---

[1]   The subject of *twēode* is almost certainly Judith; the verb probably was preceded by the negative adverb *ne*. Compare ll. 345–6, which echo this passage.

[2]   Notice the rhyme of *grunde* and *funde*. Rhyme is frequently used as an ornament in this poem (for example, in ll. 29, 63 and 113).

[3]   *ðæs . . . þe*: for this reason . . . (namely) that. . . .

[4]   The use of adjectives as nouns (see §15.2.3) is especially frequent in this poem, for example *rīċa* (l. 20), *se stīðmōda* (l. 25) and *se bealofulla* (l. 48).

[5]   The full (cups were borne) to the courtiers.

25    hū se stīðmōda    styrmde ond ġylede
      mōdiġ ond medugāl,    manode ġeneahhe
      benċsittende    þæt hī ġebǣrdon wel.
      Swā se inwidda    ofer ealne dæġ
      dryhtguman sīne    drenċte mid wīne
30    swīðmōd sinces brytta,    oð þæt hīe on swīman lāgon,
      oferdrenċte his duguðe ealle    swylċe hīe wǣron dēaðe ġesleġene,
      āgotene gōda ġehwylċes.    Swā hēt se gumena aldor
      fylġan fletsittendum    oð þæt fīra bearnum
      nēalǣhte niht sēo þȳstre.    Hēt ðā nīða ġeblonden⁶
35    þā ēadigan mæġð⁷    ofstum fetiġan
      tō his bedreste    bēagum ġehlǣste
      hringum ġehrodene.    Hīe hraðe fremedon
      anbyhtscealcas    swā him heora ealdor bebēad
      byrnwiġena brego,    bearhtme⁸ stōpon
40    tō ðām ġysterne    þǣr hīe Iūdithðe
      fundon ferhðglēawe,    ond ðā fromlīċe
      lindwiġġende    lǣdan ongunnon
      þā torhtan mæġð    tō træfe þām hēan,
      þǣr se rīca hyne    reste on symbel⁹
45    nihtes inne,¹⁰    Nerġende lāð
      Hōlofernus.    Þǣr wæs eallgylden
      flēohnet fæġer    ymbe þæs folctogan
      bed āhongen    þæt se bealofulla
      mihte wlītan þurh,    wiġena baldor
50    on ǣġhwylċne    þe ðǣrinne cōm
      hæleða bearna,    ond on hyne nǣniġ
      monna cynnes,    nymðe se mōdiga hwæne
      nīðe rōfra¹¹    him þe nēar hēte
      rinca tō rūne ġegangan.    Hīe ðā on reste ġebrōhton
55    snūde ðā snoteran idese;    ēodon ðā stercedferhðe,
      hæleð heora hēarran cȳðan    þæt wæs sēo hāliġe mēowle

---

⁶   *nīða ġeblonden*: the one corrupted by evil.

⁷   The -*þ* or dental-stem noun *mæġð* (see §6.3.4) is attested here in the nominative, accusative and genitive singular and in the nominative plural; in this poem it always lacks an ending.

⁸   *bearhtme*: with noise; with revelry (see §4.2.4). This is the same word as *breahtma* in *The Wanderer*, l. 86. Metathesis, the shift of a consonant from one end of a syllable to the other, or the reversal of consonants (see §2.1.2, item 10), is responsible for the difference. Metathesis may cause a shift of *r* when a short vowel is followed by *d*, *n*, *s* or *ht*.

⁹   *on symbel*: continuously.

¹⁰   Take *inne* with *þǣr* in l. 44: 'wherein'.

¹¹   *nīðe rōfra*: of those renowned for enmity. This phrase and *rinca* in the next line go with *hwæne* in l. 52: 'any one of those . . .'.

ġebrōht on his būrġetelde.    Þā wearð se brēma on mōde
blīðe burga ealdor,    þōhte ðā beorhtan idese
mid wīdle ond mid womme besmītan.    Ne wolde þæt wuldres Dēma
60 ġeðafian þrymmes Hyrde,    ac hē him þæs ðinges ġestȳrde
Dryhten, dugeða Waldend.    Ġewāt ðā se dēofulcunda,
gālferhð gumena * * * ðrēate,[12]
bealofull his beddes nēosan,    þǣr hē sceolde his blǣd forlēosan
ǣdre binnan ānre nihte.    Hæfde ðā his ende ġebidenne
65 on eorðan unswǣslicne,    swylċne hē ǣr æfter worhte[13]
þearlmōd ðēoden gumena    þenden hē on ðysse worulde
wunode under wolcna hrōfe.    Ġefēol ðā wīne swā druncen
se rīċa on his reste middan    swā hē nyste rǣda nānne
on ġewitlocan.[14]    Wiġġend stōpon
70 ūt of ðām inne    ofstum miċlum,
weras wīnsade    þe ðone wǣrlogan,
lāðne lēodhatan,    lǣddon tō bedde
nēhstan sīðe.    Þā wæs Nerġendes
þēowen þrymful,    þearle ġemyndiġ
75 hū hēo þone atolan    ēaðost mihte
ealdre benǣman    ǣr se unsȳfra,
womfull onwōce.    Ġenam ðā wundenlocc
Scyppendes mæġð    scearpne mēċe,
scūrum heardne    ond of sċēaðe ābrǣd
80 swīðran folme.    Ongan ðā sweġles Weard
be naman nemnan    Nerġend ealra
woruldbūendra,    ond þæt word ācwæð:
'Iċ ðē, frymða God    ond frōfre Gǣst,
Bearn Alwaldan,    biddan wylle
85 miltse þīnre    mē þearfendre,
Ðrȳnesse Ðrym.    Þearle ys mē nū ðā
heorte onhǣted    ond hiġe ġeōmor,
swȳðe mid sorgum ġedrēfed.    Forġif mē, sweġles Ealdor,
sigor ond sōðne ġelēafan,    þæt iċ mid þȳs sweorde mōte
90 ġehēawan þysne morðres bryttan.    Ġeunne mē mīnra ġesynta,
þearlmōd Þēoden gumena.    Nāhte iċ þīnre nǣfre
miltse þon māran þearfe.    Ġewrec nū, mihtiġ Dryhten,

---

[12] This line is defective in both metre and sense. Probably *gumena* is the beginning of a formula like those of ll. 9 and 32; the remainder of the line may have stated that Holofernes departed from his *ðrēat*.

[13] *swylċne hē ǣr æfter worhte*: such as he had worked for. This adjective clause modifies *ende* in l. 64.

[14] *hē nyste . . . ġewitlocan*: i.e. his senses (or reason) left him.

torhtmōd tīres Brytta,    þæt mē ys þus torne on mōde
hāte[15] on hreðre mīnum.'    Hī ðā se hēhsta Dēma
95 ædre mid elne onbryrde,    swā hē dēð ānra ġehwylċne
herbūendra    þe hyne him tō helpe sēċeð[16]
mid ræde ond mid rihte ġelēafan.    Þā wearð hyre rūme on mōde
hāliġre hyht ġenīwod.[17]    Ġenam ðā þone hæðenan mannan
fæste be feaxe sīnum,    tēah hyne folmum wið hyre weard
100    bysmerlīċe    ond þone bealofullan
listum ālēde    lāðne mannan,
swā hēo ðæs unlædan    ēaðost mihte
wel ġewealdan.    Slōh ðā wundenlocc
þone fēondsceaðan    fāgum mēċe,
105    heteþoncolne,    þæt hēo healfne forċearf
þone swēoran him,    þæt hē on swīman læġ,
druncen ond dolhwund.    Næs ðā dēad þā ġȳt,
ealles orsāwle;    slōh ðā eornoste
ides ellenrōf    ōðre sīðe
110    þone hæðenan hund    þæt him þæt hēafod wand
forð on ðā flōre.    Læġ se fūla lēap[18]
gēsne beæftan;    gæst ellor hwearf
under neowelne næs    ond ðær ġenyðerad wæs,
sūsle ġesæled    syððan æfre
115    wyrmum bewunden,    wītum ġebunden,
hearde ġehæfted    in helle bryne
æfter hinsīðe.    Ne ðearf hē hopian nō,
þȳstrum forðylmed,    þæt hē ðonan mōte
of ðām wyrmsele,    ac ðær wunian sceal
120    āwa tō aldre[19]    būtan ende forð
in ðām heolstran hām,[20]    hyhtwynna lēas.

.XI.
Hæfde ðā ġefohten    foremærne blæd
Iūdith æt gūðe,    swā hyre God ūðe
sweġles Ealdor,    þe hyre sigores onlēah.

---

[15]    In translating, the adverbs *torne* and *hāte* may be rendered as adjectives.
[16]    *þe hyne him tō helpe sēċeð*: who seeks him as a help for himself.
[17]    *hāliġre hyht ġenīwod*: hope renewed for the holy one.
[18]    Literally 'basket'; metaphorically 'the body', commonly thought of as a container for the soul.
[19]    *āwa tō aldre*: forever and ever.
[20]    The dative of *hām* sometimes lacks an ending. Some such instances are so-called 'endingless locatives' indicating location, as in the common phrase *æt hām* 'at home'. But some are not 'locative' in the usual sense, for example *siþþan hē from his āgnum hām fōr* 'after he journeyed from his own home' (*Old English Orosius*, ed. Bately [6], 14/21).

125    Þā sēo snotere mæġð   snūde ġebrōhte
       þæs herewǣðan  hēafod swā blōdiġ
       on ðām fǣtelse  þe hyre foreġenġa,
       blāchlēor ides,  hyra bēġea nest,
       ðēawum ġeðungen,  þyder on lǣdde,
130    ond hit þā swā heolfriġ  hyre on hond āġeaf
       hiġeðoncolre  hām tō berenne,
    Iūdith ġingran sīnre.  Ēodon ðā ġeġnum þanonne
       þā idesa bā  ellenþrīste,
       oð þæt hīe becōmon  collenferhðe,
135    ēadhrēðiġe mæġð,  ūt of ðām heriġe,
       þæt hīe sweotollīċe  ġesēon mihten
       þǣre wlitegan byriġ  weallas blīcan,
       Bēthūliam.  Hīe ðā bēahhrodene
       fēðelāste[21]  forð ōnettan
140    oð hīe glædmōde  ġeġān hæfdon
       tō ðām wealgate.  Wiġġend sǣton
       weras wæċċende,  wearde hēoldon
       in ðām fæstenne,  swā ðām folce ǣr
       ġeōmormōdum  Iūdith bebēad
145    searoðoncol mæġð,  þā hēo on sīð ġewāt
       ides ellenrōf.  Wæs ðā eft cumen
       lēof tō lēodum,  ond ðā lungre hēt
       glēawhydiġ wīf  gumena sumne
       of ðǣre ġinnan byriġ  hyre tōġēanes gān
150    ond hī ofostlīċe  in forlǣtan
       þurh ðæs wealles ġeat,  ond þæt word ācwæð
       tō ðām siġefolce: 'Iċ ēow secgan mæġ
       þoncwyrðe þing,  þæt ġē ne þyrfen leng
       murnan on mōde.  Ēow ys Metod blīðe
155    cyninga Wuldor;  þæt ġecȳðed wearð
       ġeond woruld wīde  þæt ēow ys wuldorblǣd
       torhtliċ tōweard  ond tīr ġifeðe
       þāra lǣðða[22]  þe ġē lange drugon.'
       Þā wurdon blīðe  burhsittende
160    syððan hī ġehȳrdon  hū sēo hāliġe sprǣc
       ofer hēanne weall.  Here wæs on lustum.[23]
       Wið þæs fæstenġeates  folc ōnette,

---

[21] *fēðelāste*: along the foot-path.
[22] The genitive phrase *þāra lǣðða* is governed by *tīr* in l. 157. Read 'as recompense for the injuries'.
[23] *on lustum*: joyfull.

weras wīf somod,   wornum ond hēapum,
ðrēatum ond ðrymmum   þrungon ond urnon
165  ongēan ðā Þēodnes mæġð   þūsendmǣlum,
ealde ġe ġeonge.   Æġhwylcum wearð
men on ðǣre medobyriġ   mōd ārēted
syððan hīe ongēaton   þæt wæs Iūdith cumen
eft tō ēðle,   ond ðā ofostlīce
170  hīe mid ēaðmēdum   in forlēton.
Þā sēo glēawe hēt,   golde ġefrǣtewod,
hyre ðīnenne   þancolmōde
þæs herewǣðan   hēafod onwrīðan
ond hyt tō bēhðe   blōdiġ ætȳwan
175  þām burhlēodum,   hū hyre æt beaduwe ġespēow.[24]
Sprǣc ðā sēo æðele   tō eallum þām folce:
'Hēr ġē magon sweotole,   siġerōfe hæleð,
lēoda rǣswan,   on ðæs lāðestan,
hǣðenes heaðorinces[25]   hēafod starian,
180  Hōlofernus[26]   unlyfiġendes,
þe ūs monna mǣst   morðra ġefremede
sārra sorga,   ond þæt swȳðor ġȳt
ȳcan wolde;   ac him ne ūðe God
lenġran līfes,   þæt hē mid lǣððum ūs
185  eġlan mōste.   Ic him ealdor oðþrong
þurh Godes fultum.   Nū ic gumena ġehwæne
þyssa burglēoda   biddan wylle
randwiġġendra,   þæt ġē recene ēow
fȳsan tō ġefeohte   syððan frymða God,
190  ārfæst Cyning,   ēastan sende
lēohtne lēoman.   Berað linde forð,
bord for brēostum   ond byrnhomas,
scīre helmas   in sceaðena ġemong.[27]
Fyllað folctogan   fāgum sweordum
195  fǣġe frumgāras.   Fȳnd syndon ēowere
ġedēmed tō dēaðe,   ond ġē dōm āgon
tīr æt tohtan,   swā ēow ġetācnod hafað
mihtiġ Dryhten   þurh mīne hand.'
Þā wearð snelra werod   snūde ġeġearewod

---

[24]  Take the hū clause with bēhðe: 'as a token of how . . .'.
[25]  The mismatch of weak lāðestan and strong hǣðenes probably indicates that we should take ðæs lāðestan and hǣðenes heaðorinces as two genitive phrases in apposition.
[26]  Latin nominatives ending in -us are often used as genitives in Old English, presumably owing to their resemblance to the Old English genitive ending -es.
[27]  in sceaðena ġemong: into the assembly of enemies; among the enemy.

200    cēnra tō campe.   Stōpon cynerōfe
secgas ond ġesīðas,   bǣron siġeþūfas,
fōron tō ġefeohte   forð on ġerihte[28]
hæleð under helmum   of ðǣre hāligan byriġ
on ðæt dæġrēd sylf.[29]   Dynedan scildas
205    hlūde hlummon.   Þæs se hlanca ġefeah
wulf in walde   ond se wanna hrefn,
wælġīfre fugel;   wiston bēġen
þæt him ðā þēodguman   þōhton tilian
fylle on fǣgum.   Ac him flēah on lāst
210    earn ǣtes ġeorn,   ūriġfeðera,
salowiġpāda   sang hildelēoð
hyrnednebba.   Stōpon heaðorincas,
beornas tō beadowe,   bordum beðeahte
hwealfum lindum,   þā ðe hwīle ǣr
215    elðēodiġra   edwit þoledon
hǣðenra hosp.   Him þæt hearde wearð
æt ðām æscplegan   eallum forgolden
Assȳrium,   syððan Ebrēas
under gūðfanum   ġegān hæfdon
220    tō ðām fyrdwīcum.   Hīe ðā fromlīċe
lēton forð flēogan   flāna scūras,
hildenǣdran   of hornbogan
strǣlas stedehearde.   Styrmdon hlūde
grame gūðfrecan,   gāras sendon
225    in heardra ġemang.[30]   Hæleð wǣron yrre,
landbūende   lāðum cynne,[31]
stōpon styrnmōde,   stercedferhðe,
wrehton unsōfte   ealdġenīðlan
medowēriġe.   Mundum brugdon
230    scealcas of sċēaðum   scīrmǣled swyrd,
ecgum ġecoste,[32]   slōgon eornoste
Assīria   ōretmæcgas;
nīðhycgende   nānne ne sparedon
þæs herefolces,   hēanne ne rīċne,
235    cwicera manna   þe hīe ofercuman mihton.

---

[28]  *forð on ġerihte*: directly.
[29]  *ðæt dæġrēd sylf*: that very dawn.
[30]  For the construction *in . . . ġemang*, see l. 193.
[31]  *lāðum cynne*: at the hateful people.
[32]  The dative *ecgum* vaguely indicates association: 'excellent with respect to their edges'.

.XII.

Swā ðā magoþeġnas   on ðā morgentīd
ēhton elðēoda   ealle þrāge
oð þæt onġēaton   ðā ðe grame wǣron,
ðæs herefolces   hēafodweardas
240   þæt him swyrdġeswing   swīðliċ ēowdon
weras Ebrisce.   Hīe wordum þæt
þām yldestan   ealdorþeġnum
cȳðan ēodon,   wrehton cumbolwigan
ond him forhtlīċe   fǣrspel bodedon,
245   medowērigum   morgencollan,
atolne ecgplegan.   Þā iċ ǣdre³³ ġefræġn
sleġefǣġe hæleð   slǣpe tōbrēdan
ond wið þæs bealofullan   būrġeteldes
wēriġferhðe   hwearfum þringan,
250   Hōlofernus.   Hogedon āninga
hyra hlāforde   hilde bodian
ǣr ðon ðe him se eġesa   onufan sǣte
mæġen Ebrēa.   Mynton ealle
þæt se beorna brego   ond sēo beorhte mæġð
255   in ðām wlitegan træfe   wǣron ætsomne,
Iūdith sēo æðele   ond se gālmōda,
eġesfull ond āfor.   Næs ðēah eorla nān
þe ðone wiġġend   āweċċan dorste
oððe ġecunnian   hū ðone cumbolwigan
260   wið ðā hālgan mæġð   hæfde ġeworden,³⁴
Metodes mēowlan.   Mæġen nēalǣhte
folc Ebrēa,   fuhton þearle
heardum heoruwǣpnum,   hæfte³⁵ guldon
hyra fyrnġeflitu,   fāgum swyrdum
265   ealde æfðoncan;   Assȳria wearð
on ðām dæġeweorce   dōm ġeswiðrod,
bælċ forbīġed.   Beornas stōdon
ymbe hyra þēodnes træf   þearle ġebylde,

---

³³ The adverb *ǣdre* goes with *tōbrēdan* in the next line rather than with *ġefræġn* here. This is a stylistic flourish that sometimes accompanies the *iċ ġefræġn* formula used by poets at narrative transitions (and already in this poem at l. 7). Compare *Beowulf* l. 2773, *Ðā iċ on hlǣwe ġefræġn hord rēafian* 'I heard that then the hoard in the mound was plundered'.

³⁴ *hū ðone cumbolwigan . . . ġeworden*: how it had turned out for the warrior with the holy maiden.

³⁵ A synecdoche, the hilt standing for all the swords of the Hebrews.

sweorcendferhðe.[36]   Hī ðā somod ealle
270  ongunnon cohhetan,   ċirman hlūde
ond gristbitian   (gōde orfeorme)
mid tōðon, torn þoliġende.   Þā wæs hyra tīres æt ende,[37]
ēades ond ellendǣda.   Hogedon þā eorlas āweċċan
hyra winedryhten;   him wiht ne spēow.
275  Þā wearð sīð ond late[38]   sum tō ðām arod[39]
þāra beadorinca   þæt hē in þæt būrġeteld
nīðheard nēðde   swā hyne nȳd fordrāf.
Funde ðā on bedde   blācne licgan
his goldġifan   gǣstes ġēsne,
280  līfes belidenne.   Hē þā lungre ġefēoll
frēoriġ tō foldan,   ongan his feax teran
hrēoh on mōde,   ond his hræġl somod,
ond þæt word ācwæð   tō ðām wiġġendum
þe ðǣr unrōte   ūte wǣron:
285  'Hēr ys ġeswutelod   ūre sylfra[40] forwyrd,
tōweard ġetācnod,   þæt þǣre tīde ys
mid nīðum nēah ġeðrungen[41]   þe wē sculon nȳde losian,
somod æt sæċċe forweorðan.   Hēr līð sweorde ġehēawen,
behēafdod healdend ūre.'   Hī ðā hrēowiġmōde
290  wurpon hyra wǣpen ofdūne,   ġewitan him wēriġferhðe
on flēam sceacan.   Him mon feaht on lāst
mæġenēacen folc   oð se mǣsta dǣl
þæs heriġes læġ   hilde ġesǣġed
on ðām siġewonge,   sweordum ġehēawen
295  wulfum tō willan   ond ēac wælġīfrum
fuglum tō frōfre.   Flugon ðā ðe lyfdon,
lāðra lindwerod.   Him on lāste fōr
swēot Ebrēa   sigore ġeweorðod,
dōme ġedȳrsod;   him fēng Dryhten God
300  fæġre on fultum,[42]   Frēa ælmihtiġ.

---

[36]  The Assyrians are encouraged to think that Holofernes will awaken and lead them to victory
– a false hope. The juxtaposition of *ġebylde* 'encouraged' and *sweorcendferhðe* 'gloomy' has
troubled editors, some of whom have suggested emending the text. But the problem is more one
for critics than for editors, since the sense is clear enough.
[37]  An impersonal construction: 'it was at the end of their glory'. The genitives in the next line
are in variation with *tīres*.
[38]  *sīð ond late*: finally.
[39]  *tō ðām arod*: bold enough.
[40]  *ūre sylfra*: our very own.
[41]  An impersonal construction: 'it has pressed near to the time'.
[42]  *him fēng . . . on fultum*: the Lord God fairly undertook (to provide) help for them.

Hī ðā fromlīċe    fāgum swyrdum
hæleð hiġerōfe    herpað worhton
þurh lāðra ġemong,    linde hēowon,
scildburh scǣron.[43]    Scēotend wǣron
305 gūðe ġegremede    guman Ebrisce;
þeġnas on ðā tīd    þearle ġelyste
gārġewinnes.    Þǣr on grēot ġefēoll
se hȳhsta dǣl    hēafodġerīmes
Assīria    ealdorduguðe,
310 lāðan cynnes.    Lȳthwōn becōm
cwicera tō cȳððe.    Ċirdon cynerōfe
wiġġend on wiðertrod,    wælscel oninnan
rēocende hrǣw.    Rūm wæs tō nimanne
londbūendum[44]    on ðām lāðestan,
315 hyra ealdfēondum    unlyfiġendum
heolfriġ hererēaf,    hyrsta scȳne,
bord ond brādswyrd,    brūne helmas,
dȳre mādmas.    Hæfdon dōmlīċe
on ðām folcstede    fȳnd oferwunnen
320 ēðelweardas,[45]    ealdhettende
swyrdum āswefede.    Hīe on swaðe reston,[46]
þā ðe him tō līfe[47]    lāðost[48] wǣron
cwicera cynna.    Þā sēo cnēoris eall,
mǣġða mǣrost,    ānes mōnðes fyrst,[49]
325 wlanc, wundenlocc,    wǣgon ond lǣddon
tō ðǣre beorhtan byriġ,    Bēthūliam,[50]
helmas ond hupseax,    hāre byrnan,
gūðsceorp gumena    golde ġefrætewod,
mǣrra mādma[51]    þonne mon ǣniġ

---

[43] This 'shield-fortification' is the shield-wall, a formation in which the men stand close enough together to present a wall of shields to the enemy. To 'cut' or 'break' the shield-wall is to create a gap in it so that warriors can attack from behind.

[44] *londbūendum*: that is, 'for the Hebrews'.

[45] The subject in this clause is *ēðelweardas*, and the object is *fȳnd*.

[46] The literal sense of *āswefede* is 'put to sleep' and that of *reston* is 'rested'; the poet employs the common figure of death as a sleep (compare *The Dream of the Rood*, l. 64).

[47] *tō līfe*: while alive.

[48] Plural adjectives are occasionally uninflected in the predicate.

[49] *ānes mōnðes fyrst*: for one month.

[50] *Bēthūliam* with its Latin accusative singular ending is here used as a dative. This happens frequently, presumably because of the resemblance between the Latin accusative and some Old English dative endings.

[51] A partitive genitive is occasionally used without a governing word: read '(a quantity of) more excellent treasures than . . .'.

330 āsecgan mæġe searoþoncelra.
Eal þæt ðā ðēodguman þrymme ġeēodon,
cēne under cumblum on compwīġe
þurh Iūdithe glēawe lāre,
mæġð mōdiġre. Hī tō mēde hyre
335 of ðām sīðfate sylfre brōhton,
eorlas æscrōfe, Hōlofernes
sweord ond swātiġne helm, swylċe ēac sīde byrnan
ġerēnode rēadum golde;[52] ond eal þæt se rinca baldor
swīðmōd sinces āhte oððe sundoryrfes,
340 bēaga ond beorhtra māðma, hī þæt þǣre beorhtan idese
āġēafon ġearoþoncolre. Ealles ðæs Iūdith sæġde
wuldor weroda Dryhtne, þe hyre weorðmynde ġeaf
mǣrðe on moldan rīċe, swylċe ēac mēde on heofonum,
sigorlēan in sweġles wuldre, þæs þe hēo āhte sōðne ġelēafan
345 tō ðām ælmihtigan; hūru æt þām ende ne twēode
þæs lēanes þe hēo lange ġyrnde. Ðæs sȳ ðām lēofan Drihtne
wuldor tō wīdan aldre,[53] þe ġesceōp wind ond lyfte,
roderas ond rūme grundas, swylċe ēac rēðe strēamas
ond sweġles drēamas, ðurh his sylfes miltse.

# Textual Notes

## 1 The Fall of Adam and Eve

**Manuscript:** London, British Library, MS Cotton Claudius B. iv (B). **Other manuscript:** Oxford, Bodleian Library, MS Laud Misc. 509 (L). B's shelfmark, 'Cotton Claudius B. iv', indicates that it was once part of the library of Sir Robert Cotton (1571–1631), a notable book collector, where it was the fourth book on the second shelf of a case topped by a bust of the emperor Claudius. All of Cotton's other manuscripts are similarly designated. In 1731 the building that housed Cotton's collection was destroyed by a fire in which some manuscripts were lost and many damaged. B escaped the fire with little

---

[52] Gold is frequently described as 'red' in medieval English texts. Many colour words have changed their meanings since Old English and Middle English times, their semantic boundaries moving on the colour spectrum. Probably 'red' then included some portion of what is now the 'yellow' section of the spectrum.

[53] *tō wīdan aldre*: forever.

damage, but several other texts in this anthology, especially 10 and 18, are from manuscripts that suffered greater damage.

3 hrepodon] repodon.    15 and hire ofspringe] *from* L; *not in* B.

# 2   The Life of St Æthelthryth

**Manuscript:** London, British Library, MS Cotton Julius E. vii. This is the best manuscript of Ælfric's collection of saints' lives.

2 hātte] hatta.    11 āwryten] awrytan.    26 formolsnodan] formolsnodon.

# 3   Ælfric on the Book of Job

**Manuscript:** Cambridge University Library MS Gg. 3 28. This manuscript is contemporary (or nearly so) with Ælfric and may be from his own scriptorium. Emendations to this text are entirely by way of normalizations for ease of reading.

8 ymbhwyrfte] ymhwyrfte.    34 fulfremedra] fulfremedre.    49 wīsan] wison.    58 ufewerdum] ufewerdan.    80 ælmihtigan] ælmihtigum.    83 ymbscrȳd] ymscryd.    89 ġewendon] gewendan.    95 maðum] maðan.    112 ūrre] ure.

# 4   Cynewulf and Cyneheard

**Manuscript:** Cambridge, Corpus Christi College, MS 173. This is the earliest manuscript of the *Chronicle*, probably written in the last decade of the ninth century or at the beginning of the tenth and continued by various hands up to the late eleventh century.

16 ryhtfæderencyn] -en- *added in a later hand.*

# 5   The Martyrdom of Ælfheah

**Manuscript:** London, British Library, MS Cotton Tiberius B. i. The manuscript is generally thought to have been written at Abingdon around the middle of the eleventh century.

2 Hæstingas] hæsting.

## 6   William the Conqueror

**Manuscript:** Oxford, Bodleian Library, MS. Laud Misc. 636. The manuscript was written at Peterborough in 1121 or shortly after; the same hand that wrote the annals up to 1121 afterwards added annals for 1122 to 1131. There- after various hands continued the chronicle up to 1154. For a facsimile of the manuscript see Whitelock [113]. The following textual notes do not report normalized spellings and endings, but only changes that are, or could be regarded as, substantive.

3 se] seo.   8 þrȳ suna] þreo sunan.   26 wæs³] not in MS; mǣst] mægest.   30 hī] heo; ġesette] gesætt.   31 hæfde þæt manncynn mid ealle on ġewealde] þet manncynn mid ealle gewealde.   32 ġecynd] gecynde; Yrland] Yrlande.   35 underþēoddan] underþēoddan man.   41 sylfne] sylf.

## 7   *Sermo Lupi ad Anglos*

**Manuscript:** London, British Library, MS Cotton Nero A. i (I). **Other manu- script:** Oxford, Bodleian Library, MS Hatton 113 (E). The homily exists in three versions, apparently representing stages of revision by the author himself. Manuscripts I and E are copies of the latest version; I has close connections to Wulfstan himself and may contain notes in his own hand.

4 spǣcan] swǣcan.   rīcsode] riosode.   5 dæġhwāmlīċe] dægliwamlice. 9 manna] mana.   13 ende] ænde.   16 bysmor] bysmora.   19 ūs unġylda] us *not in* I.   20 ġetrȳwða] getryða.   21 ne ġehādode] ne *not in* I.   27 manegan] mænege I; manegan E.   31 syllað] sylleð.   34 ġecnāwe] gecnewe.   36 hwylċ] wylc.   wǣpnġewrixl] wæþngewrixl.   43 sǣmen] sæmæn.   47 menn] mænn. 49 þurh aðbriċas] þur aðbricas.   50 on þā þing] of þa þing.   51 godfyrhte] godfyhte.   62 fordōn] fordom.   70 miċlan] miclam.

## 8   Ohthere and Wulfstan

**Manuscripts:** London, British Library, MS Additional 47967 (L); London, British Library, MS Cotton Tiberius B. i (C). MS L was written at Winchester during or shortly after the first quarter of the tenth century. For a facsimile, see Campbell [25]. C was written in the early eleventh century, possibly at Abingdon. The manuscript also contains a version of the *Anglo-Saxon Chronicle*. Eight or ten leaves are missing in L after fol. 8v, and this gap unfortunately corresponds to part of the present text, which from sentence 18 after *hyd* is printed from C.

3 þæt þæt] *from C; L has* þæt. 18 horshwælum] *from C; L has* horschwælum. 41 þone] þonne. 45 on þæt stēorbord] *not in C.* 46 līð] fylð; siððan] siðða. 59 Ēstlande] eastlande. 60 Ēstland] eastland. 66 þȳ ylcan dæġe þe] þy ylcan dæg. 67 oþ þæt] oþ þe. 69 swiftoste] swifte. 74 Ēstum] eastum. 75 fætelsas] fætels.


# 9   The Story of Cædmon


**Manuscript:** Oxford, Bodleian Library, MS Tanner 10 (T). **Other manuscripts:** Cambridge, Corpus Christi College, MS 41 (B); Oxford, Corpus Christi College, MS 279 (O); Cambridge, University Library, MS Kk. 3, 18 (Ca). T is the oldest manuscript of the Old English Bede, probably written in the first quarter of the tenth century. A manuscript of the later tenth century, London, British Library, MS Cotton Otho B. xi, was badly damaged in the Cotton Library fire of 1731. B, O and Ca all date from the eleventh century.

6 sceoldon] sealde T; sceoldon B.   11 þāra endebyrdnes] þære endebyrdnesse T; þara endebyrdnes O.   14 Gode wyrðes] godes wordes T; gode wyrðes B, Ca; gode wyrþes O.   23 þā seolfan] seolfan þa T; ða sylfan his Ca; þa sylfan his O.   31 ne wǣre] wære T; ne wære B, O.   42 onhylde] ohylde T; onhylde B, O, Ca.


# 10   Boethius on Fame


**Manuscripts:** London, British Library, MS Cotton Otho A. vi (C); Oxford, Bodleian Library, MS Bodley 180 (B); Oxford, Bodleian Library, MS Junius 12 (J). C, written in the middle of the tenth century, contains a version that includes verse renderings of the metres. The version in B, written in the twelfth century, includes prose renderings of the metres. J, written in the seventeenth century by Franciscus Junius, contains a collation of C against B and a complete copy of the Old English metres in C.

C was badly damaged in the Cotton Library fire of 1731 (see reading 1); many pages were lost altogether, while most surviving pages suffered some degree of damage. Fortunately, all of the Old English metres had been transcribed in J by Junius, who had also collated the prose sections of C against those of B. Thus the Old English metres can be restored with confidence from Junius's transcript, while the prose can be partially restored from his collation.

The present text is based on C where it is legible. Where C is not available, readings are taken from J wherever possible. Otherwise, readings are from B, but the twelfth-century spellings of that manuscript have been altered to conform to the usage that prevails in C. Such normalizations of the spellings in B are not reported in the textual notes; readers interested in studying the text of the Old English Boethius in detail should consult Sedgefield [103].

5 þissum tōlum] þissan tolan C; þissum tolum B.    16 ealre] ealræ C. ðisses] ....s C; þis B.    norðeweardne] norðeweardum C; norðeweardne B. 18 ġefaran] geferan J; gefaran B.    hǣte] hǣto B.    20 cafertūn] cauertun C; cafertun B.    21 worulde] woruld C.    cafertūn] cauertun J; cafertun B. 25 þīoda] þiod C; þeoda B.    40 lenġe] lengu C; lenge B.    41 ge eac ma gif þu wille] ge þeah þu ma wille B.    45 formǣrra] formǣra J; foremǣrena B. 55 þe] þa C.    61 of] for C; of B.    70 ġeweorðad] geweorðað J.    74 hi] in J. 82 þissum] þissum worulde C.

# 11    A Lyric for Advent

**Manuscript:** Exeter Cathedral MS 3501. This manuscript, generally called 'the Exeter Book', is a large collection of Old English poetry written in the late tenth century and donated to Exeter Cathedral (where it still resides) by Bishop Leofric in 1072. It contains such classics as *The Wanderer*, *The Seafarer* and the Riddles (see Minitext I).

# 12    The Battle of Maldon

**Manuscript:** The text formerly existed in MS Otho A. xii of the Cotton Library. At that time it was already fragmentary: an early cataloguer described it as *capite & calce mutilum* 'mutilated at head and heel'. The manuscript was destroyed in the Cotton Library fire of 1731. Fortunately, the text had already been printed by Thomas Hearne as an appendix to his *Johannis Confratris et Monachi Glastoniensis Chronica* (1726). In 1935 the transcript from which Hearne's edition was printed was discovered. This transcript was formerly thought to have been made by John Elphinston, Deputy-Library of the Cotton collection; but it is now known to have been made by David Casley, Elphinston's successor at the library. For a facsimile of the transcript, see Scragg [101], pp. 2–14.

4 tō hiġe] t hige.    5 Þā þæt] þ þæt.    10 wīġe] w...ge (*the transcriber probably indicates a space where one or more letters are not legible*).    20 randas] randan.    33 þonne] þon.    hilde] ..ulde.    61 wē] þe.    87 ūpgang]

upgangan. 103 feohte] fohte. 113 wearð] weard. 116 wearð] wærd.
160 ġefetiġan] gefecgan. 171 ġestandan] gestundan. 173 Ġeþancie]
geþance. 179 fēran] ferian. 186 wearð] wurdon. 188 mearh] mear.
191 ærndon] ærdon. 200 mōdiġlīċe] modelice. 201 þearfe] þære.
208 forlǣtan] forlætun. 212 Gemunon] ge munu. 224 ǣġþer] ægder.
292 crincgan] crintgan. 297 Forð þā] forða. 298 sunu] suna. 299 ġeþrange]
geþrang. 300 Wīġelmes] wigelines. 324 oð þæt] od þæt 325 gūðe] gude.

# 13 The Wanderer

**Manuscript:** Exeter Cathedral MS 3501.
14 healde] healdne. 22 mīnne] mīne. 24 waþema] waþena.
28 frēondlēasne] freondlease. 29 wenian] weman. 53 eft] oft. 59 mōdsefa]
modsefan. 64 weorþan] wearþan. 74 ealre] ealle. 89 deorce] deornce.
102 hrūsan] hruse.

# 14 The Dream of the Rood

**Manuscript:** Vercelli, Biblioteca Capitolare cxvii. This manuscript, generally
known as 'the Vercelli Book', is a late tenth-century manuscript of homilies
and poems preserved in the library of Vercelli Cathedral, Italy, where it was
perhaps left behind by an Anglo-Saxon on a pilgrimage to Rome.
2 hwæt] hæt. 17 Wealdendes] wealdes. 20 sorgum] surgum. 59 sorgum]
*not in MS.* 70 grēotende] reotende. 71 stefn] *not in MS.* 91 holtwudu]
holmwudu. 117 anforht] unforht. 142 mē] he.

# 15 Wulf and Eadwacer

**Manuscript:** Exeter Cathedral MS 3501.
9 hogode] dogode. 16 eargne] earne.

# 16 The Wife's Lament

**Manuscript:** Exeter Cathedral MS 3501.
20 hycgendne] hycgende. 24 ġeworden] *not in MS.* 25 Sceal] seal.
37 sittan] sittam.

## 17   The Husband's Message

**Manuscript:** Exeter Cathedral MS 3501. The folio containing this poem (123a–b) has sustained fire damage. To see the extent of the damage, consult the facsimile in Klinck [68].
21 lǣran] lǣram.    30 ġelimpan] *not in MS.*

## 18   Judith

**Manuscript:** British Library, MS Cotton Vitellius A. xv. **Other manuscript:** Oxford, Bodleian Library, MS Junius 105. The Cotton manuscript (also known as the Nowell Codex) contains *Beowulf* and several prose tracts in addition to *Judith*. The text of *Judith* has suffered various kinds of damage. First, the beginning of the poem has been missing for as long as the manuscript has been known to modern scholarship. The extent of the missing part cannot now be determined (the section numbers are no guide, for scribes sometimes numbered the sections of several consecutive poems in a single series). Second, the last six lines of the poem were on a leaf that would have contained the beginning of another text. That leaf is now missing, probably removed by an early owner of the manuscript, Sir Robert Cotton (see headnote to reading 1), who disliked fragmentary texts and sometimes mutilated his books to remove them. The missing lines were copied onto the last extant leaf, probably by one of Cotton's ammanuenses. Third, this manuscript was damaged in the Cotton Library fire of 1731, with the result that many letters and words have been lost at the edges of pages. Fortunately, most of the missing matter can be supplied from a seventeenth-century transcript by Franciscus Junius, extant in MS Junius 105.

In the present text, gaps in the Cotton manuscript have been silently supplied from the Junius transcript. Readers who wish to discover how much of the text is missing should consult Krapp and Dobbie [69], vol. 5, in which letters taken from the Junius transcript are printed in italics.

47 ymbe] and ymbe.    85 þearfendre] þearf-fendre (*with line break between the two fs*).    87 heorte] heorte ys.    134 hīe] hie hie.    142 hēoldon] heoildon (*a botched correction*).    144 Iūdith] iudithe.    150 forlǣtan] forlæton.    165 Þēodnes] þeoðnes.    179 starian] stariað.    194 Fyllað] fyllan.    201 siġeþūfas] þufas.    207 wiston] westan.    234 rīcne] rice.    247 tōbrēdan] tobredon.    249 wēriġferhðe] weras ferhðe.    251 hilde] hyldo.    287 nȳde] *not in MS.*    297 lindwerod] *only* lindw *visible at damaged edge of page.*    332 on] *abbreviation for* ond.

# Glossary

This glossary contains all words that appear in the readings and in the minitexts; it also contains all words mentioned in the book, except those that appear only in glossary-like lists such as those in chapter 14. It uses these abbreviations:

| | | | |
|---|---|---|---|
| acc. | accusative | neut. | neuter |
| adj. | adjective | nom. | nominative |
| adv. | adverb | num. | number |
| anom. | anomalous | ord. | ordinal |
| card. | cardinal | part. | participle |
| compar. | comparative | pers. | personal |
| conj. | conjunction | pl. | plural |
| dat. | dative | poss. | possessive |
| demonst. | demonstrative | prep. | preposition |
| fem. | feminine | pres. | present |
| gen. | genitive | pret. pres. | preterite-present verb |
| imp. | imperative | pron. | pronoun |
| indef. | indefinite | refl. | reflexive |
| inf. | infinitive | rel. | relative |
| infl. | inflected | sg. | singular |
| inst. | instrumental | st. + number | strong verb of class *number* |
| interj. | interjection | subj. | subjunctive |
| interrog. | interrogative | superl. | superlative |
| lit. | literally | wk. + number | weak verb of class *number* |
| masc. | masculine | | |

In addition, the sign → is used for cross-references, of which a generous number are given. In alphabetizing, æ follows a, þ/ð follows t, and the prefix ġe- is ignored; so you must seek (for example) ġefremman under f.

ā. adv. *always, forever.* ā, aa c/11, 12; f/7; 2/26, 31, etc. (14x).

a → on.

abbatissan → abbudisse.

abbodrīce. neut. *abbacy.* dat. sg. 6/24.

abbud. masc. *abbot.* acc. sg. 5/6. nom. pl. abbodas 6/21. acc. pl. abbodas 6/24.

abbudisse. wk. fem. *abbess.* nom. sg. 2/12, 20; 9/20. acc. sg. abbatissan 5/6. gen. sg. abbudissan 9/1. dat. sg. abbudissan 2/10, 17; 9/15.

ābēad → ābēodan.

ābelgan. st. 3. *anger.* subj. sg. ābelge.

ābēodan. st. 2. *command, relate, present.* past 3sg. ābēad 12/27. imp. sg. ābēod 12/49.

āberan. st. 4. *bear, carry.* 3sg. ābirð.

ābīdan. st. 1. *await* (with gen. object). inf. 16/53.

ābirþ → āberan.

ābītan. st. 1. *bite, devour, tear apart.* subj. sg. ābīte 3/20.

āblend. adj. (past part. of *āblendan* 'blind'). *blind.* dat. pl. āblendum d/2.

āblered. adj. *bare.* masc. dat. sg. ābleredum d/2.

ābregdan. st. 3. *draw, withdraw, free from.* past 3sg. ābrǣd 18/79. past part. ābrogden 10/62.

ābrēoþan. st. 2. *fail.* subj. sg. ābrēoðe 12/242.

ābrogden → ābregdan.

ābroþen. adj. (past part. of *ābrēoþan*). *degenerate, ignoble.* masc. nom. pl. ābroþene 7/50.

ac. conj. *but.* a/2, 4 (2x), 6; b/2, etc. (68x).

āc. fem. athematic. *oak.*

ācennan. wk. 1. *bring forth, give birth to, bear.* 1sg. ācenst 1/16. past part. ācenned, ācennede 11/6; 3/6.

āclǣnsian. wk. 2. *cleanse.* subj. sg. āclǣnsige 2/13.

āctrēow. neut. *oak-tree.* dat. sg. āctrēo 16/28, 36.

ācwæþ → ācweþan.

ācweald- → ācwellan.

ācweccan. wk. 1. *shake.* past 3sg. ācwehte 12/255, 310.

ācwellan. wk. 1. *kill.* past 3sg. ācwealde c/5; 3/35, 39, 93; 7/26. past pl. ācwealdon. past part. ācwealde 3/103 (2x).

ācwencan. wk. 1. *extinguish.* inf. 7/8.

ācweþan. st. 5. *say.* 3sg. ācwið 13/91. past 3sg. ācwæð 18/82, 151, 283.

ācwylman. wk. 1. *kill.* past pl. ācwylmdon 5/17.

ācȳþan. wk. 1. *reveal.* inf. 13/113.

ād. masc. *pyre.* dat. sg. āde 8/66.

ādlig. adj. *sick.* masc. nom. pl. ādlige 2/27.

ādrāf → ādrīfan.

ādrǣdan. st. 7. *be afraid.* past pl. ādrēdon.

ādrǣfan. wk. 1. *drive, exile.* past 3sg. ādrǣfde 4/2. inf. 4/3.

ādrēdon → ādrǣdan.

ādrencan. wk. 1. *flood, drown.* past 3sg. ādrencte.

ādrēogan. st. 2. *perform, commit, endure.* pl. ādrēogað 7/30.

ādrīfan. st. 1. *drive.* past 3sg. ādrāf 17/19. subj. past sg. ādrife b/5. past part. ādrifen.

ādrincan. st. 3. *drown.* past pl. ādruncon.

ādūne. adv. *down.*

ādylegian. wk. 2. *destroy.* past part. ādylegod 2/4.

āfǣran. wk. 1. *frighten.* past part. āfǣred.

āfeallan. st. 7. *fall, be defeated.* past 3sg. āfēol 3/45. past part. āfeallen 12/202.

āfēdan. wk. 1. *feed.* 3sg. āfēt.

āfēol → āfeallan.

āflīeman. wk. 1. *drive out, expel, put to flight.* past 3sg. āflȳmde 12/243. past pl. āflīemdon.

āfor. adj. *bitter, sour, fierce.* masc. nom. sg. 18/257.

āfyllan. A. wk. 1. *fill, replenish.* imp. pl. āfyllað. past part. āfylled 6/17.
　　　B. wk. 1. *fell, kill.* subj. sg. āfylle 7/36, 37.

āfȳsan. wk. 1. *urge, impel, drive away.* inf. 12/3. past part. āfȳsed 14/125.

**āgan. A.** pret. pres. *have, possess, own.* 1sg.
 āh 12/175. 3sg. āh 3/32, 33; 14/107.
pl. āgon 18/196. past 1sg. āhte 16/16.
past 3sg. āhte 7/37; 12/189; 18/3, 6, 339,
etc. (6x). subj. sg. āge м/2; 13/64. inf.
10/65; 12/87.
**B.** Negated forms. 1sg. nāh 14/131.
past 1sg. nāhte 18/91. past 3sg. nāhte
c/3. subj. sg. nāge м/2.

**āgeaf-** → āgyfan.

**āgēaton** → ongietan.

**Agelesþrep.** proper noun. *Agelesthrep.*

**āgen.** adj. *own.* fem. nom. sg. 3/82. neut.
nom. sg. 3/110; 11/9. masc. acc. sg.
āgenne 4/11; 6/24; 7/31. neut. acc. sg.
d/3; ʟa. masc. gen. sg. āgenes. masc.
dat. sg. āgenum, āgnum 7/21; 8/13;
10/34. fem. dat. sg. āgenre. neut. dat.
sg. āgnum 8/16, 20. dat. pl. āgenum
3/79; 7/35.

**āgēotan.** st. 2. *pour out, spill, drain.* past
part. āgoten, āgotene 18/32.

**āgifen** → āgyfan.

**āginnan** → onginnan.

**āglǣcan.** wk. masc. *contender, formidable
one.*

**āgnum** → āgen.

**āgon** → āgan.

**āgoten-** → āgēotan.

**āgrafan.** st. 6. *carve, inscribe.* past 3sg.
āgrōf 17/13. past part. āgrafene.

**āgyfan.** st. 5. *give, deliver, give back.* 1sg.
āgyfe ɪ/10. past 3sg. āgeaf 9/19; 12/44;
18/130. past pl. āgēafon 18/341. past
part. āgifen, āgyfen м/8; 12/116.

**āgyltan.** wk. 1. *sin.* subj. past pl. āgylton
3/9.

**āh** → āgan.

**āhafen** → āhebban.

**āhēawan.** st. 7. *cut.* past part. āhēawen
2/25; 14/29.

**āhebban.** st. 6. *raise, lift, exalt.* past 1sg.
āhōf 14/44. past 3sg. āhōf 10/49;
12/130, 244. past pl. āhōfon 12/213;
14/61. inf. в/5; 6/41. past part. āhafen
в/7; 12/106.

**āhēnge** → āhōn.

**āhōf-** → āhebban.

**āhōn.** st. 7. *hang.* subj. past sg. āhēnge
c/5. past part. āhongen 18/48.

**āhreddan.** wk. 1. *rescue.*

**ahsode** → (ge)ascian.

**āht. A.** neut. *anything.* nom. sg. āuht
10/35, 46. dat. sg. āhte 7/8.
**B.** adj. *of any account.* masc. nom.
sg. 6/27.

**āhte** → āgan.

**āhwār.** adv. *anywhere.* 7/65.

**ālǣdan.** wk. 1. *lead.* 1sg. ālǣde.

**ālǣtan.** st. 7. *give up, leave, allow.* 2sg.
ālǣtst.

**aldor** → ealdor.

**aldormon-** → ealdorman.

**aldre** → ealdor.

**ālecgan.** wk. 1. *lay, put, place.* pl. ālecgað
8/67, 72. past 3sg. ālēde 18/101. past
pl. ālēdon 14/63. past part. ālēd
8/67.

**ālēfod.** adj. *infirm.* masc. nom. pl. ālēfode.

**ālegen** → ālicgan.

**gealgean.** wk. 2. (elsewhere usually ġe-
ealgian). *defend.* inf. 12/52.

**ālicgan.** st. 5. *end, diminish.* past part.
ālegen 10/36.

**alle** → eall.

**Alwalda.** masc. nd-stem. *Almighty.* gen.
sg. alwaldan 18/84.

**alwaldend.** adj. *omnipotent.* masc. nom.
sg. 17/32.

**ālȳfan.** wk. 1. *allow.* inf. 12/90.

**ālȳsan.** wk. 1. *free, release.* past 1sg. ālȳsde
3/23.

**ālȳsend.** masc. nd-stem. *redeemer.* nom.
sg. 3/86.

**āmānsumian.** wk. 2. *excommunicate,
curse.* past part. āmānsumod d/3.

**amber.** masc. *amber* (a measure of
volume, perhaps four bushels). gen.
pl. ambra 8/29.

**ambyr.** adj. *favourable.* masc. acc. sg.
ambyrne 8/42.

**amen.** interj. *amen.* 2/31.

**āmyrran.** wk. 1. *hinder, injure, destroy.* past 3sg. **āmyrde** 12/165. past part. **āmyrrede** 3/103.

**ān. A.** adj. and card. num. *one.* masc. acc. sg. **ǣnne, ānne** 12/226; c/1; 3/44. fem. dat. sg. **ānre** 3/76, 59; 8/67 (2x); 10/17. masc. nom. sg. **ān, ōn** 6/27; 7/58; 10/20, 31. fem. nom. sg. 6/30; 8/74; 10/16, 21. neut. nom. sg. 10/13. neut. acc. sg. 8/29. masc. gen. sg. **ānes** 3/35; 18/324. masc. dat. sg. **ānum** 4/8, 15; 8/42. neut. dat. sg. **ānum** 2/11; 10/56. wk. masc. nom. sg. **āna.** *a single, the same.* masc. acc. sg. **ǣnne** H/3. neut. acc. sg. 8/17, 73; 17/18. fem. dat. sg. **ānre** 18/64. Usually weak, often interpreted as adverbial. *alone.* neut. dat. sg. **ānum** 3/33. masc. nom. sg. 10/78. wk. masc. nom. sg. **āna** 3/26, 36, 37, 38, 39, etc. (13x). **B.** card. num. as noun. *one.* nom. sg. E/1. gen. sg. **ānes.** acc. pl. 3/106. **C.** indef. pron. *a, a certain, one.* masc. nom. sg. B/2; 2/7; 4/2; 5/18; 7/30, etc. (9x). fem. nom. sg. 3/61; 8/11. neut. nom. sg. 2/12. masc. acc. sg. **ānne, ǣnne** 4/3; 10/73; 12/117. fem. acc. sg. **āne** 2/19; 7/30 (2x). neut. acc. sg. 2/20. masc. gen. sg. **ānes** 10/26, 49. fem. gen. sg. **ānre** 5/18. neut. gen. sg. **ānes** 10/35. masc. dat. sg. **ānum** 2/3; 7/30. neut. dat. sg. **ānum** 3/59. neut. acc. pl. **āne.** gen. pl. **ānra** 14/86, 108; 18/95. **D.** adv. *only.* 9/4.

**an** → on.

**(ge)anbidian.** wk. 2. *await.* 3sg. **anbidað, geanbidað** 3/80 (2x). past pl. **anbidodon.**

**anbyhtscealc.** masc. *functionary, officer.* nom. pl. **anbyhtscealcas** 18/38.

**geancsumod** → geangsumian.

**and.** conj. *and.* **and, ond** A/2 (2x), 3 (2x); B/2, etc. (987x).

**anda.** wk. masc. *enmity, anger.* acc. sg. **andan** 13/105.

**andefn.** fem. *amount.* nom. sg. 8/66.

**andettan.** wk. 1. *confess, acknowledge.* subj. sg. **andette.**

**andgiet.** neut. *understanding, intellect, meaning.* nom. sg. **andgyt** 3/88, 110. acc. sg. **andgit** 3/2. gen. sg. **andgietes, andgites** 3/3; 10/47.

**Andred.** proper noun. *The Weald, Wealden forest.* acc. sg. 4/2.

**andswarode** → ondswarian.

**andswaru.** fem. *answer.* acc. sg. **andsware** 9/11; 12/44.

**andweard.** adj. *present.* dat. pl. **ondweardum** 9/16. wk. neut. gen. sg. **andweardan** 10/39. masc. nom. sg. **anweard.**

**andweorc.** neut. *material.* nom. sg. **andweorc, ondweorc** 10/3, 4, 6. gen. sg. **andweorces** 10/2, 9. dat. sg. **andweorce** 10/3.

**andwlita.** wk. masc. *face.* gen. sg. **andwlitan** 1/19.

**andwyrdan.** wk. 1. *answer.* past 1sg. **andwyrde.** past 3sg. **andwyrde** 1/2; 3/13, 54, 61. past pl. **andwyrdon.**

**andwyrde.** neut. *answer.* dat. sg. 10/56.

**ānfeald.** adj. *single, simple.* neut. dat. sg. **ānfealdon** 3/103.

**anforht.** adj. *afraid.* masc. nom. sg. 14/117.

**ānforlǣtan.** st. 7. *let alone, relinquish.* subj. past sg. **ānforlēte** 9/20.

**angēan** → ongēan.

**Angelcynn.** neut. *the English.* gen. sg. **Angelcynnes, Angelkynnes** 5/9, 12.

**anginn.** neut. *beginning, undertaking, action.* nom. sg. **angin** 12/242. dat. sg. **anginne, angynne** 3/99; 11/8.

**Angle.** neut. *Angeln* (district on the eastern coast of the Jutland Peninsula). dat. sg. 8/48.

**geangsumian.** wk. 2. *vex, afflict.* past part. **geancsumod.**

**angynne** → anginn.

**ānhaga.** wk. masc. *solitary one.* nom. sg. 13/1.

**ānhoga.** wk. masc. *solitary thinker.* acc. sg. **ānhogan** 13/40.

**āninga.** adv. *immediately.* 18/250.

**anlīces** → onlīc.

**geanlīcian.** wk. 2. *liken.* past part. **geanlīcod** 3/84.

ānræd. adj. *single-minded.* masc. nom. sg.
ānræd 12/44, 132.

ānrædness. fem. *constancy.* dat. sg.
ānrædnysse 3/82.

anscunian. wk. 2. *avoid.* infl. inf. tō
anscunianne 10/13.

ansund. adj. *whole.* fem. nom. pl. ansunde
2/23.

ansȳn. fem. *face, presence, sight.* nom. sg.
3/95. acc. sg. ansȳne 3/92, 94, 95. dat.
sg. ansȳne 3/32, 55.

antecrist. masc. *Antichrist.* nom. sg. 3/46.
gen. sg. antecristes 7/3.

anweald. masc. *authority, power, territory.*
nom. sg. 10/9. acc. sg. anweald, anwald
10/2, 3, 9 (2x). gen. sg. anwealdes
10/2, 13, 14. dat. sg. anwealde 1/16.

anwealda. wk. masc. *ruler.* nom. sg.
14/153.

anweard → andweard.

āplantian. wk. 2. *plant.* past part.
āplantod A/3.

apostata. wk. masc. *apostate.* nom. pl.
apostatan 7/50.

apostol. masc. *apostle.* nom. sg. 3/20. gen.
pl. apostola 9/24.

ār. A. fem. *honour, favour, grace, mercy.*
acc. sg. āre 10/38; 13/114. gen. sg.
āre 13/1. *income, prosperity.* nom. sg.
8/26.
    B. masc. *messenger.* nom. sg. 12/26.

āra → ārian.

ārās → ārīsan.

āræd. adj. (past part. of *ārædan*). *resolute.*
fem. nom. sg. 13/5.

āræfnan. wk. 1. *tolerate.* past part.
āræfned.

āræran. wk. 1. *raise, build.* past 3sg.
ārærde 6/5, 15. inf. 2/26. past part.
ārǣred 14/44.

arc. masc. *ark.* dat. sg. arce.

arcebiscop. masc. *archbishop.* nom. sg.
arcebisceop, ærcebiscep 5/5. acc.
sg. arcebisceop 5/6, 8, 11. nom. pl.
arcebiscopas 6/21.

āreccan. wk. 1. *tell, expound.* past part.
āreaht 10/64.

ārētan. wk. 1. *cheer.* past part. ārēted
18/167.

ārfæst. adj. *honourable, gracious.* masc.
nom. sg. 18/190.

ārfæstness. fem. *honour, virtue, grace.*
nom. sg. ārfæstnyss 2/13. dat. sg.
ārfæstnisse 9/1.

ārian. wk. 2. *honour, be merciful to.* imp.
āra 3/85.

āriht. adv. *rightly.* 7/43.

ārīsan. st. 1. *arise.* 1sg. ārīse 3/86. 3sg.
ārīst. pl. ārīsað A/5. past 3sg. ārās 3/9,
40; 9/6, 14; 14/101. past pl. ārison. subj.
past sg. ārise c/7. inf. c/10; 9/39.

ārlēas. adj. *dishonourable, base, impious.*
wk. masc. nom. pl. ārlēasan 3/81. wk.
gen. pl. ārlēasra 3/81. gen. pl. ārlēasra.
wk. masc. nom. sg. ārlēasa.

arod. adj. *bold.* masc. nom. sg. 18/275.
wk. masc. nom. sg. aroda 10/75.

ārwurþian. wk. 2. *honour.* imp. sg.
ārwurða.

ārwurþlīce. adv. *reverently.* 2/24.

ārwurþness. fem. *honour, reverence.* dat.
sg. ārwurðnysse 2/24; 5/19.

āsāh → āsīgan.

āsǣde → āsecgan.

asca → æsc.

Ascanmynster. neut. *Axminster, Devon.*
acc. sg. 4/16.

asce. wk. fem. *ash.* dat. pl. axum 3/84.

āsceacan. st. 6. *shake.* past 3sg. āsceōc
12/230.

āscēotan. st. 2. *shoot, lance.* inf. 2/14.

(ge)ascian. wk. 2. *find out, find out about.*
past 3sg. geascode 4/4. past pl. geaxodon 3/65. past part. geaxod 3/44.

āscortian. wk. 2. *grow short, elapse.* 3sg.
āscortaþ 10/42.

āscrepan. st. 5. *scrape.* past 3sg. āscræp
3/59.

āsecgan. wk. 3. *say, tell, express.* past 3sg.
āsǣde 12/198. inf. 13/11; 18/330.

āsendan. wk. 1. *send.* 3sg. āsent 3/46. past
3sg. āsende 5/18. inf. 3/47.

āsettan. wk. 1. *set, place.* past pl. āsetton
14/32. subj. sg. āsette 8/75; 14/142.

**āsīgan.** st. 1. *sink, fall.* past 3sg. **āsāh** 5/18.

**āsingan.** st. 3. *sing, sing to.* past 3sg. **āsong** 9/19. past part. **āsungen** 10/1.

**āsmēagan.** wk. 2. *consider, investigate, search.* inf. 7/58. pres. part. **āsmēageanne.** past part. **āsmēade** 5/8.

**āsolcenness.** fem. *laziness.* acc. sg. **āsolcennesse** 7/63.

**āsong** → āsingan.

**āspendan.** wk. 1. *spend.* past part. **āspended** 8/71.

**āspryttan.** wk. 1. *sprout, bring forth.* 3sg. **āspryt** 1/18.

**assa.** wk. masc. *ass.* nom. pl. **assan** 3/36, 99. acc. pl. **assan** 3/7, 98.

**Assȳrias.** masc. *Assyrians.* gen. pl. **Assīria, Assȳria** 18/232, 265, 309. dat. pl. **Assȳrium** 18/218.

**āstāg, āstāh** → āstīgan.

**āstellan.** wk. 1. *supply, establish, institute.* past 3sg. **āstealde** 2/31.

**āstīgan.** st. 1. *climb, ascend.* past 3sg. **āstāg, āstāh** 14/103. subj. past sg. **āstige** c/8.

**āstingan.** st. 3. *put out.* past pl. **astungon.**

**āstreccan.** wk. 1. *stretch out.* subj. sg. **āstrecce** 3/33. imp. 2sg. **āstrece** 3/32, 55.

**astungon** → āstingan.

**āstyrian.** wk. 2. *move, remove.* past part. **āstyred** 14/30. *stir, excite, anger.* past 2sg. **āstyredest** 3/53. past part. **āstyred** 5/15.

**āsungen** → āsingan.

**āswebban.** wk. 1. *put to sleep, kill.* past part. **āswefede** 18/321.

**āswerian.** st. 6. *swear.* past part. **āsworene** 5/20.

**atelīce.** adv. *terribly, hideously.* 3/95.

**ātēon.** st. 2. *draw away.* subj. past sg. **ātuge** 9/26.

**ātēorian.** wk. 2. *fail, become weary.* pl. **ātēoriað.** past 2sg. **ātēorodest** 3/72.

**atol.** adj. *terrible, hideous, grisly.* masc. acc. sg. **atolne** 18/246. wk. masc. acc. sg. **atolan** 18/75.

**ātuge** → ātēon.

**āþ.** masc. *oath.* acc. sg. 7/69. dat. sg. **āþe** 17/51.

**āþbryce.** masc. *perjury.* acc. pl. **āðbricas** 7/49.

**āþecgan.** wk. 1. *serve, feed,* fig. *kill.* inf. 15/2, 7.

**āþer.** conj. in construction *āþer oððe . . . oððe, either . . . or.* 8/31.

**āþringan.** st. 3. *crowd out, push out.* past 3sg. **āþrong** 17/41.

**āuht** → āht.

**āwa.** adv. *always, forever.* 18/120.

**āwǣgan.** wk. 1. *deceive, nullify.* past part. **āwǣgede.**

**āweaxan.** st. 7. *grow.* past 1sg. **āwēox** 17/2. past part. **āweaxene** F/2.

**āweccan.** wk. 1. *awaken.* past 3sg. **āwehte** 9/26. inf. 18/258, 273.

**āwecgan.** wk. 1. *shake, dislodge.* inf. 3/82.

**āweg** → onweg.

**āwegan.** st. 5. *weigh.* past part. **āwegene** 3/76.

**āwehte** → āweccan.

**āwendan.** wk. 1. *change, transform, turn.* 3sg. **āwent** 3/81. past pl. **āwendon** 3/71. subj. sg. **āwende.** past part. **āwend** 3/44. *overthrow.* infl. inf. **tō āwendenne** 3/77.

**āwēox** → āweaxan.

**āwierged** → āwyrgan.

**āwrāt** → āwrītan.

**āwreccan.** wk. 1. *awake.* past 3sg. **āwrehte.**

**āwrēon.** st. 1. *uncover.* past part. **āwrigene.**

**āwrītan.** st. 1. *write.* past 3sg. **āwrāt** 3/22, 111; 7/62. past pl. **āwriton.** inf. 2/1; 6/12. past part. **āwriten, āwryten** 2/11; 3/95; 10/37.

**āwyrgan.** wk. 1. *curse, damn.* past part. **āwierged, āwyrged** 1/14, 17.

**geaxod, axode, geaxodon** → (ge)ascian.

**axum** → asce.

**ǣ.** fem. *law.* acc. sg. A/2. dat. sg. A/2.

**ǣcer.** masc. *field.*

**ǣdre. A.** adv. *forthwith.* 18/64, 95, 246.
    **B.** wk. fem. *vein, artery.* nom. pl. **ǣdran.**

**ǣfen.** neut. *evening.* acc. sg. G/8. dat. sg. **ǣfenne** 9/30.

**ǣfenlēoþ.** neut. *evening song.*

**ǣfentīd.** fem. *time of evening.* acc. sg. **ǣfentīde** 14/68.

**ǣfest.** adj. *pious.* masc. nom. sg. 9/26. neut. acc. pl. **ǣfeste** 9/3. wk. fem. acc. sg. **ǣfestan** 9/4.

**ǣfestness.** fem. *piety.* dat. sg. **ǣfestnesse, ǣfestnisse** 9/1, 4.

**ǣfre.** adv. *ever, always.* c/11; 2/8; 7/50; 10/73, 81, etc. (8x).

**æftan.** adv. *from behind.* 7/23.

**æfter. A.** prep. (usually with dat., sometimes with acc.). Of space or time. *after, along* (of movement). c/8; I/10; 2/17, 18; 3/34, etc. (27x). Other senses. *on account of, for the sake of, according to.* 6/17; 10/16; 13/50.

  **B.** adv. *afterwards, towards* (of purpose or intent). 9/13; 18/65.

**æfter þām þe.** conj. *after.* H/1.

**æfþonca.** wk. masc. *insult, grudge, anger.* acc. pl. **æfðoncan** 18/265.

**ǣg.** neut. es/os-stem. *egg.*

**ǣghwǣr.** adv. *everywhere.* J/88; 7/10, 20, 50; 10/80.

**ǣghwider.** adv. *in all directions.* **ǣghweder** 5/4.

**ǣghwonon.** adv. *from everywhere, everywhere.* 10/65.

**ǣghwylc.** indef. pron. *every, each.* masc. nom. sg. **ǣghwilc, ǣghwylc** 8/28; 12/234. fem. nom. sg. 14/120. masc. acc. sg. **ǣghwylcne** 14/86; 18/50. masc. dat. sg. **ǣghwylcan, ǣghwylcum** 7/13; 18/166.

**ǣgþer. A.** indef. pron. *each.* masc. nom. sg. 8/29. neut. nom. sg. 7/25; 10/40; 12/133.

  **B.** conj. *both* in construction *ǣgþer . . . and* 'both . . . and'. 12/224.

**ǣgþer ge.** conj. *both* in construction *ǣgðer ġe . . . ġe* 'both . . . and'. 1/5; 6/43; 8/16; 10/24.

**ǣgylde.** adj. *without compensation.* masc. nom. sg. 7/36.

**Ǣgypta** → Egypte.

**ǣht.** fem. *possession, cattle.* nom. pl. **ǣhta** 3/31, 102, 103. acc. pl. **ǣhta** 3/31, 35, 42, 50, 96, etc. (7x). gen. pl. **ǣhta** 3/44, 82. dat. pl. **ǣhtum** 8/22.

**ǣlc. A.** adj. *each, every, any,* in pl. *all.* masc. nom. sg. 6/17; 7/30; 10/9 (2x), 34. masc. gen. sg. **ǣlces** 10/3. neut. gen. sg. **ǣlces** 8/73; 10/15, 70, 76. masc. dat. sg. **ǣlcum** 10/58. fem. dat. sg. **ǣlcere** 8/60. neut. dat. sg. **ǣlcum, ǣlcon** 1/1; 10/33 (2x). masc. inst. sg. **ǣlce** 6/19; 8/42. gen. pl. **ǣlcra** 7/13. neut. dat. pl. **ǣlcum** 6/32.

  **B.** indef. pron. *each, everyone.* masc. nom. sg. 3/8, 79; 7/23 (2x), 40, etc. (7x). fem. nom. sg. 10/25.

**ǣlda** → ylde.

**ælfscīne.** adj. *of elven beauty.* fem. nom. sg. **ælfscīnu** 18/14.

**ælmæsriht.** neut. *right to receive alms, obligation to bestow alms.* nom. pl. 7/15.

**ælmesse.** wk. fem. *alms, charity.* acc. pl. **ælmyssan** 2/30.

**ælmihtig.** adj. *almighty.* masc. acc. sg. **ælmihtigne** c/1; 14/60. masc. nom. sg. 2/4; 9/13; 14/39, 93, 98, etc. (9x). masc. dat. sg. **ælmihtigum** 11/18. wk. masc. nom. sg. **ælmihtiga** 2/4, 8; 3/19, 21, 95, etc. (7x). wk. masc. dat. sg. **ælmihtigan** 3/80, 82; 18/7, 345.

**ælmyssan** → ælmesse.

**ælþēodig** → elþēodig.

**ǣmōd.** adj. *disheartened.* masc. nom. pl. **ǣmōde** 3/3.

**ænde** → ende.

**ǣnegum, ǣnges** → ǣnig.

**ǣnig. A.** adj. *any.* masc. nom. sg. c/11; 6/41; 8/4, 46. neut. nom. sg. 7/46. masc. acc. sg. **ǣnigne** 2/27. fem. acc. sg. **ǣnige** 7/6, 12, 43. neut. acc. sg. 9/32. masc. dat. sg. **ǣnigum** 5/7; 7/52. dat. pl. **ǣnegum** 10/46.

  **B.** indef. pron. *any.* masc. nom. sg. 6/13; 7/21, 23; 10/73, 82, etc. (8x). neut. nom. sg. 12/195. neut. acc. sg. 7/11.

neut. gen. sg. **ǣnges** 17/47. masc. dat. sg. **ǣngum, ǣnigum** 3/112; 10/72.

**ǣnne** → **ān**.

**ǣr. A.** adv. *before, early, earlier, formerly.* **ǣr, ǣrest** B/7; H/4; K/1370; 2/8, 12, etc. (38x). superl. **ǣrest, ǣrost** G/6; J/82, 89; 2/11, 27, etc. (14x). compar. **ǣror, ǣrur** 6/5, 7; 14/108. **B.** prep. *before* (in time). F/6; 3/98; 7/3, 6, 17, etc. (9x). **C.** conj. *before.* K/1371; 4/4; 8/49, 50; 12/61, etc. (9x).

**ǣr þām.** conj. *before.* **ǣr þan** 14/88.

**ǣr þām þe.** conj. *before.* **ǣr þām þe, ǣr ðon ðe** 18/252.

**ǣrænde.** neut. *message.* acc. sg. 12/28.

**ǣrcebiscep** → **arcebiscop**.

**ǣrdæg.** masc. *early day, former day.* dat. sg. **ǣrdǣge.** dat. pl. **ǣrdagum** 17/16, 54.

**ǣrendraca.** wk. masc. *messenger.* nom. sg. 3/36, 38, 39.

**ǣrest.** adj. *first.* wk. fem. nom. sg. superl. **ǣreste** 9/24. wk. masc. dat. sg. superl. **ǣrestan** 8/69.

**ǣrgewin.** neut. *former strife.* acc. sg. 14/19.

**ǣrgōd.** adj. *old and good.*

**ǣrnan.** wk. 1. *run.* pl. **ǣrnað** 8/69, 72. past pl. **ǣrndon** 12/191.

**geǣrnan.** wk. 1. *run down, reach by running.* 3sg. **geǣrneð** 8/69.

**ǣrnemerigen.** masc. *early morning.* dat. sg. 3/9.

**ǣs.** neut. *food, bait, carrion.* gen. sg. **ǣses** 12/107.

**æsc.** masc. *ash-tree, ash-wood, spear.* acc. sg. 12/43, 310. gen. pl. **asca** 13/99.

**æschere.** masc. *army armed with spears.* nom. sg. 12/69.

**æscholt.** neut. *spear of ash-wood.* acc. sg. 12/230.

**æscplega.** wk. masc. *play of spears, battle.* dat. sg. **æscplegan** 18/217.

**æscrōf.** adj. *spear-brave, brave in battle.* masc. nom. pl. **æscrōfe** 18/336.

**ǣswice.** masc. *violation of the law* (?), *adultery* (?). acc. pl. **ǣswicas** 7/48.

**æt. A.** prep. (with dat. or acc.). *at, from, by, with respect to.* 2/25; 3/1, 8, 19, 39, etc. (41x). **B.** adv. *near.* 9/7.

**ǣt.** masc. *food, meal.* gen. sg. **ǣtes** 18/210. dat. sg. **ǣte.**

**ǣt, geǣt** → **(ge)etan.**

**ætbǣrst** → **ætberstan.**

**ætberan.** st. 4. *carry* (to a place). past pl. **ætbǣron.**

**ætberstan.** st. 3. *escape.* past 1sg. **ætbǣrst** 3/36, 39.

**ǣte** → **(ge)etan.**

**ætēowed** → **ætȳwan.**

**ætflēon.** st. 2. *flee, escape.* past 1sg. **ætflēah** 3/38.

**ætforan.** prep. *before, in front of.* 3/90; 12/16.

**ætgǣdere.** adv. *together.* **ætgǣdere, ætgǣdre** 7/60; 9/32; 13/39; 14/48.

**æthrīnan.** st. 1. *touch.* past 3sg. **æthrān.**

**ætlēapan.** st. 7. *run away from, escape from.* subj. sg. **ætlēape** 7/36.

**ǣton** → **(ge)etan.**

**ætsomne.** adv. *together.* J/92; 9/29; 17/33, 50.

**ǣtt** → **(ge)etan.**

**ǣttrene.** adj. *poisonous.* masc. nom. sg. **ǣtterne** 12/146. masc. acc. sg. **ǣttrynne** 12/47.

**ætwindan.** st. 3. *escape.* past 1sg. **ætwand** 3/37.

**ætwītan.** st. 1. *reproach* someone (dat.). inf. 12/220, 250.

**ætȳwan.** wk. 1. *show, reveal to.* past 3sg. **ætȳwde.** inf. 18/174. past part. **ætēowed.**

**æþel.** adj. *noble, excellent.* fem. nom. sg. **æþelu** I/5. neut. acc. pl. **æþele** 8/18. wk. masc. nom. sg. **æðele, æðela** 10/70; 12/280. wk. fem. nom. sg. **æðele** 18/ 176, 256. wk. masc. acc. sg. **æþelan** 12/151. wk. masc. gen. sg. **æðelan.**

**æþeling.** masc. *prince, nobleman.* nom. sg. 4/8. acc. sg. 4/3, 5, 10, 15. gen. sg. **æþelinges** I/1; 4/16. dat. sg. **æðelinge** 14/58. gen. pl. **æþelinga** J/89.

**æþelo.** fem. *family, descent.* acc. sg. 12/216.

**(ge)ǣþryttan.** wk. 1. *weary.* past part. **geǣðrytte** 3/3.

**ǣwbryce.** masc. *adultery.* acc. pl. **ǣwbrycas** 7/48.

**æx.** fem. *ax.* gen. sg. **æxe** 5/18.

**bā** → **bēgen.**

**bacan.** st. 6. *bake.*

**bād, gebād** → **(ge)bīdan.**

**Baius.** masc. *Bayeux.* dat. sg. 6/26.

**baldlīce.** adv. *boldly.* superl. **baldlīcost** 12/78. 12/311.

**baldor.** masc. *lord.* nom. sg. 18/9, 49, 338.

**bān.** neut. *bone.* nom. sg. 3/83. acc. sg. 8/73. dat. sg. **bāne** 8/27. nom. pl. 10/ 71. acc. pl. 2/18, 20; 3/55; 8/18; 10/74. dat. pl. **bānum** 5/17.

**bana.** wk. masc. *killer.* nom. sg. 12/299. acc. sg. **banan** 4/12. gen. sg. **banan** 14/66. gen. pl. **banena.**

**bānlēas.** adj. *boneless.* wk. neut. acc. sg. **bānlēase** ʟb.

**bār.** masc. *boar.* acc. pl. **bāras** 6/38.

**bāt.** masc. *boat.* gen. sg. **bātes** 17/6.

**baþian.** wk. 2. *bathe.* inf. 2/11 (3x); 13/47.

**bæc.** neut. *back.* acc. sg. 12/276.

**bæcbord.** neut. *larboard.* acc. sg. 8/6, 13, 45, 49, 51, etc. (8x).

**bæd** → **biddan.**

**gebæd** → **gebiddan.**

**(ge)bǣdan.** wk. 1. *impel.* past part. **gebǣded** 17/41.

**bǣde, bǣdon** → **biddan.**

**bælc.** masc. *arrogance.* nom. sg. 18/267.

**bǣm** → **bēgen.**

**bær, gebær** → **(ge)beran.**

**gebǣran.** wk. 1. *behave.* subj. past pl. **gebǣrdon** 18/27.

**gebǣre.** neut. (indeclinable in sg.). *conduct, demeanour.* acc. sg. **gebǣro** 16/44. inst. sg. **gebǣro** 16/21. *cry.* dat. pl. **gebǣrum** 4/7.

**gebǣre** → **(ge)beran.**

**bærnan.** wk. 1. *burn.* pl. **bærnað** 7/46.

**bǣron** → **(ge)beran.**

**bærst** → **berstan.**

**be.** prep. (with dat.). *by, along.* **be, bi, big** ʙ/3; ꜰ/3; 3/96, 97, 101, etc. (25x). *about,* *with, according to.* **be, bi** 2/1, 11, 27, 29, 31, etc. (34x).

**be sūþan.** prep. *to the south of.* 5/2.

**be þām þe.** conj. *as.* 1/6.

**bēacen.** neut. *sign.* nom. sg. 14/6. acc. sg. 14/21. dat. sg. **bēacne** 14/83. gen. pl. **bēacna** 14/118.

**gebēad** → **(ge)bēodan.**

**beadolēoma.** wk. masc. *battle-light, sword.*

**beadorinc.** masc. *warrior.* gen. pl. **beadorinca** 18/276.

**beadu.** fem. *battle.* dat. sg. **beaduwe, beadowe** 12/185; 18/175, 213.

**beaducāf.** adj. *battle-quick, battle-strong, battle-bold.* wk. masc. nom. sg. **beaducāfa** 15/11.

**beadurǣs.** masc. *rush of battle.* nom. sg. 12/111.

**beaduweorc.** neut. *work of battle.* gen. pl. **beaduweorca.**

**bēag.** masc. *ring.* acc. pl. **bēagas** 12/31, 160; 17/35. gen. pl. **bēaga** 18/340. dat. pl. **bēagum** ʝ/82; 18/36.

**bēag** → **(ge)būgan.**

**bēahgifa.** wk. masc. *ring-giver, lord.* acc. sg. **bēahgifan** 12/290.

**bēahhroden.** adj. *adorned with rings.* fem. nom. pl. **bēahhrodene** 18/138.

**beald.** adj. *bold.* masc. nom. pl. **bealde** 18/17.

**bealofull.** adj. *malicious, wicked.* masc. nom. sg. 18/63. wk. masc. nom. sg. **bealofulla** 18/48. wk. masc. acc. sg. **bealofullan** 18/100. wk. masc. gen. sg. **bealofullan** 18/248.

**bealuwaru.** fem. *dweller in evil, evil one.* gen. pl. **bealuwara** 14/79.

**bēam.** masc. *tree, beam, piece of wood, cross.* nom. sg. 14/97. acc. sg. 17/13. dat. sg. **bēame** 14/114, 122. gen. pl. **bēama** 14/6.

**Bēamflēot.** masc. *Benfleet.* dat. sg. **Bēamflēote.**

**bearh** → **beorgan.**

**bearhtme** → **breahtm.**

**bearn.** neut. *child.* nom. sg. ᴍ/11; 7/21, 32; 11/23; 12/92, etc. (14x). acc. sg. 7/32.

dat. sg. **bearne** 7/21. nom. pl. 3/102, 103 (2x); 18/24. acc. pl. 3/39, 101, 106. gen. pl. **bearna** к/1367; 3/82, 103, 106; 18/51. dat. pl. **bearnum** 9/13; 18/33.

**bearn** → beirnan.

**bearnmyrþre.** wk. fem. *murderer of children.* nom. pl. **bearnmyrðran** 7/56.

**Bearrocscīr.** fem. *Berkshire.* acc. sg. **Bearrocscīre** 5/2.

**bearu.** masc. *wood, grove.* dat. sg. **bearwe** ɪ/6; 16/27; 17/23. nom. pl. **bearwas** ғ/2; к/1363. dat. pl. **bearwum** ғ/3.

**beæftan. A.** prep. (with dat.). *behind.* 4/9, 10.
**B.** adv. *behind.* 18/112.

**bebēodan.** st. 2. *command, commend.* past 1sg. **bebēad** 1/11, 17. past 3sg. **bebēad, bibēad** 1/3; 3/94; 9/31; 18/38, 144. past pl. **bebudon** 9/18. pres. part. **bebēodende** 9/44. past part. **beboden** ɢ/9; 9/7, 19; 10/2, 8.

**bebod.** neut. *command.* acc. sg. н/2.

**beboden, bebudon** → bebēodan.

**bebyrgan.** wk. 1. *bury.* past 3sg. **bebyrgde, bebyrgede, bebyrigde** c/5; 6/4. past pl. **bebyrigdon** 5/19. past part. **bebyrged** 2/16.

**bēc** → bōc.

**beceorian.** wk. 2. *murmur* about something (acc.). past pl. **beceorodon** 6/40.

**becuman.** st. 4. *come, befall.* past 3sg. **becōm, becwōm** 9/43; 18/310. past pl. **becōmon** 12/58; 18/134. subj. sg. **becume** 3/112. subj. past sg. **becōme** 3/70.

**becweþan.** st. 5. *bequeath.* past 3sg. **becwæð** 6/11.

**becwōm** → becuman.

**becyrran.** wk. 1. *turn, pass by, pervert, betray.* past 3sg. **becyrde** 5/5.

**gebed.** neut. *prayer.* acc. sg. в/6. acc. pl. **gebedu** 2/11. dat. pl. **gebedum** в/5.

**bedǣlan.** wk. 1. *deprive* of something (gen. or dat.), *separate* from something (gen. or dat.), *bereave.* past part. **bedǣled, bedǣlde, bidǣled** 3/17; 7/11; 10/15; 13/20.

**bedd.** neut. *bed.* acc. sg. **bed** 18/48. gen. sg. **beddes** 18/63. dat. sg. **bedde** 18/72, 278.

**gebedde.** wk. fem. *bedmate, wife.* acc. sg. **gebeddan** 2/7.

**bedealf** → bedelfan.

**Bedefordscīr.** fem. *Bedfordshire.* acc. sg. **Bedefordscīre** 5/2.

**bedelfan.** st. 3. *bury.* past 3sg. **bedealf** 14/75.

**bedīglian.** wk. 2. *conceal.* past 1sg. **bedīglode** 3/28.

**gebedman.** masc. athematic. *praying man, cleric.* acc. pl. **gebedmen** 10/4.

**bedrēosan.** st. 2. *deprive.* past part. **bidrorene** 13/79.

**bedrest.** fem. *bed.* dat. sg. **bedreste** 18/36.

**bedrīfan.** st. 1. *drive, assail, cover.* past part. **bedrifen, bedrifenne** 14/62.

**beēode** → begān.

**befæstan.** wk. 1. *fasten, entrust.* past part. **befæst** 10/2.

**befealdan.** st. 7. *fold up, envelop.* past part. **bifealdne** 11/14.

**befeallan.** st. 7. *fall, befall, deprive of.* subj. sg. **befealle.** past part. **befeallen** 6/36.

**befēran.** wk. 1. *overtake.* past 3sg. **befērde.**

**beflowen.** adj. *surrounded by flowing something* (dat.). masc. nom. sg. **beflōwen** 16/49.

**befōn.** st. 7. *surround, enclose.* past part. **befangen** 3/86.

**beforan.** prep. (with dat. or acc.). *before, in front of.* **beforan, biforan** 13/46.

**befrīnan.** st. 1. *question.* past 3sg. **befrān.**

**begān.** anom. verb. *traverse, surround.* past 3sg. **beēode** 3/13; 4/4.

**begeat, begēaton** → begytan.

**bēgen.** indef. pron. *both.* masc. nom. pl. 12/183, 191, 291, 305; 18/207. fem. nom. pl. **bā** 18/133. neut. nom. pl. **bū** ɪ/82. masc. acc. pl. 12/182. gen. pl. **bēgea, bēgra** 1/7; 18/128. dat. pl. **bǣm** ɪ/92.

**begēotan.** st. 2. *pour over, infuse.* past part. **begoten** 14/7, 49.

**begytan.** st. 5. *acquire, seize.* past 3sg. **begeat** 16/32, 41. past pl. **begēaton.**

**behātan.** st. 7. *promise.* past 1sg. **behēt.** past 3sg. **behēt** 2/8. past pl. **behēton, behētan** 5/1, 21; 7/68. subj. past sg. **behēte** 2/7. inf. 5/15.

**behēafdian.** wk. 2. *behead.* past part. **behēafdod** 18/289.

**behealdan.** st. 7. *hold, keep, observe, behold.* past 1sg. **behēold, behēolde** 3/52; 14/25, 58. past 2sg. **behēolde** 3/14. past pl. **behēoldon** 14/9, 11, 64.

**behēt-** → behātan.

**behofian.** wk. 2. *require.* pl. **behofigen** 10/7.

**behrēosan.** st. 2. *fall upon, cover.* past part. **bihrorene** 13/77.

**behrēowsung.** fem. *penitence.* dat. sg. **behrēowsunge** 3/96, 97.

**behrīmed.** adj. *frost-covered.* masc. nom. sg. 16/48.

**bēhþ.** fem. *token, proof.*

**behȳdan.** wk. 1. *hide.* 1sg. **behȳde** 1/10. past 1sg. **behȳdde** 3/28. past 3sg. **behȳdde** 1/8.

**beirnan.** st. 3. *run into, occur to.* past 3sg. **bearn.**

**belecgan.** wk. 1. *surround, afflict.* past 3sg. **bilegde** 15/11.

**(ge)belgan.** st. 3. *enrage.* past part. **gebolgen.**

**beliden.** adj. *deprived* (lit. abandoned by). masc. acc. sg. **belidenne** 18/280.

**belimpan.** st. 3. *pertain, belong.* 3sg. **belimpeð, belimpð** 3/111; 8/57. subj. past sg. **belumpe** 6/17. *conduce.* past pl. **belumpon** 9/4. subj. past pl. **belumpen** 9/1.

**belūcan.** st. 2. *lock.* past part. **belocen** 4/10.

**belump-** → belimpan.

**benam, benāmon** → beniman.

**benǣman.** wk. 1. *deprive* someone (acc.) of something (gen. or dat.). inf. 18/76.

**benc.** fem. *bench.* dat. sg. **bence** 12/213. dat. pl. **bencum** 18/18.

**bencsittend.** masc. nd-stem. *bench-sitter.* acc. pl. **bencsittende** 18/27.

**bend.** masc. *bond.* dat. pl. **bendum** 6/23.

**beneah** → benugan.

**benemnan.** wk. 1. *declare.* inf. 17/51.

**beniman.** st. 4. *take something* (acc.) *from someone* (dat.), *deprive someone* (acc.) *of something* (gen.). 3sg. **benimð** 8/59. past 3sg. **benam** 3/42; 4/1; 6/35. past pl. **benāmon** 3/36. inf. 10/73.

**benn.** fem. *wound.* nom. pl. **benne** 13/49.

**benorþan.** prep. *to the north of.* 8/4, 40.

**benugan.** pret. pres. (with gen. object). *enjoy, have use of, possess.* 3sg. **beneah** 17/48.

**(ge)bēodan.** st. 2. *command, proclaim, offer.* 1sg. **bēode.** pl. **bēodaþ** 7/50. past 3sg. **gebēad** 4/8, 11. past pl. **budon** 4/13. inf. **bēodon** 5/3. past part. **geboden** 4/13.

**beodan** → (ge)bīdan.

**bēodgenēat.** masc. *table-retainer, retainer who sits at his lord's table.* nom. pl. **bēodgenēatas.**

**bēon. A.** anom. verb. *be.* 1sg. **eom, bēo** I/1; 1/10; 2/13; 3/84, 86, etc. (10x). 2sg. **eart, bist** 1/14, 16, 9, 19; 3/72, etc. (7x). 3sg. **is, bið, byð, ys** A/1, 2 (2x), 3 (2x), etc. (155x). pl. **bēoð, syndan, sindon, synd, sind, sint, syn, bēo, syndon, synt** A/4 (2x), 5; E/1, 3, etc. (57x). past 1sg. **wæs** 12/217; 14/62. past 2sg. **wære** 1/19; 11/8. past 3sg. **wæs, was** B/5; F/1, 2, 4; H/1, etc. (176x). past pl. **wǣron, wǣrun, wǣran** F/2 (2x), 3, 4, 6, etc. (54x). subj. sg. **sīe, sȳ, bēo, sī, bīo** D/3; I/5; M/1, 2, 7, etc. (27x). subj. pl. **bēon, sīen, sȳn** 3/3; 10/14. subj. past sg. **wære** B/3; G/6; 1/11; 2/10, 11, etc. (42x). subj. past pl. **wǣren, wǣron** 3/76; 10/11. imp. pl. **bēoð** 3/20. inf. **bēon, bīon** B/4; J/86; M/13; 3/112 (2x), etc. (14x). infl. inf. **tō bēonne.**

**B.** Negated forms. 3sg. **nis** K/1361, 1372; 3/14, 52; 6/27, etc. (12x). past 3sg. **næs** H/4; 3/45; 6/30; 7/5; 12/325, etc. (6x). past pl. **nǣron** 3/102, 105. subj. past sg. **nǣre** 3/21; 4/12; 10/53.

**bēor.** neut. *beer.* gen. sg. **bēores.**

**beorg.** masc. *mountain, hill.* acc. sg. 14/32. dat. sg. **beorge** 14/50. dat. pl. **beorgum.**

**gebeorg.** neut. *protection, defence.* dat. sg. **gebeorge** 12/31, 131, 245.

**beorgan.** st. 3. *save something* (dat.), *spare, deliver, protect.* past 3sg. **bearh** 7/21. past pl. **burgon** 12/194. subj. sg. **beorgan, beorge** 7/16. inf. к/1372; 7/60. *guard against.* subj. pl. **beorgan** 7/70. inf. 7/54.

**beorht.** adj. *bright.* fem. nom. sg. 13/94. masc. acc. pl. **beorhte.** gen. pl. **beorhtra** 18/340. wk. fem. nom. sg. **beorhte** 18/254. wk. fem. acc. sg. **beorhtan** 11/10; 18/58. wk. masc. dat. sg. **beorhtan** 14/66. wk. fem. dat. sg. **beorhtan** 18/326, 340. masc. nom. sg. superl. **beorhtast, beorhtost** 11/1; 14/6.

**beorhtnes.** fem. *brightness.*

**Beormas.** masc. *Bjarmians* a group living on the White Sea. nom. pl. 8/14, 16, 17.

**beorn.** masc. *man, warrior.* nom. sg. 13/70, 113; 14/42. acc. sg. 12/270. gen. sg. **beornes** 12/131, 160. dat. sg. **beorne** 12/154, 245. nom. pl. **beornas** 12/92, 111; 14/32, 66; 18/213, etc. (6x). acc. pl. **beornas** 12/17, 62, 182, 277, 305, etc. (6x). gen. pl. **beorna** 12/257; 18/254. dat. pl. **beornum** 12/101.

**gebēorscipe.** masc. lit. *beer-company, banquet.* gen. sg. **gebēorscipes** 9/7. dat. sg. м/8; 9/6, 8.

**(ge)bēot.** neut. *vow, boast.* acc. sg. **bēot, gebēot** 12/15, 27; 13/70; 17/49. acc. pl. **bēot** 12/213.

**bēotian.** wk. 2. *vow, boast.* past 3sg. **bēotode** 12/290. past pl. **bēotedan** 16/21.

**bepǣcan.** wk. 1. *deceive.* past 3sg. **bepǣhte** 1/13. infl. inf. **tō bepǣcenne** 3/46.

**beprēwan.** wk. 1. *wink.* inf. 10/40.

**bera.** wk. masc. *bear.* gen. sg. **beran** 8/29.

**berād** → berīdan.

**(ge)beran.** st. 4. *bear, carry, bring, give birth to.* 3sg. **bereð, bireð, byrð** 8/71; 14/118; 15/17. pl. **berað** 8/38. past 3sg. **bær, gebær** 6/10, 19, 20; 11/20. past pl.

**bǣron** 2/24; 12/99; 14/32; 18/201. subj. past sg. **gebǣre** c/3. subj. past pl. **bēron** 12/67. imp. pl. **berað** 9/34; 18/191. inf. **beran** 2/18; 8/66; 12/12, 62. infl. inf. **berenne, tō berenne** G/7; 18/131. past part. **boren** 18/18.

**Beranburg.** fem. athematic. *Barbury Camp.* dat. sg. **Beranbyrg.**

**beren.** adj. *of bearskin.* masc. acc. sg. **berenne** 8/29.

**berīdan.** st. 1. *overtake, surround.* past 3sg. **berād** 4/4.

**bēron** → (ge)beran.

**berstan.** st. 3. *burst.* past 3sg. **bærst** 12/284. inf. 14/36.

**berȳpan.** wk. 1. *despoil, rob.* past part. **berȳpte** 7/11, 13.

**besendan.** wk. 1. *send.* 3sg. **besent** 3/112.

**besmītan.** st. 1. *soil, defile.* subj. sg. **besmīte.** inf. 18/59.

**bestandan.** st. 6. *stand on either side.* past pl. **bestōdon** 12/68.

**bestēman.** wk. 1. *drench.* past part. **bestēmed** 14/22, 48.

**bestōdon** → bestandan.

**bestrēowian.** wk. 2. *sprinkle.* past pl. **bestrēowodon** 3/69.

**bestrȳpan.** wk. 1. *strip.* past part. **bestrȳpte** 7/13.

**beswīcan.** st. 1. *deceive, betray.* 3sg. **beswīcð** 10/13. past 3sg. **beswāc** 3/64. subj. sg. **beswīce** 7/25. subj. past sg. **beswice** 3/64. inf. 3/82. past part. **beswicene** 7/14; 12/238.

**beswyllan.** wk. 1. *drench.* past part. **beswyled** 14/23.

**besyrwan.** wk. 1. *ensnare.* past part. **besyrwde** 7/14.

**bet** → wel.

**(ge)bētan.** wk. 1. *amend, make amends, atone for.* past pl. **bēttan** 7/17. subj. sg. **bēte.** subj. pl. **bētan** 7/54. inf. **bētan, gebētan** 7/67; 8/73. *pay* (as a fine). subj. sg. **gebēte** м/3, 5.

**betǣcan.** wk. 1. *commend, deliver.* past 3sg. **betǣhte.** past part. **betǣht** 7/11.

**beter-** → gōd.

betonice. wk. fem. *betony.* acc. sg. betonican.

betst → wel.

betst- → gōd.

betuh, betux → betweox.

betwēonan. prep. *among, between.* betwēonan, betwȳnan 3/51; 7/69; 8/62.

betweox. prep. (with dat. or acc.). *among, between.* betweox, betwux, betuh, betux, betwyx F/4; 1/14, 15; 2/16; 3/8, etc. (11x).

betwȳnan → betwēonan.

betȳnan. wk. 1. *enclose, close, end, conclude.* past 3sg. betȳnde 9/27, 44.

beþeccan. wk. 1. *cover over, protect.* past part. beþeahte 11/13; 18/213.

beþencan. wk. 1. (sometimes with refl. pron.). *consider, call to mind.* past pl. beðōhton. subj. pl. 7/66. inf. 7/58.

bewāwan. st. 7. *blow upon.* past part. biwāune 13/76.

beweaxen. adj. *overgrown.* masc. nom. pl. beweaxne 16/31.

beweorpan. st. 3. *surround.* past part. biworpen 15/5.

bewestan. prep. *to the west of.*

bewindan. st. 3. *wind about, wrap, surround, grasp.* past pl. bewundon 2/24. past part. bewunden 2/23, 27; 14/5; 18/115.

bewrēon. st. 1. *cover, hide.* past 1sg. biwrāh 13/23. past part. bewrigen, bewrigene 14/17, 53.

bewunden, bewundon → bewindan.

bi → be.

bi- (prefix) → be-.

bibēad → bebēodan.

gebicgan, bicgaþ → (ge)bycgan.

(ge)bīdan. st. 1. (with acc. or gen. object). *wait, wait for, experience, endure.* 3sg. gebīdeð 13/1. past 1sg. gebād 12/174; 14/125; 16/3. past 3sg. bād 8/8. past pl. beodan. inf. bīdan, gebīdan 7/6; 8/9; 9/41; 13/70. past part. gebiden, gebidenne 7/6; 14/50, 79; 18/64.

biddan. st. 5. *ask, pray.* 1sg. bidde 3/109. 3sg. bideð 11/10. past 2sg. bǣde D/1.

past 3sg. bæd 2/9, 16; 9/30; 12/20, 128, etc. (6x). past pl. bǣdon B/5; 9/36; 12/87, 262, 306. inf. F/7; 10/65; 17/13; 18/187. *ask for* something (gen.). subj. past sg. bǣde 9/31. inf. 18/84. *tell* (to do something). past 3sg. bæd 12/170.

gebiddan. st. 5. *ask, entreat, pray* (often with dat. or acc. refl.). 3sg. gebit 3/92, 97. pl. gebiddaþ 14/83. past 1sg. gebæd 14/122. past 3sg. gebæd 3/95, 96, 97; 9/42. subj. sg. gebidde.

gebiden- → (ge)bīdan.

bideþ → biddan.

bidrorene → bedrēosan.

bīegan. wk. 1. *bend.*

bifian. wk. 2. *tremble, quake.* past 1sg. bifode 14/42. inf. 14/36.

big → be.

bigspel → bīspell.

bihrorene → behrēosan.

bilewite. adj. *innocent, pure, honest.* masc. nom. sg. bilewite 3/5, 14. fem. dat. sg. bilwitre 9/43.

bilewitness. fem. *innocence, mildness.* dat. sg. bilewitnysse 3/60.

bill. neut. *sword.* acc. sg. 12/162. dat. pl. billum 12/114.

bilwitre → bilewit.

gebind. neut. *binding, freezing.* acc. sg. 13/24, 57.

(ge)bindan. st. 3. *bind.* 3sg. bindeð 13/102. pl. bindað, gebindað 13/18, 40. subj. sg. binde 13/13. inf. bindan. past part. gebunden, gebundne F/3; 18/115.

binn. fem. *bin, crib, manger.* dat. sg. binne.

binnan. prep. (with dat. or acc.). *within, in, into.* 1/1; 18/64.

bīo, bīon → bēon.

bireþ → (ge)beran.

bisceopscīre → biscopscīr.

biscepdōme → biscopdōm.

biscop. masc. *bishop.* nom. sg. bisceop, biscep, biscop 2/7, 10; 6/25. acc. sg. bisceop 5/6, 15, 17. gen. sg. biscopes. dat. sg. bisceope, biscepe. nom. pl. bisceopas 5/19. acc. pl. biscopas 6/24. gen. pl. biscopa 7/63.

**biscopdōm.** masc. *bishopric.* dat. sg. **biscepdōme.**

**biscophād.** masc. *bishopric.* dat. sg. **biscophāde.**

**biscoprīce.** neut. *bishopric.* dat. sg. 6/24.

**biscopscīr.** fem. *bishopric.* acc. sg. **bisceopscīre.**

**biscopstōl.** masc. *episcopal see.* nom. sg. 6/26.

**bismrode** → bysmerian.

**bīspell.** neut. *example, proverb, story, parable.* acc. pl. **bigspel.**

**bist** → bēon.

**gebit** → gebiddan.

**bītan.** st. 1. *bite.*

**biter.** adj. *bitter, fierce, cruel.* masc. nom. sg. 12/111. masc. gen. sg. **biteres** 14/114. masc. nom. pl. **bitre** 16/31. masc. acc. pl. **bitere** 12/85. dat. pl. **biterum** 3/81.

**biþ** → bēon.

**biwāune** → bewāwan.

**bīwist.** fem. *sustenance.* nom. sg. 10/7. acc. sg. **bīwiste** 10/6.

**biworpen** → beweorpan.

**biwrāh** → bewrēon.

**blāc.** adj. *bright, pale.* masc. acc. sg. **blācne** 18/278.

**blāchlēor.** adj. *fair-faced.* fem. nom. sg. 18/128.

**bladu** → blæd.

**blāwung.** fem. *blowing.* acc. sg. **blāwunge.**

**blǣcern.** neut. *lantern.*

**blǣd.** neut. *leaf, blade.* nom. pl. **bladu** A/3.

**blǣd.** masc. Lit. *blowing, breath. spirit, life.* acc. sg. 18/63. *glory, prosperity.* nom. sg. 13/33. acc. sg. 18/122. dat. pl. **blēdum** 14/149.

**Blecinga ēg.** proper noun. *Blekinge* (province in southern Sweden). nom. sg. 8/55.

**blēdum** → blǣd.

**blendian.** wk. 2. *make blind.* inf. 6/37.

**blēo.** neut. *colour.* gen. sg. **blēos** 2/19. dat. pl. **blēom** 14/22.

**(ge)bletsian.** wk. 2. *bless.* past 2sg. **bletsodest** 3/31. past 3sg. **bletsode** 3/99. past part. **gebletsod** 3/42.

**bletsung.** fem. *blessing.* acc. sg. **bletsunge** B/6.

**blīcan.** st. 1. *shine.* inf. 18/137.

**blind.** adj. *blind.* wk. masc. nom. sg. **blinda** 3/15, 16. wk. masc. acc. sg. **blindan** 3/16. masc. dat. sg. **blindum** 3/25. gen. pl. **blindra.**

**bliss.** fem. *bliss, merriment.* nom. sg. **blis, bliss** 3/81; 5/10; 14/139, 141. acc. sg. **blisse** 5/10. gen. sg. **blisse** 9/6. dat. sg. **blisse** 3/81; 14/149, 153.

**blissian.** wk. 2. *rejoice.* pl. **blissiað** 3/81. past 1sg. **blissode** 3/26. inf. F/7. pres. part. **blyssigende** 2/24.

**blīþe.** A. adj. *happy, friendly.* masc. nom. sg. 9/36; 18/58, 154. neut. acc. sg. 16/44. neut. inst. sg. 14/122; 16/21. masc. nom. pl. 18/159. neut. acc. pl. 9/35. masc. nom. sg. compar. **blīþra** 12/146. B. adv. *joyfully.*

**blīþelice.** adv. *joyfully.* **blȳðelīce** 2/20. compar. **blīþelīcor.**

**blīþemōd.** adj. *happy, friendly.* masc. nom. sg. 9/37. masc. nom. pl. **blīðemōde** 9/36.

**blōd.** neut. *blood.* nom. sg. 5/18. dat. sg. **blōde** 14/48.

**blōdgyte.** masc. *bloodshed.* nom. sg. 7/18.

**blōdig.** adj. *bloody.* masc. acc. sg. **blōdigne** 12/154. neut. acc. sg. 18/126, 174.

**(ge)blondan.** st. 7. *blend, corrupt.* past part. **geblonden** 18/34.

**blondenfeax.** adj. *with mixed hair, grey-haired.*

**blyssigende** → blissian.

**blȳþelīce** → blīþelice.

**bōc.** fem. athematic. *book.* nom. sg. **bōc, booc** 3/88; 9/24. acc. sg. 2/8. dat. sg. **bēc** 2/27; 10/16, 17. nom. pl. **bēc** D/3; 2/28, 30; 7/54, 57. gen. pl. **bōca** 9/24; 10/29. dat. pl. **bōcum** 2/31; 10/17.

**bōcere.** masc. *scholar, writer.* gen. sg. **bōceres.** nom. pl. **bōceras.** acc. pl. **bōceras** 9/1.

**boda.** wk. masc. *messenger.* nom. sg. 12/49. nom. pl. **bodan** 7/50.

**geboden** → (ge)bēodan.

**bodian.** wk. 2. *announce, proclaim, preach.*
1sg. **bodie.** past 3sg. **bodode** 10/49. past
pl. **bodedon** 18/244. inf. 18/251.

**bōg.** masc. *arm.* dat. pl. **bōgum** 15/11.

**boga.** wk. masc. *bows.* nom. pl. **bogan**
12/110.

**bogian.** wk. 2. *dwell, inhabit.* inf. **bōgian.**
**gebohte** → (ge)bycgan.

**bolca.** wk. masc. *gangway.* acc. sg. **bolcan.**

**boldāgend.** masc. *possessor of a hall.* dat.
pl. **boldāgendum** J/92.

**gebolgen** → (ge)belgan.

**bolla.** wk. masc. *bowl, cup.* nom. pl. **bollan**
18/17.

**bolster.** masc. *cushion.* dat. sg. **bolstre** 9/42.

**booc** → bōc.

**bord.** neut. *board, shield.* nom. sg. 12/110.
acc. sg. 12/15, 42, 131, 245, 270, etc.
(6x). gen. sg. **bordes** 12/284. acc. pl.
12/62, 283; 18/192, 317. gen. pl. **borda**
12/295. dat. pl. **bordum** 12/101; 18/213.

**bordweall.** masc. *shield-wall.* acc. sg.
12/277.

**geboren.** adj. *born.*

**boren** → (ge)beran.

**bōsm.** masc. *bosom, breast.* acc. sg. **bōsum**
6/27. dat. sg. **bōsme** 1/6; 3/28, 87.

**bōt.** fem. *help, remedy, atonement, penance.*
nom. sg. 7/8. acc. sg. **bōte** 7/5, 6, 7, 57;
13/113. gen. sg. **bōte** 7/13.

**brād.** adj. *broad.* masc. nom. sg. 8/35 (2x),
58. neut. nom. sg. 8/34, 35. neut. acc.
sg. 12/15, 163. neut. dat. sg. **brādum**
10/16. fem. nom. pl. **brāde.** fem. nom.
sg. compar. **brādre** 8/46. neut. nom. sg.
compar. **brādre, brǣdre** 8/34 (2x).
neut. nom. sg. superl. **brādost** 8/33.

**brādswyrd.** neut. *broadsword.* acc. pl.
18/317.

**gebræc.** neut. *crash.* nom. sg. 12/295.

**bræc, brǣcan** → brecan.

**brǣd.** fem. *breadth.*

**brǣd** → bregdan.

**(ge)brǣdan. A.** wk. 1. *broaden, spread.* inf.
**brǣdan** 13/47. infl. inf. **tō brǣdanne,**
**tō gebrǣdanne** 10/21, 30.
  **B.** wk. 1. *roast.* past part. **gebrǣd.**

**brǣdre** → brād.

**brǣdu.** fem. *breadth.*

**brēac** → brūcan.

**breahtm.** masc. *noise, revelry.* dat. sg.
**bearhtme** 18/39. gen. pl. **breahtma**
13/86.

**brecan.** st. 5. *break, torment* someone
with curiosity (with *fyrwit* as subject),
*transgress.* past 3sg. **bræc** 12/277. past
pl. **brǣcan** 7/17, 67. past part. **brocen**
12/1.

**bred.** neut. *surface, board.* dat. sg. **brede**
10/16.

**bregdan.** st. 3. *pull, shake, draw* (a sword).
past 3sg. **brǣd** 12/154, 162. past pl.
**brugdon** 18/229.

**brego.** masc. *ruler, lord.* nom. sg. 18/39,
254.

**brēme.** adj. *famous, glorious.* wk. masc.
nom. sg. **brēma** 18/57.

**brēmel.** masc. *bramble, brier.* acc. pl.
**brēmelas** 1/18.

**(ge)brengan.** wk. 1. *bring.* past 3sg. **brōhte,**
**gebrōhte** 18/125. past pl. **brōhton,**
**gebrōhton** 2/20; 8/18; 18/54, 335. inf.
**brengan, gebrengan** 10/80. past part.
**brōht, gebrōht** 5/16; 7/11; 18/57.

**brēost.** neut. (often pl. with sg. sense).
*breast.* dat. sg. **brēoste** 1/14. dat. pl.
**brēostum** 12/144; 13/113; 14/118;
18/192.

**brēostcearu.** fem. *sorrow in the breast.* acc.
sg. **brēostceare** 16/44.

**brēostcofa.** wk. masc. *breast-chamber.* dat.
sg. **brēostcofan** 13/18.

**(ge)brēowan.** st. 2. *brew.* past part.
**gebrowen** 8/63.

**brēr.** fem. *briar.* dat. pl. **brērum** 16/31.

**Bret.** masc. *Briton.* acc. pl. **Brettas,**
**Bryttas.** gen. pl. **Brytta** 7/61, 62. dat.
pl. **Bryttan** 7/65.

**Bretenlond.** neut. *Britain.*

**Brettisc.** adj. *British.* masc. dat. sg.
**Bryttiscum** 4/8. masc. acc. sg.
**Brettiscne.**

**Bretwēalas.** masc. *the British.* dat. pl.
**Bretwālum** 4/3.

**brēþer** → brōþor.

**bricge** → brycg.

**bricgweard.** masc. *defender of a bridge.* acc. pl. **bricgweardas** 12/85.

**brimfugol.** masc. *sea-bird.* acc. pl. **brimfuglas** 13/47.

**brimlīþend.** adj. *seafaring.* gen. pl. **brimlīþendra** 12/27.

**brimman.** masc. A/o-stem. *seaman, Viking.* nom. pl. **brimmen** 12/295. gen. pl. **brimmanna** 12/49.

**(ge)bringan.** st. 3. *bring, offer.* 3sg. **bringeð, gebringeð** 7/53; 13/54. subj. sg. **gebringe** 14/139. inf. **bringan** 10/10. past part. **brungen** 11/17.

**brocen** → brecan.

**gebrocod.** adj. *afflicted.* masc. nom. pl. **gebrocode.**

**brōga.** wk. masc. *terror.* gen. sg. **brōgan** 18/4.

**brōht-, gebrōht-** → (ge)brengan.

**brōþor.** masc. r-stem. (sometimes with neut. ending in pl.). *brother.* nom. sg. **brōðor, brōþur, brōþer** D/1; 4/3; 7/21, 32; 9/1, etc. (6x). acc. sg. 6/24. dat. sg. **brēðer** 3/39. nom. pl. **brōðor, brōðru** B/5; 9/37, 39; 12/191.

**gebrōþor.** masc. r-stem. (pl., often with neut. ending). *brothers, monks.* nom. pl. **gebrōðra, gebrōðru** B/1; 2/20; 3/1, 104; 12/305. acc. pl. **gebrōðra** 2/18.

**gebrowen** → (ge)brēowan.

**brūcan.** st. 2. (usually with gen. object, sometimes with acc.). *enjoy, use, benefit from, partake of.* past 2sg. **bruce.** past 3sg. **brēac** 13/44. past pl. **brucon.** subj. past sg. **bruce** 2/7. inf. 10/62; 14/144. *eat.* 2sg. **brȳcst** 1/19.

**brugdon** → bregdan.

**brūn.** adj. *brown, shiny.* masc. acc. pl. **brūne** 18/317.

**brūneccg.** adj. *with shiny edges.* neut. acc. sg. 12/163.

**brūnfāg.** adj. *with shiny ornaments.* masc. acc. sg. **brūnfāgne.**

**brungen** → (ge)bringan.

**bryce.** masc. *breaking, violation.* dat. sg. 7/8.

**brycg.** fem. *bridge.* acc. sg. **bricge** 12/74, 78. nom. pl. **brycga.**

**brȳcst** → brūcan.

**brȳd.** fem. *bride.* nom. sg. Lb.

**brȳdbūr.** neut. *bridal chamber.* dat. sg. **brȳdbūre.**

**brȳdguma.** wk. masc. *bridegroom.* acc. sg. **brȳdguman.**

**bryne.** masc. *fire, burning.* nom. sg. 2/13; 7/18. acc. sg. 7/70; 14/149. dat. sg. 7/8; 18/116.

**Brytland.** neut. *Britain, Wales.* nom. sg. 6/31.

**brytnian.** wk. 2. *distribute.* inf. 17/34.

**brytta.** wk. masc. *giver.* nom. sg. 18/30, 93. acc. sg. **bryttan** 13/25; 18/90.

**Brytt-** → Bret.

**Bryttiscum** → Brettisc.

**bū** → bēgen.

**būan.** anom. verb. (with strong pres. and past part. and usually weak past). *dwell, inhabit, cultivate.* past 3sg. **būde** 8/39. subj. past sg. **būde** 8/1, 2, 4, 40. inf. **būgan** 17/18. past part. **gebūn, gebūd** 8/12, 13, 14.

**būc.** masc. *vessel, container.* gen. pl. **būca.**

**Buccingahāmscīr.** fem. *Buckinghamshire.* acc. sg. **Buccingahāmscīre** 5/2.

**gebūd, būde** → būan.

**budon** → (ge)bēodan.

**bufan.** A. prep. (with dat. or acc.). *above.* 2/19, 20; 8/64.

B. adv. *above.* 2/21.

**(ge)būgan.** st. 2. *bow, bend, turn.* past 3sg. **bēag** 8/8, 9. past pl. **bugon** 12/185. inf. **būgan** 12/276; 14/36, 42. *submit.* past pl. **bugon** 5/21. inf. **gebūgan** 7/67.

**būgan** → būan.

**būgian.** wk. 2. *inhabit, dwell.* pl. **būgiað** 10/21, 22, 24, 29. inf. **gebūgian** 10/18. infl. inf. **tō būgianne** 10/7, 20.

**bugon** → (ge)būgan.

**gebūn** → būan.

**gebunden, gebundne** → (ge)bindan.

**bune.** wk. fem. *cup.* nom. sg. 13/94. nom. pl. **bunan** 18/18. dat. pl. **bunum** ʝ/82.

**būr.** masc. *chamber, cottage.* acc. sg. 4/4.

**gebūr.** masc. *freeholder, farmer.* gen. sg. **gebūres** ᴍ/6. dat. sg. **gebūre** ᴍ/7.

**burg.** fem. athematic. *fortified place, fortress, town, city.* nom. sg. **burh** 8/60. acc. sg. **burh, buruh** 5/8; 12/291. gen. sg. **burge, byrg, byrig** 10/26, 29, 31; 18/137. dat. sg. **byrig** 4/10; 5/7, 10; 8/60; 18/149, etc. (7x). acc. pl. **burga.** gen. pl. **burga** 18/58.

**Burgendan.** wk. masc. *inhabitants of Bornholm* (Danish island in the Baltic). gen. pl. **burgenda** 8/54, 55.

**būrgeteld.** neut. *tent used as a bedchamber.* acc. sg. 18/276. gen. sg. **būrgeteldes** 18/248. dat. sg. **būrgetelde** 18/57.

**burglēoda** → burhlēod.

**burgon** → beorgan.

**burgtūn.** masc. *fortified enclosure.* nom. pl. **burgtūnas** 16/31.

**burgwaru.** fem. (usually pl.; with collective sense in sg.). *populace, town-dwellers.* nom. sg. **buruhwaru** 5/19. gen. pl. **burgwara** 13/86. dat. pl. **burgwarum** 10/75.

**burhlēod.** masc. *townsperson.* gen. pl. **burglēoda** 18/187. dat. pl. **burhlēodum** 18/175.

**burhsittend.** masc. nd-stem. *city-dweller.* nom. pl. **burhsittende** 18/159.

**būrþēn.** masc. *chamber-servant, secretary.* dat. sg. **būrþēne** 12/121.

**buruhwaru** → burgwaru.

**būtan. A.** prep. (usually with dat.). *without, except, except for.* **būton, būtan** ꜰ/7; ʜ/4; 2/30; 3/23, 26, etc. (21x).

   **B.** conj. *but, unless, except, except that.* **būton, būtan** ᴅ/3; 2/11 (2x); 7/16; 8/3, etc. (10x).

**būtū.** indef. pron. *both.* masc. nom. pl. **būta** 2/30. masc. acc. pl. 14/48.

**(ge)bycgan.** wk. 1. *buy, redeem.* pl. **bicgað** 7/30. past 3sg. **gebohte** 7/31. inf. **gebicgan, bycgan** ʝ/81.

**bydel.** masc. *minister, beadle.* gen. pl. **bydela** 7/63.

**gebyldan.** wk. 1. *embolden, encourage.* past 3sg. **bylde** 12/169, 209, 320. subj. sg. **bylde** 12/234. past part. **gebylde** 18/268.

**byldu.** fem. *courage, confidence, arrogance, presumption.* acc. sg. **byldo** 11/10.

**bȳne.** adj. *inhabited, cultivated.* neut. nom. sg. 8/33. neut. dat. sg. **bȳnum** 8/32.

**gebyrd.** fem. (sometimes pl. with sg. meaning). *birth, parentage, rank.* dat. pl. **gebyrdum** 8/28.

**byrde.** adj. *of high rank.* wk. masc. nom. sg. superl. **byrdesta** 8/29.

**byre. A.** masc. *occasion, opportunity.* acc. sg. 12/121.

   **B.** masc. *son, young man.*

**gebyrede** → gebyrian.

**byrg** → burg.

**byrgan.** wk. 1. *taste.* past 3sg. **byrigde** 14/101.

**byrgen.** fem. *grave.* acc. sg. **byrgene** 2/20, 21. dat. sg. **byrgene** 2/18, 26. dat. pl. **byrgenum.**

**gebyrian.** wk. 2. *happen, pertain to.* pl. **gebyriað** 7/50. past 3sg. **gebyrede** 10/36.

**byrig** → burg.

**byrigde** → byrgan.

**byrnan.** st. 3. *burn.* pres. part. **byrnendum** ᴄ/11.

**byrne.** wk. fem. *corslet.* nom. sg. 12/144, 284. acc. sg. **byrnan** 12/163; 18/337. acc. pl. **byrnan** 18/327.

**byrnham.** masc. *corslet.* acc. pl. **byrnhomas** 18/192.

**byrnwiga.** wk. masc. *warrior in mail.* nom. sg. 13/94. gen. pl. **byrnwigena** 18/39.

**byrnwiggend.** masc. nd-stem. *warrior in a mail coat.* nom. pl. **byrnwiggende** 18/17.

**byrst.** masc. *loss, injury.* nom. sg. 7/16. gen. pl. **byrsta** 7/6.

**byrþ** → (ge)beran.

**bysen.** fem. *example.* dat. sg. **bysne** 3/29, 57. nom. pl. **bysna** 2/31.

**bysig.** adj. *busy.* masc. nom. pl. **bysige** 12/110.

**bysmer.** masc. *disgrace, insult, reproach.* acc. sg. **bysmor** 7/16, 44. dat. sg. **bysmore** 7/40. gen. pl. **bysmara** 7/6.

**bysmerian.** wk. 2. *revile, mock, put to shame.* past 3sg. **bismrode** 10/49. past pl. **bysmeredon** 14/48.

**bysmorlīce.** adv. *shamefully, irreverently, contemptuously.* **bysmerlīce, bysmorlīce** 5/17; 18/100.

**gebysnung.** fem. *example.* dat. pl. **gebysnungum** 2/10.

**byþ** → bēon.

**cāf.** adj. *quick, bold.* masc. acc. sg. **cāfne** 12/76.

**cafertūn.** masc. *vestibule, courtyard.* nom. sg. 10/20. acc. sg. 10/21.

**cāflīce.** adv. *quickly, boldly.* 12/153.

**cald. A.** adj. *cold.* neut. acc. sg. 12/91. dat. pl. **caldum.**

    **B.** neut. *cold.* dat. sg. **calde.**

**camb.** masc. *comb.*

**(ge)camp.** masc. *battle.* dat. sg. **campe, gecampe** 12/153; 18/200.

**campdōm.** masc. *warfare.* nom. sg. 3/78, 79.

**campstede.** masc. *battlefield.*

**canōn.** masc. *canon.* gen. sg. **canōnes** 9/24.

**Cantwaraburh.** fem. athematic. *Canterbury.* acc. sg. **Cantwareburuh** 5/5. dat. sg. **Cantwarebyrig** 2/17; 6/16.

**carcern.** neut. *prison.* gen. sg. **carcernes.** dat. sg. **carcerne** 10/61.

**care** → cearu.

**carlēas.** adj. *without cares, reckless.* wk. neut. nom. pl. **carlēasan.**

**carlman.** masc. athematic. *male person.* nom. sg. 6/29.

**cāsere.** masc. *Caesar, emperor.* nom. sg. H/1.

**castel.** masc. *castle.* acc. pl. **castelas** 6/31, 34.

**Caþum.** masc. *Caen.* dat. sg. 6/4.

**Caucaseas.** masc. *Caucasus Mountains.* nom. pl. 10/29.

**cǣg.** fem. *key.*

**ceaf.** neut. *chaff.* dat. sg. **ceafe.**

**ceafl.** masc. *jaw.* dat. pl. **ceaflum** 7/63.

**cealf.** neut. es/os-stem. *calf.*

**ceallian.** wk. 2. *call.* inf. 12/91.

**cēap.** masc. *commerce, price, merchandise, purchase.* acc. sg. 7/31. dat. sg. **cēape** J/81; 7/30.

**cearful.** adj. *full of care, miserable.* gen. pl. **cearfulra.**

**cearu.** fem. *care, sorrow.* nom. sg. **cearo** 13/55. acc. sg. **care, ceare** 3/112; 13/9. nom. pl. **ceare.**

**gecēas** → gecēosan.

**ceaster.** fem. *fortress, town.* dat. sg. **ceastre.**

**cellod.** adj. *meaning unknown.* neut. acc. pl. 12/283.

**cempa.** wk. masc. *warrior, soldier.* nom. sg. 3/80; 12/119. nom. pl. **cempan.**

**cende** → cennan.

**cēne. A.** adj. *brave.* masc. nom. sg. 10/76; 12/215. masc. nom. pl. 18/332. gen. pl. **cēnra** 18/200. fem. nom. sg. compar. **cēnre** 12/312.

    **B.** adv. *bravely.* 12/283.

**cennan.** wk. 1. *conceive, give birth to, produce.* past 3sg. **cende.** past part. **cenned.**

**Centingas.** masc. *the people of Kent.* acc. pl. **Kentingas** 5/2.

**cēolþel.** neut. *ship-plank, the deck of a ship.* dat. sg. **cēolþele** 17/9.

**ceorfan.** st. 3. *carve.* past pl. **curfon** 14/66.

**ceorl.** masc. *peasant, freeman, husband.* nom. sg. 12/256. gen. sg. **ceorles.** dat. sg. **ceorle** 7/14; 12/132.

**gecēosan.** st. 2. *choose, decide.* past 3sg. **gecēas** 12/113. past part. **gecoren** 9/16.

**cēpeman.** masc. athematic. *merchant.* nom. pl. **cēpemen** 10/25.

**Chaldeisce.** adj. *Chaldaean.* wk. masc. nom. pl. **Chaldeiscan** 3/38.

**(ge)cīdan.** wk. 1. *quarrel, chide.* subj. pl. **gecīden** M/8. inf. **cīdan.**

**gecierran** → (ge)cyrran.

**gecīgan.** wk. 1. *call.* past part. **gecīgde, gecīged** 3/66.

**cild.** neut. *child.* dat. sg. **cilde.** acc. pl. 1/16. dat. pl. **cildum.**

**cile.** masc. *cold.* acc. sg. **cyle** 8/74 (2x). dat. sg. 10/18.

**cirdon** → (ge)cyrran.

**cirm** → cyrm.

**cirman.** wk. 1. *cry out.* inf. 18/270.

**cirr.** masc. *occasion.* dat. sg. **cirre** 8/4.

**clāþ.** masc. *cloth, clothes* (in pl.). nom. pl. **clāþas** 10/7.

**clǣne. A.** adj. *clean, chaste, innocent.* neut. nom. sg. c/3; 9/22. *open* (of land). dat. pl. **clǣnum. B.** adv. *entirely.* 7/11, 13.

**clǣnness.** fem. *cleanness, chastity.* acc. sg. **clǣnnysse, clǣnnesse** 2/28, 31. dat. sg. **clǣnnysse** 2/4, 29, 31.

**clǣnsian.** wk. 2. *cleanse.* inf. 7/69.

**clēofan.** wk. 2. *split.* past pl. **clufon** 12/283.

**cleopedon, cleopian** → clipian.

**clif.** neut. *cliff.* dat. sg. **clife** f/3, 4 (2x).

**clipian.** wk. 2. *call, cry out.* 3sg. **clypað.** past 3sg. **clypode, clipode** 1/9; 12/25, 256. past pl. **cleopedon.** imp. sg. **clypa.** inf. **clypian, cleopian** 7/63.

**clipiend.** masc. *one who calls.* gen. sg. **clipiendes.**

**clomm.** masc. *bond, fetter.* dat. pl. **clommum.**

**clūdig.** adj. *rocky.* neut. nom. sg. 8/31.

**clufon** → clēofan.

**clumian.** wk. 2. *mumble.* past pl. **clumedan** 7/63.

**clyp-** → clipian.

**clyppan.** wk. 1. *embrace, honour, cherish.* subj. sg. **clyppe** 13/42. inf. 9/20.

**cnapa.** wk. masc. *youth, boy.*

**gecnāwan.** st. 7. *know, recognize, understand.* subj. sg. **gecnāwe** 7/16, 34. imp. pl. **gecnāwað** 7/1.

**cnēoris.** fem. *nation.* nom. sg. 18/323.

**cnēow.** neut. *knee.* dat. sg. **cnēo** LA; 13/42.

**cniht.** masc. *young man, boy, warrior.* nom. sg. M/13; 12/9, 153. in post-Conquest usage, *knight.* nom. pl. **cnihtas** 6/21.

**cnyssan.** wk. 1. *strike, crash against, beat.* pl. **cnyssað** 13/101.

**cnyttan.** wk. 1. *bind.* 3sg. **cnyt** 7/41.

**cohhetan.** wk. 1. *cough.* inf. 18/270.

**cōlian.** wk. 2. *cool.* past 3sg. **cōlode** 14/72.

**collenferþ.** adj. *proud, stout-hearted, bold.* masc. nom. sg. 13/71. fem. nom. pl. **collenferhðe** 18/134.

**cōm-** → cuman.

**compwīg.** neut. *battle.* dat. sg. **compwīge** 18/332.

**con** → cunnan.

**gecoren.** adj. (past part. of *ġecēosan*). *choice, elect, distinguished.* masc. nom. pl. **gecorene** 10/13. dat. pl. **gecorenum** 2/8. wk. masc. nom. pl. **gecorenan** 3/81.

**gecoren** → gecēosan.

**gecost.** adj. *select, tested, excellent.* neut. acc. pl. **gecoste** 18/231.

**(ge)costnian.** wk. 2. *tempt.* past part. **gecostnod** 3/64.

**costnung.** fem. *temptation, trial.* nom. sg. 3/34. nom. pl. **costnunga** 3/82. dat. pl. **costnungum** 3/30.

**cradolcild.** neut. *child in the cradle, infant.* nom. pl. 7/15.

**gecranc** → (ge)cringan.

**cræft.** masc. *strength, skill.* acc. sg. **cræftas** 10/47. dat. sg. **cræfte** 10/10. nom. pl. **cræftas** 10/9. *virtue.* nom. sg. 10/72. acc. sg. **cræftes** 10/73. gen. pl. **cræfta** 10/58. *trade.* nom. sg. 10/9. acc. sg. 10/3 (2x), 5, 10. gen. sg. **cræftes** 10/3. dat. pl. **cræftum** 10/50.

**cræftig.** adj. *strong, skilful, learned.* masc. nom. sg. 10/76.

**crēopan.** st. 2. *creep.*

**(ge)cringan.** st. 3. *fall, die.* past 3sg. **gecranc, gecrong** 12/250, 324; 13/79. past pl. **cruncon** 12/302. inf. **crincgan** 12/292.

**Cristen.** adj. *Christian.* masc. nom. sg. 2/2. neut. gen. sg. **Cristenes** 7/29. nom. pl. **Cristene** 7/12. gen. pl. **Cristenra** 7/43, 50. wk. masc. nom. pl. **Cristenan** c/12.

**Cristendōm.** masc. *Christendom.* nom. sg. 5/10; 6/17. gen. sg. **Cristendōmes** 5/9. dat. sg. **Cristendōme** 7/36.

**crocsceard.** neut. *potsherd.* dat. sg. **cro-cscearde** 3/59.

**gecrong, cruncon** → (ge)cringan.

**cuǣdon** → (ge)cweþan.

**cucan, cucen-** → cwic.

**culfre.** wk. fem. *dove.* nom. sg. G/4.

**cuman.** st. 4. *come.* 3sg. **cymð, cymeð** A/3; C/9, 11; G/5 (2x), etc. (13x). pl. **cumað** A/6; 8/59. past 1sg. **cōm** 3/41. past 2sg. **cōme** 3/12. past 3sg. **cōm, cwōm, cuōm** B/6; C/2; 1/8; 3/36, 37, etc. (24x). past pl. **cōmon, cōman, cwōman** 2/30; 3/11, 36, 38, 65, etc. (12x). subj. sg. **cyme** 11/11. subj. past sg. **cōme** B/5; 3/19; 8/49; 10/29. imp. sg. **cum.** inf. 3/47; 8/14; 10/26. pres. part. **cumende** 3/67. past part. **cumen, cumene** 9/16; 10/13; 12/104; 14/80; 17/8, etc. (7x).

**cumbol.** neut. *standard, banner.* dat. pl. **cumblum** 18/332.

**cumbolgehnāst.** neut. *clash of banners.* gen. sg. **cumbolgehnāstes.**

**cumbolwiga.** wk. masc. *warrior.* acc. sg. **cumbolwigan** 18/259. acc. pl. **cumbolwigan** 18/243.

**cunnan.** pret. pres. *know.* past pl. **cūðon** 3/104. subj. sg. **cunne** 13/69, 71. subj. pl. **cunnon** 3/110. inf. 17/9. past part. **cūþ.** As auxiliary with infinitive. *know how to, be able to, can.* 1sg. **con** 9/8. past 1sg. **cūðe** 9/8. past pl. **cūþon** 7/43. subj. sg. **cunne** 7/16, 34, 38; 13/113.

**(ge)cunnian.** wk. 2. *find out, investigate, experience.* 3sg. **cunnað** 13/29. inf. **cunnian, gecunnian** 12/215; 18/259.

**cuōm** → cuman.

**curfon** → ceorfan.

**cūþ.** adj. (past part. of *cunnan*). *known, familiar.* neut. acc. sg. **cūþe** LA. gen. pl. **cūðra** 13/55.

**cūþ-** → cunnan.

**cwalu.** fem. *killing.* nom. sg. 7/19.

**cwǣd-, cwæþ, gecwæþ** → (ge)cweþan.

**cweartern.** neut. *prison.* acc. sg. 6/24, 26. dat. sg. **cwearterne.**

**cweccan.** wk. 1. *shake.*

**gecweden** → (ge)cweþan.

**cwelan.** st. 4. *die.* 3sg. **cwelð.** pl. **cwelað.**

**cwellan.** wk. 1. *kill.*

**cwellere.** masc. *executioner.* nom. pl. **cwelleras.**

**gecwēman.** wk. 1. (with gen. object). *please, be obedient to.* past pl. **gecwēmdon** C/12.

**cwēn.** fem. *queen.* nom. sg. 1/3; 2/17. acc. sg. **cwēne** J/81. gen. sg. **cwēne.** dat. sg. **cwēne.**

**Cwēnas.** masc. *Kvens.* nom. pl. 8/37, 38. gen. pl. **Cwēna** 8/36.

**cwene.** wk. fem. *woman, wife.* acc. sg. **cwenan** 7/30.

**(ge)cweþan.** st. 5. *say, call, speak.* 3sg. **cwyð** 14/111. past 1sg. **cwæð** 10/72. past 3sg. **cwæð, gecwæð** G/2; 1/1, 4, 9, 10, etc. (57x). past pl. **cwǣdon, cuǣdon, cwǣdan** 2/14; 4/12, 13, 14; 7/49, etc. (7x). past 3pl. **cwǣdon, gecwǣdon** 3/67, 71. imp. sg. **cweð.** inf. **cweþan** 10/54; 14/116. infl. inf. **tō cweþenne** 7/15, 56. pres. part. **cweþende.** past part. **gecweden** 3/18.

**cwic.** adj. *alive.* masc. acc. sg. **cucene, cucenne** 3/44. gen. pl. **cwicera, cwicra** 13/9; 18/235, 311, 323. wk. neut. dat. sg. **cucan** 3/93.

**cwiddung.** fem. *saying, report.* dat. sg. **cwiddunge** 10/47.

**cwide.** masc. *saying.*

**cwidegiedd.** neut. *speech, song.* gen. pl. **cwidegiedda** 13/55.

**cwīþan.** wk. 1. *lament, bewail.* past pl. **cwīðdon** 14/56. inf. 13/9.

**cwōm-** → cuman.

**cwyldrōf.** adj. *slaughter-bold, bold in battle.*

**cwyþ** → (ge)cweþan.

**cȳdde** → (ge)cȳþan.

**cyle** → cile.

**cyme.** masc. *coming, advent.* dat. sg. 9/24.

**cyme, cymeþ, cymþ** → cuman.

**gecynd.** neut. *nature, character, birthright.* nom. sg. 6/32.

cynehelm. masc. *crown.* acc. sg. 6/10, 19.

cynerōf. adj. *noble and renowned.* masc. nom. pl. cynerōfe 18/200, 311.

cyning. masc. *king.* nom. sg. cyning, cyng, cynincg ᴊ/81; 2/2, 7, 10; 4/5, etc. (14x). acc. sg. cyning, cynincg, cyningc 2/9; 4/4, 6, 17; 8/23, etc. (8x). gen. sg. cyninges, cynges, cynincges ɪ/3; ᴍ/1, 2; 2/5; 4/7, etc. (9x). dat. sg. cyninge, cynge, cynincge, kyninge 2/5; 4/4, 13, 14; 5/21, etc. (8x). nom. pl. cyningas, kyningas 3/65, 70, 89; 8/64. gen. pl. cyninga 18/155.

cynn. neut. *kind, species.* acc. sg. 14/94. gen. sg. cynnes 18/52. dat. sg. cynne. *family.* gen. sg. cynnes 12/217, 266. dat. sg. cynne 12/76. *people, nation.* acc. sg. ᴅ/2, 3. gen. sg. cynnes 18/310. dat. sg. cynne 18/226. gen. pl. cynna 18/323.

cynnbān. neut. *chin bone, jawbone.* dat. sg. cynnbāne 2/12.

gecyrde → (ge)cyrran.

cyrice. wk. fem. *church.* dat. sg. cyrcan 2/18, 24.

cyrichata. wk. masc. *persecutor of the Church.* nom. pl. cyrichatan 7/50.

cyrm. masc. *uproar.* nom. sg. cyrm, cirm 12/107.

(ge)cyrran. wk. 1. *turn, return, turn back, go.* past 3sg. gecyrde 3/96, 97. past pl. cirdon 8/12; 18/311. inf. gecierran.

kyrtel. masc. *coat.* acc. sg. 8/29.

cyssan. wk. 1. *kiss.* subj. sg. cysse 13/42.

cyst. A. fem. *chest, coffin.* nom. sg. 2/27. dat. sg. cyste 2/16, 22.
  B. fem. *choicest, best.* acc. sg. 14/1.

(ge)cȳþan. wk. 1. *make known, show.* 3sg. cȳð ɢ/1. pl. cȳðaþ 2/5. past 3sg. cȳðde, cȳdde 2/2; 3/50; 9/15; 10/29, 50. past pl. cȳþdon 4/11. subj. sg. cȳþe 6/42. subj. past sg. cȳdde 3/36, 37, 38, 39. inf. cȳðan, gecȳþan 12/216; 18/56, 243. infl. inf. tō cȳðenne 3/44. past part. gecȳðed 18/155. *perform, practise.* inf. cȳðan 10/3, 5.

cȳþþ. fem. *kinship, family, homeland.* acc. sg. cȳþþe. dat. sg. cȳððe 18/311.

gedafenian. wk. 2. *befit.* 3sg. gedafenað. past 3sg. gedeofanade 9/4.

dag- → dæg.

gedāl. neut. *separation.* dat. sg. gedāle 10/59.

daroþ. masc. *spear.* acc. sg. 12/149, 255.

datarum. masc. (Latin gen. pl. used as dat. sg.). *date.* dat. sg. 5/13.

dǣd. fem. *deed.* gen. sg. dǣde 7/23, 47. nom. pl. dǣda 7/32. acc. pl. dǣda 7/65; 10/36, 37. gen. pl. dǣda 3/74; 9/26. dat. pl. dǣdum 4/1.

dæg. masc. *day.* acc. sg. ᴀ/5; ᴄ/9; 1/8; 2/26; 6/4, etc. (9x). gen. sg. dæges 3/35. dat. sg. dæge 1/5; 2/16; 3/9, 11, 51, etc. (8x). inst. sg. dæge ʙ/1; 8/42, 66. nom. pl. dagas 3/78 (2x), 83, 85. acc. pl. dagas 3/69; 8/6, 49 (2x), 51. gen. pl. daga 4/18 (2x); 14/136. dat. pl. dagum, dagan 1/14, 17; 2/8 (2x); 3/10, etc. (19x).

dæges. adv. *by day.* ᴀ/2.

dægeweorc. neut. *day's work.* gen. sg. dægeweorces 12/148. dat. sg. dægeweorce 18/266.

dæghwāmlīce. adv. *every day.* 7/5, 45.

dægrǣd. neut. *dawn.* acc. sg. dægrǣd, dægrēd 18/204.

dægweorces → dægeweorc.

dǣl. masc. *part, share.* nom. sg. 8/67; 18/292, 308. acc. sg. 2/27; 8/67, 69; 10/18, 23, etc. (6x). gen. sg. dǣles 10/18. dat. sg. dǣle 7/52, 67; 8/69; 10/19, 22.

(ge)dǣlan. wk. 1. *divide, part* (from someone). pl. gedǣlað. subj. past sg. gedǣlde 16/22. *share, distribute, dispense.* past 3sg. gedǣlde 13/83. subj. pl. dǣlon 12/33.

dēad. adj. *dead.* masc. nom. sg. 8/64; 18/107. masc. nom. pl. dēade ᴄ/10; 1/4. wk. masc. nom. sg. dēada 8/67. wk. masc. gen. sg. dēadan 8/72. wk. masc. nom. pl. dēadan 8/74.

dēaf. adj. *deaf.*

dēah → dugan.

dear → durran.

**dēaþ.** masc. *death.* nom. sg. 3/82; 6/3; 10/70, 82 (2x), etc. (6x). acc. sg. 14/101. gen. sg. **dēaþes** 11/15; 14/113. dat. sg. **dēaðe** c/5, 7, 10; 10/57; 13/83, etc. (7x). inst. sg. **dēaðe** 9/43.

**dēawigfeþere.** adj. *dewy-feathered.*

**dehter** → dohtor.

**dēma.** wk. masc. *judge.* nom. sg. 18/59, 94. gen. sg. **dēman** 18/4.

**(ge)dēman.** wk. 1. *judge, condemn.* inf. **dēman** 14/107. past part. **gedēmed** 9/6; 18/196.

**Denamearc.** fem. *Denmark.* nom. sg. 8/49. acc. sg. **Denemearce** 8/51. dat. sg. **Denemearcan** 8/53.

**Dene.** masc. *Danes.* acc. pl. 8/48. dat. pl. **Denon** 12/129.

**Denisc.** adj. *Danish.* neut. acc. sg. D/2. wk. masc. nom. pl. **Deniscan.**

**denu.** fem. *valley.* nom. pl. **dena** 16/30.

**gedeofanade** → gedafenian.

**dēofol.** masc. (often with neut. ending in pl.). *devil, demon.* nom. sg. 3/15, 17, 20, 30, 35, etc. (10x). acc. sg. 3/17, 79. gen. sg. **dēofles** 3/34, 64, 82, 103. nom. pl. **dēoflu.** dat. pl. **dēoflum** c/11.

**dēofulcund.** adj. *diabolical.* wk. masc. nom. sg. **dēofulcunda** 18/61.

**dēop.** adj. *deep.* wk. fem. acc. sg. **dēopan** 3/110. wk. masc. dat. sg. **dēopan** 14/75.

**dēope.** adv. *deeply.* 13/89.

**dēopnys.** fem. *deepness, profundity.* nom. sg. 3/2. acc. sg. **dēopnysse** 3/3.

**dēor.** neut. *animal.* acc. pl. 8/24. gen. pl. **dēora** 8/23, 27.

**deorc.** adj. *dark.* neut. acc. sg. **deorce** 13/89. neut. acc. pl. 11/15. dat. pl. **deorcan** 14/46.

**dēore.** adv. *dearly.* 7/31.

**gedeorfan.** st. 3. *labour, perish, be shipwrecked.* past pl. **gedurfon.**

**dēorfriþ.** neut. *game-preserve.* acc. sg. 6/37.

**derian.** wk. 1. (with dat. object). *harm.* 3sg. **dereð** 7/33. past 3sg. **derede, derode** 3/34; 7/19, 23. inf. 12/70.

**dēþ, gedēþ** → (ge)dōn.

**dīacon.** masc. *deacon.* nom. pl. **dīaconas.**

**didon** → (ge)dōn.

**dīgel-** → dȳgel.

**dīgelness.** fem. *secret, mystery.* acc. sg. **dīgelnysse** 3/110.

**dimm.** adj. *dark, gloomy.* fem. nom. pl. **dimme** 16/30.

**dīore.** adj. *beloved.* masc. nom. sg. 10/70.

**dōgor.** masc. *day.* inst. sg. **dōgore** 18/12. gen. pl. **dōgra** 13/63.

**dogorrīm.** neut. *count of days, lifetime.* dat. sg. **dogorrīme** 10/82.

**doht-** → dugan.

**dohtor.** fem. r-stem. *daughter.* nom. sg. I/5; Lb; 17/48. acc. sg. 7/40. dat. sg **dehter.** nom. pl. **dohtra, dohtor** 3/39, 105. gen. pl. **dohtra** 3/6, 100. dat. pl. **dohtrum.**

**dolg.** masc. *wound.* nom. sg. **dolh** 2/16. nom. pl. 14/46.

**dolhwund.** adj. *wounded.* masc. nom. sg. 18/107.

**dōm.** masc. *judgement.* acc. sg. c/10; 4/11; 7/70; 12/38. gen. sg. **dōmes** A/5; c/9; 9/24; 14/107. dat. sg. **dōme** c/9; M/2; 9/16; 10/16. dat. pl. **dōmum** 9/25. *reputation, glory.* nom. sg. 18/266. acc. sg. 12/129; 18/196. dat. sg. **dōme** 18/299.

**dōmdæg.** masc. *doomsday.* dat. sg. **dōmdæge** 14/105.

**dōmgeorn.** adj. *eager for glory.* masc. nom. pl. **dōmgeorne** 13/17.

**dōmlīce.** adv. *gloriously.* 18/318.

**(ge)dōn.** anom. verb. *do.* 3sg. **dēð** A/3; 3/15, 46; 7/12, 35, etc. (7x). pl. **dōð** D/1; 7/30. past 2sg. **dydest, dydestū** (contracted with **þū**) 1/13, 14. past 3sg. **dyde** 1/8; 2/15; 3/10, 30, 44, etc. (12x). past pl. **dydon, didon, dydan** 3/94; 6/23; 7/6; 10/37. subj. sg. **dō** 7/23. subj. pl. **dōn** 10/46. inf. **dōn, gedōn** 2/4; 6/22; 7/60, 65, 67, etc. (9x). past part. **gedōn** 3/42; 5/4; 6/12, 28; 10/10, etc. (6x). *take.* imp. sg. **dō** 10/19. inf. **dōn** 2/18. *bring about,* *cause to be.* 3sg. **gedēð** 10/70. pl. **gedōð** 8/75. past 3sg. **dyde** в/6. past pl. **gedydon** 15/14. subj. sg. **dō** 6/42. inf. **gedōn** 2/8. past part. **gedōn**.

**dorst-** → durran.

**draca.** wk. masc. *dragon.* acc. sg. **dracan.** nom. pl. **dracan.**

**drāf.** fem. *herd, company.* acc. sg. **drāfe** 7/43.

**drāf** → drīfan.

**dranc** → drincan.

**gedreag.** neut. *assembly, multitude.* nom. sg. 16/45.

**drēam.** masc. *joy, mirth, music.* nom. sg. 14/140. gen. sg. **drēames** 14/144. dat. sg. **drēame** 13/79. acc. pl. **drēamas** 18/349. dat. pl. **drēamum** 14/133.

**gedrēas** → (ge)drēosan.

**(ge)dreccan.** wk. 1. *vex, afflict, oppress, ravage.* past pl. **gedrehtan, drehton** 7/19. past part. **gedrehtan** 3/89.

**(ge)drēfan.** wk. 1. *agitate,* fig. *travel* (of rowing in the sea), *afflict.* subj. past sg. **drēfde** 17/21. past part. **gedrēfed** 14/20, 59; 18/88.

**gedrehtan, drehton** → (ge)dreccan.

**drencan.** wk. 1. *make drunk, submerge, drown.* past 3sg. **drencte** 18/29.

**dreng.** masc. *warrior.* gen. pl. **drenga** 12/149.

**drēogan.** st. 2. *perform, commit, experience, endure.* 3sg. **drēogeð** 16/50. pl. **drēogað** 7/30. past pl. **drugon** 18/158. inf. 11/15; 16/26.

**drēorig.** adj. *bloody, cruel, sorrowful.* masc. acc. sg. **drēorigne** 13/17.

**drēorighlēor.** adj. *sad-faced.* masc. nom. sg. 13/83.

**drēorsele.** masc. *dreary hall.* dat. sg. 16/50.

**(ge)drēosan.** st. 2. *fall, perish, fail.* 3sg. **drēoseð** 13/63. past 3sg. **gedrēas** 13/36.

**drīfan.** st. 1. *drive.* 1sg. **drīfe.** 2sg. **drīfst.** 3sg. **drīfð.** pl. **drīfað** 7/43. past 2sg. **drife.** past 3sg. **drāf.** past pl. **drifon.** subj. sg. **drīfe** 7/25.

**Drihten.** masc. *lord, Lord, the Lord.* nom. sg. **drihten, dryhten** 3/12, 14, 33, 42 (2x), etc. (17x). acc. sg. **dryhten, drihten** 14/64, 144. gen. sg. **dryhtnes, drihtnes** 2/30; 3/58; 10/82; 14/9, 35, etc. (9x). dat. sg. **drihtne, dryhtne** 3/30; 9/17, 43; 18/342, 346.

**drihtnē.** masc. *corpse.* dat. pl. **drihtnēum.**

**drincan.** st. 3. *drink.* pl. **drincað** 8/61 (2x). past 3sg. **dranc.** past pl. **druncon** 3/39.

**drīum** → drȳge.

**drohtnian.** wk. 2. *pass life, live, behave.* past 3sg. **drohtnode** 2/11. past pl. **drohtnodon** 2/31.

**drohtnung.** fem. *way of life, condition.* dat. sg. **drohtnunge** 2/9, 30.

**drugon** → drēogan.

**druncen.** adj. *drunk.* masc. nom. sg. 18/67, 107. masc. nom. pl. **druncene** 5/16.

**druncon** → drincan.

**drȳge.** adj. *dry.* dat. pl. **drīum.**

**Dryhten** → Drihten.

**dryhtguma.** wk. masc. *warrior.* acc. pl. **dryhtguman** 18/29.

**Dryhtn-** → Drihten.

**gedrync.** neut. *drinking.* nom. sg. 8/65. dat. sg. **gedrynce** 8/66.

**dugan.** pret. pres. *do well, prosper, be good for anything, be a benefit.* 3sg. **dēah** 12/48. past 3sg. **dohte** 7/18, 39. subj. past pl. **dohten** 10/37.

**duguþ.** fem. *body of experienced retainers, army, host.* nom. sg. 13/79. acc. sg. **dugeþe, duguðe** 7/62; 18/31. gen. sg. **duguþe** 13/97. gen. pl. **dugeða** 18/61. dat. pl. **duguðum** 10/70. *benefit.* dat. sg. **duguþe** 12/197.

**dumb.** adj. *dumb.*

**dūn.** fem. *hill.* nom. pl. **dūna** 16/30.

**dūnland.** neut. *hilly land.* dat. pl. **dūnlandum.**

**gedurfon** → gedeorfan.

**durran.** pret. pres. *dare.* 1sg. **dear** 17/11. 3sg. **dear** 7/10, 11, 12. past 1sg. **dorste** 14/35, 42, 45, 47. past 3sg. **dorste** 6/22,

28; 18/258. past pl. **dorston** 8/12, 14. subj. sg. **durre** 13/10.

**duru.** fem. u-stem. *door.* nom. sg. 3/27. acc. sg. 4/5.

**dūst.** neut. *dust.* nom. sg. 1/19. gen. sg. **dūstes** 3/83. dat. sg. **dūste** A/4; 1/19; 3/69.

**dwǣs.** adj. *foolish.* dat. pl. **dwǣsan** 7/54.

**dwelian.** wk. 2. *lead astray.* past 3sg. **dwelode** 7/4.

**dweorh.** masc. *dwarf.*

**gedwolgod.** masc. *false god.* gen. pl. **gedwolgoda** 7/10, 12. dat. pl. **gedwolgodan** 7/11.

**dyd-, gedyd-** → (ge)dōn.

**dȳgel.** adj. *secret, hidden.* neut. acc. sg. κ/1357. wk. neut. nom. sg. **dīgele** 3/88. wk. neut. dat. sg. **dīgelan** 3/103.

**dynian.** wk. 2. *resound.* past 3sg. **dynede** 18/23. past pl. **dynedan** 18/204.

**dynt.** masc. *blow.* dat. sg. **dynte** 5/18.

**dȳre.** adj. *dear, precious, expensive.* masc. nom. pl. 8/24. neut. nom. pl. 8/70. masc. acc. pl. 18/318.

**dyrne.** adj. *secret.* masc. acc. sg. 16/12.

**gedȳrsian.** wk. 2. *glorify.* past part. **gedȳrsod** 18/299.

**dysig.** A. neut. *folly.* acc. sg. 10/10. dat. sg. **dysige** 3/92. inst. sg. **dysige** 10/27.
   B. adj. *foolish.* masc. nom. pl. **dysige** 7/50.

**dyslic.** adj. *foolish.* neut. gen. sg. **dyslices** 3/43.

**dyslīce.** adv. *foolishly.* 3/49.

**ēa.** fem. athematic. *river.* nom. sg. 8/11, 57. acc. sg. 8/12. gen. sg. **ēas** 8/12. dat. sg. 8/12. nom. pl. **ēan.**

**ēac.** A. adv. *also.* A/4; B/1, 4; D/1; 1/1, etc. (45x).
   B. prep. (with dat. or inst.). *in addition to.* 12/11; 16/44.

**geēacnung.** fem. *child-bearing.* acc. pl. **geēacnunga** 1/16.

**ēad.** neut. *happiness, prosperity.* gen. sg. **ēades** 18/273.

**ēadhrēþig.** adj. *triumphantly blessed.* fem. nom. pl. **ēadhrēðige** 18/135.

**ēadig.** adj. *wealthy, prosperous, happy, blessed.* masc. nom. sg. A/1. masc. nom. pl. **ēadige.** wk. fem. nom. sg. **ēadige.** wk. fem. acc. sg. **ēadigan** 18/35. wk. masc. dat. sg. **ēadigan** 3/1, 57.

**ēage.** wk. neut. *eye.* nom. sg. 3/25. acc. sg. 10/40. nom. pl. **ēagan** 1/5, 7. acc. pl. **ēagan.** dat. pl. **ēagum** D/2; 1/6.

**eahta.** card. num. as noun. *eight.* **eahta, ehta** E/1; 5/14; 8/20. acc. pl. 3/107.

**eahtoþa.** ord. num. *eighth.* neut. dat. sg. **eahteoðan** 2/12. masc. dat. sg. **eahteoðan** 3/9.

**ēalā.** interj. *oh, alas.* **ēalā** 3/76; 6/6; 7/58; 10/2, 13, etc. (11x).

**eald.** adj. *old, ancient, senior.* masc. nom. sg. 12/310; 16/29. neut. acc. sg. 17/49. masc. nom. pl. **ealde** 18/265. neut. nom. pl. **eald, ealde** 13/87; 12/47. gen. pl. **ealdra** 7/13. dat. pl. **ealdum** 2/8; 3/70, 93. wk. masc. nom. sg. **ealda** B/4; 3/44; 12/218. wk. masc. nom. pl. **ealdan, ealde** 18/166. wk. masc. nom. sg. superl. **yldesta** 6/9. wk. masc. dat. sg. superl. **yldestan** 3/39. wk. masc. nom. pl. superl. **yldestan** 5/12. wk. masc. acc. pl. superl. **yldestan** 18/10. wk. dat. pl. superl. **yldestan** 18/242.

**ealdes.** adv. (from adj. *eald*). *formerly.* 16/4.

**ealdfēond.** masc. nd-stem. *ancient enemy.* dat. pl. **ealdfēondum** 18/315.

**ealdgenīþla.** wk. masc. *ancient enemy.* acc. pl. **ealdgenīðlan** 18/228.

**ealdgewyrht.** fem. *ancient deed.* dat. pl. **ealdgewyrhtum** 14/100.

**ealdhettend.** masc. nd-stem. *ancient adversary.* acc. pl. **ealdhettende** 18/320.

**ealdor.** A. masc. *leader, lord.* nom. sg. **ealdor, aldor** 12/202, 222, 314; 14/90; 18/32, etc. (9x). gen. sg. **ealdres** 12/53. dat. sg. **ealdre** 12/11.
   B. neut. *life, age, old age.* acc. sg. **aldor, ealdor** κ/1371; 18/185. dat. sg. **aldre, ealdre** 18/76. *eternity.* dat. sg. **aldre** 18/120, 347.

**ealdorduguþ.** fem. *body of nobles.* gen. sg. **ealdorduguðe** 18/309.

**ealdorman.** masc. athematic. *ruler, chief, overseer, nobleman.* nom. sg. **ealdorman, aldormon, ealdormon** 2/5; 4/10; 5/12; 9/15; 12/219. acc. sg. **aldormon** 4/1, 2. gen. sg. **aldormonnes, ealdormonnes** M/3; 4/15. dat. sg. **ealdormenn, ealdormen** 2/3.

**ealdorþegn.** masc. *chief thegn.* dat. pl. **ealdorþegnum** 18/242.

**eall. A.** adj. *all, each.* masc. nom. sg. **eal, eall** 2/2; 10/16. fem. nom. sg. **eal, eall** 10/66; 13/79, 115; 14/12, 55, etc. (7x). neut. nom. sg. **eall, eal** A/3; 3/95; 5/14; 7/29, 32, etc. (15x). masc. acc. sg. **ealne** 7/44; 8/6, 13, 45, 52, etc. (7x). fem. acc. sg. **ealle** 3/88; 5/8; 7/5, 29, 58, etc. (11x). neut. acc. sg. **eall, eal** c/6; 2/4; 3/44; 6/14, 16, etc. (18x). masc. gen. sg. **ealles** M/12; 10/17, 20; 16/41. fem. gen. sg. **ealre** 10/16; 13/74. neut. gen. sg. **ealles** c/2; M/1; 6/7; 10/31. masc. dat. sg. **eallum** 9/35. fem. dat. sg. **ealre, eallre** 3/105; 5/19; 7/16, 36; 10/38. neut. dat. sg. **eallum** 3/107; 5/4; 9/26. neut. inst. sg. **ealle** 7/53, 62; 10/22, 23. masc. nom. pl. **ealle, alle** c/10 (2x); H/3; M/13; 2/21, etc. (23x). fem. nom. pl. **ealle** 3/82, 103; 5/3. neut. nom. pl. **ealle, eall** F/1; 1/1; 3/33; 8/53, 68, etc. (7x). masc. acc. pl. **ealle, alle** 2/11; 3/38; 4/15; 5/2, 7, etc. (12x). fem. acc. pl. **ealle** 3/31, 35, 96; 8/72; 12/196. neut. acc. pl. **ealle, eal, eall** c/1; 2/9; 3/32, 36, 37, etc. (15x). gen. pl. **ealra, eallra** c/4; 3/113; 6/40; 7/25, 56, etc. (13x). dat. pl. **eallum** 1/14 (2x), 17; 2/22; 3/8, etc. (23x). **B.** adv. *all, entirely, just.* **eal, eall** 2/19, 23; 3/46, 59, 100, etc. (18x).

**eall swā.** conj. *as, just as.* E/3.

**ealle.** adv. *entirely, quite.* H/2.

**ealles.** adv. *all, entirely.* 7/5, 10, 13, 22, 27, etc. (13x).

**eallgylden.** adj. *entirely golden.* neut. nom. sg. 18/46.

**ealnig.** adv. *always.* 10/69.

**ealo.** masc. dental stem. *ale.* nom. sg. **ealo, ealu** 8/63; 10/7. gen. sg. **ealað** 8/75.

**eard.** masc. *country, land, homeland.* acc. sg. 5/21; 7/62, 64; 12/53, 58, etc. (7x). dat. sg. **earde** 7/14, 20, 24, 25, 29, etc. (8x).

**eardgeard.** masc. *habitation, world.* acc. sg. 13/85.

**eardian.** wk. 2. *dwell.* pl. **eardiað** 8/32. past pl. **eardedon, eardodon** 8/50; 11/22.

**eardstapa.** wk. masc. *land-traveller, wanderer.* nom. sg. 13/6.

**eardung.** fem. *dwelling.* nom. sg. F/2.

**ēare.** wk. neut. *ear.*

**earendel.** masc. *shining light, rising sun, morning star.* nom. sg. 11/1.

**earfoþe.** neut. *hardship, labour.* gen. pl. **earfeþa, earfoþa** 13/6; 16/39.

**earfoþlic.** adj. *difficult, full of hardship, laborious.* neut. nom. sg. 13/106.

**earfoþness.** fem. *hardship, affliction, difficulty.* dat. sg. **earfoþnesse** B/5. dat. pl. **earfoðnyssum** 3/57.

**earg.** adj. *wretched, vile, useless, cowardly.* neut. nom. sg. **earh** 12/238. masc. acc. sg. **eargne** 15/16.

**earhlīc.** adj. *cowardly, disgraceful.* fem. nom. pl. **earhlīce** 7/38.

**earm. A.** adj. *poor, wretched, miserable.* masc. acc. sg. **earmne** 13/40. fem. dat. sg. **earman** 7/57. masc. nom. pl. **earme** 6/40; 7/14; 14/68. masc. acc. pl. **earme** 6/34. neut. acc. pl. **earme** 5/4. gen. pl. **earmra** 14/19. wk. neut. acc. sg. **earme** 3/46. wk. fem. dat. sg. **earman** 5/10. **B.** masc. *arm.* acc. sg. 12/165.

**earmcearig.** adj. *wretchedly sorrowful.* masc. nom. sg. 13/20.

**earmlīce.** adv. *miserably.* 7/58.

**earn.** masc. *eagle.* nom. sg. 12/107; 18/210. dat. sg. **earne.**

**earnian.** wk. 2. (with gen.). *strive for, deserve.* pl. **earniað** 10/47. past pl. **geearnedan** 7/7. inf. 7/6.

**geearnian.** wk. 2. *earn, merit.* 3sg. **geearnaþ** 14/109. past pl. **geearnedon**

ᴀ/6. inf. **geearnian, geearnigan** 7/70; 10/38.

**(ge)earnung.** fem. *labour, merit, desert.* nom. pl. **geearnunga** 3/21. dat. pl. **earnungan** 7/7 (2x). *reward.* acc. pl. **geearnunga** 12/196.

**eart** → bēon.

**geearwodest** → (ge)gearwian.

**ēast.** adv. *east.* 8/8; 10/65.

**ēastan.** adv. *from the east.* 8/59 (2x); 18/190.

**Ēastengle.** masc. *East Angles.* acc. pl. 5/2. gen. pl. **Ēastengla** 2/2.

**Ēasterdæg.** masc. *Easter-day.* nom. sg. 5/13.

**ēastern.** adj. *eastern, oriental.* dat. pl. **ēasternum** 3/8.

**ēasteþe.** neut. *river-bank.* dat. sg. 12/63.

**ēasteweard. A.** adv. *in the east.* **ēasteweard, ēastewerd** 8/33, 34.
**B.** adj. *eastern part of.* masc. dat. sg. **ēasteweardum** 10/16.

**Ēastre.** fem. (always pl.). *Easter.* acc. pl. **Ēastron** 5/14. dat. pl. **Ēastron** 5/12; 6/20.

**ēastryhte.** adv. *eastwards.* 8/8.

**Ēastseaxe.** masc. *East Saxons.* acc. pl. **Ēastsexe** 5/2. gen. pl. **Ēastseaxena** 12/69.

**ēaþe.** adv. *easily.* 2/8; 7/58; 10/66; 15/18. compar. **ēð** 10/73. superl. **ēaðost** 18/75, 102.

**ēaþelīce.** adv. *easily.* 3/50, 97.

**ēaþmēdu.** fem. *humility* (pl. has sg. sense). dat. pl. **ēaðmēdum** 18/170.

**ēaþmōd.** adj. *humble.* masc. nom. sg. 14/60.

**ēaþmōdlīce.** adv. *humbly.* 9/26.

**eaxl.** fem. *shoulder.* dat. pl. **eaxlum** 14/32.

**eaxlegespann.** neut. *shoulder-span, cross-beam.* dat. sg. **eaxlegespanne** 14/9.

**eaxlgestealla.** wk. masc. *person who is by one's shoulder, companion.* nom. sg. ɪ/1.

**ebba.** wk. masc. *ebb tide.* dat. sg. **ebban** 12/65.

**Ebrēas.** masc. *the Hebrews.* nom. pl. 18/218. gen. pl. **Ebrēa** 18/253, 262, 298.

**Ebrēisc.** adj. *Hebrew.* masc. nom. pl. **Ebrisce** 18/241, 305. wk. neut. dat. sg. **Ebrēiscan.**

**ēce.** adj. *eternal.* masc. nom. sg. 9/12, 13. fem. acc. sg. 10/38. neut. acc. sg. 10/41. wk. masc. nom. sg. **ēca** 10/82. wk. neut. gen. sg. **ēcean.** wk. fem. dat. sg. **ēcan** ᴄ/11; 3/81.

**ecg.** fem. *edge, sword.* nom. sg. 12/60. acc. sg. **ecge.** dat. pl. **ecgum** 18/231.

**ecgplega.** wk. masc. *edge-play, battle.* acc. sg. **ecgplegan** 18/246.

**ēcness.** fem. *eternity.* dat. sg. **ēcnesse, ēcnysse** ᴄ/12; ꜰ/7; 2/31; 3/113.

**(ge)edcennan.** wk. 1. *bear again.* past part. **geedcenned.**

**ederas** → eodor.

**edlēan.** neut. *reward.* gen. sg. **edlēanes** 3/80 (2x).

**edwenden.** fem. *turning back, change.*

**edwit.** neut. *disgrace, blame, scorn.* nom. sg. **edwīt** 3/82. acc. sg. 18/215. dat. sg. **edwīte** 3/71.

**efenēce.** adj. *co-eternal.* masc. nom. sg. 11/19.

**efenlang.** adj. *just as long.* neut. acc. sg. ʟᴀ.

**efne.** adv. *indeed, only, just.* ʙ/3; 3/33, 39 (2x), 56, etc. (6x). *once* (in calculation). ᴇ/1.

**efnmǣre.** adj. *equally glorious.* masc. acc. sg. **efnmǣrne** 10/70.

**efstan.** wk. 1. *hurry.* past pl. **efston** 12/206. inf. 14/34. pres. part. **efstende.**

**eft.** adv. *again, afterwards, back.* 1/4, 8; 2/10, 30; 3/42, etc. (27x). *thereupon, then.* 3/83, 85, 86.

**ege.** masc. *fear, terror.* nom. sg. 3/73. acc. sg. 7/52.

**egeful.** adj. *awe-inspiring, terrible.* masc. nom. sg. **egeful, egefulle, egesful, egesfull** 10/29; 18/21, 257.

**egesa.** wk. masc. *awe, fear.* nom. sg. 14/86; 18/252.

**egesful** → egeful.

**egeslic.** adj. *terrible.* fem. nom. sg. 14/74. neut. nom. sg. 7/3, 30. fem. nom. pl.

egeslīce 7/32. wk. fem. dat. sg. egeslican. wk. masc. nom. pl. egeslice.

eglade → eglian.

eglan. wk. 1. *trouble, molest.* inf. 18/185.

eglian. wk. 2. *afflict.* past 3sg. eglade 6/2.

ēglond. neut. *island.* nom. sg. 15/5.

Egypte. masc. *Egyptians.* gen. pl. Egypta, Ægypta 9/24.

Egyptisc. adj. *Egyptian.* wk. fem. acc. sg. Egyptiscan.

ehta → eahta.

ehtan. wk. 1. *attack.* past pl. ehton 18/237.

ēhtnyss. fem. *persecution.* acc. sg. ēhtnysse 3/103. dat. sg. ēhtnysse 3/34.

Eligmynster. neut. *the monastery of Ely.* dat. sg. Eligmynstre 2/10.

ellen. neut. *zeal, strength, courage.* acc. sg. 12/211. dat. sg. elne 13/114; 18/95. inst. sg. elne 14/34, 60, 123.

ellendǣd. fem. *deed of valour.* gen. pl. ellendǣda 18/273.

ellenmǣrþu. fem. *reputation for valour.* dat. pl. ellenmǣrðum.

ellenrōf. adj. *courageous.* fem. nom. sg. 18/109, 146.

ellenþrīste. adj. *valorous.* fem. nom. pl. 18/133.

ellenwōdness. fem. *zeal.* gen. sg. ellenwōdnisse 9/27.

elles. adv. *else.* 16/23.

ellor. adv. *elsewhere.* 17/4; 18/112.

eln. fem. *ell* (unit of length). gen. pl. elna 8/19, 20 (2x), 29.

elne → ellen.

elþēod. fem. *foreign nation, foreigners* (in pl.). gen. sg. elþēode 17/37. acc. pl. elðēoda 18/237.

elþēodig. adj. *foreign.* masc. nom. sg. ælðēodig 3/27. gen. pl. elðēodigra 18/215.

embe → ymb.

emnlange. prep. *along.* 8/32.

geendade, geendaþ → geendian.

ende. masc. *end, edge, front edge.* nom. sg. c/11; 10/42. acc. sg. 10/40, 44 (2x); 18/64. dat. sg. ende, ænde F/6, 7; I/8; 3/99; 7/2, etc. (12x). inst. sg. ænde 9/27.

endebyrdness. fem. *order, series.* nom. sg. endebyrdnes 9/11. acc. sg. endebyrdnesse 9/6. dat. sg. endebyrdnysse 3/88.

endenēxt. adj. *last.* wk. masc. dat. sg. superl. endenēxtan 3/86.

geendian. wk. 2. *end.* 3sg. geendað 10/45. past 3sg. geendade 9/27, 42.

geendodlīc. adj. *finite.* wk. neut. acc. sg. geendodlīce 10/43.

geendung. fem. *ending, death.* acc. sg. geendunge. dat. sg. geendunge 2/17.

engel. masc. *angel.* acc. sg. 14/9. nom. pl. englas 2/30; 3/11, 51; 14/106. gen. pl. engla 11/1; 12/178. dat. pl. englum c/12; 1/5; 14/153.

Englaland. neut. *England.* acc. sg. 6/15, 16, 21, 30. dat. sg. Englalande 6/10, 19, 26, 30.

Engle. masc. *the English.* nom. pl. 7/39, 42; 8/50. gen. pl. Engla 7/62. dat. pl. Englum 7/65.

Englisc. adj. *English.* wk. neut. dat. sg. Engliscan 2/1. wk. masc. acc. pl. Engliscan D/1.

Engliscgereord. neut. *English language.* dat. sg. engliscgereorde 9/1.

ent. masc. *giant.* acc. pl. entas. gen. pl. enta 13/87.

ēod- → gān.

geēodon → gegān.

eodor. masc. *enclosure, dwelling.* nom. pl. ederas 13/77. fig. *lord.* acc. sg. J/89.

eodorcan. wk. 1. *chew, ruminate.* pres. part. eodorcende 9/22.

eoh. masc. *horse.* acc. sg. 12/189.

eom → bēon.

eorl. masc. *warrior, nobleman, ruler, duke.* nom. sg. 6/9; 12/6, 51, 89, 132, etc. (10x). gen. sg. eorles I/5; 12/165. dat. sg. eorle J/83; 12/28, 159; 13/12. nom. pl. eorlas 6/21; 18/273, 336. acc. pl. eorlas 6/23; 13/99. gen. pl. eorla 13/60; 18/21, 257.

eorldōm. masc. *earldom.* acc. sg. 6/26, 32.

eorlgebyrd. fem. (pl. with sg. meaning). *noble birth.* dat. pl. eorlgebyrdum 10/70.

**eorlgestrēon.** neut. *acquisition of men.* gen. pl. **eorlgestrēona** 17/47.

**eornost.** neut. *earnestness.* acc. sg. 7/43.

**eornoste.** adv. *resolutely.* 12/281; 18/108, 231.

**eornostlīce.** adv. *truly, indeed.*

**eorþbūend.** masc. nd-stem. *earth-dweller.* nom. pl. **eorðbūende** 10/70. gen. pl. **eorðbūendra** 10/72.

**eorþe.** wk. fem. *earth.* nom. sg. 1/17; 3/18; 10/66. acc. sg. **eorðan** G/2; 1/14; 3/13, 20; 5/18, etc. (10x). gen. sg. **eorðan** 1/18; 9/13; 10/16, 18, 67, etc. (8x). dat. sg. **eorðan** B/3; C/5; G/7; 1/1, 17, etc. (29x).

**eorþlic.** adj. *earthly.* wk. masc. gen. sg. **eorðlican** 10/2. wk. neut. gen. sg. **eorðlican** 10/2. wk. neut. dat. sg. **eorðlican** 10/62. wk. neut. acc. pl. **eorðlican** 10/62.

**eorþscræf.** neut. *earthen cave.* dat. sg. **eorðscræfe** 13/84; 16/28. acc. pl. **eorðscrafu** 16/36.

**eorþsele.** masc. *earthen hall.* nom. sg. 16/29.

**eorþweg.** masc. *earthly region.* dat. sg. **eorðwege** 14/120.

**ēow** → þū, gē.

**ēowan.** wk. 1. *display.* past pl. **ēowdon** 18/240.

**ēower.** adj. *your.* masc. nom. sg. 3/20; 10/22, 30. masc. acc. sg. **ēowerne** 3/77; 10/21, 23, 24, 27. fem. acc. sg. **ēowere, ēowre** 3/77; 10/21. neut. acc. sg. D/2. fem. gen. sg. **ēowre** 10/47. neut. gen. sg. **ēoweres, ēowres** 10/47 (2x). masc. dat. sg. **ēowrum** 10/68. fem. dat. sg. **ēowerre** 10/38. masc. nom. pl. **ēowre, ēowere** D/1; 4/14; 18/195. neut. nom. pl. **ēowre, ēowru** 1/5. masc. acc. pl. **ēowre** D/2. gen. pl. **ēowerra** 10/47. dat. pl. **ēowrum** 10/38.

**Eowland.** neut. *Öland* (Swedish island). nom. sg. 8/55.

**erian.** wk. 1. *plough.* past 3sg. **erede** 8/25 (2x). inf. 8/31.

**ermþe** → yrmþu.

**esne.** masc. *slave, servant, young man.* nom. sg. LA.

**Ēstas.** masc. *Ests.* dat. pl. **Ēstum** 8/57, 63, 64, 73, 74.

**Ēstland.** neut. *the land of the Ests.* nom. sg. 8/60. dat. sg. **Ēstlande** 8/59.

**Ēstmere.** masc. *Vistula Lagoon* (Zalew Wiślany; Frisches Haff). nom. sg. 8/58. acc. sg. 8/58, 59 (2x).

**(ge)etan.** st. 5. *eat.* 2sg. **etst, ytst** 1/14, 17, 18. pl. **etað** 1/2, 5; 3/83. past 1sg. **ǣt, ǣtt** 1/12, 13; 3/26. past 2sg. **ǣte** 1/17. past 3sg. **ǣt, geǣt** 1/6 (2x). past pl. **ǣton** 3/39. subj. pl. **eton, ete** 1/4. subj. past sg. **ǣte** 1/11 (2x), 17. subj. past pl. **ǣton** 1/1, 3. inf. **etan.** infl. inf. **tō etanne, tō etenne** 1/6.

**ettan.** wk. 1. *use for grazing.* inf. 8/31.

**ēþ** → ēaþe.

**ēþel.** masc. *homeland.* nom. sg. 14/156. acc. sg. 12/52; 17/26, 37. dat. sg. **ēðle** 13/20; 18/169.

**ēþelweard.** masc. *guardian of the homeland.* nom. pl. **ēðelweardas** 18/320.

**fācenful.** adj. *deceitful.*

**fāg.** adj. *variegated, adorned.* masc. nom. sg. **fāh** 13/98. masc. dat. sg. **fāgum** 18/104. dat. pl. **fāgum** 18/194, 264, 301.

**fāh.** adj. *guilty* of something (dat.), *outlawed.* masc. nom. sg. 14/13; 16/46.

**fāh** → fāg.

**Falster.** proper noun. *Falster* (Danish island). nom. sg. 8/53.

**fandian.** wk. 2. (usually with gen. object). *try, test, discover.* inf. 8/4; 10/49, 51.

**gefara** → gefēra.

**faran.** st. 6. *travel, go.* 3sg. **færð** 3/20 (2x); 10/61. pl. **faraþ** 8/6. past 3sg. **fōr** H/4; 8/5, 7, 13, 18, etc. (6x). past pl. **fōron** 18/202. imp. pl. **farað** 3/91. inf. C/11, 12; 6/27, 39; 12/88, etc. (7x).

**gefaran.** st. 6. *go, traverse,* fig. *die.* pl. **gefarað** 10/25. subj. past sg. **gefōre** 8/52. inf. 10/18. *come about, happen.* past part. **gefaren** 7/58.

fatu → fæt.

fæc. neut. *space, time.* acc. sg. 9/42. dat. sg. fæce 9/1.

fæder. masc. r-stem. *father.* nom. sg. 2/2; 3/25; 6/11, 38; 7/21, etc. (8x). gen. sg. 11/7. dat. sg. 7/21; 11/18; 13/115. nom. pl. fæderas D/1.

fǣge. adj. *about to die, doomed.* masc. nom. pl. 12/105; 18/19. wk. masc. dat. sg. fǣgean 12/125. masc. nom. sg. 12/119. masc. gen. sg. fǣges 12/297. masc. acc. pl. 18/195. dat. pl. fǣgum 18/209.

fægen. adj. *glad, joyful, rejoicing.* masc. nom. sg. 13/68.

fæger. adj. *fair, beautiful, pleasant.* neut. nom. sg. 14/73; 18/47. fem. acc. sg. fægre 17/38. masc. inst. sg. fægre 9/27. masc. nom. pl. fægere 14/8, 10. wk. fem. dat. sg. fægran 14/21.

(ge)fægnian. wk. 2. *rejoice* about something (gen.). 3sg. fægnað 10/62. past 1sg. fægnode 3/27. past 3sg. fægnode 2/24.

fægre. adv. *fairly, well.* fægere, fægre 12/22; 18/300.

fæhþo. fem. *feud, enmity.* nom. sg. 17/19. acc. sg. fæhðe 12/225; 16/26.

fæmne. wk. fem. *woman.* nom. sg. 11/20. acc. sg. fǣmnan, fēmnan 2/27. gen. sg. fǣmnan. dat. sg. fǣmnan. nom. pl. fǣmnan.

fænne → fenn.

fǣrlic. adj. *sudden.* neut. nom. sg. 3/70.

fǣrlīce. adv. *suddenly, precipitously.* 3/36, 37, 39; 13/61.

fǣrsceaþa. wk. masc. *sudden attacker.* dat. sg. fǣrsceaðan 12/142.

fǣrspel. neut. *story of an attack.* acc. sg. 18/244.

færþ → faran.

fæst. adj. *secure, fixed, enclosed.* masc. nom. sg. B/3; K/1364. neut. nom. sg. 15/5.

fæstan. wk. 1. *fast.* subj. sg. fæste. pres. part. fæstende 2/11.

fæste. adv. *firmly, securely.* 7/41; 9/14; 12/21, 103, 171, etc. (11x).

fæsten. neut. *stronghold.* acc. sg. 12/194. dat. sg. fæstenne 18/143.

fæstenbryce. masc. *failure to fast.* nom. pl. fæstenbrycas 7/49.

fæstengeat. neut. *gate to the stronghold.* gen. sg. fæstengeates 18/162.

fæstlice. adv. *firmly, resolutely.* 12/82, 254.

(ge)fæstnian. wk. 2. *fasten, secure.* past pl. gefæstnodon 14/33. inf. fæstnian 12/35.

fæstnung. fem. *stability, security, safety, protection.* nom. sg. 13/115.

fæstrǣd. adj. *steadfast.* wk. masc. nom. sg. fæstrǣda 10/76.

fæt. neut. *container, cup.* nom. pl. fatu.

fǣted. adj. *ornamented.* wk. neut. gen. sg. fǣttan 17/36.

fǣtels. masc. *vessel, pouch.* dat. sg. fǣtelse 18/127. acc. pl. fǣtelsas 8/75.

fēa. A. adj. *few.* neut. nom. pl. fēawa 2/18. dat. pl. fēawum 8/3. neut. acc. pl. fēawa.

B. adv. *little.* 14/115.

gefēa. wk. masc. *joy.* acc. sg. gefēan F/7.

gefeah → gefēon.

feaht, gefeaht → (ge)feohtan.

feala → fela.

(ge)feallan. st. 7. *fall.* 3sg. fealleþ 13/63. past 3sg. fēol, fēoll, gefēoll, gefēol 3/40; 5/18; 12/119, 126, 166, etc. (10x). past pl. fēollon 12/111. inf. feallan 12/54, 105; 14/43. pres. part. feallende.

fealohilte. adj. *yellow-hilted* (i.e. with a golden hilt). neut. nom. sg. 12/166.

fealu. adj. *yellow, tawny, dark.* masc. acc. pl. fealwe 13/46.

fealwian. wk. 2. *become yellow, wither.* pl. fealwiað A/3.

fearr. masc. *ox.* acc. pl. fearras 3/91.

feax. neut. *hair.* acc. sg. 18/281. dat. sg. feaxe 18/99.

fēdan. wk. 1. *feed.* inf. 5/21.

gefēgan. wk. 1. *join, fix, attach.* past part. gefēged 2/19.

fela. A. indef. pron. *many, much.* 6/12; 7/4 (2x), 5, 6, etc. (16x).

B. adj. (indeclinable). *many.* fela, feala 2/27, 30; 3/100; 7/20, 47, etc. (9x).

C. adv. *much.*

**felalēof.** adj. *much-loved.* wk. masc. gen. sg. **felalēofan** 16/26.

**feld.** masc. u-stem. *field.* dat. sg. **felda** м/7; 12/241.

**fell.** neut. *skin, hide.* nom. sg. **fel** 3/54. acc. sg. **fel** 8/29. dat. sg. **felle** 3/54, 86. acc. pl. 8/29. dat. pl. **fellum** 8/27.

**fēmnan** → fǣmne.

**fēng-, gefēng-** → fōn.

**fengelād.** neut. *fen-path.* acc. pl. к/1359.

**fenland.** neut. *fenland.* dat. sg. **fenlande** 2/18.

**fenn.** masc. *fen.* dat. sg. **fænne, fenne** 10/22, 23; 15/5. nom. pl. **fennas** 10/19. dat. pl. **fennum** 10/25.

**feoh.** neut. *riches, treasure, money.* nom. sg. 13/108. acc. sg. 4/8; 5/15; 8/66, 69; 12/39. gen. sg. **fēos** 4/11; 8/66. dat. sg. **fēo** 2/7; 8/68, 69, 70.

**feohgestrēon.** neut. *acquired treasure.* gen. pl. **feohgestrēona** 17/36.

**feohgīfre.** adj. *greedy for wealth.* masc. nom. sg. 13/68.

**gefeoht.** neut. *battle.* dat. sg. **gefeohte** 7/39; 12/12; 18/189, 202. dat. pl. **gefeohtum** 4/3.

**(ge)feohtan.** st. 3. *fight, obtain by fighting* (with ġe- prefix). past 3sg. **feaht, gefeaht** 4/3; 12/254, 277, 281, 298, etc. (6x). past pl. **fuhton, gefuhton** 18/262. subj. sg. **gefeohte** м/1, 3, 4, 6. inf. **feohtan, gefeohtan** 5/3; 12/16, 129, 261. pres. part. **feohtende** 4/6, 8, 15. past part. **gefohten** м/7; 18/122.

**feohte.** wk. fem. *fighting, battle.* nom. sg. 12/103.

**fēol, gefēol** → (ge)feallan.

**fēolan.** st. 3. *enter, penetrate.* past pl. **fulgon** 4/15.

**fēolheard.** adj. *file-hard* (i.e. hard as a file). neut. acc. pl. **fēolhearde** 12/108.

**fēoll-, gefēoll** → (ge)feallan.

**gefēon.** st. 5. *rejoice* about something (gen.). past 3sg. **gefeah** 18/205. pres. part. **gefēonde** 9/32.

**fēond.** masc. nd-stem. *enemy.* nom. sg. в/4. acc. sg. в/5. gen. sg. **fēondes** 3/27.

nom. pl. **fēondas, fȳnd** ꜰ/3; 14/30, 33; 18/195. acc. pl. **fȳnd, fēondas** 12/82; 14/38; 18/319. gen. pl. **fēonda.** dat. pl. **fēondum** 7/31; 12/103, 264.

**fēondrǣden.** fem. *enmity.* acc. sg. **fēondrǣdenne** 1/15.

**fēondsceaþa.** wk. masc. *enemy who does harm.* acc. sg. **fēondsceaðan** 18/104.

**feor. A.** adv. *far, long ago.* к/1361; 8/6, 7; 12/3, 57, etc. (8x). superl. **firrest** 8/6. **B.** adj. *far, distant.* neut. nom. sg. 9/40. masc. nom. sg. 13/21. neut. gen. sg. **feorres** 16/47.

**fēore, fēores** → feorh.

**feorgbold.** neut. *life-dwelling, body.* nom. sg. 14/73.

**feorh.** masc. *life.* acc. sg. к/1370; 4/8, 15; 12/125, 142, etc. (6x). gen. sg. **fēores** 12/260, 317. dat. sg. **fēore** 12/194, 259.

**feorhhord.** neut. *treasure of life, life.*

**feorhhūs.** neut. *life-house, body.* acc. sg. 12/297.

**feorhsweng.** masc. *blow that takes a life, death-blow.*

**feorran.** adv. *from afar.* к/1370; 14/57; 18/24.

**fēorþa.** ord. num. *fourth.* masc. nom. sg. 3/39. fem. nom. sg. **fēorðe.** fem. acc. sg. **fēorðan** 3/106. masc. gen. sg. **fēorðan** 10/18. masc. dat. sg. **fēorðan** 10/19. masc. inst. sg. **fēorðan** 18/12.

**fēos** → feoh.

**fēower. A.** card. num. as noun. *four.* ᴇ/1. **B.** as adj. *four.* neut. acc. pl. ʜ/1. dat. pl. 3/39; 8/8.

**fēowertig.** card. num. as noun. *forty.* ᴇ/1; 5/14, 21. gen. sg. **fēowertiges** 8/20. acc. pl. 3/106, 107.

**fēowertȳne. A.** card. num. as noun. *fourteen.* ᴇ/1. nom. pl. 3/99. **B.** as adj. *fourteen.* dat. pl. **fēowertȳnum** 9/28.

**gefēra.** wk. masc. *companion, comrade.* nom. sg. **gefara, gefēra** ɪ/2; 12/280. dat. sg. **gefēran** 1/12; 13/30. nom. pl. **gefēran** 4/14. acc. pl. **gefēran** 12/170, 229. dat. pl. **gefērum** 3/45; 4/13.

**fēran.** wk. 1. *go, journey.* past 1sg. **fērde** 3/13. past 3sg. **fērde** c/6; 2/30; 3/20. past pl. **fērdon** 3/8, 94; 5/4. inf. 12/41, 179, 221; 16/9; 18/12.

**ferdman.** masc. athematic. *man of the army, warrior.* acc. pl. **ferdmen** 10/4.

**fered-** → ferian.

**ferhþ.** masc. *spirit, life.* nom. sg. **ferð** 13/54. *mind, intellect.* dat. sg. **ferðe** 13/90.

**ferhþglēaw.** adj. *wise in mind.* wk. fem. acc. sg. **ferhðglēawe** 18/41.

**ferian.** *carry.* 1. wk. 1. past 3sg. **ferede** 13/81. past pl. **feredon** 2/30. 2. wk. 2. past 3sg. **ferode** 5/19.

**fers.** neut. *verse.* acc. pl. 9/11.

**fersc.** adj. *fresh.* masc. nom. pl. **fersce** 8/38.

**gefērscipe.** masc. *society.* nom. pl. **gefēr- scipas** 10/7. dat. pl. **gefērscipum** 10/6.

**ferþ** → ferhþ.

**ferþloca.** wk. masc. *life-enclosure.* nom. sg. 13/33. acc. sg. **ferðlocan** 13/13.

**fēseþ** → fȳsan.

**fēt** → fōt.

**(ge)fetian.** wk. 2. *fetch, seize.* subj. sg. **gefetige** 14/138. inf. **fetigan, gefetigan** 12/160; 18/35.

**fetor.** fem. *fetter.* dat. pl. **feterum** 13/21.

**fettian.** wk. 2. *contend.* past 3sg. **fettode** G/1.

**fēþa.** wk. masc. *company of foot-troops.* acc. sg. **fēþan** 12/88.

**fēþelāst.** masc. *foot-path.* dat. sg. **fēðelāste** 18/139.

**feþer.** fem. *feather, wing.* acc. pl. **feþra** 13/47. gen. pl. **feðra** 8/29. dat. pl. **feðerum** G/2; 8/27.

**fīclēaf.** neut. *figleaf.* acc. pl. 1/7.

**fielle** → fyll.

**fierd-** → fyrd.

**fīf. A.** card. num. as adj. *five.* dat. pl. 8/10, 48. neut. nom. pl. **fīfe** 14/8. masc. acc. pl. 3/7, 98. neut. acc. pl. 3/7, 98; 8/29. fem. dat. pl. 8/68.

**B.** as noun. *five.* E/1; 5/21. acc. pl. 8/66.

**fīfta.** ord. num. *fifth.* masc. nom. sg. 3/108. masc. dat. sg. **fīftan** 10/22.

**fīftig.** card. num. as noun. *fifty.* E/1. gen. sg. **fīftiges** 8/20.

**fīftȳne. A.** card. num. as noun. *fifteen.* E/3. nom. pl. **fīftēne** 8/58.

**B.** as adj. *fifteen.* acc. pl. 8/29.

**findan.** st. 3. *find.* 2sg. **findest, findst** 10/42; 17/12, 28. 3sg. **findeð** 8/73. past 1sg. **funde** 16/18. past 3sg. **funde** 18/2, 278. past pl. **fundon** 12/85; 18/41. inf. H/4; 13/26.

**finger.** masc. *finger.*

**Finnas.** masc. *Sami (the Lapps).* nom. pl. 8/13, 17, 26, 32. dat. pl. **Finnum** 8/24.

**fīras.** masc. *people.* gen. pl. **fīra** 18/24, 33. dat. pl. **fīrum** 9/13.

**firen.** fem. *crime, sin.* gen. pl. **firena** 11/20.

**(ge)firenian.** wk. 2. *commit a crime, sin, make sinful.* past part. **gefirenode** F/6.

**firenlust.** masc. *criminal desire.* dat. pl. **firenlustum** H/2.

**firenum.** adv. *criminally, sinfully.*

**firrest** → feor.

**fisc.** masc. *fish.* nom. pl. **fixas.** gen. pl. **fisca.**

**fiscaþ.** masc. *fishing.* nom. sg. 8/61. dat. sg. **fiscaþe** 8/3.

**fiscere.** masc. *fisherman.* nom. pl. **fisceras** 8/15. dat. pl. **fiscerum** 8/13.

**fixas** → fisc.

**flān.** masc. *arrow.* acc. sg. 12/269. gen. sg. **flānes** 12/71. gen. pl. **flāna** 18/221.

**flǣsc.** neut. *flesh.* nom. sg. 3/83. acc. sg. 3/55; 11/20. dat. sg. **flǣsce** 3/86.

**flēah** → flēogan.

**flēam.** masc. *flight.* acc. sg. 12/81, 254; 18/291. dat. sg. **flēame** 12/186.

**flēogan.** st. 2. *fly, flee.* past 3sg. **flēah** 18/209. past pl. **flugon** 12/194; 18/296. inf. 12/7, 109, 150, 275; 18/221.

**flēohnet.** neut. *fly-net, curtain.* nom. sg. 18/47.

**flēon.** st. 2. *flee.* inf. 12/247.

**flēotan.** st. 2. *float.* pres. part. **flēotendra** 13/54.

**flēow** → flōwan.

**flet.** neut. *floor, dwelling, hall.* acc. sg. 13/61.

**fletsittend.** masc. nd-stem. *sitter in the hall, courtier.* dat. pl. **fletsittendum** 18/19, 33.

**flocc.** masc. *company, band of men, flock.* dat. sg. **flocce.** dat. pl. **floccum** 3/38.

**flocmælum.** adv. *in troops.* 5/4.

**flōd.** masc. *water, sea.* nom. sg. κ/1361. dat. sg. **flōde** κ/1366. *tide, flood tide.* nom. sg. 12/65, 72.

**flōr.** fem. *floor.* acc. sg. **flōre** 18/111.

**flot.** neut. *sea.* acc. sg. 12/41.

**flota.** wk. masc. *ship, seafarer.* acc. sg. **flotan** 12/227. nom. pl. **flotan** 12/72.

**flotman.** masc. athematic. *seaman, Viking.* nom. pl. **flotmen** 7/39.

**flotweg.** masc. *sea-way.* acc. sg. 17/43.

**flōwan.** st. 7. *flow.* past 3sg. **flēow.** pres. part. **flōwende** 12/65.

**flugon** → flēogan.

**flyht.** masc. *flight.* acc. sg. 12/71.

**geflȳman.** wk. 1. *drive, drive out, exile.* past part. **geflȳmdum, geflȳmed** κ/1370.

**flȳs.** neut. *fleece.* dat. pl. **flȳsum** 3/26.

**foca.** wk. masc. *cake.* acc. sg. **focan.**

**fōda.** wk. masc. *food.*

**gefohten** → (ge)feohtan.

**folc.** neut. *people, army.* nom. sg. 12/45, 241; 14/140; 18/162, 262, etc. (6x). acc. sg. 10/13; 12/22, 54. gen. sg. **folces** 5/7; 7/3, 29, 64; 9/24, etc. (11x). dat. sg. **folce, folc** 10/29; 12/227, 259, 323; 18/143, etc. (6x). acc. pl. 5/4. gen. pl. **folca.**

**folclagu.** fem. *secular law.* nom. pl. **folclaga** 7/13.

**folclond.** neut. *nation.* gen. sg. **folclondes** 16/47.

**folcstede.** masc. *place for people, dwelling-place, battlefield.* dat. sg. 18/319.

**folctoga.** wk. masc. *leader of the people.* gen. sg. **folctogan** 18/47. acc. pl. **folctogan** 18/194.

**folde.** wk. fem. *earth.* acc. sg. **foldan** κ/1361; 9/13; 12/54; 17/38. gen. sg. **foldan** 13/33; 14/8, 43. dat. sg. **foldan** 12/166, 227; 14/132; 18/281.

**folgaþ.** masc. *service, office, authority.* acc. sg. 16/9.

**folgian.** wk. 2. *follow, obey, observe* a rule. past 3sg. **folgade** 6/17. inf. 4/12; 6/40.

**folm.** fem. *hand.* dat. sg. **folme** 18/80. dat. pl. **folmum** 18/99.

**folme.** wk. fem. *hand.* dat. sg. **folman** 12/150. dat. pl. **folman** 12/21, 108.

**fōn.** st. 7. *take, catch.* pl. **fōð** 8/24. past 3sg. **fēng** 12/10. *begin,* with prep. *on, undertake* something (acc.). past 3sg. **fēng** 18/299. past pl. **fēngon.** *succeed.* past 3sg. **fēng** 4/17, 18.

**gefōn.** st. 7. *seize.* past 3sg. **gefēng.**

**for.** prep. (with dat., sometimes with acc.). *for, because of.* B/5; C/2, 4; G/8; 2/28, etc. (48x). *in place of.* 2/13 (2x). *in spite of.* 5/4. *with respect to.* 5/10 (2x); 7/24 (2x). *in comparison to.* 10/21, 66. *before* (of location), *in the presence of.* J/88; 14/112; 18/192.

**fōr** → faran.

**for þām.** A. conj. *because.* **for þām, for þon, for ðæm, for ðan** A/6; G/8, 9; 5/5, 16, etc. (23x).

B. adv. *therefore, and so.* **for ðon, for þām, for þan, for ðæm** 7/6, 17, 20, 24; 9/4, etc. (19x).

**for þām þe.** conj. *because.* **for ðan ðe, for þām þe, for ðæm þe, for þon ðe** G/3; H/2; J/10, 14, 17, etc. (25x).

**for þan** → for þām.

**for þī þe.** conj. *because.* 3/102.

**for þon þe** → for þām þe.

**for þȳ.** A. adv. *therefore.* **for ðȳ, for ðī** 3/103; 8/59, 70; 10/9, 34, etc. (7x).

B. conj. *because.* 10/72.

**foran.** adv. *in front.* La.

**forbærnan.** wk. 1. *burn, cremate.* 3sg. **forbærneð** 8/71. pl. **forbærnað** 8/65. past 3sg. **forbærnde** 3/37, 45; 7/26. past part. **forbærned** 8/73.

**forbærst** → forberstan.

**forbēah** → forbūgan.

**forbēodan.** st. 2. *forbid.* past 3sg. **forbēad** J/1; 5/15; 6/38.

forberan. st. 4. *forbear, endure, tolerate.* subj. sg. forbere M/9.

forberstan. st. 3. *burst, collapse.* past 3sg. forbærst 10/56. past pl. forburston F/5.

forbīgan. wk. 1. *bend down, abase.* past part. forbīged 18/267.

forbūgan. st. 2. *refrain from, avoid, flee from.* past 3sg. forbēah 12/325. pres. part. forbūgende 3/5, 14.

forburston → forberstan.

forceorfan. st. 3. *cut out, cut through, cut off.* past 3sg. forcearf 3/40; 18/105. past pl. forcurfon. inf. H/3.

forcūþ. adj. *infamous.* wk. masc. nom. sg. superl. forcūþesta 10/14.

ford. masc. u-stem. *ford.* acc. sg. 12/88. dat. sg. forda 12/81.

fordōn. anom. verb. *ruin, destroy.* 1sg. fordō. past pl. fordydon. inf. 7/62.

fordrīfan. st. 1. *compel.* past 3sg. fordrāf 18/277.

fordyslic. adj. *very foolish.* neut. nom. sg. 10/21.

gefōre → gefaran.

forealdian. wk. 2. *decay.* past pl. forealdodon 10/37. past part. forealdod 10/9.

foregenga. wk. masc. *predecessor, ancestor, servant.* nom. sg. 18/127. gen. pl. 6/13.

foremǣre. adj. *outstanding.* masc. acc. sg. foremǣrne 18/122. masc. acc. pl. 10/80. gen. pl. formǣrra 10/45. masc. nom. pl. superl. formǣroste 10/36.

forescēawung. fem. *providence.* acc. sg. forescēawunge 2/25.

forespreca. wk. masc. *advocate, sponsor.* nom. pl. forespecan, foresprecan 7/68.

forfaran. st. 6. *perish, destroy.* past 3sg. forfor 7/27.

forgeaf, forgēafe → forgifan.

forgieldan. wk. 1. *pay for, buy off, restore.* past 3sg. forgeald 3/96. subj. pl. forgyldon 12/32. inf. forgyldan 3/101. past part. forgolden, forgoldene 3/99; 18/217.

forgietan. st. 5. *forget.* infl. inf. tō forgytanne 6/27. past part. forgitene 10/9, 80.

forgifan. st. 5. *give, grant, forgive.* past 2sg. forgēafe 1/12. past 3sg. forgeaf 3/42, 94; 12/139, 148; 14/147. imp. sg. forgif 18/88. past part. forgifen 2/3, 5; 9/17.

forgifeness. fem. *forgiveness* for something (gen.). acc. sg. forgifenesse 6/42.

forgolden-, forgyldan, forgyldon → forgieldan.

forhæfdness. fem. *abstinence, moderation.* dat. sg. forhæfdnesse.

forhealdan. st. 7. *withhold.* pl. forhealdað 7/10. inf. 7/10.

forheard. adj. of a weapon, *very hard.* masc. acc. sg. forheardne 12/156.

forheawan. st. 7. *cut down, kill by cutting.* past part. forhēawen 12/115, 223, 288, 314.

forhelan. st. 4. *conceal.* past part. forholene 10/9.

forhicgan. wk. 3. *despise.* past 3sg. forhogode 12/254.

forhogdness. fem. *contempt.* dat. sg. forhogdnisse 9/2.

forhogode → forhicgan.

forholene → forhelan.

forht. adj. *afraid, fearful, timid.* masc. nom. sg. 13/68; 14/21.

forhtian. wk. 2. *be afraid.* pl. forhtiað 14/115. subj. past pl. forhtedon 12/21.

forhtlīce. adv. *fearfully.* 18/244.

forhwæga. adv. of distance, *about.* 8/67, 68.

forlǣtan. st. 7. *let.* past 3sg. forlēt 12/149, 156, 321. *leave, leave alone, abandon, release.* 3sg. forlēt 6/3. pl. forlǣtað D/1. past 3sg. forlēt 3/50; 9/7; 10/82; 12/187. past pl. forlēton 10/36; 14/61. imp. sg. forlǣt. inf. 2/9; 3/112; 7/67; 12/2, 208. pres. part. forlǣtende 9/43. *allow, permit.* 3sg. forlǣt 10/70. past pl. forlēton 18/170. subj. sg. forlǣte. inf. 18/150.

forlēan. st. 6. *blame.* subj. pl. forlēon 6/43.

**forlegen.** adj. (past part. of *forlicgan*). *adulterous.* masc. nom. pl. **forlegene** 7/56.

**forlēogan.** st. 2. *lie, perjure, falsely accuse.* past part. **forlogen, forlogene** 7/34, 49.

**forlēosan.** st. 2. (with dat. object). *lose.* past 3sg. **forlēas** 6/29. inf. 18/63. past part. **forloren, forlorene** 3/102; 7/49.

**forlēt-** → forlǣtan.

**forliger.** neut. *fornication.* acc. pl. **forligru** 7/48.

**forlogen-** → forlēogan.

**forloren-** → forlēosan.

**forma.** ord. num. *first.* masc. acc. sg. **forman.** neut. acc. sg. **forman** 12/77. neut. dat. sg. **forman** J/90. masc. nom. sg. superl. **fyrmest** 6/26; 12/323.

**formǣroste, formǣrra** → foremǣre.

**formolsnian.** wk. 2. *decay.* inf. 2/26. past part. **formolsnodan** 2/26.

**formonig.** adj. *a great many.* masc. nom. sg. **formoni** 12/239.

**forniman.** st. 4. *take away.* past 3sg. **fornom** 13/80. past pl. **fornōman** 13/99. past part. **fornumene** 7/15.

**fornȳdan.** wk. 1. *compel.* past part. **fornȳdde** 7/14.

**foroft.** adv. *very often.* 7/19, 21, 47.

**fōron** → faran.

**forrǣdan.** wk. 1. *plot against, betray.* past 3sg. **forrǣdde** 7/26. subj. sg. **forrǣde** 7/25.

**forrotodness.** fem. *corruption.* dat. sg. **forrotodnysse** 3/83.

**forscomu.** fem. *shame, modesty.* dat. sg. **forscome** 9/6.

**forscrincan.** st. 3. *shrink,* in past participle, *shrunken, wither.* past part. **forscruncen** 3/83.

**forsēarian.** wk. 2. *dry up.* past 3sg. **forsēarode** 3/83.

**forsēon.** st. 5. *neglect, despise, scorn, reject.* 3sg. **forsihð** 10/62. pl. **forsēoð, forsīoð** D/2; 10/47. past pl. **forsāwon** H/2. past part. **forsāwene** 7/15.

**forsīþian.** wk. 2. *fare amiss.* past part. **forsīðod.**

**forspendan.** wk. 1. *expend.* pl. **forspendað** 8/72.

**forspillan.** wk. 1. *destroy, waste.* past 3sg. **forspilde** 7/27.

**forst.** masc. *frost.* dat. sg. **forste.**

**forstandan.** st. 6. *avail, benefit.* 3sg. **forstent** 10/57. past 3sg. **forstōd** 10/57.

**forstōd** → forstandan.

**forsugian, forsuwian.** wk. 2. *keep silent about, ignore, neglect, suppress.* pl. **forsuwiað** 3/49. past 3sg. **forsuwade** 3/49. past part. **forsugod** 10/9.

**forsuwade, forsuwiaþ** → forsugian, forsuwian.

**forswerian.** st. 6. *swear falsely.* past part. **forsworene** 7/34.

**forswīþe.** adv. *very much.* 10/2.

**forsworene** → forswerian.

**forsyngian.** wk. 2. *burden by sin.* past part. **forsyngod, forsyngodon** 7/47, 57.

**forþ.** adv. *forwards, forth, greatly* (in phrase *tō forþ* 'too greatly'). 7/53; 8/12; 10/80; 12/3, 12, etc. (15x).

**forþbringan.** wk. 1. *bring forth, bring about.* past 3sg. **forþbrōhte** 9/1. inf. 10/32, 35.

**forþfēran.** wk. 1. *die.* past 3sg. **forþfērde.** pres. part. **forðfērendum.**

**forþfōr.** fem. *departure, death.* nom. sg. 9/31. gen. sg. **forðfōre** 9/45, 28. dat. sg. **forðfōre** 9/29, 33.

**forþgān.** anom. verb. *go forth.* past 3sg. **forðēode** 14/54.

**forþgeorn.** adj. *eager to advance.* masc. nom. sg. 12/281.

**forþgesceaft.** fem. *the future, eternity.* acc. sg. 14/10.

**forþgewītan.** st. 1. *depart, die.* past part. **forðgewitene** 10/77.

**geforþian.** wk. 2. *carry out.* past part. **geforþod** 12/289.

**forþolian.** wk. 2. (with dat.). *do without.* inf. 13/38.

**forþsīþ.** masc. *journey forth, passing, death.* gen. sg. **forðsīþes** 17/43. dat. sg. **forðsīðe** 2/30.

forþweg. masc. *the way forward, departure, death.* dat. sg. **forðwege** 13/81; 14/125.

forþylman. wk. 1. *enclose, cover.* past part. **forðylmed** 18/118.

forwegan. st. 5. *carry off, kill.* past part. **forwegen** 12/228.

forwel. adv. *very, very well.* 10/2.

forweorþan. st. 3. *perish.* past pl. **forwurdan** 7/28, 64. subj. pl. 7/60. inf. 18/288.

forworhtan → forwyrcan.

forwundian. wk. 2. *wound severely.* past part. **forwunded, forwundod** 14/14, 62.

forwurdan → forweorþan.

forwyrcan. wk. 1. *destroy.* past pl. **forworhtan** 7/64. subj. pl. 7/53.

forwyrd. fem. *destruction, ruin.* nom. sg. 18/285. dat. sg. **forwyrde** c/11; 3/57.

forwyrnan. wk. 1. *deny.* past 1sg. **forwyrnde** 3/26.

foryrman. wk. 1. *reduce to poverty.* past part. **foryrmde** 7/14.

fōt. masc. athematic. *foot.* nom. sg. 3/25. gen. sg. **fōtes** 12/247. nom. pl. **fēt.** acc. pl. **fēt.** dat. pl. **fōtum** 12/119, 171.

fōtmǣl. neut. of measurement, *foot.* acc. sg. 12/275. acc. pl. 6/7.

fōtsceamel. masc. *footstool.* nom. sg. 3/18. dat. sg. **fōtsceamele** 3/19.

fōþ → fōn.

fracod. adj. *wicked, criminal.* masc. gen. sg. **fracodes** 14/10.

fram. A. prep. (with dat.). *from, by.* **fram, from** G/5 (2x); 1/8; 3/30, 35, etc. (27x). B. adv. *away, from there.* **fram, from** 4/13; 12/317.

franca. wk. masc. *spear.* acc. sg. **francan** 12/140. dat. sg. **francan** 12/77.

gefrægen, frægn, gefrægn → (ge)frignan.

(ge)frætwian. wk. 2. *adorn.* past 3sg. **frætwode** 2/13. past part. **gefrætewod** 18/171, 328.

frēa. wk. masc. *lord, the Lord.* nom. sg. 9/13; 18/300. acc. sg. **frēan** 12/259; 14/33. gen. sg. **frēan** J/90; La; 16/33; 17/10. dat. sg. **frēan** I/2; 12/12, 16, 184, 289.

frēcne. adj. *daring, dangerous.* neut. acc. pl. к/1359.

frēfran. wk. 1. *console.* inf. 13/28.

(ge)frēfrian. wk. 2. *console.* past 1sg. **gefrēfrode** 3/23. past pl. **gefrēfrodon** 3/104. subj. past pl. **gefrēfrodon** 3/67. infl. inf. **tō gefrēfrigenne** 3/71.

fremde. adj. *foreign, unrelated.* masc. dat. sg. **fremdan** 7/21. gen. pl. **fremdra** 10/47. dat. pl. **fremdum** 7/14, 32. wk. masc. nom. pl. **fremdan** 8/72.

fremian. wk. 2. *benefit, aid.* 3sg. **fremað** 3/97. past 3sg. **fremode** 2/27; 3/34.

(ge)fremman. wk. 1. *do.* past 3sg. **gefremede.** past pl. **fremedon** 18/37. *bring about, provide.* past 3sg. **gefremede** 18/6. inf. **gefremman** 13/16, 114. *make.* inf. **fremman** 17/19. *perpetrate.* past 3sg. **gefremede** 18/181.

fremsumness. fem. *benefit, kindness.* dat. pl. **fremsumnessum** 9/25.

frēo. adj. *free.* masc. nom. pl. 6/39.

frēod. fem. *peace.* acc. sg. **frēode** 12/39.

frēogan. wk. 2. *set free.*

frēolic. adj. *free-born, noble.* neut. nom. pl. **frēolicu.**

frēolsbryce. masc. *failure to observe a festival.* nom. pl. **frēolsbricas** 7/49.

frēolsdæg. masc. *feast day.* nom. sg. 2/11.

frēomǣg. masc. *free kinsman, noble kinsman.* dat. pl. **frēomǣgum** 13/21.

frēond. masc. nd-stem. *friend, loved one.* nom. sg. 13/108; 14/144; 16/47. acc. sg. 3/77. nom. pl. **frēondas, frīend, frȳnd** 14/76; 16/33. acc. pl. **frȳnd** 12/229. gen. pl. **frēonda** 3/82; 14/132; 16/17. dat. pl. **frēondum** 3/95, 97; 8/64.

frēondlēas. adj. *friendless.* masc. acc. sg. **frēondlēasne** 13/28.

frēondscipe. masc. *friendship, love.* nom. sg. 16/25. acc. sg. **frēondscype** 17/19.

frēorig. adj. *frozen,* fig. *unhappy.* masc. nom. sg. 13/33; 18/281.

frēoriht. neut. *rights of freemen.* nom. pl. 7/15.

frīend → frēond.

**(ge)frignan.** st. 3. *ask, hear of.* 3sg. **frīneð** 14/112. past 1sg. **gefrǣgn, gefrǣgen** Lb; 18/7, 246. past 3sg. **frǣgn** 9/32, 35, 39. past pl. **gefrūnon** 14/76.

**frīolīce.** adv. *freely.* 10/61.

**friþ.** *peace.* **1.** masc. acc. sg. 5/4; 12/39. gen. sg. **friðes** 5/1; 12/41. dat. sg. **friþe** 12/179. **2.** neut. nom. sg. 6/27.

**friþāþ.** masc. *oath of peace.* nom. pl. **friðāþas** 5/20.

**(ge)friþian.** wk. 2. *make peace with, protect, defend.* past 3sg. **gefriðode** 18/5.

**frōd.** adj. *old, mature, wise.* masc. nom. sg. κ/1366; 12/140, 317; 13/90.

**frōfor.** *consolation, help, benefit.* **1.** fem. acc. sg. **frōfre** 13/115. gen. sg. **frōfre** 18/83. dat. sg. **frōfre** 18/296. **2.** masc. acc. sg. **frōfer** 3/71.

**from** → fram.

**fromlīce.** adv. *boldly.* 18/41, 220, 301.

**fromsīþ.** masc. *journey away, departure.* nom. sg. 16/33.

**fruma.** masc. *beginning, origin.* dat. sg. **fruman** 9/24; 10/44.

**frumbearn.** neut. *first-born child.*

**frumcenned.** adj. *first-born.* masc. acc. sg. **frumcennedan.**

**frumgār.** masc. *lead-spear, leader.* acc. pl. **frumgāras** 18/195.

**frumsceaft.** masc. *first creation.* acc. sg. 9/10.

**gefrūnon** → (ge)frignan.

**frymdig.** adj. *entreating.* masc. nom. sg. **frymdi** 12/179.

**frymþ.** fem. *beginning, origin, creation.* dat. sg. **frymðe** 11/18. gen. pl. **frymða** 18/5, 83, 189.

**frȳnd** → frēond.

**fugel.** masc. *bird.* nom. sg. G/4; 13/81; 18/207. gen. pl. **fugela** 8/27. dat. pl. **fuglum** 18/296.

**fugelere.** masc. *fowler.* nom. pl. **fugeleras** 8/15. dat. pl. **fugelerum** 8/13.

**fugolcynn.** neut. *species of bird.* dat. sg. **fugolcynne.**

**fuhton, gefuhton** → (ge)feohtan.

**ful.** adv. *very, fully.* **ful, full** 7/8, 25, 38, 47, 51, etc. (17x).

**fūl.** adj. *foul.* masc. acc. sg. **fūlne** 7/64. masc. nom. pl. **fūle** 7/56. wk. masc. nom. sg. **fūla** 18/111.

**fulfremed.** adj. *perfect.* gen. pl. **fulfremedra** 10/13. masc. nom. sg. compar. **fulfremedra** 3/34.

**fulfremedness.** fem. *perfection.* nom. sg. **fulfremednys** 3/74.

**fulgon** → fēolan.

**fūlian.** st. 2. *decay.* pl. **fūliað** 8/74.

**full.** **A.** adj. *full.* masc. acc. sg. 6/27; 8/75. masc. nom. pl. **fulle** 18/19. fem. acc. pl. **fulle.**

**B.** neut. *cup.* dat. sg. **fulle** J/90.

**fullæstan.** wk. 1. *assist.*

**fullīce.** adv. *fully, completely.* 3/110; 7/36, 37.

**fūllīce.** adv. *foully.*

**fulluht-** → fulwiht.

**fultum.** masc. *help, support, protection.* acc. sg. 18/186, 300. dat. sg. **fultume** 3/23.

**gefultuman.** wk. 1. *aid.* past part. **gefultumed** 9/3.

**gefulwian.** wk. 2. *baptize.* past part. **gefulwad.**

**fulwiht.** neut. *baptism.* acc. sg. **fulluht, fulwiht** 7/68. dat. sg. **fulluhte** 7/68.

**fund-** → findan.

**fundian.** wk. 2. *come, hasten, strive.* 3sg. **fundaþ** 14/103.

**furþor.** adv. *further.* 12/247.

**furþum.** adv. *even.* 10/14, 18, 25, 26, 27, etc. (8x).

**fūs.** adj. *in a hurry, ready to go, eager, brave.* masc. nom. sg. 12/281. masc. nom. pl. **fūse** 14/57. wk. neut. acc. sg. **fūse** 14/21.

**fūslic.** adj. *ready.* neut. acc. pl. **fūslicu.**

**gefylde** → (ge)fyllan.

**fylgan.** wk. 1. (with dat. or acc. object). *follow, serve.* past 3sg. **fyligde.** inf. **fylgan, fylgean** 7/68; 18/33.

**fyll.** masc. *fall, death.* acc. sg. **fyl, fyll** 12/71, 264; 14/56. dat. sg. **fielle.**

(ge)fyllan. A. wk. 1. *fill, feed.* past 3sg. gefylde LA. inf. gefyllan. past part. gefylde, gefylled H/2.

B. wk. 1. *fell, kill.* imp. pl. fyllað 18/194. inf. fyllan, gefyllan 14/38, 73.

fyllu. fem. *fullness, feast.* gen. sg. fylle 18/209.

gefylsta. wk. masc. *helper.* dat. sg. gefylstan 3/64.

fylstan. wk. 1. *assist.* inf. 12/265.

fȳlþ. fem. *filth, immorality.* acc. sg. fȳlþe 7/30. dat. sg. fȳlþe 7/30.

fȳnd → fēond.

fȳr. neut. *fire.* nom. sg. 3/37, 45. acc. sg. K/1366; 3/46, 47; 7/8. dat. sg. fȳre C/11.

fyrd. fem. *army.* acc. sg. fierd. dat. sg. fierde, fyrde 12/221.

fyrding. fem. *expedition, army.* dat. sg. fyrdinge.

fyrdrinc. masc. *man of an army, warrior.* nom. sg. 12/140. gen. sg. fyrdrinces I/2.

fyrdsearu. neut. *army-trappings, armour.*

fyrdwīc. neut. *military encampment.* dat. pl. fyrdwīcum 18/220.

fyrgenstrēam. masc. *mountain stream.* nom. sg. K/1359.

fyrhtu. fem. *fear.* dat. sg. 9/24.

fyrmest → forma.

gefyrn. adv. *formerly, long ago.* 2/27; 10/77.

fyrngeflit. neut. *ancient quarrel.* acc. pl. fyrngeflitu 18/264.

fyrst. A. masc. *period, space of time.* acc. sg. 18/324.

B. adj. *first, principal.* wk. dat. pl. fyrstum 8/25.

fyrwit. neut. *curiosity.* nom. sg. fyrwyt.

fȳsan. wk. 1. *hasten* (often with refl. pron.). inf. 18/189. *drive off, put to flight.* 3sg. fēseð 7/39. *shoot.* past 3sg. fȳsde 12/269.

gād. neut. *lack.* nom. sg. 17/45.

(ge)gaderian. wk. 2. *gather.* past 3sg. gegaderode. subj. pl. gaderian. inf. gaderian 2/20. past part. gegaderod 5/20.

gafol. neut. *tribute.* nom. sg. 5/14, 20; 8/27. acc. sg. gafol, gofol 5/1, 3; 12/61. dat. sg. gafole 5/4; 8/26; 12/32, 46.

gafolgelda. wk. masc. *rent-payer, tenant.* gen. sg. gafolgeldan M/5.

gāl. adj. *lustful.*

galan. st. 6. *sing.* inf. 14/67; 17/23.

gālferhþ. adj. *lascivious.* masc. nom. sg. 18/62.

gālmōd. adj. *lascivious.* wk. masc. nom. sg. gālmōda 18/256.

gamol. adj. *old.* wk. masc. nom. sg. gamela.

gān. anom. verb. *go, walk.* 1sg. gā. 2sg. gǣst 1/14. 3sg. gǣð A/1; 4/16. pl. gāð. past 1sg. ēode 9/8. past 3sg. ēode 1/8; 4/5; 9/6, 19, 32, etc. (10x). past pl. ēodon B/3; 3/36; 4/10, 13; 12/260, etc. (8x). subj. pl. 6/43. subj. past pl. ēodon 12/229. imp. sg. gā. imp. pl. gāð 12/93. inf. 12/247; 18/149.

gegān. anom. verb. *arrive, obtain, conquer.* past pl. geēodon 18/331. inf. 6/15. past part. 18/140, 219.

gang. masc. *going, passage, flow.* dat. sg. gange 14/23.

(ge)gangan. st. 7. (sometimes with refl. pron.). *go, walk, get.* 1sg. gange, gonge 16/35. subj. pl. gangon, gongen M/13; 12/56. imp. sg. gang. inf. gangan, gegangan, gongan 9/28; 12/3, 40, 59, 62, etc. (7x). pres. part. gongende 9/7, 30.

gār. masc. *spear.* nom. sg. 12/296. acc. sg. 12/13, 134, 154, 237, 321. dat. sg. gāre 12/138. acc. pl. gāras 12/46, 67, 109; 18/224.

gārberend. masc. nd-stem. *spear-carrier.* nom. pl. 12/262.

gārgewinn. neut. *battle with spears.* gen. sg. gārgewinnes 18/307.

gārmitting. fem. *meeting of spears.* gen. sg. gārmittinge.

gārrǣs. masc. *rush of spears, attack by spear.* acc. sg. 12/32.

gārsecg. masc. *ocean, sea.*

gāst. masc. *spirit.* nom. sg. gǣst 18/83, 112. acc. sg. G/4; 9/44; 14/49. gen. sg. gāstes, gǣstes 9/24; 18/279. dat. sg. gāste 12/176. nom. pl. gāstas 14/11. gen. pl. gāsta 14/152.

gāstlic. adj. *spiritual, religious.* wk. masc. nom. sg. gāstlica 3/80. wk. fem. nom. sg. gāstlice 3/111. wk. neut. dat. sg. gāstlican 2/10.

gatu → geat.

gāþ → gān.

gǣlsa. wk. masc. *lust.* acc. sg. gǣlsan 7/64.

gærs. neut. *grass.*

gǣst- → gāst.

gǣstlic. adj. *spiritual.* neut. nom. sg. 13/73.

gǣþ → gān.

ge. conj. *and, both.* 1/5; 6/43; 8/16, 64; 9/28, etc. (12x).

gē → þū, gē.

gēa. adv. *yes.*

gēac. masc. *cuckoo.* acc. sg. 17/23.

geador. adv. *together.* 15/19; 17/50.

geaf, gēafon → gifan.

gealga. wk. masc. *gallows.* nom. sg. 14/10. acc. sg. gealgan 14/40.

gealgtrēow. neut. *gallows tree.* dat. sg. gealgtrēowe 14/146.

gēap. adj. *deceitful.* fem. nom. sg. compar. gēapre 1/1.

gēapscipe. masc. *cleverness, cunning.* dat. sg. 6/30.

gēar. neut. *year.* dat. sg. gēare 2/12; 5/1, 5, 12. inst. sg. gēare 4/17, 18; 6/19. acc. pl. H/1; 2/5; 6/32; 8/64; 10/44. gen. pl. gēara 2/29, 30; 3/106 (2x), 107, etc. (12x). dat. pl. gēarum 2/18.

geāra. adv. *formerly.* 13/22; 14/28.

gearcian. wk. 2. *prepare, procure, supply.* past 3sg. gearcode.

geārdæg. masc. *day of yore.* dat. pl. geārdagum 13/44.

geare. adv. *thoroughly, well.* 2/13.

gegearewod → (ge)gearwian.

gearo. adj. *ready, complete.* masc. nom. sg. 4/7; 11/6; 12/274. masc. nom. pl. gearowe 12/72, 100.

gearoþoncol. adj. *ready-witted.* fem. dat. sg. gearoþoncolre 18/341.

gearwe. adv. *readily, well, sufficiently, thoroughly.* gearwe, geare 13/69, 71; 18/2.

(ge)gearwian. wk. 2. *prepare.* past 2sg. geearwodest. past 3sg. gegearwode 9/38. subj. past sg. gegearwode 9/30. past part. gegearewod, gegearwod 7/70; 18/199.

geat. neut. *gate.* acc. sg. 18/151. acc. pl. gatu 4/10, 15.

Gēat. masc. *Geat, member of the Geatish nation.* gen. pl. Gēata.

gēat → gēotan.

gegnum. adv. *straight, directly.* 18/132.

gelp- → gielp.

gēmde → gȳman.

geō. adv. *long ago.* iū, geō 10/71; 13/22; 14/28, 87.

geoc. neut. *yoke.* acc. sg. gioc 10/68.

gēoc. fem. *help, consolation.* dat. sg. gēoce 11/21.

geocian. wk. 2. *yoke.*

geofum → gifu.

geoguþ. fem. *youth.* dat. sg. iugoðe, geoguðe 2/13; 13/35.

Geōl. neut. *Yule, Christmas, December.*

geōmor. adj. *sad.* masc. nom. sg. 16/17; 18/87. masc. acc. sg. geōmorne 17/23. fem. dat. sg. geōmorre 16/1. dat. pl. geōmrum 11/21.

geōmormōd. adj. *sad in spirit.* masc. nom. sg. 16/42. neut. dat. sg. geōmormōdum 18/144.

geōmrung. fem. *groaning, lamentation.*

geond. prep. (with acc., sometimes with dat.). *throughout, through, over.* geond, gynd 3/13, 20; 7/5, 15, 27, etc. (13x).

geondhweorfan. st. 3. *pass through, review.* 3sg. geondhweorfeð 13/51.

geondscēawian. wk. 2. *survey, examine.* 3sg. geondscēawað 13/52.

geondscīnan. st. 1. *shine over, illuminate.* inf. G/9.

geondþencan. wk. 1. *think through, ponder.* 1sg. geondþence 13/60. 3sg. geondþenceð 13/89.

**geong.** adj. *young.* masc. nom. sg. 12/210; 14/39; 16/42. fem. dat. sg. **geongre.** masc. nom. pl. **geonge** 18/166. wk. masc. nom. sg. **geonga** 12/155.

**georn.** adj. *eager* for something (gen.). masc. nom. sg. 12/107; 13/69; 17/43; 18/210. masc. nom. pl. **georne** 12/73.

**georne.** adv. *eagerly, earnestly.* 2/9; 7/5, 9, 59, 66, etc. (13x). *thoroughly, clearly.* c/2, 9; 2/22; 7/4, 8, etc. (8x). superl. **geornost** 7/60.

**geornful.** adj. *zealous.* masc. nom. sg. 12/274.

**geornfulness.** fem. *zeal, desire, diligence.* dat. sg. **geornfulnesse** 9/26.

**geornlīce.** adv. *zealously, diligently, earnestly.* ᵹ/7; 9/26; 10/15, 16; 12/265.

**gēotan.** st. 2. *pour.* past 3sg. **gēat.**

**gēsne.** adj. *barren, lacking* something (gen.), *lifeless.* masc. nom. sg. 18/112. masc. acc. sg. 18/279.

**gēt** → gīt.

**giedd.** neut. *song, poem, tale.* acc. sg. 15/19; 16/1. dat. sg. **giedde** ɪ/10.

**giefstōl.** masc. *gift-seat, throne.* gen. sg. **giefstōlas** 13/44.

**gielp.** masc. *boast, boasting, fame.* nom. sg. **gilp, gelp** 10/22, 67. acc. sg. **gelp** 10/65. gen. sg. **gelpes, gielpes, gilpes** 10/13, 57, 67; 13/69. dat. sg. **gilpe, gylpe, gelpe** 3/29; 10/50, 82.

**gielpan.** st. 3. *boast.* past pl. **gulpon.**

**gierde** → gyrd.

**gīese.** adv. *yes.*

**giestrandæg.** masc. *yesterday.*

**gīet** → gīt.

**gif.** conj. *if.* **gif, gyf** ᴍ/1, 3 (2x), 5, 8, etc. (38x).

**gifan.** st. 5. *give.* 3sg. **gyfð.** past 3sg. **geaf** 18/342. past pl. **gēafon** 3/104. subj. sg. **gife** 15/1. imp. sg. **gif.**

**gīferness.** fem. *greed, greedy deed.* acc. pl. **gīfernessa** 7/48.

**gifeþe.** adj. *given, granted.* masc. nom. sg. 18/157.

**gifu.** fem. *gift, grace.* nom. sg. 9/17. acc. sg. **gife** 9/3, 15, 20. dat. sg. **gife** 9/1. nom. pl. **gifa** 10/7. acc. pl. **gife** 3/104. gen. pl. **gifena** 18/2. dat. pl. **geofum** ᴊ/83.

**gilp-** → gielp.

**gīmelēst.** fem. *carelessness.* dat. sg. **gīmelēste** 10/36.

**gimm.** masc. *gem.* nom. pl. **gimmas** 14/7, 16. dat. pl. **gimmum** 6/7.

**gimstān.** masc. *gemstone.* dat. pl. **gymstānum** 2/13.

**gingre.** wk. fem. *maidservant.* dat. sg. **gingran** 18/132.

**ginn.** adj. *wide, spacious.* masc. acc. sg. **gynne.** wk. fem. dat. sg. **ginnan** 18/149. wk. masc. inst. sg. **ginnan** 18/2.

**gioc** → geoc.

**giōdagum.** adv. *in days of old.* 10/49.

**girnaþ, girnde** → gyrnan.

**girwan** → (ge)gyrwan.

**gīsl.** masc. *hostage.* nom. sg. **gȳsel** 12/265. dat. sg. **gīsle** 4/8.

**gist.** masc. *guest, stranger.* nom. pl. **gystas** 12/86.

**gīt.** adv. *still, yet.* **gȳt, gīt, gīet, gēt, gȳta** ᴇ/3; 2/26; 3/39, 52, 60, etc. (19x).

**git** → þū, gē.

**gītsung.** fem. *avarice, avaricious deed.* acc. sg. **gītsunge** 6/36; 7/63. gen. sg. **gītsunge** 10/67. dat. sg. **gȳtsunge** 3/50. nom. pl. **gītsung** 10/2. acc. pl. **gītsunga** 7/48.

**glæd.** adj. *bright, cheerful, glad.*

**glædlīce.** adv. *joyfully.* 9/33.

**glædmōd.** adj. *happy-minded.* fem. nom. pl. **glædmōde** 18/140.

**geglængde** → geglengan.

**glēaw.** adj. *wise.* masc. nom. sg. 13/73. fem. nom. sg. 18/13. fem. acc. sg. **glēawe** 18/333. wk. fem. nom. sg. **glēawe** 18/171.

**Glēaweceaster.** fem. *Gloucester.* dat. sg. **Glēaweceastre** 6/20.

**glēawhydig.** adj. *wise in thought.* neut. nom. sg. 18/148.

**geglengan.** wk. 1. *adorn.* past 3sg. **geglængde** 9/1. past part. **geglenged** 9/19.

**glīwian.** wk. 2. *make merry, sing.* pres. part. **glēowiende** 9/32.

**glīwstæf.** masc. *melody, joy.* dat. pl.
**glīwstafum** 13/52.

**gnæt.** masc. *gnat.*

**gnornian.** wk. 2. *mourn.* inf. 12/315.

**God.** masc. *God, god* (often with neut. ending in pl.). nom. sg. **God, Godd** A/6; G/2; 1/1 (2x), 3, etc. (42x). acc. sg. 2/2, 8; 3/5, 9, 14, etc. (19x). gen. sg. **Godes** A/2; B/5, 6; 1/8; 2/6, etc. (59x). dat. sg. **Gode** 2/12, 16, 20; 3/9, 30, etc. (19x). nom. pl. **godas, godu.** acc. pl. **godas.** dat. pl. **godum.**

**gōd. A.** adj. *good.* neut. acc. sg. 12/237. masc. nom. sg. J/83; 12/315. fem. nom. sg. **gōd, Good** I/10; 8/18. neut. nom. sg. 1/6; 12/13. masc. acc. sg. **gōdne** La; 7/40; 10/14, 38. fem. acc. sg. **gōde** 14/70. masc. gen. sg. **gōdes** 10/36. masc. dat. sg. **gōdum** 12/4. masc. acc. pl. **gōde** 12/170. neut. acc. pl. **gōde** 6/43. gen. pl. **gōdra** 9/26; 10/13, 58. dat. pl. **gōdum** 2/10; 6/14; 10/11. wk. masc. nom. sg. **gōda.** wk. neut. nom. sg. **gōde** 6/27. wk. masc. acc. sg. **gōdan** 3/44; 12/187. wk. masc. nom. pl. **gōdan** C/12; 6/43. wk. gen. pl. **gōdena** 10/47. neut. nom. sg. compar. **betere** 12/31. masc. nom. pl. compar. **beteran.** masc. nom. sg. compar. **betera** 12/276. masc. nom. sg. superl. **sēlost** G/4. fem. nom. sg. superl. **sēlost, betst** G/3 (2x), 4. neut. nom. sg. superl. **betst, sēlest** 14/118. dat. pl. superl. **betstum** 10/57. wk. masc. nom. sg. superl. **betsta, sēlesta** 8/20; 14/27. wk. neut. inst. sg. superl. **betstan** 9/19.

   **B.** neut. *good, goods, property.* acc. sg. 1/5; 3/62. gen. sg. **gōdes** 10/15; 12/176. dat. sg. **gōde** A/3; 10/46; 18/271. gen. pl. **gōda** 18/32. dat. pl. **gōdum** 3/8; 9/21.

**godbearn.** neut. *godchild.* acc. pl. 7/27.

**godcund.** adj. *divine.* fem. gen. sg. **godcundre** 9/18. fem. dat. sg. **godcundre** 9/1. gen. pl. **godcundra** 7/50. dat. pl. **godcundum** 9/1. wk. dat. pl. **godcundan** 9/25.

**godcundlīce.** adv. *divinely.* 9/3.

**gōddǣd.** fem. *good deed.* acc. pl. **gōddǣda** 7/51. dat. pl. **gōddǣdan** 7/51.

**godfyrht.** adj. *God-fearing.* masc. acc. pl. **godfyrhte** 7/51.

**(ge)gōdian.** wk. 2. *improve, endow.* past 3sg. **gegōdade** 6/5, 15. pres. part. **gōdiende** 7/7.

**gōdness.** fem. *goodness.* dat. sg. **gōdnesse** 6/43.

**godsibb.** masc. *baptismal sponsor.* acc. pl. **godsibbas** 7/27.

**godsunu.** masc. u-stem. *godson.* nom. sg. 4/15.

**gofol** → gafol.

**gold.** neut. *gold.* nom. sg. 13/32. acc. sg. 14/18. gen. sg. **goldes** 6/27, 35; 17/36. dat. sg. **golde** 2/13; 6/7; 12/35; 14/7, 16, etc. (9x).

**goldgifa.** wk. masc. *gold-giver, lord.* acc. sg. **goldgifan** 18/279.

**goldhladen.** adj. *gold-laden, wearing gold ornaments.*

**goldhord.** neut. *hoard of gold, treasure.*

**goldsmiþ.** masc. *goldsmith.* gen. sg. **goldsmiðes** 10/71.

**goldwine.** masc. *gold-friend, gold-lord, generous lord.* nom. sg. 13/35; 18/22. acc. sg. 13/22.

**gong-** → (ge)gangan.

**good** → gōd.

**Gotland.** neut. *Jutland, Gotland* (Swedish island). nom. sg. 8/46, 49, 55.

**gram.** adj. *angry, fierce.* masc. nom. sg. 3/90. masc. nom. pl. **grame** 12/262; 18/224, 238. dat. pl. **gramum** 12/100.

**Grantabricscīr.** fem. *Cambridgeshire.* acc. sg. **Grantabricscīre** 5/2.

**Grantanceaster.** fem. *Grantchester.* dat. sg. **Grantanceastre** 2/19.

**grāpian.** wk. 2. *seize.* past 3sg. **grāpode** Lb.

**grǣdig.** adj. (with gen.). *greedy.* masc. nom. sg. F/3. masc. nom. pl. **grǣdige.**

**grǣdiness.** fem. *greediness.* acc. sg. **grǣdinesse** 6/36.

**(ge)gremian.** wk. 2. *anger, provoke.* past pl. **gegræmedan** 7/62. infl. inf. **tō gremienne** 3/44. past part. **gegremede, gegremod, gegremode** 12/138, 296; 18/305.

**grēot.** neut. *earth.* acc. sg. 18/307. dat. sg. **grēote** 12/315.

**grēotan.** st. 2. *weep.* pres. part. **grēotende** 14/70.

**(ge)grētan.** wk. 1. *greet.* 3sg. **grēteð, gegrēteð** 7/52; 13/52. past 3sg. **grētte** 9/7. inf. **grētan** La, **gegrētan** J/89.

**grimlic.** adj. *fierce, cruel, terrible.* neut. nom. sg. 7/3.

**grimm.** adj. *fierce, savage.* masc. nom. sg. **grim** 12/61. masc. nom. pl. **grimme** 7/50.

**grimness.** fem. *cruelty, severity.* acc. sg. **grimnysse.**

**(ge)grindan.** st. 3. *grind.* past part. **gegrundene** 12/109.

**(ge)grīpan.** st. 1. (with acc. or gen. object). *seize, attack.* inf. **gegrīpan** 10/82. pres. part. **grīpende** F/3.

**gristbitian.** wk. 2. *gnash the teeth.* inf. 18/271.

**griþ.** neut. *truce, protection, sanctuary.* acc. sg. 5/4; 12/35. dat. sg. **griðe** 5/4; 7/28.

**griþian.** wk. 2. *make peace, protect.* inf. 7/12.

**griþlēas.** adj. *without protection.* fem. nom. pl. **griðlēase** 7/13.

**grund.** masc. *bottom.* acc. sg. K/1367. *country, earth, land.* acc. sg. 12/287. inst. sg. **grunde** 18/2. acc. pl. **grundas** 18/348.

**gegrundene** → **(ge)grindan.**

**grundwong.** masc. *ground-plain, bottom.*

**grymetan.** wk. 1. *roar.* pres. part. **grymetende** 3/20.

**gryrelēoþ.** neut. *terrifying song.* gen. sg. **gryrelēoða** 12/285.

**guldon** → **gyldan.**

**gulpon** → **gielpan.**

**guma.** wk. masc. *man, mankind.* nom. sg. 10/82; 13/45. gen. sg. **guman** 14/49, 146.

nom. pl. **guman** 12/94; 18/305. gen. pl. **gumena** K/1367; 18/9, 22, 32, 62, etc. (10x). dat. pl. **gumum.**

**gūþ.** fem. *war, battle.* nom. sg. J/83. acc. sg. **gūþe** 12/192, 325. dat. sg. **gūþe** 12/13, 94, 187, 285, 296, etc. (8x).

**gūþcræft.** masc. *war-craft, skill in fighting.*

**gūþfana.** wk. masc. *battle-standard.* dat. pl. **gūðfanum** 18/219.

**gūþfreca.** wk. masc. *warrior.* nom. pl. **gūðfrecan** 18/224.

**gūþplega.** wk. masc. *battle-play.* nom. sg. 12/61.

**gūþrinc.** masc. *warrior.* nom. sg. 12/138.

**gūþsceorp.** neut. *battle-ornament, battle-equipment.* acc. pl. 18/328.

**gyddian.** wk. 2. *speak formally, sing.* inf. 10/64.

**gyf** → **gif.**

**gyfþ** → **gifan.**

**gyldan.** st. 3. *pay, repay.* 3sg. **gylt** 8/28. pl. **gyldað** 7/44, 45; 8/26. past pl. **guldon** 18/263. subj. sg. **gylde** 7/37. inf. 8/29.

**gylden.** adj. *golden.* masc. acc. sg. **gyldenne.**

**gyllan.** wk. 1. *yell.* past 3sg. **gylede** 18/25.

**gylpe** → **gielp.**

**gylpword.** neut. *boastful word.* dat. pl. **gylpwordum** 12/274.

**gylt.** masc. *guilt, sin.* acc. sg. 2/13.

**gylt** → **gyldan.**

**gȳman.** wk. 1. *care for.* past pl. **gȳmdon** 12/192. *take care.* past 3sg. **gēmde** 9/26. *take heed of, obey.* subj. sg. **gȳme** 7/9.

**gymstānum** → **gimstān.**

**gynd** → **geond.**

**gynne** → **ginn.**

**gyrd.** fem. *rod, staff.* acc. sg. **gyrde, gierde.**

**gyrde, gegyred, gyredon** → **(ge)gyrwan.**

**gyrnan.** wk. 1. (with gen.). *yearn for, desire, ask for.* pl. **girnað** 10/27. past 3sg. **girnde, gyrnde** 10/2; 18/346. past pl. **gyrndon** 3/26; 5/1.

**(ge)gyrwan.** wk. 1. *prepare, equip* somebody (acc.) with something (dat.). past 3sg. **gyrde.** *dress, adorn.* past pl. **gyredon**

14/77. past part. **gegyred, gegyrwed** 14/16, 23. *serve* (with *ūp*, 'serve up').
inf. **girwan** 18/9.

**gȳsel** → gīsl.

**gystas** → gist.

**gystern.** neut. *guest-house.* dat. sg. **gysterne** 18/40.

**gyt** → þū, gē.

**gȳt, gȳta** → gīt.

**gytesǣl.** masc. *joy at pouring* (of drinking). dat. pl. **gytesālum** 18/22.

**gȳtsunge** → gītsung.

**habban. A.** wk. 3. *have, hold, possess.* 1sg. **hæbbe, hafu** 1/6; 14/50, 79. 2sg. **hafast, hæfst** 12/231. 3sg. **hæfð, hafað** 3/54; 7/70; 8/69; 10/18, 19, etc. (13x). pl. **habbað, hæbbe** 3/83; 6/43; 7/6, 11, 16, etc. (14x). past 1sg. **hæfde** 16/7. past 3sg. **hæfde** 2/8; 3/7, 44, 82, 98, etc. (27x). past pl. **hæfdon** 3/89; 4/6, 10; 5/2, 4, etc. (13x). subj. sg. **hæbbe** 10/4, 82. subj. pl. **hæbben** 10/38 (2x). subj. past sg. **hæfde, næfde** 3/50; 6/32. subj. past pl. **hæfden** H/3; 10/37. inf. C/12; 3/112; 6/40; 7/69; 8/70, etc. (14x). past part. **hæfd** B/3.
**B.** Negated forms. 3sg. **næfð** 10/44. pl. **nabbað.** past 3sg. **næfde** 6/7; 8/25. subj. past sg. **næfde** B/7; 6/28.

**hād.** masc. *order.* dat. sg. **hāde** 6/17.

**hādbryce.** masc. *crime against persons in orders.* acc. pl. **hādbrycas** 7/48.

**gehādian.** wk. 2. *ordain, consecrate.* past 3sg. **gehādode** 2/10. past part. **gehādod, gehādode, gehādodan** 2/10, 17; 5/7, 12; 7/21.

**hafast, hafaþ** → habban.

**hafela.** wk. masc. *head.* acc. sg. **hafelan** K/1372.

**hafenian.** wk. 2. *raise.* past 3sg. **hafenode** 12/42, 309.

**hafoc.** masc. *hawk.* acc. sg. 12/8.

**hafu** → hæf.

**hagol.** masc. *hail.* dat. sg. **hagle** 13/48.

**hagolfaru.** fem. *hailstorm.* acc. sg. **hæglfare** 13/105.

**hāl.** adj. *healthy, whole, sound.* fem. nom. sg. 2/22. neut. acc. sg. 2/26. masc. nom. pl. **hāle** 2/27; 12/292.

**hālettan.** wk. 1. *salute.* past 3sg. **hālette** 9/7.

**hālga.** wk. masc. *saint.* dat. pl. **hālgum** 2/8; 14/143, 154.

**gehālgian.** wk. 2. *consecrate, sanctify.* past 3sg. **gehālgode** 3/10.

**Hālgoland.** neut. *Hålogaland.* nom. sg. 8/39.

**hālig.** adj. *holy, saintly.* masc. nom. sg. 9/13. fem. nom. sg. **hālige** 18/160. neut. acc. sg. 9/18. fem. dat. sg. **hāligre** 18/98. masc. nom. pl. **hālige** 14/11. fem. nom. pl. **hālige** 7/28. dat. pl. **hālgum** 3/103. wk. masc. nom. sg. **hālga** 2/8. wk. fem. nom. sg. **hālige** 18/56. wk. neut. nom. sg. **hālige** 3/97; 5/18. wk. masc. acc. sg. **hālgan** G/4; 3/64. wk. fem. acc. sg. **hālgan, hāligan** 2/27; 5/18; 18/260. wk. masc. gen. sg. **hālgan** 5/19; 9/24. wk. fem. gen. sg. **hālgan.** wk. neut. gen. sg. **hālgan** 2/25; 9/21, 24. wk. fem. dat. sg. **hālgan, hāligan** 2/1; 18/203.

**hāligdōm.** masc. *holiness, chapel, relic, sacrament.*

**hāligness.** fem. *holiness, sanctuary.* nom. pl. **hālignessa** 7/13.

**hals.** masc. *neck.* acc. sg. 12/141.

**hālwende.** adj. *healing, salutary.* neut. acc. sg. 9/44.

**hām. A.** masc. *home.* acc. sg. 9/6, 19; 14/148. dat. sg. **hām, hāme** 8/13; 12/292; 18/121.
**B.** adv. *homewards, home.* 3/89; 12/251; 18/131.

**hāmfæst.** adj. *resident.* masc. nom. sg. 10/26, 36.

**Hamtūnscīr.** fem. *Hampshire.* dat. sg. **Hamtūnscīre** 4/1; 5/2 (2x).

**hand.** fem. u-stem. *hand.* nom. sg. 12/141. acc. sg. **hand, hond** 1/4; J/90; 3/32, 33, 55, etc. (8x). dat. sg. **handa, honda** 3/33, 56, 62; 9/35; 12/149, etc. (6x). nom. pl. **handa** B/4. acc. pl. **honda,**

handa 9/44; 13/43. dat. pl. **handum, handon, hondum** F/3; Lb; 12/4, 7, 14; 13/4.

handgeweorc. neut. *handiwork.* acc. sg. 3/31.

hangelle. wk. fem. *hanging thing.* gen. sg. **hangellan** La.

hangian. wk. 2. *hang.* 3sg. **hongað** La. pl. **hongiað** K/1363. past pl. **hangodon** F/3, 5.

hār. adj. *hoary, grey, old.* masc. nom. sg. 12/169. fem. acc. pl. **hāre** 18/327. wk. masc. nom. sg. **hāra** 13/82. wk. masc. acc. sg. **hārne** F/1.

hara. wk. masc. *hare.* dat. pl. **haran** 6/39.

hāt. A. neut. *heat.*
  B. adj. *hot.* wk. masc. nom. sg. **hāta** 2/13.

(ge)hātan. A. st. 7. *command, bid.* 1sg. **hāte** 14/95. pl. **hātað**. past 3sg. **hēt, heht** 2/16, 20; 9/16 (2x), 21, etc. (14x). past pl. **hēton** 12/30; 14/31. subj. past sg. **hēte** 18/53. imp. sg. **hāt**. *call, name.* 3sg. **hæt** 8/41, 48, 59. pl. **hātað** 8/24; 10/29. past part. **gehāten, hāten, hātene** 2/14; 3/4; 4/3; 6/32; 8/55, etc. (9x). *be called.* 3sg. **hātte** 8/39. past 3sg. **hēt** 6/9, 10, 11, 24. *vow, promise.* 1sg. **gehāte** 12/246. past 3sg. **gehēt** 12/289. inf. **gehātan** 17/11.
  B. Passive forms. 1sg. **hātte** I/11. 3sg. **hātte** G/3; 10/16. past 3sg. **hātte** 2/2; 7/61.

hāte. adv. *hotly.* 18/94.

hātheort. adj. *hot-hearted, angry.* masc. nom. sg. 13/66.

gehātland. neut. *promised land.* gen. sg. **gehātlandes** 9/24.

hæbbe, hæbben → habban.

hæf. neut. *sea.* acc. pl. **hafu** 17/8.

hæfd- → habban.

hæfen → hebban.

hæfst → habban.

hæft. neut. *hilt.* dat. sg. **hæfte** 18/263.

(ge)hæftan. wk. 1. *bind, imprison.* past part. **gehæfted** 18/116.

hæfþ → habban.

hæglfare → hagolfaru.

(ge)hælan. wk. 1. *heal.* 1sg. **gehæle**. past 3sg. **gehælde** 3/96, 97. inf. **hælan** 14/85. past part. **gehæled, gehælede** 2/23, 27.

hæle. masc. dental stem. *warrior, man.* nom. sg. **hæleð, hæle** 13/73; 14/39, 78, 95. nom. pl. **hæleð, hælæð** 12/214, 249; 18/56, 177, 203, etc. (7x). acc. pl. **hæleð** 18/247. gen. pl. **hæleða** 10/65, 82; 12/74; 17/39; 18/51. dat. pl. **hæleþum** 13/105.

Hælend. masc. nd-stem. *Saviour.* nom. sg. 2/31. acc. sg. 2/6. gen. sg. **hælendes** 14/25. dat. sg. **hælende** 2/31.

hælþ. fem. *health, salvation.* dat. sg. **hælðe**.

hælu. fem. *health, prosperity, salvation.* acc. sg. **hæle, hælo** 11/16.

hæman. wk. 1. *have intercourse with.* past 3sg. **hæmde** 6/29.

hæmed. neut. *sexual intercourse.* dat. sg. **hæmede** 2/4, 30.

hæmedþing. neut. *sexual intercourse, marriage.*

Hæstingas. masc. *Hastings.* acc. pl. 5/2.

hæt → (ge)hātan.

hæto. fem. *heat.* dat. sg. **hæte** 10/18.

hæþen. adj. *heathen, pagan.* masc. gen. sg. **hæðenes** 18/179. masc. nom. pl. **hæþene** 12/55, 181. masc. acc. pl. **hæþene** 7/48. gen. pl. **hæðenra** D/1, 3; 18/216. dat. pl. **hæðenum** 7/10, 11, 12. wk. fem. nom. sg. **hæðene**. wk. masc. acc. sg. **hæðenan** 18/98, 110. wk. masc. nom. pl. **hæþenan**. wk. gen. pl. **hæðenra**.

hæþenscipe. masc. *paganism, idolatry.*

hæþstapa. wk. masc. *heath-walker.* nom. sg. K/1368.

Hæþum. masc. *Hedeby.* dat. pl. 8/48, 49, 52.

hē. pron. 1. pers. *he, it.* masc. nom. sg. A/2, 3; B/3 (2x), 5, etc. (375x). masc. acc. sg. **hine, hiene, hyne** B/2; C/3, 5 (3x), etc. (63x). masc. gen. sg. **his, hys** A/2 (2x), 3 (3x), etc. (191x). masc. dat. sg. **him** A/3 (2x); B/7; H/3; 2/7, etc. (104x).

dat. pl. **him, hym** 3/11, 94; 8/51; 12/66, 197, etc. (7x). **2.** refl. *he, himself.* masc. acc. sg. **hine** 1/8; 4/5; 7/40, 59; 8/65, etc. (15x). masc. gen. sg. **his** 3/40; 6/12, 13, 14, 16, etc. (34x). masc. dat. sg. **him** 9/38, 42; 12/300; 13/1, 31, etc. (8x).

**hēadēor.** neut. *stag, deer.* acc. pl. 6/38.

**hēafod.** neut. (occasionally pl. with sg. meaning). *head.* nom. sg. 5/9; 18/110. acc. sg. 1/15; 5/18; 9/42; 13/43; 18/126, etc. (7x). dat. sg. **hēafde** Lа; 2/25 (2x). acc. pl. **hēafdu, hēafod** 3/69. dat. pl. **hēafdum** 5/17; 14/63.

**hēafodgerīm.** neut. *number of heads, number of men.* gen. sg. **hēafodgerīmes** 18/308.

**hēafodweard.** masc. *chief guardian.* nom. pl. **hēafodweardas** 18/239.

**hēah.** adj. *high, deep, great.* masc. nom. sg. 13/98. masc. acc. sg. **hēanne** 13/82; 14/40; 18/161. masc. nom. pl. **hēa.** neut. acc. pl. 17/8. dat. pl. **hēaum.** wk. neut. dat. sg. **hēan** 18/43. wk. masc. nom. sg. superl. **hēhsta, hȳhsta** 18/94, 308. wk. masc. gen. sg. superl. **hēhstan** 18/4 (2x).

**hēahfæder.** masc. r-stem. *high father, patriarch, God.* dat. sg. **hēahfædere** 3/108; 14/134.

**hēahtīd.** fem. *holy day.* dat. pl. **hēahtīdum** 2/11.

**hēahþungen.** adj. *high-ranking.* masc. nom. pl. **hēahðungene** 8/64.

**(ge)healdan.** st. 7. *hold, keep, preserve, protect, maintain.* 3sg. **hylt, gehealdeþ** D/3; 3/52; 13/112. past 3sg. **hēold, gehēold** 2/4, 6, 26; 3/64. past pl. **hēoldon** D/1; 2/28; 18/142. subj. sg. **healde** 17/37. subj. past sg. **hēolde.** subj. past pl. **hēoldon** 12/20. imp. 2sg. **heald** 3/56. inf. **healdan, gehealdan** J/86; 5/21; 10/8; 12/14, 19, etc. (10x). pres. part. **healdende.** past part. **gehealdene** 3/103 (2x). *observe.* past pl. **hēoldan** 7/22. inf. **healdan** 7/12, 69. *rule, govern.* 3sg. **hylt.** past 3sg. **hēold** 2/10; 4/17, 18 (2x). subj. sg. **healde** 13/14. *satisfy.* past part. **gehealden** 10/34.

**healdend.** masc. nd-stem. (pres. part of *healdan* 'hold'). *possessor, lord.* nom. sg. 18/289.

**healf. A.** fem. *half, side.* acc. sg. **healfe** 8/12, 36, 46; 10/29; 14/20. dat. sg. **healfe** 12/152, 318.

    **B.** adj. *half.* masc. acc. sg. **healfne** 18/105. fem. acc. sg. **healfe** 5/2. neut. acc. sg. **healf** 8/64. neut. dat. sg. **healfum** 10/22.

**hēalic.** adj. *high, noble, fine.* dat. pl. **hēalicum** 2/13.

**heall.** fem. *hall.* dat. sg. **healle** 12/214.

**healm.** masc. *straw.*

**healreced.** neut. *hall.*

**healsbēag.** masc. *necklace.*

**healt.** adj. *lame.* masc. dat. sg. **healtum** 3/25. gen. pl. **healtra.**

**hēan.** adj. *lowly, poor, wretched.* masc. nom. sg. 13/23. masc. acc. sg. **hēanne** 18/234. masc. acc. pl. **hēane** 6/3.

**hēanlic.** adj. *shameful.* neut. nom. sg. 12/55.

**hēanne** → hēah.

**hēap.** masc. *company.* dat. sg. **hēape** 2/14. dat. pl. **hēapum** 18/163.

**heard.** adj. *hard, stern, warlike, cruel.* masc. nom. sg. 12/130; 16/43. fem. nom. sg. I/8. neut. nom. sg. Lа. masc. acc. sg. **heardne** 12/167, 236; 18/79. fem. acc. sg. **hearde** 12/33. neut. acc. sg. 12/214. neut. gen. sg. **heardes** 12/266. gen. pl. **heardra** 18/225. dat. pl. **heardum** 18/263. masc. nom. sg. compar. **heardra** 12/312. neut. nom. sg. superl. **heardost** 14/87.

**hearde.** adv. *hard, firmly, painfully.* superl. **heardost** 10/67. 18/116, 216.

**heardlīce.** adv. *fiercely.* 12/261.

**heardsǣlig.** adj. *unfortunate.* masc. acc. sg. **heardsǣligne** 16/19.

**heardsǣlþ.** fem. *misfortune, misdeed.* acc. pl. **heardsǣlþa** 10/36.

**hearm.** masc. *injury.* gen. pl. **hearma** 12/223.

**hearmcwidian.** wk. 2. *slander.* inf. 10/52.

**hearpe.** wk. fem. *harp.* acc. sg. **hearpan** 9/6. gen. sg. **hearpan.** dat. sg. **hearpan** 9/6.

**hearra.** wk. masc. *lord.* nom. sg. **heorra** 12/204. dat. sg. **hearran** 18/56.

**heaþobyrne.** fem. *battle-corslet.*

**heaþorinc.** masc. *warrior.* gen. sg. **heaðorinces** 18/179. nom. pl. **heaðorincas** 18/212.

**heaþufyr.** neut. *war-fire.* gen. sg. **heaðufyres.**

**(ge)hēawan.** st. 7. *cut, hack,* fig. *kill.* 3sg. **hēaweþ** 7/23. past 3sg. **hēow** 12/324. past pl. **hēowon** 12/181; 18/303. inf. **gehēawan** 18/90. past part. **gehēawen** 18/288, 294.

**hebban.** st. 6. *lift.* 3sg. **hefeð** Lᴀ. inf. ʙ/2; 14/31. past part. **hæfen.** inf. Lb.

**hefgad** → hefigian.

**hefig.** adj. *heavy, grievous.* neut. dat. sg. **hefian** 14/61. fem. nom. pl. compar. **hefigran** 13/49. neut. nom. sg. superl. **hefegost** ɢ/7.

**hefigian.** wk. 2. *make heavy, oppress, afflict.* past part. **hefgad** 9/28.

**hefiglīce.** adv. *heavily, severely.* 10/13.

**hefigness.** fem. *heaviness, weight.* acc. sg. **hefignesse** ʙ/7.

**hefonum** → heofon.

**hege.** masc. *hedge, fence.* dat. pl. **hegum** 3/27.

**hēhst-** → hēah.

**heht** → (ge)hātan.

**hell.** fem. *hell.* acc. sg. **helle** ɢ/8. gen. sg. **helle** 18/116. dat. sg. **helle** ᴄ/6, 11.

**hellewīte.** neut. *hellish punishment.* gen. sg. **hellewītes** 7/70.

**helm.** masc. *helmet, protector.* acc. sg. 18/337. acc. pl. **helmas** 18/193, 317, 327. dat. pl. **helmum** 18/203.

**help.** fem. *help.* acc. sg. **helpe** 13/16. dat. sg. **helpe** 14/102; 18/96.

**(ge)helpan.** st. 3. (with gen. object). *help.* past 1sg. **gehēolp** 3/23. subj. sg. **helpe** 7/71. inf. **helpan.**

**helsceaþa.** wk. masc. *hellish enemy.* nom. pl. **helsceaðan** 12/180.

**gehende.** prep. (with dat. object). *near.* 12/294.

**hēo.** pron. 1. pers. *she, it.* fem. nom. sg. **hēo, hīo** ɢ/3, 4, 5, 8, 9, etc. (47x). fem. acc. sg. **hī, hīe, hȳ** 2/4, 6, 10, 22, 24, etc. (10x). fem. gen. sg. **hire, hyre** ᴊ/85; 1/6, 15 (2x); 2/2, etc. (22x). fem. dat. sg. **hire, hyre** ɢ/9 (2x); 1/6; 2/9, 10, etc. (11x). 2. refl. *she, herself.* fem. acc. sg. **hī** 2/11. fem. dat. sg. **hyre** 2/25.

**hēo** → hīe.

**heofon.** *heaven.* 1. fem. nom. sg. **heofen** 3/18. 2. masc. acc. sg. 9/13; 10/16. gen. sg. **heofenes, heofones** 10/65; 14/64. dat. sg. **heofene.** acc. pl. **heofonas, heofenas** ɢ/2; 9/24; 14/103. gen. pl. **heofona** 14/45. dat. pl. **heofenum, heofonum, hefonum** ᴄ/8, 12; 2/30; 3/37, 45, etc. (17x).

**heofone.** wk. fem. *heaven.* gen. sg. **heofonan** 6/43. dat. sg. **heofenan.** dat. pl. **heofonum.**

**heofonlic.** adj. *heavenly.* fem. nom. sg. 9/17. masc. acc. sg. **heofonlicne** 14/148. wk. neut. gen. sg. **heofonlican, heofonlecan** 9/2, 24; 10/62. wk. neut. inst. sg. **heofonlecan** 9/38.

**heofonrīce.** neut. *kingdom of heaven.* gen. sg. **heofonrīces** 9/12; 14/91.

**hēold-, gehēold** → (ge)healdan.

**heolfrig.** adj. *bloody.* neut. acc. sg. 18/130, 316.

**gehēolp** → (ge)helpan.

**heolstor.** A. masc. *darkness, concealment.* dat. sg. **heolstre** 13/23.
    B. adj. *dark.* wk. masc. dat. sg. **heolstran** 18/121.

**heonan.** adv. *hence.* **heonan, heonon** ᴋ/1361; 3/41; 12/246; 14/132; 16/6, etc. (6x).

**heonanforþ.** adv. *henceforth.* 7/7, 9.

**heora** → hīe.

**heord.** fem. *herd, keeping, care.* nom. sg. 9/7. acc. pl. **heorda.**

**heorde** → hyrde.

**hēore.** adj. *safe, pleasant.* fem. nom. sg. **hēoru** ᴋ/1372.

**heorot.** masc. *hart, stag.* nom. sg. κ/1369. acc. sg. **heort** 6/37. acc. pl. **heortas** 6/38.

**heorra** → hearra.

**heorte.** wk. fem. *heart.* nom. sg. 12/312; 18/87. acc. sg. **heortan** 3/23. gen. sg. **heortan** 13/49; 16/43. dat. sg. **heortan** 12/145. dat. pl. **heortum.**

**Heortfordscīr.** fem. *Hertfordshire.* acc. sg. **Heortfordscīre** 5/2.

**heorþgenēat.** masc. *hearth-retainer, intimate follower.* nom. pl. **heorðgenēatas** 12/204.

**heorþwerod.** neut. *troop of household retainers.* acc. sg. 12/24.

**heoruwǣpen.** neut. *sword-weapon.* dat. pl. **heoruwǣpnum** 18/263.

**hēow-** → (ge)hēawan.

**hēr.** adv. *here.* c/12; ꜰ/6; ɢ/1; 4/1; 5/1, etc. (31x).

**gehēr-** → (ge)hȳran.

**hērbūend.** masc. nd-stem. *one who dwells here.* gen. pl. **hērbūendra** 18/96.

**here.** masc. *army, Viking army, glory* (?). nom. sg. 5/15, 20; 7/18, 39; 10/78, etc. (6x). acc. sg. 7/62. gen. sg. **herges, heriges** ɪ/8; 18/293. dat. sg. **here, herige** 5/1, 21; 12/292; 18/135. nom. pl. **hergas.**

**herefolc.** neut. *army.* gen. sg. **herefolces** 18/234, 239.

**herefugol.** masc. *war-bird.* nom. pl. **herefugolas.**

**heregeatu.** fem. (pl. with sg. sense). *war-equipment.* acc. pl. 12/48.

**heregodon** → (ge)hergian.

**herehȳþ.** fem. *booty, plunder.*

**hereness.** fem. *praise.* acc. sg. **herenisse** 9/44. dat. sg. **herenesse** 9/11.

**hererēaf.** neut. *plunder from an army.* acc. sg. 18/316.

**heretoga.** wk. masc. *commander.* nom. sg. 10/75. gen. sg. **heretogan** 10/28.

**herewǣþa.** wk. masc. *warrior.* gen. sg. **herewǣðan** 18/126, 173.

**(ge)hergian.** wk. 2. *plunder, harry, seize, capture.* pl. **hergiað** 7/46; 8/37, 38. past

3sg. **gehergode** c/6. past pl. **heregodon** 5/4.

**hergung.** fem. *harrying.* acc. sg. **hergunge** 5/1.

**herheard.** masc. *residence in a pagan shrine.* acc. sg. 16/15.

**herian.** wk. 1. *praise.* subj. pl. **herien** 10/70. inf. **herian, herigean** 7/53; 9/12.

**herpaþ.** masc. *path for an army.* acc. sg. 18/302.

**hērtōēacan.** adv. *in addition.* 7/58.

**herung.** fem. *praise.* acc. sg. **herunge** 3/49.

**hēt, gehēt** → (ge)hātan.

**hete.** masc. *hate, enmity, hostile act.* nom. sg. 7/19, 39.

**hēt-** → (ge)hātan.

**hetelīce.** adv. *with enmity, violently.* 7/34.

**heteþoncol.** adj. *hostile-minded.* masc. acc. sg. **heteþoncolne** 18/105.

**hetol.** adj. *hostile.* masc. nom. pl. **hetole** 7/50.

**hī** → hēo.

**hī** → hīe.

**hicgan.** wk. 3. *think, intend.* past 1sg. **hogode** 15/9. past 3sg. **hogode** 12/133. past pl. **hogedon, hogodon** 12/123; 18/250, 273. subj. sg. **hycge** 13/14; 17/11. subj. past sg. **hogode** 12/128. inf. **hicgan, hycgan** 12/4; 16/11. pres. part. **hycgendne** 16/20.

**hīd.** fem. *hide* (unit of land). nom. sg. 6/30.

**hider.** adv. *hither, to this place.* 8/50; 9/8; 12/57; 14/103.

**hīe.** pron. **1.** pers. *they, themselves.* nom. pl. **hī, hīe, hȳ, hēo, hig** ᴀ/4; ʙ/2, 5; ꜰ/7; ʜ/2, etc. (148x). acc. pl. **hī, hīe, hȳ, hig** 2/10, 19; 3/10, 36, 42, etc. (18x). gen. pl. **heora, hyra, hiera, hiora, hira** ᴀ/1; ꜰ/3 (2x), 6; ɢ/1, etc. (69x). dat. pl. **him** ᴀ/4; ᴅ/2; ꜰ/5; ʜ/3; ᴊ/91, etc. (34x). **2.** refl. *themselves.* acc. pl. **hīe, hȳ** 4/14; 7/53. dat. pl. **him** 1/7 (2x); 3/89; 5/8; 14/31, etc. (7x).

**hīe** → hēo.

**hiene** → hē.

hiera → hīe.

hīer-, gehīer- → (ge)hȳran.

hig → hīe.

hige → hyge.

higerōf. adj. *brave-hearted*. masc. nom. pl. higerōfe 18/302.

higesnotor. adj. *wise in mind*. dat. pl. Higesnotrum 10/66.

higeþoncol. adj. *thoughtful*. fem. dat. sg. higeðoncolre 18/131.

hiht → hyht.

hild. fem. *battle*. acc. sg. hilde 12/33; 18/251. gen. sg. hilde. dat. sg. hilde 12/8, 48, 55, 123, 223, etc. (8x).

hildedēor. adj. *brave in battle*.

hildelēoþ. neut. *war-song*. acc. sg. 18/211.

hildenædre. wk. fem. *battle-serpent, arrow*. acc. pl. hildenædran 18/222.

hilderinc. masc. *warrior*. nom. sg. 12/169. nom. pl. hilderincas 14/61. gen. pl. hilderinca 14/72.

him → hīe.

hind. fem. *hind, doe*. acc. sg. hinde 6/37.

hine → hē.

hingrigendne, hingrode → hyngrian.

hinsīþ. masc. *departure, death*. dat. sg. hinsīðe 18/117.

hīo → hēo.

hiora, hira → hīe.

hire → hēo.

gehīre → (ge)hȳran.

hīred. masc. *household, family, company*. acc. sg. 3/7. gen. sg. hīredes M/12. dat. sg. hīrede 6/12.

hīredman. masc. athematic. *household retainer*. nom. pl. hīredmen 12/261.

hisping. fem. *scorn, mockery*. acc. sg. hispinge 10/53.

hit. pron. 1. pers. *it*. neut. nom. sg. hit, hyt B/1, 4; M/7, 9; 2/1, etc. (50x). neut. acc. sg. hit, hyt A/4; H/2, 3; 2/4, 5, etc. (19x). 2. refl. *it*. neut. gen. sg. his 8/31.

hīw. neut. *colour*. gen. sg. hīwes.

hīwcūþ. adj. *familiar*. masc. acc. pl. hīwcūðe 10/80.

(ge)hīwian. wk. 2. *form, feign*. past part. gehīwod 3/45.

hlāf. masc. *bread, loaf*. acc. sg. 3/26. gen. sg. hlāfes 1/19. acc. pl. hlāfas. gen. pl. hlāfa. dat. pl. hlāfum.

hlāford. masc. *lord, the Lord*. nom. sg. 4/12; 6/7, 12; 7/41; 12/135, etc. (10x). acc. sg. 7/25; 14/45. gen. sg. hlāfordes G/7; 7/25. dat. sg. hlāforde 7/36; 8/1; 12/318; 18/251. acc. pl. hlāfordas.

hlāfordlēas. adj. *lordless*. masc. nom. sg. 12/251.

hlāfordswica. wk. masc. *traitor to one's lord*. nom. pl. hlāfordswican 7/24.

hlāfordswice. masc. *betrayal of one's lord*. nom. sg. 7/25 (2x).

hlagol. adj. *inclined to laugh*.

hlanc. adj. *lank, lean*. wk. masc. nom. sg. hlanca 18/205.

hlæfdige. wk. fem. *lady*. acc. sg. hlæfdigan.

gehlæstan. wk. 1. *load*. past part. gehlæste 18/36.

hlǣw. masc. *burial mound*. gen. pl. hlǣwa 10/74.

gehlēapan. st. 7. *leap onto, mount*. past 3sg. gehlēop 12/189.

hlehhan. st. 6. *laugh*. past 3sg. hlōh 12/147; 18/23.

hlēo. masc. *shelter, protector*. nom. sg. 12/74.

gehlēop → gehlēapan.

hlēoþrian. wk. 2. *speak*. past 3sg. hlēoðrode 14/26.

hlīfian. wk. 2. *rise high, tower*. 1sg. hlīfige 14/85.

hlimman. st. 3. *resound*. past pl. hlummon 18/205.

hlīsa. wk. masc. *fame, approbation*. nom. sg. 10/30, 31, 45, 55, 78, etc. (6x). acc. sg. hlīsan 10/14, 21, 31, 32, 38, etc. (6x). gen. sg. hlīsan 10/13, 57, 58, 65, 67. dat. sg. hlīsan 10/15, 46, 59.

hliþ. neut. *cliff, hill, slope*. gen. sg. hliþes 17/22.

hlōh → hlehhan.

hlūde. adv. *loudly*. 18/205, 223, 270.

**hlummon** → hlimman.

**hlūtor.** adj. *pure, bright, sincere.* neut. inst. sg. **hlūttre** 9/43.

**hlyd.** neut. *covering, lid, roof.* acc. sg. 2/19.

**hlȳdan.** st. 1. *make a loud noise, shout.* past 3sg. **hlȳdde** 18/23.

**hlynnan.** wk. 1. *make noise, shout.* past 3sg. **hlynede** 18/23.

**(ge)hlystan.** wk. 1. *listen.* past pl. **gehlyston** 12/92. imp. sg. **hlyst.**

**(ge)hlȳwan.** wk. 1. *warm.* past part. **gehlȳwde** 3/26.

**hnāg** → hnīgan.

**hnecca.** wk. masc. *neck.* dat. sg. **hneccan** D/2.

**hnīgan.** st. 1. *bend, bow.* past 1sg. **hnāg** 14/59.

**hnoll.** masc. *top of the head.* dat. sg. **hnolle** 3/58.

**hnutu.** fem. athematic. *nut.* nom. pl. **hnyte.**

**hocor.** masc. *derision.* dat. sg. **hocere** 7/51.

**hocorwyrde.** adj. *derisive.* masc. nom. pl. 7/50.

**hogedon, hogod-** → hicgan.

**hōh.** masc. *heel.* dat. sg. **hō** 1/15.

**hol.** neut. *hole.* acc. sg. La.

**hōl.** neut. *slander.* nom. sg. 7/19.

**gehola.** wk. masc. *confidant.* gen. pl. **geholena** 13/31.

**hold.** adj. *friendly, gracious, loyal.* gen. pl. **holdra** 16/17. neut. acc. sg. superl. **holdost** 12/24.

**holm.** masc. *sea.* acc. sg. 13/82.

**holmclif.** neut. *sea-cliff.* acc. pl. **holmclifu.**

**holt.** neut. *forest.* gen. sg. **holtes** 12/8; 14/29.

**holtwudu.** masc. *wood of the forest.* acc. sg. K/1369; 14/91.

**hōn.** st. 7. *hang.*

**hond-** → hand.

**hongaþ, hongiaþ** → hangian.

**hopian.** wk. 2. *hope, expect.* 1sg. **hopie.** 2sg. **hopast.** 3sg. **hopað.** pl. **hopiað.** past 2sg. **hopodest.** past 3sg. **hopode.** past pl. **hopodon.** inf. 18/117.

**hordcofa.** wk. masc. *hoard-chamber, breast, thought.* acc. sg. **hordcofan** 13/14.

**hordwela.** wk. masc. *hoarded wealth.* acc. sg. **hordwelan.**

**horh.** masc. *defilement* (in pl. with sg. sense). dat. pl. **horwum** 3/83.

**hōring.** masc. *fornicator.* nom. pl. **hōringas** 7/56.

**horn.** masc. *horn.* dat. pl. **hornum** K/1369.

**hornboga.** wk. masc. *bow* (tipped with horn or curved like a horn). dat. sg. **hornbogan** 18/222.

**hors.** neut. *horse.* acc. sg. 8/69; 12/2. nom. pl. 8/70. acc. pl. 8/68. dat. pl. **horsan** 8/25.

**horshwæl.** masc. *walrus.* dat. pl. **horshwælum** 8/18.

**hosp.** masc. *reproach, contempt.* acc. sg. 18/216.

**gehradian.** wk. 2. *hasten, further, prosper.* past 3sg. **gehradode** 2/19.

**hrān.** masc. *reindeer.* gen. sg. **hrānes** 8/29. acc. pl. **hrānas** 8/24 (2x).

**hraþe, raþe, rade.** adv. *quickly.* superl. **radost, raþost** H/3; 4/7. **raðe, hraðe, hræðe** 10/15; 12/30, 164, 288; 18/37.

**hræd.** adj. *quick, brief.* neut. nom. sg. superl. **hrædest, hraðost** 7/15, 56; 10/11.

**hræding.** fem. *haste, brevity.* acc. sg. **hrædinge** 7/58.

**hrædlīce.** adv. *quickly.*

**hrædness.** fem. *quickness, speed.* dat. sg. **hrædnesse** B/7.

**hrædwyrde.** adj. *hasty of speech.* masc. nom. sg. 13/66.

**hræfen** → hrefn.

**hrægl.** neut. *cloth, sheet.* dat. sg. **hrægle.** dat. pl. **hreglum.** *clothing, garment.* acc. sg. La; Lb; 18/282. dat. sg. **hrægle** 8/71. *sail.*

**hræþe** → hraþe, raþe, rade.

**hrēw.** neut. *body.* nom. sg. 14/72. acc. sg. 14/53. acc. pl. 18/313.

**hrēam.** masc. *outcry, tumult.* nom. sg. 12/106.

hrēaw. adj. *raw.* neut. gen. sg. hrēawes.

hrefn. masc. *raven.* nom. sg. hrefn, hræfen 18/206. nom. pl. hremmas 12/106.

hreglum → hrægl.

hrēoh. adj. *rough, fierce.* fem. acc. sg. hrēo 13/105. *disturbed, troubled.* masc. nom. sg. 18/282. wk. masc. nom. sg. hrēo 13/16.

Hrēopadūn. fem. *Repton, Derbyshire.* dat. sg. Hrēopadūne 4/17.

hrēopon → hrōpan.

hrēosan. st. 2. *fall.* inf. 13/48. pres. part. hrēosende 3/39; 13/102.

hrēowcearig. adj. *sorrowful.* masc. nom. sg. 14/25.

hrēowigmōd. adj. *regretful, sorrowful.* masc. nom. pl. hrēowigmōde 18/289.

hrēowlīce. adv. *sadly.* 7/14.

hrepian. wk. 2. *touch.* past 3sg. hrepode 3/72. past pl. hrepodon 2/27. subj. past pl. hrepodon 1/3. imp. 2sg. hrepa 3/55.

hrēran. wk. 1. *move, stir.* inf. 13/4.

hreþer. masc. *breast, heart, mind.* dat. sg. hreðre 18/94. gen. pl. hreþra 13/72.

hrīm. masc. *frost.* acc. sg. 13/48. dat. sg. hrīme 13/77.

hrīmceald. adj. *frost-cold.* fem. acc. sg. hrīmcealde 13/4.

hrīmig. adj. *frosty.* masc. nom. pl. hrīmige F/2.

hrind. adj. *frost-covered.* masc. nom. pl. hrinde K/1363.

hring. masc. *ring.* acc. pl. hringas 12/161. dat. pl. hringum 18/37.

hringed. adj. *made of rings.* fem. acc. sg. hringde.

hringedstefna. wk. masc. *ring-prow, ship with ringed prow.*

hringloca. wk. masc. (apparently pl. with sg. sense). *ring-enclosure,* fig. *mail-coat.* acc. pl. hringlocan 12/145.

hrīþ. masc. *frost.* nom. sg. 13/102.

hrīþig. adj. *snow-swept.* masc. nom. pl. hrȳðge 13/77.

(ge)hroden. adj. *adorned.* fem. acc. sg. gehrodene 18/37.

hrōf. masc. *roof, summit.* dat. sg. hrōfe 9/13; 10/13; 18/67.

hrōpan. st. 7. *shout, cry out, scream.* past pl. hrēopon.

hrūse. wk. fem. *earth* (sometimes pl. with sg. sense). acc. sg. hrūsan 13/102. gen. sg. hrūsan 13/23. nom. pl. hrūsan 10/74.

hrycg. masc. *ridge, back.*

hrȳman. wk. 1. *cry, wail.* past pl. hrȳmdon 3/68. pres. part. hrȳmende 3/23.

hryre. masc. *fall, death.* dat. sg. 3/27. gen. pl. 13/7.

hrȳþer. neut. *cow.* gen. pl. hrȳþera 5/17; 8/25.

hrȳþge → hrīþig.

hū. A. adv. *how.* 6/2, 6 (2x), 12 (2x), etc. (19x).

   B. conj. *how.* G/1; 2/31; 5/7; 9/39; 13/30, etc. (9x).

hund. A. card. num. as noun. *hundred.* E/2; 8/47. acc. pl. 3/106, 107; 8/23.

   B. as adj. *hundred.* masc. acc. pl. hund, hunde H/1; 3/7, 98. neut. acc. pl. 3/7, 98.

   C. masc. *dog.* acc. sg. G/6; 18/110. dat. pl. hundum K/1368; 7/30.

hundeahtatig. card. num. as noun. *eighty.* E/2.

hundnigontig. card. num. as adj. *ninety.* masc. acc. pl. H/1.

hundred. card. num. as noun. *hundred.* E/2; 6/35.

hundseofontig. card. num. as noun. *seventy.* E/1; 10/25.

hundtwelftig. card. num. as noun. *one hundred and twenty.*

hungor. masc. *hunger, famine.* nom. sg. hunger 7/18.

hunig. neut. *honey.* nom. sg. 8/61.

hunta. wk. masc. *hunter.* nom. pl. huntan 8/15. dat. pl. huntum 8/13.

Huntadūnscīr. fem. *Huntingdonshire.* acc. sg. Huntadūnscīre 5/2.

huntoþ. masc. *hunting.* dat. sg. huntoðe 8/3.

**hupseax.** neut. *sword worn on the hip, short-sword.* acc. pl. 18/327.

**hūru.** adv. *indeed, certainly.* 7/3, 23, 59; 8/58; 14/10, etc. (6x).

**hūs.** neut. *house.* nom. sg. 9/29. acc. sg. B/1; 3/39; 9/7. gen. sg. **hūses** B/2. dat. sg. **hūse** M/1, 4, 6; 3/8; 9/6, etc. (7x). nom. pl. 7/13. acc. pl. 7/11. dat. pl. **hūsum** 8/64.

**hūsl.** neut. *eucharist.* acc. sg. 9/32, 34. gen. sg. **hūsles** 9/33.

**hūsting.** neut. *court.* dat. sg. **hūstinge** 5/17.

**hwā.** pron. **1.** interrog. *who, what.* masc. nom. sg. 1/11; 6/30; 10/74; 12/95, 124, etc. (6x). neut. nom. sg. **hwæt** G/7; I/11; 6/17; 7/46; 8/16, etc. (15x). neut. acc. sg. **hwæt** 6/3; 7/47; 9/10; 10/31, 82, etc. (7x). masc. gen. sg. **hwæs** 6/30. neut. inst. sg. **hwan, hwon** G/8; 9/31; 10/23; 13/59. **2.** indef. *any, anyone, anything.* masc. nom. sg. M/1, 3 (2x), 11; 10/70. neut. nom. sg. **hwæt** 10/35. masc. acc. sg. **hwone** 10/65. neut. acc. sg. **hwæt** 9/1. masc. nom. pl. 6/12. *something, someone, a certain one.* masc. nom. sg. 12/71. masc. acc. sg. **hwæne** 3/20; 12/2; 18/52. neut. acc. sg. **hwæt** 3/2. masc. dat. sg. **hwām** 3/70. In phrases *swā hwā swā, swā hwæt swā. whoever, whatever.* masc. nom. sg. 6/37. neut. nom. sg. **hwæt** 10/10. neut. acc. sg. **hwæt** 3/54.

**gehwā.** indef. pron. *every, everyone, everything.* masc. nom. sg. 3/47; 7/59. neut. nom. sg. **gehwæt** 10/7. fem. acc. sg. **gehwane, gehwæne** 11/4; 18/186. neut. gen. sg. **gehwæs** 9/12. masc. dat. sg. **gehwām** 13/63. fem. dat. sg. **gehwǣre.** neut. dat. sg. **gehwǣm** K/1365.

**hwal-** → hwæl.

**hwan** → hwā.

**gehwane** → gehwā.

**hwanon.** adv. *whence.* **hwanon, hwonon** G/5; 3/12, 19; 9/16.

**hwæl.** masc. *whale.* nom. sg. 8/19. gen. sg. **hwæles, hwales** 8/27 (2x), 29. nom. pl. **hwalas** 8/19.

**hwælhunta.** wk. masc. *whale-hunter.* nom. pl. **hwælhuntan** 8/6.

**hwælhuntaþ.** masc. *whale-hunting.* nom. sg. 8/20.

**gehwǣm** → gehwā.

**hwæne** → hwā.

**gehwæne** → gehwā.

**hwænne** → hwonne.

**hwǣr. A.** adv. *where.* 1/9; 3/73, 74; 10/71, 75, etc. (12x).

**B.** conj. *where.* G/2; 7/32; 13/26; 14/112; 16/8.

**gehwǣre** → gehwā.

**hwæs** → hwā.

**gehwæs** → gehwā.

**hwæt. A.** interj. *lo, behold.* 3/40, 52, 104; 7/8; 10/2, etc. (14x).

**B.** adj. *vigorous.*

**hwæt** → hwā.

**gehwæt** → gehwā.

**hwæthwugu.** indef. pron. *something.* neut. acc. sg. 9/7; 10/40.

**hwæþer. A.** conj. *whether.* **hwæðer, hweðer** G/9; M/2; 8/4; 9/32, 35, etc. (8x).

**B.** interrog. pron. *which* of two. neut. acc. sg. 8/8, 9.

**gehwæþer. A.** indef. pron. *both.*

**B.** adj. *either.* fem. acc. sg. **gehwæðere** 12/112.

**hwæþre.** adv. *however, nevertheless, yet.* **hwæðre, hweðere** 9/3, 9, 28, 31; 14/18, etc. (14x).

**hwealf. A.** fem. *vault.* nom. pl. **hwealfe** 10/65.

**B.** adj. *concave.* dat. pl. **hwealfum** 18/214.

**hwearf.** masc. *crowd.* dat. pl. **hwearfum** 18/249.

**hwearf** → hweorfan.

**hwelc.** pron. **1.** interrog. *which, what, what kind of.* masc. nom. sg. G/4, 6. fem. nom. sg. **hwelc, hwylc** G/3; 9/33. masc. acc. sg. **hwelcne, hwilcne** A/6; 6/12. fem. acc. sg. **hwylce** 9/15. neut. inst. sg. **hwelce** 10/27. dat. pl. **hwelcum.** **2.** indef. *which.* masc. dat. sg. **hwelcum** 10/74. *any.* masc. nom. sg. **hwilc, hwelc,**

hwylc 3/109; 6/29; 7/36; 10/32. In phrase *swā hwelć swā. whatever, whoever.* masc. nom. sg. 4/7. masc. dat. sg. hwylcum 1/5. masc. nom. pl. hwylce.

gehwelc. indef. pron. *each, every.* masc. nom. sg. gehwylc 12/128, 257. masc. acc. sg. gehwylcne 18/95. neut. gen. sg. gehwylces 18/32. masc. dat. sg. gehwelcum, gehwilcum, gehwylcum 4/8; 7/9; 14/108. masc. inst. sg. gehwylce 13/8; 14/136.

hwelp. masc. *cub, young of an animal.* acc. sg. 15/16.

hwemm. masc. *corner.* dat. pl. hwemmum 3/39.

hwēne. adv. *somewhat.* 8/34.

hweorfan. st. 3. *turn, change, go.* past 3sg. hwearf 18/112. inf. 13/72.

gehwerfde → gehwyrfan.

hwettan. wk. 1. *urge.*

hweþer → hwæþer.

hwī → hwȳ.

hwider. conj. *to where, whither.* 13/72.

hwīl. fem. *time, space of time.* acc. sg. hwīle 2/21; 4/17; 6/12; 7/29, 58, etc. (12x). gen. sg. hwīle 10/40. nom. pl. hwīla 10/40. acc. pl. hwīla 10/39 (2x).

hwilc- → hwelc.

gehwilc- → gehwelc.

hwīle. adv. *for a while.* 14/64, 84; 18/214.

hwīlendlic. adj. *transitory.* wk. neut. gen. sg. hwīlendlican 10/39.

hwīlum. adv. *sometimes, formerly, at times.* hwīlum, hwīlon, hwȳlum 1/3, 7; 2/8; 6/7; 7/21, etc. (21x).

hwīt. adj. *white.* neut. gen. sg. hwītes 2/19. masc. dat. sg. hwītum 2/19.

hwītlocced. adj. *fair-haired.* fem. nom. sg. hwītloccedu 1/4.

hwomm. masc. *corner.* dat. sg. hwomme.

hwōn. adv. *little, a little.* 3/32; 8/8; 10/80.

hwon, hwone → hwā.

hwonne. A. adv. *when.* hwænne 14/136. B. conj. *when, until.* hwænne 12/67.

hwonon → hwanon.

hwȳ. adv. (inst. of *hwā*). *why.* hwī, hwȳ G/9; 1/1, 13; 3/62, 101, etc. (7x).

hwylc- → hwelc.

gehwylc- → gehwelc.

hwȳlum → hwīlum.

gehwyrfan. wk. 1. *turn, convert, move.* past 3sg. gehwerfde, gehwyrfde 9/18, 22.

hȳ → hīe.

hycg- → hicgan.

hȳd. fem. *hide, skin.* nom. sg. 3/83; 8/18. dat. sg. hȳde 8/27, 29.

gehȳdan. wk. 1. *hide.* past 3sg. gehȳdde 13/84.

gehygd. fem. *mind, thought, intention.* nom. sg. 13/72.

hyge. masc. *thought, mind, heart.* nom. sg. hige, hyge 12/312; 13/16; 16/17; 18/87. dat. sg. hige, hyge 12/4; 17/11.

hygegeōmor. adj. *sad in mind.* masc. acc. sg. hygegeōmorne 16/19.

hygewlonc. adj. *proud in mind.* fem. nom. sg. Lb.

hȳhsta → hēah.

hyht. masc. *hope.* nom. sg. hiht, hyht 3/87; 14/126, 148; 18/98.

hyhtful. adj. *hopeful.* masc. nom. pl. hyhtfulle 11/16.

hyhtwynn. fem. *the joy of hope.* gen. pl. hyhtwynna 18/121.

hyldan. wk. 1. *lean, bend* (transitive). inf. 14/45.

hyldo. fem. *favour, grace, protection.* acc. sg. 18/4.

hylt → (ge)healdan.

hym → hē.

(ge)hȳnan. wk. 1. *humiliate, oppress, condemn, lay low.* pl. hȳnað 7/45. past 3sg. hȳnde 12/324. inf. hȳnan 12/180. past part. gehȳnede 7/14.

hyne → hē.

hyngrian. wk. 2. (impersonal). *be hungry.* past 3sg. hingrode. pres. part. sg. hingrigendne.

hyra → hīe.

(ge)hȳran. wk. 1. *hear, listen to.* 1sg. hīere, gehīre, gehȳre 1/10; 17/50. 2sg. gehȳrst, hīerst, gehȳrest 12/45; 15/16. 3sg. hīerð. pl. hīerað, gehȳrað. past 1sg. gehȳrde 14/26. past 2sg. gehērdest, hīerdest,

gehȳrdest 1/17; 10/49. past 3sg.
gehērde, hīerde, gehȳrde 9/11; 10/53.
past pl. gehȳrdon, hīerdon, gehīerdun,
gehȳrdan, hȳrdon 1/8; 2/27; 4/9; 7/65;
9/45, etc. (6x). subj. sg. gehȳre 3/109.
subj. past sg. gehȳrde 12/117; 17/22.
imp. pl. gehȳrað. inf. gehȳran, gehēran
3/22; 14/78; 18/24. infl. inf. tō gehȳ-
ranne, tō gehȳrenne 2/28; 9/23. past
part. gehēred 10/53. *hear of.* 3sg. gehērð
10/26. past 3sg. gehērde 10/31. past pl.
gehērdon 10/29. *obey* (with dat.). past
3sg. hīerde. inf. hȳran. in phrases *hȳran
in (on), hȳran to, be subject to.* 3sg. hȳrð
8/48. pl. hȳrað 8/51, 53, 55.
**hyrde.** masc. *shepherd, guide, guardian.*
nom. sg. 10/76; 18/60. dat. sg. **heorde.**
nom. pl. **hyrdas.** acc. pl. **hyrdas** 3/37,
38.
**hyre** → hēo.
**hȳrman.** masc. ᴀ/o-stem. *hired man.* nom.
sg. 3/80.
**hyrnednebb.** adj. *horny-beaked.* wk. masc.
nom. sg. **hyrnednebba** 18/212.
**gehȳrness.** fem. *hearing.* dat. sg. **gehȳ-
rnesse** 9/22.
**hyrst.** fem. *ornament, trappings.* acc. pl.
**hyrsta** 18/316.
**hyrwan.** wk. 1. *deride, slander.* 3sg.
**hyrweð** 7/51, 53.
**hys** → hē.
**hyse.** masc. *young man.* nom. sg. 12/152.
gen. sg. **hysses** 12/141. nom. pl. **hysas,
hyssas** 12/112, 123. acc. pl. **hyssas**
12/169. gen. pl. **hyssa** 12/2, 128.
**hyspan.** wk. 1. *scorn, revile, mock.* past pl.
**hyspton** ʜ/2. inf. 10/52.
**hyt** → hit.
**hȳþ.** fem. *harbour.* dat. sg. **hȳðe.**
**ic, wē.** pron. **1.** pers. *I, myself.* nom. sg.
**Ic** ᴅ/1, 3; ɢ/2, 3, 4, etc. (155x). acc. sg.
**mē, mec** ɪ/3; 1/13; 3/53, 83 (2x), etc.
(27x). gen. sg. **mīn** 10/11. dat. sg. **mē**
ᴅ/1; ɢ/2, 3, 4, 5, etc. (47x). nom. pl. **wē**
ᴄ/1, 2, 3, 4, 5, etc. (74x). acc. pl. **ūs**
6/43; 7/19, 44, 45, 57, etc. (12x). gen.

pl. **ūre** ᴄ/4; 3/112; 7/21, 71; 12/234. dat.
pl. **ūs** ᴅ/3; 1/3; 2/28, 30; 3/36, etc. (36x).
nom. dual **wit** 16/13, 21. acc. dual **unc**
14/48; 16/12, 22. dat. dual **unc. 2.** refl.
*I, myself.* acc. sg. **mē** 1/10; 14/45. dat.
sg. **mē** 12/318; 14/122; 16/9. acc. pl. **ūs**
7/65, 66, 70. dat. pl. **ūs** 7/60, 70; 12/40.
**īcan.** wk. **1.** *increase, augment.* past 3sg.
**īhte** 7/5. inf. **īecan, ȳcan** 18/183.
**īdel.** adj. *void, empty, idle, vain.* neut. nom.
sg. 13/110. neut. acc. sg. 3/31. masc.
gen. sg. **īdelan** 10/57. neut. gen. sg. **īdles**
9/4. neut. nom. pl. **īdlu** 13/87. dat. pl.
**īdelan** 7/54.
**ides.** fem. *woman, lady.* nom. sg. 18/14,
109, 128, 146. acc. sg. **idese** 18/55, 58.
dat. sg. **idese** 18/340. nom. pl. **idesa**
18/133.
**īdles, īdlu** → īdel.
**īecan** → īcan.
**īeg.** fem. *island.* dat. sg. **īege, īge** 15/4, 6.
**ierfe.** neut. *property, inheritance.* gen. sg.
**ierfes** ᴍ/2.
**iermþa** → yrmþu.
**īge** → īeg.
**īgland.** neut. *island.* nom. pl. 8/44, 51. gen.
pl. **īglanda** 8/49.
**īhte** → īcan.
**ilca.** indef. pron. *same.* masc. nom. sg. **ylca**
3/64. neut. nom. sg. **ilce** 4/13. masc.
acc. sg. **ylcan** 2/8. neut. acc. sg. **ilce** 9/
14. neut. gen. sg. **ilcan** 10/14. masc. dat.
sg. **ilcan** 6/15. fem. dat. sg. **ilcan** 10/36.
neut. dat. sg. **ylcan.** masc. inst. sg. **ylcan**
8/66. neut. inst. sg. **ilcan** 4/17, 18.
**ile.** masc. *sole* of the feet. acc. pl. **ilas**
3/58.
**Ilfing.** masc. *Elbląg River.* nom. sg. 8/59
(3x).
**in. A.** prep. (with dat. or acc.). *in, on.* ʙ/3;
ᴊ/83; 8/59; 9/1 (2x), etc. (35x). *into, to.*
8/51, 58, 59 (2x); 9/18, etc. (10x).
 **B.** adv. *in, inland.* **in, inn** ᴋ/1371;
3/39; 8/8, 9, 11, etc. (12x).
**inbryrdness.** fem. *inspiration, ardour.* acc.
sg. **inbryrdnisse** 9/1.

inc → þū, gē.

inca. wk. masc. *question, grievance*. acc. sg. **incan** 9/36. dat. sg. **incan** 9/35.

incer → þū, gē.

indryhten. adj. *noble, excellent*. masc. nom. sg. 13/12.

ingeþanc. neut. *thought, conscience*. acc. sg. 7/69. gen. sg. **ingeðonces** 10/47.

ingong. masc. *entrance, entering*. acc. sg. 9/38. dat. sg. **ingonge** 9/24.

inlǣdan. wk. 1. *lead in*. inf. **inlǣdon** 9/29.

inlīhtan. wk. 1. *illuminate*. 2sg. **inlīhtes** 11/5. subj. sg. **inlēohte** 11/12.

inn. neut. *dwelling*. dat. sg. **inne** 18/70.

innan. A. prep. (with dat. or acc.). *in, into*. 6/30; 7/13.

   B. adv. *from within, within*. 7/13.

inne. adv. *in, inside, within*. 5/7; 7/11 (2x), 18, 39, etc. (12x).

innoþ. masc. *womb*. dat. sg. **innoðe** 3/41.

intinga. wk. masc. *cause*. nom. sg. 9/6.

intō. A. prep. (usually with dat., sometimes with acc.). *into*. c/12; 2/18, 24.

   B. adv. *into the place*. 5/5.

inwidda. wk. masc. *wicked one*. nom. sg. 18/28.

inwidhlemm. masc. *hostile wound*. nom. pl. **inwidhlemmas** 14/47.

īow → þū, gē.

Iraland. neut. *Ireland*. nom. sg. 8/44. acc. sg. **Ȳrland** 6/32. dat. sg. **Īralande** 8/44.

īren. neut. *iron*. nom. sg. 12/253.

irnan. st. 3. *run, flow*. pl. **irnað**. past pl. **urnon** 4/7; 18/164. pres. part. **irnende, yrnende** 8/52.

īs. neut. *ice*.

is → bēon.

īsen. adj. *iron*. dat. pl. **īsenum**.

īsig. adj. *icy*. wk. dat. pl. **īsigean** f/3.

Israhēla. masc. *of the Israelites*. gen. pl. 9/24.

Israhēlisc. adj. *Israelite*. wk. neut. acc. sg. **Israhēlisce**.

iū → geō.

Iūdēisc. adj. *Jewish*. wk. masc. nom. pl. **Iūdēiscan**.

iugoþe → geoguþ.

lā. interj. *O, Oh, indeed*. 3/14, 52; 6/41; 7/8, 35, etc. (9x).

lāc. neut. *offering, sacrifice, gift*. acc. sg. 15/1. acc. pl. 3/9, 91, 93. dat. pl. **lācum** 7/11.

gelāc. neut. *motion, commotion, tossing* (of waves). acc. sg. 16/7.

lād. fem. *course, way, journey*. gen. sg. **lāde** 17/25.

lāf. fem. *remainder, widow*. acc. sg. **lāfe**. dat. sg. **lāfe** e/3, 4; 8/66.

gelagian. wk. 2. *decree by law*. past part. **gelagod** 7/10.

lāgon → licgan.

lagu. A. fem. *law*. acc. sg. **lage** 7/9, 12, 22. dat. sg. **lage** 7/22, 50. nom. pl. **laga** 7/15, 38. acc. pl. **laga** 6/37. dat. pl. **lagum** 7/68.

   B. masc. u-stem. *water, sea*. acc. sg. 17/21.

gelagu. fem. *of the sea, expanse*. acc. sg. 17/42.

lagulād. fem. *sea-way*. acc. sg. **lagulāde** 13/3.

lagustrēam. masc. *sea current*. nom. pl. **lagustrēamas** 12/66.

lahbryce. masc. *violation of the law*. acc. pl. **lahbrycas** 7/48.

lahlīce. adv. *according to law*. 7/21.

lām. masc. *clay, earth*. dat. sg. **lāme** 3/84.

lamb. neut. *lamb*.

gelamp → (ge)limpan.

land. neut. *land, nation*. nom. sg. 6/17, 32; 8/3, 4, 8, etc. (15x). acc. sg. **land, lond** k/1357; 6/40 (2x); 8/6, 8, etc. (16x). gen. sg. **landes, londes** 4/11; 6/7 (2x), 30; 8/18, etc. (10x). dat. sg. **lande, londe** 2/7; 3/4; 6/26, 27; 7/4, etc. (29x). nom. pl. 8/53, 55 (2x). acc. pl. **lond** h/4. gen. pl. **landa** 6/12. dat. pl. **landum, londum** 8/16, 50; 10/25.

landbūend. masc. nd-stem. *inhabitant*. nom. pl. **landbūende** 18/226. dat. pl. **londbūendum** 18/314.

**landlēode.** masc. *tenant.* dat. sg. 6/35.
**lang.** adj. *long, tall.* masc. nom. sg. 8/19, 29;
  10/45. neut. nom. sg. 8/3, 30; 10/42,
  82; 12/66. fem. acc. sg. **lange** 10/81;
  14/24. masc. nom. pl. **lange** 8/20 (2x).
  neut. acc. sg. 2/10. nom. pl. **lange.** wk.
  masc. nom. sg. **langa** 12/273. wk. neut.
  dat. sg. **langan** 8/72. neut. gen. sg.
  compar. **lengran** 18/184. masc. nom.
  sg. compar. **lengra** 8/19.
**Langaland.** neut. *Langeland* (Danish
  island). nom. sg. 8/53.
**lange.** adv. *long, for a long time.* superl.
  **lengest** 4/1. **lange, longe** 5/7, 11, 14;
  7/13, 18, etc. (15x). compar. **leng, lencg**
  7/2; 8/64; 12/171; 18/153.
**langian.** wk. 2. (impersonal, with acc.).
  *long, yearn.* past 3sg. **longade** 16/14.
**langoþ.** masc. *longing.* gen. sg. **longaþes**
  16/41. dat. sg. **langoþe** 16/53.
**langsum.** adj. *long-lasting, tedious.* masc.
  nom. sg. 10/55. neut. nom. sg. 3/108.
  fem. acc. sg. **langsume** 3/89.
**langsumnyss.** fem. *length, tediousness.* acc.
  sg. **langsumnysse** 3/3.
**langunghwīl.** fem. *time of longing.* gen.
  pl. **langunghwīla** 14/126.
**lār.** fem. *learning, doctrine, teaching,
  instruction.* acc. sg. **lāre** 7/22; 18/333.
  gen. sg. **lāre** 9/18. dat. sg. **lāre** 9/24.
  nom. pl. **lāra** 7/15. acc. pl. **lāra.**
**lārcwide.** masc. *lore-speech, teaching.* dat.
  pl. **lārcwidum** 13/38.
**lārēow.** masc. *teacher.* nom. sg. 2/27. nom.
  pl. **lārēowas** 3/111; 9/23. gen. pl.
  **lārīowa** 10/79. dat. pl. **lārēowum.**
**lārlic.** adj. *instructive, doctrinal.* wk. neut.
  acc. sg. **lārlican.**
**lāst.** masc. *track.* acc. sg. 18/209, 291. dat.
  sg. **lāste** 13/97; 18/297.
**late.** adv. *late.* 18/275.
**latian.** wk. 2. *tarry, delay* (with gen.
  object). subj. sg. **latige** 7/59.
**lāþ. A.** adj. *hateful, hated, hostile.* masc.
  nom. sg. 18/45. neut. nom. sg. 7/29.
  masc. acc. sg. **lāðne** 18/72, 101. fem. dat.

sg. **lāþere** 12/90. neut. dat. sg. **lāðum**
  18/226. nom. pl. **lāðe** H/3. masc. nom.
  pl. **lāðe** 12/86. fem. nom. pl. **lāðe** 7/15.
  gen. pl. **lāðra** 18/297, 303. wk. neut.
  gen. sg. **lāðan** 18/310. neut. acc. sg.
  compar. **lāþre** 12/50. masc. gen. sg.
  superl. **lāðestan** 18/178. masc. nom. pl.
  superl. **lāðost** 18/322. neut. nom. sg.
  superl. **lāðost** 14/88. wk. masc. dat. sg.
  superl. **lāðestan** 18/314.
  **B.** neut. *pain, harm, injury, misfortune.* nom. sg. 15/12.
**lāþettan.** wk. 1. *hate.* 3sg. **lāðet** 7/53.
**(ge)laþian.** wk. 2. *invite.* past pl.
  **gelaðodon** 3/8.
**lāþlice.** adv. *wretchedly.* superl. **lāðlicost**
  16/14.
**gelaþung.** fem. *congregation, church.* dat.
  sg. **gelaðunge** 3/111.
**gelæccan.** wk. 1. *seize.* past pl. **gelæhton**
  3/38.
**lǣce.** masc. *physician.* nom. sg. 2/14 (2x),
  22, 23.
**(ge)lǣdan.** wk. 1. *lead, bring.* 1sg. **gelǣde.**
  3sg. **lǣtt** 6/43. pl. **lǣdað** 7/46. past 3sg.
  **lǣdde, gelǣdde** 9/15; 18/129. past
  pl. **lǣddon, gelǣddon** 5/8, 17; 18/72,
  325. subj. sg. **gelǣde** F/7. inf. **lǣdan,
  gelǣdan** 12/88; 14/5; 18/42.
**Lǣden.** neut. *Latin.* acc. sg. **Lȳden.**
**lǣfan.** wk. 1. *leave.* past 3sg. **lǣfde** 3/44;
  4/10; 6/8. infl. inf. **tō lǣfanne** 10/11.
  past part. **lǣfed** 10/20.
**læg, lǣg-** → licgan.
**lægde** → (ge)lecgan.
**gelæhton** → gelæccan.
**Lǣland.** neut. *Lolland* (Danish island).
  nom. sg. 8/53.
**lǣndagas.** masc. *transitory days.* gen. pl.
  **lǣndaga.**
**lǣne.** adj. *transitory.* masc. nom. sg.
  10/15; 13/108, 109 (2x). neut. nom. sg.
  13/108. neut. dat. sg. **lǣnum** 14/109.
  wk. neut. dat. sg. **lǣnan** 14/138.
**(ge)lǣran.** wk. 1. *teach, advise, exhort,
  persuade.* past 3sg. **lǣrde** 9/20; 12/311.

inf. **lǽran** 2/7; 9/21; 17/21. pres. part.
**lǽrende.** past part. **gelǽred** 9/3.
**gelǽred.** adj. (past part. of *lǽran*). *learned.*
masc. nom. sg. 3/109. wk. masc. acc.
pl. superl. **gelǽredestan** 9/16.
**lǽrig.** masc. *rim.* nom. sg. 12/284.
**lǽs.** neut. (indeclinable). *less.* 7/39.
**lǽssa, lǽst-** → **lȳtel.**
**(ge)lǽstan.** wk. 1. *follow, perform, abide
by.* past 3sg. **gelǽste** 12/15. subj. pl.
**gelǽstan** 7/68. inf. **lǽstan** 17/53. *pay.*
subj. sg. **gelǽste** 7/9. past part. **gelǽst**
5/14, 20. *serve* someone (dat.). inf.
**gelǽstan** 12/11.
**lǽswian.** wk. 2. *graze.* past pl. **lǽswodon**
3/36.
**lǽtan.** st. 7. *let, allow.* past 3sg. **lēt** 7/62;
12/7, 140. past pl. **lēton** 5/6; 12/108;
18/221. imp. sg. **lǽt** 17/24. *cause* to do
something. past 3sg. **lēt** 6/34. *keep,
consider.* past 3sg. **lǽt, lēt** 7/40; 8/6.
**gelǽte.** wk. neut. *meeting.* dat. pl.
**gelǽtum.**
**lǽtt** → **(ge)lǽdan.**
**lǽþþ.** fem. *injury, malice.* gen. pl. **lǽððа**
18/158. dat. pl. **lǽððum** 18/184.
**lǽwede.** adj. *lay, unlearned.* dat. pl.
**lǽwedum** 3/3, 110. masc. nom. pl.
5/12; 7/21. wk. neut. dat. sg. **lǽwedum.**
**lēaf. A.** fem. *leave, permission.* acc. sg. **lēafe**
10/82.
**B.** neut. *leaf.* nom. pl. ʌ/3.
**gelēafa.** wk. masc. *faith.* acc. sg. **gelēafan**
18/6, 89, 344. dat. sg. **gelēafan** 3/20, 82.
inst. sg. **gelēafan** 18/97.
**gelēafful.** adj. *faithful.* dat. pl. **gelēaffullum**
3/57. wk. masc. dat. sg. **gelēaffullum**
2/14.
**lēah.** masc. *pasture, meadow.*
**lēan.** neut. *reward, gift, loan.* gen. sg.
**lēanes** 18/346.
**lēap.** masc. *basket,* fig. *body.* nom. sg.
18/111.
**lēas.** adj. *lacking, false.* masc. nom. sg. 6/6;
18/121. neut. nom. sg. 16/32. neut. acc.
sg. 11/20. neut. nom. pl. **lēas, lēase**

13/86. masc. gen. sg. **lēases** 10/13, 58.
masc. dat. sg. **lēasum** 10/50.
**lēasbregdness.** fem. *deception, falsehood.*
acc. pl. **lēasbregdnessa.**
**lēasung.** fem. *falsehood.* gen. sg. **lēasunge**
9/4. acc. pl. **lēasunga** 7/49. dat. pl.
**lēasungum** 10/55.
**(ge)lecgan.** wk. 1. *lay, place,* of laws,
*institute.* 3sg. **legeð** ɪ/4. past 3sg. **lægde**
6/37. past pl. **lēdon** 2/24. subj. sg. **lecge**
13/42. past part. **gelēd** 3/87.
**lēdon** → **(ge)lecgan.**
**leg** → **licgan.**
**leger.** neut. *bed, lying.* dat. sg. **legere** 8/72.
acc. pl. 16/34.
**legeþ** → **(ge)lecgan.**
**lehtrian.** wk. 2. *accuse, revile.* 3sg. **lehtreð**
7/51.
**lencg** → **lange.**
**lenctenfæsten.** neut. *Lenten fast.*
**leng.** fem. *length.*
**leng, lengest** → **lange.**
**lengra, lengran** → **lang.**
**lengþu.** fem. *length.*
**lengu.** fem. *length.* acc. sg. **lenge** 10/40.
**lēo.** wk. masc. *lion.* nom. sg. 3/20. nom.
pl. **lēon.**
**lēod. A.** masc. *person.* gen. pl. **lēoda**
18/178. dat. pl. **lēodum, lēodon** ɪ/85;
12/23; 14/88; 15/1; 16/6, etc. (6x).
**B.** fem. (often pl. with sg. sense).
*nation, people.* gen. sg. **lēode** 7/63. acc.
pl. **lēoda** 12/37. dat. pl. **lēodum** 7/12;
12/50.
**lēodbiscop.** masc. *provincial bishop.* nom.
pl. **lēodbiscopas** 6/21.
**lēodfruma.** wk. masc. *leader of the people,
lord.* nom. sg. 16/8.
**lēodhata.** wk. masc. *tyrant.* acc. sg.
**lēodhatan** 18/72. nom. pl. **lēodhatan**
7/50.
**lēodmægen.** neut. *might of a people, army.*
gen. sg. **lēodmægnes.**
**lēof. A.** adj. *beloved, dear.* masc. nom. sg.
ɪ/2. fem. nom. sg. ɪ/85; 18/147. masc.
acc. sg. **lēofne** 12/7, 208. masc. gen. sg.

**lēofes** 13/38; 16/53. fem. gen. sg. **lēofre** 13/97. masc. nom. pl. **lēofe** 16/34. gen. pl. **lēofra** 13/31; 16/16. wk. masc. nom. sg. **lēofa** 14/78, 95. wk. masc. dat. sg. **lēofan** 12/319; 18/346. wk. masc. nom. pl. **Lēofan** 7/1; 9/37. masc. nom. sg. compar. **lēofra** 4/12. *pleasant, agreeable*. neut. nom. sg. superl. **lēofost** 12/23.
B. masc. *sir*. nom. sg. 1/10.
**leofaþ** → libban.
**lēoflic**. adj. *beloved*.
**lēoflīce**. adv. *lovingly*.
**leofod-** → libban.
**lēoht**. A. neut. *light*. dat. sg. **lēohte** 14/5.
B. adj. of weight, *light*. neut. acc. pl. **lēohte** 8/38.
C. adj. *bright*. masc. acc. sg. **lēohtne** 18/191.
**lēohte**. adv. *brightly*.
**leohtmōd**. adj. *lighthearted, easygoing*. fem. nom. sg. J/85.
**lēoma**. wk. masc. *light, radiance*. nom. sg. 11/3. acc. sg. **lēoman** 3/16; 18/191.
**leomu** → lim.
**leornere**. masc. *scholar*. acc. pl. **leorneras** 9/16.
**(ge)leornian**. wk. 2. *learn*. past 2sg. **leornodest, liornodest** 10/16, 17. past 3sg. **leornade, geleornade, geleornode** 9/1, 3, 5. past pl. **leornodon** 9/23. inf. **geleornian** 9/22.
**leorningcniht**. masc. *disciple*. nom. pl. **leorningcnihtas**. acc. pl. **leorningcnihtas**. dat. pl. **leorningcnihtum**.
**leornung**. fem. *learning*.
**lēoþ**. neut. *song*. nom. sg. 9/23. acc. sg. 9/5, 16, 22, 24; 10/1. gen. sg. **lēoþes** 9/4. inst. sg. **lēoðe** 9/19. acc. pl. 9/1, 3.
**lēoþcræft**. masc. *art of poetry, art of song*. acc. sg. 9/3.
**lēoþsang**. masc. *song, poem, poetry*. gen. sg. **lēoþsonges** 9/18. dat. pl. **lēoþsongum** 9/2.
**lēt-** → lǣtan.

**gelettan**. wk. 1. *hinder, prevent* someone from going on a journey (gen.). past 3sg. **gelette** 12/164. inf. 17/25.
**lēw**. fem. *injury*. acc. sg. **lēwe** 7/54.
**gelēwian**. wk. 2. *injure*. past part. **gelēwede** 7/55.
**libban**. wk. 3. *live*. 3sg. **leofað, lifað** κ/1366; 3/86. pl. **lifiaþ** 14/134. past 1sg. **lifde** 10/11. past 3sg. **leofode, lifode** 3/106, 107. past pl. **leofodan, lifdon, lifodon, lyfdon** 6/17; 16/14; 18/296. inf. 6/32, 40; 10/81. infl. inf. **tō libbanne** 10/11. pres. part. **libbende, libbendum, lifgende, lifgendne, lifgendum, lifiendne, lifigendan, lifigendum** 7/25; 10/60; 16/34; 17/25, 53.
**līc**. neut. *body, corpse*. nom. sg. 3/95; 4/16, 17; 8/65. acc. sg. 2/11, 26. gen. sg. **līces** 14/63. dat. sg. **līce** 3/59.
**gelīc**. adj. *like, similar, equal*. neut. acc. sg. **gelic** 10/33. masc. nom. pl. **gelīce** 1/5. masc. acc. pl. **gelīce** 10/70. wk. masc. nom. pl. **gelīcan** 10/80. masc. nom. pl. compar. **gelīcran** A/4.
**gelīca**. wk. masc. *equal*. nom. sg. 3/14, 21, 52.
**gelīce**. adv. *similarly, equally, like*. superl. **gelīccast** 7/30. 7/54; 9/3.
**līcettan**. wk. 1. *pretend*. subj. past sg. **līcette** 10/53.
**licgan**. st. 5. *lie, be situated*. 3sg. **līð, ligeð** 2/24; 4/16, 17; 8/31, 64, etc. (11x). pl. **licgað** 8/32, 64, 74; 13/78. past 3sg. **læg, leg** B/2; 2/22, 27; 3/27; 4/10, etc. (14x). past pl. **lāgon, lǣgon** 4/8; 12/112, 183; 18/30. subj. sg. **licge** 7/36. subj. past sg. **lǣge** 2/22; 8/4; 12/279. inf. 12/319; 18/278. pres. part. **licgende** 14/24. with refl. pron. *lie down*. subj. past sg. **lǣge** 12/300. of a road or waterway, or veins in the body, *run*. 3sg. **līð, ligeð** 8/46, 47, 58 (2x), 59. past 3sg. **læg** 8/11.
**līchama**. wk. masc. *body, corpse*. nom. sg. 2/26. acc. sg. **līchaman** 2/24; 5/19. gen. sg. **līchoman** 10/59, 61. nom. pl. **līchaman**. acc. pl. **līchaman** 2/26.

līchamlic. adj. *bodily.* fem. dat. sg. līchomlicre 9/28.

līchomlīce. adv. *in the flesh.* 10/60.

(ge)līcian. wk. 2. *please.* 3sg. līcað 10/33 (2x). past 3sg. līcode, gelīcode 3/42; 10/2, 32, 34. subj. sg. licige 10/35.

līcsang. masc. *dirge.* acc. sg. 2/21.

lidman. masc. athematic. *seafarer.* nom. pl. lidmen 12/99. gen. pl. lidmanna 12/164.

līf. neut. *life.* nom. sg. 3/78, 79, 108. acc. sg. M/2; 6/17; 7/21; 9/27, 42, etc. (10x). gen. sg. līfes D/1; F/6; 1/14, 17; 9/2, etc. (12x). dat. sg. līfe D/3; 2/10; 3/54, 79, 103, etc. (13x). acc. pl. 13/60.

lifaþ, lifd-, lifgend-, lifiaþ, lifiend-, lifigend-, lifod- → libban.

ligetu. fem. *lightning.* nom. sg. līgetu G/5.

ligeþ → licgan.

līhtan. wk. 1. *alight.* past 3sg. līhte 12/23.

līhting. fem. *shining, illumination.* dat. sg. līhtinge.

lilige. wk. fem. *lily.* nom. sg. G/3.

lim. neut. *limb.* acc. pl. leomu, limu 6/29; 9/7. dat. pl. limum 2/22.

gelimp. neut. *event, good fortune, misfortune.* dat. sg. gelimpe. dat. pl. gelimpum 7/46.

(ge)limpan. st. 3. *happen, befall.* 3sg. limpð, gelimpð A/4; 7/38. past 3sg. gelamp, gelomp B/1; 3/11, 111; 6/1; 10/49. past pl. gelumpon 5/3. inf. gelimpan 7/35; 17/30.

gelimplic. adj. *suitable.* fem. acc. sg. gelimplice 9/7.

gelimplīce. adv. *fittingly, suitably.* 2/19.

limwērig. adj. *weary in limb.* masc. acc. sg. limwērigne 14/63.

lind. fem. *linden, shield.* acc. sg. linde 12/244. acc. pl. linde 12/99; 18/191, 303. dat. pl. lindum 18/214.

lindwerod. neut. *shield-bearing army.* nom. sg. 18/297.

lindwiggend. masc. nd-stem. *warrior bearing a linden shield.* nom. pl. lindwiggende 18/42.

liornodest → (ge)leornian.

listum. adv. *skilfully.* 18/101.

līþ → licgan.

lōca, lōcaþ → lōcian.

locc. masc. *lock* of hair. acc. pl. loccas 3/40.

lōcian. wk. 2. *look.* 3sg. lōcað G/8; 7/40. past 3sg. lōcude 4/5. past pl. lōcodon 6/12. imp. sg. lōca.

lof. neut. *praise.* nom. sg. 10/36. acc. sg. 9/39, 44; 10/33. dat. sg. lofe 10/46.

(ge)lōgian. wk. 2. *place, lodge.* past 3sg. gelōgode 7/28. *arrange,* of rhetoric, *order.* pl. lōgiað 3/77.

gelōme. adv. *often.* 2/1, 5; 7/10, 16, 18, etc. (15x).

gelōmlīce. adv. *often, frequently, repeatedly.*

gelomp → (ge)limpan.

lond- → land.

londbūendum → landbūend.

londstede. masc. *place in the land, country.* dat. sg. 16/16.

gelong. adj. *dependent on* (with æt). fem. nom. sg. 16/45.

longade → langian.

longaþes → langoþ.

longe → lange.

lor. neut. *loss.*

losian. wk. 2. *be lost, perish.* past pl. losodon 10/37. inf. 10/72; 18/287.

lūcan. st. 2. *lock.* past pl. lucon 12/66.

lufian. wk. 2. *love.* 3sg. lufað. pl. lufiað D/1; 7/52. past 3sg. lufode 2/6, 7, 11; 6/36, 38. past pl. lufodon 6/14. subj. pl. lufie. inf. lufian, lufigean 7/53, 68; 9/20.

lufu. *love.* 1. fem. dat. sg. lufe 2/28. 2. wk. fem. dat. sg. lufan 9/26 (2x).

gelumpon → (ge)limpan.

Lunden. proper noun. *London.* dat. sg. Lundene 5/19.

Lundenburg. fem. athematic. *London.* dat. sg. Lundenbyrig 5/12.

lungre. adv. *quickly.* 18/147, 280.

lūs. fem. athematic. *louse.*

**lust.** masc. *desire, lust, pleasure.* acc. sg. 7/22. dat. pl. **lustum** 3/79; 18/161.

**lustbǣre.** adj. *desirable, pleasant.* neut. nom. sg. 1/6.

**lustum.** adv. *with pleasure.* 17/21.

**Lȳden** → Lǣden.

**lȳfan.** wk. 1. *allow, grant* something (gen.). past 3sg. **lȳfde** 2/10.

**gelȳfan.** wk. 1. *believe.* 3sg. **gelȳfð.** pl. **gelȳfað** c/1; 11/16. subj. sg. **gelȳfe** 7/29.

**lyfdon** → libban.

**gelȳfed.** adj. (past part.). *advanced.* fem. gen. sg. **gelȳfdre** 9/5.

**lyft.** fem. *air.* acc. sg. **lyft, lyfte** 14/5; 18/347. dat. sg. **lyfte.**

**lyre.** masc. *loss.* nom. sg. 3/82. acc. sg. 3/44. dat. sg. 3/64.

**lȳsan.** wk. 1. *release, liberate, redeem.* inf. 12/37; 14/41.

**gelystan.** wk. 1. (impersonal). *desire* something (gen.), with acc. of person. 3sg. **lysteð** 10/67. past 3sg. **gelyste** 18/306. subj. sg. **lyste** 10/65, 68.

**lȳt.** adj. *little, few.* neut. acc. sg. 13/31; 16/16.

**lytegian.** wk. 2. *act cunningly.* inf. 12/86.

**lȳtel. A.** adj. *little, small.* fem. acc. sg. **lȳtle** 4/17. masc. nom. sg. 10/15, 20, 79. fem. nom. sg. **lȳtel, lȳtlu** 10/16, 66. neut. nom. sg. 10/40. neut. gen. sg. **lȳtles** 3/2. fem. dat. sg. **lȳtelre** 6/35; 7/15. masc. inst. sg. **lȳtle** 4/4. fem. nom. pl. **lȳtle** 7/4. neut. acc. pl. **lȳtle** 8/38. wk. neut. acc. sg. **lȳtle** 8/25. wk. masc. dat. sg. **lȳtlan** 10/24. wk. neut. dat. sg. **lȳtlan** 10/46. masc. nom. sg. compar. **lǣssa** 8/19. wk. masc. nom. sg. superl. **lǣsta** 8/67. wk. masc. acc. sg. superl. **lǣstan** 8/69.

    **B.** indef. pron. *little.* neut. acc. sg. 7/10.

**lȳthwōn.** adv. *a little,* as pron *few.* 18/310.

**lȳtle.** adv. *a little.*

**lȳtlian.** wk. 2. *diminish.* 3sg. **lȳtlað** 12/313.

**lȳþre.** adj. *wicked.* fem. acc. sg. 7/63.

**mā.** neut. (indeclinable). *more.* B/3; 6/35; 7/39, 49; 8/25, etc. (7x).

**mā** → micle.

**macian.** wk. 2. *make.* past 3sg. **macode** 2/19; 6/27. past pl. **macodon.**

**mādm-** → māþum.

**māg-** → mǣg.

**magan.** pret. pres. *be able to, can, may.* 1sg. **mæg** 6/3; 13/58; 14/85; 16/2, 38, etc. (7x). 2sg. **meaht, miht** 9/9; 10/16, 18, 20; 14/78. 3sg. **mæg, mag** G/9 (2x); K/1365; M/13; 2/4, etc. (25x). pl. **magon, magan** 3/22, 88; 7/54, 58, 60, etc. (12x). past 1sg. **meahte, mihte** 13/26; 14/18, 37. past 3sg. **mihte, meahte, mehte** B/4; H/4; 2/7, 8, 16, etc. (28x). past pl. **mihton** B/2, 4; 2/28; 3/82. subj. sg. **mǣge** 7/23; 8/46; 10/31, 40; 12/235, etc. (6x). subj. pl. **mǣgen** 10/38. subj. past sg. **meahte, mihte** H/3; 8/35; 10/54. subj. past pl. **mihten** B/5; 18/24, 136.

**mago.** masc. *kinsman, young man, warrior.* nom. sg. 13/92.

**magorinc.** masc. *man.* nom. pl. **magorincas** 10/79.

**maguþegn.** masc. *noble kinsman.* nom. pl. **magoþegnas, maguþegnas** 13/62; 18/236.

**man. A.** masc. athematic. *man, person, husband.* nom. sg. **man, mon, mann** G/6; 2/2; 3/14 (2x), 27, etc. (37x). acc. sg. **man, mon, monn** 3/30, 44; 6/28; 9/3; 12/77, etc. (7x). gen. sg. **mannes, monnes** G/7; 3/21, 78, 79; 8/72, etc. (10x). dat. sg. **men** 3/25; 5/7; 9/20; 10/58, 66, etc. (7x). nom. pl. **men, menn** B/2; c/10; 2/27; 3/49; 4/4, etc. (26x). acc. pl. **men, menn** 4/15; 5/7; 6/3, 34, 41, etc. (10x). gen. pl. **manna, monna** B/3; D/1, 3; 6/26; 7/5, etc. (15x). dat. pl. **mannum, monnum** c/2; 2/24; 3/3, 29, 57, etc. (21x).

    **B.** indef. pron. *one, someone.* masc. nom. sg. **man, mon** c/5; 2/21; 3/3, 54, 93, etc. (57x).

**mān.** neut. *evil deed, crime, sin.* gen. pl. **māna** 7/56.

**geman** → gemunan.

**gemāna.** wk. masc. *company, companionship, intercourse.* acc. sg. **gemānan** c/3.

**mancynn.** neut. *mankind.* nom. sg. **moncynn** 10/18. acc. sg. **mancynn, mancyn, manncynn** 3/46; 6/31; 14/41, 104. gen. sg. **mancynnes, moncynnes, monncynnes** c/2; 9/13, 24; 14/33, 99. dat. sg. **mancynne** 3/108.

**māndǣd.** fem. *evil deed.* acc. pl. **māndǣda** 7/48. gen. pl. **māndǣda** 9/26.

**mānfordǣdla.** wk. masc. *evil-doer.* nom. pl. **mānfordǣdlan.**

**mānful.** adj. *wicked, evil.* wk. masc. nom. sg. **mānfulla** 3/30. wk. masc. nom. pl. **mānfullan.**

**gemang** → gemong.

**(ge)manian.** wk. 2. *admonish, exort, advise.* past 2sg. **gemanode** 12/231. past 3sg. **manode, monade** 9/20; 18/26. inf. **manian** 12/228.

**manig. A.** adj. *many, much.* fem. nom. pl. **manega, manege, manige** F/3; 2/31; 7/28; 10/24. masc. acc. pl. **manega, manege, manige** 6/33; 3/69; 7/53. masc. nom. sg. **mænig, monig** 12/282. fem. nom. sg. 8/60. neut. nom. sg. **mænig.** masc. acc. sg. **manigne, mænigne** 12/188, 243. neut. acc. sg. **monig** 9/24, 25, 44. neut. gen. sg. **maniges** 6/7. neut. dat. sg. **manegum** 10/29. masc. nom. pl. **manege, manige, mænege, mænige, monige** 7/14, 24, 30, 34, 50, etc. (9x). neut. nom. pl. 6/16. fem. acc. pl. **manega, manege** 2/10; 7/5; 10/25. neut. acc. pl. **monig, manig, mænig** 6/35; 8/47; 9/14; 10/70. gen. pl. **manigra, monigra** B/4; 9/2; 14/41. dat. pl. **manegum, monegum, manegan** 2/4, 27; 3/75; 7/27; 9/24, etc. (8x).

**B.** indef. pron. *many.* masc. nom. pl. **manega** 12/200.

**manigeo** → menigu.

**manigfeald.** adj. *manifold, various, numerous.* fem. acc. pl. **mænigfealde** 7/47, 64. dat. pl. **mænigfealdum** 2/13. wk. dat. pl. **menigfealdum** 3/26. neut. nom. sg. compar. **mænigfealdre** 7/33.

**manna.** wk. masc. *man.* acc. sg. **mannan, monnan** 16/18; 17/28; 18/98, 101.

**manncynn** → mancynn.

**mannslaga.** wk. masc. *killer.* nom. pl. **mannslagan** 7/56.

**mannsylen.** fem. *sale of men.* acc. pl. **mannsylena** 7/48.

**manode, gemanode** → (ge)manian.

**Mans.** neut. *Maine.* nom. sg. 6/32.

**manslyht.** masc. *manslaughter.* acc. pl. **manslyhtas** 7/48.

**mānswora.** wk. masc. *swearer of false oaths.* nom. pl. **mānsworan** 7/56.

**māra.** indef. pron. *more.* neut. nom. sg. **māre** 7/33; 10/20, 23. neut. acc. sg. **māre** 7/23. neut. gen. sg. **māran** 10/35, 79.

**mār-** → micel.

**marc.** neut. *mark (monetary unit).* acc. pl. 6/35.

**marmstān.** masc. *marble.* dat. sg. **marmstāne** 2/19 (2x).

**gemartiredon** → gemartyrian.

**martyr.** masc. *martyr.* gen. sg. **martires** 5/19.

**gemartyrian.** wk. 2. *martyr.* past pl. **gemartiredon** 5/11. past part. **gemartyrode.**

**maþa.** wk. masc. *maggot, worm.* dat. pl. **maðum** 3/95.

**maþelian.** wk. 2. *speak* (formally). past 3sg. **maþelode** 12/42, 309.

**māþþumgyfa.** wk. masc. *treasure-giver.* nom. sg. 13/92.

**māþum.** masc. *treasure.* acc. pl. **mādmas** 18/318. gen. pl. **māðma, mādma** 17/46; 18/329, 340. dat. pl. **māþmum** J/87.

**gemǣc.** adj. *equal, similar, suitable.* masc. acc. sg. **gemǣcne** 16/18.

**mǣd.** fem. *meadow.* nom. pl. **mǣdwa.** dat. pl. **mǣdum.**

**mǣden-** → mægden.

**mǣg.** masc. *kinsman.* nom. sg. 4/12; 12/5, 114, 224, 287, etc. (6x). dat. sg. **mǣge** 3/94. nom. pl. **māgas, mǣgas** 4/11; 16/11. gen. pl. **māga** 13/51. dat. pl. **māgum, mǣgum** 3/96; 4/13; 8/64.

**mǣg-** → magan.

**mǣgden.** neut. *maiden, virgin.* nom. sg. **mǣden** c/3; 2/1, 5, 8, 26. acc. sg. **mǣden, mægden.** gen. sg. **mǣdenes** 2/25. dat. sg. **mǣdene** 2/1. gen. pl. **mǣgdena.**

**mǣgen.** neut. *might, army, virtue.* nom. sg. 12/313; 18/253, 261. gen. pl. **mǣgena** 10/13.

**mǣgenēacen.** adj. *mighty.* neut. nom. sg. 18/292.

**mǣgrǣs.** masc. *attack on relatives.* acc. pl. **mǣgrǣsas** 7/48.

**mǣgslaga.** wk. masc. *killer of a kinsman.* nom. pl. **mǣgslagan** 7/56.

**mǣgþ.** fem. dental stem. *maiden.* nom. sg. 18/78, 125, 145, 254. acc. sg. 18/35, 43, 165, 260. gen. sg. 18/334. nom. pl. 18/135.

**mǣgþ.** fem. *family, tribe, nation.* nom. sg. 8/74. dat. sg. **mǣgðe** 7/36. gen. pl. **mǣgða** 18/324. dat. pl. **mǣgþum.** *generation.* acc. sg. **mǣgðe** 3/106.

**gemǣgþ.** fem. *longing* for something (gen.). nom. sg. 10/2.

**mǣgþhād.** masc. *virginity.* nom. sg. 2/4. acc. sg. 2/5.

**mǣl.** neut. *occasion, season, meal.* dat. sg. **mǣle** 2/11. acc. pl. **mǣla** 12/212.

**mǣlan.** wk. 1. *speak.* past 3sg. **mǣlde, gemǣlde** 12/26, 43, 210, 230, 244.

**mǣnan.** wk. 1. *tell, intend, complain* about something (acc.). past 3sg. **mǣnde** H/4. past pl. **mǣndon** 6/40.

**gemǣne.** adj. *common, joint, universal.* masc. nom. sg. 7/16. neut. nom. sg. 7/36. fem. acc. sg. 7/30. masc. dat. sg. **gemǣnum** 7/30. neut. nom. pl. 7/38.

**mǣnege** → manig.

**mǣnifealdlīce.** adv. *in many ways.* 6/5.

**mǣnig-** → manig.

**mǣnigfeald-** → manigfeald.

**gemǣnigfyldan.** wk. 1. *multiply, increase.* 1sg. **gemǣnifylde** 1/16. past part. **gemenifylde.**

**gemǣran.** wk. 1. *glorify.* past part. **gemǣred** 9/1.

**mǣre.** adj. *famous, glorious, excellent, great.* masc. nom. sg. 3/8. neut. nom. sg. 6/16. masc. acc. sg. **mǣrne** 3/30. fem. acc. sg. 2/19. wk. fem. nom. sg. 13/100; 14/12, 82. wk. neut. acc. sg. 6/15. wk. masc. gen. sg. **mǣran** 3/112. wk. masc. dat. sg. **mǣran** 14/69; 18/3. gen. pl. compar. **mǣrra** 18/329. masc. nom. sg. superl. **mǣrost** 10/71. fem. nom. sg. superl. **mǣrost** 18/324.

**(ge)mǣrsian.** wk. 2. *make famous, glorify.* past part. **gemǣrsod** 3/57.

**mǣrþ.** fem. *fame, glory.* acc. sg. **mǣrðe** 18/343. acc. pl. **mǣrða** 2/5; 7/70.

**mǣsse.** wk. fem. *mass.* dat. sg. **mǣssan** 5/5.

**mǣssedæg.** masc. *mass-day, feast.*

**mǣsseprēost.** masc. *mass-priest.*

**mǣsserbana.** wk. masc. *killer of a priest.* nom. pl. **mǣsserbanan** 7/56.

**mǣst.** indef. pron. *most, greatest.* neut. nom. sg. 12/223. neut. acc. sg. 5/4.

**mǣst-** → micel, micle.

**(ge)mǣtan.** wk. 1. *dream* (impersonal). past 3sg. **mǣtte, gemǣtte** 14/2.

**mǣte.** adj. *poor, inferior, small.* neut. inst. sg. 14/69, 124.

**gemǣte. A.** adv. *suitably.* 2/25.
**B.** adj. *suitable.* masc. nom. sg. 2/25.

**mǣþ.** fem. *ability, propriety, honour.* nom. sg. 12/195. acc. sg. **mǣðe** 3/88; 7/28. dat. sg. **mǣðe** 3/3; 7/11.

**mǣw.** masc. *mew, sea-gull.* gen. sg. **mǣwes** 17/26.

**mē** → ic, wē.

**meaht** → magan.

**meahte** → miht.

**mēar-** → mearh.

**mearcweard.** masc. *border-warden.* nom. pl. **mearcweardas.**

**mearh.** masc. *horse.* nom. sg. **mearg** 13/92. acc. sg. 12/188. dat. sg. **mēare**

12/239. gen. pl. **mēara** 17/46. dat. pl.
**mēarum** ɪ/87.

**mearþ.** masc. *marten.* gen. sg. **mearðes**
8/29.

**mearu.** adj. *tender, delicate.* masc. acc. sg.
**mearune.**

**mec** → ic, wē.

**mēce.** masc. *sword.* acc. sg. **mēce** 12/167,
236; 18/78. dat. sg. 18/104.

**mēd.** fem. *reward, payment.* acc. sg. **mēde**
10/47; 18/343. gen. sg. **mēde** 10/48. dat.
sg. **mēde** 18/334.

**mēdgilda.** wk. masc. *hireling, mercenary.*
gen. sg. **mēdgildan** 3/78.

**medmicel.** adj. *moderate, short.* neut. acc.
sg. 9/42. neut. dat. sg. **medmiclum** 9/1.

**medoærn.** neut. *mead-hall.*

**medobyrig** → meoduburg.

**medowērig.** adj. *weary from drinking mead,*
*hung over.* masc. acc. pl. **medowērige**
18/229. dat. pl. **medowērigum** 18/245.

**medu.** masc. u-stem. *mead.* nom. sg.
**medu, medo** 8/63. acc. sg. **medo** 8/61.
dat. sg. **meodo** 12/212.

**medudrēam.** masc. *mead-joy, joy in the*
*mead-hall.* gen. pl. **meododrēama** 17/46.

**medugāl.** adj. *drunk with mead.* masc.
nom. sg. 18/26.

**meduheall.** fem. *mead-hall.* dat. sg.
**meoduhealle** 13/27.

**mehte** → magan.

**men** → man.

**(ge)mengan.** wk. 1. *mix, mingle, stir up.*
inf. **mengan** 17/44. past part. **gemenged**
13/48.

**gemenifylde** → gemænigfyldan.

**menigfealdum** → manigfeald.

**menigu.** fem. *multitude.* dat. sg. **manigeo,**
**mænige** 14/112, 151.

**menn** → man.

**menniscness.** fem. *humanity, incarnation.*
dat. sg. **menniscnesse, menniscnysse**
3/111; 9/24.

**meodo** → medu.

**meododrēama** → medudrēam.

**meodorǣden.** fem. *mead-drinking,* fig.
*assembly.* dat. sg. **meodorǣdenne** ɪ/87.

**meodosetl.** neut. *mead-seat, seat in a*
*mead-hall.* gen. pl. **meodosetla.**

**meoduburg.** fem. athematic. *mead-town,*
*happy town.* dat. sg. **medobyrig** 18/167.
dat. pl. **meoduburgum** 17/17.

**meoduhealle** → meduheall.

**meolc.** fem. athematic. *milk.* acc. sg. 8/61.

**Meore.** proper noun. *Möre* (district in
Småland, southern Sweden). nom. sg.
8/55.

**Meotod-** → Metod.

**mēowle.** wk. fem. *woman.* nom. sg. 18/56.
acc. sg. **mēowlan** 18/261.

**Merantūn.** masc. *Merton.* dat. sg.
**Merantūne** 4/4.

**mere.** masc. *sea, lake.* nom. sg. κ/1362.
acc. sg. 8/59; 17/26. dat. sg. 8/59. nom.
pl. **meras** 8/38. acc. pl. **meras** 8/38.

**merelād.** fem. *sea-way.* acc. sg. **merelāde**
17/28.

**merestrēam.** masc. *sea-stream.* acc. pl.
**merestrēamas** 17/44.

**mergen** → morgen.

**gemet.** neut. *measure, measurement,*
*boundary.* acc. sg. **gemet, gemett** 6/14;
10/17. *meter.* acc. sg. 9/14. *ability.*

**metan.** st. 5. *measure.* subj. sg. **mete** 10/
44. infl. inf. **tō metanne** 10/16, 43, 45.

**(ge)mētan.** wk. 1. *meet, encounter, find.*
pl. **gemētað.** past 3sg. **mētte** 8/13. past
pl. **gemētton, mētton** 2/19; 4/10. past
part. **gemētte** 3/105.

**mete.** masc. *food.* nom. sg. 10/7.

**metelēas.** adj. *without food.*

**metelīst.** fem. *lack of food.* dat. sg.
**metelīeste.** nom. pl. **metelīste** 15/15.

**gemetgung.** fem. *temperance, moderation.*

**gemetlīce.** adv. *moderately.* 9/28.

**Metod.** masc. *God, Creator.* nom. sg.
12/175; 18/154. gen. sg. **Meotodes,**
**Meotudes, Metodes, Metudes** 9/12;
11/23; 13/2; 18/261. dat. sg. **Metode**
12/147.

**metsung.** fem. *provision.* acc. sg. **met-**
**sunge** 5/1.

**mēþe.** adj. *weary, dejected.* masc. nom. sg.
14/65. masc. nom. pl. 14/69.

meþelstede. masc. *meeting-place*. dat. sg. 12/199.

micclum → miclum.

micel. A. adj. *much, large, big, great, vast*. masc. nom. sg. micel, mycel 7/25; 14/130. fem. nom. sg. micel, mycel 3/88; 7/8, 9, 66; 8/11, etc. (8x). neut. nom. sg. mycel, micel 2/12; 8/60, 61, 62; 10/28. masc. acc. sg. micelne, mycelne 3/7; 10/31 (2x). fem. acc. sg. micle, mycele 6/31; 16/51. neut. acc. sg. mycel, miccle 3/57; 6/28, 33, 37. fem. gen. sg. micelre 9/27. neut. gen. sg. micles 10/32. masc. dat. sg. miclan, mycelum 7/8 (2x). fem. dat. sg. micelre, mycelre в/7; 2/24. neut. dat. sg. myclum 6/35. neut. inst. sg. mycle 14/34, 60, 123. masc. nom. pl. micle 8/38. fem. nom. pl. micle, micele 3/21; 7/24, 32. fem. acc. pl. micele 3/50. dat. pl. micelan, miclan, miclum 4/3; 7/7 (2x). wk. masc. nom. sg. micla. wk. neut. nom. sg. mycele. wk. masc. acc. sg. miclan c/10; 7/70. wk. fem. acc. sg. miclan. wk. masc. dat. sg. micclan, miclan c/9; 3/82. wk. fem. dat. sg. miclan 14/102. wk. neut. dat. sg. miclan 14/65. wk. dat. pl. micclum 3/30. masc. nom. sg. compar. māra 17/31. fem. nom. sg. compar. māre 10/58; 7/35. neut. nom. sg. compar. māre 12/313. fem. acc. sg. compar. māran 8/64; 18/92; 3/112. masc. acc. sg. compar. māran. neut. acc. sg. compar. māre D/3. masc. nom. sg. superl. mǣst 6/26; 7/25. neut. nom. sg. superl. mǣst 18/181. fem. acc. sg. superl. mǣste 12/175; 18/3. wk. masc. nom. sg. superl. mǣsta 18/292. wk. masc. acc. sg. superl. mǣstan 8/67; 10/18. wk. fem. acc. sg. superl. mǣstan 9/1. wk. masc. dat. sg. superl. mǣstan 8/69. wk. masc. nom. pl. superl. mǣstan 8/20.

B. indef. pron. *a great deal*. neut. nom. sg. 5/7. neut. acc. sg. micel, mycel c/4; 2/7; 5/2 (2x); 7/10, etc. (6x).

micellic. adj. *great, magnificent*. neut. gen. sg. micellices 10/22.

micle. adv. *much, almost* (superl. mǣst only). compar. mā 4/14; 7/21; 10/41, 69; 16/4. superl. mǣst 7/23 (2x); 8/26. miccle, micle 8/19, 64; 12/50.

miclum. adv. *greatly, very*. miclum, micclum, mycclum 2/20, 27; 3/97, 104; 4/5, etc. (9x).

mid. A. prep. (usually with dat., sometimes with acc.). *with, among*. в/5, 7; c/11, 12 (2x), etc. (154x).

B. adv. *with*. 2/23, 27; 8/24; 14/106.

mid þām þe. conj. *when, as soon as*. 3/37.

midd. adj. *middle*. fem. acc. sg. midde 9/32. masc. dat. sg. middum м/7. masc. acc. sg. midne 1/8. fem. dat. sg. midre 14/2. dat. pl. middum. wk. fem. dat. sg. middan 18/68.

middangeard. masc. *world*. nom. sg. 13/62. acc. sg. middangeard, middaneard F/1; G/9; 9/13, 43; 11/2, etc. (7x). gen. sg. middangeardes, middaneardes 6/6; 9/24; 10/16, 17, 44. dat. sg. middanearde.

middanwintre → midewinter.

Middelseaxe. masc. *Middle Saxons*. acc. pl. Middelsexe 5/2.

middeweard. adv. *in the middle*. 8/34.

midewinter. masc. u-stem. *midwinter, Christmas*. dat. sg. middanwintre 6/20.

Mierce. wk. masc. *the Mercians*. gen. pl. Miercna 4/17. dat. pl. Myrcon 12/217.

miht. fem. athematic. *might*. nom. sg. 2/26. acc. sg. meahte, mihte 2/4; 9/12. dat. sg. mihte 14/102. acc. pl. mihta 5/19.

miht- → magan.

mihtig. adj. *mighty*. masc. nom. sg. 11/23; 14/151; 18/92, 198. masc. nom. pl. mihtige.

mīl. fem. *mile*. dat. sg. mīle 8/67 (2x). gen. pl. mīla F/4; 8/34, 35, 47, 58. dat. pl. mīlum 8/68 (2x).

milde. adj. *mild, kind*. masc. nom. sg. 6/14; 12/175.

mildheort. adj. *merciful, compassionate*. masc. nom. pl. mildheorte.

**mildheortness.** fem. *mercy.* acc. sg.
**mildheortnisse** 6/42.

**mīlgemearc.** neut. *distance in miles.* gen.
sg. **mīlgemearces** κ/1362.

**milts.** fem. *compassion, mercy.* acc. sg.
**miltse** 18/349. gen. sg. **miltse** 13/2;
18/85, 92.

**gemiltsian.** wk. 2. *have mercy on.* imp. sg.
**gemiltsa.**

**mīn.** adj. *my, mine.* masc. nom. sg. 14/78,
95; 2/13; 3/86, 92, etc. (20x). fem. nom.
sg. 14/130; 1/8, 10; 3/27, 76, etc. (7x).
masc. dat. sg. **mīnum** 14/30; 18/94; 1/2;
3/28, 87, etc. (8x). neut. nom. sg. 3/83
(2x). masc. acc. sg. **mīnne** 2/13; 3/14,
26, 52; 12/248, etc. (8x). fem. acc. sg.
**mīne** 3/28; 12/216; 13/9. masc. gen. sg.
**mīnes** 3/27; 12/53; 15/9; 16/26; 17/10.
fem. gen. sg. **mīnre** 3/41; 16/2, 10, 40.
neut. dat. sg. **mīnum** 3/86 (2x); 10/11.
masc. nom. pl. **mīne** 3/1, 85; 9/37 (2x);
10/9. fem. nom. pl. **mīne** 3/76. neut.
nom. pl. **mīne.** masc. acc. pl. **mīne**
13/27; 16/38. fem. acc. pl. **mīne** 3/28.
gen. pl. **mīnra** 3/26; 16/5; 18/90. dat.
pl. **mīnum** 3/26, 27; 15/1.

**misbēodan.** st. 2. (with dat. object).
*mistreat.* inf. 7/12.

**misdǣd.** fem. *misdeed.* acc. pl. **misdǣda**
7/47, 54. gen. pl. **misdǣda** 7/56. dat.
pl. **misdǣdan, misdǣdum** 7/51, 62.

**mislic.** adj. *various, diverse.* fem. nom. pl.
**mislica** 10/24, 32. masc. acc. pl. **mislice.**
fem. acc. pl. **mistlice** 7/24, 49. neut.
acc. pl. **mistlice** 7/48. dat. pl. **mislicum**
10/25.

**mislīce.** adv. *variously.*

**mislimpan.** st. 3. *turn out badly.* subj. sg.
**mislimpe** 7/47.

**missenlic.** adj. *various, manifold, diverse.*
neut. gen. sg. **missenlices.** gen. pl.
**myssenlicra.**

**missenlīce.** adv. *variously, here and there.*
13/75.

**mistlice** → mislic.

**mīþan.** st. 1. *conceal, be concealed, refrain
from.* pres. part. **mīþendne** 16/20.

**mixen.** fem. *dung heap.* dat. sg. **mixene**
3/59.

**mōd.** neut. *heart, mind, spirit, courage.*
nom. sg. 2/9; 3/44; 10/1, 12, 13, etc.
(11x). acc. sg. 16/20. gen. sg. **mōdes**
3/82. dat. sg. **mōde** 10/19; 13/41, 111;
14/130; 18/57, etc. (9x). inst. sg. **mōde**
9/32, 43; 14/122. nom. pl. 9/2. acc. pl.
9/35; 10/13.

**mōdcearig.** adj. *sorrowful at heart.* masc.
nom. sg. 13/2.

**mōdcearu.** fem. *sorrow of mind.* acc.
sg. **mōdceare** 16/51. gen. sg. **mōdceare**
16/40.

**mōdgehygd.** fem. *mind's thought.* dat. pl.
**mōdgehygdum.**

**mōdgeþanc.** masc. *thought, conception,
purpose.* acc. sg. 9/12.

**mōdig.** adj. *spirited, brave, proud.* masc.
nom. sg. **mōdig, mōdi** 12/147; 14/41;
18/26. fem. gen. sg. **mōdigre** 18/334.
masc. nom. pl. **mōdge, mōdige** 12/80;
13/62. gen. pl. **mōdigra.** wk. masc. nom.
sg. **mōdiga** 18/52.

**mōdigan.** st. 2. *become proud.* inf. 6/41.

**mōdiglīce.** adv. *proudly, bravely.* 12/200.

**mōdignyss.** fem. *pride.* acc. sg. **mōdi-
gnysse** 3/45.

**mōdlufu.** wk. fem. *heart's love.* acc. sg.
**mōdlufun** 17/10.

**mōdor.** fem. *mother.* acc. sg. 7/32; 14/92.
gen. sg. 3/41.

**mōdorlīce.** adv. *in motherly fashion.*
2/10.

**mōdsefa.** wk. masc. *mind, spirit, soul.*
nom. sg. 13/59; 14/124. acc. sg. **mōdsefan** 13/10, 19.

**molde.** fem. *earth.* acc. sg. **moldan** 14/12,
82. gen. sg. **moldan** 18/343. dat. sg.
**moldan** 6/7.

**moldern.** neut. *earthen house, sepulchre.*
acc. sg. 14/65.

**mon** → man.

**gemon** → gemunan.

**mōna.** wk. masc. *moon.* dat. sg. **mōnan.**

**monade** → (ge)manian.

**Mōnandæg.** masc. *Monday.*

**mōnaþ.** masc. *month.* acc. sg. 8/64. gen. sg. **mōnðes** 18/324. dat. sg. **mōnðe** 8/42. acc. pl. 2/10.

**moncynn-** → mancynn.

**mondryhten.** masc. *lord of men.* nom. sg. 17/7. acc. sg. 13/41.

**monegum** → manig.

**gemong.** neut. *multitude, assembly.* acc. sg. **gemong, gemang** 18/193, 225, 303.

**monig-** → manig.

**monn-** → man.

**monnan** → manna.

**monncynnes** → mancynn.

**monnian.** wk. 2. *man.* past part. **monnad** 10/4.

**mōr.** masc. *moor.* nom. sg. 8/35. acc. sg. 8/37. gen. sg. **mōres** 8/36. dat. sg. **mōre** 8/35. nom. pl. **mōras** 8/32; 10/19. acc. pl. **mōras** 8/38. dat. pl. **mōrum** 8/32.

**morgen.** masc. *morning.* dat. sg. **morgenne, mergen, morgene** G/9; 4/9; 5/19; 9/15, 19.

**morgenceald.** adj. *morning-cold.*

**morgencollen.** wk. masc. (attested only here). *morning terror*(?). acc. sg. **morgencollan** 18/245.

**morgenswēg.** masc. *morning-sound.*

**morgentīd.** fem. *morning.* acc. sg. 18/236.

**morþdǣd.** fem. *murderous deed.* acc. pl. **morðdǣda** 7/48.

**morþor.** neut. *murder.* acc. sg. 16/20. gen. sg. **morðres** 18/90. gen. pl. **morðra** 18/181.

**morþorwyrhta.** wk. masc. *one who causes death.* nom. pl. **morþorwyrhtan** 7/56.

**mōst-** → mōtan.

**gemōt.** neut. *assembly,* (military) *encounter.* nom. sg. 12/301. acc. sg. 12/199. gen. sg. **gemōtes.**

**mōtan.** pret. pres. *may, can, must.* 1sg. **mōt** 14/142; 16/37. 2sg. **mōst** 12/30. 3sg. **mōt** 3/47; 10/62, 82. pl. **mōtan, mōte, mōton** F/7; 7/6, 7; 8/70. past sg. **mōste** 5/15. past 3sg. **mōste** 6/15; 12/272; 18/185. past pl. **mōston** 6/40;

12/83; 17/17. subj. sg. **mōte** 12/95, 177; 14/127; 18/89, 118. subj. pl. **mōtan, mōten, mōton** 10/81; 12/180; 17/33. subj. past sg. **mōste** 2/9; 6/32. subj. past pl. **mōston** 6/39; 12/87, 263.

**gemunan.** pret. pres. *think of, remember.* 1sg. **geman** 14/28. 3sg. **gemon** 13/34, 90; 16/51. past 3sg. **gemunde** 12/225. subj. pl. **gemunon** 12/212. subj. past sg. **gemunde** 17/14. subj. past pl. **gemundon** 12/196.

**mund.** fem. u-stem. *hand, protection.* dat. sg. **munde** 7/11. dat. pl. **mundum** 18/229.

**mundbyrd.** fem. *protection.* nom. sg. 14/130. acc. sg. 18/3.

**munt.** masc. *mountain.* dat. sg. **munte.** acc. pl. **muntas** 10/29. gen. pl. **munta** 10/29. dat. pl. **muntum** 10/25.

**munuc.** masc. *monk.* acc. pl. **munecas** 6/15. dat. pl. **munecum** 6/17.

**munuchād.** masc. *monastic orders.* acc. sg. 9/20.

**munuclic.** adj. *monastic.* fem. dat. sg. **munuclicere** 2/30.

**murnan.** st. 3. *be anxious, be fearful.* past pl. **murnon** 12/96. inf. 12/259; 18/154. pres. part. **murnende** 15/15.

**mūþ.** masc. *mouth.* dat. sg. **mūðe** 9/23.

**mycclum** → miclum.

**mycel-, mycl-** → micel.

**myltestre.** fem. *prostitute.* nom. pl. **myltestran** 7/56.

**gemynd.** fem. *memory, thought, mind.* acc. sg. 13/51. dat. sg. **gemynde** 9/14. dat. pl. **gemyndum** 17/31.

**gemyndgian.** wk. 2. *remember.* past 3sg. **gemyndgade** 9/22.

**gemyndig.** adj. *mindful, remembering.* masc. nom. sg. 13/6. fem. nom. sg. 18/74. masc. nom. pl. **gemyndig, gemyndige** 3/112; 10/11.

**mynecen.** fem. *nun.* dat. sg. **mynecene** 2/10. acc. pl. **mynecena** 2/10.

**mynster.** neut. *monastery.* nom. sg. 6/16. acc. sg. M/3; 6/15; 9/21. gen. sg.

mynstres в/1. dat. sg. **mynstre** 2/10, 11, 20; 5/19; 6/4, etc. (6x).

**mynsterhata.** wk. masc. *persecutor of monasteries.* nom. pl. **mynsterhatan** 7/56.

**mynsterlic.** adj. *monastic.* fem. dat. sg. **mynsterlicre** 2/9.

**myntan.** wk. 1. *intend, suppose.* past pl. **mynton** в/2; 18/253.

**Myrcon** → Mierce.

**myre.** wk. fem. *mare.* gen. sg. **myran** 8/61.

**myrhþa.** fem. *joy.* acc. pl. 7/70.

**myrran.** wk. 1. *hinder.* pl. **myrrað.**

**myssenlicra** → missenlic.

**nā.** adv. *no, not at all, never.* **nā, nō** а/4; D/3; к/1366; 3/45, 86, etc. (23x).

**nabbaþ** → habban.

**naca.** wk. masc. *ship.* acc. sg. **nacan** 17/41. gen. sg. **nacan.**

**nacod.** adj. *naked.* masc. nom. sg. 1/10, 11; 3/41 (2x). masc. nom. pl. **nacode** 1/7.

**nāge, nāh** → āgan.

**nāht. A.** indef. pron. *nothing.* neut. nom. sg. **nāuht** 10/44. neut. acc. sg. **nōht, nāht, nāuht** 9/4, 8 (2x); 10/42. masc. nom. pl. **nāhte** 3/85.

**B.** adv. *not at all.* 3/34.

**nāhte** → āgan.

**nāhwǽr.** adv. *nowhere, not at all.* **nāwer** 10/18, 27.

**nales.** adv. *not at all, emphatically not.* **nales, nalæs, nalles** 9/3; 13/32, 33; 15/15.

**nam, genam, nām-, genām-** → (ge)niman.

**nama.** wk. masc. *name.* nom. sg. 3/4, 42; 10/26, 29, 76, etc. (6x). acc. sg. **naman** 8/59; 10/23, 24, 26, 27, etc. (7x). dat. sg. **naman, noman** 7/60; 9/7; 14/113; 18/81. inst. sg. **naman** 10/28. nom. pl. **naman** 3/66. acc. pl. **naman.**

**namian.** wk. 2. *name, appoint.* subj. sg. **namige.**

**nān. A.** adj. *no.* masc. nom. sg. **nān, nōn** 3/14; 6/28; 8/40; 10/3, 5, etc. (7x). neut. nom. sg. 7/47. masc. acc. sg. **nǽnne, nānne** 10/3 (2x), 10, 44. neut. acc. sg.

3/43, 47; 5/15 (2x); 6/22, etc. (6x). dat. pl. **nǽnum** 10/50.

**B.** indef. pron. *none, no one.* masc. sg. 10/42. masc. nom. sg. 13/9; 18/257. masc. acc. sg. **nānne** 18/68, 233. neut. acc. sg. 10/8. masc. acc. pl. **nāne** 10/82.

**nāp, genāp** → (ge)nīpan.

**nāt** → (ge)witan.

**nāteshwōn.** adv. *not at all.* 1/4.

**nāthwā.** indef. pron. *something.* neut. acc. sg. **nāthwæt** Lb.

**nāthwelc.** indef. pron. *I don't know which, one or another.* masc. gen. sg. **nāthwylces.**

**naþelǽs.** adv. *nevertheless.* 5/4.

**nāþor.** conj. *neither.* 7/22.

**nāuht** → nāht.

**nāwer** → nāhwǽr.

**nǽdre.** wk. fem. *snake, serpent.* nom. sg. **nǽddre, nǽdre** 1/1 (2x), 4, 13. dat. sg. **nǽddran** 1/14. nom. pl. **nǽdran.**

**næfde** → habban.

**nǽfre.** adv. *never.* c/3; 3/45; 4/12; 6/28; 9/4, etc. (16x).

**næfþ** → habban.

**nǽgan.** wk. 1. *approach, attack.*

**nægl.** masc. *nail.* dat. pl. **næglum** 14/46.

**næglian.** wk. 2. *nail.* past part. **næglede** 17/35.

**nǽnig.** indef. pron. *none, no one, no.* masc. nom. sg. 4/8, 12; 8/63; 9/3; 10/77, etc. (6x). masc. acc. sg. **nǽnigne** 9/36. fem. acc. sg. **nǽnige** в/7. neut. acc. sg. 9/5. masc. dat. sg. **nǽnigum** 14/47. neut. inst. sg. **nǽnige** 10/67.

**nǽnne, nǽnum** → nān.

**nǽre, nǽron** → bēon.

**næs. A.** masc. *headland, ground.* acc. sg. 18/113. acc. pl. **næssas** к/1358. gen. pl. **næssa** к/1360.

**B.** adv. *not at all.*

**næs** → bēon.

**ne. A.** conj. *neither, nor.* а/1 (3x), 3, 4, etc. (49x).

**B.** adv. *not.* а/1 (2x), 4 (2x), 5, etc. (128x).

**ne ne.** conj. *nor.* A/3.

**nēah. A.** adj. *near,* in superlative *last, next.* fem. nom. sg. **nēah, nēh** 9/31; 12/103. neut. nom. sg. 9/33, 39. masc. nom. sg. compar. **nēar** 3/34. neut. dat. sg. superl. **nȳhstan** 7/62. wk. masc. nom. sg. superl. **nȳhst** 8/67. wk. masc. acc. sg. superl. **nēxtan** 6/4. wk. neut. dat. sg. superl. **nēxtan** 6/24. wk. masc. dat. sg. superl. **nēhstan** 18/73. **B.** adv. *near, almost.* A/3; 8/17; 10/18, 21, 27, etc. (8x). superl. **nȳhst** 8/69. compar. **nēar** 18/53. **C.** prep. *near.*

**geneahhe.** adv. *sufficiently, abundantly, often.* **geneahhe, genehe** 12/269; 13/56; 18/26.

**neaht-** → niht.

**(ge)nēalǣcan.** wk. 1. *approach.* 3sg. **nēalǣcð** 7/2. past 3sg. **nēalǣhte, nēalǣcte, genēalǣhte** 9/28; 18/34, 261. inf. **genēalǣcan, nēalēcan** 9/6.

**nearo.** adj. *narrow, limited.* masc. nom. sg. 10/30. masc. acc. pl. **nearowan** 10/67.

**nēat.** neut. *animal, cattle.* gen. pl. **nēata** 9/7.

**genēat.** masc. *retainer.* nom. sg. 12/310.

**nēawest.** fem. *neighbourhood.* dat. sg. **nēaweste** 9/29.

**nēh** → nēah.

**genehe** → geneahhe.

**nēhstan** → nēah.

**nell-** → willan.

**nemnan.** wk. 1. *name, call.* 3sg. **nemneð.** past 3sg. **nemnde** 9/7. inf. 18/81. past part. **nemned** 10/75.

**nemne. A.** prep. *except for.* 16/22. **B.** conj. *unless.*

**nemþe.** conj. *unless.* **nemþe, nymðe** 13/113; 18/52.

**nēod.** fem. *necessity, business, difficulty.* nom. sg. **nēod, nȳd** 7/60; 18/277. dat. sg. **nēode, nȳde** C/4; 2/18; 6/35; 17/41.

**nēode.** adv. *necessarily.*

**neorxnawang.** masc. *Paradise.* gen. sg. **neorxnawonges** 1/8. dat. sg. **neorxnawange** 1/3, 8, 10.

**nēosan.** wk. 1. (with gen. object). *seek, go to.* inf. 18/63.

**(ge)nēosian.** wk. 2. *seek, visit.* subj. past pl. **genēosodon** 3/65, 67.

**nēotan.** st. 2. *make use of* something (gen.). inf. 12/308.

**neoþan.** adv. *from beneath, below.* **neoðan, nēoðan** F/4.

**neoþeweard.** adj. *nethermost.* masc. acc. pl. **neoðewerde** 3/58.

**neowol.** adj. *prostrate, deep.* masc. acc. sg. **neowelne** 18/113.

**nered-, genered-, genereþ** → (ge)nerian.

**Nergend-** → Neriend.

**(ge)nerian.** wk. 1. *save, rescue, defend.* 3sg. **genereþ.** past 1sg. **nerede.** past 2sg. **neredest.** past 3sg. **generede** 4/15; 5/5. past pl. **neredon.**

**Neriend.** masc. nd-stem. *Saviour.* acc. sg. **nergend** 18/81. gen. sg. **nergendes** 18/73. dat. sg. **nergende** 18/45.

**generwed** → genyrwan.

**nese.** adv. *no.*

**nest.** neut. *provisions.* acc. sg. 18/128.

**nēten-** → nȳten.

**nēþan.** wk. 1. *dare, risk.* past 3sg. **nēðde** 18/277.

**nēxta.** wk. masc. *neighbour.* acc. pl. **nēxtan.**

**nēxtan** → nēah.

**nicor.** masc. *water-monster.* nom. pl. **nicras** F/5. gen. pl. **nicra** F/2, 3.

**nīetenum** → nȳten.

**nigon.** card. num. as noun. *nine.* E/1.

**niht.** fem. athematic. *night.* nom. sg. 18/34. acc. sg. **niht, neaht** 3/83; 8/42; 9/32. gen. sg. **neahte** 9/30. dat. sg. **nihte, neahte** 9/7; 14/2; 18/64. gen. pl. **nihta** K/1365. dat. pl. **nihtum** 8/52.

**nihtes.** adv. *by night.* A/2; 18/45.

**nihthelm.** masc. *cover of night.* acc. sg. 13/96.

**nihtscūa.** wk. masc. *night-shadow.* nom. sg. 13/104.

**nihtwæcce.** cs. *night-watch.* **nihtwæccan.**

**(ge)niman.** st. 4. *take, take from.* 3sg. **nimð** 8/69. pl. **nimað** 8/72. past 3sg. **genam, nam** 1/6; 3/64; 5/4; 6/3, 35, etc. (7x).

past pl. **genāmon, genāman, nāman**
2/20; 5/6, 7, 17; 14/30, etc. (6x). subj.
pl. **nimon** 6/43. subj. past sg. **genāme**
12/71. imp. sg. **nim, nym**. imp. pl.
**nimað** 3/91. inf. **niman** 12/252; 16/15.
infl. inf. **tō nimanne** 18/313. past part.
**genumen** 1/19; 8/69; 10/19 (2x). *seize,
capture*. past 3sg. **nam**. *accept*. inf.
**niman** 12/39.

**genip**. neut. *mist, darkness*. nom. pl.
**genipu** F/2. acc. pl. **genipu** K/1360.

**(ge)nīpan**. st. 1. *grow dark*. 3sg. **nīpeð**
13/104. past 3sg. **nāp, genāp** 13/96.

**nis** → bēon.

**nīþ**. masc. *strife, enmity, evil*. acc. sg. 6/40.
dat. sg. **nīðe** 18/53. gen. pl. **nīða** 18/34.
dat. pl. **nīðum** 18/287.

**niþer**. adv. *down, downwards*. **niðer,
nyþer** F/1, 5; K/1360; 5/18.

**nīþheard**. adj. *fierce in strife*. masc. nom.
sg. 18/277.

**nīþhycgende**. adj. *intending malice*. masc.
nom. pl. 18/233.

**nīþwundor**. neut. *evil wonder*. acc. sg.
K/1365.

**genīwad** → genīwian.

**nīwe**. adj. *new, recent*. masc. nom. sg.
10/29. fem. nom. pl. 2/23. dat. pl.
**nīwum** 2/24.

**nīwes**. adv. (from adj. *nīwe*). *recently*.
16/4.

**genīwian**. wk. 2. *renew, restore*. past part.
**genīwad, genīwod** 13/50, 55; 14/148;
18/98.

**nō** → nā.

**genōg**. adj. *enough, many, much*. masc.
nom. pl. **genōge** 14/33. masc. nom.
sg. **genōh** 8/63. neut. nom. sg. **genōh**
3/110. neut. acc. sg. **genōh** 17/35.

**genōh**. adv. *sufficiently, very*. 7/40.

**genōh** → genōg.

**nōht** → nāht.

**nold-** → willan.

**noman** → nama.

**nōn** → nān.

**Normandige**. neut. *Normandy*. nom. sg.
6/32. dat. sg. 6/4, 9, 25, 26.

**norþ**. adv. *north*. F/2; 8/3, 6, 59; 10/70.
superl. **norþmest** 8/1. compar. **norðor**
8/33.

**norþan**. adv. *from the north*. 8/8; 13/104.

**norþanweard**. adj. *northern part of*. masc.
acc. sg. **norðanweardne, norðeweardne**
F/1; 10/16. neut. acc. sg. **norðeweard**
8/36. neut. dat. sg. **norðeweardum,
norþweardum** 8/36, 2.

**norþdæl**. masc. *northern region*. dat. sg.
**norþdæle**.

**norþeweard**. adv. *in the north*. 8/35.

**norþeweard-** → norþanweard.

**Norþhymbre**. wk. masc. *the Northumbrians*.

**Norþmen**. masc. *Norwegians*. nom. pl.
8/37. acc. pl. 8/37, 38. gen. pl.
**Norðmanna, Norðmonna** 8/1, 30.

**norþryhte**. adv. *northwards*. 8/4, 5, 7.

**norþweardum** → norþanweard.

**Norþweg**. masc. *Norway*. nom. sg. 8/45.

**notian**. wk. 2. *make use of* something
(gen.). pl. **notigað** 10/18.

**nū**. **A**. adv. *now*. E/4; F/7; 2/1, 8 (2x), etc.
(57x).

　　**B**. conj. *now that, since*. D/1; 9/33;
10/23; 12/57, 222, etc. (7x).

**genumen** → (ge)niman.

**nȳd-** → nēod.

**nȳde**. adv. *necessarily*. 7/3, 8; 18/287.

**nȳdgyld**. neut. *forced payment*. nom. pl.
7/38.

**nȳdmāge**. wk. fem. *near kinswoman,
female cousin*. acc. sg. **nȳdmāgan** 7/40.

**nȳdþearf**. fem. *necessity*. nom. sg. 7/9.

**nȳhst-** → nēah.

**nylle** → willan.

**nym** → (ge)niman.

**nymþe** → nemþe.

**genyrwan**. wk. 1. *narrow, restrict*. past
part. **generwed, genyrwde** 7/15; 10/22.

**nysse, nyste, nyte** → (ge)witan.

**nȳten**. neut. *beast, animal*. nom. sg. **nēten**
9/22. nom. pl. **nȳtenu, nētenu** 1/1;
10/18. dat. pl. **nīetenum, nȳtenum**
1/14.

**nyþer** → niþer.

(ge)nyþerian. wk. 2. *bring low.* past part.
genyðerad 18/113.

of. prep. (with dat.). *from, of, out of.* c/7,
10; f/2; 1/1, 2, etc. (79x).

ofdūne. adv. *down.* 18/290.

ofer. prep. (with dat. or acc.). *over, beyond,
upon.* b/4; f/1; g/2; k/1363; 1/1, etc.
(39x). of time, *after.* 1/8; 5/14; 9/32.
*against.* 14/35. *concerning.* 17/49.

ōfer. masc. *bank, shore.* dat. sg. ōfre
k/1371; 12/28.

ofercuman. st. 4. *overcome, overtake.* inf.
18/235.

oferdrencan. wk. 1. *give too much to drink.*
past 3sg. oferdrencte 18/31.

oferfēran. wk. 1. *traverse.* inf. 8/35 (2x).

oferfrēosan. st. 2. *freeze.* past part.
oferfroren 8/75.

oferfyll. fem. *overeating.* acc. pl. oferfylla
7/64.

ofergān. anom. verb. *conquer.* past part.
5/2.

oferhelmian. wk. 2. *cover over.* 3sg.
oferhelmað k/1364.

oferhoga. wk. masc. *despiser* (with gen. of
what one despises). nom. pl. oferhogan
7/50.

oferlīce. adv. *excessively.* 7/62.

ofermōd. A. neut. *excessive pride.* dat. sg.
ofermōde 12/89.

　　B. adj. *proud.* wk. masc. nom. pl.
ofermōdan 10/68.

ofermōdlic. adj. *proud.* masc. dat. sg.
ofermōdlicum 10/50.

oferrǣdan. wk. 1. *read over.* subj. sg.
oferrǣde 3/109.

ofersēon. st. 5. *observe, see over.* past pl.
ofersēgon. inf. 8/46.

ofersittan. st. 5. *occupy.* past part.
oferseten, ofseten 10/18, 19.

oferstīgan. st. 1. *exceed.* 3sg. oferstīhð
3/2.

oferswīþan. wk. 1. *overpower.* past part.
oferswīðed.

oferwinnan. st. 3. *overcome.* past part.
oferwunnen 17/45; 18/319.

oferwrēon. st. 2. *cover over.* past part.
oferwrogen 6/7.

oferwunnen → oferwinnan.

(ge)offrian. wk. 2. *offer.* past 3sg. offrode
3/9, 93. past pl. offrodon. imp. pl.
geoffriað 3/91. inf. offrian.

offrung. fem. *offering, sacrifice.* nom. sg.
3/93.

ofgifan. st. 5. *give up, leave.* past pl.
ofgēafon 13/61.

ofhrēowan. st. 2. *cause pity for someone*
(gen.). 3sg. ofhrīewð.

oflongad. adj. (past part. of -*longian*).
*seized with longing.* fem. nom. sg. 16/29.

ofost. fem. *haste.* dat. sg. ofste 7/2.

ofostlīce. adv. *quickly.* ofostlīce, ofstlīce
12/143; 18/150, 169.

ōfre → ōfer.

ofscēotan. st. 2. *kill by shooting.* past 3sg.
ofscēat 12/77.

ofseten → ofersittan.

ofslēan. st. 6. *kill, slay.* 1sg. ofslēa. past
3sg. ofslōg 4/1, 17. past pl. ofslōgon
3/36, 38; 4/15. subj. past sg. ofslōge
8/21. past part. ofslǣgen, ofslǣgene,
ofslǣgenne, ofslegen 4/6, 9, 10, 14.

ofspring. masc. *offspring.* dat. sg.
ofspringe 1/15 (2x).

ofst- → ofost.

ofstingan. st. 3. *stab to death.* past 3sg.
ofstang 4/2.

ofstum. adv. *hastily.* 18/10, 35, 70.

oft. adv. *often.* h/3, 4 (2x); i/9; 2/7, etc.
(41x). compar. oftor 7/17; 14/128.
superl. oftost 7/50.

oftēon. st. 2. *deprive* someone (dat.) of
something (gen.), *withhold.* past 3sg.
oftēah.

oftorfian. wk. 2. *pelt to death.* past pl.
oftorfedon 5/17.

ofþryccan. wk. 1. *crush.* past 3sg. ofðrihte
3/39.

ofþyncan. wk. 1. *seem displeasing, be a
matter of regret.* past 3sg. ofðūhte.

olfend. masc. *camel.* acc. pl. olfendas
3/38. gen. pl. olfenda 3/7, 98, 99.

**oll.** neut. *scorn.* dat. sg. **olle** 7/52.

**ombeht.** masc. *officer, retainer.*

**on. A.** prep. (with dat. or acc.). *on, in, upon.* **on, a, an** A/1 (3x), 2, 5, etc. (405x). *to, towards, into, onto, at.* F/1, 7; H/4; M/13; 1/6, etc. (57x). *against.* 4/6. *at the time of, during, in the course of.* B/2; D/3; 2/30. *because of, from.* 4/7; 12/125, 129; 14/138. **B.** adv. *on, in.* 1/4; 10/18; 14/34, 98.

**on ān.** adv. *continuously, at once.* C/11, 12.

**ōn** → **ān.**

**onbærnan.** wk. 1. *kindle, inspire.* past part. **onbærnde, onbærned** 9/2, 27.

**onbryrdan.** wk. 1. *inspire.* past 3sg. **onbryrde** 18/95.

**onbūtan.** adv. *about.* 3/20.

**onbyrigan.** wk. 1. (with gen. or dat. object). *taste.* inf. 14/114.

**oncerran.** wk. 1. *divert.* inf. 10/73.

**oncnāwan.** st. 7. *recognize, perceive.* past pl. **oncnēowon** 1/7; 3/68. inf. 12/9. *disclose.* past pl. **oncnēowon.**

**oncweþan.** st. 5. *answer.* past 3sg. **oncwæð** 12/245.

**ond** → **and.**

**ondrædan.** st. 7. (frequently with refl. pron.). *be afraid, dread.* 1sg. **ondræde** 1/10. 3sg. **ondræt** 3/31. past 1sg. **ondrēd.** pres. part. **ondrædende** 3/5, 14.

**ondswarian.** wk. 2. *answer.* past 3sg. **andswarode, ondswarade, ondswarede** 9/8, 37; 10/1, 54. past pl. **ondswaredon, ondswarodon** 9/33, 36, 40.

**ondweardum** → andweard.

**ondweorc** → andweorc.

**onemn.** prep. *beside.* 12/184.

**ōnettan.** wk. 1. *hasten.* past 3sg. **ōnette** 18/162. past pl. 18/139.

**onfindan.** st. 3. *find out, discover.* past 3sg. **onfand, onfunde** 12/5. past pl. **onfundon** 4/7. subj. past pl. **onfunden** 4/4.

**onfōn.** st. 7. (with acc., gen. or dat. object). *receive, succeed to, take.* past 3sg. **onfēng** 9/3, 11, 15, 21; 12/110. past pl. **onfēngon** F/5. subj. past sg. **onfēnge** 9/20. past part. **onfongne** 9/19.

**onfund-** → onfindan.

**ongan** → onginnan.

**ongēan. A.** prep. (with dat. or acc.). *against, towards, opposite.* **ongēan, angēan** 1/15; 3/43, 49, 79; 5/15, etc. (9x). **B.** adv. *back, again.* 3/91, 94; 12/49, 137, 156. *opposite, in opposition.* 8/46; 10/53.

**ongeat, ongēaton** → ongietan.

**Ongelþēod.** fem. *English people, England.* dat. sg. **Ongelþēode** 9/3.

**ongietan.** st. 5. *understand, perceive.* 3sg. **ongit** 10/15. pl. **ongite** 10/30. past 3sg. **ongeat** 4/5. past pl. **ongēaton, āgēaton** 6/12; 12/84; 18/168, 238. inf. **ongetan, ongietan, ongitan, ongytan** 10/16, 20; 13/73; 14/18. past part. **ongieten** B/4.

**onginnan.** st. 3. *begin, endeavour, undertake.* past 3sg. **ongan, ongon** 9/11, 20; 10/12, 49, 52, etc. (17x). past pl. **ongunnon** 9/3; 12/86, 261; 14/65, 67, etc. (8x). subj. pl. **āginnan, onginnen** 7/57; 14/116. subj. past sg. **ongunne.** imp. sg. **ongin** 17/26.

**ongit-** → ongietan.

**ongyrwan.** wk. 1. *undress.* past 3sg. **ongyrede** 14/39.

**ongytan** → ongietan.

**onhætan.** wk. 1. *heat, inflame.* past part. **onhæted** 18/87.

**onhrēran.** wk. 1. *arouse.* past part. **onhrēred.**

**onhweorfan.** st. 3. *change.* past part. **onhworfen** 16/23.

**onhyldan.** wk. 1. *bend down, lower.* past 3sg. **onhylde** 9/42.

**oninnan.** prep. *within, in the middle of, in the midst of.* 18/312.

**onlænan.** wk. 1. *lend, grant.* 3sg. **onlænð** 10/72.

**onlēon.** st. 2. *lend* something (gen.) to someone (dat.), *give* something (gen.)

to someone (dat.). past 3sg. **onlēah** 18/124.

**onlēsed** → onlȳsan.

**onlīc.** adj. *similar.* neut. gen. sg. **anlīces, onlīces** 10/40, 42, 44.

**onlīcness.** fem. *likeness.* dat. sg. **onlīcnesse** F/3.

**onlȳsan.** wk. 1. *release, redeem.* past 3sg. **onlȳsde** 14/147. past part. **onlēsed** 10/61.

**onmiddan.** prep. (with dat.). *in the middle of.* 1/3, 8.

**onmunan.** pret. pres. *consider worthy of something* (gen.). subj. past pl. **onmunden** 4/14.

**onsǣge.** adj. *falling upon, attacking.* neut. nom. sg. 7/17.

**onsǣgedness.** fem. *offering, sacrifice.* acc. pl. **onsǣgednessa.**

**onscyte.** masc. *attack, calumny.* dat. pl. **onscytan** 7/23, 54.

**onsendan.** wk. 1. *send.* 3sg. **onsendeð** 13/104. past 3sg. **onsende** 17/7. subj. sg. **onsende** 11/11. past part. **onsended** 14/49.

**onsittan.** st. 5. *occupy, oppress, fear* (with refl.). 3sg. **onsit** 7/34. pl. **onsittað** 7/7. imp. sg. **onsite** 17/27.

**onslēpan.** wk. 1. *go to sleep, sleep.* past 3sg. **onslēpte** 9/7, 42.

**onstellan.** wk. 1. *institute, establish.* past 3sg. **onstealde** 9/12.

**onstyrian.** wk. 2. *move, budge, rouse, disturb.* inf. B/2, 4.

**onsundran.** adv. *singly, apart, privately.* 17/1.

**onswīfan.** st. 1. *turn, turn aside.* inf. 10/73.

**ontīgan.** wk. 1. *untie.* past part. **ontīged** 10/61.

**onufan.** prep. (with dat.). *upon.* 18/252.

**onwacan.** st. 6. *awake.* subj. past sg. **onwōce** 18/77.

**onwæcnan.** wk. 1. *awake.* 3sg. **onwæcneð** 13/45.

**onweg.** adv. *away.* **āweg, onweg** B/5; 5/6.

**onwendan.** wk. 1. *change, overturn.* 3sg. **onwendeð** 13/107.

**onwōce** → onwacan.

**onwrēon.** st. 1. *uncover, reveal.* imp. sg. **onwrēoh** 14/97.

**onwrīþan.** st. 1. *unwrap.* inf. 18/173.

**open.** adj. *open.* masc. nom. pl. **opene** 14/47. wk. masc. nom. sg. **opena.**

**geopenian.** wk. 2. *open.* past 3sg. **geopenode** 2/21, 22; 3/27. past part. **geopenode, geopenod** 1/5, 7; 2/16.

**openlīce.** adv. *openly, plainly.* B/4; 10/80.

**ōr.** neut. *beginning, origin.* acc. sg. 9/12.

**ōra.** wk. masc. *border, edge, shore.* dat. sg. **ōran** 17/22.

**orc.** masc. *cup.* nom. pl. **orcas** 18/18.

**ord.** masc. *point* of a spear, *vanguard.* nom. sg. 12/60, 69, 146, 157, 253. acc. sg. 12/47, 110. dat. sg. **orde** 12/124, 226, 273.

**ōretmæcg.** masc. *combatant.* acc. pl. **ōretmæcgas** 18/232.

**orf.** neut. *cattle.* dat. sg. **orfe** 3/93.

**orfcwealm.** masc. *murrain, pestilence of cattle.* nom. sg. 7/19.

**orfeorme.** adj. *destitute of, lacking.* masc. nom. pl. 18/271.

**orgellīce.** adv. *proudly, arrogantly.* 10/49.

**ormǣte. A.** adv. *immensely.* 3/7.
   **B.** adj. *great, immense.* wk. fem. dat. sg. **ormǣtan** 3/68.

**orsāwle.** adj. *without a soul, dead.* masc. nom. sg. 18/108.

**geortrūwian.** wk. 2. *despair.*

**orþung.** fem. *breath.* gen. sg. **orðunge.**

**oþ. A.** prep. (usually with acc., sometimes with dat.). *until, to, up to, as far as.* 2/24, 26; 3/58, 106; 5/11, etc. (13x).
   **B.** conj. *until.* 4/1, 5, 8; 5/14; 8/69, etc. (7x).

**oþ þæt.** conj. *until.* 1/19; 2/30; 4/2, 6, 15, etc. (12x).

**oþberan.** st. 4. *bear away.* past 3sg. **oþbær** 13/81.

**ōþer. A.** indef. pron. *other, another, one* (of two things). masc. nom. sg. 3/86;

6/10; 8/29 (2x), 75, etc. (6x). neut. nom. sg. 7/46. masc. acc. sg. **ōðerne** 6/28; 7/23 (2x), 32; 12/143. neut. acc. sg. 9/25; 10/21, 66; 12/207. neut. gen. sg. **ōðres** 10/42. masc. dat. sg. **ōðrum** 8/69; 12/70, 133. fem. dat. sg. **ōþerre** 15/4. neut. dat. sg. **ōðrum** 7/5, 23, 30, 40; 12/64. masc. nom. pl. **ōðer, ōðre** M/9 (2x); 3/103; 9/3. neut. nom. pl. 6/16. neut. acc. pl. **ōðre** E/3. dat. pl. **ōðrum, ōðran** 3/8, 97; 7/27; 10/33.

**B.** adj. and ord. num. *other, another, second.* masc. nom. sg. 3/37. masc. acc. sg. **ōðerne** 6/28; 8/67; 12/234. fem. acc. sg. **ōðre** 6/12; 8/12, 36, 46; 9/27, etc. (6x). neut. acc. sg. **oþer** M/5. masc. gen. sg. **ōðres** M/4. neut. gen. sg. **ōðres** 9/38. masc. dat. sg. **ōþrum** 7/21. neut. dat. sg. **ōðrum** 10/32 (2x). masc. inst. sg. **ōðre** 10/28; 18/109. masc. nom. pl. **ōðre** 8/19, 64. masc. acc. pl. **ōðre.** neut. acc. pl. **ōþra** H/4. dat. pl. **ōþrum** 8/7; 9/24; 10/46. neut. dat. pl. **ōðrum** 6/27. neut. nom. pl. **ōðre** 1/1.

**ōþr-** → ōþer.

**oþþe.** conj. *or.* G/9; M/4, 6; 3/49, 109, etc. (40x).

**oþþon.** conj. *or.* 7/25, 68.

**oþþringan.** st. 3. *force out.* past 1sg. **oðþrong** 18/185.

**ōwiht.** neut. *anything.* nom. sg. 16/23.

**oxa.** wk. masc. *ox.* gen. sg. **oxan.** acc. pl. **oxan.** gen. pl. **oxena** 3/7, 98, 99.

**Oxenafordscīr.** fem. *Oxfordshire.* acc. sg. **Oxenafordscīre** 5/2.

**Pante.** wk. fem. *the River Blackwater.* acc. sg. **Pantan** 12/68, 97.

**pāpa.** wk. masc. *pope.* dat. sg. **pāpan.**

**Paradīsus.** noun. *Paradise.* dat. sg. **paradīsum** 1/1, 2.

**Parþas.** masc. *Parthians.* dat. pl. **Parðum** 10/29.

**pearroc.** masc. *enclosure.* dat. sg. **pearroce** 10/24.

**Pentecosten.** masc. *Pentecost.* dat. sg. 6/20.

**pleagian** → plegian.

**plega.** wk. masc. *play, sport.* nom. sg. 8/65. dat. sg. **plegan** 8/66.

**plegian.** wk. 2. *play.* past 3sg. **plegode** 6/29.

**plegode** → pleagian.

**port.** masc. *port.* nom. sg. 8/41. dat. sg. **porte** 8/48.

**portic.** masc. *vestibule.* dat. sg. **porticum.**

**prass.** masc. *pomp* (?). dat. sg. **prasse** 12/68.

**prēost.** masc. *priest.* nom. pl. **prēostas.**

**price.** wk. fem. *point.* nom. sg. 10/16, 21.

**Pryfetesflōde.** wk. fem. *Privett, Hampshire.* dat. sg. **Pryfetesflōdan** 4/2.

**prȳte.** wk. fem. *pride.* dat. sg. **prȳtan** 7/54.

**pund.** neut. *pound.* gen. pl. **punda** 5/14; 6/35.

**racu.** fem. *story.* acc. sg. **race** 3/88, 109. gen. sg. **race** 3/2.

**gerād.** adj. *conditioned, circumstanced, wise.*

**rād** → rīdan.

**radost** → hraþe, raþe, rade.

**ramm.** masc. *ram.* acc. pl. **rammas** 3/91.

**ranc.** adj. *proud, haughty, arrogant.* masc. acc. sg. **rancne** 7/40.

**rand.** masc. *edge,* (metonymically) *shield.* acc. pl. **randas** 12/20.

**randwiggendra** → rondwiggend.

**raþe, raþost** → hraþe, raþe, rade.

**geræcan.** wk. 1. *reach, obtain.* past 3sg. **geræhte** 12/142. inf. 7/7. fig. *wound.* past 3sg. **geræhte** 12/158, 226. present. inf. J/91.

**ræd.** masc. *advice, sense, reason.* acc. sg. J/91. gen. sg. **rædes.** dat. sg. **ræde** 18/97. gen. pl. **ræda** 18/68.

**(ge)rædan.** wk. 1. *read, advise, decide.* 2sg. **gerædest** 12/36. pl. **rædað** 3/1. past 3sg. **rædde** 12/18. imp. sg. **ræd.** inf. **rædan** 3/109.

**rædend.** masc. (pres. part. of *rǣdan*). *ruler.*

**gerædu.** neut. (always pl.). *equipage for a horse.* dat. pl. **gerædum** 12/190.

ræfnan. wk. 1. *perform*. past pl. ræfndon 18/11.

geræhte → geræcan.

ræpling. masc. *prisoner*. nom. sg. 5/9.

ræran. wk. 1. *raise, offer up*. inf. 9/39. *promote, commit*. past 3sg. rærde 7/5.

ræsan. wk. 1. *rush*. past 3sg. ræsde 4/5.

ræswa. wk. masc. *leader, ruler*. dat. sg. ræswan 18/12. nom. pl. ræswan 18/178.

rēad. adj. *red*. neut. dat. sg. rēadum 18/338. wk. fem. nom. sg. G/8. wk. fem. dat. sg. Rēadan.

rēade. adv. *redly*. G/9.

Rēadingas. masc. *people of Reading, Reading*. dat. pl. Rēadingum.

rēaf. neut. *garment*. acc. sg. 3/70; 12/161. gen. sg. rēafes 2/27. acc. pl. 3/69.

rēafere. masc. *plunderer*. nom. pl. rēaferas 7/56.

rēafian. wk. 2. *plunder*. pl. rēafiað 7/46. past 3sg. rēafode.

rēaflāc. neut. *plundering*. nom. sg. 7/19. acc. sg. 7/63.

rēcan, reccan. wk. 1. *care, care for, care about* something (gen. or acc.). pl. reccað 10/46. past 3sg. rōhte 6/40. past pl. rōhton, rōhtan 2/28; 7/47; 12/260. subj. sg. recce. inf. reccan 10/2, 3. infl. inf. tō reccenne 10/9.

(ge)reccan. wk. 1. *tell, reckon, count as*. past pl. rehton 9/18. inf. reccan, gereccan, gerēccan 2/28; 3/2; 10/10.

reccan → rēcan, reccan.

gerēccan, reccaþ, recce → (ge)reccan.

gereccednyss. fem. *narrative*. gen. sg. gereccednysse 3/111.

reccelēst. fem. *negligence*. dat. sg. reccelēste 10/36.

reced. neut. *hall*.

recene → rycene.

gerēfa. wk. masc. *reeve, sheriff*. acc. sg. gerēfan 5/6. dat. sg. gerēfan.

regollic. adj. *regular*. dat. pl. regollecum 9/26.

regollīce. adv. *according to rule*. 7/21.

regul. masc. *rule*. dat. sg. regule 6/17.

rehton → (ge)reccan.

reliquias. masc. *relics*.

gerēnian. wk. 2. *arrange, ornament*. past part. gerēnod, gerēnode 12/161; 18/338.

rēnig. adj. *rainy*. neut. nom. sg. 15/10.

rēnscūr. masc. *rain shower*.

rēocan. st. 2. *reek, steam*. pres. part. rēocende 18/313.

gereord. neut. *meal, feast, banquet*. dat. sg. gereorde.

reordberend. masc. nd-stem. *speech-bearer, person*. nom. pl. 14/3. dat. pl. reordberendum 14/89.

reordian. wk. 2. *speak*.

gereordian. wk. 2. *feed, eat* (with refl.). past pl. gereordodon.

rēotig. adj. *wailing, lamenting*. fem. nom. sg. rēotugu 15/10.

rēowan → rōwan.

rēowlic. adj. *grievous, cruel*. neut. acc. sg. 6/1. neut. nom. sg. compar. rēowlicor 6/2, 1.

rest. fem. *rest, bed*. acc. sg. reste 9/32; 14/3; 18/54. dat. sg. reste 9/7; 18/68.

restan. wk. 1. *rest*. past 3sg. reste 14/64, 69; 18/44. past pl. reston 18/321.

gerestan. wk. 1. *rest, find rest* from something (gen.). inf. 9/30; 16/40.

rēþe. adj. *fierce, cruel, raging, severe*. masc. nom. sg. 6/22. masc. acc. pl. 18/348. masc. nom. sg. superl. rēðost.

rīce. A. adj. *powerful, noble, wealthy*. masc. nom. sg. 6/7, 13, 25, 40; 10/49. masc. acc. sg. rīcne 7/40; 14/44; 18/234. masc. gen. sg. rīces 10/26. masc. nom. pl. 6/21. masc. acc. pl. 6/3. gen. pl. rīcra 7/63; 14/131. wk. masc. nom. sg. rīca 10/75; 18/20, 44, 68. wk. masc. dat. sg. rīcan 18/11. masc. nom. sg. superl. ricost 12/36. wk. masc. nom. pl. superl. rīcostan 8/61.

B. neut. *rule, authority*. acc. sg. 6/27. gen. sg. rīces 10/2. *kingdom, empire*. nom. sg. 10/28; 13/106. acc. sg. 4/3; 14/119, 152. gen. sg. rīces 4/1, 11; 9/24.

dat. sg. 3/65; 4/17, 18; 5/18; 6/43, etc. (6x).

ricene → rycene.

rīcsian. wk. 2. *rule, prevail.* past 3sg. rīcsode, rīxade 4/16; 6/30, 32; 7/4. infl. inf. tō rīcsianne 10/4.

rīdan. st. 1. *ride.* 1sg. rīde ɪ/7. 3sg. rīdeð 8/70. past 3sg. rād 12/18, 239. past pl. ridon 4/10. inf. 12/291.

riht. adj. *correct, fitting.* neut. nom. sg. 12/190. masc. acc. sg. rihtne, ryhtne 14/89. fem. dat. sg. rihtre ᴀ/3. masc. inst. sg. rihte 18/97.

(ge)riht. neut. *straight line.* dat. sg. gerihte 18/202. *law, justice.* acc. sg. riht 3/49; 7/52. dat. sg. rihte 7/9, 50, 67. *obligation, dues* (always pl.). nom. pl. gerihta 7/13. acc. pl. gerihta 7/9, 10. *privilege.* gen. pl. gerihta 7/13.

(ge)rihtan. wk. 1. *guide, direct.* past part. geriht 14/131.

rihte. adv. *correctly, justly.* 7/23; 12/20.

rihtfæderencyn. neut. *direct paternal ancestry.* nom. sg. ryhtfæderencyn 4/16.

rihtlagu. fem. *law.* gen. pl. rihtlaga 7/50.

gerihtlǣcan. wk. 1. *correct, amend.*

rihtlīce. adv. *rightly, justly, correctly.* 3/90, 92; 7/69.

rihtryne. masc. *correct course.* dat. sg. 10/73.

rihtwīs. adj. *righteous.* masc. nom. sg. 3/5, 14. wk. masc. nom. pl. rihtwīsan ᴀ/6. wk. gen. pl. rihtwīsena, rihtwīsra ᴀ/5; 3/81.

rihtwīsness. fem. *righteousness.* nom. sg. rihtwīsnys. dat. sg. rihtwīsnysse 3/24.

rīnan. st. 1. *rain.* subj. pl. rīnon.

rinc. masc. *man, warrior.* gen. pl. rinca 10/73; 18/54, 338. dat. pl. rincum 12/18.

rīsan. st. 1. *rise.*

gerisene. neut. *what is fitting, dignity.* gen. pl. gerisena 7/13.

gerisenlic. adj. *suitable, becoming.* neut. acc. pl. gerisenlice 9/1.

gerisenlīce. adv. *fittingly.* 10/2.

rīxade → rīcsian.

rōd. fem. *cross, crucifix.* nom. sg. 14/44, 136. acc. sg. rōde 14/119. dat. sg. rōde c/5; 14/56, 131.

rōdetācn. neut. *sign of the cross.* dat. sg. rōdetācne 9/42.

rodor. masc. *sky, heaven.* acc. sg. 10/73. acc. pl. roderas 18/348. gen. pl. rodora 10/70. dat. pl. roderum 18/5.

rōf. adj. *brave, renowned.* masc. nom. pl. rōfe 18/20. gen. pl. rōfra 18/53.

rōht- → rēcan, reccan.

Rōmāne. masc. *Romans.* nom. pl. ʜ/2, 3. gen. pl. Rōmāna 10/28, 29, 75.

Rōmānisc. adj. *Roman.* masc. nom. sg. 10/31.

Rōmeburg. fem. athematic. *Rome.* nom. sg. ʜ/1.

Rōmweg. masc. *road to Rome.* dat. sg. rōmwege.

rondbēag. masc. *boss.* nom. sg. 10/16.

rondwiggend. masc. nd-stem. *warrior armed with a shield.* nom. pl. rondwiggende 18/11, 20. gen. pl. randwiggendra 18/188.

rōtlīce. adv. *cheerfully.* 9/33.

rōwan. st. 7. *row.* past pl. rēowan 2/19.

gersuma. wk. masc. *treasure.* acc. pl. gersuman 6/11.

rūm. A. masc. *space, opportunity.* nom. sg. 18/313. acc. sg. 10/70.
B. adj. *spacious.* masc. acc. pl. rūme 18/348.

rūme. adv. *abundantly.* 18/97.

rūmedlic. adj. *generous.* neut. gen. sg. rūmedlices 10/22.

rūmheort. adj. *generous-hearted.* fem. nom. sg. ᴊ/86.

rūn. fem. *mystery, secret.* acc. sg. rūne ᴊ/86. *counsel.* dat. sg. rūne 13/111; 18/54.

rycene. adv. *quickly, hastily.* ricene, recene, rycene ᴊ/91; 12/93; 13/112; 18/188.

ryhtfæderencyn → rihtfæderencyn.

ryhtne → riht.

ryhtnorþanwind. masc. *wind from due north.* gen. sg. ryhtnorþanwindes 8/9.

(ge)rȳman. wk. 1. *make room, clear a way, yield.* past 1sg. gerȳmde 14/89. past part. gerȳmed 12/93.

ryne. masc. *course, flow, stream.* dat. pl. rynum A/3.

rȳpan. wk. 1. *plunder, rob.* pl. rȳpaþ 7/46. past pl. rȳpton 5/4.

rȳpere. masc. *robber.* nom. pl. rȳperas 7/56. gen. pl. rȳpera 7/19.

Sabei. masc. *Sabaeans.* nom. pl. 3/36.

sācerd. masc. *priest.* nom. pl. sācerdas.

sacu. fem. *strife, dispute, battle.* nom. sg. H/4. dat. sg. sæcce 18/288.

sadol. masc. *saddle.*

saga → secgan.

sāh → sīgan.

salo. adj. *dark, sallow.* masc. nom. sg. I/11.

salowigpād. adj. *dark-coated.* wk. masc. nom. sg. salowigpāda 18/211.

sam. conj. (correlative conj.). in construction *sam . . . sam, whether . . . or.* 8/75 (2x).

same. adv. in phrase *swā same swā. just as.* some 10/37.

gesamnode → gesomnian.

samod → somod.

sanctus. adj. *saint.* masc. gen. sg. sancte, sanctes, sanctus 6/17, 4; 5/5, 19. masc. nom. sg. F/1; G/6. masc. acc. sg. F/7. fem. dat. sg. sancte 2/1.

sandcorn. neut. *grain of sand.* nom. pl. 3/76.

sang. masc. *song.* nom. sg. song 9/23. gen. sg. songes 9/14. dat. sg. sange 2/30. dat. pl. sangum 2/24.

sang → singan.

sangcræft. masc. *art of song.* acc. sg. songcræft 9/3.

sār. A. adj. *sore, painful, grievous, sorrowful.* fem. nom. pl. sāre 13/50. gen. pl. sārra 14/80; 18/182.

　　B. neut. *pain, illness, affliction.* nom. sg. 3/70.

sāre. adv. *painfully, grievously.* 7/14, 55; 14/59.

sārlīce. adv. *painfully, grievously.* 3/59; 10/36.

sārness. fem. *pain.* nom. sg. sārnys 3/72. dat. sg. sārnysse 1/16; 3/83. dat. pl. sārnyssum 3/81.

sāule → sāwol.

gesāw- → (ge)sēon.

sāwllēas. adj. *soulless, lifeless.* wk. masc. acc. sg. sāwllēasan 2/24.

sāwol. fem. *soul.* nom. sg. sāwl, sāwul 10/60, 61; 12/177; 14/120. acc. sg. sāwle, sāule 2/30; 3/56; 5/18; 7/25. gen. sg. sāwle 3/64; 10/59. dat. sg. sāule, sāwle 3/112; 6/42. nom. pl. sāwla F/3, 5, 6. acc. pl. sāwla F/7. dat. pl. sāwlum 3/103.

sǣ. fem. *sea.* nom. sg. 8/8, 9, 46, 47; 10/18, etc. (6x). acc. sg. 8/31, 59; 13/4. dat. sg. 3/76; 7/43 (2x); 8/3; 10/22, etc. (7x). dat. pl. sǣm.

sæcce → sacu.

sǣd-, gesǣd- → secgan.

sǣfæreld. neut. *sea-journey.* dat. sg. sǣfærelde.

sǣflōd. neut. *flood.*

(ge)sǣgan. wk. 1. *lay low, destroy.* past part. gesǣged 18/293.

sǣgd- → secgan.

sǣgrund. masc. *sea-floor.* dat. sg. sǣgrunde.

sǣl. masc. *time, occasion.* nom. sg. 14/80.

(ge)sǣlan. A. wk. 1. *fasten, bind, confine.* inf. sǣlan 13/21. past part. gesǣled 18/114.

　　B. wk. 1. *happen.* subj. sg. gesǣle 10/70.

sǣlida. wk. masc. *seafarer.* nom. sg. 12/45. acc. sg. sǣlidan 12/286.

gesǣlþ. fem. *prosperity.* dat. sg. gesǣlðe 3/112.

sǣman. masc. athematic. *seaman, viking.* nom. pl. sǣmen 7/43; 12/29. dat. pl. sǣmannum 12/38, 278.

sǣnaca. wk. masc. *sea-going ship.* acc. sg. sǣnacan 17/27.

gesǣne → gesȳne.

**sǣrinc.** masc. *seaman, Viking.* nom. sg. 12/134.

**sæt, sætt, gesæt, sæt-** → (ge)sittan.

**Sæternesdæg.** masc. *Saturday.* nom. sg. 5/15.

**scamian.** wk. 2. (impersonal, with acc. of person). *shame, be ashamed* of something (gen.). 3sg. **scamaδ** 7/51, 53, 54, 57 (2x). inf. 10/67.

**scamu.** fem. *shame, disgrace.* nom. sg. 7/35.

**scandlic.** adj. *shameful.* neut. nom. sg. 7/30. neut. nom. pl. **scandlīce** 7/38. dat. pl. **sceandlican** 7/23. wk. fem. acc. sg. **sceandlican** D/3.

**scǣron** → scyran.

**sceacan.** st. 6. *shake, depart.* inf. 18/291.

**scead.** neut. *shadow.* acc. pl. **sceadu** 11/15.

**sceadu.** fem. *shadow.* nom. sg. 14/54.

**gesceādwīsnes.** fem. *reason.* nom. sg. 10/2, 12. gen. sg. **gesceādwīsnesse** 10/47.

**sceaf** → scūfan.

**sceaft.** masc. *shaft.* nom. sg. 12/136.

**gesceaft.** fem. *creature, creation.* nom. sg. 14/12, 55, 82. acc. sg. **gesceafte** 7/31. *destiny.* nom. sg. 13/107.

**sceal, sceall, scealt** → sculan.

**scealc.** masc. *servant, retainer, warrior, man.* gen. sg. **scealces.** nom. pl. **scealcas** 12/181; 18/230. gen. pl. **scealca.**

**sceandlican** → scandlic.

**gesceap.** neut. *form, creature, creation.* dat. sg. **gesceape** 9/24.

**scēap.** neut. *sheep.* acc. pl. **scēp** 3/37, 45. gen. pl. **scēapa** 3/7, 26, 98, 99; 8/25.

**gesceapen** → (ge)scyppan.

**sceard.** neut. *shard, gap.* acc. pl. 10/19.

**scearp.** adj. *sharp,* fig. *cruel.* masc. acc. sg. **scearpne** 18/78. wk. masc. nom. sg. **scearpa** 6/3.

**scēat.** masc. *region.* acc. pl. **scēatas** 10/67. *surface.* acc. pl. **scēatas** 14/37. dat. pl. **scēatum** 14/8, 43. *garment.* dat. sg. **scēate** LA.

**scēat** → scēotan.

**sceatt.** masc. *coin, treasure.* dat. pl. **sceattum** 12/40, 56.

**scēaþ.** fem. *sheath.* dat. sg. **scēaðe, scēðe** 12/162; 18/79. dat. pl. **sceaðum** 18/230.

**sceaþa.** wk. masc. *criminal, enemy.* gen. pl. **sceaðena** 18/193.

**scēaþum** → scēaþ.

**scēawian.** wk. 2. *look, see, examine.* past 1sg. **scēawode** 14/137. past 3sg. **scēawode** 2/22.

**scēawung.** fem. *examination.* dat. sg. **scēawunge** 8/18.

**scel** → sculan.

**scelde** → scild.

**scendan.** wk. 1. *injure, disgrace.* pl. **scendaδ** 7/40, 44.

**sceocc-** → scucca.

**sceol-, sceold-** → sculan.

**sceōp, gesceōp** → (ge)scyppan.

**scēotan.** st. 2. *shoot, rush, contribute.* pl. **scēotaδ** 7/30. past 3sg. **scēat** 12/143, 270.

**scēotend.** masc. nd-stem. *archer, warrior.* nom. pl. 18/304.

**sceþþan.** wk. 1. (with dat. object). *injure.* pl. **sceþþaδ.** inf. 14/47.

**sciell.** fem. *shell.* acc. sg. **scielle.**

**scild.** masc. *shield.* dat. sg. **scelde, scylde** 10/16; 12/136. nom. pl. **scildas** 18/204. acc. pl. **scyldas** 12/98.

**scildburh** → scyldburh.

**Scildinga** → Scylding.

**scilling.** masc. *shilling.* nom. pl. **scillingas.** acc. pl. **scillingas** M/3, 5, 6, 7, 8, etc. (7x).

**scīma.** wk. masc. *brightness, splendour.* acc. sg. **scīman** 14/54.

**scīnan.** st. 1. *shine.* 3sg. **scīnδ, scȳnδ** G/9; 2/13. pl. **scīnaδ.** past pl. **scinon.** inf. 14/15.

**scip.** neut. *ship.* nom. sg. 8/52. dat. sg. **scipe, scype** 7/46; 12/40, 56. nom. pl. **scipu.** acc. pl. **scipu, scypa, scypu** 8/38 (2x). gen. pl. **scypa** 5/21. dat. pl. **scypan** 5/8.

**scipen.** fem. *stall, shed.* dat. sg. **scipene** 9/7.

**sciprāp.** masc. *ship's rope.* acc. pl. **sciprāpas** 8/29. dat. pl. **sciprāpum** 8/18, 27.

**scīr. A.** adj. *shining, resplendent.* masc. acc. sg. **scīrne** 14/54. neut. acc. sg. 12/98. masc. acc. pl. **scīre** 18/193. **B.** fem. *district.* nom. sg. 8/39.

**Scīringesheal.** masc. *Skiringssal* (an area in Vestfold, formerly with a market town). acc. sg. 8/41, 46. dat. sg. **Scīringesheale** 8/45, 48, 49.

**scīrmǣled.** adj. *brightly adorned.* neut. acc. pl. 18/230.

**Sciþþeas.** masc. *Scythians* (inhabiting much of eastern Europe and Russia in ancient times). nom. pl. 10/29.

**scold-** → sculan.

**Scōneg.** proper noun. *Skåne* (province in southern Sweden). nom. sg. 8/53.

**scopgereord.** neut. *poetic language.* dat. sg. **scopgereorde** 9/1.

**scort.** adj. *short.* masc. nom. sg. 10/45. wk. masc. dat. sg. **scortan** 10/46. wk. fem. dat. sg. **scortan** 3/112.

**Scotland.** neut. *Scotland.* acc. sg. 6/31.

**gescrīd** → (ge)scrȳdan.

**scrīfan.** st. 1. *care* about something (gen. or prepositional phrase). pl. **scrīfað, scrīfeð** 7/30; 10/70.

**scrift.** masc. *penance, confessor.* dat. sg. **scrifte.**

**scrīn.** neut. *shrine, reliquary.*

**(ge)scrȳdan.** wk. 1. *clothe.* inf. **scrȳdan** 5/21. past part. **gescrīd** 6/7.

**scucca.** wk. masc. *demon, devil.* nom. sg. **scucca, sceocca** 3/11, 13, 19, 51, 54, etc. (6x). gen. sg. **sceoccan** 3/34. dat. sg. **sceoccan, scuccan** 3/33, 56.

**scūfan.** st. 2. *shove, push.* past 3sg. **scēaf** 12/136.

**sculan.** pret. pres. *be obliged, must, have to, ought to, should.* 1sg. **sceal** 3/41; 9/10; 16/25; 17/3. 2sg. **scealt.** 3sg. **sceal, sceall, scel** ɪ/81, 83; 3/3, 54; 7/3, etc.

(22x). pl. **sceolon, sculon, sceole, sceolan** c/10, 11, 12; ɪ/82; 3/62, etc. (14x). past 1sg. **sceolde** 13/8, 19; 14/43. past 3sg. **sceolde, scolde** 2/14; 5/21; 6/37; 7/5, 21, etc. (15x). past pl. **sceoldon, scoldan, sceoldan** 7/12, 22, 63; 9/6, 29, etc. (9x). subj. sg. **scule, scyle** 16/42. subj. past sg. **sceolde** 6/41. subj. past pl. **sceoldon, sceolden, scolden** 9/39; 10/48; 12/291, 307. *will, shall.* 2sg. **scealt** 17/9. 3sg. **sceal** 7/7, 8; 8/65; 12/252; 14/119. subj. sg. **scyle** 10/32. subj. pl. **scylan, scylen** 7/6; 10/24.

**scūr.** masc. *shower, storm,* fig. *battle.* acc. pl. **scūras** 18/221. dat. pl. **scūrum** 18/79.

**scylan** → sculan.

**scyldan.** wk. 1. *shield, defend.* past 3sg. **scylde** 10/53.

**gescyldan.** wk. 1. *shield, protect.* subj. sg. **gescylde.**

**scyld-** → scild.

**scyldburh.** fem. athematic. *shield-fortification, shield-wall.* acc. sg. **scildburh, scyldburh** 12/242; 18/304.

**scyldig.** adj. *guilty, liable.* masc. nom. sg. ᴍ/1.

**Scylding.** masc. *descendant of Scyld, Dane.* gen. pl. **Scildinga, Scyldinga.**

**scyl-** → sculan.

**gescyndan.** wk. 1. *drive away.* past part. **gescynd** 3/82.

**scȳne.** adj. *beautiful.* fem. acc. sg. 18/316.

**scynscaþa.** wk. masc. *demonic foe.*

**scȳnþ** → scīnan.

**scyp-** → scip.

**(ge)scyppan.** st. 6. *make.* past 3sg. **gesceōp, sceōp** c/1; 9/13; 18/347. past part. **gesceapen** 2/25.

**Scyppend.** masc. nd-stem. *Creator.* nom. sg. 9/13; 13/85. gen. sg. **scyppendes** 9/11, 44; 18/78. dat. sg. **scyppende** 3/113.

**scyran.** st. 4. *cut.* past pl. **scǣron** 18/304.

**scyrting.** fem. *summary.* acc. sg. **scyrtinge** 3/109.

scytta. wk. masc. *archer*. gen. pl. scyttena.

se. pron. 1. demonst. *the, that*. masc. nom. sg. A/1; B/4, 6, 7; K/1362, etc. (109x). fem. nom. sg. sēo, sīo G/3, 8; 1/1 (2x), 4, etc. (36x). neut. nom. sg. þæt, tæt A/3; F/4; K/1361, 1372; 1/2, etc. (52x). masc. acc. sg. þone, þæne B/5 (2x); C/10; G/4; K/1367, etc. (67x). fem. acc. sg. ðā D/3; 1/14; 2/20 (2x), 21, etc. (48x). neut. acc. sg. ðæt, þat 1/3, 13; 2/14, 19, 22, etc. (68x). masc. gen. sg. þæs 2/5; 3/34 (2x), 64, 103, etc. (28x). fem. gen. sg. ðǣre 1/18; 3/2, 16, 111; 7/13, etc. (9x). neut. gen. sg. þæs B/1, 2; C/11; D/1; F/6, etc. (36x). masc. dat. sg. þām, þǣm, ðān A/1; B/4, 5; C/9; F/2, etc. (56x). fem. dat. sg. þǣre B/3, 5; 1/14, 17; 2/1, etc. (37x). neut. dat. sg. þām, ðǣm, ðān A/3; C/8; D/2; F/1, 3, etc. (83x). masc. inst. sg. þȳ 18/12. neut. inst. sg. þȳ, þon, þē 4/14, 17, 18; 7/21; 8/66, etc. (18x). nom. pl. þā A/4, 5 (2x), 6 (2x), etc. (65x). acc. pl. ðā D/1; E/3 (2x); 2/11, 18, etc. (55x). gen. pl. þāra, þǣra A/5; F/3; 1/2; 2/7; 3/2, etc. (18x). dat. pl. þām, þǣm D/2, 3; F/3, 5; 3/30, etc. (32x). *that one, he, it*. masc. nom. sg. D/3; 3/47; 4/8; 6/3; 7/62, etc. (13x). fem. nom. sg. sēo 8/46. masc. acc. sg. þone. masc. dat. sg. ðām 3/12, 20; 16/52. nom. pl. þā 6/17; 8/54. *this, the aforementioned*. masc. nom. sg. 3/5, 8; 4/3 (2x), 16, etc. (8x). fem. nom. sg. sēo 2/18. neut. nom. sg. þæt 8/57. masc. gen. sg. þæs 4/3. 2. rel. *who, which, that which, that*. masc. nom. sg. 2/29; 4/3, 15; 6/9; 8/69, etc. (12x). neut. nom. sg. þæt A/3 (2x); I/6; 6/2, 30, etc. (15x). masc. acc. sg. þone B/2, 4; 8/41. fem. acc. sg. ðā. neut. acc. sg. þæt 2/4; 6/35; 7/1, 53 (2x), etc. (12x). masc. dat. sg. þām 2/31; 6/11. neut. dat. sg. þǣm 9/29, 45. nom. pl. ðā 8/24, 55; 12/81, 184. acc. pl. þā 9/22. gen. pl. þāra 9/7, 11.

se þe. rel. pron. *that, which, that which, who, he who, whoever*. masc. nom. sg. 2/26; 3/47, 97, 113; 5/9, etc. (22x). fem.

nom. sg. sēo ðe 2/17; 14/121. masc. acc. sg. ðone þe 10/45; 13/27. masc. gen. sg. ðæs þe 10/18. neut. gen. sg. þæs þe 2/10; 3/26; 7/58; 8/72; 10/7. masc. dat. sg. þām þe 13/31, 56, 114. fem. dat. sg. ðǣre ðe 1/19. nom. pl. þā þe F/5, 6; 2/27; 3/83, 104, etc. (11x). acc. pl. þā þe 9/14. gen. pl. þāra þe, ðǣra ðe 3/79; 14/86. dat. pl. þām þe, þǣm þe 10/57; 14/149, 154.

geseah → (ge)sēon.

seald-, geseald- → (ge)sellan.

sealm. masc. *psalm*. acc. pl. sealmas 2/21.

sealobrūn. adj. *deep brown*.

sealt. adj. *salt*. masc. acc. pl. sealte 17/5.

searacræftas → searocræft.

sēarian. wk. 2. *become sere, wither*. pl. sēariað A/3.

searocræft. masc. *art, artifice, wile*. acc. pl. searacræftas 7/48.

searoþoncol. adj. *shrewd, wise*. fem. nom. sg. 18/145. gen. pl. searoþoncelra 18/330.

searowrenc. masc. *trick*. acc. pl. syruwrencas 5/5.

sēaþ. masc. *pit*. dat. sg. sēaþe 14/75.

Seaxe. wk. masc. *Saxons* (i.e. the continental Saxons). dat. pl. Seaxum 8/48.

(ge)sēcan. wk. 1. *seek*. 3sg. sēceð 13/114; 18/96. past 1sg. sōhte, gesōhte 13/25; 17/6. past 3sg. gesōhte, sōhte 8/23; 12/287; 18/14. past pl. sōhton 12/193; 14/133. subj. sg. sēce K/1369. inf. sēcan, gesēcan C/10; 12/222; 14/104, 119, 127, etc. (7x). infl. inf. tō sēcenne 2/18. pres. part. sēcende 3/20.

Seccandūn. fem. *Seckington, Warwickshire*. dat. sg. Seccandūne 4/17.

secg. masc. *man*. nom. sg. 12/159. nom. pl. secgas 18/201. acc. pl. secgas 12/298. gen. pl. secga 13/53. dat. pl. secgum 14/59; 17/34.

secgan. wk. 3. *say, tell*. 1sg. secge D/1, 3; G/2, 3, 4, etc. (12x). 3sg. segeð, segð 3/97; 12/45. pl. secgað D/3; 2/29, 28, 30; 3/88. past 3sg. sǣde, sægde, gesǣde

1/11; 2/7, 27; 3/29, 37, etc. (19x). past
pl. **sǣdon, sǣgdon** 3/88; 8/16; 9/18.
subj. sg. **secge** 14/96. imp. sg. **saga, sege**
G/2, 3, 4, 5, 6, etc. (10x). inf. 3/3, 88,
110; 9/16, 45, etc. (11x). infl. inf. **tō**
**secganne** 10/11. past part. **gesǣd**.
**sefa.** wk. masc. *mind, spirit*. acc. sg. **sefan**
13/57.
**sege** → secgan.
**segen.** masc. *banner, standard*.
**gesegen** → (ge)sēon.
**segeþ** → secgan.
**segl.** masc. *sail*. dat. sg. **segle** 8/52.
**(ge)seglian.** wk. 2. *sail*. past 3sg. **seglode**
8/49. subj. past sg. **seglode** 8/48. inf.
**seglian, geseglian** 8/42, 43.
**(ge)segnian.** wk. 2. *sign, cross*. past 3sg.
**gesegnode** 9/42. pres. part. **segniende**
9/44.
**segþ** → secgan.
**seht.** fem. *friendship*. acc. sg. **sehte** 6/40.
**geselda.** wk. masc. *hall-companion*. nom.
sg. I/3. acc. pl. **geseldan** 13/53.
**seldcyme.** masc. *seldom coming*. nom. pl.
**seldcymas** 15/14.
**seldhwænne.** adv. *seldom*. **seldhwænne,**
**seldhwonne** 2/11; 10/35.
**seledrēam.** masc. *hall-joy, hall-revelry*.
nom. pl. **seledrēamas** 13/93.
**seledrēorig.** adj. *hall-sorrowful, sorrowful*
*at separation from the hall*. masc. nom.
sg. 13/25.
**selesecg.** masc. *man of the hall, retainer*.
acc. pl. **selesecgas** 13/34.
**sēlesta** → gōd.
**seleþ** → (ge)sellan.
**self.** pron. **1.** indef. (usually adding emphasis to a pron. or noun). *self, himself,*
*herself, itself, myself, yourself*. masc. nom.
sg. **sylf, self, sylfa** H/4; I/11; 2/8; 3/47,
111, etc. (11x). fem. nom. sg. **sylf** 2/16;
17/14. masc. acc. sg. **sylfne** 6/41; 7/53,
66. fem. acc. sg. **sylfe** 14/92. masc. gen.
sg. **seolfes** 9/45. fem. gen. sg. **sylfre**
16/2. dat. sg. **sylfum** 11/5. masc. dat.
sg. **sylfum, selfum** C/12; 3/22, 33, 97;

9/17, etc. (6x). fem. dat. sg. **sylfre**
18/335. neut. dat. sg. **selfum** 10/63.
masc. nom. pl. **sylf, seolfan** 8/54; 9/23.
gen. pl. **sylfra, selfra** 10/68; 12/38;
18/285. **2.** refl. *self, himself, herself,*
*myself*. masc. nom. sg. **sylf, sylfa** 3/86.
masc. acc. sg. **sylfne, selfne, seolfne**
7/40, 59; 9/44; 11/26. fem. acc. sg. **sylfe**
2/11. fem. dat. sg. **sylfre** 2/25. masc.
nom. pl. **selfe** 7/64. dat. pl. **sylfum**
7/60.
**(ge)sellan.** wk. 1. *give, sell, yield* (of crops).
3sg. **seleð, selð, sylð** A/3; K/1370; 3/54.
pl. **syllað** 7/31. past 3sg. **sealde, gesealde**
1/6, 12; 7/29, 32 (2x), etc. (7x). past pl.
**sealdon, gesealdon** 12/184. subj. sg.
**geselle** M/5, 6, 9, 11. subj. pl. **syllon**
12/61. imp. pl. **sille**. inf. **syllan** 5/15;
12/38, 46. past part. **gesealde** 7/14.
**sēlost** → gōd.
**selþ** → (ge)sellan.
**(ge)sēman.** wk. 1. *reconcile*. inf. **gesēman**
12/60.
**sencan.** wk. 1. *submerge*.
**(ge)sendan.** wk. 1. *send*. 3sg. **sendeð**. past
3sg. **sende** 2/18; 5/1; 12/134. past pl.
**sendon** 12/29; 18/224. subj. sg. **sende**
18/190. imp. sg. **gesend**. inf. **sendan**
11/26; 12/30; 13/56. past part. **sended**
B/5; 11/2.
**gesēne** → gesȳne.
**sengan.** wk. 1. *singe*.
**sēo þe** → se þe.
**sēo** → se.
**sēoc.** adj. *sick*. fem. acc. sg. **sēoce** 15/14.
**seofian.** wk. 2. *sigh*. past pl. **seofedun**.
**seofon.** **A.** card. num. as adj. *seven*. acc.
pl. 3/7. masc. acc. pl. H/1; 3/91 (2x).
neut. acc. pl. 6/7. dat. pl. **seofon, syfan**
3/9; 8/52.
    **B.** noun. *seven*. E/1 (2x). nom. pl.
**seofan, syfan** 3/6; 8/19. acc. pl. 3/98,
100.
**seofonfeald.** adj. *sevenfold*. neut. acc. pl.
**seofonfealde** 3/9.
**geseoh** → (ge)sēon.

**sēoles** → seolh.

**seolf-** → self.

**seolfor.** neut. *silver*. gen. sg. **seolfres** 6/35. dat. sg. **seolfre** 14/77.

**seolh.** masc. *seal*. gen. sg. **sēoles, sīoles** 8/27, 29.

**(ge)sēon.** st. 5. *see, look*. 1sg. **gesēo** 3/86. 2sg. **gesihst, gesīhst** 3/55. 3sg. **gesihð** 3/16; 13/46. past 1sg. **geseah** 14/14, 21, 33, 36, 51. past 3sg. **geseah** F/1, 3; 1/6; 3/17, 106, etc. (8x). past pl. **gesāwon, gesāwe** 12/84, 203. subj. past sg. **gesāwe** 14/4. imp. sg. **geseoh**. inf. **gesēon, sēon** K/1365; 5/10; 10/18; 18/136. pres. part. **gesēonde** F/1. past part. **gesegen, gesewen, gesewene** 3/76; 9/17, 45; 11/22.

**sēoþan.** st. 2. *boil*.

**geset.** neut. *seat, habitation*. nom. pl. **gesetu** 13/93.

**geseted** → (ge)settan.

**geseten** → (ge)sittan.

**geseteness.** fem. *institution, law*. nom. pl. **gesetenessa** 10/32.

**setl.** masc. *seat, throne, see*. dat. sg. **setle** A/1.

**(ge)settan.** wk. 1. *set, put, place*. past 1sg. **gesette**. past 3sg. **gesette, sette** 6/15, 26, 30; 9/7. past pl. **setton, gesetton** 14/67. inf. **settan** 17/4. past part. **geset, geseted** 3/29; 14/141. with prep. *of, depose*. past 3sg. **sette** 6/24. *establish, institute*. 1sg. **sette** 1/15. past 3sg. **sette** 6/37, 39. past part. **geset, geseted** 9/5. *compose*. past 3sg. **gesette** 2/8, 27; 9/44.

**gesewen-** → (ge)sēon.

**sī** → bēon.

**sibb.** fem. *peace*. dat. sg. **sibbe** H/4.

**gesibb.** adj. *related*. masc. nom. sg. **gesib** 7/21. masc. dat. sg. **gesibban** 7/21. masc. nom. pl. **gesibbe** 3/65.

**sibleger.** neut. *incest*. acc. pl. **siblegeru** 7/48.

**sīd.** adj. *broad*. fem. acc. sg. **sīde** 18/337.

**sīde. A.** wk. fem. *side*. dat. sg. **sīdan** 14/49. nom. pl. **sīdan** 3/26.

**B.** adv. *amply, widely*. 7/51; 14/81.

**sidu.** masc. u-stem. *manners, morality*. dat. pl. **sidum** 10/24.

**sīe, sīen** → bēon.

**gesīene** → gesȳne.

**sīgan.** st. 1. *descend, issue*. past 3sg. **sāh** 2/15.

**sigebēam.** masc. *tree of victory*. nom. sg. 14/13. acc. sg. 14/127.

**sigedryhten.** masc. *lord of victory*. dat. sg. **sigedryhtne** 11/25.

**sigefolc.** neut. *victorious people*. dat. sg. **sigefolce** 18/152.

**sigelēas.** adj. *without victory*. masc. nom. pl. **sigelēase** 7/39.

**sigerōf.** adj. *renowned in victory*. masc. nom. pl. **sigerōfe** 18/177.

**sigeþēod.** fem. *victorious people*. dat. sg. **sigeþēode** 17/20.

**sigeþūf.** masc. *victory-banner*. acc. pl. **sigeþūfas** 18/201.

**sigewong.** masc. *field of victory*. dat. sg. **sigewonge** 18/294.

**(ge)siglan.** wk. 1. *sail*. past 3sg. **siglde** 8/8, 10. inf. **gesiglan, siglan** 8/7, 8, 10, 12.

**sigor.** masc. *victory*. acc. sg. 18/89. gen. sg. **sigores** 18/124. dat. sg. **sigore** 18/298. gen. pl. **sigora** 14/67.

**sigorfæst.** adj. *secure in victory*. masc. nom. sg. 14/150.

**sigorlēan.** neut. *reward of victory*. acc. sg. 18/344.

**gesihst** → (ge)sēon.

**gesihþ.** fem. *sight*. acc. sg. **gesyhðe** 14/96. gen. sg. **gesihðe** 3/17. dat. sg. **gesihðe, gesyhðe** 1/6, 8; 3/11, 15, 35, etc. (11x).

**gesihþ** → (ge)sēon.

**sille** → (ge)sellan.

**Sillende.** neut. *district in the Jutland Peninsula*. nom. sg. 8/46, 49.

**simle** → symble.

**sīn.** adj. *his, her, its, their*. fem. dat. sg. **sīnre** 18/132. neut. dat. sg. **sīnum** 18/99. masc. acc. pl. **sīne** 18/29.

**sinc.** neut. *treasure*. acc. sg. 12/59; 17/34. gen. sg. **sinces** 13/25; 18/30, 339. dat. sg. **since** 14/23.

**sincgyfa.** wk. masc. *treasure-giver, lord.* acc. sg. **sincgyfan** 12/278.

**sinchroden.** adj. *adorned with treasure.* fem. nom. sg. 17/14.

**sincþegu.** fem. *receiving of treasure.* acc. sg. **sincþege** 13/34.

**sind, sindon** → bēon.

**singal.** adj. *everlasting.* fem. nom. sg. 14/141.

**singallīce.** adv. *constantly.* 7/45; 10/13.

**singan.** st. 3. *sing.* past 3sg. **sang, song** 9/14, 24; 12/284; 18/211. past pl. **sungon** 2/21. imp. sg. **sing** 9/7, 10. inf. 9/4, 6, 8 (2x), 9, etc. (9x). pres. part. **singende** 10/64.

**sinneahtes.** adv. *in perpetual night.* 11/14.

**sinsorg.** fem. *everlasting sorrow, huge sorrow.* gen. pl. **sinsorgna** 16/45.

**sint** → bēon.

**sīo** → se.

**sīoles** → seolh.

**(ge)sittan.** st. 5. *sit,* in past part. *situated.* 3sg. **siteð, sitt** A/1; 16/47. past 1sg. **sæt** 15/10. past 3sg. **sæt, gesæt, sætt** B/4; G/2; 3/59; 13/111. past pl. **sǣton** 3/69; 11/14; 18/141. subj. past sg. **sǣte** G/2; 18/252. inf. **sittan** 16/37; 18/15. past part. **geseten** 3/4.

**sīþ. A.** masc. *journey, undertaking.* acc. sg. 18/145. gen. sg. **sīþes** 17/24. fig. *plight.* acc. sg. 16/2. *time* i.e. occasion. dat. sg. **sīðe** 18/73. inst. sg. **sīðe** 18/109.
    **B.** adv. *late.* 18/275.

**gesīþ.** masc. *companion, retainer.* nom. pl. **gesīðas** 18/201. dat. pl. **gesīþum** 17/34.

**sīþfæt.** neut. (often with neut. ending in pl.). *journey.* dat. sg. **sīðfate** 14/150; 18/335.

**sīþian.** wk. 2. *travel, journey.* subj. sg. **sīðie** 12/251. inf. 12/177; 14/68.

**gesīþmægen.** neut. *band of retainers.* acc. sg. J/88.

**siþþan. A.** adv. *afterwards.* **syððan, siððan** c/5, 7, 11, 12; 2/10, etc. (21x).
    **B.** conj. *after, since.* **siððan, syððan** 2/12, 16; 3/45; 8/13; 10/53, etc. (13x).

**sīþum.** adv. (dat. pl. of *sið*). *times.* **sīðon** E/1.

**six** → syx.

**slāpaþ** → slǣpan.

**slǣp.** masc. *sleep.* nom. sg. 13/39. dat. sg. **slǣpe** 2/22; 9/14; 18/247.

**slǣpan.** st. 7. *sleep.* pl. **slāpað** 3/83. pres. part. **slǣpende** 9/14.

**slǣwþ.** fem. *sloth, laziness.* dat. sg. **slǣwðe** 10/36.

**(ge)slēan.** st. 6. *strike, kill, pitch* (a tent). past 3sg. **slōh** 3/58; 5/18; 12/163, 285; 18/103, etc. (6x). past pl. **slōgon** 5/4; 18/231. subj. past sg. **slōge** 6/37; 12/117. inf. **slēan** 2/20; 6/28. past part. **geslegene** 18/31.

**slegefǣge.** adj. *doomed to death.* masc. acc. pl. 18/247.

**geslegene** → (ge)slēan.

**slīþen.** adj. *cruel.* fem. nom. sg. 13/30.

**slōg, slōh** → (ge)slēan.

**smæl.** adj. *narrow.* neut. nom. sg. 8/30. neut. nom. sg. compar. **smælre** 8/33. neut. nom. sg. superl. **smalost** 8/35.

**smēagan.** wk. 2. *ponder, meditate.* past 3sg. **smēade** 7/5. subj. sg. **smēage** 7/59. inf. 10/16. infl. inf. **tō smēagenne** 3/88. pres. part. **smēagende** A/2.

**smolt.** adj. *peaceful, gentle.* neut. acc. pl. 9/35.

**smylte.** adj. *mild, peaceable, calm, cheerful.* fem. dat. sg. **smyltre** 9/43. masc. inst. sg. 9/43.

**snāw.** masc. *snow.* acc. sg. 13/48.

**snell.** adj. *quick, bold.* masc. nom. pl. **snelle** 12/29. gen. pl. **snelra** 18/199.

**snīwan.** wk. 1. *snow.* past 3sg. **snīwde.**

**Snotengahām.** masc. *Nottingham.*

**snotor.** adj. *wise.* masc. nom. sg. **snottor** 13/111. wk. masc. nom. sg. **snotera.** wk. fem. nom. sg. **snotere** 18/125. wk. fem. acc. sg. **snoteran** 18/55.

**snotorness.** fem. *wisdom.* nom. sg. **snoternys.** acc. sg. **snotornesse.**

**snūde.** adv. *quickly.* 18/55, 125, 199.

**gesoden.** adj. *boiled.*

**sōfte.** adv. *softly, easily.* 12/59.

**sōht-, gesōht-** → (ge)sēcan.

**some** → same.

**gesomnian.** wk. 2. *assemble, collect, unite, gather.* inf. 9/16. past part. **gesamnode, gesomnad** 8/68; 15/18.

**gesomnung.** fem. *assembly, company.* dat. sg. **gesomnunge** 9/21.

**somod.** adv. *simultaneously, together, also.* **somod, samod** 3/37, 67; 8/59; 11/22; 13/39, etc. (9x).

**sōna.** adv. *soon, immediately.* в/6; 2/15, 19, 27; 6/29, etc. (9x).

**song-** → singan.

**songcræft** → sangcræft.

**sorg.** fem. *sorrow, pain.* nom. sg. 13/30, 39, 50. acc. sg. **sorge.** gen. pl. **sorga** 14/80; 18/182. dat. pl. **sorgum** 14/20, 59; 18/88.

**sorhlēoþ.** neut. *sorrowful song, dirge.* acc. sg. 14/67.

**sōþ.** **A.** adj. *true.* neut. nom. sg. 7/1, 13, 65. masc. acc. sg. **sōðne** 18/89, 344. wk. masc. gen. sg. **sōþan** 11/7. wk. masc. dat. sg. **sōðan.**
   **B.** neut. *truth.* gen. sg. **sōþes** 7/63; 8/16. dat. sg. **sōþe** 13/11.

**sōþfæst.** adj. *true, righteous, truthful.* wk. masc. nom. sg. **sōðfæsta** 11/3.

**sōþlīce.** adv. *truly.* 1/5; 2/26; 3/9, 86, 92, etc. (7x).

**spanan.** st. 7. *urge.* past 3sg. **spēon** 2/9.

**sparian.** wk. 2. *spare.* past 3sg. **sparode** 6/24. past pl. **sparedon** 18/233.

**spǣcan, specaþ** → (ge)sprecan.

**spēd.** fem. (sometimes pl. with sg. sense). *wealth.* nom. pl. **spēda** 8/22. acc. pl. **spēda** 8/64, 72.

**spēdan.** wk. 1. *be prosperous.* pl. **spēdaþ** 12/34.

**spēdig.** adj. *successful, prosperous.* masc. nom. sg. 8/22; 14/151.

**spell.** neut. *story, narrative, homily.* acc. sg. **spell, spel** 9/18; 10/64; 12/50. gen. sg. **spelles** 9/21. gen. pl. **spella** 8/16. dat. pl. **spellum** 9/24.

**spēon** → spanan.

**spēow, gespēow** → (ge)spōwan.

**spere.** neut. *spear.* acc. sg. 12/137. acc. pl. **speru** 12/108.

**spillan.** wk. 1. *destroy, kill.* inf. 12/34.

**(ge)spōwan.** st. 7. (impersonal). *succeed.* past 3sg. **spēow, gespēow** 18/175, 274.

**sprang** → springan.

**sprǣc.** fem. *speech, statement, saying.* nom. sg. 10/25. acc. sg. **sprǣce** 3/77. dat. sg. **sprǣce** 10/24. gen. pl. **sprǣca** 10/25. *conversation.* acc. sg. **sprǣce** 3/89.

**(ge)sprecan.** st. 5. *speak, converse.* 3sg. **spriceð** 13/70. pl. **sprecað, specað** 3/49; 6/13; 10/75. past 2sg. **sprǣce** 3/61. past 3sg. **spræc, gespræc** 3/43, 49, 90; 12/211, 274, etc. (7x). past pl. **sprǣcon, spǣcan, gesprǣcon, gesprǣconn** 3/90, 92; 7/4; 8/17; 10/24, etc. (10x). inf. **sprecan** 9/28; 10/12; 14/27. infl. inf. **tō specenne** 7/30. pres. part. **sprecende** G/6; 9/9, 32, 33. past part. **gesprecen** 10/12.

**sprengan.** wk. 1. *make spring.* past 3sg. **sprengde** 12/137.

**spriceþ** → (ge)sprecan.

**springan.** st. 3. *spring.* past 3sg. **sprang** 12/137.

**spyrian.** wk. 2. *track, enquire, strive to attain.* inf. 10/15.

**spyrte.** wk. fem. *basket.* acc. pl. **spyrtan.**

**stafum** → stæf.

**gestāh** → (ge)stīgan.

**stalian.** wk. 2. *steal.* subj. sg. **stalie** м/11, 12.

**stalu.** fem. *theft, stealing.* nom. sg. 7/19. acc. pl. **stala** 7/48.

**stān.** masc. *stone.* nom. sg. в/2, 7; 2/25. acc. sg. в/5; ʀ/1; 2/18. dat. sg. **stāne** в/4; ʀ/2 (2x); 14/66.

**(ge)standan.** st. 6. *stand, exist.* 3sg. **stondeð, standeð, stent, stynt** ʌ/1; ĸ/1362; 8/48, 59; 12/51, etc. (8x). pl. **stondaþ** 13/76. past 1sg. **stōd** 14/38. past 3sg. **stōd** 3/15, 19; 9/7; 12/25, 28, etc. (8x). past pl. **stōdon, gestōdon** 3/11, 51; 12/63, 72, 79, etc. (14x). imp.

sg. **stand**. inf. **standan, gestandan** 12/19, 171; 14/43, 62. pres. part. **standende** 2/19.

**stang** → stingan.

**stānhliþ**. neut. *stony cliff, stony slope*. dat. sg. **stānhliþe** 16/48. acc. pl. **stānhleoþu** 13/101.

**starian**. wk. 2. *gaze*. inf. 18/179.

**staþe** → stæþ.

**staþol**. masc. *foundation, place, condition*. dat. sg. **staðole** 14/71.

**stædefæste** → stedefæst.

**stæf**. masc. *staff, letter, writing*. dat. pl. **stafum** 9/1.

**stælhrān**. masc. *decoy reindeer*. nom. pl. **stælhrānas** 8/24.

**stæppan**. st. 6. *go, step*. past 3sg. **stōp** 12/8, 78, 131. past pl. **stōpon** 18/39, 69, 200, 212, 227.

**stǣr**. neut. *story, history*. acc. sg. 9/24. gen. sg. **stǣres** 9/21.

**stæþ**. neut. *shore*. dat. sg. **staðe, stæðe** 8/59; 12/25.

**steall**. masc. *place, position*.

**gesteall**. neut. *foundation*. nom. sg. **gesteal** 13/110.

**stēam**. masc. *steam, moisture, blood*. dat. sg. **stēame** 14/62.

**stēap**. adj. *deep, tall*. masc. nom. pl. **stēape** 18/17.

**stearc**. adj. *stern*. masc. nom. sg. 6/14, 22, 35.

**stede**. masc. *place, position, stability*. acc. sg. ʟᴀ; 12/19. dat. sg. 6/15; 10/66.

**stedefæst**. adj. *steadfast*. masc. nom. pl. **stædefæste, stedefæste** 12/127, 249.

**stedeheard**. adj. *of enduring hardness*. masc. acc. pl. **stedehearde** 18/223.

**stefn**. A. fem. *voice*. nom. sg. 14/71. acc. sg. **stemne** 1/8, 10, 17.
   B. masc. *root, branch, trunk*. dat. sg. **stefne** 14/30.

**stemnettan**. wk. 1. *stand firm* (?). past pl. **stemnetton** 12/122.

**stenc**. masc. *odour, fragrance*. dat. sg. **stence**.

**stent** → (ge)standan.

**stēopbearn**. neut. *orphan*. dat. sg. **stēopbearne** 3/23, 26.

**stēoran** → (ge)stȳran.

**stēorbord**. neut. *starboard*. acc. sg. 8/6, 13, 44, 45, 49, etc. (8x).

**steorfa**. wk. masc. *pestilence*. nom. sg. 7/19.

**stēorlēas**. adj. *without guidance*. masc. dat. sg. **stēorlēasum** 10/66.

**steorra**. wk. masc. *star*. nom. pl. **steorran**.

**stercedferhþ**. adj. *courageous, cruel-minded*. masc. nom. pl. **stercedferhðe** 18/55, 227.

**(ge)stīgan**. st. 1. *ascend, climb*. past 3sg. **gestāh** 14/40. inf. **gestīgan** 14/34.

**stihtan**. wk. 1. *direct, exhort*. past 3sg. **stihte** 12/127.

**stilness**. fem. *stillness, quiet, peace*. dat. sg. **stilnesse** 9/42.

**stincan**. st. 3. *stink*. 3sg. **stincð**.

**stingan**. st. 3. *sting, pierce*. past 3sg. **stang** 12/138.

**stīoran** → (ge)stȳran.

**stīþ**. adj. *stiff, firm*, of battle, *fierce*. masc. nom. sg. 6/40. neut. nom. sg. ʟᴀ; 12/301.

**stīþhicgende**. adj. *resolute*. masc. nom. pl. **stiðhirgende** 12/122.

**stīþlīce**. adv. *firmly, severely, sternly*. ᴄ/4; 12/25.

**stīþmōd**. adj. *resolute, courageous*. masc. nom. sg. 14/40. wk. masc. nom. sg. **stīðmōda** 18/25.

**stōd-, gestōd-, stond-** → (ge)standan.

**stōp-** → stæppan.

**storm**. masc. *storm*. dat. sg. **storme** 16/48. nom. pl. **stormas** 13/101.

**stōw**. fem. *place*. nom. sg. ᴋ/1372. acc. sg. **stōwe** 9/30. dat. sg. **stōwe**. nom. pl. **stōwa** 7/28. dat. pl. **stōwum** 8/3, 31, 35 (2x).

**strang**. adj. *strong*. masc. nom. sg. 14/40. masc. nom. pl. **strange** 3/20; 7/39; 14/30. masc. nom. sg. compar. **strengra** 6/13.

**stranglīce**. adv. *strongly, severely*. 6/2.

**strǣl.** masc. *arrow*, fig. *nail.* acc. pl. **strǣlas** 18/223. dat. pl. **strǣlum** 14/62.

**strēam.** masc. *stream, current*, in pl. *sea.* acc. sg. 12/68. acc. pl. **strēamas** 17/5; 18/348.

**strengra** → strang.

**strengþ.** fem. *strength.* nom. sg. **strencð, strengð** 3/73. acc. sg. **strengþe** 6/31.

**gestrēon.** neut. *property.* nom. pl. 8/71.

**strīc.** neut. *sedition* (?), *pestilence* (?). nom. sg. 7/19.

**stronglic.** adj. *strong, stable.* fem. sg. 10/66.

**strūdung.** fem. *robbery.* acc. pl. **strūdunga** 7/48.

**gestrȳnan.** wk. 1. *beget.* past 3sg. **gestrȳnde** 2/30.

**stund.** fem. *period of time, moment.* acc. sg. **stunde** 12/271.

**stunt.** adj. *foolish.* fem. nom. sg. 3/61.

**Stūrmere.** masc. *Sturmer, Essex.* acc. sg. 12/249.

**styccemǣlum.** adv. *here and there.* 8/3.

**stynt** → (ge)standan.

**stȳpel.** masc. *steeple.* nom. pl. **stȳplas.**

**(ge)stȳran.** wk. 1. *steer, guide, restrain from something* (gen.). past 3sg. **gestȳrde** 18/60. inf. **stēoran, stīoran** 10/2, 3.

**styrman.** wk. 1. *storm, rage.* past 3sg. **styrmde** 18/25. past pl. **styrmdon** 18/223.

**styrnmōd.** adj. *stern-minded.* masc. nom. pl. **styrnmōde** 18/227.

**gesūg-** → (ge)swīgian.

**sulh.** fem. athematic. *plough.* dat. sg. **sylh.** nom. pl. **syll** 3/36.

**sum.** indef. pron. *a certain, one, some.* masc. nom. sg. 2/14; 3/4, 36, 37; 8/21, etc. (12x). neut. nom. sg. 3/70, 112. masc. acc. sg. **sumne** F/1; 2/18; 13/81, 82, 83, etc. (6x). fem. acc. sg. **sume** 10/53; 12/271. neut. acc. sg. I/9; 2/12; 9/18; 12/285. masc. dat. sg. **sumum, suman** 2/29; 3/11, 51; 7/67; 8/4. fem. dat. sg. **sumre** 9/7; 10/29. masc. inst.

sg. **sume** B/1. masc. nom. pl. **sume** 2/14; 10/80. masc. acc. pl. **sume** 3/22; 7/28; 8/18; 13/80. fem. acc. pl. **sume** 7/69. neut. acc. pl. **sumu** 9/32. dat. pl. **sumum** 8/31, 35 (2x). *about.* masc. acc. pl. **sume** 2/10.

**sumor.** masc. u-stem. *summer.* nom. sg. 8/75. dat. sg. **sumera** 8/3.

**sumorlang.** adj. *summer-long* (i.e. extra long as in summer). masc. acc. sg. **sumorlangne** 16/37.

**gesund.** adj. *sound, whole, healthy.* masc. nom. pl. **gesunde** 4/13.

**sundor.** adv. *apart.* 13/111.

**sundoryrfe.** neut. *private inheritance* (presumably as opposed to the public treasury). gen. sg. **sundoryrfes** 18/339.

**sungon** → singan.

**Sunnanǣfen.** masc. *Sunday eve, Saturday evening.* acc. sg. 5/17.

**Sunnandæg.** masc. *Sunday.*

**sunne.** wk. fem. *sun.* nom. sg. G/8; 3/16. acc. sg. **sunnan** 10/73; 11/11. gen. sg. **sunnan** 3/16; 11/3. dat. sg. **sunnan** 3/15.

**sunu.** masc. u-stem. *son.* nom. sg. C/2; 4/18; 11/7, 23; 12/76, etc. (8x). nom. pl. **suna, suno** 3/8, 39. acc. pl. **suna** 2/30; 6/8. gen. pl. **suna** 3/6, 100. dat. pl. **sunum** 3/9, 10.

**sūsl.** neut. *torment.* dat. sg. **sūsle** 18/114.

**sutelaþ** → (ge)swutelian.

**sūþ.** adv. *south.* 10/65, 70; 17/27.

**sūþan.** adv. *from the south.* 5/16; 8/59.

**sūþerne.** adj. *southern.* masc. acc. sg. 12/134.

**sūþeweard.** adj. *southern part of.* masc. dat. sg. **sūðeweardum** 10/16. neut. dat. sg. **sūðeweardum** 8/36, 41.

**Sūþrīge.** proper noun. *Surrey.* acc. sg. 5/2.

**sūþryhte.** adv. *southwards.* 8/9, 10.

**Sūþsexe.** masc. *the South Saxons.* acc. pl. 5/2.

**swā. A.** adv. *so, thus, in such a way, such.* A/4; B/4, 7; F/1; G/9, etc. (87x). In construction *swā . . . swā . as.* 2/23; 5/7; 7/5, 23; 8/6, etc. (9x).

   **B.** conj. *as, as if, so that.* A/3; B/6; G/9; M/11; 1/5, etc. (42x).

**swā swā.** conj. *as, just as, as far as.* F/3; 2/1, 2, 5, 8, etc. (48x).

**swā þēah.** adv. *nevertheless.* B/3; 2/1, 29; 3/17, 95, etc. (7x).

**swā þēah hwæþere.** adv. *nevertheless.* 3/56.

**swān.** masc. *swineherd.* nom. sg. 4/2.

**swāse** → swǣs.

**swāt.** neut. *sweat, blood.* gen. sg. **swātes** 14/23. dat. sg. **swāte** 1/19.

**swātig.** adj. *sweaty, bloody.* masc. acc. sg. **swātigne** 18/337.

**swaþu.** fem. *path.* dat. sg. **swaðe** 18/321.

**swæc.** masc. *flavour, taste, fragrance.* gen. sg. **swæcces.**

**swǣr.** adj. *heavy, oppressive.* wk. neut. acc. sg. **swǣre** 10/68. fem. nom. pl. compar. **swǣrran** 3/76.

**swǣs.** adj. *intimate, beloved, gentle, sweet.* masc. acc. sg. **swǣsne** 13/50. fem. nom. pl. **swāse.**

**swǣsende.** neut. nd-stem. (often pl. with singular sense). *food, meal, banquet.* acc. pl. **swǣsendo** 18/9.

**swǣtan.** wk. 1. *sweat, bleed.* inf. 14/20.

**swealt** → sweltan.

**sweart.** adj. *black, dark.* wk. masc. dat. sg. **sweartan.** neut. nom. sg. F/4. fem. nom. pl. **swearte** F/3.

**swebban.** wk. 1. *put to sleep, kill.*

**swefn.** neut. *dream.* acc. sg. 9/7, 16. gen. pl. **swefna** 14/1.

**sweg.** masc. *sound.* nom. sg. **swēg.** acc. sg. **swēg.** dat. sg. **swege.**

**swēgan.** wk. 1. *sound, roar.* past 3sg. **swēgde** 3/39.

**swegl.** neut. *sky, heaven.* gen. sg. **swegles** 11/7; 18/80, 88, 124, 344, etc. (6x).

**geswel.** neut. *tumour.* nom. sg. 2/12, 13. acc. sg. **geswell** 2/14, 22.

**swelc.** pron. 1. indef. *such.* masc. nom. sg. **swilc** 6/17. masc. acc. sg. **swelcne** 10/21. fem. dat. sg. **swilcere, swylcere** 2/13, 18. neut. dat. sg. **swilcan** 7/65.

masc. nom. pl. **swelce** A/4. gen. pl. **swelcra** 10/79. dat. pl. **swylcum** 2/31. 2. rel. *such as,* in construction *swelc . . . swelc, such . . . as.* fem. nom. sg. H/4. masc. acc. sg. **swylcne** 18/65.

**swelce. A.** adv. *likewise, also.* **swylce, swelce, swilce** 1/1, 16; 2/23; 3/11; 6/22, etc. (15x). *as it were, approximately.* **swelce, swilce** F/4; 10/20, 21.

   **B.** conj. *as if, as, like.* **swilce, swelce, swylce** B/3, 7; H/2; 2/16, 22, etc. (14x).

**sweltan.** st. 3. *die, perish.* pl. **sweltað** 10/60. past 3sg. **swealt** 6/4. subj. pl. **swelton** 1/3. imp. 2sg. **swelt** 3/60. inf. 12/293.

**geswencan.** wk. 1. *trouble, torment, afflict, pursue.* past 1sg. **geswencte** 3/53. past pl. **geswencton** 3/75. past part. **geswenct, geswenced** K/1368; 2/13.

**swencean.** wk. 1. *oppress.* inf. 6/34.

**geswencedness.** fem. *affliction.* gen. sg. **geswencednysse** 3/83.

**sweng.** masc. *blow, stroke.* gen. sg. **swenges** 12/118.

**Swēoland.** neut. *Sweden.* nom. sg. 8/36.

**Swēon.** masc. *the Swedes.* dat. pl. 8/55.

**swēoran** → swūra.

**gesweorcan.** st. 3. *become dark.* subj. sg. **gesweorce** 13/59.

**sweorcendferhþ.** adj. *dark in mind, gloomy.* masc. nom. pl. **sweorcendferhðe** 18/269.

**sweord.** neut. *sword.* nom. sg. **sweord, swurd** 12/166. acc. sg. **swurd, sweord** 12/15, 237; 18/337. gen. sg. **sweordes.** dat. sg. **swurde, sweorde** 3/38; 12/118; 18/288. inst. sg. **sweorde** 18/89. acc. pl. **swurd, swyrd** 12/47; 18/230. gen. pl. **sweorda.** dat. pl. **swyrdum, sweordum** 18/194, 264, 294, 301, 321.

**sweostor.** fem. r-stem. *sister.* nom. sg. **sweostor, swuster, swustor** 2/17, 24. acc. sg. **swustor.** gen. sg. **swuster, swustor** 2/18; 12/115. acc. pl. **swustru** 3/8.

**gesweostor.** fem. (pl. only). *sisters.* nom. pl. **gesweostor, geswustru** 3/104. dat. pl. **geswustrum** 2/16.

**swēot.** neut. *army.* nom. sg. 18/298.

**sweotole** → swutole.

**sweotollīce.** adv. *clearly.* 18/136.

**sweotule** → swutole.

**swer.** masc. *column.* nom. pl. **sweras.**

**geswētan.** wk. 1. *sweeten.* past 3sg. **geswētte.**

**swēte.** adj. *sweet.* wk. neut. acc. sg. superl. **swēteste** 9/22.

**swētness.** fem. *sweetness.* acc. sg. **swētnisse** 9/1. dat. sg. **swētnesse** 9/24.

**swica.** wk. masc. *deceiver, traitor.*

**geswīcan.** st. 1. *depart, cease* (with gen. or dat. object), *betray.* past pl. **geswicon** 5/1. inf. F/6.

**swicdōm.** masc. *deception, betrayal.* acc. pl. **swicdōmas** 7/48.

**swician.** wk. 2. *wander, deceive.* past 3sg. **swicode** 7/23.

**swicol.** adj. *cunning, false, deceitful.* wk. masc. nom. sg. **swicola** 3/64.

**geswicon** → geswīcan.

**swift.** adj. *swift.* wk. masc. acc. sg. **swiftan** 10/73. wk. neut. nom. pl. **swiftan** 8/70. neut. acc. pl. superl. **swyftoste** 8/68. wk. neut. acc. sg. superl. **swiftoste** 8/69.

**(ge)swīgian.** wk. 2. *fall silent, be silent* about something (gen.). past 3sg. **gesūgode** 10/1, 12. past pl. **geswugedan** 7/63. inf. **gesūgian, swīgian** 10/54.

**swilc-** → swelc.

**swīma.** wk. masc. *swoon.* dat. sg. **swīman** 18/30, 106.

**swimman.** st. 3. *swim.* pl. **swimmað** 13/53.

**geswinc.** neut. *labour, hardship.* nom. sg. 10/21. acc. sg. 2/12; 6/33. dat. pl. **geswyncum** 1/17.

**swincan.** st. 3. *labour* (with *ymb,* for something). pl. **swincað** 10/30. subj. pl. **swincen** 10/69.

**swingan.** st. 3. *beat, flog.* past pl. **swungon.**

**swingel.** fem. *scourging, affliction.* dat. sg. **swingle** 3/106.

**swinsung.** fem. *sound, melody.* acc. sg. **swinsunge** 9/18.

**swīran** → swūra.

**swīþ.** adj. *strong,* in comparative *right* (hand, side). fem. acc. sg. compar. **swīðran** 14/20. fem. dat. sg. compar. **swīðran** 18/80.

**swīþe.** adv. *very, very much, greatly, strongly.* **swīðe, swȳðe** F/2; H/2, 3; 2/2, 7, etc. (70x). compar. **swīðor, swȳþor** 3/2, 57, 99; 7/51; 18/182. superl. **swīþost, swȳþost** 7/50, 52; 8/18, 72. *severely.* 4/8; 6/34; 12/115, 118.

**swīþlic.** adj. *very great, violent, intense.* masc. nom. sg. 3/39. neut. acc. sg. 18/240.

**swīþmōd.** adj. *stout-hearted, arrogant.* masc. nom. sg. 18/30, 339.

**geswiþrian.** wk. 2. *decrease, end.* past part. **geswiðrod** 18/266.

**swōt.** adj. *sweet.* dat. pl. **swōtum.**

**geswugedan** → (ge)swīgian.

**swungon** → swingan.

**swūra.** wk. masc. *neck.* nom. sg. 2/13. acc. sg. **swēoran, swūran** H/3; 2/13; 18/106. dat. sg. **swūran, swīran** 2/12 (2x); 10/68.

**swūrbēag.** masc. *torque, necklace.* dat. pl. **swūrbēagum** 2/13.

**swurd-** → sweord.

**swuster, swustor, swustru** → sweostor.

**geswustru, geswustrum** → gesweostor.

**(ge)swutelian.** wk. 2. *reveal, prove.* 3sg. **sutelað, geswutelað** 2/4; 5/19. pl. **geswuteliað** D/2; 2/1. past part. **geswutelod** 2/26; 18/285.

**swutol.** adj. *evident, manifest.* neut. nom. sg. 2/26; 7/17, 46. neut. nom. pl. **swutele** 2/5.

**swutole.** adv. *clearly, plainly, openly.* **sweotole, sweotule** 10/65; 13/11; 18/177.

**swyftoste** → swift.

**swylc-** → swelce.

**swȳn.** neut. *pig, swine.* gen. pl. **swȳna** 8/25.

**geswyncum** → geswinc.

**swyrd-** → sweord.

**swyrdgeswing.** neut. *striking with swords.* acc. sg. 18/240.

**swȳþe, swȳþor, swȳþost** → swīþe.

**sȳ** → bēon.

**syfan** → seofon.

**sȳfre.** adj. *pure, chaste.* masc. nom. pl. 3/20.

**gesyhþe** → gesihþ.

**sylf-** → self.

**sylh, syll** → sulh.

**syll-** → (ge)sellan.

**syllic.** adj. *rare, wonderful.* masc. nom. sg. 14/13. neut. acc. sg. compar. **syllicre** 14/4.

**sylþ** → (ge)sellan.

**symbel. A.** neut. *feast, banquet.* dat. sg. **symle, symble** 9/6; 14/141; 18/15. gen. pl. **symbla** 13/93.

   **B.** adj. *continuous.* neut. acc. sg. 18/44.

**symble.** adv. *always, continuously.* **symle, simle, symble** J/88; 3/27, 44, 82; 4/8, etc. (9x).

**syn.** fem. *sin.* acc. sg. **synne** 3/94. nom. pl. **synna** G/7; 3/76. acc. pl. **synna** 3/28; 7/47, 64. gen. pl. **synna** 6/42; 9/26. dat. pl. **synnum, synnan** 3/71; 7/3, 39, 62; 11/14, etc. (9x).

**syn, sȳn, synd-** → bēon.

**synderlīce** → syndriglīce.

**syndrig.** adj. *private.* neut. acc. pl. **syndrige** 2/11.

**syndriglīce.** adv. *specially.* **synderlīce, syndriglīce** 9/1; 10/26.

**gesȳne.** adj. *visible, evident.* neut. nom. sg. **gesȳne, gesǣne, gesēne** 7/17, 34, 46, 57. neut. nom. pl. **gesīene** 14/46.

**synfull.** adj. *sinful.* masc. nom. sg. **synful.** gen. pl. **synfulra** A/1. wk. masc. nom. pl. **synfullan** A/5; C/11.

**syngian.** wk. 2. *sin.* pl. **syngiað** 3/49. past 3sg. **syngode** 3/43, 48, 49, 63. subj. pl. 7/53.

**synlēaw.** fem. *injury of sin.* acc. pl. **synlēawa** 7/55.

**synscipe.** masc. *marriage, sexual intercourse.* gen. sg. **synscipes** 2/7. dat. sg. **synscipe, synscype** 2/5, 28.

**synt** → bēon.

**gesynto.** fem. (sometimes pl. with sg. sense). *health, salvation.* gen. pl. **gesynta** 18/90.

**syruwrencas** → searowrenc.

**(ge)syrwan.** wk. 1. *contrive, plot, arm.* 2sg. **syrwst** 1/15. past part. **gesyrwed** 12/159.

**syrwung.** fem. *treachery.* dat. pl. **syrwungum** 3/64.

**syþþan** → siþþan.

**sȳwian.** wk. 2. *sew.* past pl. **sȳwodon** 1/7.

**syx. A.** card. num. as noun. *six.* E/1. nom. pl. **six, syx** 3/99; 8/24. acc. pl. 8/23, 66. gen. pl. **syxa** 8/21.

   **B.** as adj. *six.* pl. 8/35. fem. dat. pl. 8/68.

**syxtig.** card. num. as noun. *sixty.* E/1. nom. pl. 8/29, 34. acc. pl. 8/21.

**syxtȳne.** card. num. as adj. *sixteen.* 2/18.

**tācen.** neut. *sign.*

**getācnian.** wk. 2. *betoken, represent, show, signal.* 3sg. **getācnað** G/3, 4. past 3sg. **getācnode.** past part. **getācnod** 18/197, 286.

**getācnung.** fem. *sign, meaning.* nom. sg. 3/111.

**taltrigan** → tealtrian.

**tam.** adj. *tame.* gen. pl. **tamra** 8/23.

**tǣcan.** wk. 1. *teach, instruct.* 3sg. **tǣcð.** past 3sg. **tǣhte** 12/18. subj. sg. **tǣce.** subj. pl. 7/54, 57.

**getæl.** neut. *number, account.* acc. sg. **getæl, getæll, getel** 3/103; 9/21.

**tǣlan.** wk. 1. *scold, slander, despise, deride.* 3sg. **tǣleð** 7/52. subj. sg. **tǣle** 3/109.

**tǣlwyrþlic.** adj. *blameworthy.* neut. nom. sg. superl. **tǣlwyrðlicosð** 10/32.

**tǣsan.** wk. 1. *wound.* past 3sg. **tǣsde** 12/270.

**tæt** → se.

**tēah** → tēon.

**teala** → tela.

**geteald** → (ge)tellan.

**tealt.** adj. *unsteady, wavering.* fem. nom. pl. **tealte** 7/20.

**tealtrian.** wk. 2. *stumble, become unstable.* inf. **taltrigan.**

**tēam.** masc. *family.* nom. sg. 2/2.

**tēdre.** adj. *weak, infirm.* masc. nom. sg. 10/15.

**getel** → getæl.

**tela.** interj. *good!.* **Teala** 9/41.

**geteld.** neut. *tent.* acc. sg. 2/20.

**tele** → (ge)tellan.

**(ge)tellan.** wk. 1. *count.* 2sg. **getelest** 10/39. subj. sg. **telle** 10/44. imp. sg. **tele** 10/40, 41. inf. **tellan.** *consider.* inf. **tellan** 6/41. past part. **geteald** 3/92. *tell, relate.* inf. **tellan** 6/3.

**Temes.** proper noun. *Thames.* dat. sg. **Temese** 5/2.

**tempel.** neut. *temple.* dat. sg. **temple.**

**tēn** → tȳn.

**tēon. A.** st. 2. *draw, pull.* past 3sg. **tēah** 18/99.

    **B.** wk. 1. *prepare, furnish, adorn, create.* past 3sg. **tēode** 9/13.

    **C.** st. 1. *accuse.*

**tēona.** wk. masc. *injury, insult, anger.* acc. sg. **tēonan** D/2. acc. pl. **tēonan** 6/33.

**tēoþa.** ord. num. *tenth.* masc. acc. sg. **tēoðan** 10/23.

**teran.** st. 4. *tear.* inf. 18/281.

**Terfinnas.** masc. *Ter Sami* (Lapps of the eastern Kola Peninsula). gen. pl. **Terfinna** 8/15.

**tēþ** → tōþ.

**tīd.** fem. *time, hour, season.* nom. sg. 12/104. acc. sg. **tīd, tīde** 9/5, 7, 28; 10/81; 18/306. gen. sg. **tīde** 9/41. dat. sg. **tīde** A/3; 9/7, 28, 39; 18/286. nom. pl. **tīda.** gen. pl. **tīda** 11/4. dat. pl. **tīdum** 7/61.

**tīenwintre.** adj. *ten-year-old.* masc. nom. sg. M/13.

**tigolgeweorc.** neut. *brick-making.* dat. sg. **tigolgeweorce.**

**tihte** → tyhtan.

**til.** adj. *good.* masc. nom. sg. 13/112.

**tilian.** wk. 2. *endeavour, procure, provide* something (gen.) for someone (dat.). pl. **tiliað, tioliað** 10/30, 69. inf. 18/208.

**getillan.** wk. 1. *touch.* imp. 2sg. **getill** 3/32.

**tīma.** wk. masc. *time.* acc. sg. **tīman** 5/11. dat. sg. **tīman** 3/108; 5/3; 6/33.

**getimbran.** wk. 1. *build.* past part. **getimbred** H/1.

**(ge)timbrian.** wk. 2. *build.* past pl. **timbredon** B/1. past part. **getymbrad** 6/16.

**timbrung.** fem. *building, construction.* dat. sg. **timbrunge** B/2.

**getīmian.** wk. 2. *happen.* past 3sg. **getīmode** 2/8.

**tintreglic.** adj. *full of torment, infernal.* wk. neut. gen. sg. **tintreglican** 9/24.

**tioliaþ** → tilian.

**tīr.** masc. *glory, fame.* nom. sg. 12/104; 18/157. acc. sg. 18/197. gen. sg. **tīres** 18/93, 272.

**tīrfæst.** adj. *glorious.* fem. acc. sg. **tīrfæste** 17/12.

**tirgan.** wk. 1. *worry, provoke.* past pl. **tirigdon** 3/71.

**tīþ.** fem. *permission, grant, favour.* acc. sg. **tīðe** 18/6.

**tō. A.** prep. (usually with dat.). *to, towards, into.* A/3, 6; B/5; C/2, 5, etc. (141x). *against.* 4/10. *as a.* E/3, 4; M/5, 6, 8, etc. (32x). *at* (of time). A/3; 12/12; 14/2, 43. *on, for, from.* 2/11, 18; 7/6, 8 (2x), etc. (12x).

    **B.** adv. *too, in addition.* 3/91; 7/4 (2x), 5, 10, etc. (45x). *to, to that place.* B/3; 2/9; 3/30, 51, 60, etc. (8x).

**tōberstan.** st. 3. *break apart.* past 3sg. **tōbærst** 12/136, 144.

**tōblāwan.** st. 7. *blow apart, scatter.* 3sg. **tōblǣwð** A/4.

**tōbræc** → tōbrecan.

**tōbrǣdan.** wk. 1. *spread out.* subj. pl. **tōbrǣden** 10/23. inf. **tōbrǣdan, tōbrēdan** 10/24, 27, 32, 67.

**tōbrecan.** st. 4. *break.* past 3sg. **tōbræc.** past part. **tōbrocen, tōbrocene** 7/34; 12/242.

**tōbrēdan.** st. 3. *tear apart, awaken from.* inf. 18/247.

**tōbrēdan** → tōbrǣdan.

**tōbrocen-** → tōbrecan.

**tōbrȳtan.** wk. 1. *crush.* 3sg. **tōbrȳtt** 1/15.

**tōcyme.** masc. *arrival, advent.* dat. sg. 7/3.

**tōdæg.** adv. *today.*

**tōdǣlan.** wk. 1. *divide.* subj. past pl. **tōdǣlden** 16/12. imp. pl. **tōdǣlaÞ** E/3; 8/66. past part. **tōdǣled, tōdǣlda** 10/25 (3x).

**tōēacan.** prep. *in addition to, aside from.* 6/26; 7/27; 8/18.

**tōemnes.** prep. *alongside.* 8/36 (2x).

**tōfēran.** wk. 1. *disperse.* past 3sg. **tōfērde** 5/20.

**tōforan.** prep. (with dat.). *before.* 5/12.

**tōgædere.** adv. *together.* **tōgǣdere, tōgædre** 7/30, 43; 12/67.

**tōgēanes.** prep. *towards.* 3/53; 18/149.

**tōgeþēodan.** wk. 1. *add.* past 3sg. **tōgeþēodde** 9/14.

**getoht.** masc. *battle.* dat. sg. **getohte** 12/104.

**tohte.** wk. fem. *battle.* dat. sg. **tohtan** 18/197.

**tōl.** neut. *tool.* nom. sg. 10/4. acc. pl. 10/8. gen. pl. **tōla** 10/2. dat. pl. **tōlum** 10/3, 5, 6, 8.

**tōlicgan.** st. 5. *divide, separate.* 3sg. **tōlīÞ** 8/57. past part. **tōlegena** 10/25.

**tōmiddes.** adv. *in the middle.* B/2.

**tōmorgen.** adv. *tomorrow.*

**tōniman.** st. 4. *divide.* past part. **tōnumen.**

**torht.** adj. *bright, beautiful.* masc. nom. sg. 11/4. wk. fem. acc. sg. **torhtan** 18/43.

**torhtlic.** adj. *bright, beautiful.* masc. nom. sg. 18/157.

**torhtmōd.** adj. *noble-minded, glorious.* masc. nom. sg. 18/6, 93.

**torn.** neut. *anger, grief, suffering.* acc. sg. 13/112; 18/272.

**torne.** adv. *grievously.* 18/93.

**tōslēan.** st. 6. *break in pieces, destroy.* past 3sg. **tōslōh** 3/39.

**tōslītan.** st. 1. *tear apart.* 3sg. **tōslīteÞ** 15/18.

**tōswellan.** st. 3. *swell.* past part. **tōswollen** 3/95.

**tōtær-, tōtǣre** → tōteran.

**tōteran.** st. 4. *tear apart.* past 3sg. **tōtær** 3/40. past pl. **tōtǣron** 3/69. subj. past sg. **tōtǣre** 3/70.

**totwǣman.** wk. 1. *divide.* past part. **totwǣmed** 12/241.

**tōþ.** masc. athematic. *tooth.* acc. pl. **tēÞ** 8/18. gen. pl. **tōÞa.** dat. pl. **tōÞon, tōþum** 8/18; 18/272.

**tōweard.** A. adj. *future, impending, heading.* masc. nom. sg. 18/157. fem. nom. sg. 18/286. wk. masc. gen. sg. **tōweardan** 9/24.
B. prep. *towards.* 8/69.

**tōwrītan.** st. 1. *describe.* past 3sg. **tōwrāt** 10/17.

**trahtnian.** wk. 2. *expound.* past pl. **trahtnodon** 3/111.

**træf.** neut. *tent.* acc. sg. 18/268. dat. sg. **træfe** 18/43, 255.

**trēocyn.** neut. *kind of tree.* nom. sg. 17/2.

**trēow.** A. neut. *tree.* nom. sg. 1/6. acc. sg. 1/3; 14/4, 14, 17, 25. gen. sg. **trēowes** 1/3, 6. dat. sg. **trēowe** A/3; 1/1, 4, 5, 8, etc. (8x). gen. pl. **trēowa** 1/2.
B. fem. *faith, promise, trust.* acc. sg. **trēowe** 13/112; 17/12.

**getrēowe.** adj. *true, faithful.* wk. masc. nom. sg. **getrēowa.**

**trēowen.** adj. *wooden.* fem. dat. sg. **trēowenre** 2/16.

**getrēowþ.** fem. (often pl. with sg. sense). *truth, honour, loyalty.* nom. pl. **getrēowþa, getrȳwÞa** 7/4, 20. acc. pl. **getrȳwÞa** 7/69.

**trēowwyrhta.** wk. masc. *carpenter.*

**trum.** adj. *firm, strong.* masc. nom. sg. K/1369. masc. acc. sg. **trumne** 18/6.

**Truso.** proper noun. *Truso* (probably on Lake Druzno in present-day Poland). nom. sg. 8/59. dat. sg. 8/52.

**trym.** neut. *short length,* in phrase *fōtes trym. step.* acc. sg. 12/247.

**trymian.** wk. 2. *encourage, arrange.* past pl. **trymedon** 12/305. inf. 12/17.

**getrymman.** wk. 1. *strengthen, arrange.* pres. part. **getrymmende** 9/38. past part. **getrymmed** 12/22.

**getrȳwlīce.** adv. *loyally.* 7/23.

**getrȳwþa** → getrēowþ.

**tū** → twēgen.

**(ge)tūcian.** wk. 2. *torment.* past part. **getūcod** 3/71.

**tūdor.** neut. *offspring, fruit.* dat. sg. **tūdre** 17/2.

**tūn.** masc. *enclosure, dwelling, village, town.* dat. sg. **tūne** 8/67 (2x), 69. gen. pl. **tūna.**

**tunece.** wk. fem. *tunic, coat.* acc. sg. **tunecan** 3/40.

**tunge.** wk. fem. *tongue.* nom. sg. ɪ/8; 9/44. acc. sg. **tungan** 9/4.

**tūngerēfa.** wk. masc. *town reeve.* dat. sg. **tūngerēfan** 9/15.

**tungol.** masc. *star.* gen. sg. **tungles.** acc. pl. **tunglas** 11/4.

**tūsc.** masc. *tusk.*

**twā.** card. num. as noun. *two.* ᴇ/1. nom. pl. **twēgen** 12/80. acc. pl. 3/107. gen. pl. **twēga** 12/207.

**twā, twām** → twēgen.

**getwǣfan.** wk. 1. (with gen.). *separate from, deprive of, hinder.* inf. 17/24.

**twēga** → twā.

**twēgen.** card. num. as adj. *two.* masc. nom. pl. ʙ/2; 7/43. fem. nom. pl. **twā.** masc. acc. pl. 8/29, 49, 51, 64, 75. fem. acc. pl. **tū, twā** 3/49. neut. acc. pl. **twā** 6/32; 10/25. gen. pl. **twēga** 17/49. dat. pl. **twām** 2/1; 8/21, 35.

**twēgen** → twā.

**twelf. A.** card. num. as noun. *twelve.* **twelf, twelfe** ꜰ/4; 7/40.

**B.** as adj. *twelve.* masc. acc. sg. 2/10. neut. acc. pl. 2/5.

**twēntig. A.** card. num. as noun. *twenty.* ᴇ/1. acc. pl. **twentig** 8/25.

**B.** as adj. *twenty.*

**twēogan.** wk. 2. *doubt* something (gen.). past 3sg. **twēode** 18/1, 345.

**twēone.** card. num. as adj. (only in construction *be* + noun + *twēonum* = between two of a thing). *two.* dat. pl. **twēonum.**

**twēonian.** wk. 2. *be doubtful.* 3sg. **twēonað** ɢ/9.

**twīa.** adv. *twice.* ᴇ/1.

**twig.** neut. *twig, branch.* nom. pl. **twigu** ꜰ/5. dat. pl. **twigum** ꜰ/5.

**twyfeald.** adj. *double.* neut. dat. sg. **twyfealdum** 3/96, 101.

**tyhtan.** wk. 1. *stretch, incite, persuade.* past 3sg. **tihte.**

**tȳman.** wk. 1. *have children.* past 3sg. **tȳmde.**

**getymbrad** → (ge)timbrian.

**getȳme.** neut. *team.* nom. pl. 3/99. acc. pl. **getȳme, getȳmu** 3/7, 98.

**tȳn. A.** card. num. as noun. *ten.* **tēn, tȳn, tȳne** ᴇ/1; 7/39, 40; 8/29; 10/40, etc. (7x).

**B.** as adj. *ten.* neut. nom. pl. 3/103.

**tyslian.** wk. 2. *dress.* pl. **tysliað** ᴅ/2.

**tyslung.** fem. *fashion* (in clothing). acc. sg. **tyslunge** ᴅ/3.

**þā. A.** adv. *then.* ʙ/2, 3, 5, 6, 7, etc. (183x).

**B.** conj. *when.* ɢ/2; 3/21; 5/8, 20; 7/68, etc. (30x).

**þā hwīle þe.** conj. *while, for as long as.* 3/79; 12/14, 83, 235, 272.

**þā þā.** conj. *when.* 1/8; 2/5; 3/11, 19, 44, etc. (10x).

**þā þe** → se þe.

**þā** → se.

**(ge)þafian.** wk. 2. *allow, consent to.* past 3sg. **geðafode, þafode** 3/57, 64; 9/20. inf. **geðafian** 18/60.

**þafung.** fem. *consent.* acc. sg. **þafunge** 7/39.

**þāh** → (ge)þēon.

**þām þe** → se þe.

**þām, þān** → se.

**(ge)þanc.** *thought, purpose, design, mind, thanks* for something (gen.). **1.** masc. acc. sg. **þanc, þonc** 11/24; 12/120, 147. dat. sg. **geðance, geðonce** 3/9; 7/53; 18/13. **2.** neut. acc. sg. **geþanc** 12/13.

**(ge)þancian.** wk. 2. *thank* someone (dat.) for something (gen.). 1sg. **geþancie** 12/173. past 3sg. **þancode** 2/12. pres. part. **ðancigende** 2/20.

**þancolmōd.** adj. *thoughtful.* fem. acc. sg. **þancolmōde** 18/172.

þanon. A. adv. *thence.* þonan, þanon
c/11; 3/45; 8/3, 10, 38, etc. (7x).
B. conj. *from which, whence.* 5/10.

þanonne. adv. *thence.* 18/132.

þār → þǣr.

þāra þe → se þe.

þāra → se.

þās → þes.

þat → se.

þǣm þe → se þe.

þǣm, þæne → se.

þænne → þonne.

þǣr. A. conj. *where.* F/1, 7; K/1359; 1/8;
4/10, etc. (24x).
B. adv. *there.* þǣr, þār B/2, 3, 6;
c/11, 12, etc. (99x).

þǣr þǣr. conj. *where.* 2/24.

þǣra þe → se þe.

þǣra → se.

þǣre þe → se þe.

þǣre → se.

þǣrinne. adv. *therein, inside.* 4/15; 6/31;
18/50.

þǣrof. adv. *from there.* c/6.

þǣron. adv. *therein.* 3/110; 8/14; 14/67.

þǣrrihte. adv. *instantly.* 3/68; 10/56.

þǣrtō. adv. *thereto, to it, from there.* 2/19;
3/8; 4/10; 10/48.

þǣrwiþ. adv. *in addition.* 6/37.

þǣrymbūtan. adv. *thereabouts.* 10/29.

þæs. adv. *afterwards. accordingly, therefore.*
10/49. *to that extent, so.* K/1366.

þæs þe. conj. *after, because, as.* 4/3; 7/63;
11/26; 17/31; 18/13, etc. (6x).

þæs þe → se þe.

þæs → se.

þæt. conj. *that, so that, because.* B/1, 4, 5
(2x); c/2, etc. (238x).

þæt → se.

þætte. A. conj. *that, when.* 9/1, 23, 39, 43;
10/5, etc. (12x).
B. rel. pron. *that, which.* neut. nom.
sg. 10/13; 15/18.

þe. A. rel. pron. *that, which, who.* A/1, 3;
c/1, 3, 12, etc. (137x). *when.* 8/65, 66;
18/287.

B. conj. *when, where, than, or.* M/2;
4/14; 5/11; 6/15; 7/21, etc. (8x).

þe lǣs → þȳ lǣs.

þe → se.

þē → þȳ.

þēah. A. adv. *though, nevertheless.* 4/15;
8/3, 25, 31; 10/2, etc. (12x).
B. conj. *though, although.* þēah, þēh
I/5; M/7; 7/4, 16, 36, etc. (12x).

þēah þe. conj. *although, even if.* K/1368;
1/4; 2/1, 8, 10, etc. (10x).

geþeaht. neut. *counsel, advice.* acc. sg.
A/1. dat. sg. geþeahte A/5.

þeahte → þeccan.

þearf. fem. *need* for something (gen.), *benefit, distress.* nom. sg. 7/13, 65, 66, 67;
9/33, etc. (8x). acc. sg. þearfe 12/175;
18/3, 92. dat. sg. ðearfe c/2; 12/201, 232,
307. dat. pl. þearfum 11/9.

þearf → þurfan.

þearfa. wk. masc. *pauper.* acc. pl. þearfan
3/23. gen. pl. þearfena 3/25, 26. dat. pl.
ðearfum 3/26.

þearfende. adj. (past part. of þearfan
'be in need'). *needy.* fem. dat. sg.
þearfendre 18/85.

þearflēas. adj. *without need.* masc. nom.
sg. 3/53.

þearle. adv. *severely, exceedingly, vigorously.* 7/19; 12/158; 14/52; 18/74, 86,
etc. (8x).

þearlmōd. adj. *severe.* masc. nom. sg.
18/66, 91.

þēaw. masc. *custom, habit, morals.* nom.
sg. 8/64, 73; 9/29; 13/12. nom. pl.
þēawas 10/32. acc. pl. þēawas D/1 (2x);
3; 3/22; 10/36. gen. pl. þēawa 7/50. dat.
pl. þēawum 10/24; 18/129.

þec → þū, gē.

þeccan. wk. 1. *cover.* past 3sg. þeahte Lb.
subj. pl. þeccen 10/74.

þecen. fem. *roof.* acc. sg. þecene Lb.

þegengylde. neut. *wergild for a thegn.* acc.
sg. 7/37.

þegenlīce. adv. *as a thane would do,
loyally.* 12/294.

þegn. masc. *servant.* nom. sg. ðegen, þegn 3/90; 9/31. acc. sg. þegen, þegn 9/30; 12/151. nom. pl. þegnas 14/75. acc. pl. ðegnas 18/10, 306. dat. pl. þēnan 7/12. *retainer, nobleman, master.* nom. sg. þegen, þegn 4/10; 7/37. acc. sg. þegen 7/36, 41. gen. sg. þegenes 7/40. dat. sg. ðegne, þegene 2/29; 7/36. nom. pl. þegnas, þegenas 4/7, 9; 6/21; 12/205, 220. acc. pl. þegenas, þegnas 6/24; 12/232. dat. pl. þēnum.

þegnian. wk. 2. *serve.* inf. 9/29.

þēgon → (ge)þicgan.

þēh → þēah.

þēn- → þegn.

(ge)þencan. wk. 1. *think of, imagine, consider.* pl. þencaþ 14/115. imp. pl. geðencað 10/24. inf. geþencan 13/58. *intend.* 1sg. þence 12/319. 3sg. þenceð 12/258, 316; 14/121. pl. ðencað 3/77. past 3sg. þōhte 7/23; 18/58. past pl. þōhton 18/208.

þenden. conj. *while.* 17/17; 18/66.

þenian. wk. 2. *stretch out.* inf. 14/52.

þēnian. wk. 2. *serve.* past 3sg. ðēnode 3/8. inf. 2/11.

þēnung. fem. *service.* dat. pl. ðēnungum 3/1.

þēod. fem. *nation, people, country.* acc. sg. þēode 7/4, 5, 15, 27, 43, etc. (7x). gen. sg. þēode 10/26. dat. sg. þēode 7/13, 16, 17, 34, 38, etc. (11x). nom. pl. þēoda 10/24. acc. pl. þīoda 10/25, 69. gen. pl. þēoda 10/24, 32; 12/173. dat. pl. þēodum, þēode, þīodum 7/10, 11, 33; 10/19.

geþēodan. wk. 1. *join.* past 3sg. geþēodde 9/21.

geþēode. neut. *language, nation.* acc. sg. 8/17. gen. sg. geðēodes 8/73.

þēode → þēowan.

þēoden. masc. *ruler, king.* nom. sg. 12/120, 178, 232; 17/29; 18/66, etc. (6x). acc. sg. 12/158. gen. sg. þēodnes ʟb; 13/95; 17/48; 18/165, 268. dat. sg. ðēodne 12/294; 14/69; 18/3, 11.

þēodguma. wk. masc. *man of a nation.* nom. pl. þēodguman 18/208, 331.

geþēodness. fem. *joining, association.* dat. sg. geþēodnisse 9/2.

þēodscipe. masc. *nation.* nom. sg. 7/47. *discipline.* dat. pl. þēodscipum 9/26.

þēodwita. wk. masc. *scholar.* nom. sg. 7/61.

þēoh. neut. *thigh.* dat. sg. þēo ʟa.

(ge)þēon. st. 1. *prosper, benefit* someone (dat.), *find favour with* someone (dat.). 3sg. geðīhð 3/79. past 3sg. ðāh. subj. sg. ðīo 10/70. inf. geþēon ɪ/84.

þēos, þeosse, þeossum → þes.

þēostrum → þўstru.

þēow. masc. *servant, slave.* nom. pl. þēowas 7/11. acc. pl. ðēowas 2/6; 7/12. gen. pl. þēowa 9/21. dat. pl. þēowum 7/12.

þēowa. wk. masc. *servant, slave.* nom. sg. ðēowa 3/92 (2x). acc. sg. ðēowan 3/14, 52. dat. sg. ðēowan 3/91. nom. pl. þēowan 8/61.

þēowan. wk. 1. *serve.* past 3sg. þēode 9/43.

þēowen. fem. *female servant, handmaiden.* nom. sg. 18/74.

(ge)þēowian. wk. 2. *serve, enslave.* past 3sg. þēowode. inf. þēowian 2/9. past part. geþēowede 7/15.

þēowot. neut. *servitude, slavery.* acc. sg. ᴍ/13.

þes. demonst. pron. *this.* masc. nom. sg. 2/13; 3/87; 7/47; 13/62; 16/29. fem. nom. sg. ðēos 7/2; 10/66; 14/12, 82. neut. nom. sg. ðis ꜰ/6; 2/13; 3/110; 6/17; 8/45, etc. (9x). masc. acc. sg. þisne, þysne ꜰ/1; ɢ/9; 2/26; 5/21; 10/73, etc. (12x). fem. acc. sg. þās 2/8; 3/13, 20, 88, 109, etc. (16x). neut. acc. sg. ðis 1/14; 2/24; 3/29, 36, 37, etc. (14x). masc. gen. sg. þises, þisses, þysses 3/21, 112; 6/6; 10/2, 16, etc. (7x). fem. gen. sg. þisse, ðeosse, þisere 9/1; 10/16, 18, 21; 13/74. neut. gen. sg. þisses ᴅ/1; 10/2, 39 (2x). masc. dat. sg. þysan,

**ðisum, þeossum, þissum** 7/14, 20, 25, 29; 9/8, etc. (8x). fem. dat. sg. **þysse, ðisse, ðyssere** 3/81; 7/13, 16, 17, 33, etc. (10x). neut. dat. sg. **þissum, ðisum, þysan, þyssum, ðysum, þysson** 2/27; 3/97, 110; 5/1, 4, etc. (17x). masc. inst. sg. **ðȳs** 18/2. neut. inst. sg. **þȳs** 18/89. nom. pl. **ðās** 3/70, 82; 5/3; 8/53, 55, etc. (6x). acc. pl. **þās** 3/91; 6/43; 10/8, 62, 67, etc. (9x). gen. pl. **þyssa** 18/187. dat. pl. **ðisum, þissum** 3/43, 48, 63; 10/5, 8, etc. (6x).

**þī lǣs þe** → **þȳ lǣs þe.**

**(ge)þicgan.** st. 5. *accept, receive, consume, eat.* past pl. **þēgon** 18/19. inf. **geþicgean** 4/8.

**þider.** adv. *thither, to that place.* **þider, þyder** B/6; 4/7, 10; 8/18, 42, etc. (6x).

**þider þe.** conj. *whither, towards the place where.*

**þiderweard.** adv. *towards that place.* 8/49.

**þīefþ.** fem. *theft.* dat. sg. **ðīefðe, þȳfþe** M/13; 7/15.

**þīestru** → **þȳstru.**

**geþīhþ** → **(ge)þēon.**

**þīn.** adj. *your, of you.* masc. nom. sg. 3/73. fem. nom. sg. 3/73. neut. nom. sg. 3/74; 11/9. masc. acc. sg. **þīnne.** fem. acc. sg. **ðīne** 3/32, 33, 55; 1/10. neut. acc. sg. 10/40; 12/178; 1/15. masc. gen. sg. **þīnes** 1/19 (2x). fem. gen. sg. **þīnre** 18/85, 91. masc. dat. sg. **þīnum** 1/15. fem. dat. sg. **ðīnre** 3/33, 56, 60; 9/33. neut. dat. sg. **þīnum** 10/19; 1/14, 17. masc. nom. pl. **Ðīne** 3/39; 15/14. fem. nom. pl. **ðīne** 3/39; 15/13. masc. acc. pl. **ðīne** 3/36. fem. acc. pl. **þīne** 12/37; 1/16 (2x). neut. acc. pl. **ðīne** 3/37, 39. gen. pl. **ðīnra** 3/74. dat. pl. **þīnum** 12/50. neut. gen. sg. **ðīnes** 1/14, 17 (2x).

**þīn** → **þū, gē.**

**þinc-** → **þyncan.**

**geþincþum** → **geþyncþ.**

**þindan.** st. 3. *swell.* inf. ᴌb.

**þīnen.** fem. *maid-servant, handmaid.* acc. sg. **þīnene, ðīnenne** 18/172. dat. pl. **þīnenum** 2/11.

**þing.** neut. *thing.* acc. sg. 3/43; 5/15; 6/1, 22; 18/153. gen. sg. **þinges** 10/70, 76; 18/60. nom. pl. 3/33. acc. pl. C/1; 3/32; 6/43; 7/50 (2x), etc. (7x). gen. pl. **þinga** 7/11; 10/8. dat. pl. **ðingum** 3/43, 48, 63; 6/27. *motive.* dat. pl. **þingum** 10/46. *reason.* dat. pl. **þingum.** *means.* gen. pl. **ðinga** 10/67.

**geþinge.** neut. *agreement, result.*

**þingian.** wk. 2. *settle.* subj. pl. 7/66.

**þingrǣden.** fem. *intercession.* dat. sg. **ðingrǣdene** 3/94.

**þīo** → **(ge)þēon.**

**þīod-** → **þēod.**

**þīodisc.** neut. *language.* acc. pl. 10/70.

**þis, þiss-** → **þes.**

**geþōht.** masc. *thought.* nom. sg. 16/43. acc. sg. 16/12. inst. sg. **geþōhte** 13/88. nom. pl. **geþōhtas.**

**þōht-** → **(ge)þencan.**

**(ge)þolian.** wk. 2. *suffer, endure, remain.* 1sg. **ðolige** 3/76. pl. **þoliað** 7/44. past 3sg. **þolode, geðolode** C/4; 2/12. past pl. **þoledon, þolodan** 14/149; 18/215. inf. **þolian** 12/201, 307. pres. part. **þoligende** 18/272. *tolerate.* inf. **geþolian** 12/6.

**þolmōdan.** adj. *patient.* wk. masc. nom. pl. 3/81.

**þolod-, geþolod** → **(ge)þolian.**

**þon** → **se.**

**þonan** → **þanon.**

**þonc-, geþonc-** → **(ge)þanc.**

**þoncwyrþe.** adj. *deserving of thanks, acceptable, memorable.* neut. acc. sg. 18/153.

**þone þe** → **se þe.**

**þone** → **se.**

**þonēcan þe.** conj. *whenever, as soon as.* 10/37.

**þonne. A.** adv. *then.* **þonne, þænne** C/10, 12; F/5, 6; M/5, etc. (50x).

　　**B.** conj. *when, whenever.* A/4; D/2; F/5; 2/13, 26, etc. (21x). *than, than that.* 1/1; 3/76, 99, 112; 4/12, etc. (23x).

**þorftun** → **þurfan.**

**þorn.** masc. *thorn.* acc. pl. **ðornas** 1/18.

þracu. fem. *power, violence, attack*. acc. sg. þræce.

þrafung. fem. *reproof*. dat. pl. ðrafungum 3/75.

þrāg. fem. *time, period*. nom. sg. 13/95. acc. sg. þrāge 18/237.

geþrang. neut. *throng*. dat. sg. geþrange 12/299.

þrang → (ge)þringan.

þræce → þracu.

þræl. masc. *slave*. nom. sg. 7/36, 41. acc. sg. 7/37. dat. sg. þræle 7/36, 41. gen. pl. þræla 7/36.

þrælriht. neut. *rights of slaves*. nom. pl. 7/15.

þrē → þrīe.

þrēagan. wk. 2. *chastise*. infl. inf. tō ðrēagenne 3/77.

þrēat. masc. *band of men, army, violence, cruelty*. acc. sg. 15/2, 7. dat. sg. ðrēate 18/62. dat. pl. ðrēatum 18/164.

þrēo. A. card. num. as noun. *three*. nom. pl. 3/6. acc. pl. 3/7, 98, 100. gen. pl. þrēora 8/35; 12/299.
  B. as noun. *three*. E/1.

þrēo → þrīe.

þridda. ord. num. *third*. masc. nom. sg. 3/38; 6/11. fem. nom. sg. þridde. masc. acc. sg. þriddan 8/67. masc. dat. sg. ðriddan 2/16. masc. inst. sg. þriddan 10/28.

þrīe. card. num. as adj. *three*. masc. nom. pl. þrīe, þrē, þrȳ B/2; 7/43; 10/7. masc. acc. pl. þrȳ, þrīe 2/30; 3/65, 70, 89; 6/8, etc. (7x). fem. acc. pl. þrēo. neut. acc. pl. þrēo. dat. pl. ðrim 3/38, 90; 8/7; 10/6.

þrindan. st. 3. *swell*. pres. part. þrindende Lb.

(ge)þringan. st. 3. *crowd, press, oppress*. past 3sg. þrang. past pl. þrungon 18/164. inf. þringan 18/249. past part. geðrungen 18/287.

þrīttig. card. num. as noun. *thirty*. þrīttig, þrȳttig E/1; 2/29, 30. nom. pl. þrītig 8/34.

þrīwa. adv. *thrice*. E/1; 6/19.

þrosm. masc. *smoke, darkness*. dat. sg. þrosme 11/13.

þrōwian. wk. 2. *suffer*. past 3sg. þrōwode C/4; 14/84, 98, 145. subj. past sg. þrōwade.

þrōwung. fem. *passion*. dat. sg. ðrōwunge 3/93; 9/24.

þrūh. fem. athematic. *coffin*. nom. sg. 2/25. acc. sg. 2/19, 20. dat. sg. þrȳh 2/24.

geþrungen, þrungon → (ge)þringan.

þrȳ → þrīe.

þryccan. wk. 1. *oppress, afflict*. past part. þrycced 9/28.

þrȳh → þrūh.

þrym. masc. *army, might, splendour*. nom. sg. 13/95; 18/86. gen. sg. þrymmes 18/60. dat. sg. þrymme 18/331. dat. pl. ðrymmum 18/164.

þrymfæst. adj. *glorious*. masc. nom. sg. 14/84.

þrymful. adj. *filled with glory*. fem. nom. sg. 18/74.

þrymlic. adj. *glorious*. neut. acc. pl. 18/8.

þrymsetl. neut. *throne*. nom. sg. 3/18.

Þrȳness. fem. *Trinity*. gen. sg. Ðrȳnesse 18/86.

þrȳttig → þrīttig.

þrȳþ. fem. *multitude, host*. nom. pl. þrȳþe 13/99.

þū, gē. pron. 1. pers. *you, yourself*. nom. pl. gē 1/4 (2x), 5 (2x); D/1, etc. (39x). acc. pl. ēow D/2; 10/68, 70; 12/41. nom. sg. ðū D/1; 1/9, 11 (3x), etc. (56x). acc. sg. ðē, þec 3/32, 55, 72 (2x); 11/9, etc. (8x). gen. sg. þīn 17/29, 48. dat. sg. ðē D/1; G/2, 3, 4, 6, etc. (27x). dat. pl. ēow, īow D/1; 1/1; 3/2, 88 (2x), etc. (19x). nom. dual git, gyt 17/16, 17, 33, 54. gen. dual incer 17/49. dat. dual inc 17/32. 2. refl. *you*. dat. sg. þē 11/11.

geþūht, þūhte → þyncan.

geþungen. adj. *accomplished, senior, noble*. fem. nom. sg. 18/129. masc. gen. sg. geðungenes M/4.

þunian. wk. 2. *stand out, be prominent*. inf. Lb.

**þunorrād.** fem. *peal of thunder.* nom. pl. **ðunorrāda.**

**þurfan.** pret. pres. *have need, have occasion.* 3sg. **þearf** 14/117; 18/117. pl. **þurfe, þurfon** 12/34, 249. past pl. **þorftun.** subj. pl. **þyrfen** 18/153.

**þurh.** prep. (usually with acc., sometimes with dat. or gen.). *through, by, by means of, because of.* **þurh, þuruh** 2/2, 8, 25, 26, 27, etc. (76x).

**þurhdrīfan.** st. 1. *drive through.* past pl. **þurhdrifan** 14/46.

**þurhfaran.** st. 6. *pass through, penetrate, pierce.* 3sg. **þurhfærð.**

**þurhsmēagan.** wk. 2. *investigate.* past 3sg. **þurhsmēade** 6/30.

**þurhþyddan.** wk. 1. *pierce.* past part. **ðurhðyd** 3/83.

**þurhwadan.** st. 6. *go through, pierce.* past 3sg. **þurhwōd** 12/296.

**þurhwunian.** wk. 2. *remain, persevere.* 2sg. **þurhwunast** 3/60. 3sg. **þurhwunað** 2/8. past 3sg. **þurhwunode** 2/8. subj. sg. **þurhwunige** 10/45.

**þus.** adv. *thus, so.* **ðus, þuss** 3/10, 30, 66, 111; 8/71, etc. (9x).

**þūsend. A.** card. num. as noun. *thousand.* 5/14; 10/40, 41, 42. nom. pl. **þūsend, þūsenda, þūsendu** 3/99 (2x). acc. pl. 3/7 (2x), 98 (2x).

**B.** as adj. *thousand.* masc. nom. pl. 3/99. neut. nom. pl. 3/99.

**þūsendmǣlum.** adv. *by thousands.* 18/165.

**geþwǣre.** adj. *harmonious.* masc. nom. pl. 11/24.

**þwēan.** st. 6. *wash.* past pl. **þwōgon** 2/24.

**þwȳrness.** fem. *perversity, adversity.* dat. pl. **ðwȳrnyssum** 3/112.

**þȳ. A.** adv. *therefore.* **þȳ, þē** A/5; 7/2, 17, 51, 66, etc. (12x).

**B.** conj. *because.* **þē** 10/14; 12/313.

**þȳ lǣs.** conj. *lest.* **þe lǣs, þȳ lǣs** 7/60.

**þȳ lǣs þe.** conj. *lest.* **ðī lǣs ðe, ðȳ lǣs ðe** 1/3; 3/9.

**þȳ** → **se.**

**þyder** → **þider.**

**þȳfþe** → **þīefþ.**

**geþyld.** neut. *patience.* nom. sg. 3/74. acc. sg. 3/57. dat. sg. **geðylde** M/9.

**geþyldelīce.** adv. *patiently.* 10/53.

**geþyldig.** adj. *patient.* masc. nom. sg. 10/54; 13/65. masc. nom. pl. **geðyldige** 3/112.

**þyllic.** adj. *such.* neut. acc. pl. **ðyllice** 3/93.

**þyncan.** wk. 1. *seem* to someone (dat.). 3sg. **þinceð, þincð** 10/38; 12/55; 13/41. past 3sg. **ðūhte** 1/6; 8/17; 9/31; 12/66; 14/4. subj. sg. **ðince** 10/42, 66, 81, 82. subj. past sg. **þūhte** 10/53. inf. **þincan** 7/20, 47, 55; 10/66. past part. **geþūht** 2/13, 16.

**geþyncþ.** fem. *dignity, rank.* dat. pl. **geðincðum, geþyncðum** 3/34.

**þyrel.** adj. *pierced.* neut. nom. sg. LA.

**þyrfen** → **þurfan.**

**þyrstan.** wk. 1. (impersonal). *be thirsty.* past 3sg. **þyrste.** pres. part. sg. **þyrstendne.**

**þys-, þyss-, þȳs-** → **þes.**

**þȳstre.** adj. *dark.* neut. nom. pl. **þȳstru** F/2. wk. fem. nom. sg. 18/34.

**þȳstru.** fem. (often pl. with sg. sense). *darkness.* nom. sg. **þīestru.** nom. pl. **þȳstro** 14/52. dat. pl. **þēostrum, þȳstrum** 11/13; 18/118.

**ufan.** adv. *from above.* 3/45, 46.

**ufeweard.** adj. *uppermost.* masc. dat. sg. **ufewerdum** 3/58.

**ūhtcearu.** fem. *dawn-care, sorrow at dawn.* acc. sg. **ūhtceare** 16/7.

**ūhte.** wk. fem. *dawn.* dat. sg. **ūhtan** 16/35. gen. pl. **ūhtna** 13/8.

**ūhtsang.** masc. *lauds, nocturns.* acc. sg. **ūhtsong** 9/39.

**unālȳfedlic.** adj. *unlawful.* fem. nom. sg. 3/93.

**unārīmedlic.** adj. *innumerable.*

**unāsecgendlic.** adj. *inexpressible.* neut. nom. sg. 5/7.

**unateallendlic.** adj. *innumerable.* masc. acc. pl. **unātellendlice** 6/11.

**unbeboht.** adj. *not yet bought.* gen. pl. **unbebohtra** 8/23.

**unbefohten.** adj. *unfought.* masc. nom. pl.
  **unbefohtene** 12/57.

**unc** → ic, wē.

**uncer.** adj. *our, of us two.* masc. nom. sg.
  16/25. masc. acc. sg. **Uncerne** 15/16.
  neut. acc. sg. 15/19.

**unclǣne.** adj. *unclean.* masc. dat. sg.
  **unclǣnum.**

**uncoþu.** fem. *disease.* nom. sg. 7/19.

**uncræft.** masc. *evil practice.* dat. pl.
  **uncræftan** 7/69.

**undǣd.** fem. *misdeed.* dat. sg. **undǣde**
  7/53.

**under.** prep. (with dat. or acc.). *under.*
  F/2, 4; к/1360, 1361; 1/16, etc. (14x).

**underfōn.** st. 7. *receive, accept.* 1sg.
  **underfō** 3/92. 2sg. **underfēhst.** past 3sg.
  **underfēng** 3/94, 95, 103. past pl.
  **underfēngon, underfēngan** 3/62; 5/19;
  7/68. inf. 3/62.

**underlūtan.** st. 2. *bow under.* inf. 10/68.

**underniman.** st. 4. *receive.* past 3sg.
  **undernam.**

**understandan.** st. 6. *understand.* subj.
  sg. **understande** 7/32, 38. imp. pl.
  **understandað** 7/4. inf. 7/43, 70. infl.
  inf. **tō understandenne** 3/97.

**underþēod.** adj. *subjected.* wk. masc. dat.
  pl. **underþēoddan** 6/35.

**underþēodan.** wk. 1. *add, subjugate,*
  *subject.* past 3sg. **underþēodde** 6/31.
  past part. **underþēoded** 9/26.

**undyrne.** adj. *not secret, manifest.*

**unearg.** adj. *not cowardly.* masc. acc. sg.
  **uneargne.** masc. nom. pl. **unearge**
  12/206.

**unforbærned.** adj. *uncremated.* masc.
  nom. sg. 8/64 (2x). neut. acc. sg.
  8/73.

**unforcūþ.** adj. *not infamous.* masc. nom.
  sg. 12/51.

**unforht.** adj. *unafraid.* masc. nom. sg.
  14/110. masc. nom. pl. **unforhte** 12/79.

**unforworht.** adj. *innocent.* masc. nom. pl.
  **unforworhte** 7/14.

**unfracoþlīce.** adv. *not ignominiously,*
  *honourably.* 10/2.

**unfriþ.** masc. *hostility, strife.* dat. sg.
  **unfriþe** 8/12.

**ungedafenlīce.** adv. *improperly.* 10/32.

**ungederad.** adj. *unharmed.* masc. nom. sg.
  6/27.

**ungeendod.** adj. *unending.* wk. neut. acc.
  sg. **ungeendode** 10/41. wk. neut. gen.
  sg. **ungeendodan** 10/39.

**ungeendodlic.** adj. *eternal.* wk. neut. acc.
  sg. **ungeendodlīce** 10/43.

**ungefēalīce.** adv. *unhappily.* 4/17.

**ungefēre.** adj. *impassable.* dat. pl.
  **ungefērum** 10/25.

**ungefōge.** adv. *excessively.* 8/70.

**ungelǣred.** adj. *unlearned.* gen. pl.
  **ungelǣredra** 3/2.

**ungelīc.** adj. *different.* neut. nom. sg. 15/3.
  masc. nom. pl. **ungelīce** 10/32. fem.
  nom. pl. **ungelica** 10/24.

**ungelīce.** adv. *differently.* 15/8.

**ungelimp.** neut. *misfortune.* nom. sg.
  3/112. acc. pl. 3/44, 65. gen. pl.
  **ungelimpa** 7/38.

**ungemet. A.** neut. *lack of moderation.* dat.
  sg. **ungemete** H/4.
  **B.** adv. *immeasurably.* **unigmet** 10/66.

**ungemetlic.** adj. *immeasurable.* masc. gen.
  sg. **ungemetlices** 10/13.

**ungemetlīce.** adv. *immeasurably.* 10/21,
  23, 24, 32.

**ungerīm.** neut. *a countless number.* nom.
  sg. 7/56.

**ungesǣlþ.** fem. *misfortune.* nom. pl.
  **ungesǣlða** 5/3.

**ungesewenlic.** adj. *invisible.* wk. masc. acc.
  sg. **ungesewenlican** 3/79.

**ungetrȳwþ.** fem. *treachery, disloyalty.*
  nom. pl. **ungetrȳwþa** 7/24.

**ungeþyldelīce.** adv. *impatiently.* 10/53.

**ungewemmed.** adj. (past part.). *undefiled,*
  *pure.* fem. nom. sg. 2/5, 8, 26.

**ungylde.** neut. *excessive tax.* nom. pl.
  **ungylda** 7/19.

**unhēanlīce.** adv. *not ignobly.* 4/5.

**unigmet** → ungemet.

**unlagu.** fem. *illegal act, crime.* acc. pl.
  **unlaga** 7/5, 15, 63.

unlǣd. adj. *wretched, evil.* wk. masc. gen. sg. unlǣdan 18/102.

unlond. neut. *not-land, useless land.* gen. sg. unlondes 10/22.

unlyfigende. adj. *not living.* masc. gen. sg. unlyfigendes 18/180. dat. pl. unlyfigendum 18/315.

unlȳtel. adj. *not a little.* neut. nom. sg. 7/8.

(ge)unnan. pret. pres. (with gen. object). *grant, give, allow.* pl. unnon D/1. past 3sg. ūðe, geūðe 6/15; 18/123, 183. past pl. ūþon 4/11. subj. sg. geunne 12/176; 17/32. imp. sg. geunne 18/90.

unnyt. adj. *useless.* masc. nom. sg. unnet 10/67. masc. acc. sg. unnytne 10/65. neut. acc. sg. unnet 10/69.

unorne. adj. *simple, humble.* masc. nom. sg. 12/256.

unrǣd. masc. *folly, crime, treachery.* acc. pl. unrǣdas 5/3.

unriht. A. neut. *injustice, vice, sin.* acc. sg. 3/49; 7/5, 67. dat. sg. unrihte F/6; 6/35. nom. pl. 7/20. gen. pl. unrihta 7/4.

  B. adj. *illegal, unjust, wicked, sinful.* neut. acc. sg. 7/14. masc. gen. sg. unryhtes 10/13. dat. pl. unryhtum 4/1.

unrihtlīce. adv. *wrongly, unjustly.* D/1; 7/23; 10/30.

unrihtwīs. adj. *unrighteous.* gen. pl. unrihtwīsra A/1. wk. masc. nom. pl. unrihtwīsan A/4, 5, 6.

unrihtwīsnys. fem. *unrighteousness.* acc. sg. unrihtwīsnysse 3/28.

unrōt. adj. *dejected.* masc. nom. pl. unrōte 18/284.

unrōtness. fem. *unhappiness.* dat. sg. unrōtnysse 3/50.

(ge)unrōtsian. wk. 2. *make unhappy.* past part. geunrōtsod 3/72.

unryht- → unriht.

unscæþþigness. fem. *innocence.* acc. sg. unscæððignysse 3/52.

unscyldig. adj. *innocent.* masc. acc. pl. unscyldige 7/27.

unsidu. masc. u-stem. *bad custom.* acc. pl. unsida 7/48.

unsōfte. adv. *ungently.* 18/228.

unspēdig. adj. *not prosperous, poor.* wk. masc. nom. pl. unspēdigan 8/61.

unstilness. fem. *lack of quiet, tumult.* acc. sg. unstilnesse 4/7.

unswǣslic. adj. *ungentle, cruel.* masc. acc. sg. unswǣslicne 18/65.

unsȳfre. adj. *unclean.* wk. masc. nom. sg. unsȳfra 18/76.

untrum. adj. *infirm, sick.* gen. pl. untrumra 9/29. masc. acc. pl. compar. untrumran 9/29.

geuntrumian. wk. 2. *make sick.* past 3sg. geuntrumode 3/97.

untrumness. fem. *illness.* nom. sg. untrumnys 3/82. dat. sg. untrumnysse, untrymnesse 2/13; 3/68, 98; 9/28. dat. pl. untrumnyssum 3/96.

geuntrumod. adj. (past part.). *sick.* fem. nom. sg. 2/12.

untrymnesse → untrumness.

unþanc. masc. *displeasure.* gen. sg. unðances 6/29.

unþances. adv. *unwillingly.*

unþēaw. masc. *vice, sin.* dat. pl. unþēawum D/2; H/2.

unwāclīce. adv. *bravely.* 12/308.

unwǣstm. masc. *failure of crops.* gen. pl. unwǣstma 7/19.

unweaxen. adj. *ungrown, young.* masc. nom. sg. 12/152.

unweder. neut. *bad weather* (pl. with sg. sense). nom. pl. unwedera 7/19.

unwemme. adj. *undefiled, pure.* fem. acc. sg. 2/6.

unwendedlic. adj. *unchangeable.* masc. nom. sg. B/3.

unweorþian. wk. 2. *dishonour.* 3sg. unwurþað D/3.

unwīs. adj. *unwise.* dat. pl. unwīsum 10/66.

unwrēst. adj. *untrustworthy.* masc. nom. sg. 6/6.

unwriten. adj. *unwritten.* masc. acc. pl. 10/36.

unwurþaþ → unweorþian.

**unwyrþe.** adj. *unworthy* of something (gen.). masc. nom. pl. 10/14.

**ūp.** adv. *up.* **ūp, ūpp** B/2, 5, 7; 2/18; 6/41, etc. (11x).

**ūpāstīgness.** fem. *ascension.* dat. sg. **ūpāstīgnesse** 9/24.

**ūpgang.** masc. *landing-place.* acc. sg. 12/87.

**ūphēah.** adj. *high, lofty.* fem. nom. pl. **ūphēa** 16/30.

**ūplic.** adj. *high, lofty, supreme.* dat. pl. **ūplicum.**

**uppan.** prep. *upon.* **upon, uppon** 3/19, 59.

**uppe.** adv. *up.* 14/9.

**ūre.** adj. *our, ours.* neut. acc. sg. 7/69; 3/2. masc. nom. pl. 7/68. masc. nom. sg. 2/31; 12/232, 240, 314; 18/289. fem. nom. sg. 18/285. neut. nom. sg. 12/313. masc. acc. sg. **ūrne** 12/58. fem. acc. sg. 3/88. masc. gen. sg. **ūres.** fem. dat. sg. **ūrre** 3/112. masc. acc. pl. 3/38. fem. acc. pl. F/7. neut. acc. pl. 5/4. dat. pl. **ūrum** 2/8; 7/39; 12/56.

**ūre** → ic, wē.

**ūrigfeþere.** adj. *dewy-winged.* wk. masc. nom. sg. **ūrigfeðera** 18/210.

**urnon** → irnan.

**ūs** → ic, wē.

**ūt.** adv. *out.* 2/15; 4/5; 7/14, 29, 43, etc. (12x).

**ūtan.** adv. *from outside, outside,* in construction *ymb . . . utan, around.* 4/4; 8/16; 10/65.

**utan** → uton.

**ūte.** adv. *outside, without.* 7/11 (2x), 18, 39; 18/284.

**ūtgān.** anom. verb. *go out.*

**ūtgang.** masc. *departure.* dat. sg. **ūtgonge** 9/24.

**uton.** *let us.* **uton, utun, utan.** subj. pl. **utan, uton, wutan, wuton** F/7; 7/60, 65, 67, 68, etc. (8x).

**ūþe, geūþe, ūþon** → (ge)unnan.

**ūþwita.** wk. masc. *philosopher.* nom. sg. 10/49, 53 (3x), 54, etc. (6x). gen. sg. **ūðwitan** 10/49.

**uuiþ** → wiþ.

**wā. A.** interj. *alas.* 6/41 (2x); 7/42 (2x). **B.** masc. *woe.* nom. sg. 16/52.

**wāc.** adj. *weak, cowardly,* of a spear, *slender.* masc. nom. sg. 13/67. masc. acc. sg. **wācne** 12/43.

**wacian.** wk. 2. *be awake, keep watch.* pres. part. **waciende.**

**wācian.** wk. 2. *weaken, lose courage.* inf. 12/10.

**wacol.** adj. *wakeful, vigilant.* masc. nom. pl. **wacole** 3/20.

**(ge)wadan.** st. 6. *go, advance, travel.* past 1sg. **wōd** 13/24. past 3sg. **wōd, gewōd** 12/130, 157, 253. past pl. **wōdon** 12/96, 295. inf. **wadan** 12/140; 13/5.

**wald.** masc. *forest.* dat. sg. **walde** 18/206.

**waldend** → wealdend.

**wand** → windan.

**wandian.** wk. 2. *flinch.* past 3sg. **wandode** 12/268. inf. 12/258.

**wandrian.** wk. 2. *wander.* past 3sg. **wandrode.**

**wanedan** → (ge)wanian.

**wange.** wk. neut. *cheek.*

**wanhȳdig.** adj. *careless, rash, reckless.* masc. nom. sg. 13/67.

**(ge)wanian.** wk. 2. *diminish* (transitive), *lessen, dwindle.* past pl. **wanedan** 7/13. inf. **gewanian** 7/11. past part. **gewanode** 7/15.

**wann.** adj. *dark.* masc. nom. sg. **won, wonn** 13/103. fem. nom. sg. 14/55. wk. masc. nom. sg. **wanna, wonna** 18/206.

**warian.** wk. 2. *guard, defend, hold, possess.* 3sg. **warað** 13/32. pl. **warigeað** K/1358.

**warnian.** wk. 2. (sometimes with refl. pron.). *warn, take warning.* inf. 7/65.

**was** → bēon.

**wāst, wāt, gewāt** → (ge)witan.

**waþum.** masc. *wave.* gen. pl. **waþema** 13/24, 57.

**wæccan.** wk. 1. *watch, wake.* pres. part. **wæccende** 18/142.

**wǣd.** fem. *clothing.* dat. pl. **wǣdum** 14/15, 22.

**gewǣd.** fem. *clothing, garment.* nom. pl. **gewǣda** 2/23. dat. pl. **gewǣdum** 2/24.

**wǣdbrēc.** fem. athematic. (always pl.). *breeches.* acc. pl. 1/7.

**wǣdla.** adj. *poor.* dat. pl. **wǣdlum** 10/70.

**wǣfersȳn.** fem. *spectacle.* dat. sg. **wǣfersȳne** 14/31.

w̄ǣge. wk. fem. *scale.* dat. sg. **wǣgan** 3/76.

**wægn.** masc. *waggon, cart, carriage.*

**wǣgon** → wegan.

**wæl.** neut. *slaughter,* collectively *the slain.* nom. sg. 12/126. acc. sg. 12/303. dat. sg. **wæle** 12/279, 300.

**wælcēasega.** wk. masc. *chooser of the slain, corpse-picker.*

**wælcyrie.** wk. fem. *sorceress.* nom. pl. **wælcyrian** 7/56.

**wælgīfre.** adj. *greedy for slaughter.* masc. nom. sg. 18/207. neut. nom. pl. **wælgīfru** 13/100. dat. pl. **wælgīfrum** 18/295.

**wælhrēow.** adj. *slaughter-cruel, blood-thirsty, savage.* masc. nom. pl. **wælrē-owe** 15/6. fem. acc. pl. **wælhrēowe** 7/15.

**wælrǣste.** fem. *bed of slaughter,* fig. *place to die.* acc. sg. 12/113.

**wælrēowe** → wælhrēow.

**wælscel.** masc. *company of the slain*(?). acc. sg. 18/312.

**wælsliht.** masc. *slaughter.* gen. pl. **wælsleahta** 13/7, 91.

**wælspere.** neut. *deadly spear.* acc. sg. 12/322.

**wælstōw.** fem. *place of slaughter, battle-field* (*wealdan wælstōwe* = win the battle). gen. sg. **wælstōwe** 12/95. dat. sg. **wælstōwe** 12/293.

**wælwulf.** masc. *wolf of slaughter,* fig. *warrior.* nom. pl. **wælwulfas** 12/96.

**wǣpen.** neut. *weapon.* nom. sg. 12/252. acc. sg. 12/130, 235. gen. sg. **wǣpnes** 12/168. dat. sg. **wǣpne** 12/228. nom. pl. **wǣpen, wǣpnu** 10/7; 13/100. acc. pl. 18/290. gen. pl. **wǣpna** 12/83, 272,

308. dat. pl. **wǣpnum** 6/32; 8/71; 12/10, 126.

**wǣpengewrixl.** neut. *exchange of weapons, battle.* nom. sg. **wǣpngewrixl** 7/36. gen. sg. **wǣpengewrixles.**

**wǣr.** fem. *faith, agreement, protection.* acc. sg. **wǣre** 17/52.

**wǣr-** → bēon.

**wǣrlīce.** adv. *carefully.* 7/69.

**wǣrloga.** wk. masc. *breaker of pledges, treacherous person.* acc. sg. **wǣrlogan** 18/71.

**wǣs** → bēon.

**wæstm.** masc. *fruit.* dat. sg. **wæstme** 1/2, 3, 6. acc. pl. **wæstmas** A/3.

**wǣta.** wk. masc. *moisture.* dat. sg. **wǣtan** 14/22.

**wæter.** neut. *water.* nom. sg. F/4; 7/8. acc. sg. κ/1364; 12/91, 98. gen. sg. **wæteres** 8/75. dat. sg. **wætere, wætre** F/1, 4; G/5; 12/64, 96, etc. (6x). nom. pl. **wæteru** F/1. acc. pl. **wæteru.** gen. pl. **wætera** A/3.

**wæterǣdre.** wk. fem. *vein of water, artery of water, spring.* nom. pl. **wæterǣdran.**

**wē** → ic, wē.

**wēa.** wk. masc. *misfortune, misery.* acc. pl. **wēan** 17/45.

**wēagesīþ.** masc. *companion in woe, companion in crime.* nom. pl. **wēagesīðas** 18/16.

**geweald.** neut. *power.* acc. sg. 12/178; 14/107. dat. sg. **gewealde** 6/31 (2x); 7/14, 31, 32.

**(ge)wealdan.** st. 7. (with gen. or dat. object). *rule, control.* 3sg. **gewylt** 1/16. past pl. **wēoldon.** inf. **wealdan, gewealdan** 12/95; 18/103. *wield* a weapon. inf. **wealdan** 12/83, 168, 272. *bring about.* past pl. **wēoldan** 7/19.

**wealdend.** masc. nd-stem. *ruler, the Lord.* nom. sg. **waldend, wealdend** 10/70; 12/173; 14/111, 155; 18/5, etc. (6x). acc. sg. 14/67. gen. sg. **wealdendes** 14/17, 53. dat. sg. **wealdende** 14/121. nom. pl. **waldend** 13/78.

**wealgeat.** neut. *wall-gate* (i.e. city gate). dat. sg. **wealgate** 18/141.

**weall.** masc. *wall*. nom. sg. **weal** 13/98. acc. sg. 2/19; 18/161. gen. sg. **wealles** 18/151. dat. sg. **wealle** 13/80. nom. pl. **weallas** 13/76. acc. pl. **weallas** 18/137.

**weallan.** st. 7. *boil, well, swarm*. subj. past sg. **wēolle** 3/95. pres. part. **weallendan** 7/70.

**wealsteal.** masc. *wall-place, foundation*(?). acc. sg. 13/88.

**weard. A.** masc. *guard, guardian, guardianship*. nom. sg. 9/13. acc. sg. 9/12; 14/91; 18/80. dat. sg. **wearde** 18/142. **B.** adv. (with prep. *tō* or *wið*). *towards*. 18/99.

**weardian.** wk. 2. *guard, occupy, inhabit*. pl. **weardiað** 16/34. inf. **weardigan** 17/18.

**wearg.** masc. *criminal, monster, evil spirit*. acc. pl. **wergas** 14/31. gen. pl. **wearga** F/2.

**wearm.** adj. *warm*.

**wearme.** adv. *warmly*.

**wearþ, gewearþ** → (ge)weorþan.

**wēaþearf.** fem. *woeful need*. dat. sg. **wēaþearfe** 16/10.

**(ge)weaxan.** st. 7. *grow, increase*. past 1sg. **wēox** 16/3. past 3sg. **wēox, gewēox** 1/6; 2/12. past pl. **wēoxon** 3/31. imp. pl. **weaxað**. inf. **weaxan, geweaxan** J/84; Lb.

**weccan.** wk. 1. *wake*. inf. **weccean.**

**wedbryce.** masc. *violation of an agreement*. acc. pl. **wedbrycas** 7/49.

**wedd.** neut. *agreement, covenant*. acc. sg. **wed** 7/69. gen. sg. **weddes**. nom. pl. **wed** 7/34.

**weder.** neut. *weather*. nom. sg. 15/10.

**weg.** masc. *way, road*. acc. sg. A/6; 6/43; 8/6, 13, 45, etc. (9x). gen. sg. **weges** 8/70. dat. sg. **wege** A/1. gen. pl. **wega**. dat. pl. **wegum** 8/72.

**wēg.** masc. *wave*. acc. pl. **wēgas** 13/46.

**wegan.** st. 5. *carry, bring, weigh*. past pl. **wǣgon, wēgon** 12/98; 18/325.

**wegfērend.** masc. nd-stem. *wayfarer*. dat. pl. **wegfērendum** 3/27.

**wegnest.** neut. *journey-food*. inst. sg. **wegneste** 9/38.

**wēgon** → wegan.

**wel.** adv. *well, fully, indeed*. **wel, well** c/12 (2x); 2/11, 13; 6/15, etc. (16x). compar. **bet** 7/6; 10/81. superl. **betst** 10/32.

**wela.** wk. masc. *wealth, prosperity, riches*. nom. sg. 6/6; 13/74. acc. sg. **welan.** dat. pl. **welum** 3/26; 10/70.

**weldǣd.** fem. *good deed*. gen. pl. **weldǣda** 3/113.

**weldōnd.** masc. *performer of good deeds, benefactor*. dat. pl. **weldōndum.**

**gewelede** → gewelian.

**weler.** masc. *lip*. dat. pl. **welerum** 3/43, 48, 49 (2x), 63.

**(ge)welgian.** wk. 2. *make prosperous*. 3sg. **gewelgað** 3/81.

**gewelhwǣr.** adv. *everywhere*. 7/11.

**gewelhwelc.** indef. pron. *every*. masc. dat. sg. **gewelhwilcan, gewelhwylcan** 7/18, 39.

**gewelian.** wk. 2. *bind*. past part. **gewelede** 7/43.

**welig.** adj. *wealthy*. wk. masc. acc. sg. **welegan** 10/70.

**welm.** masc. *boiling, burning, fervour*. dat. sg. **welme** 9/27.

**welwyllende.** adj. *benevolent*. wk. masc. dat. sg. **welwyllendan** 3/113.

**gewēman.** wk. 1. *persuade, lead astray*. inf. 3/30.

**wēn.** fem. *hope, expectation* (with gen. of what is expected). nom. pl. **wēna** 15/13. dat. pl. **wēnum** 15/9; 17/29.

**wēna.** wk. masc. *idea, opinion, hope, expectation*. dat. sg. **wēnan.**

**wēnan.** wk. 1. (with gen.). *expect, suspect, believe, think*. 1sg. **wēne** 14/135. 2sg. **wēnstū** 10/31 (contracted with *þū*). past 3sg. **wēnde** 10/51; 12/239; 18/20. past pl. **wēndon.** subj. sg. **wēne** 7/16. subj. pl. **wēnen** 10/81.

**(ge)wendan.** wk. 1. (frequently with refl. pron.). *turn, change, go, return.* past 3sg. **gewende, wende** 3/35, 58. past pl. **wendon, gewendan** 3/89; 5/8; 12/193, 205. subj. sg. **wende, gewende** 1/19; 12/252. inf. **wendan, gewendan** 3/41; 12/316; 14/22.

**Wendle.** masc. *Wendels* (an unidentified nation). gen. pl. **Wendla.**

**wenian.** wk. 2. *accustom, entertain.* past 3sg. **wenede** 13/36. inf. 13/29.

**wēold-** → (ge)wealdan.

**wēolle** → weallan.

**Weonodland** → Weonoþland.

**Weonoþland.** neut. *the land of the Wends.* nom. sg. **Weonodland, Weonoðland** 8/53, 56. acc. sg. **Weonodland** 8/57. dat. sg. **Weonodlande, Winodlande** 8/58, 59.

**wēop** → wēpan.

**weorc.** neut. *work, labour, workmanship, deed.* acc. sg. 9/12. dat. sg. **weorce** 1/17; 10/2. acc. pl. 7/69; 14/79. gen. pl. **weorca** 10/13, 47. dat. pl. **weorcum** 2/2; 10/11.

**geweorc.** neut. *work, construction, fortification.* nom. sg. 11/9. nom. pl. 13/87.

**weorcgerēfa.** masc. *overseer.* dat. pl. **weorcgerēfum.**

**weorcman.** masc. athematic. *working man.* acc. pl. **weorcmen** 10/4.

**weorcstān.** masc. *hewn stone.* gen. pl. **weorcstāna** 2/18.

**weorod-** → werod.

**weorpan.** st. 3. *throw, cast.* past pl. **wurpon** 18/290. imp. sg. **wurp.**

**weorþ. A.** neut. *value, price, money.* dat. sg. **weorðe** 7/31, 32.

    **B.** adj. of price, *worth* something (gen.). fem. nom. sg. **wurð** 6/30.

**(Ge)weorþan.** st. 3. *become.* 3sg. **weorþeð, wyrð** 7/3; 13/110. past 3sg. **wearð, gewearð** B/7; 2/12; 4/7; 7/47, etc. (9x). past pl. **wurdon, wurdun** 2/27; 18/159. inf. **weorðan** 7/7; 13/64. past part. **geworden** 9/43; 14/87; 16/24. *turn,*

*change, convert.* 2sg. **gewyrst** 1/19. 3sg. **wyrð.** past 3sg. **geweard.** subj. sg. **weorþe** 7/36. past part. **geworden** 7/51. *happen, turn out.* past 3sg. **geweard** 7/32. subj. sg. **weorðe, geweorþe** 7/36 (2x). subj. past sg. **gewurde** 7/40. past part. **geworden** 7/25, 30, 63; 18/260. *be* (frequent with past part. in passive constructions). 3sg. **wyrð** 7/16; 10/36. past 3sg. **wearð** 2/2, 3, 5, 10, 16, etc. (18x). past pl. **wurdon** 1/7. subj. past sg. **wurde** 2/4; 3/44, 57; 12/1. subj. past pl. **wurden** 10/9.

**weorþfullic.** adj. *worthy.* neut. gen. sg. **weorðfullices** 10/22.

**weorþfullīce.** adv. *worthily.* 10/11.

**weorþgeorn.** adj. *desirous of honour, ambitious.* wk. masc. nom. sg. **weorðgeorna** 10/76. masc. nom. pl. superl. **weorðgeornuste** 10/36.

**(ge)weorþian.** wk. 2. *honour, worship, exalt.* pl. **weorðiað** 14/81. past 3sg. **geweorðode, wurðode** 2/6; 14/90, 94. past pl. **wurþodon.** imp. pl. **weorða.** inf. **weorþian** 14/129. infl. inf. **tō weorðianne.** past part. **geweorðad, geweorðod, geweorðode, gewurðod** 2/2; 9/1; 10/70; 14/15; 18/298.

**weorþlīce.** adv. *worthily, splendidly.* **weorðlīce, wurðlīce** 12/279; 14/17.

**weorþmynt.** fem. *honour, glory.* nom. sg. **wurðmynt** 2/31; 3/113. acc. sg. **weorðmynde** 18/342.

**weorþscipe.** masc. *honour, respect.* acc. sg. **weorðscipe, wurðscipe** 6/12; 10/31. dat. sg. 7/44.

**weorþung.** fem. *honour, veneration, worship.* dat. sg. **weorðunge** 7/10.

**weoruld** → woruld.

**weoruldhāde** → woruldhād.

**wēox-, gewēox-** → (ge)weaxan.

**wēpan.** st. 7. *weep.* past 3sg. **wēop** 14/55. inf. 16/38. pres. part. **wēpende** 3/68.

**wer.** masc. *man, husband.* nom. sg. A/1; B/6; 2/30; 3/4, 5, etc. (7x). acc. sg. 2/8; 3/64. gen. sg. **weres** C/3; La; 1/16; 3/112.

dat. sg. **were** B/5; 1/6; 3/1, 57. nom. pl.
**weras** 2/31; 15/6; 18/71, 142, 163, etc.
(6x). acc. pl. **weras** 5/7; 10/80. gen. pl.
**wera** B/4. dat. pl. **werum** 2/1.

**wergas** → wearg.

**werian.** A. wk. 1. *defend.* 3sg. **wereð.** past
3sg. **werede** 4/5. past pl. **weredon**
12/82, 283.
B. wk. 2. *wear.* past 3sg. **weorode**
2/11.

**wērig.** adj. *weary.* neut. nom. sg. 13/15.
masc. acc. sg. **wērigne** 13/57. neut.
nom. pl. **wērige** 12/303.

**wērigferhþ.** adj. *weary in spirit.* masc.
nom. pl. **wērigferhðe** 18/290. masc. acc.
pl. **wērigferhðe** 18/249.

**wērigmōd.** adj. *weary in spirit.* masc. nom.
sg. 16/49.

**werod.** neut. *army, host, troop, multitude.*
nom. sg. 12/64, 97; 18/199. acc. sg.
12/102. dat. sg. **weorode, werode**
12/51; 14/152. inst. sg. **weorode,**
**werede, werode** 4/4; 14/69, 124. gen.
pl. **weroda, weruda** 14/51; 18/342. dat.
pl. **weorodum** 11/17.

**werscipe.** masc. *cunning.* dat. sg. 6/32.

**wesan.** anom. verb. *be.* 2sg. **wes.** inf. J/83,
85; 14/110, 117; 16/42.

**west.** adv. *west.* 8/59; 10/65; 12/97.

**westanwind.** masc. *westerly wind.* gen. sg.
**westanwindes** 8/8.

**wēste.** adj. *waste, uncultivated, barren,*
*ruined.* masc. nom. sg. 8/3; 13/74. neut.
nom. sg. 8/13, 15. neut. gen. sg. **wēstes**
10/19. wk. neut. acc. sg. 8/6.

**wēsten.** neut. *wilderness, desert.* dat. sg.
**wēstene, wēstenne** 3/39; 8/4. dat. pl.
**wēstenum** 10/25.

**westeweard.** adj. *western part of.* masc.
acc. sg. **westeweardne** 10/16.

**Westmynster.** neut. *Westminster.* dat. sg.
**Westmynstre** 6/20.

**Westsǣ.** fem. *Western Sea* (i.e. the sea west
of Norway). acc. sg. 8/2.

**Westseaxe, Westseaxan.** wk. masc. *West*
*Saxons.* gen. pl. **Westseaxna** 4/1.

**wīc.** neut. *habitation.* nom. sg. 16/32. dat.
sg. **wīce.** acc. pl. 16/52.

**wicca.** wk. masc. *witch.* nom. pl. **wiccan**
7/56.

**wicg.** neut. *horse.* dat. sg. **wicge** I/7;
12/240.

**(ge)wīcian.** wk. 2. *camp, dwell, live.* pl.
**wīciað** 8/3. past 3sg. **wīcode** 8/42. past
pl. **gewīcodon** 8/15. past part. **gewīcode.**

**wīcing.** masc. *Viking.* acc. sg. 12/139. dat.
sg. **wīcinge** 7/36. acc. pl. **wīcingas**
12/322. gen. pl. **wīcinga** 12/26, 73, 97.
dat. pl. **wīcingum** 12/116.

**wīd.** adj. *wide, long* (of time). wk. neut.
dat. sg. **wīdan** 18/347.

**wīde.** adv. *widely.* 5/20; 7/3, 5, 12, 13, etc.
(19x).

**gewīde.** adv. *far apart.* superl. **gewīdost**
16/13.

**wīdgil.** adj. *broad, extensive.* fem. nom.
sg. **wīdgel** 10/66. fem. nom. pl. 10/65.

**wīdl.** masc. *filth.* dat. sg. **wīdle** 18/59.

**wīdlāst.** masc. *long journey.* dat. pl.
**wīdlāstum** 15/9.

**wīdsǣ.** fem. *open sea.* nom. sg. 8/13, 49.
acc. sg. 8/6.

**wīf.** neut. *woman, wife.* nom. sg. J/84;
M/11; 1/2, 6, 8, etc. (9x). acc. sg. 3/64.
gen. sg. **wīfes** 1/17; 3/82; 4/7. dat. sg.
**wīfe** 1/1, 4, 13, 15, 16, etc. (7x). nom.
pl. 2/31; 18/163. acc. pl. 5/7. gen. pl.
**wīfa** 14/94. dat. pl. **wīfum.**

**wīfcȳþþu.** fem. *company of a woman.* dat.
sg. **wīfcȳþþe** 4/4.

**gewīfian.** wk. 2. *marry.* past 3sg. **gewīfode.**

**wīfman.** masc. athematic. *woman.* acc.
sg. **wimman** 6/29. nom. pl. **wimmen**
3/105.

**gewīfode** → gewīfian.

**wīg.** neut. *war, battle.* nom. sg. J/84;
13/80. gen. sg. **wīges** 12/73, 130. dat.
sg. **wīge** 12/10, 128, 193, 235, 252.

**wiga.** wk. masc. *warrior.* nom. sg. 12/210;
13/67. acc. sg. **wigan** 12/75, 235. dat. sg.
**wigan** 12/126. nom. pl. **wigan** 12/79,
302. gen. pl. **wigena** 12/135; 18/49.

**wīgend. A.** masc. nd-stem. *warrior.* acc. sg. **wiggend** 18/258. nom. pl. **wiggend, wīgend** 12/302; 18/69, 141, 312. dat. pl. **wiggendum** 18/283. **B.** adj. *fighting.* gen. pl. **wīgendra.**

**wiggendum** → wīgend.

**wīgheard.** adj. *fierce in battle.* masc. acc. sg. **wīgheardne** 12/75.

**wīgplega.** wk. masc. *battle-play.* dat. sg. **wīgplegan** 12/268, 316.

**wīhaga.** wk. masc. *battle-hedge*, fig. *shield-wall.* acc. sg. **wīhagan** 12/102.

**wiht. A.** fem. *weight.* dat. sg. **wihte** 6/35. **B.** adv. *at all.* 18/274.

**wiites** → wīte.

**wilddēor.** neut. *wild beast, wild animal.* dat. pl. **wildēorum, wildrum** 1/14; 8/22.

**wilde.** adj. *wild.* masc. nom. pl. 8/32. wk. masc. acc. pl. **wildan** 8/24.

**wildēorum, wildrum** → wilddēor.

**wile** → willan.

**will.** neut. *desire.* gen. sg. **willes.**

**willa.** wk. masc. *will, purpose, desire.* nom. sg. 14/129. acc. sg. **willan** 6/40; 7/70. gen. sg. **willan** 10/63. dat. sg. **willan** 6/14, 22, 23. dat. pl. **willum** 10/68. *pleasure.* nom. sg. A/2; 17/30. dat. sg. **willan** 18/295. gen. pl. **wilna** 17/45.

**willan. A.** anom. verb. *wish, be willing, desire, intend.* 1sg. **wille, wylle** 12/221, 317; 14/1; 17/1; 18/84, etc. (6x). 2sg. **wylt.** 3sg. **wile** La; 2/4; 10/15; 12/52. pl. **willað, wille, wyllað** 2/1; 3/2; 12/35, 46; 15/2, etc. (6x). past 3sg. **wolde** c/6; H/4; 2/5, 9, 18, etc. (20x). past pl. **woldon** 5/7; 6/40; 9/27; 10/14, 27, etc. (8x). subj. sg. **wille** K/1371; 7/29, 32; 10/41, 65, etc. (7x). subj. pl. 7/54. subj. past sg. **wolde** 8/4. Expressing futurity. *will.* 1sg. **wille, wylle** 12/216, 247. 2sg. **wilt** 10/16 (2x). 3sg. **wile** 10/30; 14/107. pl. **willaþ, wille, wyllað** 6/12; 8/66; 12/40. past 1sg. **wolde** 10/54, 65. past 3sg. **wolde** 2/11 (3x). past pl. **woldon** 5/21. subj. sg. **wille** 12/37. **B.** Negated forms. 1sg. **nelle, nylle** 12/246. pl. **nellað** 7/54. past 3sg. **nolde**

2/4; 3/101, 102; 4/8; 5/3, etc. (9x). past pl. **noldon** F/6; 4/11, 12; 12/81, 185, etc. (6x). subj. past pl. **noldon.**

**wilnian.** wk. 2. *desire* something (gen.), *seek* something (gen.) from (*tō*) some source. 3sg. **wilnað, gewilnigað** 6/12; 10/14. pl. **wilniað, wilnigað, wilnige** 10/14, 21, 23, 24, 48. past 1sg. **wilnode** 10/2, 9, 11. past 3sg. **wilnode** 10/55, 58. past pl. **wilnodon** 10/57. subj. sg. **wilnige** 10/32, 35. subj. pl. **wilnigen** 10/81.

**gewilnian.** wk. 2. *wish, ask.* past 3sg. **gewilnode** 2/10.

**wilnung.** fem. *desire* for something (gen.). nom. sg. 10/13.

**wilsumness.** fem. *devotion.* dat. sg. **wilsumnesse** 9/43.

**wilt** → willan.

**Wiltūnscīr.** fem. *Wiltshire.* dat. sg. **Wiltūnscīre** 5/2.

**wimman, wimmen** → wīfman.

**wīn.** neut. *wine.* nom. sg. 5/16. dat. sg. **wīne** 18/29, 67.

**Winceasterlēode.** fem. *the people of Winchester.*

**Winceastre** → Wintanceaster.

**wincel.** masc. *corner.* dat. sg. **wincle** Lb.

**wind.** masc. *wind.* nom. sg. A/4; 3/39. acc. sg. 8/42; 18/347. dat. sg. **winde** G/5; 13/76. gen. pl. **winda** G/2.

**windan.** st. 3. *wind, twist.* past pl. **wundon.** past part. **wunden** 13/32. *fly, fly in a circle.* past pl. **wundon** 12/106. inf. 12/322. *roll.* past 3sg. **wand** 18/110. *brandish.* past 3sg. **wand** 12/43.

**windig.** adj. *windy.* masc. acc. pl. **windige** K/1358.

**wine.** masc. *friend, lord, husband.* nom. sg. 12/250; 16/49, 50; 17/39. acc. pl. **winas** 12/228.

**Winedas.** masc. *Wends* (i.e. the Slavs). dat. pl. **Winedum** 8/48.

**winedryhten.** masc. *friend and lord.* acc. sg. **winedrihten, winedryhten** 12/248, 263; 18/274. gen. sg. **winedryhtnes** 13/37.

**winelēas.** adj. *friendless.* masc. nom. sg. 13/45; 16/10.

**winemǣg.** wk. masc. *dear kinsman.* acc. pl. **winemāgas** 12/306. gen. pl. **winemǣga** 13/7.

**winetrēow.** fem. *conjugal fidelity, conjugal agreement.* acc. sg. **winetrēowe** 17/52.

**wīngeard.** masc. *vineyard.* dat. sg. **wīngearde.**

**wīngedrinc.** neut. *wine-drinking.* dat. sg. **wīngedrince** 18/16.

**wīnhāte.** wk. fem. *invitation to wine.* acc. sg. **wīnhātan** 18/8.

**gewinn.** neut. *strife, battle.* nom. sg. 3/81; 8/62. acc. sg. **gewin, gewinn** H/4; 12/214. dat. sg. **gewinne** 3/79, 81; 12/248, 302; 14/65.

**winnan.** st. 3. *labour, struggle, contend.* pl. **winnað** 10/21. subj. past sg. **wunne.** *suffer.* past 1sg. **wonn** 16/5.

**gewinnan.** st. 3. *win, conquer.* inf. 7/62; 12/125. past part. **gewunnen** 6/32.

**Winodlande** → Weonoþland.

**wīnsǣd.** adj. *satiated with wine.* masc. nom. pl. **wīnsade** 18/71.

**wīnsǣl.** neut. *wine-hall.* nom. pl. **wīnsalo** 13/78.

**Wintanceaster.** fem. *Winchester.* acc. sg. **Wintanceastre** 4/16. dat. sg. **Winceastre** 6/20.

**winter.** masc. u-stem. *winter, year.* nom. sg. 8/75. gen. sg. **wintres** 13/103. dat. sg. **wintra** 8/3. gen. pl. **wintra** H/1; 4/3, 16, 18; 10/40, etc. (6x). dat. pl. **wintrum** 12/210.

**wintercearig.** adj. *sorrowful as winter.* masc. nom. sg. 13/24.

**wiotan** → wita.

**wirigþ** → wyrigan.

**gewis.** adj. *certain, aware.* masc. nom. sg. 9/45.

**wīs.** adj. *wise.* masc. nom. sg. 6/13; 10/49, 51; 12/219; 13/64. masc. inst. sg. **wīse** 13/88. gen. pl. **wīsra** 10/16. dat. pl. **wīsum.** wk. masc. nom. sg. **wīsa** 10/51, 54, 76. wk. masc. acc. sg. **wīsan** 10/67.

wk. masc. gen. sg. **wīsan** 10/53, 71, 74. masc. nom. sg. compar. **wīsra.**

**wīsdōm.** masc. *wisdom.* nom. sg. 10/1, 64. acc. sg. G/1. dat. sg. **wīsdōme** 10/9, 10.

**wīse.** wk. fem. *manner, way, subject matter.* nom. sg. I/10. acc. sg. **wīsan** 7/12; 9/19, 27. acc. pl. **wīsan** 3/49; 7/24. dat. pl. **wīsum** 2/4.

**wīsian.** wk. 2. *guide.* past 3sg. **wīsode** 12/141.

**Wisle.** wk. fem. *Vistula.* nom. sg. 8/57, 58, 59. dat. sg. 8/59.

**Wislemūþa.** wk. masc. *the mouth of the Vistula.* nom. sg. 8/59. dat. sg. **Wislemūðan** 8/56.

**wīslīce.** adv. *wisely.* 10/15.

**wisse** → (ge)witan.

**wist.** fem. *abundance, nourishment, feast.* dat. sg. **wiste** 13/36.

**wist-** → (ge)witan.

**wit** → ic, wē.

**wita.** wk. masc. *wise man, counsellor,* (Roman) *senator.* nom. sg. 10/75; 13/65. gen. sg. **witan** M/4. nom. pl. **witan, wiotan** 4/1; 5/1, 12.

**gewita.** wk. masc. *witness, one with knowledge* of something (gen.), *accomplice.* nom. sg. M/13; 10/63.

**(ge)witan.** A. pret. pres. *know, understand.* 1sg. **wāt** 2/13; 3/86; 13/11. 2sg. **wāst** 10/2, 3, 5, 17, 28. 3sg. **wāt** A/6; 1/5; 10/74; 12/94; 13/29, etc. (6x). pl. **witan, witon** C/2, 9; 7/8, 32, 47, etc. (7x). past 3sg. **wisse, wiste** 8/8; 12/24; 13/27. past pl. **wiston** 9/36; 18/207. subj. sg. **wite** K/1367; 3/47. inf. **witan** J/91; 7/28; 10/16. infl. inf. **tō gewitanne, tō witanne** 6/12; 7/30. pres. part. **witende** 1/5.

B. Negated forms. 1sg. **nāt** 10/27. 3sg. **nāt** 10/77. past 3sg. **nyste, nysse** 6/30; 8/8, 9, 16; 18/68. subj. sg. **nyte** M/11.

**gewītan.** st. 1. (sometimes with refl. pron.). *depart.* 3sg. **gewīteð** K/1360. pl. **gewītað** F/1. past **gewiton.** past 1sg. **gewāt** 9/8; 16/9. past 3sg. **gewāt** 2/5,

16; 12/72, 150; 13/95, etc. (9x). past pl.
gewiton, gewitan F/5; 14/133; 18/290.
imp. sg. gewīt.

wīte. neut. *punishment, perdition, torment.*
nom. sg. 3/72. acc. sg. 16/5. gen. sg.
wiites, wītes 9/24; 10/32. dat. sg. M/5,
6, 8, 10, 12, etc. (6x). gen. pl. wīta
14/87. dat. pl. wītum A/6; 18/115.

wītega. wk. masc. *prophet.*

wītegian. wk. 2. *prophesy, predict.* past 3sg.
wītegode 2/12.

gewīteness. fem. *departure.* gen. sg.
gewītenesse 9/28.

Witland. neut. *Witland* (area east of the
Vistula). nom. sg. 8/57. acc. sg. 8/57.

gewitlēast. fem. *folly.* nom. sg. 3/82.

gewitloca. wk. masc. *container of intellect,
mind.* dat. sg. gewitlocan 10/67; 17/15;
18/69.

gewitness. fem. *knowledge* (*on gewitnesse*
= with the complicity of), *witness.* dat.
sg. gewitnesse M/12.

witod. adj. *decreed.*

witodlīce. adv. *truly, indeed.* 3/65; 6/33.

gewiton → gewītan.

wiþ. A. prep. (with acc., dat. or gen.).
*towards.* 6/29; 7/23; 9/27; 12/8, 131.
*against.* wið, uuiþ 2/19; 3/9, 64 (2x),
79, etc. (14x). *near.* 3/36; 8/2, 31. *in
exchange for.* 5/15; 7/31, 32; 12/31, 35,
etc. (6x). of personal interaction, *with.*
G/6; 3/89; 5/4; 7/30, 66, etc. (7x).
   B. adv. *towards, against.* 5/3.

wiþ þām þe. conj. *on condition that,
provided that.* 5/1.

wiþcweþan. st. 5. *contradict, oppose.* past
pl. wiðcwǣdon 6/14.

wiþēastan. adv. *to the east.* 8/32.

wiþerlēan. neut. *repayment.* nom. sg.
12/116.

wiþertrod. neut. *the way back.* acc. sg.
18/312.

wiþerwinna. wk. masc. *adversary.* nom.
sg. 3/20.

wiþmetan. st. 5. *compare with.* past part.
wiðmeten 3/84.

wiþstondan. st. 6. *withstand.* imp. pl.
wiðstandað 3/20. inf. 13/15.

Wiþsūþan. prep. *to the south of.* 8/46.

wiþuppon. adv. *above* (at higher eleva-
tions). 8/32.

wiþūtan. prep. *without, outside of.* 3/27;
6/32.

wlanc- → wlonc.

wlāt → wlītan.

wlenco. fem. (pl. with sg. sense). *pride,
splendour.* dat. pl. wlencum 10/70.

wlītan. st. 1. *look.* past 3sg. wlāt 12/172.
inf. 18/49.

wlitig. adj. *beautiful.* neut. nom. sg. 1/6.
masc. nom. pl. wlitige 3/105. wk. fem.
gen. sg. wlitegan 18/137. wk. neut. dat.
sg. wlitegan 18/255.

wlonc. adj. *splendid, lofty, proud, arrogant.*
fem. nom. sg. wlanc, wlonc 13/80;
18/325. masc. acc. sg. wlancne 12/139.
neut. dat. sg. wloncum 1/7. nom. pl.
wlance 18/16. masc. nom. pl. wlance
12/205. wk. neut. dat. sg. wlancan
12/240.

wōd-, gewōd- → (ge)wadan.

wōdlīce. adv. *madly.*

wōh. adj. *crooked, depraved, evil, unjust.*
wk. masc. nom. sg. wō.

wōhdōm. masc. *wrongful judgement.* acc.
pl. wōhdōmas 7/63.

wōhgestrēon. neut. *ill-gotten gains.* gen.
pl. wōhgestrēona 7/63.

wōlberend. adj. *pestilential.* neut. dat. sg.
wōlbǣrendum A/1.

wolcen. neut. *cloud, sky, heaven.* dat. sg.
wolcne. gen. pl. wolcna 18/67. dat. pl.
wolcnum 10/65; 14/53, 55.

wold- → willan.

wōma. wk. masc. *noise, tumult.* nom. sg.
13/103.

womful. adj. *impure, criminal, sinful.*
masc. nom. sg. womfull 18/77.

womm. masc. *stain, defilement, sin.* dat.
sg. womme 18/59. dat. pl. wommum
14/14.

won → wann.

**wonn** → winnan.

**wonna** → wann.

**wōp.** masc. *weeping, lamentation.*

**word.** neut. *word.* acc. sg. 9/44; 11/17; 12/168; 14/35; 18/82, etc. (7x). gen. sg. **wordes** 7/23, 47. dat. sg. **worde** 14/111. acc. pl. 7/69; 9/11, 14, 18, 44, etc. (8x). dat. pl. **wordum, wordon** 3/71; 9/14; 10/65; 12/26, 43, etc. (10x).

**wordbēotung.** fem. *promise in words.* acc. pl. **wordbēotunga** 17/15.

**geworden** → (ge)weorþan.

**wordlēan.** neut. *reward for words.* gen. pl. **wordlēana** 1/9.

**worht-, geworht-** → (ge)wyrcan.

**wōrian.** wk. 2. *wander, decay.* pl. **wōriað** 13/78.

**worn.** masc. *multitude.* acc. sg. 13/91. dat. pl. **wornum** 18/163.

**woroldscamu.** fem. *worldly shame, public disgrace.* dat. sg. **woroldscame** 7/42, 43.

**woroldstrūdere.** masc. *robber of worldly goods.* nom. pl. **woroldstrūderas** 7/56.

**woruld.** fem. *world.* nom. sg. **worold** 7/2. acc. sg. **woruld, weoruld, worulde** 10/21; 13/58, 107; 18/156. gen. sg. **worulde** 9/2; 10/21; 13/74; 14/133; 16/46, etc. (6x). dat. sg. **worulde, worolde** c/11, 12; F/6; 2/16; 3/81, etc. (17x).

**woruldbūend.** masc. nd-stem. *dweller in the world.* gen. pl. **woruldbūendra** 18/82.

**woruldgesǣlig.** adj. *prosperous in worldly possessions.* masc. nom. sg. 12/219.

**woruldhād.** masc. *secular life.* acc. sg. 9/20. dat. sg. **weoruldhāde** 9/5.

**woruldlic.** adj. *worldly.* dat. pl. **woruldlicum.**

**woruldman.** masc. athematic. *layman.* nom. pl. **woruldmen, woruldmenn** 2/28; 10/14.

**woruldrīce.** neut. *kingdom of the world.* dat. sg. 13/65; 16/13.

**woruldþing.** neut. *worldly thing, worldly affair.* acc. pl. **woruldþincg** 2/9.

**wōþ.** fem. *noise, speech, song.*

**wōþbora.** wk. masc. *orator, singer, poet.* dat. sg. **wōðboran** 1/9.

**wrāþ.** adj. *angry, terrible, grievous, cruel.* gen. pl. **wrāþra** 13/7; 14/51.

**wrāþe.** adv. *fiercely, cruelly.* 16/32.

**wræc** → (ge)wrecan.

**wræcca.** wk. masc. *exile, wretch.* nom. sg. 16/10. acc. sg. **wræccan** 10/73.

**wrǣce** → (ge)wrecan.

**wræclāst.** masc. *path of exile.* nom. sg. 13/32. acc. pl. **wræclāstas** 13/5.

**wræcmæcg.** masc. *exile, outcast, wretch, devil.* nom. sg. **wræcmæcgas.**

**wræcsīþ.** masc. *journey of exile.* acc. pl. **wræcsīþas** 16/38. gen. pl. **wræcsīþa** 16/5.

**wrǣtlic.** adj. *ornamental, curious, wondrous.* neut. nom. sg. La.

**(ge)wrecan.** st. 5. *avenge, take revenge.* past 3sg. **wræc** H/3. *tell, relate.* 1sg. **wrece** 16/1.

**wreccan.** wk. 1. *awaken.* past pl. **wrehton** 18/228, 243.

**wreoton** → (ge)wrītan.

**gewrit.** neut. *writing, scripture, book.* nom. sg. 3/97. acc. sg. 6/30. gen. sg. **gewrites** 9/24. nom. pl. **gewritu** 10/37.

**(ge)wrītan.** st. 1. *write.* past pl. **wreoton, writon** 9/23; 10/37. past part. **gewritene** 6/43.

**wrītere.** masc. *writer.* nom. pl. **wrīteras** 10/37. gen. pl. **wrītera** 10/36.

**writon** → (ge)wrītan.

**wrīþan.** st. 1. *twist, bind, torture.*

**wrixendlīce.** adv. *in turn.* 9/36.

**gewrohte** → (ge)wyrcan.

**wucu.** wk. fem. (with nom. sg. -*u* from the strong fem. declension ). *week.* dat. pl. **wucum** 8/35.

**wudu.** masc. u-stem. *wood, forest.* nom. sg. κ/1364; 14/27. acc. sg. 12/193. gen. sg. **wuda** 16/27. dat. sg. **wuda** 15/17. dat. pl. **wudum** 10/25.

**wuldor.** neut. *glory.* nom. sg. 2/26, 31; 3/113; 18/155, 347. acc. sg. 18/342. gen.

sg. **wuldres** 3/17; 14/14, 90, 97, 133, etc. (6x). dat. sg. **wuldre** 2/16, 31; 11/7; 14/135, 143, etc. (7x).

**wuldorblæd.** masc. *glorious success.* nom. sg. 18/156.

**wuldorfæder.** masc. *Father of glory.* gen. sg. 9/12.

**wulf.** masc. *wolf.* nom. sg. ꜰ/3; 13/82; 15/17; 18/206. nom. pl. **wulfas.** dat. pl. **wulfum** 18/295.

**wulfhliþ.** neut. *wolf-slope, wild land.* acc. pl. **wulfhleoþu** ᴋ/1358.

**gewuna.** wk. masc. *custom, habit.* dat. sg. **gewunan.** dat. pl. **gewunan** 7/51.

**wund. A.** fem. *wound.* nom. sg. 2/23. acc. sg. **wunde** 12/139, 271. dat. sg. **wunde** 3/58, 59. dat. pl. **wundum** 12/293, 303. **B.** adj. *wounded.* masc. nom. sg. 12/113, 144.

**wunden** → windan.

**wundenlocc.** adj. *wavy-haired.* fem. nom. sg. 18/77, 103, 325.

**gewundian.** wk. 2. *wound.* past 3sg. **gewundode** 4/5. past part. **gewundad, gewundod** 4/8, 15; 12/135.

**wundon** → windan.

**wundor.** neut. *wonder, miracle.* nom. sg. 7/47. nom. pl. **wundra** 2/1, 5. gen. pl. **wundra** 3/113; 9/12.

**wundorlic.** adj. *wonderful, strange.* neut. nom. sg. 2/1, 25.

**wundorlīce.** adv. *wonderfully, miraculously.* 2/31.

**wundrian.** wk. 2. *wonder, be astonished at someone* (gen.). past 3sg. **wundrode** 9/31. past pl. **wundrodon** 3/104.

**wundrum.** adv. *wondrously.* 13/98; 18/8.

**wundrung.** fem. *wonder, spectacle.* dat. sg. **wundrunge** 2/24.

**wunedon** → (ge)wunian.

**gewunelic.** adj. *customary.* neut. nom. sg. 3/70, 93.

**(ge)wunian.** wk. 2. *live* (in a place), *dwell, remain.* pl. **wuniaþ** 14/135. past 3sg. **wunode, wunade** ʙ/3; 2/1, 5, 10; 4/1, etc. (7x). past pl. **wunedon, wunodon**

2/31; 6/12; 14/3, 155. inf. **wunian** ᴄ/11; 14/121, 143; 16/27; 18/119. pres. part. **wunigende** 2/30. *be accustomed.* past 3sg. **gewunade** 9/1.

**wunne, gewunnen** → winnan.

**wunung.** fem. *dwelling.* acc. sg. **wununge** ᴄ/12.

**wurd-, gewurd-** → (ge)weorþan.

**wurp-** → weorpan.

**gewurpan.** wk. 1. *recover.* inf. 2/16.

**wurþ** → weorþ.

**wurþful.** adj. *worthy, magnificent.* masc. nom. sg. compar. **wurðfulra** 6/13.

**wurþlīce** → weorþlīce.

**wurþmynt** → weorþmynt.

**wurþod-, gewurþod-** → (ge)weorþian.

**wurþscipe** → weorþscipe.

**wutan, wuton** → uton.

**wydewe.** wk. fem. *widow.* gen. sg. **wydewan** 3/23. nom. pl. **wydewan** 7/14.

**wyll-** → willan.

**wyllen.** adj. *woollen.* neut. acc. sg. 2/11.

**wylspring.** masc. *spring.* nom. pl. **wylspringas.**

**wylt** → willan.

**gewylt** → (ge)wealdan.

**wynlic.** adj. *joyful.* neut. acc. pl. compar. **wynlicran** 16/52.

**wynn.** fem. *joy, pleasure.* nom. sg. **wyn** 13/36; 15/12; 16/46. gen. pl. **wynna** 12/174; 16/32. dat. pl. **wynnum** 13/29; 14/15.

**wynsum.** adj. *pleasant, delightful, joyful.* masc. gen. sg. **wynsumes.** neut. nom. pl. **wynsumu** 9/23. wk. fem. acc. sg. **wynsuman.**

**(ge)wyrcan.** wk. 1. *make, create.* 3sg. **wyrcð** 7/41. pl. **wyrcað** 8/74. past 3sg. **geworhte, worhte** ᴄ/1; ɢ/2; 1/1; 2/23; 9/24, etc. (6x). past pl. **worhton, worhtan, geworhton** 1/7; 7/22; 14/31; 18/302. imp. sg. **wyrc.** inf. **wyrcan, gewyrcan, wyrcean** 8/74; 9/1, 3, 4; 12/81, etc. (8x). past part. **geworht** 2/19, 25; 8/27, 29; 9/1. *build.* past 3sg. **gewrohte** 6/31. past pl. **worhton** 2/30.

inf. **wyrcean** 6/34. *work* towards some end (acc.). past 3sg. **worhte** 18/65. *perform* a task. 3sg. **wyrcð** 2/1. pl. **gewyrcað** 7/70. past pl. **worhtan** 7/47. inf. **wyrcan** 10/3, 8. infl. inf. **tō wyrcanne, tō wyrcenne** 10/2, 8. past part. **geworhte** 7/49. *bring about.* inf. **gewyrcan** 12/264.

**wyrd.** fem. *event, fate, fortune, destiny.* nom. sg. 13/5, 100; 14/74. gen. sg. **wyrde.** dat. sg. **wyrde** 13/15. gen. pl. **wyrda** 13/107; 14/51.

**gewyrht.** fem. *deed, merit.* dat. pl. **gewyrhtum** 7/35; 11/25.

**wyrigan.** wk. 1. *curse.* 3sg. **wirigð, wyrigð** 3/32, 55. imp. 2sg. **wyrig** 3/60.

**wyrm.** masc. *serpent, snake, dragon, worm.* nom. pl. **wyrmas.** dat. pl. **wyrmum** 18/115.

**wyrmlīc.** neut. *likeness of a serpent.* dat. pl. **wyrmlīcum** 13/98.

**wyrms.** masc. *pus.* nom. sg. 2/15. acc. sg. 3/59.

**wyrmsele.** masc. *hall of serpents* (i.e. hell). dat. sg. 18/119.

**wyrnan.** wk. 1. *withhold* something (gen.). past 3sg. **wyrnde** 12/118.

**wyrs-** → yfel.

**wyrsian.** wk. 2. *worsen.* past pl. **wyrsedan** 7/13.

**gewyrst** → (ge)weorþan.

**wyrstan** → yfel.

**wyrt.** fem. *plant, herb, vegetable.* nom. sg. G/3 (2x). nom. pl. **wyrta.** acc. pl. **wyrta** 1/18. dat. pl. **wyrtum.** *root.* dat. pl. **wyrtum** K/1364.

**wyrtwala.** wk. masc. *root.* dat. sg. **wyrtwalan** B/3.

**wyrþ** → (ge)weorþan.

**wyrþe.** adj. *worth, worthy, deserving.* fem. nom. sg. 2/13. neut. nom. sg. 10/32. masc. gen. sg. **wyrðes** 9/14. masc. nom. pl. H/2; 10/79.

**wȳscan.** wk. 1. *wish.* 1sg. **wȳsce.** past 3sg. **wȳscte** H/3.

**ȳcan** → īcan.

**yfel. A.** adj. *bad, evil, wretched.* masc. dat. sg. **yfelum.** neut. acc. pl. **yfele** 6/43. dat. pl. **yfelan** 7/51, 53. wk. masc. nom. pl. **yfelan.** neut. nom. sg. compar. **wyrse** 10/80. fem. acc. pl. compar. **wyrsan** 7/65. wk. fem. dat. sg. superl. **wyrstan** 3/58. **B.** neut. *evil, harm.* nom. sg. 10/13. acc. sg. 1/5; 3/5, 14, 62; 6/28, etc. (6x). gen. sg. **yfeles** 12/133. dat. sg. **yfele** 5/4. gen. pl. **yfela.**

**yfelian.** wk. 2. *become worse, become sick* (impersonal with dat.). past 3sg. **geyfelade** 6/2. inf. 7/3.

**yfelness.** fem. *evilness.* nom. sg. **yfelnes.** acc. sg. **yfelnesse** 6/43.

**yfle.** adv. *badly.* compar. **wyrse** 7/2.

**ylc-** → ilca.

**ylde.** masc. (pl. only). *men.* gen. pl. **ælda, yldo** 13/85; 17/3. dat. pl. **yldum.**

**yldest-** → eald.

**yldo.** fem. *age.* gen. sg. **ylde** 9/5.

**yldra.** wk. masc. (compar. of *eald*). *elder.* acc. pl. **yldran** D/2.

**ymb.** prep. (usually with acc., sometimes with dat.). *around, near.* **ymb, embe** 4/15; 8/16; 12/249. *about, concerning.* **ymb, ymbe, embe** A/2; D/3; G/1; 6/13; 7/5, etc. (9x). Of time, *after.* **embe, ymb** 2/10; 4/3; 12/271.

**ymbclyppan.** wk. 1. *embrace.* past 3sg. **ymbclypte** 14/42.

**ymbescīnan.** st. 1. *shine about.* past 3sg. **ymbescān.**

**ymbesittan.** st. 5. *sit around, surround, besiege.* past pl. **ymbsǣton** 5/5.

**ymbeþencan.** wk. 1. *consider, ponder.* subj. past sg. **ymbeþōhte** 10/65.

**ymbhwyrft.** masc. *circle, extent.* acc. sg. 10/16. *alternation, turn.* dat. sg. **ymbhwyrfte** 3/8.

**ymbsǣton** → ymbesittan.

**ymbscīnan.** st. 1. *surround with light.* 3sg. **ymbscīnð** 3/16.

**ymbscrȳdan.** wk. 1. *clothe.* past part. **ymbscrȳd** 3/24, 83.

**ymbsēon.** st. 5. *look about.* subj. past sg. **ymbsāwe** 10/65.

**ymbsprǣce.** adj. *spoken of.* masc. nom. pl. 10/80.

**ymbstandan.** st. 6. *stand around.* past pl. **ymbstōdan.**

**ymbtrymman.** wk. 1. *fortify, protect.* past 2sg. **ymbtrymedest** 3/31.

**ymbūtan.** prep. *about, around.* 10/65.

**ȳr.** noun. *back*(?). dat. sg. **ȳre** 5/18.

**yrfenuma.** wk. masc. *heir.*

**yrfeweardness.** fem. *inheritance.* nom. sg. **yrfweardnyss.**

**geyrgan.** wk. 1. *intimidate.* past part. **geyrigde** 7/39.

**yrgþo.** fem. *cowardice, slackness.* acc. sg. **yrhðe, yrhðo** 7/63; 12/6.

**geyrigde** → geyrgan.

**Ȳrland** → Īraland.

**yrmþu.** fem. *misery, poverty, crime.* nom. sg. **yrmð** 3/76; 7/32. acc. sg. **yrmðe, ermðe** 5/10; 7/30. dat. sg. **yrmðe** 7/42.

acc. pl. **yrmða, iermða** 1/16; 7/7. gen. pl. **yrmþa** 16/3.

**yrnende** → irnan.

**yrre. A.** neut. *anger.* nom. sg. G/7; 7/34. acc. sg. 7/16, 35, 38, 39, 41, etc. (6x). dat. sg. 7/46.
   **B.** adj. *angry.* masc. nom. sg. 12/44, 253. masc. nom. pl. 18/225.

**yrþling.** masc. *ploughman.* nom. sg. 3/37. acc. pl. **yrðlingas** 3/36.

**ys** → bēon.

**ysl.** fem. *ember.* dat. pl. **yslum** 3/84.

**yteren.** adj. *of sealskin.* masc. acc. sg. **yterenne** 8/29.

**ȳtmǣst.** adj. *uttermost, last.* wk. masc. nom. pl. **ȳtmestan** 10/70. wk. neut. acc. pl. superl. **ȳtmæstan** 9/44.

**ytst** → (ge)etan.

**ȳþ.** fem. *wave.* gen. pl. **ȳþa** 16/7; 17/42.

**ȳþan.** wk. 1. *lay waste, devastate.* past 3sg. **ȳþde** 13/85.

# References

[1] Alexander, J. J. G. *Insular Manuscripts, 6th to the 9th Century*. Vol. 1 of Survey of Manuscripts Illuminated in the British Isles. London: Harvey Miller, 1978.

[2] Alexander, Michael. *Old English Literature*. History of Literature Series. New York: Schocken Books, 1983.

[3] Assmann, Bruno, editor. *Angelsächsische Homilien und Heiligenleben*. Reprint with supplementary introduction by Peter Clemoes. Vol. 3 of Bibliothek der angelsächsischen Prosa. Darmstadt: Wissenschaftliche Buchgesellschaft, 1964.

[4] Baker, Peter S., editor. *The Beowulf Reader*. First published in 1995 as *Beowulf: Basic Readings*. Vol. 1 of Basic Readings in Anglo-Saxon England. New York: Garland Press, 2000.

[5] Baker, Peter S. and Michael Lapidge, editors. *Byrhtferth's Enchiridion*. Vol. 15 of Early English Text Society, Supplementary Series. Oxford: Oxford University Press, 1995.

[6] Bately, Janet, editor. *The Old English Orosius*. Vol. 6 of Early English Text Society, Supplementary Series. London: Oxford University Press, 1980.

[7] Bately, Janet, editor. *The Anglo-Saxon Chronicle: A Collaborative Edition*. Vol. 3, MS A. Cambridge: D. S. Brewer, 1986.

[8] Bessinger, Jess B. *A Concordance to the Anglo-Saxon Poetic Records*. Programmed by Philip H. Smith, Jr. The Cornell Concordances. Ithaca, NY: Cornell University Press, 1978.

[9] Bethurum, Dorothy, editor. *The Homilies of Wulfstan*. Oxford: Clarendon Press, 1957.

[10] Bischoff, Bernhard. *Latin Palaeography: Antiquity and the Middle Ages*. Trans. Dáibhí Ó Cróinín and David Ganz. Cambridge: Cambridge University Press, 1990.

[11]    Bjork, Robert E., editor. *Cynewulf: Basic Readings*. Vol. 4 of Basic Readings in Anglo-Saxon England. New York: Garland Press, 1996.

[12]    Bjork, Robert E. and John D. Niles, editors. *A Beowulf Handbook*. Exeter: University of Exeter Press, 1997.

[13]    Bliss, A. J. *The Metre of Beowulf*. 2nd edition. Oxford: Blackwell, 1967.

[14]    Blockley, Mary E. *Aspects of Old English Poetic Syntax: Where Clauses Begin*. Urbana: University of Illinois Press, 2001.

[15]    Bosworth, Joseph, T. Northcote Toller and Alistair Campbell. *An Anglo-Saxon Dictionary*. Vol. 2: *Supplement* by T. N. Toller; Vol. 3: *Enlarged Addenda and Corrigenda* by A. Campbell to the *Supplement* by T. N. Toller. Oxford: Oxford University Press, 1882–98, 1908–21, 1972.

[16]    Bradley, S. A. J. *Anglo-Saxon Poetry*. Everyman's Library. London: Dent, 1982.

[17]    Bredehoft, Thomas A. *Early English Metre*. Toronto: University of Toronto Press, 2005.

[18]    Brown, Michelle P. *Understanding Illuminated Manuscripts: A Guide to Technical Terms*. Malibu: J. Paul Getty Museum and British Library, 1994.

[19]    Brunner, Karl. *Altenglische Grammatik nach der angelsächsischen Grammatik von Eduard Sievers*. 3rd edition. Tübingen: Max Niemeyer Verlag, 1964.

[20]    Cable, Thomas. *The English Alliterative Tradition*. Middle Ages Series. Philadelphia: University of Pennsylvania Press, 1991.

[21]    Calder, Daniel G. and Michael J. Allen, editors. *Sources and Analogues of Old English Poetry: The Major Latin Texts in Translation*. Cambridge: D. S. Brewer, 1976.

[22]    Calder, Daniel G. et al., editors. *Sources and Analogues of Old English Poetry II: The Major Germanic and Celtic Texts in Translation*. Cambridge: D. S. Brewer, 1983.

[23]    Cameron, Angus, Ashley Crandell Amos, Sharon Butler, Christine Franzen, Antonette diPaolo Healey, Joan Holland, Ian McDougall, David McDougall, Nancy Porter, Nancy Speirs and Pauline Thompson. *Dictionary of Old English*. Not yet complete. Toronto: Pontifical Institute of Medieval Studies, from 1986.

[24]    Cameron, Angus, Allison Kingsmill and Ashley Crandell Amos. *Old English Word Studies: A Preliminary Author and Word Index*. Vol. 8 of Toronto Old English Series. Toronto: University of Toronto Press, 1983.

[25]    Campbell, A. *The Tollemache Orosius*. Vol. 3 of Early English Manuscripts in Facsimile. Copenhagen: Rosenkilde and Bagger, 1953.

[26]    Campbell, A. *Old English Grammar*. Oxford: Clarendon Press, 1959.

[27]    Campbell, Jackson J., editor. *The Advent Lyrics of the Exeter Book*. Princeton: Princeton University Press, 1959.

[28]    Campbell, James, Eric John and Patrick Wormald. *The Anglo-Saxons*. Oxford: Phaidon, 1982.

[29]    Chambers, R. W., Max Förster and Robin Flower, editors. *The Exeter Book of Old English Poetry*. London: P. Lund, 1933.

[30]    Clark Hall, John R. *A Concise Anglo-Saxon Dictionary*. With a supplement by Herbert D. Meritt. 4th edition. Cambridge: Cambridge University Press, 1960.

[31]    Clayton, Mary. 'An Edition of Ælfric's Letter *to Brother Edward*.' *Early Medieval English Texts and Interpretations: Studies Presented to Donald G. Scragg*. Ed.

by Elaine Treharne and Susan Rosser. Tempe, Arizona: Arizona Center for Medieval and Renaissance Studies, 2002, pp. 263–83.

[32] Colgrave, Bertram, editor. *The Life of Bishop Wilfrid by Eddius Stephanus*. Cambridge: Cambridge University Press, 1927.

[33] Crawford, Samuel J., editor. *The Old English Version of the Heptateuch, Ælfric's Treatise on the Old and New Testament, and His Preface to Genesis*. Reprint of 1922 ed. with additional material by N. R. Ker. Vol. 160 of Early English Text Society. London: Oxford University Press, 1969.

[34] Cross, James E. and Thomas D. Hill, editors. *The Prose Solomon and Saturn and Adrian and Ritheus*. Vol. 1 of McMaster Old English Texts and Studies. Toronto: University of Toronto Press, 1982.

[35] Dodwell, C. R. and P. A. M. Clemoes, editors. *The Old English Illustrated Hexateuch*. Vol. 18 of Early English Manuscripts in Facsimile. Copenhagen: Rosenkilde and Bagger, 1974.

[36] Donoghue, Daniel. *Style in Old English Poetry: The Test of the Auxiliary*. Vol. 196 of Yale Studies in English. New Haven: Yale University Press, 1987.

[37] Donoghue, Daniel. *Old English Literature: A Short Introduction*. Oxford: Blackwell, 2004.

[38] Dunning, T. P. and A. J. Bliss, editors. *The Wanderer*. New York: Appleton-Century-Crofts, 1969.

[39] Fell, Christine E. *Women in Anglo-Saxon England*. London: British Museum Publications, 1984.

[40] Flower, Robin and Hugh Smith, editors. *The Parker Chronicle and Laws*. Vol. 208 of Early English Text Society. London: Oxford University Press, 1941.

[41] Fulk, R. D., editor. *Interpretations of Beowulf: A Critical Anthology*. Bloomington and Indianapolis: Indiana University Press, 1991.

[42] Fulk, R. D. *A History of Old English Meter*. Middle Ages Series. Philadelphia: University of Pennsylvania Press, 1992.

[43] Fulk, R. D. and Christopher M. Cain. *A History of Old English Literature*. Oxford: Blackwell, 2003.

[44] Garmonsway, G. N. and Jacqueline Simpson, editors. *Beowulf and Its Analogues*. London: Dent, 1969.

[45] Godden, Malcolm and Michael Lapidge, editors. *The Cambridge Companion to Old English Literature*. Cambridge: Cambridge University Press, 1991.

[46] Godden, Malcolm, editor. *Ælfric's Catholic Homilies: The Second Series*. Vol. 5 of Early English Text Society, Supplementary Series. London: Oxford University Press, 1979.

[47] Godden, Malcolm. *Ælfric's Catholic Homilies: Introduction, Commentary and Glossary*. Vol. 18 of Early English Text Society, Supplementary Series. Oxford: Oxford University Press, 2000.

[48] Gollancz, Israel, editor. *The Cædmon Manuscript of Anglo-Saxon Biblical Poetry*. Oxford: Oxford University Press, 1927.

[49] Gordon, R. K. *Anglo-Saxon Poetry*. Everyman's Library. London: Dent, 1954.

[50] Greenfield, Stanley B. and Daniel G. Calder. *A New Critical History of Old English Literature*. Includes a survey of the Anglo-Latin background by Michael Lapidge. New York and London: New York University Press, 1986.

[51]    Greenfield, Stanley B. and Fred C. Robinson. *A Bibliography of Publications on Old English Literature to the End of 1972.* Toronto: University of Toronto Press, 1980.

[52]    Griffith, Mark, editor. *Judith.* Exeter Medieval English Texts and Studies. University of Exeter Press, 1997.

[53]    Griffiths, Bill, editor. *Alfred's Metres of Boethius.* 2nd edition. Pinner, Middlesex: Anglo-Saxon Books, 1994.

[54]    Hasenfratz, Robert J. *Beowulf Scholarship: An Annotated Bibliography, 1979–1990.* Vol. 14 of Garland medieval bibliographies. New York: Garland Press, 1993.

[55]    Healey, Antonette diPaolo and Richard L. Venezky. *A Microfiche Concordance to Old English.* Toronto: Dictionary of Old English Project, 1980.

[56]    Hecht, Hans, editor. *Bischof Wærferths von Worcester Übersetzung der Dialoge Gregors des grossen.* 2nd edition. Vol. 5 of Bibliothek der angelsächsischen Prosa. Darmstadt: Wissenschaftliche Buchgesellschaft, 1965.

[57]    Henel, Heinrich, editor. *Aelfric's De Temporibus Anni.* Vol. 213 of Early English Text Society. London: Oxford University Press, 1942.

[58]    Hogg, Richard M. *A Grammar of Old English.* Oxford and Cambridge, Mass.: Blackwell, 1992.

[59]    Holthausen, F. *Altenglisches etymologisches Wörterbuch.* 2nd edition. Heidelberg: Carl Winter, 1963.

[60]    Hunter Blair, Peter. *An Introduction to Anglo-Saxon England.* 2nd edition. Cambridge: Cambridge University Press, 1977.

[61]    Irvine, Susan, editor. *The Anglo-Saxon Chronicle: A Collaborative Edition.* Vol. 7, MS E. Cambridge: D. S. Brewer, 2004.

[62]    Karkov, Catherine E., editor. *The Archaeology of Anglo-Saxon England: Basic Readings.* Vol. 7 of Basic Readings in Anglo-Saxon England. New York: Garland Press, 1999.

[63]    Ker, N. R. *Catalogue of Manuscripts Containing Anglo-Saxon.* Oxford: Clarendon Press, 1957. See also Ker 1976.

[64]    Ker, N. R. 'Supplement to Catalogue of Manuscripts Containing Anglo-Saxon.' *Anglo-Saxon England* 5 (1976): 121–31.

[65]    Keynes, Simon. *Anglo-Saxon History: A Select Bibliography.* A more current version is on line at http://www.wmich.edu/medieval/research/rawl/keynesbib/index.html. Vol. 13 of Old English Newsletter Subsidia. Binghamton, N.Y.: Center for Medieval and Early Renaissance Studies, 1987.

[66]    Kiernan, Kevin S., editor. *The Electronic Beowulf.* Ann Arbor: University of Michigan Press, 2000.

[67]    Klaeber, F., editor. *Beowulf and the Fight at Finnsburg.* Includes two supplements. 3rd edition. Boston: D.C. Heath, 1950.

[68]    Klinck, Anne L., editor. *The Old English Elegies: A Critical Edition and Genre Study.* Montreal: McGill-Queen's University Press, 1992.

[69]    Krapp, George Philip and Elliott Van Kirk Dobbie, editors. *The Anglo-Saxon Poetic Records.* New York: Columbia University Press, 1931–53.

[70]    Lapidge, Michael, John Blair, Simon Keynes and Donald Scragg, editors. *The Blackwell Encyclopaedia of Anglo-Saxon England.* Oxford: Basil Blackwell, 1999.

[71]    Lapidge, Michael and Michael Herren. *Aldhelm: The Prose Works.* Ipswich and Cambridge: D. S. Brewer, 1979.

[72]  Lapidge, Michael and James L. Rosier. *Aldhelm: The Poetic Works*. Cambridge: D. S. Brewer, 1985.

[73]  Lass, Roger. *Old English: A Historical Linguistic Companion*. Cambridge: Cambridge University Press, 1994.

[74]  Leslie, R. F., editor. *Three Old English Elegies*. 2nd edition. Exeter Medieval English Texts and Studies. Exeter: University of Exeter Press, 1988.

[75]  Liuzza, R. M., editor. *Old English Literature: Critical Essays*. New Haven and London: Yale University Press, 2002.

[76]  Liuzza, R. M., editor. *The Poems of MS Junius 11: Basic Readings*. Vol. 8 of Basic Readings in Anglo-Saxon England. New York: Routledge, 2002.

[77]  Magoun, Francis P. 'The Oral-Formulaic Character of Anglo-Saxon Narrative Poetry.' *Speculum* 28 (1953): 446–67.

[78]  Marsden, Richard, editor. *The Cambridge Old English Reader*. Cambridge: Cambridge University Press, 2004.

[79]  Miller, Thomas, editor. *The Old English Version of Bede's Ecclesiastical History of the English People*. Vol. 95, 96, 110, 111 of Early English Text Society. London: Oxford University Press, 1890–8.

[80]  Mitchell, Bruce. *Old English Syntax*. Oxford: Clarendon Press, 1985.

[81]  Mitchell, Bruce and Fred C. Robinson. *A Guide to Old English*. 5th edition. Oxford: Blackwell, 1992.

[82]  Mitchell, Bruce and Fred C. Robinson, editors. *Beowulf: An Edition with Relevant Shorter Texts*. Includes 'Archaeology and Beowulf' by Leslie Wesbster. Oxford: Blackwell, 1998.

[83]  Morrell, Minnie Cate. *A Manual of Old English Biblical Materials*. Knoxville: University of Tennessee Press, 1965.

[84]  Morris, R., editor. *The Blickling Homilies*. First published 1874–80. Vol. 58, 63, 73 of Early English Text Society. London: Oxford University Press, 1967.

[85]  Muir, Bernard J., editor. *The Exeter Anthology of Old English Poetry*. 2nd edition. Exeter Medieval English Texts and Studies. Exeter: University of Exeter Press, 2000.

[86]  Muir, Bernard J., editor. *A Digital Facsimile of Oxford, Bodleian Library, MS. Junius 11*. Oxford: Bodleian Library, 2004.

[87]  O'Donnell, Daniel Paul, editor. *Cædmon's Hymn: A Multimedia Study, Archive and Edition*. Society for Early English and Norse Electronic Editions. Cambridge: D. S. Brewer, 2005.

[88]  O'Keeffe, Katherine O'Brien, editor. *Old English Shorter Poems: Basic Readings*. Vol. 3 of Basic Readings in Anglo-Saxon England. New York: Garland Press, 1994.

[89]  O'Keeffe, Katherine O'Brien, editor. *Reading Old English Texts*. Cambridge: Cambridge University Press, 1997.

[90]  O'Keeffe, Katherine O'Brien, editor. *The Anglo-Saxon Chronicle: A Collaborative Edition*. Vol. 5, MS C. Cambridge: D. S. Brewer, 2001.

[91]  O'Neill, Patrick P. editor. *King Alfred's Old English Prose Translation of the First Fifty Psalms*. Vol. 104 of Medieval Academy Books and Monographs. Cambridge, Mass.: Medieval Academy of America, 2001.

[92]  Orchard, Andy. *A Critical Companion to Beowulf*. Cambridge: D. S. Brewer, 2003.

[93]   Pelteret, David A. E. *Slavery in Early Medieval England*. Vol. 7 of Studies in Anglo-Saxon History. Woodbridge, Suffolk: Boydell Press, 1995.

[94]   Pelteret, David A. E., editor. *Anglo-Saxon History: Basic Readings*. Vol. 6 of Basic Readings in Anglo-Saxon England. London: Routledge, 2000.

[95]   Pope, John C. and R. D. Fulk, editors. *Eight Old English Poems*. 3rd edition. New York: W. W. Norton, 2000.

[96]   Pulsiano, Phillip, A. N. Doane, and Ronald Buckalew, editors. *Anglo-Saxon Manuscripts in Microfiche Facsimile*. In progress. Tempe, Arizona: Medieval and Renaissance Texts and Studies, from 1994.

[97]   Pulsiano, Phillip. *A Companion to Anglo-Saxon Literature*. Oxford: Blackwell, 2001.

[98]   Richards, Mary P., editor. *Anglo-Saxon Manuscripts: Basic Readings*. Vol. 2 of Basic Readings in Anglo-Saxon England. New York: Garland Press, 1994.

[99]   Robinson, Orrin W. *Old English and Its Closest Relatives: A Survey of the Earliest Germanic Languages*. Stanford: Stanford University Press, 1992.

[100]  Russom, Geoffrey. *Old English Meter and Linguistic Theory*. Cambridge: Cambridge University Press, 1987.

[101]  Scragg, Donald G., editor. *The Battle of Maldon*. Old and Middle English Texts. Manchester: Manchester University Press, 1981.

[102]  Scragg, Donald G., editor. *The Battle of Maldon, AD 991*. Oxford: Blackwell, 1991.

[103]  Sedgefield, Walter John, editor. *King Alfred's Old English Version of Boethius De Consolatione Philosophiae*. Oxford: Clarendon Press, 1899.

[104]  Sherley-Price, Leo. *Bede: Ecclesiastical History of the English People*. rev. edition. London: Penguin, 1990.

[105]  Short, Douglas D. *Beowulf Scholarship: An Annotated Bibliography*. Vol. 193 of Garland reference library of the humanities. New York: Garland Press, 1980.

[106]  Skeat, Walter W., editor. *Ælfric's Lives of Saints*. Vols. 76, 82, 94, 114 of Early English Text Society. London: Oxford University Press, 1881–1900.

[107]  Stenton, F. M. *Anglo-Saxon England*. 3rd edition. Vol. 2 of The Oxford History of England. Oxford: Clarendon Press, 1971.

[108]  Swanton, Michael, editor. *The Dream of the Rood*. 2nd edition. Exeter Medieval English Texts and Studies. Exeter: University of Exeter Press, 1987.

[109]  Swanton, Michael. *Anglo-Saxon Prose*. 2nd edition. London: Dent, 1993.

[110]  Szarmach, Paul E. et al., editors. *Medieval England: An Encyclopedia*. New York: Garland, 1998.

[111]  Szarmach, Paul. E., editor. *Old English Prose: Basic Readings*. Vol. 5 of Basic Readings in Anglo-Saxon England. London: Routledge, 2000.

[112]  Temple, E. *Anglo-Saxon Manuscripts, 900–1066*. Vol. 2 of Survey of Manuscripts Illuminated in the British Isles. London: Harvey Miller, 1976.

[113]  Whitelock, Dorothy, editor. *The Peterborough Chronicle*. Vol. 4 of Early English Manuscripts in Facsimile. Copenhagen: Rosenkilde and Bagger, 1954.

[114]  Whitelock, Dorothy, editor. *Sermo Lupi ad Anglos*. 3rd edition. Methuen's Old English Texts. London: Methuen, 1963.

[115]  Whitelock, Dorothy, editor. *Sweet's Anglo-Saxon Reader in Prose and Verse*. 15th edition. Oxford: Oxford University Press, 1975.

[116]   Williamson, Craig, editor. *The Old English Riddles of the Exeter Book*. Chapel Hill: University of North Carolina Press, 1977.

[117]   Wilson, David M., editor. *The Archaeology of Anglo-Saxon England*. Cambridge: Cambridge University Press, 1981.

[118]   Wilson, David M. *Anglo-Saxon Art from the Seventh Century to the Norman Conquest*. Woodstock, NY: Overlook Press, 1984.

[119]   Zupitza, Julius and Norman Davis, editors. *Beowulf. Reproduced in Facsimile from the Unique Manuscript, British Museum Ms. Cotton Vitellius A. XV*. 2nd edition. Vol. 245 of Early English Text Society. London: Oxford University Press, 1967.

# Index